American Indian Treaties

The History of a Political Anomaly

Francis Paul Prucha

UNIVERSITY OF CALIFORNIA PRESS

Berkeley / Los Angeles / London

University of California Press
Berkeley and Los Angeles, California

University of California Press, Ltd.
London, England

© 1994 by
The Regents of the University of California

Library of Congress Cataloging-in-Publication Data

Prucha, Francis Paul.
    American Indian treaties : the history of a political anomaly /
Francis Paul Prucha
        p.   cm.
    Includes bibliographical references and index
    ISBN 0-520-08531-0 (alk. paper)
    1. Indians of North America—Treaties—History.   I. Title.
KF8205.P75   1994
341′.026673—dc20   93-36297
                                                        CIP

Printed in the United States of America
9 8 7 6 5 4 3 2 1

The condition of the Indians in relation to the United States is perhaps unlike that of any other two people in existence.

Cherokee Nation v. Georgia (1831)

We have in theory over sixty-five independent nations within our borders, with whom we have entered into treaty relations as being sovereign peoples; and at the same time the white agent is sent to control and supervise these foreign powers, and care for them as wards of the Government. This double condition of sovereignty and wardship involves increasing difficulties and absurdities.

Edward P. Smith, commissioner
of Indian affairs (1873)

The relation of the Indian tribes living within the borders of the United States, both before and since the Revolution, to the people of the United States has always been an anomalous one and of a complex character.

United States v. Kagama (1886)

The publisher gratefully acknowledges the contribution provided by the General Endowment Fund of the Associates of the University of California Press.

Contents

Illustrations

Preface

I have long been interested in American Indian treaties, for they were one of the principal instruments by which the United States government dealt with the Indian nations. For the Indians, too, the treaties were of tremendous importance historically, and they continue today as the basis, in large measure, for the Indians' land claims, hunting and fishing rights, and distinct political status.

Although much attention has been paid to the treaties in histories of Indian policy and in legal studies, I felt a need for a substantial volume that would deal specifically with the treaties and with what might be called the treaty system—to discuss how and why the treaties were negotiated, to uncover the historical arguments for and against their use (which culminated with the ending of treaty making in 1871), and to look at the vicissitudes in the continuing history of the treaties that had been ratified before that date. It is my hope that such a volume will help toward a fuller understanding of a part of United States history about which there is still much misunderstanding, emotional disturbance, and wishful thinking. The account of two centuries of treaty history should at least make clear the complexity of the historical record and promote an appreciation that goes deeper than popular stereotypes and slogans.

This is primarily a chronological account of treaty making and of the subsequent history of the treaties. Yet as I wrote the narrative I was plagued by two problems that were hard to shake. One was the urge to write a treaty-by-treaty account, because nearly every treaty had unique features, and accurate generalizations, even narrowly defined ones, proved difficult to construct. The other was the danger of launching once again into a general history of American Indian policy, because the treaties played a large role in giving flesh to that policy. I am not sure that I have solved the problems. Scholars who have studied a particular treaty intensively will no doubt be disappointed that I did not treat that one more fully. As for Indian policy, I have tried to keep my eye on the treaty *process,* with reference to the formulation of policy only as needed to give the treaties a historical context.

Although treaties are thought of as contracts between independent states, in the case of the treaties of the United States with the Indian nations it is necessary to remember that formal written treaties were an Anglo-American, not an Indian, device. And as the decades passed, the United States played an increasingly dominant role, making use of the treaty process for its own purposes. These two facts make it appropriate—and even necessary—to consider American Indian treaties largely from the white perspective. Such a course, I know, slights Indian views of the treaties—stories that remain to be told in some detail as more scholars turn their attention to them and as more materials become available. Here I work, as in previous studies, on the national level, leaving for others to supply the detailed knowledge and corrected impressions that can come only from tribal or other particular investigations.

In the appendixes the book has reference materials that may be used independently of the narrative, especially the complete and careful lists of ratified treaties and ratified agreements, which contain basic information about each document.

I owe a debt to many people for assistance: to librarians and archivists for locating, retrieving, and helping to assemble the necessary documents; to scholars and other friends who have listened to my problems and have offered information and advice; and to my colleagues at Marquette University and my fellow Jesuits there, who have been generous and patient as I concentrated on this project. I thank, also, the University of Nebraska Press for permission to copy some brief sections from my book *The Great Father*.

Francis Paul Prucha, S.J.
Marquette University

Abbreviations Used in Footnotes

ASPIA   *American State Papers: Indian Affairs*. 2 vols. Washington: Gales and Seaton, 1832–34.

CIA AR   Annual Report of the Commissioner of Indian Affairs. For the period 1824–1920, the edition in the Congressional Serial Set is used, and the serial number is given.

Documents   Documents Relating to the Negotiation of Ratified and
(T494)   Unratifed Treaties with Various Indian Tribes, 1801–1869. National Archives Record Group 75 (T494).

GPO   United States Government Printing Office.

JCC   *Journals of the Continental Congress*. 34 vols. Washington: United States Government Printing Office, 1904–37.

Kappler   Charles J. Kappler, comp. *Indian Affairs: Laws and Treaties*. 5 vols. Washington: United States Government Printing Office, 1904–41.

OIA LS   Office [Bureau] of Indian Affairs, Letters Sent. National Archives Record Group 75 (M21).

Ratified Treaties Ratified Indian Treaties, 1722–1869. General Records of the United States Government. National Archives Record Group 11 (M668).

Royce, *Cessions* Charles C. Royce, *Indian Land Cessions in the United States*. Eighteenth Annual Report of the Bureau of American Ethnology, 1896–1897, part 2. Washington: United States Government Printing Office, 1899.

Senate Ex. Proc.	*Journal of the Executive Proceedings of the Senate of the United States of America.* Vols. 1–3, Washington: Duff Green, 1828; vols. 4—, Washington: United States Government Printing Office, 1887—. Reprint, New York: Johnson Reprint Corporation, 1969.
Senate (RG 46)	Records of Executive Proceedings, Presidents' Messages— Indian Relations. Records of the United States Senate. National Archives Record Group 46.
Terr. Papers	Clarence E. Carter, ed., *The Territorial Papers of the United States.* 26 vols. Washington: United States Government Printing Office, 1934–56; National Archives, 1958–62.
WD LS	Letters Sent by the Secretary of War Relating to Indian Affairs, 1800–1824. National Archives Record Group 75 (M15)

For documents in the Congressional Serial Set the numbers of the Congress and session are given in this abbreviated form: 46-2. The abbreviations used in the citations to some legal sources follow the forms given in *The Bluebook: A Uniform System of Citation*, 15th ed. (Cambridge: Harvard Law Review Association, 1991).

Introduction

The Anomaly of Indian Treaties

The formal treaties made by the United States government and various Indian tribes and bands have a complex history. They served many purposes for both the United States and the tribes, and they were negotiated by a great array of federal commissioners and Indian chiefs and warriors. Between 1778, when the first treaty was signed with the Delawares, and 1868, when the final one was completed with the Nez Perces, there were 367 ratified Indian treaties and 6 more whose status is questionable. In addition, a considerable number of treaties that were signed by the Indian chiefs and the federal commissioners were never ratified by the Senate and the president.[1] For both sides, conditions at the time of treaty signing called for pragmatic decisions, and it is dangerous to approach the treaties and their history with a priori patterns into which the actual events are squeezed to fit. Nor has the understanding of the old treaties in newer times followed a single pattern.

Indian treaties, when all is said and done, were a political anomaly. Chief Justice John Marshall hit it right when he wrote in *Cherokee Nation v. Georgia* (1831): "The condition of the Indians in relation to the United States is perhaps unlike that of any other two people in existence. . . . The relation of the Indians to the United States is marked by peculiar and cardinal distinctions which exist nowhere else." More than half a

---

1. Appendix B provides a list of the ratified treaties with basic information about each one.

1

century later the Supreme Court in *United States v. Kagama* (1886) echoed Marshall's sentiment: "The relation of the Indian tribes living within the borders of the United States . . . to the people of the United States has always been an anomalous one and of a complex character."[2] What was true about Indian-white relations in general was especially true about the Indian treaties.

The general rule is that a treaty is a formal agreement between two or more fully sovereign and recognized states operating in an international forum, negotiated by officially designated commissioners and ratified by the governments of the signatory powers. But American Indian treaties have departed from that norm in numerous ways, as their history shows. They exhibited irregular, incongruous, or even contradictory elements and did not follow the general rule of international treaties. It will not do to insist on univocal definitions while ignoring the multifaceted historical reality of the use of treaties in the relationships between the United States and the Indian communities. Only a detailed historical account will display the nature of the treaties and the many changes through which the understanding and use of the treaties passed in the course of American history.

Sovereignty

Indian treaties had certain characteristics or elements that, although appearing paradoxical or even incompatible, did not cancel each other out but existed together in an anomalous whole.

The United States, from the beginning of its political existence, recognized a measure of autonomy in the Indian bands and tribes. Treaties rested upon a concept of Indian sovereignty or quasi sovereignty and in turn greatly contributed to that concept. Treaties, as it was repeatedly pointed out in discourse about the relations between the United States and the Indians, made no sense unless based on recognition of some kind of special legal status of the Indians. In their actions, whites frequently enough disregarded Indian rights, but both theoretically and in practice the treaties gave the Indians a protected existence. Often this recognition of independence meant more to Indian groups than did their lands, and tribes eagerly sought treaties in order to gain

2. 5 Peters 16; 118 U.S. 381.

political recognition and not just to acquire the economic benefits that came from presents and from annuities paid for land.

The autonomous status was seen in the early treaties of "peace and friendship," for declaring war and peace were functions of sovereign nations. The first United States treaty—that with the Delawares in 1778 while the Revolutionary War was still raging—declared that "a perpetual peace and friendship shall henceforth take place, and subsist between the contracting parties . . . through all succeeding generations," and at the end of the war, treaties with all the onetime hostile Indians were designed to establish peace. The preambles to the treaties spoke of the United States "giving peace" to the Indians and receiving them into its favor and protection, but it was to be a mutual understanding of peace; the formula used in 1785–86 with the Cherokees and other southern tribes at Hopewell, in South Carolina, made this evident:

> The hatchet shall be forever buried, and the peace given by the United States, and friendship re-established between the said states on the one part, and all the Cherokees on the other, shall be universal; and the contracting parties shall use their utmost endeavors to maintain the peace as aforesaid, and friendship re-established.[3]

Similarly, after the War of 1812, the treaties at Portage des Sioux with the western tribes declared: "There shall be perpetual peace and friendship between all the citizens of the United States of America, and all the individuals composing [the particular tribe]." And the post–Civil War treaties made with the Five Civilized Tribes, who had aligned themselves with the Confederacy, reestablished "permanent peace and friendship" between the United States and each tribe; some of the tribes agreed, as the Creek treaty read, "to remain firm allies and friends of the United States, and never to take up arms against the United States, but always faithfully to aid in putting down its enemies."[4] In between such times of return to peace after a war, countless treaties issued or renewed declarations of peace between the United States and the Indian tribes.

Treaties also dealt with other aspects of the quasi-international status of the Indian tribes. Boundaries were established between the tribes and the United States and in some cases, notably in the Treaty of Prairie du Chien of 1825 and the Treaty of Fort Laramie of 1851, between the

3. Kappler, 2:3, 10–11.
4. Ibid., 110, 932.

various tribes as well. The lands of the Indian groups, although within the territorial limits of the United States recognized by European nations, were considered to be apart from the lands of the whites. This was a carryover from the concept of Indian country that was found in the Proclamation of 1763 with its line dividing Indian lands from areas of white settlement, a concept more sharply institutionalized by the federal trade and intercourse laws between 1790 and 1834. Treaties reinforced and amplified this principle of the separateness of tribal territory, especially in the initial years of treaty making. Early treaties with the Creeks and with the Cherokees, for example, required passports for United States citizens to enter Indian lands. There were, in addition, provisions in the treaties for the extradition of criminals, requiring the Indian tribes to deliver up Indians or other persons who committed crimes against United States citizens, so that they could be duly punished by the federal government. The cession of Indian lands, a prominent feature of Indian treaties, was an indication of Indian sovereignty over those lands, and the recognition by the United States of Indian ownership to the lands remaining strengthened the concept.[5]

Combined with the idea of separate Indian lands was the recognition of Indian autonomy within those lands. The language of the treaties is unmistakable in this regard. The first treaty was made with the Delaware "nation," and subsequent treaties followed that terminology, although little by little, especially with the Indians north of the Ohio River, the term "tribe" replaced "nation" or was used alternately with it. Even when "tribe" became common, the Creeks, Cherokees, and others of the southern tribes were still usually denominated "nations."[6]

John Marshall in the Cherokee cases of 1831 and 1832 argued the point at some length. In *Cherokee Nation v. Georgia* (1831) he declared that there was no doubt that the Cherokees were a state, "a distinct political society, separated from others, capable of managing its own affairs and governing itself." They had always been considered a state, he said, and the numerous treaties made with them by the United States had recognized them as "a people capable of maintaining the relations of peace and war, of being responsible in their political character for any violation of their engagements, or for any aggression committed on the citizens of the United States by any individual of their community."[7] Though Marshall balked at defining Indian tribes as foreign nations

5. See the discussion, pp. 226–34, on land cessions and payment therefor.
6. See discussion of the concept of "tribe," pp. 211–13.
7. 5 Peters 16.

able to bring suit before the Supreme Court, calling them instead domestic dependent nations, in *Worcester v. Georgia* (1832) he repeated and amplified his argument that the Indian nations were distinct, independent political communities. He concluded: "The words 'treaty' and 'nation' are words of our own language, selected in our diplomatic and legislative proceedings, by ourselves, having each a definite and well understood meaning. We have applied them to Indians as we have applied them to the other nations of the earth. They are applied to all in the same sense."[8]

Erosion of Sovereignty

If the matter had stopped there with "the 'platonic notions of Indian sovereignty' that guided Chief Justice Marshall"—to which the United States Supreme Court recently referred—all might be simple enough.[9] The anomaly in treaty making, however, soon appeared. Indian tribal sovereignty had gradually eroded, until the tribes became the dependent nations Marshall also spoke of. The treaties both reflected and contributed to the inequality and dependency with which the Indian negotiators faced the federal treaty commissioners. They rested on the assumption that the Indian tribes were not independent nations on the international scene. The treaties of peace after the Revolutionary War not only spoke of the United States as giving peace to the Indians but also included some such phrases as the following: "The said Indian nations do acknowledge themselves and all their tribes to be under the protection of the United States and of no other sovereign whatsoever."[10]

The same formula was used by the United States in treaties with the western tribes who signed treaties at Portage des Sioux after the War of 1812; the Missouri River tribes encountered by General Henry Atkinson and Indian Agent Benjamin O'Fallon in 1825 (which admitted that they resided within the territorial limits of the United States, acknowl-

8. 6 Peters 559–60.

9. *County of Yakima v. Confederated Tribes and Bands of the Yakima Nation*, 112 S. Ct. 687. The phrase "platonic notions of Indian sovereignty" was used in *McClanahan v. Arizona State Tax Commission*, 411 U.S. 172 (1973).

10. Treaty of January 21, 1785, with Wyandots and others, Kappler, 2:7. A similar phrase appears in the treaties with the southern tribes at Hopewell in 1785–86, the Treaty of Fort Harmar of 1789, the 1790 treaty with the Creeks, and on and on through the subsequent decades.

edged its supremacy, and claimed its protection); the tribes of the Pacific Northwest met by Governor Isaac I. Stevens in the mid-1850s; and the northern plains tribes with whom the Edmunds Commission dealt at Fort Sully in 1865. In such treaties the Indians agreed to submission to the United States in their external political affairs. John Marshall called such submission the "single exception" to tribal independence, "imposed by irresistible power, which excluded them [the tribes] from intercourse with any other European potentate than the first discoverer of the coast of the particular region claimed." In declaring that the Indians were not *foreign* nations, Marshall spoke bluntly:

> They look to our government for protection; rely upon its kindness and its power; appeal to it for relief of their wants; and address the President as their great father. They and their country are considered by foreign nations, as well as by ourselves, as being so completely under the sovereignty and dominion of the United States, that any attempt to acquire their lands, or to form a political connection with them, would be considered by all as an invasion of our territory, and an act of hostility.[11]

In fact, even though in the beginning the treaties were of a diplomatic nature—being negotiated by separate political powers dealing with each other on grounds of rough equality—very soon the United States came to negotiate the treaties from a position of overwhelming strength. Thomas Jefferson wrote to William Henry Harrison as early as 1803 regarding the Indians, "We presume that our strength and their weakness is now so visible that they must see we have only to shut our hand to crush them." Secretary of War John C. Calhoun, less than two decades later, could say of the Indians: "They are not, in fact, an independent people, (I speak of those surrounded by our population,) nor ought they to be so considered. They should be taken under our guardianship; and our opinion, and not theirs, ought to prevail, in measures intended for their civilization and happiness." William Clark, Indian superintendent at St. Louis, spoke in 1826 of the Indians as once a "formidable and terrible enemy," whose "power has been broken, their warlike spirit subdued, and themselves sunk into objects of pity and commiseration."[12]

11. *Worcester v. Georgia*, 6 Peters 559; *Cherokee Nation v. Georgia*, 5 Peters 17–18.
12. Jefferson to Harrison, February 27, 1803, *The Writings of Thomas Jefferson*, ed. Andrew A. Lipscomb, 20 vols. (Washington: Thomas Jefferson Memorial Association, 1903–4), 10:370–71; Calhoun report of January 15, 1820, *ASPIA*, 2:200–201; Report of Clark, March 1, 1826, *House Report* no. 124, 19-1, serial 138.

"The practical inequality of the parties," the legal scholar Felix Cohen once warned, "must be borne in mind in reading Indian treaties."[13]

The political dependence of the tribes was matched by economic dependence. In fact, economic dependence was in large part the reason that the Indians were forced to accept United States suzerainty. Since the Indians were dependent upon the whites for trade goods, control of that trade was a primary means for putting political pressure upon the tribes, and elimination of abuses in the trade was a means for preserving peace on the frontiers. The details of trading relations were worked out in a series of trade and intercourse laws, stretching from 1790 to 1834, and between 1795 and 1822 the federal government itself managed trading houses (called factories) in the Indian country to satisfy the Indians' wants and tie them to the United States. But the treaties were another means, for in them the Indians themselves agreed to give Congress the exclusive right to regulate trade with them. Some treaties repeated the provisions of the trade and intercourse laws requiring a license from a United States official for citizens or others trading in the Indian country, and the Treaty of Greenville in 1795, for example, specified in considerable detail the measures to control the trade.[14]

The treaties signed by tribes along the Missouri River in 1825 contained this clause: "The said bands also admit the right of the United States to regulate all trade and intercourse with them." And as the United States domain expanded west to the Pacific, the Indians newly encountered agreed by treaty to the extension of the trade and intercourse laws over their territories.[15] The Indians' continuing, increasing, and in many cases nearly absolute dependence upon white citizens for necessary goods was an important factor in the growing conviction that Indians were wards of the government, not members of independent sovereignties with whom the United States should deal by means of formal treaties.

Moreover, the sovereignty of the tribes was seriously compromised by repeated provisions in the treaties that left many stipulations to be carried out at the discretion of Congress, the Senate, or the executive.

---

13. Felix S. Cohen, *Handbook of Federal Indian Law* (Washington: GPO, 1942), 41. There is discussion of Indian dependency in Francis Paul Prucha, *The Indians in American Society: From the Revolutionary War to the Present* (Berkeley: University of California Press, 1985), chap. 2.

14. Kappler, 2:10, 42–43.

15. Ibid., 230ff., 583, 585.

In a number of cases, when articles in the treaties specified payments or grants to individuals, the treaties themselves provided that if these articles were not ratified, the rest of the treaty would not be affected. The treaties at Fort Sully in 1865 with the northern plains tribes carried this principle to an extreme, for each of those nine treaties provided:

> Any amendment or modification of this treaty by the Senate of the United States shall be considered final and binding upon the said band, represented in council, as a part of this treaty, in the same manner as if it had been subsequently presented and agreed to by the chiefs and head-men of said band.[16]

The 1842 treaty with the Chippewas allowed the Indians to hunt on the territory ceded by the treaty "until required to remove by the President of the United States" and stipulated that the trade and intercourse laws would continue to be in force with respect to Indian intercourse with whites "until otherwise ordered by Congress." The treaties with the eastern Sioux in 1851 declared that "rules and regulations to protect the rights and persons and property among the Indians, parties to this treaty, and adapted to their condition and wants, may be prescribed and enforced in such manner as the President or the Congress of the United States, from time to time, shall direct."[17] When a treaty was signed with the Delawares in 1854, a practically open provision for federal action was included in these words:

> A primary object of this instrument being to advance the interests and welfare of the Delaware people, it is agreed, that if it prove insufficient to effect these ends, from causes which cannot now be foreseen, Congress may hereafter make such further provision, by law, not inconsistent herewith, as experience may prove to be necessary to promote the interests, peace, and happiness of the Delaware people.[18]

The president, again and again, was given discretionary authority in treaties to establish trading posts and military posts at locations of his choice, designate places in the Indian country at which trade could be conducted, appoint agents to advise and direct the Indians, arbitrate claims between whites and Indians, decide territorial claims between Indian tribes and arbitrate other such claims, determine the time at

16. For example, treaty with Lower Brulé Sioux, October 14, 1865, ibid., 886.
17. Ibid., 542–43, 589, 592.
18. Treaty of May 6, 1854, ibid., 617.

which a tribe should remove from ceded lands, fix the size of annuity payments and the nature of such payments (in goods or in cash), determine lands for the Indians in exchange for cessions, convey parts of Indian lands to individual Indians as private reserves, approve sale of reserves by the Indians, dispose of lands held within reservations by missionary groups, decrease annuities as tribal population decreased, approve attorneys chosen by Indian chiefs, invest tribal moneys, and extend benefits to Indian tribes as he might think just and proper.[19]

Such authority placed in the hands of the president (usually to be exercised by the secretary of war or the secretary of the interior) indicated not only the respect that the Indians had for the Great Father but also the ability of the federal government by means of treaties to set its will as the determining factor in many elements of Indian life.

Civilization

Many grants of authority given to the president or Congress in the treaties were business or administrative matters, which by a stretch of the imagination might be seen as proper in the relations between a sovereign and a dependent protectorate. Much more powerful in contributing to the anomalous character of the Indian treaties was the persistent drive of white society and its government to change— indeed, to revolutionize—Indian societies by the promotion of white civilization. The treaties themselves, to a remarkable degree, were instruments intended to transform the cultures of the tribes. Building upon a long history of colonial precedents, federal leaders beginning with George Washington sought to change the Indians from hunters and gatherers to agriculturalists and herdsmen. It is not surprising that the treaties were full of provisions designed explicitly to enhance this process.

The treaty with the Creeks in 1790 declared: "That the Creek nation may be led to a greater degree of civilization, and to become herdsmen

19. I have been helped in summarizing elements of treaty making by the section "The Scope of Treaties," in Cohen, *Handbook of Federal Indian Law*, 38–46. Similar material is carried over into later works based on Cohen's book; see Office of the Solicitor, Department of the Interior, *Federal Indian Law* (Washington: GPO, 1958), 148–64; *Felix S. Cohen's Handbook of Federal Indian Law*, 1982 ed. (Charlottesville, Va.: Michie Bobbs-Merrill, 1982), 62–70.

and cultivators, instead of remaining in a state of hunters, the United States will from time to time furnish gratuitously the said nation with useful domestic animals and implements of husbandry."[20] Such items would weaken communal ties, or so Secretary of War Henry Knox hoped when he spoke in 1789 of instilling in the Indians a "love of exclusive property" and recommended that gifts of sheep and other domestic animals be presented to the chiefs and their wives. Knox instructed General Rufus Putnam, who was sent in 1792 to treat with the Indians near Lake Erie, to make clear the desire of the United States to impart to the Indians "the blessings of civilization, as the only mean[s] of perpetuating them on the earth," and that the government was willing to teach them to read and write and to practice the agricultural arts of the whites.[21]

It became common in the treaties for the United States to promise clothing, implements of husbandry, domestic animals, spinning wheels, and looms; to provide blacksmiths to repair agricultural implements as well as guns; and to build mills—all designed to promote the movement toward white ways of subsistence (although often the dispensing of these goods and services was left to the discretion of the president). It is easy to concentrate on the land cession provisions of the treaties and see the treaties simply as a means of territorial aggrandizement, as a "license for empire," and thus to miss the overwhelming obsession of the United States with changing the cultures of the Indians from communally to individually based systems of property ownership and from hunting or mixed economies to yeomanry.[22]

When treaties were made in the 1850s with the tribes in the newly acquired territories in the West, the same concern for civilization was evident, even though many of the Indians were not ready for it and hardly understood what it meant. The Treaty of Fort Laramie of 1851,

20. Kappler, 2:28.
21. Knox to Washington, July 7, 1789, *ASPIA*, 1:53–54; Knox to Putnam, May 22, 1792, ibid., 235.
22. The term "license for empire" comes from Dorothy V. Jones, *License for Empire: Colonialism by Treaty in Early America* (Chicago: University of Chicago Press, 1982), 186. An example of overly harsh concentration on the land provisions of the treaties is Ronald N. Satz's statement: "As the demand for Indian lands grew, American officials increasingly resorted to bribery, deception, economic coercion, threats, and sometimes brute force to secure Indian signatures on land cession treaties. The treaty-making process served as a convenient means of sanctioning federal land grabs under the guise of diplomacy." *Chippewa Treaty Rights: The Reserved Rights of Wisconsin's Chippewa Indians in Historical Perspective*, Transactions of the Wisconsin Academy of Sciences, Arts and Letters, vol. 79, no. 1 (Madison: Wisconsin Academy of Sciences, Arts and Letters, 1991), 6.

for example, provided annuities in "provisions, merchandise, animals, and agricultural implements." In justifying the payment of $50,000 a year for fifty years (a duration drastically cut by the Senate to fifteen years), one of the commissioners of the treaty remarked, "Humanity calls loudly for some interposition on the part of the American government to save, if possible, some portion of these ill-fated tribes; and this, it is thought, can only be done by furnishing them the means, and gradually turning their attention to agricultural pursuits."[23]

The much-criticized treaties signed with the eastern Sioux in 1851, in which the bands ceded large sections of land in Minnesota and adjacent regions of Dakota and Iowa in order to make room for expectant settlers and to acquire funds to wipe out large debts to traders, were also seen as a means to acculturate the Indians to agricultural life. "Unknown to most Dakota [Sioux]," a recent historian of those Indians writes, "the treaties of 1851 were tools of reform rather than examples of reciprocity." Even the abortive treaties with the Apaches, Navajos, and Utes in New Mexico Territory embodied civilizing principles, for the Indians agreed to cultivate the soil and raise flocks and herds, and they accepted gradually reduced annuities, which the president, at his discretion, could use in part for the Indians' moral improvement and civilization.[24]

The treaties in the same decade signed by Commissioner of Indian Affairs George W. Manypenny with the eastern tribes that had been moved west of the Mississippi in earlier decades—Indians who, for the most part, had long been in contact with whites—adopted the ultimate provision for changing the Indians into yeoman farmers: allotment of reservation lands in separate agricultural parcels to individual families. The treaties with the Pacific Northwest tribes in the same years spoke specifically of "civilization" and contained stipulations toward that end.

The treaties signed in 1867 and 1868 by the United States Indian Peace Commission at the very end of the treaty-making era were civilizing documents. One needs only to read the treaties—with their extensive provision for arable land for farming; construction of warehouses, mechanics shops, and other buildings; a "land book" to record individual allotments; domestic clothing; compulsory education; seeds

---

23. David D. Mitchell to Luke Lea, November 11, 1851, CIA AR, 1851, serial 613, pp. 289–90.

24. Gary Clayton Anderson, *Kinsmen of Another Kind: Dakota-White Relations in the Upper Mississippi Valley, 1650–1862* (Lincoln: University of Nebraska Press, 1984), 203. Two of the treaties with Indians in the southwest are printed in Kappler, 5:686–92.

and agricultural implements; and farmers, blacksmiths, and physicians—to see the strong thrust toward civilization that dominated them. By then the treaties had long since ceased to be simple political agreements between equal sovereigns, as some present-day Indian writers still see them.

Aside from the change to an agricultural mode of subsistence, formal schooling was the principal vehicle for modifying Indian cultures. The United States encouraged the educational efforts of missionary groups among the Indians and in 1819 formalized its support of these groups by providing an annual "civilization fund" to support their schools. It is understandable, then, that the treaties, too, made provision for schools and teachers. It was another element in the contract: the United States promised to furnish the means, and the Indians, explicitly or implicitly, agreed to send their children to school.

The Treaty of Doak's Stand with the Choctaws in 1820 provided that fifty-four sections of good land out of the ceded territory should be sold "for the purpose of raising a fund, to be applied to the support of the Choctaw schools, on both sides of the Mississippi," and a subsequent treaty in 1825 added an annuity of $6,000, to be applied for twenty years "to the support of schools in said nation, and extending to it the benefits of instruction in the mechanic and ordinary arts of life." Between 1817 and 1852 Congress appropriated more than $500,000 for Choctaw education under treaty provisions.[25]

Other tribes, too, benefited from education provisions in the treaties, for the treaty commissioners repeatedly entered such stipulations into the treaties.[26] By 1834 fourteen treaties provided an annual total of $35,500 for schools, with payments to run for limited periods of time or at the pleasure of Congress. By 1845 the annual sum (in twenty-four treaties) reached $68,195.[27]

Farther west, the story was the same. The treaties made by Manypenny in the 1850s included stipulations for schools and education, and in Governor Stevens's Treaty of Medicine Creek of 1854 with Puget Sound Indians, the government agreed to furnish an agricultural and

25. Kappler, 2:193, 212. Calculations on money for Choctaw education are given in George D. Harmon, *Sixty Years of Indian Affairs: Political, Economic, and Diplomatic, 1789–1850* (Chapel Hill: University of North Carolina Press, 1941), 357–58.

26. See Kappler, 2:270 (Chippewas, 1826), 274 (Potawatomis, 1826), 282 (Chippewas, 1827), 287 (Miamis, 1828), 304 (Delawares, 1829), 307 (Sacs and Foxes, 1830).

27. Harmon, *Sixty Years of Indian Affairs*, tables VI and VII, 380–81. Harmon estimates that in the first seventy-five years of the United States about $3 million was stipulated in treaties for Indian education. Ibid., 360.

industrial school for twenty years.[28] The Indian Peace Commission treaties of 1867–68, of course, made sure that education was attended to. All its treaties included this article:

> In order to insure the civilization of the Indians entering into this treaty, the necessity of education is admitted, especially of such of them as are or may be settled on said agricultural reservations, and they therefore pledge themselves to compel their children, male and female, between the ages of six and sixteen years, to attend school; and it is hereby made the duty of the agent for said Indians to see that this stipulation is strictly complied with; and the United States agrees that for every thirty children between said ages who can be induced or compelled to attend school, a house shall be provided and a teacher competent to teach the elementary branches of an English education shall be furnished, who will reside among said Indians, and faithfully discharge his or her duties as a teacher. The provisions of this article to continue for not less than twenty years.[29]

It must be noted that these and other educational provisions were not always carried out to the letter. The United States was remiss in fulfilling its promises for schools and teachers and the Indians in sending their children to school. Still, the presence of such provisions in the political treaties enhanced their anomalous character.

Another thrust toward bettering the condition of the Indians came in treaty provisions to prohibit or restrict the use of spirituous liquors by the Indians. Control of the liquor trade, with its deleterious effects on Indian society, was a fundamental element of American Indian policy. The trade and intercourse laws became increasingly severe in the matter, and those statutes were augmented by specific treaty provisions. Many chiefs recognized the evil of the liquor traffic and easily acquiesced in restrictive articles entered in the treaties. Thus, in some of the Manypenny treaties of the 1850s the Indians promised "to use their best efforts to prevent the introduction and use of ardent spirits in their country; to encourage industry, thrift, and morality; and by every possible means to promote their advancement in civilization." The Chippewa treaty of 1854 said bluntly, "No spirituous liquors shall be made, sold, or used on any of the lands herein set apart for the residence of the Indians, and the sale of the same shall be prohibited in the Territory hereby ceded, until otherwise ordered by the President." In

---

28. Kappler, 2:613, 663.
29. See, for example, the Fort Laramie Treaty of 1868, ibid., 1000.

some cases, as a motivation for enforcement, the treaties provided for withholding annuities (for as long as the president would determine) from Indians who drank liquor or brought it into the reservations.[30]

The desire to direct the Indians into the path of peaceable white civilization was well summed up in an article inserted in Manypenny's treaty with the Winnebagos signed in Washington in 1855:

> The said tribe of Indians, jointly and severally, obligate and bind themselves, not to commit any depredation or wrong upon other Indians, or upon citizens of the United States; to conduct themselves at all times in a peaceable and orderly manner; to submit all difficulties between them and other Indians to the President, and to abide by his decision; to respect and observe the laws of the United States, so far as the same are to them applicable; to settle down in the peaceful pursuits of life; to commence the cultivation of the soil; to educate their children, and to abstain from the use of intoxicating drinks and other vices to which many of them have been addicted. And the President may withhold from such of the Winnebagos as abandon their homes, and refuse to labor, and from the idle, intemperate, and vicious, the benefits they may be entitled to under these articles of agreement and convention, or under articles of former treaties, until they give evidences of amendment and become settled, and conform to, and comply with, the stipulations herein provided.[31]

Such provisions, of course, cut deeply into the lives of the Indians and subjected them almost completely to the will of the dominant partner in the treaties. The treaties, in fact, became social documents as well as political ones, a catch-all for legislating a good life for the reservation Indians.

Domestic Policy

Running through the anomaly of Indian treaties and going directly counter to the notion that a treaty is an *international* agreement between independent sovereign states was the hard fact that the Indians were ultimately a domestic issue for the United States. This was evident from the start, as Indian affairs were made the responsibility

30. Ibid., 193, 556, 633, 650, 660, 663.
31. Ibid., 692–93.

of the War Department (and later the Interior Department) rather than the State Department. When interference in Indian affairs by the separate states of the Union was condemned as a violation of the Articles of Confederation, it was because it went against the "sole and exclusive right and power" of Congress to regulate trade and manage all affairs with Indians (Article IX) rather than because it violated the prohibition upon the states against entering into "any conference, agreement, or alliance or treaty with any King, prince, or state" (Article VI). It is instructive to note, too, that Lewis and Clark, who met many Indian tribes on their cross-continental journey in 1804–6 and freely distributed peace medals to the chiefs, did not enter into treaty negotiations with them. President Jefferson, who was an aggressive treaty maker with Indians within the territorial boundaries of the United States, thought of dealing with the distant tribes only through trade, not through the political arrangements of formal treaties. This may have been because, when he planned the "voyage of discovery," the Louisiana Purchase had not yet been consummated and the Indians were not yet within United States territory.[32]

Even John Marshall, for all his talk about autonomous political entities and the meaning of the words *treaty* and *nation,* said that the relation of the Indians and the United States "resembles that of a ward to his guardian." The bold act of the southern tribes in throwing off their allegiance to the Union in the Civil War and joining the South has the appearance of an international act (although the Confederacy was never recognized as independent), but the Confederate States themselves, in their treaties with the Indian tribes, adopted Marshall's usage and spoke of recognizing the Indians "as their wards." By the time the treaties were being used to regulate Indian trade, provide for Indian education, and transform the Indians from hunters to full-time agriculturalists, the domestic nature of Indian affairs was fully confirmed. The post–Civil War drive to detribalize the Indians and assimilate them as individuals into the dominant white society was a culmination of a movement that had long been under way. Resolution of disputes between the tribes and the United States has always been the business of federal courts, not international tribunals.

It is true that some Indians in the twentieth century have demanded

---

32. There is nothing about formal treaty making in James P. Ronda, *Lewis and Clark among the Indians* (Lincoln: University of Nebraska Press, 1984), although Ronda discusses Jefferson's concern to bring the western Indians into America's political orbit by making trading arrangements with them.

international status and have sought recognition by the League of Nations or the United Nations, but they have been little heeded.[33]

Faith and Honor

What kept the anomaly of the treaties alive was the enduring quality in the American character that upheld the faith and honor of the nation. Government officials, in the early years of the republic especially, were conscious that the United States was an experiment in republican government, watched by the whole world. If the treaty contracts were not lived up to by the federal government, there would be an indelible stain on the honor of the country and its citizens. Moreover, there was a deep consciousness that the United States was a Christian nation and that not only would it lose its religious innocence by dealing unfairly with the Indians but that God in his justice would punish the nation if it left the path of righteousness by violating "sacred" treaties. Evangelical leaders tried hard to prevent the commission of such a national sin by arousing the conscience of the citizenry.

Many Indians relied on this concept of national honor in dealing with the United States, asserting their belief in honorable treatment by the federal government (even though long experience might have cautioned them against it), and they pleaded with the government not to violate its plighted faith and the national honor. Such tactics had considerable influence, for they touched a sympathetic chord among many white citizens and their official leaders. The cry for living up to treaty stipulations made by the articulate opponents of Indian removal in the 1820s and 1830s, for example, softened the blow of removal and left the southern Indian nations intact. The reliance on the honor of the nation in respect to treaty rights prevented the organization of territorial government in the Indian Territory in the decades immediately following the Civil War, for the sanctity of property rights acquired by contract

33. An interesting case is that of the Canadian Iroquois named Deskaheh, who in 1923 and 1924 sought recognition for the Six Nations of Canada from the League of Nations and a hearing of grievances against the Canadian government, only to be completely rebuffed in the end. See Joëlle Rostkowski, "The Redman's Appeal for Justice: Deskaheh and the League of Nations," in Christian F. Feest, ed., *Indians and Europe: An Interdisciplinary Collection of Essays* (Aachen: Rader Verlag, 1987), 435–53. There is discussion of the International Indian Treaty Council and the Geneva Conference it organized in the 1970s on pp. 418–19 below.

was a principle that neither the legislators nor the courts could openly reject.

After powerful arguments against signing any more treaties with Indian groups because they had lost the attributes of sovereignty, Congress in 1871 declared an end to such treaty making. But it could not disregard arguments about the sanctity of the treaties already signed and ratified, and confirmation of those treaties appeared side by side with the prohibition against making any more. On one hand the sovereign political character of Indian communities was denied; on the other, the tribes continued to exist as subjects of the rights the old treaties promised.

In the twentieth century a renewed popular movement in support of treaty rights, although not uniformly successful, brought forward the strong sense of conscience relative to contractual obligations that imbued the American ethos; some observers saw its strength or virulence resting upon a guilt complex over the treatment accorded the Indians in the past.

The Supreme Court in upholding Indian treaty rights in modern times has reflected anew (but again not uniformly) the noble ideal of living up to the obligations of formal contracts with the Indians. The statement of Justice Hugo Black in dissenting in a case in which it seemed to him the majority of the Court had temporarily lost its way, has become an oft-repeated motif for Indians and their advocates: "Great nations, like great men, should keep their word."[34]

This reliance on faith and honor has been mocked by the "broken treaty" syndrome that has become a pervasive part of pro-Indian rhetoric in the later twentieth century. There is a widely held sentiment that the federal government has consciously and intentionally broken all the treaties it signed with the Indian tribes. Such a view was dramatically expressed and widely circulated in the 1969 book by Vine Deloria, Jr., *Custer Died for Your Sins*. "America has yet to keep one Indian treaty or agreement," Deloria said, "despite the fact that the United States government signed over four hundred such treaties and agreements with Indian tribes." And he concluded that "it is doubtful that any nation will ever exceed the record of the United States for perfidy." He added: "In looking back at the centuries of broken treaties, it is clear that the United States never intended to keep any of its promises."[35] The refrain

34. 362 U.S. 142 (1960).
35. Vine Deloria, Jr., *Custer Died for Your Sins: An Indian Manifesto* (New York:

has been a common one, repeated so often that scholars as well as the man in the street accept it as conventional wisdom.[36]

The matter is not that simple, as the historical narrative below will demonstrate. There certainly are well-confirmed cases in which the federal government failed to live up to the stipulations of the treaties, just as there are cases in which the Indian signatories "broke" the treaties. Neither the United States nor the Indian tribes were able to control the actions of their subjects, as aggressive white settlers moved illegally into lands reserved for the Indians and as young Indian warriors continued their raids on white settlements after the chiefs had agreed to permanent peace. On the side of the whites the governmental system contributed to the problem, for treaties negotiated and signed in good faith by the executive branch were delayed, amended, or rejected by the Senate, and Congress was often slow or negligent in appropriating the funds needed to implement the treaties. But it is not proper to maintain, as some Indian groups have done, that an initial treaty is absolute and that any subsequent treaty, agreement, or statute that changes its provisions is an illegal abrogation of the original treaty.

The anomaly of Indian treaties would be ended if the treaties could be wiped out—totally abrogated—because of the historical changes that time has brought. Some Americans think that would be the answer, and their representatives in Congress have introduced bills to that effect, but the demand for an absolute end to Indian treaty rights on the basis of "equal rights for all citizens" has made little headway, and it is not likely to. Treaties are on the books, and the courts have supported them. In mulling over the reasons *why* "the Supreme Court has refused to allow American Indian tribes to be engulfed by the passage of time," the legal historian Charles F. Wilkinson offers a thoughtful conclusion:

Macmillan Company, 1969; reprint, with a new preface, Norman: University of Oklahoma Press, 1988), 28, 48.

36. The first question I am asked by persons who hear I am studying Indian treaties is usually, "Is it true that the United States broke every Indian treaty it signed?" The noted legal scholar at the University of Washington, Ralph W. Johnson, in a 1991 article includes the subheading "All Indian Treaties Have Been at Least Partially Abrogated." "Fragile Gains: Two Centuries of Canadian and United States Policy toward Indians," *Washington Law Review* 66 (July 1991): 685. He explains the phrase, however, to mean treaties were "entered on the assumption that Indian tribes were sovereign entities" and that that sovereignty has been weakened or otherwise modified since. Letter to author, December 12, 1991.

These old laws emanate a kind of morality profoundly rare in our jurisprudence. It is far more complicated than a sense of guilt or obligation, emotions frequently associated with Indian policy. Somehow, those old negotiations—typically conducted in but a few days on hot, dry plains between midlevel federal bureaucrats and seemingly ragtag Indian leaders—are tremendously evocative. Real promises were made on those plains, and the Senate of the United States approved them, making them real laws. My sense is that most judges cannot shake that. Their training, experience, and, finally, their humanity—all of the things that blend into the rule of law—brought them up short when it came to signing opinions that would have obliterated those promises.[37]

The judges are not alone. Many Americans would be brought up short if asked to support unilateral obliteration of Indian treaty rights. So the anomaly continues in the final decade of our century, for as Indian tribes have renewed the exercise of their inherent sovereignty in limited forms and speak much about self-determination, they simultaneously demand the continuation and amplification of the trust responsibility of the federal government for education, health services, and social welfare—both demands based on their reading of the old treaties.[38]

To ignore the political anomaly that has arisen during two centuries of Indian treaty making is to ignore the actual history of Indian-white relations and to destroy any realistic foundation for future programs and development based on that history.

37. Charles F. Wilkinson, *American Indians, Time, and the Law: Native Societies in a Modern Constitutional Democracy* (New Haven: Yale University Press, 1987), 121–22. Wilkinson's "hot, dry plains" were not a typical site for treaty councils, as a glance at the map in appendix B will show.

38. I have written before about this strange juxtaposition, speaking of it as a "paradox." See, for example, Prucha, *Indians in American Society*. But the combination of the two elements—enhanced tribal sovereignty and increased dependence on a paternal government—is part of the anomaly of Indian treaties.

PART ONE

A Treaty System

The Indian treaty system of the United States did not spring forth full-blown from some statesman's brow. No federal commission or task force proposed a blueprint for relations with the Indians who inhabited aboriginal lands within the territorial boundaries of the United States. To be sure, there were precedents of colonial and British imperial policy, and the idea of formal treaties with Indian tribes had roots in European practice. But the United States worked out a set of procedures on its own, reacting to the crisis on its frontiers (where white settlers encroaching on Indian lands roused Indian resistance and retaliation) and mindful of the high republican principles it was testing under the eyes of the rest of the world. Practical decisions were made by the federal legislature and its committees; then by the president, his advisers, and the treaty commissioners; and finally, after the Constitution was adopted, by the Senate. State governments, too, sought to protect their interests touched by treaty making, and the Indian leaders, astute and resourceful, fought to preserve their lands and their autonomy within a context of intertribal and intratribal divisions.

The decisions made were not inevitable. Many of them could have gone some other way, but by the end of the eighteenth century certain patterns became accepted and the procedures standardized. Thus, management of Indian affairs fell to the federal government, not to the states (although the relationships between the two levels of government were not always smooth). The general stipulations on treaty making embodied in the Constitution were specified in practice by George Washington and the Senate. Indian protocol and ceremonies, at first adopted by United States commissioners, were cast aside as the power of the new nation increased in comparison with that of the Indians and it was no longer necessary to defer to Indian customs. And the treaties began to serve as vehicles for "reforming" the cultures of the Indians to bring them into conformity with white society. Though not yet perfected, a treaty system was in place by the time Thomas Jefferson assumed the presidency.[1]

1. For an alternate approach to the creation of a treaty system, see Dorothy V. Jones, *License for Empire: Colonialism by Treaty in Early America* (Chicago: University of Chicago Press, 1982).

CHAPTER ONE

The Revolutionary War Years

During the Revolutionary War, as the Continental Congress groped its way toward a satisfactory procedure for dealing with the Indian tribes within the boundaries of the nation, the United States got its first taste of treaty making with the Indians. The Congress hoped to gain the friendship or at least the neutrality of the tribes in the war with Great Britain, to ease the continuing pressure of white settlement on Indian lands, and withal to maintain a posture of justice and humanity that would win the support and admiration of the whole civilized world. It was not an easy task for the weakly united colonies, which were intent first of all on vindicating by military force the independence from Great Britain that they had so eloquently proclaimed in the Declaration of Independence.

The colonies, of course, did not lack precedents on which to base their actions. The Mother Country, against whom they were now rebelling, had dealt with the American Indians for almost two centuries. The two cultures—marked by distinct races—had worked out patterns of accommodation for coexistence. Colonial governors, assemblies, and other agencies spent a good deal of time on problems concerning the struggle for control of America's lands. The Indians, on their side, followed diplomatic and economic interests of their own and were not merely passive recipients of European initiatives. Out of the joint concerns, as a means of diplomatic engagement, came numerous treaties and treaty councils.[1]

The Role of Indian Treaties

Confusion about the initial dealings of the Congress with the Indians arises from reading back into the past our modern understandings of the word *treaty*. The current prevailing sense is a contract between two or more states, relating to peace, alliance, commerce, or other international relations, and also, the document embodying such a contract, formally signed by plenipotentiaries appointed by the government of each state. But in the colonial and early national periods of United States history the term also had an alternate meaning, now considered rare or obsolete, that was widely used; a "treaty" in that sense was the "act of negotiating," the discussion aimed at adjustment of difference or the reaching of an agreement, and by extension the

1. Alden T. Vaughan, ed., *Early American Indian Documents: Treaties and Laws, 1607–1789*, 20 vols. projected (Washington: University Publishers of America, 1979—), 1: xiii. This series, when completed, will be an invaluable source for the colonial period, presenting reliable texts of key documents, including treaties and reports of treaty councils.

There is a small corpus of scholarly works on colonial treaties, mostly British treaties. See references in Francis Paul Prucha, *A Bibliographical Guide to the History of Indian-White Relations in the United States* (Chicago: University of Chicago Press, 1977), 119, and its supplement, *Indian-White Relations in the United States: A Bibliography of Works Published 1975–1980* (Lincoln: University of Nebraska Press, 1982), 30. Recent studies include Dorothy V. Jones, *License for Empire: Colonialism by Treaty in Early America* (Chicago: University of Chicago Press, 1982), which discusses a treaty system of accommodation between Great Britain and the Indians, 1763–68, the transformation of that system, 1768–86, and the emergence of a "colonial" treaty system, 1787–96; Francis Jennings, ed., *The History and Culture of Iroquois Diplomacy: An Interdisciplinary Guide to the Treaties of the Six Nations and Their League* (Syracuse: Syracuse University Press, 1985), which accompanies an extensive microfilm edition of Iroquois treaty documents, *Iroquois Indians: A Documentary History of the Diplomacy of the Six Nations and Their League*, ed. Francis Jennings (Woodbridge, Conn.: Research Publications, 1984), for which there is a printed guide; and Dorothy V. Jones, "British Colonial Indian Treaties," in *Handbook of North American Indians*, vol. 4, *History of Indian-White Relations*, ed. Wilcomb E. Washburn (Washington: Smithsonian Institution, 1988), 185–90, which appends a table of "Indian Treaties with Britain and British Colonies," 1607–1775, prepared by George Chalou.

meeting itself at which such negotiations took place.[2] The language of the Continental Congress and its contemporaries makes it clear enough from the context which sense of the word is meant. The documents are full of such terminology as "holding a treaty" with the Indians, "inviting Indians to a treaty," providing military support and purchasing presents "for a treaty," or greeting Indians as they arrived "at a treaty."

These gatherings or councils, following British colonial custom, had a number of purposes. The open discussion itself was of primary importance, for it was a vehicle for expressing or developing mutual friendship. In an exchange of views, usually expressed according to the style, rubrics, and protocol of the Indians, the commissioners of the Congress (or those of the states interested in the issues) made known their concerns and demands, while in turn the Indians' spokesmen voiced their complaints, grievances, and desires. There could be a beneficial clearing of the air, and such parleying was an end in itself, as each side expressed its friendship for the other, past wrongs were forgiven, and promises of one sort or another were firmly made. Especially among the Iroquois and the northwestern tribes, speeches were confirmed by exchange of strings or belts of wampum (or hostile positions were maintained by rejection of the symbolic wampum). The meetings sometimes brought to light divisions between the tribes, a diplomatic fact that the United States commissioners learned to appreciate and even to encourage.[3]

A second purpose or function of the councils was the presentation of gifts to the assembled Indians. The exchange of presents was a part of Indian protocol, but in many cases it became a one-way street, as the Congress provided presents—often goods badly needed by the Indians—to win or keep the friendship of the tribes. The Indians depended upon the articles provided, and the United States early learned the importance of finding appropriate goods to supply the Indians in order to keep their loyalty. Attempts were made to gain the support of influential chiefs by special presents and by marks of authority and

2. *The Oxford English Dictionary*, 2d ed. (1989); *The American Heritage Dictionary*, 3d ed. (1992). *Webster's Third New International Dictionary of the English Language, Unabridged* (1981) gives as a specific additional meaning: "A formal meeting between representatives of the U.S. government and of one or more Indian tribes designed to produce settlement (as of issues in dispute)."

3. The use of wampum and the protocol at Iroquois treaty councils is discussed in William N. Fenton, "Structure, Continuity, and Change in the Process of Treaty Making," and Mary A. Druke, "Iroquois Treaties: Common Forms, Varying Interpretations," in Jennings, ed., *Iroquois Diplomacy*, 3–36, 85–98.

esteem such as silver medals, ornamental gorgets, and wrist bands, which had also been the custom among the European nations in their dealings with the Indians.

Meetings, moreover, were an opportunity to overawe hesitant tribes by a display of military force. Many of the councils, sometimes to the dismay of the Indians, were held at established forts, and for some, additional troops or state militia were at hand or in readiness for any overt hostility on the part of the Indians.

In the beginning, the production of a written agreement signed by the negotiators and ratified by the governments—a treaty in the modern sense—was not a primary consideration; the meeting itself was the significant event, and for the Indians the exchange and acceptance of wampum strings and belts confirmed the decisions at the council. The belts with their designs were memory aids in recalling the contents of the conferences, and such oral tradition was considered a suitable substitute for paper documents. Of the numerous "treaties" held with Indians by commissioners of the Continental Congress during the Revolutionary War (1775 to 1783), only *one*—the treaty with the Delawares at Fort Pitt in 1778—resulted in a formal document, the first in the standard collections of United States–Indian treaties.

The united colonies faced a severe challenge from the Indians in the north, where the powerful league of the Iroquois leaned toward its old friends, the British; in the south, where Cherokees, Creeks, Choctaws, and Chickasaws adhered to the British cause or engaged in friendly intercourse with the Spanish; and in the west, where tribes across the Appalachians in the Kentucky district of Virginia and in the region northwest of the Ohio River resisted the encroachment of white settlers with open hostility.[4]

Individual colonies sent commissioners to the tribes, but relations with the Indians could not be handled adequately by disparate provincial actions. On July 12, 1775, therefore, the Continental Congress established three departments for Indian affairs: northern, for the Six Nations of the Iroquois and Indians to the north of them; southern, for the

---

4. For a solid account of Indian affairs in the upper Ohio valley from 1755 to 1795, see Randolph C. Downes, *Council Fires on the Upper Ohio: A Narrative of Indian Affairs in the Upper Ohio Valley until 1795* (Pittsburgh: University of Pittsburgh Press, 1940). Iroquois Indian affairs are treated in Barbara Graymont, *The Iroquois in the American Revolution* (Syracuse: Syracuse University Press, 1972); those in the south, in James H. O'Donnell III, *Southern Indians in the American Revolution* (Knoxville: University of Tennessee Press, 1973). See also Walter H. Mohr, *Federal Indian Relations, 1774–1788* (Philadelphia: University of Pennsylvania Press, 1933).

Cherokees and all others to the south of them; and middle, for the tribes living in between. For each department Congress appointed commissioners of Indian affairs, who were to treat with the Indians "in the name, and on behalf of the united colonies"; the commissioners were to work to preserve peace and friendship with the Indians and, in a quaint understatement, "to prevent their taking any part in the present commotions." The appointment of Benjamin Franklin, Patrick Henry, and James Wilson for the middle department indicates the importance attached to the matter.[5]

The commissioners (who were a fluid group, with frequently changing membership), aided or substituted for by military commanders on the frontiers, called numerous councils with the Indian nations. Given the slowness in communications between Philadelphia and the frontiers and the involvement of the Continental Congress in the complexities of carrying on a war, engaging in diplomatic negotiations with European nations, and attempting to solve or prevent domestic problems, the commissioners were allowed considerable discretion in their handling of Indian matters. They tested the attitude of the Indians, picked suitable spots for the meetings, called the chiefs and warriors to the councils, arranged for presents for the Indians and for military presence at the councils (under general or particular authorization by Congress), and reported regularly to the lawmakers in Philadelphia.

Indian Affairs in the North

Major General Philip Schuyler was the dominant commissioner in the northern department. Together with other commissioners appointed by Congress and those appointed by the government of New York to represent that state's interests, Schuyler held conferences with the various tribes of the Iroquois at Albany in 1775, at German Flats in 1776, at Albany again in 1777 (with mostly Oneidas and Tuscaroras), and at Johnstown, New York, in 1778 (with Oneidas, Tuscaroras, and Onondagas).[6]

5. *JCC,* 2:174–77, 183, 192, 194.
6. There is a good account of Schuyler's work and of his meetings with the Indians, set in a broad perspective of northern Indian affairs, in Graymont, *Iroquois in the American Revolution*. See also Don R. Gerlach, *Proud Patriot: Philip Schuyler and the War of Independence, 1775–1783* (Syracuse: Syracuse University Press, 1987). The minutes of the

The northern councils represented the changing character of the war as both the British and the Americans deserted the policy of Indian neutrality and actively sought and gained military support from the tribes. For the Johnstown council Congress instructed the commissioners "to speak to the Indians . . . in language becoming the representatives of free, sovereign, and independent states, and in such a tone as will convince them that we feel ourselves to be so," but the commissioners were granted discretion about whether to insist upon active aid from the Indians or merely neutrality. Governor George Clinton of New York was empowered to select a suitable commissioner to attend the meeting. A report of the council, held on March 7, 1778, with "a number of Sachems and Warriors of the Six Nations" was referred to the Board of War, but no formal treaty document came out of the meeting.[7]

Another series of treaty councils was held at Pittsburgh (Fort Pitt), under the auspices of the commissioners of the middle department. These were for the western tribes, although on occasion Indians from the Six Nations also attended.

In September and October 1775 the first of five councils was held, with some Indians from the Six Nations, Delawares, Shawnees, and Wyandots in attendance. Virginia sent five commissioners; two more came from Philadelphia to represent the united colonies. The commissioners reassured the Indians that the boundary lines established at the Treaty of Fort Stanwix in 1768 would hold, and they sought to convince them that the patriots' cause would succeed.[8]

As various Indian delegations arrived at the meeting place, they were formally greeted by the commissioners with prepared speeches, to which they responded with similar ceremonial talk, the usual fare of treaty councils carried over from British practice.[9] Condolence ceremonies were performed for the Wyandots and others, who had "never been

---

councils at German Flats and Albany are printed in E. B. O'Callaghan, ed., *Documents Relative to the Colonial History of the State of New-York*, 15 vols. (Albany: Weed, Parsons and Company, 1853–87), 8:605–31. For other actions, see *JCC,* 5:651; 7:166.

7. *JCC,* 10:105–6, 110–11, 291. See also Graymont, *Iroquois in the American Revolution,* 162–63. Graymont emphasizes how these events split and destroyed the old Iroquois Confederacy, as some of the Six Nations joined the British, others the United States.

8. The proceedings of the treaty are printed in Reuben Gold Thwaites and Louise Phelps Kellogg, eds., *The Revolution in the Upper Ohio, 1775–1777* (Madison: Wisconsin Historical Society, 1908), 74–127.

9. Ibid., 76.

condoled with Agreeable to their Custom since the last War for the loss of their freinds who fell in Battle." Strings of wampum were presented and goods were delivered "as a present of Condolence," comprising four black strouds, four ruffled shirts, four pairs of leggings, four matchcoats, and a blanket. Then came more speeches, which went in part:

> It is from that Council [the Continental Congress] we are sent to renew and more perfectly Establish the Antient Friendship that has Subsisted between you and us we therefore Bretheren bid you Welcome to this Council Fire and with these strings we wipe the Dust and Sweat Occasioned by the Fatigue of your Journey   we likewise wipe off from your Memories and Clear your Ears from any Wicked reports which may have Tended to Interrupt you and our peace and the peace of our Wives and Childeren that you may Plainly hear and Understand what we say to you   *A String to Each Nation*
>
> *Bretheren* with these strings we dry up your Tears for the Loss of your Freinds who have died since your last assembly at this Place we remove all Greif from your hearts on this Account that your minds may be at ease whilst we deliver our Embassy to you from our great United Council of Wise men now Assembled at Philadelphia which we hope you will hear with as much pleasure as we shall deliver it and we Collect the Bones of your Deceased freinds and Bury them deep in the Earth and Transplant the Tree of Peace over them that our Freindship may not be Interrupted nor our Minds disturbed at the Sight of them   *A Large String to Each Nation*   with these strings we Clear our Council House and desire no discontent may be allowed to Enter therein but that we may Consult together with Honest Hearts for your and our Mutual Peace and Happiness   *A String to Each Nation*[10]

Such speeches of good will, interspersed with similar orations from the Indian leaders, occupied a good many days. On October 10, the united colonies' commissioners withdrew so that those from Virginia could conduct their business, which dealt in large measure with the return of white captives, blacks, and horses that the Indians had not yet searched out and given up. In the end, on October 19, agents were appointed to make sure that the agreements about return of prisoners and property would be carried out. There was no signed treaty, and none of the participants seemed to have expected one.[11]

News from the west of continuing Indian unrest, often exaggerated

10. Ibid., 82–83.
11. Ibid., 93–127.

as it spread eastward, moved the Continental Congress to provide for a second council at Pittsburgh in 1776. George Morgan, the Pennsylvania land speculator and trader who had been appointed agent for the Indians of the middle department, spread the alarm, and Congress responded with a series of resolutions providing funds for a new gathering of the tribes. Congress directed on April 10 "that so soon as conveniently may be, a treaty be held between the commissioners for Indian affairs in the middle department, and the nations of Indians to the westward; and that the said commissioners be desired to appoint the time and place of meeting for that purpose, and give the Indians information thereof." A month later, on May 6, it extended its plan to all the departments and urged that treaties be held with the Indians as soon as practicable, and it appropriated $10,000 to the commissioners of each department for presents to the Indians and other expenses. It instructed the standing Committee on Indian Affairs to carry into execution the resolution of May 6, and it specified that July 20 be set as the date for holding a treaty at Pittsburgh with the Indians of the middle department. As might be expected, affairs did not move very quickly, and on July 4, new commissioners for the middle department were appointed.[12]

There was continuing fear that the Indians were forming a confederacy to resist the Americans, but new information from the frontier dissipated to a large extent the panic of the spring. On August 19, after a report on the state of Indian affairs on the western frontier from the standing Committee on Indian Affairs, Congress granted discretion to the commissioners about when to hold the new treaty and where, and instructed them to make the treaty as general as possible. Representatives of only the Senecas, Delawares, and Shawnees appeared at Pittsburgh, but Morgan was able to report to Congress on November 8 that the cloud that had threatened from the west "appears now to be nearly dispersed."[13]

The third council at Pittsburgh in 1777 was intended as a similar event. On the urging of Morgan, who had invited the Delawares, Shawnees, and the Six Nations to assemble again at Fort Pitt in July, Congress appropriated funds for the meeting. The Delawares were on hand, and on Morgan's urging some Senecas, too, appeared. But frontiersmen at Pittsburgh, holding the Senecas accountable for recent murders and captures, killed several of the Indians when they arrived

12. *JCC*, 4:267–68, 330, 347–48; 5:517.
13. Ibid., 5:668. Morgan is quoted in Downes, *Council Fires*, 194.

for the council, thus destroying any good that might have been expected from the meeting.[14]

In 1778 a fourth council at Pittsburgh with the western Indians was prepared. On June 4 Congress authorized three commissioners (two to be appointed by Virginia and one by Pennsylvania) and agreed to the necessary expenses. On June 20 it appropriated $10,000 for procuring goods and presents for the Indians and set July 23 as the date for the treaty. The commissioners were directed to dispose of the goods among the Indians "in such manner as they shall judge will best conduce to conciliate their affection and secure them in the interest of these states."[15]

The plan did not work out quite as intended, for the meeting did not commence until September 12. Only the two Virginia commissioners appeared, General Andrew Lewis and his brother Thomas Lewis, and only the Delaware Indians, but it was a significant parley nonetheless, for it resulted in the only written agreement made with the Indians during the Revolutionary War.

In 1778 preparations had begun for an attack on Detroit, and Delaware friendship was essential for its success, since the expedition was to proceed through Delaware territory. That friendship was successfully sought at Pittsburgh, for some Delawares had been strongly influenced toward friendship with the Americans by the Moravian missionaries, especially David Zeisberger and John Heckewelder, who worked among them. In the ceremonial language demanded by the occasion, the Delawares at the council were told by the commissioners:

> You alone of all the Western Indians seem inclined to hold fast the Chain of friendship and even in this instance it has Contracted some Rust, of a very Dangerous Nature. The paths between us are grown up with Bushes, so that they can scarce be seen. They are Bloody, your and our peoples Bones are scattered thro' the Woods, our people Stumble over them. Black Heavy Clouds hang over our heads. . . . We present you with this Belt of Wampum, by which we open the path between us, once more, and wash away the Blood that has been Spilt on it, we Bury the scattered Bones of our Deceased Relations, and Dispel the Black Clouds, and wipe the tears from your Eyes, we remove all sorrow from your hearts, that joy and the Bright Sun of friendship may shine on you with greater Lustre than ever.[16]

14. *JCC*, 8:478, 493–94; Downes, *Council Fires*, 201–4.

15. *JCC*, 11:568, 626.

16. The minutes of the council are published in David I. Bushnell, Jr., "The Virginia Frontier in History—1778," pt. 5, "The Treaty of Fort Pitt," *Virginia Magazine of History*

Then, with a belt of white wampum showing in black the thirteen
United States and the Delaware Nation holding to the same chain of
friendship, the commissioners presented their arguments to the Indian
delegates. They offered friendship, wishing to consider the Delawares
as their own people; they noted the American alliance with France,
which would soon enable the United States "to trample all our Enemies
under our feet"; they promised no obligations to the Indians except
such as would be "for mutual Good and Happiness" and that "would
secure future peace whilst the Sun or the Earth endures," but they clearly
intended the Delawares to be active allies against the British. After the
Indians agreed to their presentation, the United States commissioners
drew up a document, which was read and explained to the Indians on
September 14. Three days later these "Articles of Confederation &
Union" were read and interpreted again, and the Indians gave their
assent. The document was then signed in triplicate.[17]

The signing was witnessed by a number of military men, including
General Lachlan McIntosh, the commandant at Fort Pitt, who entertained the Indians with a parade of his troops in celebration and delivered
a speech to the assembly, in which he told the Delawares it was time to
show their friendship "by taking up this Hatchet like men determined
to be free with us, against all our Enemies and your Enemies. And this
Belt [of wampum] to Confirm it, expecting when I go over this river
your Warriors will join me, that we may grow great together, and be
one people (as you have declared this Day) Whilst the Sun and Moon
Shines or the Waters Run."[18]

The Treaty of Fort Pitt was a treaty of formal alliance, a fact which
perhaps explains why it was produced in written form. After asserting
perpetual peace and friendship, the document said: "And if either of the
parties are engaged in a just and necessary war with any other nation or
nations, that then each shall assist the other in due proportion to their
abilities, till their enemies are brought to reasonable terms of accommodation." The Delawares agreed to allow free passage of United States
troops through their country and to ally their warriors with the Amer-

and Biography 24 (April 1916): 168–79. The quotation is on 170–71. A similar version
of the negotiations is printed in Louise Phelps Kellogg, ed., *Frontier Advance on the Upper
Ohio, 1778–1779* (Madison: State Historical Society of Wisconsin, 1916), 138–45.

17. Bushnell, "Treaty of Fort Pitt," 171, 174–78.

18. Ibid., 178. McIntosh's speech is not included in Kellogg, *Frontier Advance*.

ican troops. The United States agreed to build a fort in Delaware country "for the better security of the old men, women and children . . . [of the Delaware Nation], whilst their warriors are engaged against the common enemy."[19]

In the final article the United States agreed to guarantee the territorial rights of the Delawares. Then it provided for other friendly tribes to join with the Delawares and "to form a state whereof the Delaware nation shall be the head, and have a representation in Congress." The origin of this extraordinary provision is unknown, and the extant treaty proceedings make no mention of it.[20]

Nothing in the treaty was to be considered conclusive until Congress approved. The treaty was received by Congress with a letter from the commissioners on October 6 and referred to a committee, but there is no indication of any action taken.[21]

The treaty on the surface seemed to be a great success, but in the end it accomplished little, and it left a bad taste in the mouths of the Delawares. John Killbuck, one of the three Delaware signers, on January 20, 1779, wrote to George Morgan that he had been deceived because he had not understood the interpreter. He asserted that he had been determined "to continue in that what I was so often told to do by you, which was to sit quite still & let you & the English make out the matter together; but was very much surprized when I found after my return from the Treaty, that I was looked upon as a Warrior." He claimed that when the tomahawk was handed to him at Fort Pitt it was done "not in a Warlike manner" and that he had contracted only to lead the United States troops through his country as they sought the enemy. Colonel

19. Kappler, 2:3–5.

20. C. A. Weslager, *The Delaware Indians: A History* (New Brunswick: Rutgers University Press, 1972), 305, says that it was the idea of the Delaware chief White Eyes: "He came to the conference to obtain support for a unique proposition—namely that the Delaware Indians should be permitted *to form the fourteenth state in the American union.* White Eyes may have felt that, if he could persuade the commissioners to accept this new and unprecedented proposal, he could agree to almost anything, including going on the warpath against the English. In the absence of detailed information, one can only speculate about his motives." Annie H. Abel says, "The permission thus granted was entirely a matter of military expediency; yet it was never acted upon, very probably because the Indians had no adequate conception of its significance, were unprepared to take the initiative, and the white men disinclined to do so." "Proposals for an Indian State, 1778–1878," *Annual Report of the American Historical Association for the Year 1907*, 2 vols. (Washington: GPO, 1908), 1:89.

21. *JCC*, 12:986.

Morgan, himself, said later, "There never was a Conference with the Indians so improperly or villainously conducted as the last one at Pittsburgh—I am only surprised it has not had worse Effects."[22]

Morgan, in the spring of 1779, arranged for a Delaware delegation to Philadelphia, where the Indians could explain to the Continental Congress their dissatisfaction with the Treaty of Fort Pitt, but it availed nothing, and peace and friendship between the United States and the Delawares collapsed. The best friend of the United States among the tribe, Chief White Eyes, was murdered by frontiersmen, and eventually the tribe's council decided to join the British in fighting the United States.[23]

Before that eventuality, however, still another council was held at Pittsburgh in September 1779, this time with the Wyandots, who, unlike the Delawares in 1778, were unwilling to let American troops pass through their lands in the projected attack on Detroit. There was a good deal of wampum exchanged in pledges of friendship and condolences for past enmities in speeches by Daniel Brodhead, who had replaced McIntosh in command of Fort Pitt, and Half King, the Wyandot chief, but nothing else was accomplished.[24]

Indian Affairs in the South

Meanwhile, a comparable series of councils was held on the southern frontiers, where conditions were as unsettled as those in the north but where more initiative was left in the hands of the states of Virginia, North Carolina, South Carolina, and Georgia.[25] The states appointed commissioners, including well-established Indian traders, to deal with the tribes, and the Continental Congress in the beginning

22. John Killbuck to George Morgan, January 20, 1779, in Kellogg, *Frontier Advance*, 203–4; George Morgan to Daniel Brodhead, January 31, 1779, ibid., 217.

23. Weslager, *Delaware Indians*, 307–17. There was a great deal of factionalism within the Indian tribes, especially between those favorable to the Americans and those who hoped to unite against American advance toward the west. See the account in Gregory Evans Dowd, *A Spirited Resistance: The North American Indian Struggle for Unity, 1745–1815* (Baltimore: Johns Hopkins University Press, 1992).

24. The exchange of speeches is printed in Louise Phelps Kellogg, ed., *Frontier Retreat on the Upper Ohio, 1779–1781* (Madison: State Historical Society of Wisconsin, 1917), 66–72. See also Downes, *Council Fires*, 253–55.

25. I follow here for the most part the account in O'Donnell, *Southern Indians*, which provides extensive documentation.

authorized five commissioners for the southern department. Congress appointed John Walker of Virginia and Willie Jones of North Carolina, to whom were added George Galphin and Edward Wilkinson of South Carolina and Robert Rae of Georgia.[26] The plans for parleys with the Indians to maintain their neutrality, however, were aggressively countered by the British Indian superintendent John Stuart, and in 1776 the Cherokees (acting against the advice of Stuart) took up arms against the colonists.

The resounding defeat of the Cherokees in this Cherokee War of 1776 by patriot forces from Virginia, the Carolinas, and Georgia had a lasting effect and substantially removed the threat of major Indian uprisings in the south. Negotiations for a formal treaty of peace after the patriot victory were initiated by Virginia, which appointed special commissioners to meet with Cherokee delegates to draw up a preliminary agreement. The initial discussions in April 1777 with the Overhill Cherokees dealt with declarations of peace, the return of prisoners, and the protection of the Indians' lands from white incursions. Meanwhile South Carolina and Georgia negotiated with other groups of Cherokees at DeWitt's Corner, South Carolina. In the treaty drawn up there with the Lower Cherokees on May 20, 1777, the Indians admitted their defeat, ceded their lands east of the Unicoi Mountains, and agreed to deliver up prisoners, both white and black. The states promised to provide trade goods and to keep whites east of the new boundary line. The hatchet was to be forever buried.[27]

Then, two months later, a formal council at Long Island of the Holston began between the Overhill Cherokees and four commissioners from North Carolina and three from Virginia. After some days of speeches from both sides, confirmed by strings of wampum, separate "Articles of a Treaty of Peace" were signed on July 20, 1777, between the Virginia and North Carolina delegates and the Cherokees. The

---

26. *JCC*, 2:192, 194. Congress delegated the nomination of the other three commissioners to the council of safety of South Carolina. The early work of these men is described in O'Donnell, *Southern Indians*, 23–28.

27. O'Donnell, *Southern Indians*, 34–58. There is a brief account of the proceedings with the Overhill Cherokees in Draper Manuscripts, 4 QQ 122–49 (microfilm edition, 1980), State Historical Society of Wisconsin. The treaty of DeWitt's Corner, with the commissions to the commissioners of North Carolina and of Virginia, is printed in *American State Papers: Public Lands*, 8 vols. (Washington: Gales and Seaton, 1832–61), 1:59–60. The treaty also appears in Archibald Henderson, ed., "The Treaty of Long Island of Holston, July, 1777," *North Carolina Historical Review* 8 (January 1931): 76–78.

treaties provided for the cessation of hostilities, return of prisoners, and cessions of land with new boundary lines. No whites were to be allowed to settle or graze cattle on the Indian lands, and whites residing in or passing through the Overhill towns were required to have a license.[28] At the same time George Galphin conferred with potentially hostile Creeks, hoping to maintain peace by promises of trade.[29]

But during much of the Revolutionary War, southern Indian affairs were in control of the British, who maintained their influence with the tribes, upon whose loyalty they depended. Indians were stirred up against the patriots, and sporadic raids and counterraids continued, including an invasion of Cherokee lands from Virginia in 1780. Then, as the patriot military cause succeeded in the area, the Indians lost their British support. By 1782 the Cherokees and Chickasaws sought to make peace with the Americans. Only the Creeks stood by the British, bolstered by the emergence of Alexander McGillivray as leader of the Creek confederation; but some dissident Creeks, importuned by Georgia, ceded lands in a treaty with the state at Augusta in 1783.[30]

The Continental Congress, acting for the united colonies, appeared to take little or no part in these southern affairs. No formal treaties negotiated and signed by special commissioners of the Congress appeared until after the Treaty of Paris in 1783.[31]

The Articles of Confederation

The action of the southern states in dealing with the Cherokees and Creeks during the Revolutionary War pointed up a persistent problem in treaty making in the early years of the new nation: Should treaties be made by the separate states, who inherited the

28. Henderson, "Treaty of Long Island of Holston," 103–5 (Virginia treaty); 107–10 (North Carolina treaty). The document includes the commissions from the governors of North Carolina and Virginia and a transcription of the speeches.

29. See O'Donnell, *Southern Indians*, 59–60, and citations given there.

30. See O'Donnell, *Southern Indians*, chaps. 4–6; Randolph C. Downes, "Creek-American Relations, 1782–1790," *Georgia Historical Quarterly* 21 (June 1937): 142–84.

31. There is no compilation of official minutes of these early councils. The Continental Congress received reports from the commissioners and from the special committees appointed from time to time to consider Indian affairs. The records that exist of descriptions of the ceremonies and transcripts of the speeches survived in private hands for the most part and were ferreted out in later times by diligent historians and antiquarians.

sovereignty of the British Crown and who were intimately concerned with the Indians on their borders, or was treaty making an exclusive power of the Continental Congress, representing the confederated states? It was a question of states' rights versus the central government, and it was not easily settled either in theory or in practice, although from the beginning (following late imperial practice) the decision moved toward central control of Indian affairs.

Benjamin Franklin's Albany Plan of Union of 1754 had provided that the president-general with the advice of the grand council should "hold or order all Indian Treaties, Regulate all Indian Trade, make Peace and Declare war with Indian Nations, [and] Make all Indian Purchases of Lands not within the Bounds of Perticular Colonies."[32] When Franklin in the Continental Congress drew up a draft for a confederation on July 21, 1775, he relied upon the Albany ideas. He offered two articles. First, no colony could engage in offensive war against the Indians without the consent of Congress, which would be the judge of the justice and necessity of the war. Second, a perpetual alliance, both offensive and defensive, should be made with the Six Nations. For them, as well as for all other tribes, boundaries should be drawn, their land protected against encroachments, and no purchases of land made except by contract drawn between the great council of the Indians and the Congress. Agents residing among the tribes would prevent injustices in the trade and provide for the "personal Wants and Distresses" of the Indians by occasional presents. The purchase of land from the Indians was to be "by Congress for the General Advantage and Benefit of the United Colonies."[33]

The committee appointed to draft the Articles of Confederation put the task into the hands of the able writer John Dickinson, a Pennsylvanian like Franklin and an advocate of congressional control of the western lands. His draft, submitted on July 12, 1776, elaborated Franklin's plan; in the general enumeration of powers granted the central government, Dickinson included "Regulating the Trade, and managing all Affairs with the Indians."[34]

This centralized control of Indian affairs did not appeal to all the

32. "Short Hints toward a Scheme for a General Union of the British Colonies on the Continent," drawn up by a committee of the Albany Congress, *The Papers of Benjamin Franklin*, ed. Leonard W. Labaree, 28 vols. to date (New Haven: Yale University Press, 1959—), 5:361–64; it is based on an earlier sketch of a union drawn up by Franklin, June 8, 1754, ibid., 335–38.

33. The 1775 draft is in *JCC*, 2:195–99.

34. *JCC*, 5:550.

states; South Carolina, for example, wanted to handle Indian affairs herself. But the overall necessities of controlling the Indians prevailed, for, as James Wilson pointed out, the Indians refused to recognize any superior authority, and only the United States in Congress assembled could hope to deal with them effectively. Above all else, rivalries between colonies in treating with the Indians had to be avoided.[35]

When Congress accepted an amended draft on August 20, the Franklin-Dickinson articles about alliance, maintaining boundaries, and purchase of the lands were omitted. Only a simple statement appeared: "The United States Assembled shall have the sole and exclusive right and power of . . . regulating the trade, and managing all affairs with the Indians, not members of any of the States."[36]

Even this did not satisfy the advocates of state control, who were jealous of individual state authority within their own territories, and corrective amendments were offered. Congress rejected two alternative amendments before agreeing to the provision that appeared in the ratified document. In its long enumeration of the powers of Congress, the Articles of Confederation declared: "The United States in Congress assembled shall also have the sole and exclusive right and power of . . . regulating the trade and managing all affairs with the Indians, not members of any of the States, provided that the legislative right of any State within its own limits be not infringed or violated."[37] The document was approved by Congress on November 15, 1777, but not ratified until March 1, 1781, because Maryland held out until the landed states agreed to transfer their western lands to the national government.

Thus the principle was enunciated that the management of Indian affairs and the regulation of Indian trade belonged to the federal government, but it was far from clear what was meant in practice by "Indians, not members of any of the States" or what would infringe or violate the legislative right of any state within its own boundaries. New York continued to deal with the Iroquois and the southern states with the Indians on their frontiers, each interpreting the Articles according to its own interests.

A second question, closely tied to state-versus-federal control of Indian affairs, was whether the Indian tribes were to be considered the same as foreign nations or whether they were primarily a domestic

35. Ibid., 6:1077–79. The debate is summarized in Mohr, *Federal Indian Relations*, 182–84.
36. *JCC*, 5:681–82.
37. Ibid., 9:845

issue? If they were "members of any of the States," they could hardly be considered foreign states, and "treaties" signed with them would be domestic conventions. If, however, the tribes transcended state authority and could be dealt with only by the national Congress, their status as international bodies would be considerably advanced. There was little consistency in the actions of European nations during the colonial period or of the states and the Continental Congress during the Revolutionary War. In some cases the Indians were described as dependent or subjects; at other times they were addressed in councils as allies.[38]

The situation becomes clearer, however, when one considers the sections of the Articles of Confederation and the practice of the Continental Congress concerning treaties with European nations. Procedures for dealing with established foreign nations were quite different from those for dealing with the Indian nations, although eventually the patterns of the former crept into those of the latter. Article VI of the Articles of Confederation declared: "No state without the Consent of the united states in congress assembled, shall send any embassy to, or receive any embassy from, or enter into any conference, agreement, or alliance or treaty with any King, prince, or state. . . . " Article IX provided: "The united states in congress assembled, shall have the sole and exclusive right and power of determining on peace and war . . .— of sending and receiving ambassadors—entering into treaties and alliances . . . "; in the case of imminent danger of an Indian invasion, however, war could be engaged in by a state. The provision in Article IX about the sole and exclusive right and power of the Congress to regulate trade and manage all affairs with the Indians was tucked away in a list of exclusive powers that included regulating the value of coins, fixing weights and measures, establishing post offices, and appointing officers of the army and navy—domestic questions all.

The Continental Congress during the Revolutionary War made elaborate preparations for treaties of alliance or commerce with European nations. A detailed "Plan of a Treaty" was drawn up, discussed, and amended in Congress, and specific instructions were issued to specially appointed agents.[39] For Indian councils, however, the commissioners for the several Indian departments were usually granted wide discretion

---

38. See Henry S. Manley, *The Treaty of Fort Stanwix, 1784* (Rome, New York: Rome Sentinel Company, 1932), 23–24; and James Duane to George Clinton, quoted ibid., 57–58.

39. See, for example, *JCC*, 5:431, 575–90, 709–10, 718, 768–79, 813–17, 827–28.

for inviting Indians to council and negotiating with them, and, except for the case of the Delawares in 1778, no formal documents resulted.

During the Revolutionary War, Indian affairs were considered and treated as a domestic (and largely military) matter, not a foreign (or diplomatic) question, and most of the documents refer to "Indian tribes within the limits of the United States." The Indian tribes were treated to some extent as independent but at the same time in some way subject to the United States because they were within its boundaries. Treaties with the Indians fell under the jurisdiction of the Board of War, those with foreign nations under that of the Committee on Foreign Affairs. At Indian treaties presents for distribution to the chiefs and warriors were a major concern, and it was the practice to provide military troops at or near the council grounds to overawe the Indians and to protect the commissioners of the United States, if necessary, from Indian attack. Expenses of the treaty—often considerable because of the large numbers of Indians attending—were borne solely by the United States or by the individual state.

When the war ended, the United States, still uncertain about the responsibilities of its new independent status, continued to rely upon this legacy of Indian relations from the colonial and revolutionary periods.

CHAPTER TWO

Treaties of Peace
after the Revolution

The Treaty of Paris of 1783, by which Great Britain recognized the independence of the colonies and their sovereignty over the western lands reaching to the Mississippi, made no mention of the Indians, who for the most part had sided with the British. The tribes, in effect, were deserted by their ally in war, and in their discouragement and disarray had to make peace separately with the new nation. The Indians did not think that they had been militarily defeated, but the United States looked upon itself as a conqueror and counted the Indians among the conquered.[1]

1. The treaties with the Indians after the Revolutionary War are discussed, among other accounts, in Walter H. Mohr, *Federal Indian Relations, 1774–1788* (Philadelphia: University of Pennsylvania Press, 1933), chaps. 3–5; Reginald Horsman, *Expansion and American Indian Policy, 1783–1812* (East Lansing: Michigan State University Press, 1967); Dorothy V. Jones, *License for Empire: Colonialism by Treaty in Early America* (Chicago: University of Chicago Press, 1982), chaps. 6 and 7; and Joyce G. Williams and Jill E. Farrelly, *Diplomacy on the Indiana-Ohio Frontier, 1783–1791* (Bloomington: Indiana University Bicentennial Committee, 1976). An excellent account of the Indian background on which treaties with the northwestern tribes rested can be found in Richard White, *The Middle Ground: Indians, Empires, and Republics in the Great Lakes Region, 1650–1815* (New York: Cambridge University Press, 1991).

Plans for Peace

The Congress under the Articles of Confederation acted quickly and responsibly to ensure peace. On May 1, 1783, it directed the secretary of war to inform the Indian nations that preliminary articles of peace had been agreed on and that hostilities had ceased with Great Britain. He was to tell the Indians that the British forts would soon be evacuated and to intimate to the Indians that the United States were "disposed to enter into friendly treaty with the different tribes." But unless hostile Indians stopped their attacks upon citizens of the states and accepted the offers of peace, Congress would take strong measures to compel them. Congress was concerned also about the steady encroachment onto Indian land by whites. A proclamation of September 22 forbade settlement on lands inhabited or claimed by the Indians outside of state jurisdiction and purchase or other receipt of such lands without the express authority and direction of Congress. It declared, moreover, that any such purchases or cessions were null and void.[2]

A report submitted on October 15 by a committee headed by James Duane of New York proposed a policy for dealing with the Indians of the northern and middle departments. The committee argued strongly against any action that would result in war, but it nevertheless proposed drawing proper boundary lines that would restrict the Indians enough so that lands would be available to fulfill pledges of land bounties made to soldiers during the war and to provide for expanding population. The committee spoke of the Indians as conquered nations, whose lands could be taken by right of conquest. And even if the right of conquest were waived, it said, the destruction wrought by Indians and the outrages and atrocities they had committed required atonement and a reasonable compensation for the expenses incurred by the United States.[3]

The committee proposed a general conference with the tribes in order

2. *JCC*, 24:264, 319–20; 25:602.
3. Ibid., 25:680–94. The committee relied heavily on the opinions and advice of George Washington, expressed in a letter to the committee head, James Duane, September 7, 1783, *The Writings of George Washington from the Original Manuscript Sources, 1745–1799*, ed. John C. Fitzpatrick, 39 vols. (Washington: GPO, 1931–44), 27:133–40. Much of the wording of the report is identical with that in Washington's letter. Washington, in turn, relied on a letter of General Philip Schuyler, July 29, 1783.

to receive them back into the favor and friendship of the United States and to determine the boundary lines that would divide the white settlements from the villages and hunting grounds of the Indians. The government commissioners, the committee said, should demand hostages for the return of all prisoners but should indicate at the same time the nation's preference for clemency instead of rigor in dealing with the defeated Indians. And the importance of the Indian trade was not forgotten; to prevent violence, fraud, and injustice toward the Indians, the trade must be regulated and the traders required to give security that they would follow the regulations.

The question of whether there should be just one general convention with the Indians or whether separate treaties should be sought from the different tribes was answered first one way and then another. Duane's committee favored a general treaty and would yield to separate conventions only "in case of inevitable necessity." But Congress on occasion had to fall back on separate councils and in fact signed two treaties with the Six Nations, three with western tribes, and three more with southern Indians.

The Treaty of Fort Stanwix

Congress began first in the north, hoping for a settlement with the Iroquois and the western tribes together. In February 1784 it directed General Philip Schuyler to send notice to the Indians that Congress was seeking a comprehensive treaty with them "as soon as the season and other necessary circumstances will permit" and that in the meantime, if they maintained peace, they could depend on the protection of the United States. On March 4 it elected five commissioners to negotiate with the western Indians as far south as the Cherokees. In what amounted to prior ratification of whatever treaties might be signed, Congress gave authority to any three of the commissioners (later reduced to two) to treat with the Indians and promised to hold valid and to carry out whatever might be agreed upon.[4]

4. *JCC*, 26:73–74, 123–24, 135–36. To equalize the commissioners among the states, Congress directed that one commissioner from each of the following groups of states be selected: New Hampshire, Massachusetts, and Rhode Island; Connecticut, New York, and New Jersey; Pennsylvania, Delaware, and Maryland; Virginia and North Carolina; and South Carolina and Georgia. The men first appointed were George Rogers

Meanwhile, a good deal of activity was taking place on the frontiers.[5] On January 11, 1784, General Schuyler met with tribal leaders at Schenectady and spoke strongly to them. He reminded them that they had not kept their promises of peace in 1776, but he added: "And yet Congress with a magnanimity and a generosity peculiar to a free people, are willing to forget the injuries and give peace to the Indians." He gave the Indians a copy of the peace treaty with Great Britain to convince them that the treaty contained no stipulations for the Indians. "They are not even so much as mentioned," he said of the Indians, "they are therefore left to settle matters with Congress." He added that the "conditions will be doubtless such as Congress have a right to insist upon and as the Indians out of regard to their future welfare ought to accept."[6]

The state of New York was making its own plans for treating with the Indians. In this regard, Governor Clinton in the summer of 1784 received advice from James Duane about interpreting the rights of Congress in Indian affairs under the Articles of Confederation. "If the Tribes are to be considered as *independent Nations*, detached from the State, and absolutely unconnected with it," Duane wrote, "the Claim of Congress would be uncontrovertible." On the other hand, the state could treat them as *"antient Dependants"* of New York. "On this Ground," Duane argued, "the Tribes in question may fall under the Character of *Members of the State* with the management of whom Congress hath no concern." He thought the Indians should be reconciled to that idea, and he urged careful consideration to the "Stile as well as the Substance" of the state's communications with them. To that end,

---

Clark, Oliver Wolcott, Nathaniel Greene, Richard Butler, and Stephen Higginson; late in April, Benjamin Lincoln and Arthur Lee were chosen to replace Greene and Higginson, who declined to serve. Ibid., 273–74, 282. A vivid, candid picture of the interstate rivalries that plagued the dealings with the Indians is given in a letter of Charles Thomson, secretary of Congress, to his wife, October 21, 1783, *Congress at Princeton: Being the Letters of Charles Thomson to Hannah Thomson, June-October 1783*, ed. Eugene R. Sheridan and John M. Murrin (Princeton: Princeton University Library, 1985), 82–83.

5. The fullest historical account of the activities leading up to the Treaty of Fort Stanwix and of the treaty itself is Henry S. Manley, *The Treaty of Fort Stanwix, 1784* (Rome, N.Y.: Rome Sentinel Company, 1932), which is based on extensive primary sources, both Canadian and American. For General Schuyler's work in the preliminary discussions, see also Don R. Gerlach, *Proud Patriot: Philip Schuyler and the War of Independence, 1775–1783* (Syracuse: Syracuse University Press, 1987), 504–6, 513–17.

6. Manley, *Treaty of Fort Stanwix*, 30–31, 34–35, quoting from Schuyler manuscripts in the New York Public Library. Schuyler was not appointed as an official commissioner for the formal negotiations.

he advised that the Indians should not be addressed as "nations," and he objected to the use of the word *treaty,* "which seems too much to imply Equality."[7]

At the end of August and in the early part of September 1784, the New York governor and three state commissioners met with representatives of the Six Nations at Fort Stanwix. The Indians listened to the commissioners, but in the end, influenced by the Mohawk leader Joseph Brant, they refused to deal with the state until they had met first with the commissioners of the thirteen states.[8] The western Indians, insisting that the negotiations be at Niagara, refused to go to Fort Stanwix to treat with Governor Clinton, and it was impossible to assemble them for a council with the United States so late in the season. The negotiations of the commissioners of Congress at Fort Stanwix were thus limited to the Six Nations, with only a few Shawnees as spectators.[9]

The council at Fort Stanwix in October was a dramatic encounter, with forceful statements on each side accompanied by the exchange of wampum strings and belts. The United States commissioners—Oliver Wolcott, Richard Butler, and Arthur Lee—issued a formal statement, which set forth their authority and asserted that the Indians should treat only with them. They recalled the error the tribes had made in going to war on the side of Great Britain and how they had in the end been abandoned. Peace, they noted, was necessary for the Indians and that it could be obtained by giving up their prisoners and by making an appropriate cession of land.[10]

The Indian reply was made by the Mohawk chief Aaron Hill, who adopted a strong and arrogant tone, speaking, he said, not only for the Six Nations "but also in the names of all the other tribes." He declared:

7. Duane's letter is printed in Franklin B. Hough, ed., *Proceedings of the Commissioners of Indian Affairs, Appointed by Law for the Extinguishment of Indian Titles in the State of New York,* 2 vols. (Albany: Joel Munsell, 1861), 1:21–24n. See also Manley, *Treaty of Fort Stanwix,* 57–58.

8. Manley, *Treaty of Fort Stanwix,* 68–72. The minutes of the meeting are printed in Hough, *Proceedings of the Commissioners of Indian Affairs,* 1:35–66.

9. Manley, *Treaty of Fort Stanwix,* 73–75.

10. The proceedings for the Treaty of Fort Stanwix are published in *The Olden Time; a Monthly Publication, Devoted to the Preservation of Documents and Other Authentic Information in Relation to the Early Explorations, and the Settlement and Improvement of the Country around the Head of the Ohio,* ed. Neville B. Craig (Pittsburgh, 1846 [vol. 1] and 1848 [vol. 2]; reprint, Millwood, N.Y.: Kraus Reprint Company, 1976). The commissioners' speech, prepared on October 11, is in 2:413–15. See Manley, *Treaty of Fort Stanwix,* 76–93, for an account of the negotiations with extensive quotations from the proceedings.

"We are free, and independent, and at present under no influence. We have hitherto been bound by the Great King, but he having broke the chain, and left us to ourselves, we are again free, and independent." In regard to the prisoners, he suggested that the commissioners themselves send a delegation back to the tribes to pick them up. The next day the Seneca half blood Cornplanter spoke. He excused the actions of the Indians in the war and then, with some hesitation, set forth a proposed boundary line, which, however, was about the same as that fixed at Fort Stanwix by the treaty in 1768.[11]

On October 20 the commissioners replied in a dictatorial speech, probably delivered by General Butler. Butler found it "extraordinary" that the Six Nations should speak for the western Indians, because only the Six Nations had been summoned to treat, and he asked for some authority, either in writing or in wampum belts, without which "your words will pass away like the winds of yesterday that are heard no more." He dismissed the claim that the Indians had merely been fulfilling their covenants with Great Britain in warring against the colonists. "Where was your sense of covenants," he asked, "when after solemnly covenanting with us in 1775, and again as solemnly in 1776, receiving our presents to cover you, to comfort, and to strengthen you—immediately you took up the hatchet against us, and struck us with all your might?" Then he rejected the claim to independence made by Hill: "It is not so. You are a subdued people; you have been overcome in a war which you entered into with us, not only without provocation, but in violation of most sacred obligations."[12]

On the questions of prisoners and of the boundary line, Butler declared that the Indians had not given "the smallest satisfaction." He asserted that only the Indians could collect and deliver up the prisoners and that they were obliged to do so. And he rejected the boundary line proposed by the Indians. "We shall now therefore," he concluded, "declare to you the condition, on which alone you can be received into the peace and protection of the United States." He then read to the Indians the four articles the commissioners had drawn up and commented briefly on each one.

1. The United States would retain six hostages, to be held until the prisoners were delivered.

11. *Olden Time*, 2:418–23.
12. Ibid., 423–25.

2. The Oneidas and Tuscaroras (who had sided with the colonists) would be secured in the possession of their lands.

3. A new boundary line would be drawn, by which the western limit of the Six Nations' lands was set roughly at a line running north and south from the eastern tip of Lake Erie. In commenting upon this article, the commissioners made explicit reference to the right of conquest: "The line proposed, leaves as extensive a country to the remaining four nations, as they can in reason desire, and more than, from their conduct in the war, they could expect. The King of Great Britain ceded to the United States *the whole*, by the right of conquest they might *claim the whole*. Yet they have taken but a small part, compared with their numbers and their wants. Their warriors must be provided for. Compensations must be made for the blood and treasures which they have expended in the war. The great increase of their people, renders more lands essential to their subsistence. It is therefore necessary that such a boundary line should be settled, as will make effectual provisions for these demands, and prevent any future cause of difference and dispute."

4. "In consideration of the present circumstances of the Six Nations, and in execution of the humane and liberal views of the United States," goods for the use and comfort of the Indians would be given upon the signing of the articles.[13]

At the end the Indians were told, "They are the terms on which you may obtain perpetual peace with the United States, and enjoy their protection. You must be sensible that these are blessings, which can not be purchased at too high a price. Be wise, and answer us accordingly." Cornplanter answered meekly: "You have this day declared your minds to us fully, and without disguise. We thank you for it; this is acting like men, for thus men speak. We will take what you have said into our most serious consideration, and when we shall have prepared ourselves to answer to what you have proposed, you shall hear our voice."[14]

On October 22 the treaty was signed by the cowed Indians exactly as it had been presented to them. Aaron Hill and five lesser chiefs were taken as hostages, to the great indignation of the Indians.[15]

13. Ibid., 425–27.
14. Ibid., 427.
15. Kappler, 2:5–6. Note that Aaron Hill did not sign the treaty. On the hostages, see Manley, *Treaty of Fort Stanwix*, 101–4.

Special claims of Pennsylvania were handled at Fort Stanwix immediately after the treaty with the United States. On October 23 Pennsylvania commissioners, who had attended the general treaty councils, got the agreement of the Six Nations to relinquish all their claims to land in Pennsylvania except for eight hundred acres on the Allegheny River reserved for Cornplanter and his heirs. In return Pennsylvania provided a large quantity of trade goods for the Indians.[16]

The Treaty of Fort Stanwix was not an auspicious beginning of treaty making by the independent United States. The United States used the procedural forms of treaty negotiations to force unilaterally upon the Indians the demands of the United States—in this case return of prisoners and, most important, land cessions. It did this under an umbrella of magnanimity; it spoke of giving peace to the tribes and of receiving them into the protection of the United States; and it delivered goods to the Indians "in consideration of their present circumstances" and to carry out its "humane and liberal views." But the blatant reliance on the principle of conquest set a bad tone, and in fact the claim of conquest later had to be abandoned.

The failure to include western Indians in the treaty gave substance to the Indians' claim that the treaty was invalid since it provided for land cessions without the approval of all the tribes. Nor did the preliminary action of New York in meeting with the Indians and the subsequent agreement of Pennsylvania with the Six Nations do anything to dispel the cloud of confusion about the precise line of jurisdiction between the United States and the individual states in treating with the Indians. After Fort Stanwix the state of New York, by numerous state treaties with the Six Nations, managed to acquire most of the Indian lands within New York.[17]

16. Manley, *Treaty of Fort Stanwix*, 95. Pennsylvania, unlike New York, acted with due deference to the Continental Congress. See *JCC*, 25:595, 717–18, 766–67.

17. Barbara Graymont, "New York State Indian Policy after the Revolution," *New York History* 57 (October 1976): 438–74, shows how New York continued to treat with the Indians within its borders, contrary to federal policy, and in the end largely stripped the Indians of their lands. She notes the provision in Article I of the Constitution that said that "no State shall enter into any Treaty, Alliance, or Confederation" and remarks, "These Constitutional provisions the State of New York blithely ignored throughout much of the remainder of the eighteenth century and the early years of the nineteenth century as it proceeded to make a multitude of treaties with the Six Nations or separately with their constituent nations" (p. 458). Of the 1790 trade and intercourse law, which forbade purchase of land from Indians without federal concurrence, she says, "This provision New York would ignore continually well on into the nineteenth century as it conducted Indian treaties" (p. 460).

Treaties with the Western Indians

The United States commissioners turned next to deal with the Wyandots and Delawares and with attending Ottawas, Chippewas, Munsees, and Senecas. At Fort McIntosh (on the Ohio below Pittsburgh at the mouth of the Beaver River) a treaty was signed on January 21, 1785, by "commissioners plenipotentiary" of the United States George Rogers Clark, Richard Butler, and Arthur Lee and by tribal representatives, including the Wyandot Half King (Daunghquat) and the Delaware Captain Pipe (Hobocan).[18]

The council and the treaty followed closely those at Fort Stanwix, exacting from the Indian signers present a cession of land that should have had the approval of the confederated northwest tribes. At the opening of the conference on January 8, 1785, the commissioners made it clear to the Indians present that they stood alone against the United States. They read the treaty of alliance with France, in which the French king had renounced all claims to lands within the United States, and the treaty of peace with Great Britain. "The King of Great Britain in his treaty with the U. States," they told the Indians, "has not stipulated any thing in favour of you & of the other Indian Nations who joined him in the war against us. You are therefore left to obtain peace from the U. States, & to be received under their government and protection, upon such conditions as seem proper to Congress, the Great Council of the U. States."[19]

The Indians pleaded to retain the lands on which they lived and which had been handed down to them by their fathers, but their pleas were brushed aside by the commissioners, who replied:

> You have been particular in describing to us the claim and title of each particular tribe. . . . The detail of these claims and title may appear to be of consequence among yourselves. But to us & to the business of the Council Fire to which we have called you, they have

18. I follow here the account in Randolph C. Downes, *Council Fires on the Upper Ohio: A Narrative of Indian Affairs in the Upper Ohio Valley until 1795* (Pittsburgh: University of Pittsburgh Press, 1940), 292–95. See also Williams and Farrelly, *Diplomacy on the Indiana-Ohio Frontier*, 14–16.

19. "Memorandum of the Proceedings at Treaty of Fort McIntosh," Timothy Pickering Papers, quoted in Downes, *Council Fires*, 293.

no relation; *because* we claim the country by conquest; and are to give not to receive. It is of this that it behooves you to have a clear and distinct comprehension.[20]

The treaty document, signed on January 21, 1785, described a boundary line between the Wyandot and Delaware Indians and the United States. Within the lines, the United States "allotted" the lands to those tribes and to Ottawas who lived there; outside the lines, the lands belonged to the United States, and the Indians were forbidden to settle on them. The first article of the treaty provided for hostages—one Wyandot chief and two Delaware chiefs—to be retained until prisoners were given up. In the second article the Indians acknowledged themselves and all their tribes "to be under the protection of the United States and of no other sovereign whatsoever." Other sections reserved lands for United States trading posts and military forts, withdrew American protection from whites who might settle on the Indian lands, and directed the handing over of Indians who committed robbery or murder against citizens of the United States. As at Fort Stanwix, the treaty provided for the distribution of goods to the Indians upon its being signed.[21]

The Treaty of Fort McIntosh reinforced the blustering attitudes that the United States had displayed at Fort Stanwix. Instead of assuring peace, the treaty increased the Indians' discontent and resentment and strengthened their desire to unite in defense of the Ohio River boundary. The British agent Alexander McKee wrote to Sir John Johnson on May 29, 1785, "The impolicy of exacting or enforcing such terms upon the Indians was visible by the disgust shown upon this occasion by all Nations."[22]

Congress still needed to deal with the more western tribes—the Shawnees, Miamis, Weas, Piankashaws, Potawatomis, Kickapoos, and others. To provide for them, it adopted a formal resolution for holding

20. Ibid., 294.
21. Kappler, 2:6–8. On the same day, following the official United States treaty, came a separate convention between the Wyandot and Delaware Indians and two commissioners of Pennsylvania, in which the Indians agreed to deed to the state "all that part of the said Commonwealth not yet purchased of the Indians" for the consideration of $2,000. The proceedings of the treaty with Pennsylvania are printed in Joseph H. Bausman, *History of Beaver County, Pennsylvania, and Its Centennial Celebration*, 2 vols. (New York: Knickerbocker Press, 1904), appendix IV-A, 2:1203–10.
22. Quoted in Downes, *Council Fires*, 295, from Draper Manuscripts, 23 U 17, 22, 23.

a treaty conference at Vincennes on the Wabash, gave specific authority to the commissioners, and instructed them to make the contemplated cession of land "as extensive and liberal as possible." The continuing hostility of the tribes, however, made it impossible for the commissioners to hold negotiations as far in the interior as Vincennes, and recognizing the obstacles, Congress directed that the council be held on the western bank of the Ohio, at the rapids or at the mouth of the Great Miami, and it provided for troops to be present at the negotiations.[23]

Again the United States failed in its hope of making a general treaty with the western confederacy, for many Indians opposed the partial treaties signed at Fort Stanwix and Fort McIntosh and rejected the invitations of the United States commissioners. Only the Shawnees arrived to treat at Fort Finney, which had been established at the mouth of the Miami. When the council began at the end of January 1786, the commissioners (George Rogers Clark, Richard Butler, and Samuel H. Parsons) presented the usual terms—recognition of United States sovereignty over the lands ceded by Great Britain, acceptance of the protection of the United States, surrender of hostages for the return of prisoners, relinquishment of claims to their lands east of the Miami River, and agreement to punish, under American law, crimes against whites in the Shawnee country. These exorbitant demands the Shawnee chief Kekewepellethe rejected outright:

> By what you have said to us yesterday, we expected every thing past would be forgotten; that our proposals for collecting the prisoners were satisfactory, and that we would have been placed on the same footing as before the war. To-day you demand hostages till your prisoners are returned. You next say you will divide the lands. I now tell you it is not the custom of the Shawnese to give hostages, our words are to be believed, when we say a thing we stand to it, we are Shawnese—and as to the lands, God gave us this country, we do not understand measuring out the lands, it is all ours. You say you have goods for our women and children; you may keep your goods, and give them to the other nations, we will have none of them. Brothers, you seem to grow proud, because you have thrown down the King of England; and as we feel sorry for our past faults, you rise in your demands on us. This we think hard.[24]

23. *JCC*, 28:172–74, 180–81, 431, 487.
24. A detailed account of the treaty council is given as part of General Richard Butler's

Such a tone only irritated the American commissioners. General Butler answered the Indians belligerently: "You have addressed us with great warmth. We think the answer unwise and ungrateful; and in return for just and generous proposals, you have not only given us improper language, but asserted the greatest falsehoods." He warned that the United States intended to hold firm to its conditions and that refusal of the terms would mean war. "The destruction of your women and children or their future happiness," he said, "depends on your present choice. Peace or war is in your power; make your choice like men, and judge for yourselves." The Indians were chastened and meekly agreed. "Brethren . . . ," Kekewepellethe said, "you have every thing in your power—you are great, and we see you own all the country; we therefore hope, as you have everything in your power, that you will take pity on our women and children. . . . and we agree to all you have proposed, and hope, in future, we shall both enjoy peace, and be secure."[25]

The treaty signed by Kekewepellethe and the other Shawnee chiefs on January 31, 1786, was more like a dictated peace treaty than the result of negotiations between two sovereign powers. It called for three hostages; the Shawnees acknowledged the United States to be "the sole and absolute sovereigns" of all the territory ceded to it by Great Britain; the United States granted peace to the Shawnee Nation and received the Indians into its friendship and protection and "allotted" lands to them within specified boundaries. Indian criminals against whites were to be delivered up for punishment, and whites illegally settling on the Indians' lands forfeited their government's protection.[26]

The treaty at the mouth of the Great Miami did no more to assure peace than had that at Fort McIntosh. The Shawnees had been intimidated into agreeing to its terms and felt justified in repudiating the treaty. Attacks and reprisals continued to mark the relations between the Shawnees and the Kentucky frontiersmen.

Even though the United States had failed to achieve its goals in the three treaties signed between October 1784 and January 1786 in the north, the nation acted as though the Indian cessions of much of Ohio

---

journal, published in *Olden Time*, 2:518–25, 529–31. Kekewepellethe's speech is on page 522.

25. *Olden Time*, 2:523–24 (Butler); 524 (Kekewepellethe). For a different version of the exchange, based on the journal of Major Ebenezer Denny, see Williams and Farrelly, *Diplomacy on the Indiana-Ohio Frontier*, 26, n. 74.

26. Kappler, 2:16–18. The treaty was entered in the *Journals* of Congress on April 17, 1786. *JCC*, 30:185–87.

were an accomplished fact and passed ordinances for surveying, selling, and governing the land. Yet the national government could not restrain the eager speculators and settlers who sought the lands still in Indian hands. After a tour of the West in 1784, George Washington had reported the extent of the menace. "Such is the rage for speculating in, and forestalling of Lands on the No. West side of the Ohio," he said, "that scarce a valuable spot within any tolerable distance of it, is left without a claimant. Men in these times talk with as much facility of fifty, a hundred, and even 500,000 Acres as a Gentleman formerly would do of 1000 acres. In defiance of the proclamation of Congress, they roam over the Country on the Indian side of the Ohio, mark out Lands, Survey, and even settle them. This gives great discontent to the Indians, and will unless measures are taken in time to prevent it, inevitably produce a war with the western Tribes."[27]

The United States, however, was not yet ready to go to war, and it began to soften the arrogant position of conquerors that had been behind the dictated treaties and which, it became increasingly clear, had not solved the problem of Indian hostility on the frontier nor guaranteed the peaceful expansion of white settlers. As an alternative to war it sought to better organize its trade and other relations with the Indians. In fact, on May 17, 1786, Congress disbanded the treaty commissions established in the previous year because "the future connection and intercourse with the several Indian nations, may, at less expence, be maintain'd by a proper organization of the Indian department."[28] Such action indicated that the Congress thought of treaties with the Indians as only *one* way of proceeding—and an expensive way. Its belief that it would be better to rely on a well-organized Indian department pointed up the fact that the Indians were considered chiefly a domestic matter.

After considerable attention to alternatives, Congress on August 7, 1786, enacted an Ordinance for the Regulation of Indian Affairs, which reasserted the sole and exclusive right of Congress to deal with Indian affairs. The ordinance provided for southern and northern districts with a superintendent in each to carry out the instructions of Congress and to report, through the secretary of war, to Congress. Special regulations requiring licenses and bonds were established to govern the trade with the Indians. In a set of instructions issued to the superintendents in February 1787, Congress recalled the republican principles of the new

27. Washington to Jacob Read, November 3, 1784, *Writings of George Washington*, ed. Fitzpatrick, 27:486.
28. *JCC*, 30:286–87, 397.

nation and sought to allay Indian resentment and hostility. "The United States are fixed in their determination," the instructions read in part, "that justice and public faith shall be the basis of all their transactions with the Indians. They will reject every temporary advantage obtained at the expence of these important national principles." Congress directed the superintendents to seek out the causes of Indian unrest and correct them as far as possible. Abuses irritating to the Indians could be checked by controlling the traders, and military commanders on the frontier were to be called upon to help enforce the ordinance.[29]

The Treaties of Fort Harmar

Although there still were cries from many for military action against the Indians, Secretary of War Henry Knox in July 1787 urged new treaties instead of military action. He spoke of the "strong principles of humanity which ever forbid a war for an object which may be obtained by peaceable and honorable means," and he argued that the nation was "utterly unable to maintain an Indian war with any dignity or prospect of success." Even if a war were successful, he noted, peace must ultimately be accomplished by a treaty with the Indians. Knox did not want the United States to seem to prefer war to peace and thus arouse "the verdict of mankind" against it, for, he shrewdly noted, "men are ever ready to espouse the cause of those who appear to be oppressed provided their interference may cost them nothing." A warlike attitude on the part of the United States would stain its reputation, and Knox wanted to follow the British custom of paying for the lands ceded by the Indians rather than take them by right of conquest. The British, he said, "thought a treaty and purchase money for land, was the most prudent measure and in no degree dishonorable to the nation." He realized that in a new treaty with the northern tribes the boundaries fixed in the original treaties might have to be discussed again and payment made for the cessions. On July 21 Congress officially resolved to pursue a treaty with the Indians to be held at Vincennes.[30]

A report in August 1787 from the Committee on Indian Affairs in the Northern Department showed a considerable softening of Con-

29. Ibid., 31:490–93; 32:66–69.
30. Ibid., 33:388–91.

gress's views about Indian relations. The committee saw that either a war or a treaty to adjust difficulties had to occur soon; it opted for a treaty, but it recommended a change in treaty practice. Instead of holding frequent and separate treaties with the various tribes—"which can have no permanent effect upon the temper of the Indians, or tendency to produce a general acquiescence in them to the cessions made of any of their lands"—the committee wanted general treaties with chiefs of many tribes at the same treaty, for such treaties would not only be able to adjust all issues relative to the same subject but would be less frequent and less expensive. It wanted to give durable gifts to the chiefs instead of lavishing presents upon all kinds of Indians, and it admonished: "Instead of a language of superiority and command; may it not be politic and Just to treat with the Indians more on a footing of equality, convince them of the Justice and humanity as well as power of the United States and of their disposition to promote the happiness of the Indians." Finally it recommended the "principle of fairly purchasing" the Indian lands.[31]

In October 1787 Congress directed the governor of the Northwest Territory, Arthur St. Clair, to hold a general treaty with the Indians north of the Ohio. But the instructions drawn up on October 26 showed the ambivalence of the lawmakers.[32] The governor was to remove "all causes of controversy, so that peace and harmony may continue between the United States and the Indian tribes," to regulate trade, and to settle boundaries. The boundary line to be proposed was an extension to the Mississippi of the east-west line stipulated in the land ordinance of 1785—a line that began where the Ohio crossed the western boundary of Pennsylvania and considerably north of the rest of the Ohio River, which the Indians wanted to be the boundary.[33] These were incompatible ends, for the boundary line specified was precisely what was rejected by the Indians, still supported in their claims by the British, who retained the northwest forts on United States soil.

So the matter dragged on. Congress appropriated considerable sums of money for the treaty and modified some of its instructions to St.

31. Ibid., 477–80.
32. Ibid., 611–12, 666, 696. The instructions are printed in *Terr. Papers*, 2:78–79. They are also in *JCC*, 33:711–12.
33. St. Clair was instructed to act if possible in conjunction with the superintendent of Indian affairs for the northern department, Richard Butler. By the time the treaty was finally negotiated, the office of superintendent had been combined with that of governor of the Northwest Territory, so St. Clair became the sole commissioner. Butler, whose relations with St. Clair were sometimes strained, signed the treaty as a witness.

Clair, directing him on July 2 to fix the boundary even farther to the north at the forty-first parallel rather than at the line stipulated in his original instructions.[34] St. Clair, to his credit, objected to the boundary lines proposed by Congress. Even the first line, he wrote to Secretary Knox in July 1788, would not be agreed to without much difficulty, for the land to be thus acquired contained the principal hunting grounds of the Indians and was the home of some tribes not well disposed toward the United States. To extend the boundary to the forty-first parallel he thought completely out of the question. The Indians would not give up the lands for any sum that the United States could afford to offer. If, by chance, the Indians did sign a treaty with such boundary stipulations, they would never consider themselves bound by it, "so that instead of establishing a solid and permanent peace, a foundation may probably be laid for irreconcilable hatred and wasting Wars and the money be thrown away into the Bargain."[35]

St. Clair was unable to get any Indians to appear for a treaty until the final days of 1788, when Iroquois, Wyandots, Delawares, Ottawas, Chippewas, Potawatomis, and Sacs came to Fort Harmar, a fort that had been established in 1785 at the mouth of the Muskingum River (present-day Marietta, Ohio).

Despite Knox's strong advice and the changed tone in Congress's deliberations about dealing with the northwest Indians, the council at Fort Harmar was little more than a repetition of those of the earlier treaties. St. Clair discovered that the Indians were not united, and he brushed aside their renewed proposal of the Ohio boundary; the Indians' willingness to settle for the Muskingum River as the western line of white settlement was ignored. Irritated by Indian resistance, St. Clair on January 6 assumed some of the air of superiority that had marked the earlier treaty negotiations.

The United States would have been justified to all the World to have Marched their Armies into Your Country and punished you in an exemplary manner, but they Chose to give an example of Clemency. They considered that the War had Spread Misery enough over many country's and were desirous to prevent its Spreading wider. They offered You peace upon the Condition of Surrendering a Part of Your Country. You accepted it upon that condition, and a boundary was Established [at the treaties of Fort McIntosh and the mouth of the

34. *JCC*, 34:286–87; additional instructions to Governor St. Clair, July 2, 1788, in *Terr. Papers*, 2:117–18.
35. St. Clair to the secretary of war, July 16, 1788, *Terr. Papers*, 2:130–32.

Great Miami]. . . . If there were ever engagements that Should be binding upon Mankind, they were these, for the U. States, not only buried the remembrance of past injuries but made a generous division of the Ceded Country, with You and made you very valuable Presents of Goods besides.

St. Clair told the Indians they could have either peace or war. If they would renew and confirm the boundary set at Fort McIntosh, he would insert in the treaty a provision allowing them to hunt on the land they had ceded and make a payment in goods. He did not have the nerve to propose the boundary lines set forth in his instructions from Congress.[36]

The Indians were not prepared to stand up to St. Clair, and two treaties were signed at Fort Harmar on January 9, 1789. The first, with the Wyandots and other western tribes present, reconfirmed the Fort McIntosh boundary line, and for the ceded lands the United States now agreed to pay goods worth $6,000. The new treaty was considerably longer than the one it confirmed. There were renewed provisions for hostages, for trading posts and military forts, and a renewal of peace and friendship, but there was in addition an amplification of provisions to ease the contacts between the Indians and the whites. The treaty specified punishment for crimes committed, established punishment for stealing horses (by either side) and demanded return of the stolen animals, set up regulations for opening trade with the Indians, sought to forestall Indian hostilities, and restricted white settlements.[37]

The second treaty was with the representatives of the Six Nations (excluding the Mohawks, who did not come). It repeated the Treaty of Fort Stanwix of 1784 and confirmed the boundary line "in consideration of the peace then granted to them, the presents they then received, as well as in consideration of a quantity of goods, to the value of three thousand dollars, now delivered to them by . . . Arthur St. Clair."[38]

Not until May 2 did Governor St. Clair forward the treaties to President Washington (who had been inaugurated on April 30, 1789),

36. The Fort Harmar council proceedings are in Draper Manuscripts, 23 U 75–142 (microfilm edition, 1980), State Historical Society of Wisconsin. Quotations are from 134–35.

37. Kappler, 2:18–23. For questions about the authenticity of the "separate article" appended to both this treaty and the one with the Six Nations, dealing with punishment of Indians who committed robbery or murder against whites, see *Terr. Papers*, 2:181n. The treaty was signed in duplicate, one copy for the United States and one for the Indians. St. Clair presented belts of wampum to the Indians and promised that new belts would be forwarded to them in the spring. Draper Manuscripts, 23 U 141–43.

38. Kappler, 2:23–25.

pleading in justification of the long delay his own indisposition and the severity of the winter, which had made communication impracticable. He explained the impossibility of setting the northern boundary at the forty-first parallel (as he had been directed by Congress), for any efforts to extend the limits of the previous cession would have been "very ill received" and might have defeated entirely the treaty of peace. "The negotiation," he told Washington, "was both tedious and troublesome, and, for a long time, had an unpromising aspect, but it came, at last, to as favorable an issue as could have been expected." But he noted that several Indian tribes along the Wabash, who had not come to Fort Harmar, were still ill-disposed and likely to make trouble. The two separate treaties, with the Six Nations and the more western Indians, he explained, had been signed because there was "a jealousy that subsisted between them, which I was not willing to lessen by appearing to consider them as one people." St. Clair was persuaded that the Indians' general confederacy was entirely broken, and he thought "it would not be very difficult, if circumstances required it, to set them at deadly variance."[39]

On January 18, shortly after the signing of the treaties, St. Clair had written to Knox that the Indians "seem to be very well satisfied, and if they are not sincere in their professions, they know very well how to put on the appearance of it," but in fact the treaties accomplished no more than had the previous ones. St. Clair had not carried out his instructions, for there was no "general treaty," and he had not even been able to broach the subject of extending the earlier cessions. Although he had spoken boldly to the Indians, he had not overly impressed them. They resented all the treaties, including the ones just signed at Fort Harmar, and Indian hostilities along the western frontiers of settlement continued. Not until the Ohio Indians were roundly defeated by Anthony Wayne in 1794 did they give up claim to the ceded lands.[40]

39. St. Clair to the president, May 2, 1789, *The St. Clair Papers: The Life and Public Services of Arthur St. Clair*, ed. William Henry Smith, 2 vols. (Cincinnati, 1882; reprint, New York: Da Capo Press, 1971), 2:111–13. The ratification and proclamation instruments for the treaty with the western tribes are printed in *Terr. Papers*, 2:219–20. The treaty with the Six Nations was never approved by the Senate or proclaimed by the president, and only belatedly was it added to the official collection of Indian treaties. See *Terr. Papers*, 2:183n.

40. St. Clair to secretary of war, January 18, 1789, *St. Clair Papers*, 2:108–9. Charles C. Royce, in his authoritative book on Indian land cessions, remarks that the treaties of Fort McIntosh, the mouth of the Great Miami, and Fort Harmar were never carried into effect because of Indian hostility and were ultimately superseded by the treaty of August 3, 1795, at Greenville, and he does not show the cessions stipulated by the three treaties

The Treaties at Hopewell

In the south, the difficulties in dealing with the Indians after the Revolutionary War were, if anything, even greater than in the north. It was not clear how far the authority of Congress extended, because the states of Virginia, North Carolina, South Carolina, and Georgia aggressively pushed their own interests; they strove to satisfy the demands of their citizens for more land and were imbued with a strong sense of their state sovereignty. This continual clash between the states and Congress seriously weakened the possibilities for firm action on the part of the national government. In the south, moreover, the four principal Indian nations—Cherokee, Creek, Choctaw, and Chickasaw—had organized governments and astute leaders, who put forth their rights to land and who could field sizable military forces. Added to these complications was the presence of the Spanish, who had regained Florida in the peace of 1783 and who sought to promote their interests by diplomatic connections with the Indian nations. The Spanish signed treaties with the Creeks, Choctaws, and Chickasaws in the summer of 1784, and these Indians submitted to Spanish protection and trading dominance. The Indians, especially the Creeks, continued to play the Spanish against the Americans in their diplomatic game.[41]

Congress moved slowly in extending its treaty policy to the south. A committee appointed to consider southern Indian affairs returned a report in May 1784, which argued that Congress should have exclusive control of Indian affairs, and which otherwise offered proposals about the same as those put forth in October 1783 for the northern and middle departments. Opposition to centralized control from southern delegates and the fear that excessive land cessions from the southern Indians would benefit land speculators caused continuing delay, and

on his detailed maps of land cessions. Royce, *Cessions*, 649, 651. See also White, *Middle Ground*, chap. 10. White describes the politics of the Indians' confederations and shows why the Indians did not present a united front to the Americans.

41. A good brief discussion of Indian affairs in the south is Kenneth Coleman, "Federal Indian Relations in the South, 1781–1789," *Chronicles of Oklahoma* 35 (Winter 1957–58): 435–58. See also the detailed account in Mohr, *Federal Indian Relations*, 139–72.

Congress adjourned in June 1784 without attending to the southern problems.[42]

The delegates met again in November, but it was not until March 15, 1785, that Congress adopted a report about dealing with the southern Indians. The report asked for the appointment of commissioners "to form a treaty or treaties with the Indians in the southern department, for the purpose of making peace with them, receiving them into the favor of the United States, and ascertaining the boundary lines by which the settlements of the citizens of the United States are or ought to be separated and divided from the Indian villages and hunting grounds; and thereby if possible extinguishing animosity, and preventing in future any contention or disquiet." It contained a number of specific instructions for commissioners concerning prisoners, notice to the Indians that they were now at the mercy of the United States (which, the report stated, nevertheless intended to treat them kindly), investigation of the boundaries of lands already ceded, notice to the states of times and places of meetings, restriction of settlement on Indian lands, and agents for the tribes.[43]

Congress chose five commissioners, any three of whom were empowered to treat: Benjamin Hawkins, Andrew Pickens, Joseph Martin, Lachlan McIntosh, and William Peery (although Peery never attended any council sessions).

Negotiations with the Creeks were scheduled for Galphinton on the Ogeechee River in Georgia, but when the commissioners arrived there on October 24, they found Indians from only two of the one hundred towns and refused to treat with such a small number, suspecting that others had not appeared because of the intrigues of the Spanish and the influence of Alexander McGillivray, the shrewd mixed blood who had risen to top leadership among the Creeks. They explained their mission and gave presents to those on hand and then departed. Commissioners of Georgia, who visited the United States commissioners, protested the projected treaty, and after the latter had left, signed a treaty of their own with the Indians for a cession of land (the Treaty of Galphinton).[44]

The four federal commissioners arrived at Hopewell (the plantation of Andrew Pickens on the Keowee River in northwestern South Carolina) on November 17 and on November 21 began negotiations with

42. *JCC*, 27:398, 453–64, 550–51.

43. Ibid., 28:118–20, 126–39, 159–62.

44. The commissioners reported this information to Charles Thomson, secretary of Congress, on November 17 and again on December 30, 1785. *ASPIA*, 1:16, 49.

the Cherokees. North Carolina and Georgia had representatives on hand, but they took no active part.

In an opening statement the commissioners reminded the Indians that they had sided with Great Britain in the war, that the king had been defeated and compelled to withdraw, and that Congress was now the sovereign of the whole country. But the tone was conciliatory, and the commissioners, noting the "humane and generous" policy of the United States, expressed a desire to promote the happiness of the Indians, "regardless of any distinction of color, or of any difference in our customs, our manners, or particular situation." There was no mistaking the reply of the Indians, who insisted on the boundary line established in 1777 and who wanted the whites removed who had settled across that line. "Are Congress, who conquered the King of Great Britain," asked The Tassel, "unable to remove these people?" The commissioners countered that many of the intruders had been there a long time, that they were numerous, and that it was impossible to remove them. After some days of forthright give and take, the commissioners drew up the treaty with the boundary lines stipulated. The treaty was "read, and interpreted to them [the Indians] with great attention, so that they agreed that they perfectly understood every article, and would with pleasure unanimously sign the same." On November 28, 1785, two copies were signed, one for the Cherokees, the other for the United States. The next day presents worth $1,200 were delivered for the 918 Indians at the council.[45]

This treaty, like those in the north, contained more than provisions for boundary lines. It spoke of the United States giving peace to the Cherokees and receiving them under its protection, and the Indians acknowledged themselves "to be under the protection of the United States of America, and of no other sovereign whosoever." The boundary line was "allotted to the Cherokees for their hunting grounds." Both sides agreed to restore prisoners, and whites intruding on Indian lands would forfeit the protection of the United States if they did not leave within six months of the ratification of the treaty.

Two articles dealt with trade. One read: "For the benefit and comfort of the Indians, and for the prevention of injuries or oppression on the part of the citizens or Indians, the United States in Congress assembled shall have the sole and exclusive right of regulating the trade with the

45. The minutes of the council are in *ASPIA*, 1:40–43. The treaty is in Kappler, 2:8–11.

Indians, and managing all their affairs in such manner as they think proper" (an echo of Article IX of the Articles of Confederation); in the other, all citizens of the United States were authorized to trade with the Cherokees until Congress decided otherwise.

Another article, about which there was no indication in the minutes of the council and which was never acted upon, gave the Indians "the right to send a deputy of their choice, whenever they think fit, to Congress." This was an indication that, whatever the language in the negotiations, the tribe was considered a domestic, not a foreign nation.

The land provisions of the treaty were in general accord with the existing situation and by no means satisfied white speculators and eager settlers. Nor was the "sole and exclusive right of Congress" in Indian affairs clearly vindicated. Before the treaty document was presented for the Indians' agreement, William Blount (attending the council as an agent of North Carolina) issued a formal protest to the commissioners against the treaty, "as containing several stipulations which infringe and violate the legislative rights of the State" (another echo of Article IX). The commissioners replied bluntly: "We are certain that a steady adherence to the treaty alone, can ensure confidence in the justice of Congress, and remove all causes of future contention or quarrels. The local policy of some States is certainly much opposed to federal measures, which can only, in our opinion, make us respectable abroad and happy at home."[46]

The United States commissioners, not expecting to see the Choctaws or Chickasaws, were preparing to adjourn when word came that the Choctaws were on their way, having been delayed by Creek attempts to prevent them and by the theft of their horses. They arrived without needed clothing and provisions—"the whole of them almost naked"—and had to be cared for before the negotiations could begin. The council got under way at the end of December, and a treaty was signed on January 3, 1786, which set the boundary of Choctaw lands where it had been on November 29, 1782, the day before the signing of the preliminary peace with Great Britain. Otherwise the treaty was very similar to that with the Cherokees, although no mention was made of a delegate to Congress.[47]

46. Both the protest and the response, dated November 28, 1785, are in *ASPIA*, 1:44. The commissioners reported that they had also received a protest from the commissioners of Georgia who were at the council. Benjamin Hawkins and Andrew Pickens to Charles Thomson, December 30, 1785, ibid., 49.

47. Hawkins, Pickens, and Martin to Thomson, December 30, 1785, and the same

Meanwhile the Chickasaw delegation arrived, and negotiations began at once with them. The commissioners, who reported that in the negotiations they paid "particular attention to the rights and interests of the United States . . . regardless of the protests of the adjoining States against us," gave their set speech about the change in sovereignty that came with Great Britain's defeat and about the humanity and generosity of the United States. They presented a draft of a treaty, and the Indians examined and discussed it. On January 10 "the treaty was then read over again, and every article explained with great attention, and the Indians acquiesced with them"; and the treaty was signed. It was very much like those with the Cherokees and with the Choctaws. Two days later presents were given to the Indians. As before, William Blount submitted a protest against the treaty for North Carolina.[48]

On April 17 the treaties were entered into the *Journals* of Congress, an act that was intended to signify ratification.[49] The three treaties themselves referred to "commissioners plenipotentiary" of the United States, and at the end of each was the statement that the commissioners "by virtue of our full powers, have signed the definitive treaty, and have caused our seals to be herewith affixed."

The matter of settlement with the obstreperous Creeks was left hanging. The years 1786 to 1790 were full of trouble between the Creeks and Georgia, which wanted no federal interference in its interests but at the same time looked to the federal Congress for protection. Georgia signed a new treaty at Shoulderbone in November 1786 with a few Creek chiefs, confirming the cessions made to the state earlier, and McGillivray insisted again that the Indian signers did not represent the Creek Nation.[50]

Congress was aware that the treaties were not well received by North Carolina and Georgia and that the boundary provisions were not observed by white citizens. Henry Knox in July 1787 reported to

---

to John Hancock, January 4, 1786, ibid., 1:49–50. McIntosh had departed Hopewell before word of the approach of the Choctaws and could not be recalled in time for the treaty. The minutes of the council are in Draper Manuscripts 14 U 56–92. The treaty is in Kappler, 2:11–14.

48. Hawkins, Pickens, and Martin report, January 4, 1786, *ASPIA*, 1:50. The minutes of the council appear ibid., 50–53. The treaty is in Kappler, 2:14–16.

49. *JCC*, 30:185.

50. There is a discussion of Creek-American relations in Coleman, "Federal Indian Relations in the South," 447–58. See also the older article, Randolph C. Downes, "Creek-American Relations, 1782–1790," *Georgia Historical Quarterly* 21 (June 1937): 142–84.

Congress on the southern situation and pointed to the weakness of Article IX, wondering about Congress's power to deal with the Creeks within Georgia. The article, he thought, was "perhaps, too inexplicit to be applied as a remedy," because the Indians seemed to be members of the state, and the same held true for North Carolina. He recommended that the states cede their western territories to the United States, so that Congress could then manage the land and its Indian inhabitants.[51]

A special committee (to which were referred Knox's report as well as a plea from Georgia delegates for help in case of a war with the Creeks), on August 3, 1787, delivered a ringing rebuke to the southern states and demanded that Congress give serious attention to the repeated complaints of the Indians about encroachments upon their lands, "as well because they [the encroachments] may be unjustifiable as on account of their tendency to produce all the evils of a general Indian war on the frontiers." Its strongest statement came in support of federal control of Indian affairs:

> The committee conceive that it has been long the opinion of the country, supported by Justice and humanity, that the Indians have just claims to all lands occupied by and not fairly purchased from them; and that in managing affairs with them, the principal objects have been those of making war and peace, purchasing certain tracts of their lands, fixing the boundaries between them and our people, and preventing the latter settling on lands left in possession of the former. The powers necessary to these objects appear to the committee to be indivisible, and that the parties to the confederation must have intended to give them entire to the Union, or to have given them entire to the State; these powers before the revolution were possessed by the King, and exercised by him nor did they interfere with the legislative right of the colony within its limits. ... It cannot be supposed, the state has the power mentioned without making the recited clause [in the Articles of Confederation] useless, and without absurdity in theory as well as in practice.[52]

Still the encroachments continued. Knox reported to Congress in July 1788 the unprovoked and direct outrages against the Cherokee Indians by the inhabitants on the frontiers of North Carolina in open violation of the Treaty of Hopewell. The outrages were of such extent, Knox declared, "as to amount to an actual although informal war," and

51. Knox report of July 18, 1787, *JCC*, 32:365–69.
52. *JCC*, 33:455–62.

he urged Congress to take action to uphold the treaty provisions and thus the reputation and dignity of the Union. Congress, at Knox's behest, issued a proclamation on September 1, which cited the provisions of the Treaty of Hopewell and the boundary lines it provided and which ordered the intrusions and outrages to cease. It directed the secretary of war to have troops ready to disperse the intruders.[53]

That Knox and Congress were not sure of their ground is shown by the deference they both paid to the state of North Carolina. Knox stated in his report his assumption that North Carolina would place no obstruction in the way of federal action, but he recommended nevertheless that a special request of concurrence be made of the state. Congress sent special copies of the proclamation to the executives of North Carolina and Virginia, asking their cooperation.

As the days of the Confederation came to a close, it was clear that Congress in its treaty making with the Indians had not had substantial success. The treaties made with the Indians in the north had been largely repudiated by the Indians, and those in the south Congress found impossible to enforce against citizens of the states.

It was not a good foundation for subsequent treaty making, but at least the problems had been pointed up and some patterns developed that persisted—for good or for bad—into the new era. For one thing, there was no turning back from the policy of dealing with the Indian tribes through formal treaties. Consideration of the Indians as "nations" not as members of the states seemed essential if congressional authority was to prevail over that of states like New York, North Carolina, and Georgia. Knox made the position clear in a report shortly after the inauguration of the new government under the Constitution: "The independent nations and tribes of Indians ought to be considered as foreign nations, not as subjects of any particular State. Each individual State, indeed, will retain the right of pre-emption of all lands within its limits, which will not be abridged; but the general sovereignty must possess the right of making all treaties, on the execution or violation of which depend peace and war."[54]

Yet, despite the expediency of considering the Indians "foreign nations," treaty making was the white man's device, not the Indian's.

53. Ibid., 34:342–44, 476–79. A committee of Congress on July 30, 1788, made a similar plea because of continuing violations of the Treaty of Hopewell with the Cherokees, urging Congress to "enforce a due observance of the said treaty." Ibid., 34:369–71.

54. Henry Knox to the president, July 7, 1789, *ASPIA*, 1:53.

Indians were called or invited to a treaty council by white government officials or agents. Even though the whites adopted Indian protocol at the early councils, as time passed the procedures became more clearly white-driven. The white agents started the proceedings, drew up the treaty drafts, explained them (through interpreters) to the Indians. They also provided food for the Indians attending (often in large numbers) and clothing when it was required, and they presented gifts at the conclusion of the deliberations. There were exchanges of strings and belts of wampum in the early treaties, but the giving of gifts and goods was not reciprocal. And the Indians agreed to a considerable diminution of their autonomy when they accepted peace given by the United States, agreed to be under its protection, and acquiesced in the treaty provisions that Congress would have "the sole and exclusive right of regulating the trade with the Indians, and managing all their affairs in such manner as they think proper."

CHAPTER THREE

Treaty-Making Procedures under the Constitution

The rough edges in treaty making with the Indians were smoothed out when the Constitution replaced the Articles of Confederation. The uncertainty about which Indians would attend the councils and whom they represented, the indecision between "treaties" as councils for discussion and "treaties" as formal written covenants, the lack of clarity about how far the powers of the Continental Congress reached, and the opportunity that such confusion gave to states to act independently of Congress in Indian affairs disappeared to a large extent. The provisions in the Constitution about trade and about treaty making vindicated centralized control, and the new government, with its stronger executive, could hope to make the provisions effective. George Washington worked out in practice what the constitutional provisions for senatorial advice and consent meant, and his decision to consider Indian treaties on a par with foreign treaties formalized Indian treaty making and provided an important means for the United States to manage Indian relations. Not all the problems were resolved, of course, and the basic anomaly of dealing by treaty with groups of limited autonomy within the territorial jurisdiction of the United States never went away, but in the first decade under the Constitution regularization of the process and continuing dependence upon treaties to carry out federal Indian policy set a pattern for future decades.

The Constitutional Convention

In spite of the ambiguity in the Articles of Confederation about federal or state management of Indian affairs, very little attention was paid to the issue in the Constitutional Convention, and there was no extensive statement about Indians in the Constitution itself. The lack of prolonged debate on the question was a sign of agreement within the convention that Indian affairs should be left in the hands of the federal government.

Since the Constitutional Convention had been called to consider weaknesses in the Articles, the question of federal authority over Indian affairs, of course, did find some place in the discussion. James Madison well understood the problem, and when the Committee of the Whole discussed the Paterson plan on June 19, he asked, "Will it prevent encroachments on the federal authority? A tendency to such encroachments has been sufficiently exemplified among ourselves, as well [as] in every other confederated republic antient and Modern." His first example was the following: "By the federal articles, transactions with the Indians appertain to Congs. Yet in several instances, the States have entered into treaties & wars with them."[1] When the draft of the Committee on Detail submitted on August 6 said nothing about Indians in its listing of the powers of the legislature, Madison on August 18 proposed adding to the list of such powers: "To regulate affairs with the Indians as well within as without the limits of the United States." The proposal was referred to the Committee on Detail.[2]

This broad grant, touching internal state affairs as well as affairs beyond the territory of the states, was cut down by the committee, which merely added to the clause granting Congress the power "to

1. Max Farrand, ed., *The Records of the Federal Convention of 1787*, rev. ed., 4 vols. (New Haven: Yale University Press, 1937), 1:316. Madison had Georgia specifically in mind. In his journal after the word "States" he had entered and then crossed out "in question Georgia." And in his rough "Preface to Debates in the Convention of 1787," in writing about disregard of the authority of the Confederacy, he said: "In other cases the Fedl authy was violated by Treaties & wars with Indians, as by Geo." Ibid., 3:548. Robert Yates reported Madison as saying, "Has not Georgia, in direct violation of the confederation made war with the Indians, and concluded treaties," and Rufus King gave a similar report. Ibid., 1:326, 330.
2. Ibid., 2:181–82, 321, 324.

regulate commerce with foreign nations, and among the several States" the words "and with Indians, within the Limits of any State, not subject to the laws thereof." Then on September 4 the Committee of Eleven reduced the clause still further to the simple five-word phrase "and with the Indian tribes." The convention agreed to this wording on the same day without debate.[3]

The convention in its long deliberations over the treaty-making power did not mention Indian treaties specifically, but the power of states to make any treaties was repeatedly denied. As a further protection against state usurpation, the convention declared federal laws and treaties superior to those of the states. The Paterson plan on June 15 offered a detailed proposal to make federal laws and treaties superior to state laws and to authorize the central government to use force to compel obedience. There was considerable discussion on the matter. Madison considered "the negative on the laws of the States as essential to the efficacy & security of the Genl. Govt," because the "necessity of a general Govt. proceeds from the propensity of the States to pursue their particular interests in opposition to the general interest." He insisted that the power to overrule laws of the states was "the most mild & certain means of preserving the harmony of the system." The Committee on Detail on August 6 reported the provision from the Paterson plan as it stood, except that it omitted the section authorizing forceful execution of the laws or treaties. A small amendment was made on August 23, and on August 25 action was taken "to obviate all doubt concerning the force of treaties preexisting," by inserting after "all treaties made" the words "or which shall be made," so that the first phrase would refer to past treaties and the inserted words to future treaties. In the final version, the Constitution included this statement in Article VI: "This Constitution, and the Laws of the United States which shall be made in Pursuance thereof; and all Treaties made, or which shall be made, under the Authority of the United States, shall be the supreme Law of the Land; and the Judges in every State shall be bound thereby, any Thing in the Constitution or Laws of any State to the Contrary notwithstanding."[4]

3. Ibid., 2:367, 493, 495, 497, 499.
4. Ibid., 1:245; 2:27–28, 132, 183, 417, 663. George Mason objected to the provision, in words that foreshadowed the debates over treaty making in 1871: "By declaring all treaties supreme laws of the land, the Executive and the Senate have, in many cases, an exclusive power of legislation; which might have been avoided by proper distinctions with respect to treaties, and requiring the assent of the House of Representatives, where it could be done with safety." Ibid., 2:639. Note that some Indians have

There was considerable debate about which branch of the government should have the responsibility for making treaties and the power to do so. Was treaty making an executive function, a legislative function, or a joint function? The Convention opted for the third choice, and the Constitution in Article II provided: "He [the president] shall have Power, by and with the Advice and Consent of the Senate, to make Treaties, provided two thirds of the Senators present concur."[5] But how this was to be carried out in practice was not clear from the Constitution itself. Two questions arose: How precisely did the Senate advise and consent in regard to treaties, and were agreements with Indian tribes to follow regular treaty procedures?

Washington and the Senate

Both questions were answered in 1789 and 1790, as President Washington and Secretary of War Henry Knox dealt with the Senate concerning the treaties signed at Fort Harmar in 1789 and the treaty made with the Creeks in New York in August 1790. The answers worked out at that time set the procedures for future Indian treaties.[6]

---

misinterpreted the supremacy clause and wrongly asserted that treaties are on a par with the Constitution and above federal statutes.

5. Recent scholars have been concerned about the growth of executive power in treaty making and have sought to show that treaty making as a joint function of the president and the Senate was the intent of the framers. An excellent discussion of the issue is found in Jack N. Rakove, "Solving a Constitutional Puzzle: The Treatymaking Clause As a Case Study," *Perspectives in American History*, n.s., 1 (1984): 233–81. See also two long articles by Arthur Bestor: "Separation of Powers in the Domain of Foreign Affairs: The Intent of the Constitution Historically Examined," *Seton Hall Law Review* 5 (Spring 1974): 527–665, and "Respective Roles of Senate and President in the Making and Abrogation of Treaties—The Original Intent of the Framers of the Constitution Historically Examined," *Washington Law Review* 55 (1979): 1–135. There is useful discussion, also, in Abraham D. Sofaer, *War, Foreign Affairs, and Constitutional Power: The Origins* (Cambridge, Mass.: Ballinger Publishing Company, 1976), but the book does not deal specifically with Indian treaties.

6. I have been guided in my treatment of this matter by Ralston Hayden, *The Senate and Treaties, 1789–1817: The Development of the Treaty-Making Functions of the United States Senate during Their Formative Period* (New York: Macmillan Company, 1920), especially chap. 2, "Development of Treaty-Making Power through Action on Treaties with Indian Tribes, 1789–1795," 11–39. The best source of documentation for Washington's dealings with the Senate is *Documentary History of the First Federal Congress of the United States of America*, ed. Linda Grant De Pauw, vol. 2, *Senate Executive Journal and*

Although negotiated and signed before the new government under the Constitution was set up, the Fort Harmar treaties were submitted by President Washington to the Senate on May 25, 1789. The treaties and related documents were delivered to the Senate and placed in the hands of the vice president by Henry Knox, "under whose official superintendence the business was transacted," as Washington noted, "and who will be ready to communicate to you any information on such points as may appear to require it." With the treaties, the president sent a report by Knox, dated May 23, which explained the nature of the treaties and their authorization by the Continental Congress, and which recommended, if the Senate "should concur in their approbation of the said treaties," their ratification and publication, with a proclamation enjoining their observance. To his report Knox appended a statement of Indian opposition to the earlier treaties of Fort Stanwix and Fort McIntosh, and he included the treaty instructions sent by Congress to Governor Arthur St. Clair.[7]

The Senate was in no hurry. It put the material aside for future consideration, and not until June 12 did it appoint a committee of three to deal with the treaties. The committee made its report on August 12, and the Senate considered it on August 26. The committee noted that the Fort Harmar treaties contained "a more formal and regular convey-ance to the United States of the Indian Claims to the Lands yielded" by the treaties of Fort Stanwix and Fort McIntosh and submitted a reso-lution to the effect that the Senate accept the treaties and advise the president "to execute and enjoin the observance of the same." The committee apparently felt that its duty was to see that the treaty had been negotiated according to the instructions given, and its formulation of its recommendation followed the suggestion of Knox's report. On September 8, the Senate again considered the report and duly resolved that the president "be advised to execute and enjoin an observance" of the Fort Harmar treaty with the Wyandots and other western Indians.[8]

This rather vaguely worded approval of the treaty did not satisfy

---

Related Documents (Baltimore: Johns Hopkins University Press, 1974). It is skillfully edited and includes a considerable number of related documents. I have cited this work whenever possible rather than the earlier printings of the same materials in *JCC, Annals of Congress, ASPIA,* and James D. Richardson's *A Compilation of the Messages and Papers of the Presidents.*

7. *Senate Executive Journal and Related Documents,* 3. Knox's report (without the appended documents) is on pages 3–6.

8. Ibid., 7–8, 26, 37, 38.

Washington, who on September 17 sent Henry Knox again to the Senate with another message, which elaborated the president's views on Indian treaties.[9]

First of all, Washington stated his general opinion about procedures in handling Indian treaties:

> It is said to be the general understanding and practice of Nations, as a check on the mistakes and indiscretions of Ministers or Commissioners, not to consider any treaty, negociated, and signed by such Officers, as final and conclusive until ratified by the sovereign or government from whom they derive their powers: this practice has been adopted by the United States, respecting their treaties with European Nations, and I am inclined to think it would be adviseable to observe it in the conduct of our treaties with the Indians: for tho' such treaties, being on their part, made by their Chiefs or Rulers, need not be ratified by them, yet being formed on our part by the agency of subordinate Officers, it seems to be both prudent and reasonable, that their acts should not be binding on the Nation until approved and ratified by the Government. It strikes me that this point should be well considered and settled, so that our national proceedings in this respect may become uniform, and be directed by fixed, and stable principles.

He noted that he had forwarded the Fort Harmar treaties with two questions for the Senate to resolve: "1st. Whether those Treaties were to be considered as perfected, and consequently as obligatory, without being ratified, if not, then 2ndly. whether both, or either, and which of them ought to be ratified?" He was not satisfied with the Senate's action of September 8, with its advice "to execute and enjoin an observance of" the Wyandot treaty, for it seemed ambiguous. "To execute" could mean either that the treaty was to be ratified by the president as a new act of government, that it was already perfected and obligatory and that he was only to carry it out, or that the treaty would "derive its completion and obligation from the silent approbation and ratification which my Proclamation may be construed to imply." He thought that all doubts about the Senate's intention ought to be removed. He asked, also, for some action on the treaty with the Six Nations.

The committee of the Senate to whom Washington's letter was referred reported the following day: "That the Signature of treaties with the Indian Nations has ever been considered as a full completion thereof,

9. Ibid., 40–41. Material in the following paragraphs is taken from that message.

and that such treaties have never been solemnly ratified by either of the contracting Parties as hath been commonly practised among the civilized Nations of Europe." The committee, therefore, did not consider formal ratification of the treaty either "expedient or necessary," and it thought that the Senate's resolution of September 8 was sufficient. As to the Six Nations treaty, no action had been recommended because of "particular circumstances affecting a part of the ceded lands." This report, however, was rejected by the full Senate, which on September 22 resolved "that the Senate do advise and consent that the President of the United States ratify" the Wyandot treaty. It postponed action on the Six Nations treaty because the treaty might "be construed to prejudice the claims of the States of Massachusetts and New York and of the Grantees under the said States."[10]

Washington was satisfied, and on September 29 he issued an instrument of ratification for the treaty with the Wyandots and other western Indians, in which he noted that the treaty had been made in proper form by Governor St. Clair, who had been duly authorized. He added: "Now Know Ye That I having seen and considered the said Treaty, do by and with the advice and consent of the Senate, Accept, ratify, and confirm the same, and every article and clause thereof." On the same day, he issued a public proclamation of like effect, in which he enjoined and required "all officers of the United States civil and military and all other citizens and inhabitants thereof faithfully to observe and fulfill the same."[11]

Thus the precedent was established, in accordance with Washington's views, that Indian treaties—like those with foreign nations—be formally approved by the Senate before they took effect. The Senate "advised and consented" that the president "ratify" the treaty, which he did in a formal instrument of ratification. The standard construction of treaties was that ratification was retroactive; a treaty took effect from the date of the signing.[12]

The second Fort Harmar treaty (with the Six Nations) indicated that not all the confusion about the ratification of treaties had been dissipated. Although the Senate and the president failed to ratify the agreement and although the treaty was not forwarded to the Department of State to become part of its official treaty archives until 1797, officials of the federal government acted as though the treaty were valid. Washington

10. Ibid., 42–43.
11. *Terr. Papers*, 2:219–20.
12. Ratification and proclamation documents are found in Ratified Treaties.

himself, writing to Seneca chiefs in January 1791, referred to the boundary set at Fort Stanwix and "confirmed by the Treaty of Fort Harmar upon the Muskingum, so late as the 9th. of January 1789," and he asserted that "the lines fixed at Fort Stanwix and Fort Harmar, must therefore remain established." Peace commissioners to the confederated Indians in the northwest on July 31, 1793, noted that the Six Nations had "renewed and confirmed the treaty of fort Stanwix" at the Fort Harmar council.[13]

The Fort Harmar treaties had been signed before the inauguration of the new government under the Constitution. The Senate did not, therefore, have any part in the negotiations of the treaties but was presented with them as a fait accompli. It could only judge whether they had been completed in due form and according to the instructions drawn up by the Congress under the Articles of Confederation. It was quite otherwise with negotiations for a treaty with the Creeks initiated by President Washington in 1789, for the new president took seriously the prescription to act "with the advice and consent" of the Senate, which he at first took to mean using the Senate as a sort of council with whom to discuss the negotiations. He expected to talk with the senators in person, to get their advice about proposed strategies, and to receive prior approval and confirmation of his actions.

Even before the Fort Harmar treaties were disposed of, the Senate and the president began to work out procedures for treaty making (and for confirmation of appointments, the other executive action where the Senate's advice and consent was mandated by the Constitution). On August 6 the Senate appointed a committee "to wait on the President of the United States, and confer with him on the mode of communication proper to be pursued between him and the Senate, in the formation of Treaties, and making appointments to Offices."[14]

The committee members and the president met on August 8 and again on August 10. The matter of confirming nominations was easily disposed of. Washington believed that in these cases written communications alone would serve and that the presence of the president when

13. The transfer of the treaty to the State Department is noted in John Stagg, Jr., to George Taylor, May 9, 1797, in Ratified Treaties, roll 2, frame 210. For Washington's references to the treaty, see Washington to Cornplanter, Half-Town, and the Great Tree, Chiefs of the Seneca Nation, January 19, 1791, *The Writings of George Washington from the Original Manuscript Sources, 1745–1799*, ed. John C. Fitzpatrick, 39 vols. (Washington: GPO, 1931-44), 31:197–98; *ASPIA*, 1:353. See also *Terr. Papers*, 2:186n.

14. *Senate Executive Journal and Related Documents*, 24.

the Senate considered his nominations would be improper and unpleas-
ant for both parties—"as the President has a right to nominate without
assigning his reasons, so has the Senate a right to dissent without giving
theirs." In the matter of treaties, however, Washington thought that
"oral communications seem indispensably necessary; because in these a
variety of matters are contained, all of which not only require consideration, but some of them may undergo much discussion; to do which
by written communications would be tedious without being satisfactory." He was also concerned about the proper protocol. Where should
the oral communications take place, and if in the Senate chamber, how
would the president and the vice president (who presided over the
Senate) be positioned? "These are matters," he said, "which require
previous consideration and adjustment for meetings in the Senate
Chamber or elsewhere."[15]

At the second meeting, Washington was more forceful in asserting
his prerogatives. The time and place of consultation, he thought, should
rest with the president, who could summon the Senate to his house,
but he was willing to make a distinction between confirmation of
nominations (a purely executive function of the Senate, in which case
that body could be summoned to the president) and treaty business
(which was a legislative matter and could more properly be handled in
the Senate chamber). Washington did not want any hard and fast rules,
however, for "the *manner* of consultation may also vary" according to
the nature of the business and the inclinations or dispositions of the
two parties. And experience might well suggest modifications. The
Senate, he thought, should provide "for the reception of either oral [or]
written propositions, and for giving their consent and advice in either
the *presence* or *absence* of the President." In a letter to James Madison on
August 9, Washington said the committee had informed him that the
Senate wanted to accommodate the wishes of the president, but that he
sensed "oral communications was the point they aimed at." The president's views met approval in the Senate, and on August 21 it set up the
protocol to be followed.[16]

The theory was soon tested in practice, for on August 21 Washington
sent a message to the Senate that he would meet with them the next
morning at 11:30 "to advise with them on the terms of the Treaty to

15. *Writings of George Washington*, 30:373–74.
16. Ibid., 374–75, 377–78; *Senate Executive Journal and Related Documents*, 29–30.

be negotiated with the Southern Indians."[17] The Senate was then a small body; since Rhode Island and North Carolina were late in ratifying the Constitution, it had only twenty-two members.

Washington went to the Senate in good faith. Two weeks earlier he had sent the Senate information about the critical state of affairs existing between Georgia and the Indians, which seemed "to require the immediate interposition of the General Government." He was looking for action that would be fair to both sides. "While measures of Government ought to be calculated to protect its citizens from all injury and violence," he told the Senate, "a due regard should be extended to those Indian tribes whose happiness, in the course of events, so materially depends on the national justice and humanity of the United States." The president asked for authority, too, to appoint a three-man commission to arrange for a treaty with the Indians. Congress appropriated $20,000 for such a treaty and provided pay for commissioners to carry out the negotiations. Washington nominated Benjamin Lincoln, Cyrus Griffin, and David Humphries, and the Senate quickly confirmed the nominations.[18]

On August 22, accompanied by Henry Knox, Washington went to the Senate chamber, where he took his place in the vice president's seat, while John Adams, who presided over the Senate, sat with the rest of the senators. In a written statement the president summarized the state of affairs respecting the southern Indians (which had been the burden of the reports he had earlier submitted to the Senate). He noted the military power of the tribes and asserted that the fate of the southern states "may principally depend on the present measures of the Union towards the southern Indians." He called attention to the violations of the Treaty of Hopewell with the Cherokees by citizens of North Carolina but thought no solution could be proposed until that state had ratified the Constitution and joined the Union. For the Cherokees and the more distant Choctaws and Chickasaws he advocated no more than messages of assurance and friendship and plans for trade.[19]

That left the powerful Creeks, on whom Washington then centered his attention. Their case he said was of the highest importance and required an immediate decision, and he referred to the fundamental cause of conflict between the tribe and the state of Georgia: the difference

17. *Senate Executive Journal and Related Documents*, 30.

18. *Annals of Congress*, 1:58–59; 1 Stat. 54 (1789); *Senate Executive Journal and Related Documents*, 30.

19. *Senate Executive Journal and Related Documents*, 31–35. Material in the following paragraphs is taken from this statement.

of judgment about the Georgia treaties of Augusta (1783), Galphinton (1785), and Shoulderbone (1786), with their land cessions to Georgia. The only solution was to have United States commissioners investigate the problem and seek some agreement with Georgia and the Creeks.

But what should the commissioners be instructed to do? It was on this point that Washington sought the senators' advice, and he proposed seven specific questions to which he wanted their answers. The first two questions concerned the Cherokees and the Choctaws and Chickasaws and were quickly passed over. The remaining five questions set forth a series of either/or proposals for the Senate's judgment:

Question 3. If the commissioners judged that the Creek Nation had been fully represented at the three Georgia treaties and that the treaties were "just and equitable," should the commissioners insist on a confirmation of their provisions, and if the Creeks refused, should military force be used to compel them?

Question 4. If, on the other hand, the commissioners judged that the three treaties had not been proper, should they attempt to obtain a cession of the lands, offering (if less would not suffice):

- compensation in goods and money up to an amount to be specified.

- a secure port on the Altahama or St. Mary's rivers through which the Creeks could obtain trade goods.

- payment and honorary military distinctions to Creek chiefs.

- solemn guarantee of remaining Creek lands—with a line of military posts if necessary.

Question 5. If such offers did not induce the Creeks to make the desired cession to Georgia, should the commissioners issue an ultimatum?

Question 6. Or should a treaty be made with the Creeks, with the disputed lands retained by them? Or should a temporary boundary be drawn at the Oconee River and should other provisions of the treaty conform to those in the Treaties of Hopewell with the Cherokees, Choctaws, and Chickasaws?

Question 7. Could all of the $20,000 appropriated for treaties be spent on a treaty with the Creeks? If not, what proportion of it?

Two days later, August 24, on Washington's second visit (again attended by Knox) the Senate replied to these questions. Question 3 was answered in the affirmative, as was question 4, with the sum of money to be determined by the president. Question 5, about issuing an ultimatum to the Creeks, was answered in the negative. The first part of question 6 was likewise answered negatively, while the rest was confirmed. On question 7 the Senate approved use of the full $20,000 for a Creek treaty, at the discretion of the president.[20]

If one relies solely on the Senate journal, the conclusion must be that the conferences progressed smoothly, with the questions proposed by Washington answered quickly, precisely, and amicably by the senators. The idea of the Senate as a council to advise the executive about specific proposals for treaty negotiations seemed to be off to a good start. The reality, however, was quite the opposite, and Washington never again went to confer with the Senate in person (nor did any of his successors). What happened during those two days in the Senate chamber?

The answer appears in the detailed private journal of the Senate proceedings kept by William Maclay, a senator from Pennsylvania. It is obvious from Maclay's account that the meetings were not pleasant for either the president or the senators. Washington's seven questions were read by the vice president from his chair on the floor, but carriages passing by outside made so much noise that the senators could not understand what was being read. The president was fretful and the senators seemed overawed and reluctant at first to speak; the Senate asked for the reading of the earlier treaties and other documents alluded to in Washington's statement. "I cast an Eye at the President of the United States," Maclay recorded. "I saw he wore an aspect of Stern displeasure." When a proposal was made to commit all the papers to a committee for further study, Maclay noted: "the President of the U.S. started up in a Violent fret. *This defeats every purpose of my coming here,* were the first words that he said.   he then went on that he had brought his Secretary at War with him to give every necessary information, that the Secretary knew all about the Business—and yet he was delayed and could not go on with the Matter—" Washington "cooled however by degrees" and agreed to postponement of further discussion until Monday, two days hence. At the reconvening of the Senate, Maclay reported: "The President wore a different aspect from What he did Saturday.   he was placid and Serene, and manifested a Spirit of Accommodation." There was "tedious debate," but in the end all the questions were answered, and the president withdrew.[21]

20. Ibid., 35–36.
21. The journal or diary of Maclay, covering actions of the First Congress from April 24, 1789, to March 3, 1791, has been newly edited and published in *Documentary History*

The president had wanted a full and immediate discussion, with problems in the senators' minds answered at once by the knowledgeable Knox. The senators, however, wanted more time to study the supporting documents and were irked when they were rushed ahead without time to examine the evidence. The beautiful theory of a Senate council advising the president in a face-to-face discussion fell apart. The story circulated in the capital that on leaving the Senate, Washington declared that "he would be damned if he ever went there again." Washington, nevertheless, continued to keep the Senate informed in writing about the negotiations with the Creeks.[22]

The Creek Treaty of 1790

With the advice of the Senate in his pocket, Washington undertook negotiations with the Creeks. The three commissioners were given instructions that closely paralleled the agreement reached between the president and the Senate. "The first great object of your Commission," they were told, "is to negociate and establish peace between the State of Georgia and the Creek Nation. The whole Nation must be represented and solemnly acknowledged to be so by the Creeks themselves." They were instructed to meet the Indians at Rock Landing of the Oconee River in Georgia on September 15, where the Indians were expected to assemble.[23]

The commissioners, when they arrived in Georgia, sent messages of friendship to the Cherokees, Choctaws, and Chickasaws, dealt extensively with the governor of Georgia, and notified Creek chief Alexander

---

of the First Federal Congress of the United States of America, vol. 9, The Diary of William Maclay and Other Notes on Senate Debates, ed. Kenneth R. Bowling and Helen E. Veit (Baltimore: Johns Hopkins University Press, 1988). It supersedes earlier editions of the manuscript, which are not as accurate, complete, or well documented. Maclay's account of Washington's visits to the Senate on August 22 and 24 appears on pages 128–32.

22. The story about Washington's reaction was told by Secretary of the Treasury William H. Crawford in a cabinet meeting on November 10, 1824, reported in Memoirs of John Quincy Adams, ed. Charles Francis Adams, 12 vols. (Philadelphia: J. B. Lippincott and Company, 1874–77), 6:427. For Washington's dealings with the Senate on the Creek treaty, see Senate Executive Journal and Related Documents, 55, 86–87, 88–89, 90–91, 92–93, 96–97.

23. The instructions, dated August 29, 1789, are printed in Senate Executive Journal and Related Documents, 202–10, and in ASPIA, 1:65–68.

McGillivray of their coming and their hopes for peace. On September 20 they arrived at Rock Landing, and the negotiations began. The spokesman for the Creeks was, of course, McGillivray, but some two thousand Indians were on hand.[24]

Despite all the preparations and the desire of the Washington administration to find some means to assure peace on the Georgia frontier, the council came to nothing. The commissioners presented a draft of a treaty, but the boundary line it stipulated (leaving the occupied Oconee lands in the possession of Georgia) did not satisfy McGillivray. He abruptly departed the conference on September 25 without submitting his own position on the boundary nor discussing fully with the commissioners his objections to the former treaties. In reply to the entreaties of the commissioners, he wrote on September 27: "We expected ample & full Justice should be given us in restoring to us the encroachments we complained of, in which the Oconee Lands are included, but finding that there was no such Intention and that a restitution of territory hunting Grounds was not to be the Basis of a Treaty of Peace between us, I resolved to return to the nation. . . . We sincerely desire a Peace, but we cannot sacrifice much to obtain it." The next day the commissioners ruefully wrote to the secretary of war: "We have the Mortification to inform you that the Parties have separated without forming a Treaty. The Terms which were offered by us at the commencement of the Negotiation were not agreeable to Mr. McGillevray; but neither would he come forward with written objections or propose any Conditions of his own."[25]

In early 1790 Washington tried again. He sent a special emissary to McGillivray, Colonel Marinus Willett, a Revolutionary War veteran. Willett carried a letter from Benjamin Hawkins, then a senator from North Carolina, who candidly chided the Creek leader for having rejected the peaceful overtures of the United States and warned him of the calamities that would follow a war with the United States.[26] Willett

24. Reports of the commissioners to Henry Knox, November 17 and 20, 1789, are in *Senate Executive Journal and Related Documents*, 210–41, and in *ASPIA*, 1:68–80. This documentation, which includes correspondence and other papers, gives a full picture of the negotiations. A useful secondary account is Lucia Burk Kinnaird, "The Rock Landing Conference of 1789," *North Carolina Historical Review* 9 (October 1932): 349–65. McGillivray's correspondence about the Rock Landing conference is printed in John Walton Caughey, *McGillivray of the Creeks* (Norman: University of Oklahoma Press, 1938).

25. Draft of treaty, *Senate Executive Journal and Related Documents*, 224–25; McGillivray to commissioners, September 27, 1789, ibid., 229; commissioners to Knox, September 28, 1789, ibid., 230.

26. Hawkins to McGillivray, March 6, 1790, in Caughey, *McGillivray*, 256–59.

persuaded the Creek chief to reconsider his rejection of the proposed treaty and to come to New York to deal directly with Washington and Henry Knox. Escorted by Willett, McGillivray and some thirty Creeks made a celebrated journey through the Carolinas, Virginia, and Pennsylvania (where they were entertained by local officials) and a dramatic entry into New York for treaty negotiations.[27]

The Creeks in New York were attended by federal officials, and they made a good impression. But they were not all as acculturated to white ways as McGillivray was. The Revolutionary War soldier and artist John Trumbull told how Washington was interested to see in what manner Trumbull's recently completed portrait of the president would be received by the Indians.

> He therefore directed me to place the picture in an advantageous light, facing the door of entrance of the room where it was, and having invited several of the principal chiefs to dine with him, he, after dinner, proposed to them a walk. He was dressed in full uniform, and led the way to the painting-room, and when the door was thrown open, they started at seeing another "Great Father" standing in the room. One was certainly with them, and they were for a time mute with astonishment. At length one of the chiefs advanced towards the picture, and slowly stretched out his hand to touch it, and was still more astonished to feel, instead of a round object, a flat surface, cold to the touch. He started back with an exclamation of astonishment— "Ugh!" Another then approached, and placing one hand on the surface and the other behind, was still more astounded to perceive that his hands almost met. I had been desirous of obtaining portraits of some of these principal men, who possessed a dignity of manner, form, countenance and expression, worthy of Roman senators, but after this I found it impracticable; they had received the impression, that there must be magic in an art which could render a smooth flat surface so like to a real man; I however succeeded in obtaining drawings of several by stealth.[28]

It was the first treaty negotiations set, not in the Indian country, but in the capital of the United States, and Secretary of War Knox himself

27. There is a brief account of Willett's mission in Caughey, *McGillivray*, 40–43. An excellent account of the business, which emphasizes the diplomatic implications, is J. Leitch Wright, Jr., "Creek-American Treaty of 1790: Alexander McGillivray and the Diplomacy of the Old Southwest," *Georgia Historical Quarterly* 51 (December 1967): 379–400. See also the popular article by Gary L. Roberts, "The Chief of State and the Chief," *American Heritage* 26 (October 1975): 28–33, 86–89.

28. *The Autobiography of Colonel John Trumbull, Patriot-Artist, 1765–1843*, ed. Theodore Sizer (New Haven: Yale University Press, 1953), 166–67.

was designated the official commissioner for the United States. Washington informed the Senate on August 4 that the treaty negotiations were "far advanced," but that trade arrangements were causing embarrassment. He noted that the Creeks got their trade goods from British merchants operating in Spanish ports, and he declared: "As the trade of the Indians is a main means of their political management, it is therefore obvious, that the United States cannot possess any security for the performance of treaties with the Creeks, while their trade is liable to be interrupted or withheld, at the caprice of two foreign Powers." He therefore asked the Senate to approve a secret article for the treaty that authorized trade goods for the Creeks to pass through United States ports free of duty if their regular channels of trade became obstructed, consent that the Senate immediately gave. By August 6 Washington, who indicated that the negotiations to that point had been informal, was ready to draw up the treaty in proper form, and on August 7 the treaty was signed by Knox and twenty-four Creek representatives. The president laid the completed treaty before the Senate on the same day, the Senate gave its consent by a vote of fifteen to four on August 12, and on August 13 Washington formally ratified it.[29]

A ratification ceremony took place in Federal Hall before a large assembly, including the vice president, the governor of New York, and several members of Congress. Washington addressed the Creeks, declaring the treaty "just and equal," and presented a string of beads and a paper of tobacco to McGillivray as tokens of peace. McGillivray made a short reply, the Creeks sang a song of peace, and the parties exchanged handshakes, ending the "highly interesting, solemn and dignified transaction."[30]

The treaty was similar to those signed in 1785–86 with the Cherokees, Choctaws, and Chickasaws.[31] It spoke of perpetual peace and friendship between the citizens of the United States and the Creeks, and it stipulated that the Creek Nation was under the protection of the United States and that it would not hold any treaty with a state or with individuals of a state. Provisions were made for return of prisoners, for punishment of crimes, and for discouraging white settlement on Creek lands. In a foreshadowing of later and persistent use of treaties as

29. *Senate Executive Journal and Related Documents*, 86–87, 88–89, 90–91, 96–97. The treaty and the presidential ratification are printed on pages 241–48 and the secret articles on pages 248–50.

30. *Pennsylvania Packet and Daily Advertiser*, August 18, 1790, in Caughey, *McGillivray*, 278.

31. Kappler, 2:25–29.

vehicles for promoting the civilization of the Indians, Article XII stipulated:

> That the Creek nation may be led to a greater degree of civilization and to become herdsmen and cultivators, instead of remaining in a state of hunters, the United States will from time to time furnish gratuitously the said nation with useful domestic animals and implements of husbandry. And further to assist the said nation in so desirable a pursuit, and at the same time to establish a certain mode of communication, the United States will send such and so many persons to reside in said nation as they may judge proper, and not exceeding four in number, who shall qualify themselves to act as interpreters.

The key item, of course, was the boundary line specified, which validated some, but not all, of the earlier cessions made to Georgia that McGillivray had so adamantly opposed. In return, trade goods were delivered to the Creeks and a $1,500 annuity was provided. The United States solemnly guaranteed the remaining Creek lands. Instituting a practice that became common in subsequent treaties, the treaty stipulated that it would "take effect and be obligatory on the contracting parties, as soon as the same shall have been ratified by the President of the United States, with the advice and consent of the Senate of the United States."

According to secret articles, McGillivray got control of the trade for the Creeks through United States ports (as he had control of such trade through Spanish ports), and he was made an agent of the United States in the Creek Nation with the rank of brigadier general and pay of $1,200 a year. Commissions, large medals, and $100 a year were allowed for six "great medal chiefs." There is no doubt that these perquisites helped incline McGillivray to sign, especially the placing of a trade monopoly in his hands, for his status among the Creeks rested largely on his ability to control the influx of essential goods, and he had begun to question the ability of his agreements with Spain to maintain that flow. But there were other factors as well. His connections with the Spanish were weakening, and the danger of a British-Spanish war arising out of a conflict involving Nootka Sound in the Pacific Northwest made reliance on Spain even more problematic. The Yazoo land grants, made by Georgia to speculators, threatened Indian claims, and McGillivray saw that it was in his interest as well as that of the federal government to thwart those schemes.[32]

32. See the discussion in Wright, "Creek-American Treaty of 1790," 384–87. The

Both sides seemed pleased. The United States had publicly won the loyalty of the Creek leader, confirmed its authority to deal with the Indians, and provided for Georgia citizens who had settled on lands claimed by the Creeks. McGillivray won United States acceptance of his office as head chief of the Creeks and gained control of trade, to say nothing of his commission and annual stipend.

But in fact the treaty never took full effect. Georgia was dissatisfied because not all her claims were met; dissident Creeks who disputed McGillivray's leadership were not appeased; and Spain threatened to replace McGillivray as its agent if he did not repudiate the concessions he had made and the ties to the United States he had agreed to in New York. The boundary line was not surveyed and marked because the Indians would not join the American surveyors. Restlessness and hostility persisted on the Creek-Georgia frontier.

Yet this first foray of President Washington into treaty making was a significant beginning. He had felt his way toward a fixed procedure for sharing his responsibility with the Senate, and he had persuaded the powerful Creek Nation to come to his seat of government for treaty negotiations. He was now more confident in dealing with other tribes that called for his attention.

---

article analyzes the influence of the Nootka Sound controversy between England and Spain and the Yazoo land grants in McGillivray's decision to go to New York to treat with the United States, and it traces the activities of Spanish and British agents in New York during the time of the treaty negotiations.

CHAPTER FOUR

Confirming the Procedures

Other Treaties in the 1790s

After negotiating with the Creeks in 1790, Washington turned to the Cherokees, whose complaints about violations of the Treaty of Hopewell by citizens of North Carolina he had forwarded to the Senate in 1789.[1] At the time, he had noted the impossibility of taking firm action because North Carolina had not yet joined the Union, but that state ratified the Constitution on November 21, 1789, and its cession of western lands was accepted on April 2, 1790. The president now felt empowered to act, and in August 1790 he sent a written message to the Senate, asserting: "I shall conceive myself bound to exert the powers entrusted to me by the Constitution in order to carry into faithfull execution the treaty of Hopewell, unless it shall be thought proper to attempt to arrange a new boundary with the Cherokees, embracing the settlements, and compensating the Cherokees for the cessions they shall make on the occasion." He therefore proposed three questions to the Senate:

---

1. *Documentary History of the First Federal Congress of the United States of America*, ed. Linda Grant De Pauw, vol. 2, *Senate Executive Journal and Related Documents* (Baltimore: Johns Hopkins University Press, 1974), 31; the documents are printed 185–88, 199–201. There is an account of the dealings with the Cherokees in Ralston Hayden, *The Senate and Treaties, 1789–1817: The Development of the Treaty-Making Functions of the United States Senate during Their Formative Period* (New York: Macmillan Company, 1920), 30–34.

1. Should an attempt be made to arrange a new boundary with the Cherokees, to include the white settlements made since the Treaty of Hopewell?
2. Should payment be made to the Cherokees—an annuity or a gross sum—for land relinquished, with the settlers held liable for the value of the land?
3. Should the United States solemnly guarantee any new boundary arranged?[2]

The Senate immediately considered the message and resolved "to advise and consent" that the president, at his discretion should either enforce the Treaty of Hopewell or undertake to gain a new cession from the Cherokees "as the Tranquillity and Interest of the United States may require." It authorized in payment an annuity not to exceed $1,000 and agreed to solemnly guarantee any new boundary that might be drawn. Washington in this case avoided the awkward face-to-face confrontation with the Senate that he had found so unsatisfactory in the case of the Creek treaty, and he asked the Senate's advice in very general terms, unlike the specific either/or proposals he had sent about Creek negotiations. The Senate, on its part, moved quickly, and it seemed not to hesitate in giving prior consent to guarantee a new boundary without knowing precisely what the provisions might be. Congress had already voted funds for a treaty on July 22, 1790.[3]

New Treaties with the Cherokees

William Blount, the newly appointed governor of the Territory Southwest of the Ohio who was instructed to conduct the treaty, met some 1,200 Cherokees on the banks of the Holston River at the present site of Knoxville in June 1791. Blount had a flair for ceremony, and the assembly was a colorful event; the governor sat under a marquee in full uniform, with civil and military officers at his side, and the Indians in ranks faced the marquee. Blount, looking out for his own land interests as well as the interests of the United States, wanted to expand his instructions and acquire greater cessions, but Secretary of

2. *Senate Executive Journal and Related Documents*, 94–95.
3. Ibid., 95–97; 1 Stat. 136.

War Knox objected, and the Indians insisted on cutting back his proposals for the boundary.[4]

The treaty, signed on July 2, 1791, contained an affirmation of peace and friendship, the acknowledgment by the Cherokees of the protection of the United States, and provisions dealing with prisoners and prohibition of settlement on Indian lands similar to those in the Treaty of Hopewell. It added an article on promoting the acculturation of the Cherokees like that in the Creek treaty of 1790. The boundary line, over which Blount and the Indians had argued, was set to include in the cession the lands on which the whites had settled in force. After Washington submitted the document to the Senate, a committee that studied the treaty reported that it considered the treaty to be in accord with the president's instructions and the Senate's advice given on August 11, 1790, and it recommended approval. Whereupon the Senate gave its advice and consent. Washington issued a statement of ratification and a separate proclamation on November 11, 1791.[5]

The Cherokees were dissatisfied with the treaty and sent a delegation to Philadelphia, which arrived in the capital on December 28, 1791. The delegates met with the president and made known their complaints to the secretary of war. Their spokesman, Bloody Fellow, related the arguments with Blount about the boundary and how the Cherokees had finally given in. "At the time of the treaty," he said, "we objected to giving up so much land; but, for the sake of peace and quietness, we did it. But we object to the little money given for so much land." It was not enough, he lamented, even to buy a breech clout for each one in the nation; he asked that the $1,000 annuity be raised to $1,500. Knox signed an agreement with the Indians to that effect on January 17, 1792, and the next day Washington sent the agreement to the Senate as an additional article to the original treaty, which the Senate approved.[6]

4. There is a description of the negotiations in William H. Masterson, *William Blount* (Baton Rouge: Louisiana State University Press, 1954), 203–6. See also Knox to Washington, March 10, 1791, in *Terr. Papers*, 4:50–52. For other accounts of the negotiations, see the remarks of Bloody Fellow on January 7, 1792, *ASPIA*, 1:203–4, and a statement of Blount, July 15, 1791, ibid., 628–29.

5. Kappler, 2:29–32; the cession is shown in Royce, *Cessions*, plate 54, area no. 8. The actions of Washington and the Senate are in *Senate Ex. Proc.*, 1:85, 88–89. The statements of ratification and proclamation are in *Terr. Papers*, 4:67–68.

6. *ASPIA*, 1:204–5; *Senate Ex. Proc.*, 1:98, 99. The additional article is printed in Kappler, 2:32–33. Charles C. Royce, in "The Cherokee Nation of Indians: A Narrative of Their Official Relations with the Colonial and Federal Governments," *Fifth Annual Report of the Bureau of Ethnology*, 1883–1884 (Washington: GPO, 1887), 169–71, considers it a separate treaty. Royce's study was reprinted as Charles C. Royce, *The*

The Treaty of Holston still did not bring satisfaction to the Cherokees and even less to the white citizens who had continued to encroach upon Cherokee lands despite threats from the federal government, and actual hostilities broke out. Another treaty was negotiated in Philadelphia on June 26, 1794, by Knox and a delegation of Cherokees. The Senate was in recess at the time, and Washington did not submit it to the Senate, as "certain additional articles" to the Treaty of Holston, until December 30, almost two months after the opening of the second session of the Third Congress. After referring the message to a committee and hearing its report, the Senate gave its approval on January 8, 1795.[7]

The treaty was primarily a renewal of the Treaty of Holston. Both parties declared that the former treaty was "to all intents and purposes in full force and binding upon the said Parties as well in respect to the boundaries therein mentioned as in all other respects whatever," and it prescribed that the boundaries be marked. The compensations set forth in the the Hopewell and Holston treaties were replaced by a more generous annuity of goods valued at $5,000. To deal with the serious problem of horse stealing, the Cherokees agreed in the treaty to a deduction of fifty dollars from the annuity for every horse stolen from whites by Cherokees.[8]

The ineffectiveness of treaties can be seen in the fact that these agreements with the Cherokees in 1791, 1792, and 1794 did not end the encroachment upon Indian lands that had been guaranteed by the United States in the treaties. The boundary line specified in the Treaty of Holston and reconfirmed in 1794 was not finally marked until late in 1797, with a result that numerous whites were found across the line. They were removed, but to correct that "inconvenience" George Walton of Georgia and Lieutenant Colonel Thomas Butler, commanding United States troops in Tennessee, were appointed commissioners to negotiate yet another treaty. Secretary of War James McHenry sent detailed instructions, and he told the commissioners, "Should the Indians not incline to sell the whole quantity of land therein specified, you will endeavor to obtain as much of it as you possibly can." President Adams sent a talk to the Cherokees about the negotiations, full of reminders of the

---

Cherokee Nation of Indians (Chicago: Aldine Publishing Company, 1975), with different pagination.

7. *Senate Ex. Proc.*, 1:168, 169, 170; *Terr. Papers*, 4:348. Washington proclaimed the treaty on January 21.

8. Kappler, 2:33–34.

goodwill of the United States toward their nation, but noting too that he had to look out for the interests of "my white children, the citizens of the United States."[9]

A treaty was signed at Tellico in eastern Tennessee on October 2, 1798. It renewed the previous treaties, but it also stipulated new land cessions by the Cherokees, for which $5,000 worth of goods was delivered at once, and an annuity of $1,000 added to the annuities already promised.[10]

The Northwest Territory

The decade of the 1790s was a time of troubles in the Northwest Territory, where there were continuing hostilities. Washington and Knox wanted to avoid war, not only because war was so expensive but also because "the blood and injustice which would stain the character of the nation, would be beyond all pecuniary calculation." But the Americans were intent on settling north of the Ohio, and the Indians were equally resolved that the Ohio was to be a permanent and irrevocable boundary between the whites and themselves. Pressure for war became too strong for Knox to resist as reports of Indian incursions and atrocities poured in from the west.[11]

In September 1790 General Josiah Harmar launched an attack from Fort Washington (the site of Cincinnati) against the Miami towns, only to be roundly defeated by the Indians. The next year Arthur St. Clair, the territorial governor, tried in turn to pacify the Indians; his command was attacked on November 4, 1791, and destroyed. Washington next appointed General Anthony Wayne to command a new expedition, but

9. Two of the three original commissioners appointed by President Adams and approved by the Senate dropped out, and the president appointed Walton and Butler as a new commission. The instructions to the original commissioners, dated March 30, 1798, are in *ASPIA*, 1:639–40; those to Walton and Butler, August 27, 1798, ibid., 640. Adams's talk, August 27, 1798, appears ibid., 640–41.

10. Kappler, 2:51–55; Royce, *Cessions*, plate 54, area no 42; *Senate Ex. Proc.*, 1:307. See also the discussion of the treaty in Royce, "Cherokee Nation of Indians," 174–83.

11. Knox to Washington, June 15, 1789, *ASPIA*, 1:12–14; reports of disturbances, ibid., 84–96.

while the general trained and disciplined his troops, one more attempt was made for peace.[12]

In May 1792 Secretary of War Knox instructed General Rufus Putnam to call a general council with the hostile tribes in order to bring them to understand the peaceful intentions of the United States. "As the basis . . . of your negociation," Knox said, "you will, *in the strongest and most explicit terms*, renounce on the part of the United States, all claims to any Indian land which shall not have been ceded by fair treaties, made with the Indian nations." Putnam was to inform the Wabash Indians, with whom no treaty had yet been made, about the new and stronger government under the Constitution and that now all the Indians could "rest with great confidence upon the justice, the humanity, and the liberality, of the United States" and that the United States wanted to advance their well-being. He was to convince the Indians that the United States wanted "not a foot of their land" and that they had "the right to sell and the right to refuse to sell."[13]

In mid-September Putnam met the Indians at Vincennes and persuaded them to agree to a peace. He read the treaty articles to them and confirmed the agreement with wampum belts, telling the Indians, "The White People commit to writing what they transact, that the paper may speak when they are dead. Your custom is to record by Belts. We shall do it both ways."[14] The treaty, signed on September 27, 1792, reflected Knox's instructions to Putnam, from which the fourth article was taken almost verbatim:

> The United States solemnly guaranty to the Wabash, and Illinois nations, or tribes of Indians, all the lands to which they have a just claim; and no part shall ever be taken from them, but by a fair purchase, and to their satisfaction. That the lands originally belonged to the Indians; it is theirs, and theirs only. That they have a right to

12. For a summary of the military action, see Francis Paul Prucha, *The Sword of the Republic: The United States Army on the Frontier, 1783–1846* (New York: Macmillan Company, 1969), 17–38.

13. Knox to Putnam, May 22, 1792, in *The Memoirs of Rufus Putnam and Certain Official Papers and Correspondence*, ed. Rowena Buell (Boston: Houghton, Mifflin and Company, 1903), 257–67, and in *ASPIA*, 1:234–36. An account of Putnam's negotiations is provided in R. David Edmunds, "'Nothing Has Been Effected': The Vincennes Treaty of 1792," *Indiana Magazine of History* 74 (March 1978): 23–35.

14. "Journal of the Proceedings at a Council Held with the Indians of the Wabash and Illinois, at Post Vincents, by Brigadier General Putnam," in *Memoirs of Rufus Putnam*, 335–62. The quotation is on 361.

sell and a right to refuse to sell. And that the United States will protect them in their said just rights.[15]

This article proved to be the undoing of the treaty, for when Washington submitted it to the Senate in February 1893, he suggested approval but with an amendment that would "guard, in the ratification, the exclusive pre-emption of the United States to the lands of the said Indians." A Senate committee, later in the month, recommended postponement of further consideration of the treaty until the next session of Congress and that in the meantime the executive should negotiate a new article with the Indians that would provide for United States preemption rights, as Washington had suggested. Such action proved impossible, however, because many of the principal Wabash chiefs had died of smallpox.[16]

On January 9, 1794, almost a year after the treaty had been submitted, the Senate considered it again, and an attempt was made to accept the treaty with an amendment providing for preemption, but when the vote was finally taken on the simple question of approving the treaty as it stood, the Senate voted it down, twenty-one to four.[17] It was the first instance in which the Senate refused to agree to an Indian treaty or even to amend it according to the president's recommendation. But by that time the signatory Indians had renewed hostilities, and the treaty was a dead issue. Meanwhile, a new peace initiative had been undertaken in 1793, and commissioners appointed to treat with the northwest Indians went to Detroit. The Indians, however, refused to deal with them, and the peace movement fell apart.[18]

A new military expedition was the result. General Wayne moved north against the Indians the next summer, and on August 20, 1794,

15. The treaty is printed in *ASPIA*, 1:338; it also appears in *Memoirs of Rufus Putnam*, 363–66.

16. *Senate Ex. Proc.*, 1:128, 135; Knox to Washington, January 2, 1794, *ASPIA*, 1:470.

17. *Senate Ex. Proc.*, 1:146.

18. *ASPIA*, 1:340–60. Timothy Pickering was one of the commissioners, and there are accounts of the episode in Edward Hake Phillips, "Timothy Pickering at His Best: Indian Commissioner, 1790–1794," *Essex Institute Historical Collections* 102 (July 1966): 185–92, and Gerard H. Clarfield, *Timothy Pickering and the American Republic* (Pittsburgh: University of Pittsburgh Press, 1980), 137–44. For a detailed account that emphasizes British action and influence, see Reginald Horsman, "The British Indian Department and the Abortive Treaty of Lower Sandusky, 1793," *Ohio Historical Quarterly* 70 (July 1961): 189–213.

the American troops decisively defeated the Indians at the Battle of
Fallen Timbers on the Maumee. The British at Fort Miami, not willing
to risk an open conflict with the United States, closed their gates in the
face of the retreating Indians, and the hope of British aid collapsed. The
following summer the Indians gathered at Fort Greenville to accept the
terms of the victor. Wayne received a draft of a treaty to be presented
to the Indians and instructions for his negotiations.[19]

The various Indian delegates arrived over a period of days in June.
They were greeted by Wayne with brief speeches and gifts of wampum,
but it was not until July 13 that the formal council with all the assembled
tribes got under way. A good bit of time was spent explaining the earlier
treaties and their land cessions, and Wayne remarked about the ceded
lands, "Younger Brothers: Notwithstanding that these lands have been
twice paid for, by the Fifteen Fires, at the places I have mentioned, yet,
such is the justice and liberality of the United States, that they will now,
a third time, make compensation for them." And he continued the
Indian protocol:

> We have nothing to do but to bury the hatchet, and draw a veil over
> past misfortunes. As you have buried our dead with the concern of
> brothers, so I now collect the bones of your slain warriors, put them
> into a deep pit, which I have dug, and cover them carefully over with
> this large belt, there to remain undisturbed. I also dry the tears from
> your eyes, and wipe the blood from your bodies, with this soft, white
> linen: no bloody traces will ever lead to the graves of your departed
> heroes; with this, I wipe all such entirely away. I deliver it to your
> uncle the Wyandot, who will send it round amongst you. [A large
> belt, with a white string attached.]
>
> I now take the hatchet out of your heads, and with a strong arm
> throw it into the centre of the great ocean, where no mortal can ever
> find it; and I now deliver to you the wide and straight path to the
> Fifteen Fires, to be used by you and your posterity for ever. So long
> as you continue to follow this road, so long will you continue to be
> a happy people: you see it is straight and wide, and they will be blind
> indeed, who deviate from it. I place it also in your uncle's hands, that
> he may preserve it for you. [A large road belt]
>
> I will, the day after to-morrow, shew you the cessions you have
> made to the United States, and point out to you the lines which may,
> for the future, divide your lands from theirs; and, as you will have

19. For a brief analysis of the treaty, see Dwight L. Smith, "Wayne and the Treaty of
Greene Ville," *Ohio State Archaeological and Historical Quarterly* 63 (January 1954): 1–7.

to-morrow to rest, I will order you a double allowance of drink; because we have now buried the hatchet, and performed every necessary ceremony, to render propitious our renovated friendship.[20]

Later he pointed out the cessions that were to be confirmed and read the articles of the treaty to the Indians. Indian spokesmen replied, some with suggestions for changes, but Wayne was unmoved. In the end the Indians indicated their assent and on August 3 signed the treaty. Presents and medals were distributed, and the council adjourned on August 10.

The treaty established the well-known Treaty of Greenville line, by which the Indians relinquished claim to the southern two-thirds of Ohio and a slim triangle of land in what is now Indiana. It was similar to the Fort Harmar line but with considerable extension to the west, and it enclosed more land than Wayne's instructions had prescribed. In addition, the Indians approved a number of parcels of land for military or trading posts beyond the line. Remaining lands were guaranteed to the Indians, but there was a clear statement that when the tribes disposed of any of them the lands were to be sold only to the United States. In return for the cessions the United States delivered to the Indians $20,000 worth of goods and promised a $9,500 perpetual annuity of "like useful goods, suited to the circumstances of the Indians." A tribe could ask that a part of the annuity be commuted to "domestic animals, implements of husbandry, and other utensils convenient for them, and in compensation for useful artificers who may reside with or near them, and be employed for their benefit." The Indians got the right to hunt in the ceded territory "without hindrance or molestation, so long as they demean themselves peaceably, and offer no injury to the people of the United States." The treaty contained the usual statements about peace and friendship and acceptance by the Indians of the protection of the United States and included provisions for a licensed trade.[21]

The Treaty of Greenville was a good example of independent executive action in Indian treaty making. When considering a new treaty with the western Indians in early 1793, Washington had proposed questions to his cabinet about such a treaty, especially about retroceding lands to the Indians already acquired by treaty, and he asked "whether the Senate shall be previously consulted on this point." Jefferson, then secretary of state, reported that the unanimous opinion was that it would be better

20. The minutes of the council are printed in *ASPIA*, 1:564–82. The quotations are from 573. The brackets are in the original.
21. Kappler, 2:39–45.

not to consult the Senate, giving as a reason that news of it might leak out to the British.[22] The Senate apparently was not asked to approve Wayne as commissioner, and it received no communications from Washington about the Treaty of Greenville until December 9, 1795, two days after the opening of the Fourth Congress, when the president submitted the treaty, the instructions given Wayne, and the council proceedings. On December 22 the senators unanimously approved the treaty without any apparent concern that they had not been consulted ahead of time. Washington proclaimed the treaty on the same day.[23]

Treating with the Six Nations

The hostility of the Wabash River tribes and the military expeditions against them in 1790, 1791, and 1794 created serious worry about the Indians of the Six Nations. How could their neutrality be assured, so that they did not militarily aid the western Indians in their struggle against the United States? And was there even a possibility that some of the Iroquois might be recruited to assist the American forces? These concerns led to a number of councils with the Six Nations and ultimately to the Treaty of Canandaigua in 1794, which were the work primarily of Timothy Pickering as United States commissioner.[24]

Pickering had been active in the Revolutionary War as adjutant general, quartermaster general, and member of the Board of War, but he had had no direct experience with Indians until Washington in September 1790 appointed him commissioner to treat with the Seneca Indians, who were incensed by the recent murder of two of their number by white brigands. It was essential to United States policy to keep the Indians at peace, and Pickering met with the Senecas at Tioga Point, a frontier post on the Susquehanna River above Wilkes-Barre near the northern boundary of Pennsylvania. Here, in November 1790, he successfully redressed the Indians' grievances with mourning belts of wam-

22. Thomas Jefferson, "Anas," in *The Writings of Thomas Jefferson*, ed. Andrew A. Lipscomb, 20 vols. (Washington: Thomas Jefferson Memorial Association, 1903–4), 1:338–43.
23. *Senate Ex. Proc.*, 1:193, 197; *Terr. Papers*, 2:534.
24. I follow here largely the accounts in Phillips, "Timothy Pickering at His Best," 163–202, and Clarfield, *Timothy Pickering*. Both rely heavily on the Pickering Papers in the Massachusetts Historical Society.

pum, an array of presents, and promises to investigate problems in the land purchases that had been made from the Senecas.[25]

In 1791, after General Harmar's defeat, Washington sent Pickering to deal with the combined Six Nations to hold them to the line of peace. In late June and early July, the commissioner met the Indians at New-town Point on the Chemung River in southern New York State, some forty miles west of Tioga Point. A large gathering of Indians assembled (finally more than a thousand), and Pickering sparred with the Seneca orator Red Jacket. Ignoring his instructions to attempt to recruit warriors to aid the United States in its campaign against the western Indians, Pickering managed to quiet the Indians' fears and misgivings. He promised, too, to promote their adoption of the arts of husbandry, a policy that became increasingly important in his mind. After distribution of generous gifts, Pickering closed the conference on July 17, with the neutrality of the Six Nations assured.[26]

After the unsuccessful peace attempts in the west in 1792 and 1793, the Six Nations again became a center of attention, especially as they challenged the development of white settlements at Presque Isle, and Pickering once more was delegated to treat with them. He met with the Indians in October 1794 at Canandaigua, the home of General Israel Chapin (the United States agent to the Iroquois) at the northern point of Lake Canandaigua. As usual, the Indians were slow to assemble, but eventually about 1,600 appeared, and the conference opened on October 18. Amid delays caused by Indian drunkenness, Pickering conducted the negotiations with reliance on Indian protocol, and—aided by the news of Wayne's victory at Fallen Timbers, which arrived on October 27—he was able, after considerable haggling, to get agreement of the Indians to a formal treaty on November 11.[27] It was the last treaty with the Iroquois in which the American commissioners followed the ancient forms of the native protocol. After that the United States no longer felt bound to observe the Indian customs.[28]

25. Phillips, "Timothy Pickering at His Best," 166–71; Clarfield, *Timothy Pickering*, 117–18.

26. Phillips, "Timothy Pickering at His Best," 173–77; Clarfield, *Timothy Pickering*, 124–29.

27. Phillips, "Timothy Pickering at His Best," 193–99; Clarfield, *Timothy Pickering*, 149–52. The importance of the Treaty of Canandaigua as a culmination of dealings with the Iroquois is clearly noted in Jack Campisi, "From Stanwix to Canandaigua: National Policy, States' Rights, and Indian Land," in Christopher Vecsey and William A. Starna, eds., *Iroquois Land Claims* (Syracuse: Syracuse University Press, 1988), 49–65.

28. William N. Fenton, "Structure, Continuity, and Change in the Process of Iroquois

The treaty settled a long-standing Seneca complaint about the boundary established at Fort Stanwix in 1784 and reconfirmed at Fort Harmar, for Pickering redrew the line, returning to the Senecas more than a million acres, and the treaty acknowledged the land of the Oneidas, Onondagas, and Cayugas reserved in their treaties with New York. The United States agreed not to claim any of the Indian lands until the Indians themselves chose to sell them to the United States, and the Indians gave up claims to any other lands. The United States won the right to build a road from Lake Ontario to Buffalo Creek on Lake Erie and free passage of American citizens through Indian lands. The Indians received goods valued at $10,000, and their annuity was raised to $4,500, to be spent "yearly forever, in purchasing clothing, domestic animals, implements of husbandry, and other utensils suited to their circumstances, and in compensating useful artificers, who shall reside with or near them, and be employed for their benefit." The treaty reaffirmed perpetual peace and friendship and condemned private revenge or retaliation for injuries.[29]

In addition, Pickering concluded a treaty on December 2 with the Oneida, Tuscarora, and Stockbridge Indians; it provided compensation to those loyal Indians for property lost during the Revolutionary War—in the form of $5,000 to be distributed to individuals, gristmills and sawmills with persons to run them for three years, and $1,000 to build a church. In return the Indians relinquished all claims for losses and services during the war.[30]

The Creeks

In the summer of 1795 President Washington turned his attention again to the Creeks and at the request of Georgia planned

Treaty Making," in Francis Jennings, ed., *The History and Culture of Iroquois Diplomacy: An Interdisciplinary Guide to the Treaties of the Six Nations and Their League* (Syracuse: Syracuse University Press, 1985), 27.

29. Kappler, 2:34–37; Royce, *Cessions*, plate 47. The article about the yearly grant of clothing, domestic animals, and implements of husbandry had been planned ahead of time by President Washington, who on March 23, 1792, had asked the Senate for approval of such a provision. The Senate gave its consent on March 26. *Senate Ex. Proc*, 1:116.

30. Kappler, 2:37–39. Both treaties were sent to the Senate by Washington on January 2, 1795, and the Senate quickly approved them on January 9. They were proclaimed on January 21. *Senate Ex. Proc.*, 1:168, 170.

another treaty with them, seeking to discover and to settle the reasons for Creek dissatisfaction with the Treaty of New York. To that end he appointed Benjamin Hawkins, Andrew Pickens, and George Clymer commissioners to hold a treaty with the nation. Washington wanted the treaty to follow the general terms of the Treaty of New York, and he expected Georgia to bear half the cost of the provisions for the Indians who assembled for the council.[31]

Almost a year passed before the commissioners met the Indians in May and June 1796 at Coleraine, on Georgia's southern boundary, on land held by the Creeks but vehemently claimed by Georgia.[32] Three commissioners from Georgia were on hand, but the federal commissioners refused to let them land the militia they brought up the river and in other ways put obstacles in their path. Fending off rumors that the Georgia militia intended to force a land cession from the Creeks, the federal commissioners established stringent regulations for the council grounds:

> The commissioners for holding a treaty with the Creek nation of Indians, in order to prevent quarrels, improper behavior, or malpractices, during the negotiation, have judged proper, in virtue of the powers and authorities vested in them, to make the following regulations:
>
> 1. The Indians are to encamp on the river bank, above the garrison, convenient to the spring and the river.
> 2. The superintendent is to fix his residence within the Indian encampment.
> 3. No citizen of the United States is to be permitted to encamp with, or near to, the Indians, except such as are under the direction of the superintendent.
> 4. No citizen is to be permitted to enter the Indian camp in arms.
> 5. No citizen is to visit the Indians, or hold conversation with them, except with a permit from the commissioners of the United States, or either of them.
> 6. No citizen is to be in arms in the garrison, or neighborhood of it; and, on the arrival of any visiters, who may travel with arms,

31. Washington to the Senate, June 25, 1795, *Senate Ex. Proc.*, 1:189–91. The Senate confirmed the nominations of the commissioners on June 26. Ibid., 192.

32. Documents relating to the Coleraine council and treaty, including reports of the negotiations, are printed in *ASPIA*, 1:586–616. An excellent article, which recounts in detail the role of the Georgia commissioners and the opposition to them by the federal commissioners, is Clyde R. Ferguson, "Confrontation at Coleraine: Creeks, Georgians, and Federalist Indian Policy," *South Atlantic Quarterly* 78 (Spring 1979): 224–43. See also Hayden, *Senate and Treaties*, chap. 5, "The Creek Treaty of 1796," 95–106.

they are to be informed of this order, and required to conform thereto.

7. No citizen is to be permitted to furnish, by sale or gift, any spirituous liquors to the Indians, or to have any commercial traffic with them.

8. These regulations are to be posted up at the two gates of the garrison, and at the residence of the superintendent.[33]

The Georgia commissioners were outraged, for they believed that the actions of Hawkins and his colleagues were an unconstitutional assumption of power. "The ground they [the Creeks] encamp on, and the ground the treaty is to be held on, is within the limits, and under the actual jurisdiction of the State of Georgia . . . , " they complained. "We know of no power on earth, competent to hinder a citizen of Georgia, observing the laws of his country, from exercising the loco-motive faculty, within the limits of the State, in the most liberal extent." But the federal commissioners would not budge, and in the end the Georgians acquiesced.[34] The federal government under Washington was concerned to protect Indian rights against aggressive state citizens, and it would not be cowed by Georgia. When the Creeks rejected a cession to Georgia, the commissioners upheld them, and the Georgians were frustrated.

The Treaty of Coleraine, signed on June 29, 1796, reaffirmed the Treaty of New York and provided for the running of the boundary under the eyes of the Indians, and the Creeks relinquished any claims they had to lands ceded by the Cherokees, Choctaws, and Chickasaws at Hopewell. Articles III and IV allowed the United States to establish trading posts and military posts in the Creek country and authorized annexing to each post a tract of land five miles square for use of the United States, which land was to revert to the Indians when it was no longer needed by the federal government. The Indians received goods valued at $6,000 and were promised two blacksmiths.[35]

The Georgia commissioners issued a long and strongly worded protest against the treaty the day before the signing. They objected to the restrictions on their freedom in dealing with the Indians, to the place and manner of the negotiations, to the commissioners' open rejection of the treaties of Augusta, Galphinton, and Shoulderbone, to

33. *ASPIA*, 1:589.
34. Ibid., 591–94. The quotation is on 591.
35. Kappler, 2:46–50.

the grant of land to the United States for posts without the consent of Georgia (as violating Article I, section 8, of the Constitution), and to being liable for half the provisions supplied at the council. They claimed that the United States commissioners knew *before* the treaty council met that the Creeks had adamantly decided against any land cessions and that sticking the state with payment for the council was a "fraud on the State, and a trick, unworthy of the dignity and honor of the United States," for the treaty was to serve federal purposes and the state would reap no benefits from it.[36]

These complaints were considered by the Senate, for Washington, on January 4, 1797, laid the treaty before the Senate with the bulky correspondence and other papers relating to it. The Senate spent a good deal of time on the matter, showing special concern for Georgia's protest against the grant of land around the posts without its consent. In the end, the Senate agreed to the treaty with the following proviso: "That nothing . . . shall be construed to affect any claim of the State of Georgia to the right of pre-emption in the land therein set apart for military or trading posts; or to give to the United States, without the consent of the said State, any right to the soil, or to the exclusive legislation over the same, or any other right than that of establishing, maintaining, and exclusively governing, military and trading posts within the Indian territory . . . as long as the frontier of Georgia may require these establishments." Thus the Senate, mindful of Georgia's claims, amended the treaty, although there is no evidence that the executive was not in accord with the changes.[37]

Despite the conflicts between the federal government and Georgia, the Treaty of Coleraine, unlike that of New York, was effective, and peace was finally established on the southern frontiers, the result of changed circumstances between 1790 and 1796 that strengthened the federal government's position. Alexander McGillivray had died in February 1793. Defeat of the Indians in the Northwest Territory by Anthony Wayne in 1794 removed one obstacle to forceful United States action in the south, and the Treaty of San Lorenzo (Pinckney Treaty) with Spain in 1794 ended American-Spanish rivalry in the southwest. The firm resolve of Washington's administration to protect the Indians from avaricious whites strengthened its hand in dealing with the Indians. That the executive was more confidant in its treaty making was shown,

36. *ASPIA,* 1:613–14.
37. *Senate Ex. Proc.,* 1:219, 222, 223, 225, 226, 227, 229, 231 (for quoted section). See also the discussion in Hayden, *Senate and Treaties,* 97–100.

too, by its proceedings in the second Creek treaty. Whereas the Treaty of New York had been preceded by extensive collaborative discussion with the Senate, that of Coleraine was simply presented to the Senate as an established fact.

Provisions for Trade

Treaties by themselves were not sufficient for managing relations with the Indians. The constant complaints from the Indians of violation of the boundaries set by the treaties and the simultaneous cries from settlers about Indian depredations convinced Washington and Knox that something more was needed if the promises made to the Indians about guaranteeing their lands were to be kept and the honor of the republic thus preserved. The president's insistent call upon Congress to take some action was met by a series of laws "to regulate trade and intercourse with the Indian tribes." These laws, which were originally designed to implement the treaties and enforce them against obstreperous whites, gradually came to embody the basic features of federal policy and became a means parallel to treaties for governing Indian affairs. The first of the laws (July 22, 1790) continued the pattern set by the Ordinance of 1786 by establishing a licensing system for trade with the Indians. But it also struck directly at the frontier difficulties. To prevent the steady eating away at the Indian lands by individual or by state acquisitions, the law explicitly stated in section 4:

> No sale of lands made by any Indians, or any nation or tribe of Indians within the United States, shall be valid to any person or persons, or to any state, whether having the right of pre-emption to such lands or not, unless the same shall be made and duly executed at some public treaty, held under the authority of the United States.

And to put a stop to the outrages committed on the Indians by whites who aggressively invaded the Indian country, the law provided punishment for murder and other crimes committed by whites against the Indians.[38]

38. 1 Stat. 137–38.

The law did not prove strong enough to restrain the whites and defend the Indians, and Washington continued his campaign to provide a rule of law and justice in dealing with the Indians. In his annual message to Congress on October 25, 1791, he outlined his basic principles for advancing the happiness of the Indians and attaching them firmly to the United States. He had a six-point program:

1. An "impartial dispensation of justice" toward the Indians.
2. A carefully defined and regulated method of purchasing lands from the Indians, in order to avoid imposition on the Indians and controversy about the reality and extent of the purchases.
3. Promotion of commerce with the Indians, "under regulations tending to secure an equitable deportment toward them."
4. "Rational experiments" for imparting to the Indians the "blessings of civilization."
5. Authority for the president to give presents to the Indians.
6. An "efficacious provision" for punishing those who infringed Indian rights, violated treaties, and thus endangered the peace of the nation.[39]

In 1793 Congress replaced the first trade and intercourse law (which had been authorized to run for only three years) with a second and stronger measure, and three years later still another law was enacted. The 1796 act provided the first designation of the boundaries of the Indian country in statute law. This delineation was meant to indicate with added clarity the government's intention to uphold the treaties. There was opposition in Congress to this provision and to the strong measures to prevent encroachment on the Indian lands, but the law emerged unscathed. In 1799 the law was reenacted with only minor changes.[40]

Much of Washington's program for Indian affairs was contained in these intercourse laws, and the statutory measures were continued into the nineteenth century with important new laws in 1802 and in 1834. But Washington had another plan as well. "Next to a rigorous execution of justice on the violators of peace," he told Congress on December 3, 1793, "the establishment of commerce with the Indian nations in behalf

39. James D. Richardson, comp., *A Compilation of the Messages and Papers of the Presidents*, 10 vols. (Washington: GPO, 1896–99), 1:104–5.

40. See Francis Paul Prucha, *American Indian Policy in the Formative Years: The Indian Trade and Intercourse Acts, 1790–1834* (Cambridge: Harvard University Press, 1962).

of the United States is most likely to conciliate their attachment." And the president proposed a system of government trading houses (called factories) to offer competition to the profit-seeking private traders and thus eliminate fraud and extortion in the trade. Congress heeded the president's advice and in 1795 provided a tentative system of trading houses and in 1796 established the program firmly as an essential element in American Indian policy that lasted until 1822, when it was crushed by the power of private fur traders.[41]

Treaties were covenants with the Indians that bound the tribes and the United States government to carry out the stipulations set forth. The trade and intercourse laws were aimed not at the Indians but at white citizens of the United States, but they had many of the same ends as the treaties. The factory system sought to benefit the Indians and promote peaceful relations with the white society by eliminating abuses in the trade and ultimately advancing the civilization programs already enunciated in the treaties and in the intercourse laws.

The century ended with this tripartite policy in place. The intercourse laws and those establishing the trading houses were unilateral actions on the part of the United States in regulating the relations between its citizens and the Indians. The treaties, on the other hand, were bilateral agreements, ostensibly based on negotiations between the two parties, and an honest diplomatic give and take can be found from time to time in future decades of treaty making. But in the new century, treaties to a large extent became merely another means for the United States government to carry out the domestic Indian policy it had adopted—not unmindful, to be sure, of the Indians' welfare (as whites conceived it) but primarily concerned with the interests of the rapidly expanding white population of the United States.

41. Fifth Annual Message, Richardson, *Messages and Papers*, 1:141. There is full discussion of the trading houses in Francis Paul Prucha, *The Great Father: The United States Government and the American Indians*, 2 vols. (Lincoln: University of Nebraska Press, 1984), 1:115–34.

PART TWO

Instruments of Federal Policy

Between the beginning of Thomas Jefferson's administration and the end of the 1860s the United States engaged in six decades of active, and in some cases almost frenetic, treaty making with the Indians. The bulk of the ratified Indian treaties—348 of them—were negotiated in that period, and they exhibited a great variety in purpose and scope. Along with the series of trade and intercourse laws, which regulated by statute the relations between white citizens and the Indians, treaties became primary instruments for carrying out federal Indian policy. As that policy developed in complexity, so too did the intercourse laws and the treaty system. It is not true that the treaties were simply imposed upon the Indians—although there were examples of such action—for the Indians, too, saw benefits in the system. But the treaties were European instruments, and their history is heavy with white designs.

Of signal importance were the massive land transfers by which the Indians lost title to most of the continental United States. By 1860, cessions of land made by the Indians in the treaties had cleared the eastern half of the nation of Indian title (roughly to the ninety-eighth meridian, well west of the Mississippi River), and the Indians had lost as well most of the Pacific slope. In the next decade much of the remaining trans-Mississippi West passed into white hands.[1]

1. A dramatic view of the transfer of lands from Indians to whites can be seen in the series of maps showing Indian land cessions decade by decade in Francis Paul Prucha, *Atlas of American Indian Affairs* (Lincoln: University of Nebraska Press, 1990), 22–30.

A good deal of the land transfer occurred during the period of Indian removal in the 1830s, when eastern lands of the Indians were exchanged for lands beyond the Mississippi, with the fatuous hope among federal officials that west of the Great Lakes and west of Arkansas and Missouri the Indians would be secure from white pressures and white vices. Then the great territorial acquisitions of the 1840s—Texas, Oregon, and the Mexican Cession—upset that vision, and the United States suddenly had to deal with new communities of Indians on the plains, in the mountains, and beyond the Sierras and Cascades. Although these western Indians differed in marked respects from those who had originally lived east of the Mississippi, the old treaty patterns were used to deal with them. As westering white citizens moved to Oregon and California and onto the plains, they aroused Indian resentment and resistance that led to two and a half decades of Indian wars. The Civil War, too, in which the southern Indians in what is now Oklahoma joined the Confederacy, brought new problems.

The convenient solution for all the western problems was to extend the trade and intercourse laws to the new regions and to sign treaties with the newly encountered Indian inhabitants. The treaties in the new West recapitulated in their reformist and civilizing tendencies the old treaties, which were in fact consciously adopted as patterns.

There was occasional criticism of the treaty system from United States officials and voicing of doubts by them and other Americans about whether treaties were a legitimate form of agreement between an increasingly dominant white society and the increasingly weakened and dependent Indian tribes. During the debate over Indian removal, especially, were the pros and cons of treaty making vigorously debated, but there was no concerted drive yet to end the system.

CHAPTER FIVE

Testing the Treaty System

1800 to the War of 1812

Jefferson's administration continued the process of treaty making, accepting without question what by then had become the traditional method of dealing with the Indian tribes. Between 1800 and the War of 1812 the treaty system was well tested, as treaties were negotiated with the southern Indians, with the Six Nations in New York, and with the tribes in the Old Northwest—altogether some thirty treaties. These documents specified and confirmed the uses to which treaties were put by the United States government.

Treaties with the Southern Indians

The treaties with the southern tribes before the War of 1812 were generally well ordered. The commissioners had clear instructions (even though they were given a good deal of discretion), and they dealt with established chiefs of tribes that already had been recognized as nations in treaties concluded at the end of the Revolutionary War. And except for some overlapping of claims, the different tribes had clearly defined territories. The Indians, of course, were not easily swayed to part with lands they did not want to sell, so the goals of the United States were only partially obtained. Nevertheless, the continual pressure from white settlers, the decrease in game on Indian hunting lands, the heavy debts the Indians owed to merchants and traders, and some judicious attention to pliant chiefs enabled the United States to acquire extensive new lands.[1]

The treaties were short documents and primarily land cession instruments, and the chief American motive for the cessions was to satisfy the expanding white population seeking new lands. "Our seventeen States compose a great and growing nation," Jefferson told visiting Choctaws in Washington at the end of 1803, "Their children are as the leaves of the trees, which the winds are spreading over the forest."[2] But Jefferson had other concerns, as well. Out of fear of foreign invasion up the Mississippi Valley, he was determined to obtain possession of lands bordering the river on the east. In addition, roads through the Indian country were needed to tie the sections of the nation together.

The Indians—especially the Creeks and the Cherokees—strongly resisted selling more land, though little by little they gave in. The Choctaws and to some extent the Chickasaws, burdened by debts owed to the British trading firm of Panton, Leslie and Company, were more willing to cede lands so that they could obtain funds to pay their creditors. Jefferson's remarks about encouraging the Indians to run up debts at United States factories because they would then be willing to "lop them off" by cessions of land have been frequently quoted as an indication of the president's cynicism.[3] But in fact the Indians needed little encouragement to run into debt. As hunting for furs and pelts declined, cession of lands was the only way at hand to pay for trade goods that had become necessary for their well-being.

In May 1800 Congress authorized $15,000 "to defray the expense of such treaty or treaties, as the President of the United States shall deem it expedient to hold with the Indians south of the river Ohio." Jefferson acted quickly, and through Secretary of War Henry Dearborn he made preparations to deal with those tribes. Postponing action with

1. The story of Indian policy in regard to the southern tribes in this period is told critically in Reginald Horsman, *Expansion and American Indian Policy, 1783–1812* (East Lansing: Michigan State University Press, 1967), chap. 8, "The South, 1799–1809," 115–41. A more favorable view of the government's policy and action is presented in Thomas D. Clark and John D. W. Guice, *Frontiers in Conflict: The Old Southwest, 1795–1830* (Albuquerque: University of New Mexico Press, 1989), 29–39.

2. *The Writings of Thomas Jefferson*, ed. Andrew A. Lipscomb, 20 vols. (Washington: Thomas Jefferson Memorial Association, 1903–4), 16:401.

3. The Jefferson texts cited are "Hints on the Subject of Indian Boundaries, suggested for Consideration," December 29, 1802, *Writings of Thomas Jefferson*, ed. Lipscomb, 17:374, and Jefferson to Harrison, February 27, 1803, ibid., 10:370. There is a sprightly refutation of the charges in Clark and Guice, *Frontiers in Conflict*, 37–38.

the Creeks for the time being, Dearborn in mid-June 1801 called the Cherokees to a conference at Southwest Point in eastern Tennessee on August 1, the Chickasaws at Chickasaw Bluffs on September 1, and the Choctaws at Natchez on October 1, urging them to send their principal men as representatives of the whole tribe.[4]

In instructions of June 24 to William R. Davie, James Wilkinson, and Benjamin Hawkins, the United States commissioners, Dearborn outlined what they were to seek from each of the tribes and what compensation might be paid. Above all, the commissioners were cautioned to proceed diplomatically. They were told to pay careful attention to the disposition of the Indians and to introduce the wishes of the government in such a way that they could drop them quietly in the face of Indian objections "without giving the Indians an opportunity to reply with a decided negative, or raising in them unfriendly and inimical dispositions." None of the propositions were to be stated in a "tone of demands," and the commissioners were to proceed according to their judgment of the prospects of success of the various items they proposed.[5]

Less than a month later, Dearborn sent the commissioners special instructions for dealing with the Creeks, whom they were to meet at Fort Wilkinson in Georgia after dealing with the other tribes. He charged them to obtain the area known as Tallassee County and to investigate the possibility of gaining land also between the Oconee and the Ocmulgee rivers. "The Creeks being a powerful and proud nation, and great jealousies having at different times arisen between them and the frontier inhabitants," Dearborn told the commissioners, "all prudent means in your power should be exerted to reconcile them, and to remove every obstacle to their mutual friendship."[6]

The results of this first round of nineteenth-century treaties were mixed. "Our applications to the Cherokees failed altogether," Jefferson admitted. "Though our overtures to them were moderate, and respectful of their rights, their determination was, to yield no accommodation." The commissioners' request for a road through Cherokee country and

4. 2 Stat. 82; Dearborn to Cherokees, Chickasaws, and Choctaws, June 18, 1801, WD LS, Book A, 55–56 (M15, roll 1). The invitations were to be delivered to the Indians by their agents; see Dearborn to John McKee, June 18, 1801, and Dearborn to Return J. Meigs, June 18, 1801, ibid., 54–55.

5. Dearborn to Davie, Wilkinson, and Hawkins, June 24, 1801, *ASPIA*, 1:649–50. Davie was replaced by Andrew Pickens on July 16. Dearborn to Pickens, July 16, 1801, and Dearborn to Wilkinson and Hawkins, July 16, 1801, WD LS, Book A, 101–2 (M15, roll 1).

6. Dearborn to Wilkinson, Hawkins, and Pickens, July 17, 1801, *ASPIA*, 1:651.

for sites for houses of entertainment and ferries was met curtly by the Indians: "The roads you propose, we do not wish to have made through our country."[7]

The Chickasaws and the Choctaws were more obliging and allowed roads through their lands. The Choctaws pleased the commissioners by indicating a willingness to consider agriculture and domestic manufactures and by rejecting the whiskey that was intended as presents for them.[8] The Creeks, in delayed negotiations, in June 1802 ceded two narrow strips of land in exchange for sizable annuities, goods, and payment of debts and allowed the United States to establish military posts within their country.[9]

The first round of treaties with these southern tribes was quickly followed by another stretching from 1802 to 1806 that provided a series of land cessions. The initial treaties, with the Choctaws, were simple "conventions" formally specifying boundaries for lands previously ceded by the Indians to Great Britain. These were routine matters, hardly calling for formal treaty procedures, but there seemed to be no other way to accomplish the business.[10]

More complicated was a "treaty of limits" negotiated with the Choctaws by Silas Dinsmoor, a New Hampshire Yankee who was their agent, and James Robertson, a Tennessee soldier and land speculator. President Jefferson, eager to build up settlements along the Mississippi, wanted land for that purpose held by the Choctaws, and the Choctaws, heavily in debt to Panton, Leslie and Company, were willing to sell. At the instigation of the company, the Indians in 1803 and 1804, knowing that they could not alienate their land to the company directly, petitioned the president to buy enough land to provide money to cancel the debts.[11]

7. Jefferson to Senate, December 23, 1801, *ASPIA*, 1:648; Jefferson to House of Representatives, February 9, 1802, ibid., 656; extract of speeches at Southwest Point, September 4, 1801, ibid., 656–57.

8. The Chickasaw and Choctaw treaties are in Kappler, 2:55–58; the minutes of the conferences are in *ASPIA*, 1:652 and 660–63. See also Wilkinson, Hawkins, and Pickens to Dearborn, October 25 and December 18, 1801, ibid., 651–52, 658–59. The roadways conceded are shown by a dotted line in Royce, *Cessions*, plates 36 and 54.

9. Kappler, 2:58–59; Wilkinson and Hawkins to Dearborn, July 15, 1802, *ASPIA*, 1:669–70. The journal of the conference appears ibid., 672–81. Jefferson submitted the Chickasaw, Choctaw, and Creek treaties in December 1801 and March and December 1802; all were unanimously approved by the Senate and duly ratified and proclaimed by the president. *Senate Ex. Proc.*, 1:399–429 passim.

10. Kappler, 2:63–64, 69–70; Royce, *Cessions*, plates 1 and 36, area no. 46. General Wilkinson was the sole United States commissioner for these treaties; both were approved unanimously by the Senate. *Senate Ex. Proc.*, 1:430–36, 452–55.

11. Choctaw petitions of September 20, 1803, and August 23, 1804, Documents

A preliminary meeting with the Choctaws at Fort St. Stephens in the summer of 1805 produced no results.[12] Then, in November 1805, a treaty was signed at Mount Dexter in the Choctaw country. The Indians were unwilling to cede the lands along the Mississippi, but with the heavy debt resting upon them and Panton, Leslie and Company more insistent on payment, they made a large cession of lands in southern Mississippi Territory. In compensation the United States agreed to pay $50,000, of which $48,000 was "to enable the Mingoes to discharge the debt due to their merchants and traders, and also, to pay for the depredations committed on stock, and other property by evil disposed persons of the said Chaktaw nation."[13]

Jefferson still clung to his desire to gain lands along the Mississippi and lamented the fact that the Choctaws had won out at Mount Dexter

---

(T494), roll 1, frames 136–37; undated memorial of John Forbes, head of the company, to the president (which gives a detailed history of the Choctaw debts), ibid., frames 140–46. Jefferson's views on acquiring lands along the Mississippi are expressed in "Hints on the Subject of Indian Boundaries," December 29, 1802, *Writings of Thomas Jefferson*, ed. Lipscomb, 17:373–77. See also Dearborn to Wilkinson, April 16, 1803, in *Terr. Papers*, 5:214, in which he remarked, "If the debt [of the Choctaws to Panton, Leslie and Company] should prove very large nothing could tempt the Government to meddle with it but the acquisition of Country on the Mississippi. Our views are to plant on the Mississippi a population equal to its own defence." The complicated story of Indian indebtedness to Panton, Leslie and Company and action to cover the debts by cessions of land is told in detail with full documentation in Robert S. Cotterill, "A Chapter of Panton, Leslie and Company," *Journal of Southern History* 10 (August 1944): 275–92. Forbes had extended dealings with Secretary of War Dearborn, some of which appear in *ASPIA,* 1:750–71.

12. This conference drew a sharp rebuke from the secretary of war because of the extravagance of the provisions charged to the treaty negotiations. Dearborn wrote to Dinsmoor to criticize him for ordering such supplies for the commissioners' use and to question his prudence and discretion:

> The quantity and expense of articles of the highest luxury, such as could not have been intended for the Indians, exceed all reasonable bounds. The amount of the most delicate spices, anchovies, raisins, almonds, hyson tea, coffee, mustard, preserves, English cheese, segars, brandy, wine, etc. etc. could not have been either necessary or useful. Many of the articles ought never to have appeared on a bill of expenses for an Indian Treaty, especially in the wilderness. . . . Such accounts of expenses at an Indian Treaty, have, I presume, never before been exhibited to our Government and, it is to be wished that we may never have a second exhibition of the Kind.

Dearborn to Dinsmoor, August 28, 1805, WD LS, Book B, 101–2 (M15, roll 2).

13. Kappler, 2:87–88; Royce, *Cessions,* plates 1 and 36, area no. 61. Some historians have considered the grant in the treaty to John Pitchlynn as simply a present for favorable work as interpreter, but that charge has been refuted in Samuel J. Wells, "Rum, Skins, and Powder: A Choctaw Interpreter and the Treaty of Mount Dexter," *Chronicles of Oklahoma* 61 (Winter 1983–84): 422–28.

and ceded alternate lands instead to cover their debts. He stubbornly refused to send the treaty to the Senate. As he later told that body, "[Because the treaty was] against express instructions, and not according with the object then in view, I was disinclined to its ratification, and therefore did not, at the last session of Congress, lay it before the Senate for their advice, but have suffered it to lie unacted on." But conditions changed, as tension arose between the United States and Spain over West Florida, and Jefferson reconsidered. "It is now, perhaps," he said at the beginning of 1808, "become as interesting to obtain footing for a strong settlement of militia along our southern frontier, eastward of the Mississippi, as on the west of that river; and more so than higher up the river itself. The consolidation of the Mississippi territory, and the establishing a barrier of separation between the Indians and our southern neighbors, are also important objects." So he finally submitted the treaty to the Senate on January 15, 1808, and the Senate approved it unanimously on January 27.[14]

The Chickasaws, too, were indebted to Panton, Leslie and Company and agreed to a land cession in 1805; the treaty provided $20,000 "for the use of the nation at large, and for the payment of the debts due to their merchants and traders." As was common in the treaties, the United States provided special payments for the chiefs.[15]

The United States, pressed by Georgia, did not give up its intention to gain from the Creeks the lands in Georgia between the Oconee and the Ocmulgee rivers, but it was a long process, for the Indians did not want to give up the lands. A conference in 1803 failed to gain Indian assent, and Dearborn informed Governor John Milledge of Georgia that the boundary would be marked in conformity with the stipulations of the 1802 Treaty of Fort Wilkinson. But soon new negotiations were undertaken, and in November 1804 the Indians granted land west to the Ocmulgee and were promised payment of $200,000 to be held in trust by the secretary of war, with 6 percent interest paid to the Indians semiannually.[16] It was a high price, but a necessary one, as the president explained to the Senate when he submitted the treaty for its approval in December 1804.[17]

14. Jefferson to Senate, January 15, 1808, *ASPIA*, 1:748–49; *Senate Ex. Proc.*, 2: 65–67.

15. Kappler, 2:79–80; Royce, *Cessions*, plate 56, area no. 55. Instructions to the treaty commissioners are in Dearborn to Robertson and Dinsmoor, March 20, 1805, *ASPIA*, 1:700.

16. The treaty and related documents are printed in *ASPIA*, 1:690–93.

17. Jefferson to Senate, December 13, 1804, ibid., 690–91.

The Senate refused its sanction. On February 2, 1805, after an unsuccessful attempt to send the treaty back to the president for "such modification of the terms contemplated by said treaty, as well relative to price, as to the mode of payment, as may be more conformable to the policy and interest of the United States," it rejected the treaty by a vote of nineteen to twelve. When the Senate returned the treaty, however, it sent along a special resolution requesting the president "to cause a further and immediate negotiation to be entered into, for the procuring of the lands between the Oconee and Oakmulgee rivers, not already obtained, together with such other lands as the said Creeks may be disposed to relinquish."[18]

Finally, in Washington, on November 14, 1805, Dearborn signed the desired treaty with the Creeks, in which the Ocmulgee became the boundary and a horse path was authorized from the Ocmulgee to Mobile through the Creek country. The Creeks accepted an annuity of "money or goods, and implements of husbandry, at the option of the Creek nation"—$12,000 worth for eight years and then $11,000 worth for ten succeeding years—a little more than half as much as the original treaty had provided. The Senate approved the treaty twenty-eight to one on December 23, 1805.[19] Although they were urged to do so, the Creeks refused to specify in the treaty any use of the money to pay their debts to Panton, Leslie and Company.[20]

At length the Cherokees, who had refused to consider the proposals of the United States commissioners in 1801, signed a series of four treaties in 1804–6.[21] In the first of these, on October 24, 1804, the Cherokees agreed to no more than the relinquishment of a small tract in Georgia known as Wafford's Settlement, for a payment of $5,000 in goods and an additional annuity of $1,000.[22]

The subsequent history of this treaty is a good indication of the less than sacrosanct character with which the documents were endowed, for

18. *Senate Ex. Proc.*, 1:483–84.

19. Kappler, 2:85–86; Royce, *Cessions*, plate 15, area no. 60; *Senate Ex. Proc.*, 2:3–4, 9.

20. See the discussion of Creek debts to the company in Cotterill, "A Chapter of Panton, Leslie and Company," especially 287–88.

21. There is useful information on the provisions and the historical background of these treaties in Charles C. Royce, "The Cherokee Nation of Indians: A Narrative of Their Official Relations with the Colonial and Federal Governments," *Fifth Annual Report of the Bureau of Ethnology*, 1883–1884 (Washington: GPO, 1887), 183–97. This report was reprinted as Charles C. Royce, *The Cherokee Nation of Indians* (Chicago: Aldine Publishing Company, 1975), with different pagination.

22. Kappler, 2:73–74; Royce, *Cessions*, plate 15, area no. 52.

the treaty was lost in the War Department files for twenty years. It was not received by President Jefferson and thus not sent to the Senate for its action. The Indians received the $5,000 payment on the spot and relinquished the land (which, in fact, was already well settled by whites), but the promised annuity was not forthcoming. Then, in January 1824, a Cherokee delegation in Washington brought up the question of the treaty, but the War Department, after a search of its files, could find no record of it. At that point the Cherokees produced their copy of the treaty and asked that it be sent to the Senate to complete the process of ratification. John McKee, one of the witnesses of the signing of the treaty in 1804 and then a member of the House of Representatives from Alabama, attested to the genuineness of the treaty, and Secretary of War John C. Calhoun sought information as well from Thomas Jefferson, who called the document genuine and asserted that his careful records of correspondence indicated that he had never received the treaty or laid it before the Senate; he apologized deeply for this "slip of the executive functionaries." The Cherokees' copy of the treaty was sent to the Senate, which gave its consent to ratification on May 13, 1824.[23]

Since the ill-fated treaty of 1804 had not obtained cession of all the lands that the federal government had instructed the treaty commissioners to acquire, three additional treaties were negotiated, one at Tellico, another in Washington, and a third at Chickamauga. In the first two the Cherokees ceded land, the successful negotiations being aided by gifts to the chiefs who signed the treaties (in the second treaty by means of secret articles). Return J. Meigs, the Cherokee agent, who was one of the commissioners, later wrote to the secretary of war, "With respect to the chiefs who have transacted the business with us, they will have their hands full to satisfy the ignorant, the obstinate, and the cunning of some of their own people, for which they well deserve this *silent* consideration."[24]

On December 2, 1807, Meigs negotiated another treaty with Cherokees, this time at Chickamauga on the Tennessee River, to purchase

23. The documents on this embarrassing situation are printed in *ASPIA*, 2:506–11. The Senate's action is in *Senate Ex. Proc.*, 3:374, 376–77. A note attached to the letter printed in the *American State Papers* from the secretary of war to the Cherokees reporting that the treaty could not be found reads: "Some time after this letter was written, a copy of the treaty referred to by the Cherokee delegation, with a copy of the communication from Daniel Smith, one of the commissioners by whom it was concluded, was accidentally found in a bundle of old miscellaneous papers." *ASPIA*, 2:507.

24. Kappler, 2:82–84; Royce, *Cessions*, plate 54, area nos. 57, 64. Meigs's letter is quoted in Royce, "Cherokee Nation of Indians," 197n.

from the Indians a tract of land six miles square as a site for iron works, although the Indians agreed as well that if the ore should give out in the ceded tract, "the United States shall have full liberty to get ore off their land in the most suitable place." Jefferson, in transmitting the brief treaty to the Senate, spoke strongly of the advantages of the measure, not least because the iron works would create a demand for corn and other provisions and would "immediately draw around it a close settlement of the Cherokees, would encourage them to enter on a regular life of agriculture, familiarize them with the practice and value of the arts, attach them to property, lead them, of necessity, and without delay, to the establishment of laws and government, and thus make a great and important advance towards assimilating their condition to ours." The Senate, apparently not moved by this prospective utopia and not convinced by the advantages Jefferson pointed out of producing cast and wrought iron in close proximity to the Indians, after considerable delay rejected the treaty unanimously on January 10, 1812.[25]

Land Transfers in New York

Land transfers accomplished in New York in the first years of the new century illustrate the wide latitude of Indian treaty procedures under the Constitution, for some documents in the official collection of Indian treaties are a far cry indeed from conventions between sovereign nations.

The sale of Indian lands to the state of New York or to individuals or land companies within the state had begun at the end of the eighteenth century. A notable example was the sale on September 15, 1797, by the Senecas to the land speculator Robert Morris of all the country in western New York assigned to the Indians by the Treaty of Canandaigua in 1794, except for certain reserved parcels. This was done by an "indenture." Although the document described the sale as done "at a treaty held under the authority of the United States," this transaction was not treated as an official treaty.[26]

25. The treaty and an explanatory letter from Meigs are printed with Jefferson's message to the Senate, March 10, 1808, *ASPIA,* 1:752–53. The action of the Senate is in *Senate Ex. Proc.,* 2:72, 73, 204, 205.

26. The document is printed in *Report of Special Committee to Investigate the Indian Problem of the State of New York, Appointed by the Assembly of 1888* [Whipple Report]

Then, in order to exchange tracts of land and to cede some of the reserved lands, new negotiations were undertaken in 1802 at the instigation of Governor George Clinton of New York. To handle them on the part of the United States, Thomas Jefferson appointed John Tayler of New York.[27] Secretary of War Dearborn sent instructions to Tayler on March 17, which made clear the commissioner's subordinate role to Governor Clinton: "Governor Clinton will notify you of the time and place of holding any such Conventions. You will act in some measure in the character of an umpire between the State and the said Indians in any bargains which may be made between the parties, and you will of course pay due attention to the interests of the Indians, and see that all transactions relative to our bargains are explicit and fair." Tayler's compensation was to come from New York, or, in case of cessions to the Holland Land Company, from the company. At the same time Dearborn wrote to Clinton about the proposed negotiations. "It has been considered," he said, "that all such bargains, between Individuals and any of the Indian Nations should be made under the direction of the Governor of the State in which such Indians reside. Mr. Taylor [sic] will therefore attend to the negociations between the aforesaid Agent [of the Holland Land Company] and the Senecas, by instructions from your Excellency when convenient for the parties."[28]

Out of the negotiations came four documents, which President Jefferson on December 28, 1802, laid before the Senate as treaties, asking "whether you will advise and consent to their respective ratifications."[29]

1. Between the state of New York (through agents Ezra L'Hommedieu and Simon De Witt) and the Oneida Indians, dated June 4,

---

(Albany: Troy Press Company, 1889), 131–34, and it appears in Ratified Treaties as no. 27, but both the *United States Statutes at Large* and Kappler print it only as an appendix. Royce, *Cessions*, 658–60, enters it as a "contract" and shows the cession on plate 47, area bounded by a red line.

27. Jefferson to Senate, March 10, 1802, *Senate Ex. Proc.*, 1:408. This nomination superseded a similar nomination of Tayler for more restricted negotiations made on February 10, 1802; both nominations were confirmed by the Senate. Ibid., 406, 407, 409. The first nomination of Tayler with accompanying documents was referred to a committee for study, and the consideration and approval of the nomination appear to have served as preliminary Senate approval of the negotiations to be undertaken.

28. Dearborn to Tayler, March 17, 1802, and Dearborn to Clinton, March 17, 1802, WD LS, Book A, 194–95 (M15, roll 1).

29. Jefferson to Senate, December 27, 1802, *ASPIA*, 1:663–64. The treaties and related papers are printed ibid., 664–68.

1802, by which the tribe ceded tracts of land to the state for an immediate sum plus a perpetual annuity to be paid by the state.

2. Between the state of New York (represented by Governor Clinton) and the Seneca Indians, dated August 20, 1802, by which the Indians sold to the state lands along the Niagara River.

3. Between the Holland Land Company and the Seneca Nation, dated June 30, 1802, in which an exchange of parcels of land was negotiated. The heading of this document calls it an "indenture," but the body of the document speaks of "a treaty, held under the authority of the United States." The document was signed by only the Senecas and the Holland agents, but Tayler attested that it was done "at a full and general treaty . . . under the authority of the United States."[30]

4. Between the Seneca Indians and Oliver Phelps and his associates Isaac Bronson and Horatio Jones, dated June 30, 1802, by which the Indians sold the men a tract of land along the Genessee River known as Little Beard's Reservation. The document speaks of "a treaty held under the authority of the United States . . . in the presence of John Tayler, Esquire, commissioner, appointed by the President of the United States for holding said treaty." Actually, Tayler had some doubts about whether his commission included this action, but apparently those doubts were resolved positively.[31]

The Senate on receipt of the four treaties from the president considered them over a period of days from December 28, 1802, to February 4, 1803, referring some of them to a committee for study; in the end it advised and consented to them *all* and so informed the president.[32]

But of the four documents only two—those with Oliver Phelps and with the Holland Land Company—were finally ratified by the president, the first on January 12 and the second on February 7, 1803. They were incorporated into the State Department's official collection of treaties (nos. 33 and 34), printed in the *United States Statutes at Large*, and entered into Charles J. Kappler's official compilation.[33] The treaties between the Oneidas and the Senecas and the state of New York were dropped for reasons that cannot now be ascertained.[34]

30. Ibid., 665–66.

31. Tayler to Dearborn, July 19, 1802, and Oliver Phelps to Dearborn, July 24, 1802, ibid., 666–67.

32. *Senate Ex. Proc.*, 1:427–31, 442. The vote was unanimous in all cases save that of the Holland Land Company, in which there was one negative vote.

33. Ratified Treaties (M668, roll 3); 7 Stat. 70–73; Kappler, 2:60–62.

34. They are printed in *ASPIA*, 1:664–66, and appear also in an appendix to *Report*

William Henry Harrison

Treaty making in the Old Northwest was more compli-
cated and confused than that with the established tribes in the south
and in New York. The Treaty of Greenville in 1795, with its effective
land grants north of the Ohio, had not settled affairs as firmly as General
Wayne had imagined. The line established by the treaty was not immediately marked, and the press of settlers to the north and west created
new troubles with the resident Indians. Parcels of land granted to the
United States at Greenville beyond the principal boundary, especially
that at Vincennes, needed specification. Some tribes in the area, like the
Sacs and Foxes, moreover, had not signed treaties with the United
States, and others, like the Kaskaskias, had wasted away until their land
claims seemed out of proportion to their small numbers. To add to the
difficulties, in the first decade of the new century, the Indian tribes of
the region showed a restlessness, aggravated by British intrigue, that
could easily have led to war.

Responsibility for Indian affairs in this cauldron rested largely on
William Henry Harrison, who on May 13, 1800, at the age of twenty-
seven, was appointed governor of the newly created Indiana Territory.[35]
Harrison, when he arrived at Vincennes in January 1801 to assume his
new duties, faced the difficulties realistically. He noted the near impossibility of bringing white murderers of Indians to justice, the need to
remove white settlers who had settled beyond the treaty lines, the illegal
destruction of game on the Indian lands by whites, the necessity to
conciliate the Indians lest the abuses lead them to war against the United

of Special Committee to Investigate the Indian Problem of the State of New York, 214–15,
256–59.

35. Sources on Harrison's Indian policy and actions, including treaty making, are
extensive. The best collection of published papers is Logan Esarey, ed., *Messages and
Letters of William Henry Harrison*, 2 vols., Indiana Historical Collections, vols. 7 and 9
(Indianapolis: Indiana Historical Commission, 1922), which can be supplemented by
Terr. Papers, vol. 7, and *ASPIA*, vol. 1. An old but generally balanced account of Harrison's
Indian work is Dorothy Burne Goebel, *William Henry Harrison: A Political Biography*,
Indiana Historical Collections, vol. 14 (Indianapolis: Historical Bureau of the Indiana
Library and Historical Department, 1926), chap. 4, "Superintendent of Indian Affairs,"
89–127. For a brief and somewhat hostile account, see Horsman, *Expansion and American
Indian Policy*, chap. 9, "The Old Northwest, 1795–1809," 142–57.

States, the immense and destructive problem of drunkenness among the Indians, and the difficulty of dealing effectively with Indian groups that had not yet entered into any treaty relationship with the United States.[36]

For the next two years a heavy correspondence about Indian affairs passed between Harrison at Vincennes and the secretary of war and the president. The governor made clear the needs and offered his suggestions for action. He depended closely on the directions he received from his superiors in Washington, but they in turn gave him almost total discretion in handling specific affairs with the Indians.

Three particular elements in the relations with the Indians in the Old Northwest called for new treaties with the tribes.

Foremost was the matter of land. The United States wanted new cessions to satisfy the pressure of white settlers and to consolidate the settlements already begun, as, for example, between the Greenville cession and the growing settlement at Vincennes. And when news reached the United States of the transfer of Spanish Louisiana to France, Jefferson and others became alarmed about American security and sought land cessions from the Indians that would give the United States control of land along the upper Mississippi. Jefferson in February 1803 remarked on the importance of gaining the whole eastern border of the Mississippi. "The crisis is pressing," he wrote. "Whatever can now be obtained must be obtained quickly. The occupation of New Orleans, hourly expected, by the French, is already felt like a light breeze by the Indians. You know the sentiments they entertain of that nation. Under the hope of their protection, they will immediately stiffen against cessions of land to us. We had better therefore do at once what can now be done."[37]

Before new cessions could be negotiated, however, precise boundaries needed to be established and marked for lands already ceded (especially at Greenville in 1795), and the continual and often bitter controversies among the different tribes about joint or independent

36. Harrison to Dearborn, July 15, 1801, Esarey, *Messages and Letters*, 1:25–31.

37. Jefferson to Harrison, February 27, 1803, ibid., 73. Harrison was well aware of the Indians' fondness for the French. Of a later conference with Indians, he reported: "One of their orators at the breaking up of the Council assured me in the name of the rest that they would in future look upon the United States in the same light that they had formerly done their fathers the French—An unexpected Compliment and one which I never supposed I should hear from an Indian—They almost universally consider the era of the French establishment in this Country as their golden Age—And time has not deminished the ardour of their attachment to that Nation." Harrison to Jefferson, August 29, 1805, *Terr. Papers*, 7:301–2.

ownership of particular areas had to be resolved. Such resolution of disputed boundaries and disputed ownership was needed not only to maintain peace but to facilitate new cessions of land for white occupancy. As Harrison candidly reported to the secretary of war near the end of his tenure as governor: "It was at once determined, that the community of interests in the land amongst the Indian tribes, which seemed to be recognized by the treaty of Greenville, should be objected to; and that each individual tribe should be protected in every claim that should appear to be founded in reason and justice." Harrison also wanted to provide compensation to Indians who lived on lands to be ceded, even though they did not have claim to the land, and he admitted such Indians as parties to the treaties. In addition he sought to get recognition of particular tribal claims by the other tribes, so that there would be no grounds for complaint when the lands were transferred.[38]

A second strong element of Jeffersonian policy to be incorporated into treaties was the program of civilization that sought to turn the Indians from hunters into farmers.[39] Secretary of War Dearborn reminded Harrison that the intention of Congress in establishing trading houses was to promote "the introduction of civilization, by encouraging and gradually introducing the arts of husbandry and domestic manufactures among them." And Jefferson himself repeatedly preached this doctrine to Indian groups who visited Washington. The president told Harrison, "The decrease of game rendering their subsistence by hunting insufficient, we wish to draw them to agriculture, to spinning and weaving."[40]

Harrison in turn harangued the Indians on the same point when he met them in council. He told a group of Kaskaskias, Kickapoos, Weas, Eel River Miamis, Piankashaws, and Potawatomis whom he met at

38. Harrison to the secretary of war, March 22, 1814, Esarey, *Messages and Letters*, 2:639. The complexity of determining just which tribes owned which tract and what proportion of ownership each joint owner could claim is clearly shown in the deliberations and findings of the Indian Claims Commission, which in the 1950s handled claims for additional compensation for the lands ceded in the Harrison treaties. See Indian Claims Commission, *Indians of Ohio, Indiana, Illinois, Southern Michigan, and Southern Wisconsin: Commission Findings*, 3 vols. (New York: Garland Publishing, 1974).

39. See the instructions sent to the Indian agent in the Northwest, Dearborn to William Lyman, July 14, 1801, *Terr. Papers*, 7:26–29. A copy of these instructions was sent on September 6, 1802, to Lyman's successor, Charles Jouett.

40. Dearborn to Harrison, February 23, 1803, Esarey, *Messages and Letters*, 1:39; Jefferson to Miamis, Potawatomis, and Weas, January 7, 1802, WD LS, Book A, 142–43 (M15, roll 1); Jefferson to Delawares, December 1808, Esarey, *Messages and Letters*, 1:333–35; Jefferson to Harrison, February 27, 1803, ibid., 70–71.

Vincennes in August 1802 that the president wanted them "to assemble your scattered warriors, and to form towns and villages, in situations best adapted to cultivation; he will cause you to be furnished with horses, cattle, hogs, and implements of husbandry, and will have persons provided to instruct you in the management of them." Harrison told the Indians of God's command for men to increase and multiply and that that divine command "could not be obeyed if we were all to depend upon the chase for our subsistence." In the minds of the Jeffersonians, adoption of white civilization and the cession of lands went hand in hand, for as Jefferson told Harrison, "When they [the Indians] withdraw themselves to the culture of a small piece of land, they will perceive how useless to them are their extensive forests, and will be willing to pare them off from time to time in exchange for necessaries for their farms and families."[41]

A third factor that led to treaties with the Indians under Harrison's jurisdiction was the patent needs of the Indians. Their dependence upon white goods, like that of Indian groups in other regions of the United States, became increasingly manifest, as advancing white settlement and a decrease in fur-bearing animals made reliance on the fur trade insufficient for their needs. Many Indians were eager enough for presents and annuity goods to be willing to cede lands, again and again, to the Americans. As Harrison noted when he explained to the secretary of war why he had included the Potawatomis in the Treaty of Fort Wayne, "The poverty and wretchedness of the Potawatomies made them extremely desirous of a treaty at which they expected to have their most pressing wants relieved."[42]

For these reasons treaty making proceeded rapidly under Harrison's direction. On February 8, 1803, Jefferson sent the governor a special commission, "with full power to conclude and sign any Treaty or Treaties, which may be found necessary with any Indian Tribes North West of the Ohio, and within the Territory of the United States, on the subject of their boundaries or Lands."[43] Between that date and the conclusion of treaties at the end of 1809, Harrison negotiated eleven treaties with the Indians.[44]

41. Harrison's address to Indian council, August 12, 1802, Esarey, *Messages and Letters*, 1:53–55; Jefferson to Harrison, February 27, 1803, ibid., 71.

42. Harrison to the secretary of war, November 3, 1809, ibid., 388.

43. *Terr. Papers*, 7:84–85.

44. Information on these treaties and citations to the *Statutes at Large* and to Kappler's compilation of treaties can be found in appendix B. The treaty with the Kaskaskias reserved for the United States the right to apportion the annuities among individual

Harrison succeeded in his mission, cajoling the tribes and playing upon their dependency for goods. He specified boundary lines for the tract at Vincennes ceded by the fourth article of the Treaty of Greenville and acquired a valuable salt spring in southern Indiana and sites for houses of entertainment along roads through Indian lands. The cessions made by the Indians stretched west to the Mississippi. By the end of 1805, in fact, he had gained for the United States a margin of land north of the Ohio above the mouth of the Wabash in present-day Indiana, roughly fifty miles in width. And in what is now Illinois he gained a large central area from the Kaskaskias and a connecting link with the Indiana lands from the Piankashaws—to say nothing of a huge cession made at St. Louis in 1804 by the Sacs and Foxes, who gave up their claims to the territory between the Mississippi and Illinois rivers, running north as far as Wisconsin and including a segment of land across the Mississippi in what is now Missouri. To make these cessions more secure, the governor obtained a release from other tribal claimants to some of these lands.[45]

In return the United States paid small sums in accordance with what it was accustomed to pay for Indian title. These were in the form of goods or money, paid on the spot or provided as annuities. Payments were intended to ease the hardships and suffering of the Indians, but the treaties also vigorously pushed a civilization program for the Indians. A good example is the treaty with the Delawares at Vincennes in 1804, in which the official rationale was explicitly set forth in the preamble:

---

families. Such a division may have been proposed by Harrison because of the small number of Kaskaskias still living, but it became a somewhat tricky maneuver on the part of the United States as it was included in later treaties. Dearborn wrote to Harrison on June 27, 1804: "It is suggested by the President of the United States, for your consideration and opinion, whether it would not be expedient to give certain annuities, to each actual family, during the existence of said family, even if the aggregate to a nation, should be increased 15 to 20 per cent. For instance, we give the Piankeshaws five hundred dollars per annum; suppose they have fifty families, we agree to give the nation twelve dollars for each family annually and when a family becomes extinct, the annuity to cease, or if, when its members decrease, the annuity to decrease in proportion." Esarey, *Messages and Letters*, 1:101.

45. The various cessions can be followed in Royce, *Cessions*. Of the Sac and Fox cession, Jefferson said, "This cession, giving us a perfect title to such a breadth of country on the eastern side of the Mississippi, with a command of the Ouisconsin, strengthens our means of retaining exclusive commerce with the Indians on the western side of the Mississippi; a right indispensable to the policy of governing those Indians by commerce, rather than by arms." Jefferson to the Senate, December 31, 1804, *Senate Ex. Proc.*, 1:478–79. The Sac and Fox treaty of 1804 is used as a case study of Jefferson's Indian policy in Donald Jackson, *Thomas Jefferson and the Stony Mountains: Exploring the West from Monticello* (Urbana: University of Illinois Press, 1981), 203–22.

The Delaware tribe of Indians finding that the annuity which they receive from the United States, is not sufficient to supply them with the articles which are necessary for their comfort and convenience, and afford the means of introducing amongst them the arts of civilized life, and being convinced that the extensiveness of the country they possess, by giving an opportunity to their hunting parties to ramble to a great distance from their towns, is the principal means of retarding this desirable event; and the United States being desirous to connect their settlements on the Wabash with the state of Kentucky . . .

The tribe ceded the land along the Ohio that the United States wanted, and the United States promised on its side to increase the tribe's annuity by $300, "to be exclusively appropriated to the purpose of ameliorating their condition and promoting their civilization." In addition the United States agreed to employ persons for five years to teach the Indians how to build fences, cultivate the earth, and perform "such of the domestic arts as are adapted to their situation," and $400 worth of draft horses, cattle, hogs, and implements of husbandry were to be delivered in the course of the next spring. All of this, plus $800 worth of goods delivered at once was the payment for the ceded tract.[46]

After Harrison's treaties of 1803, 1804, and 1805, conditions in the Old Northwest were not conducive to treaty making. Increasing hostility of the tribes, many of whom supported The Prophet (Tenskwatawa) and his brother Tecumseh, and the continuing British agitation convinced Harrison to lie low for the time being. But by the summer of 1809, the governor noted more peaceful circumstances, and he wrote to the secretary of war from Vincennes: "I have for several years considered a further extinguishment of Indian title . . . as a most desirable object. And it appears to me that the time has arrived when the purchase may be attempted with a considerable prospect of success."[47]

President Madison's secretary of war, William Eustis, quickly gave his approval: "The President of the United States," he wrote in mid-July, "authorizes and instructs you to take advantage of the most favorable moment for extinguishing the Indian title to Lands lying east of the Wabash and adjoining south on the lines of the Treaties of Fort Wayne [1803] and Grouseland. The compensation to be paid for this extinguishment should not exceed the rate heretofore given for the Indian title to Lands in that quarter; to prevent any future dissatisfaction,

46. Kappler, 2:70–72.
47. Harrison to the secretary of war, May 16, 1809, Esarey, *Messages and Letters*, 1:346.

Chiefs of all the Nations who have or pretend right to these lands, should be present at the Treaty; and, if practicable, the cession should be obtained without leaving any reservations." It was left to the governor to decide the method of payment—a gross sum at the signing of the treaty, installment payments, an annuity for a set number or years or in perpetuity, or a combination of these modes.[48]

Harrison decided to hold the treaty at Fort Wayne, rather than at Vincennes, "where the facility of procuring spirits and the constant intrusion of bad men amongst them would probably render them unmanageable." He met the various groups as they arrived, explained his purposes, and tried to calm the jealousies between tribes. In general meetings he pressed the Indians for a new cession, pointing to "the vast benefit which they derived from their annuities without which they would not be able to cloathe their woman & children," and that the proposed addition to these annuities would enable them to acquire domestic animals and begin raising them on a large scale. But he held firm against Indian demands for a higher price for their lands. He spoke to them, also, of the purposes and importance of treaties:

> No other power but the United States had ever Treated with them. Other Civilized Nations considered the lands of the Indians as their own and appropriated them to their own use whenever they pleased. A Treaty was considered by white people as a most solemn thing and those which were made by the United States with the Indian Tribes were considered as binding as those which were made with the most powerful Kings on the other side of the Big Water. They were all concluded with the same forms and printed in the same Book so that all the world might see them and brand with infamy the party which violated them. The United States would always adhere to their engagements. To do otherwise would be offensive to the great spirit and all the world would look upon them as a faithless people.[49]

The Miamis were the hardest to convince, but at length after a private conference with Harrison they too joined in signing the treaty, which took place on September 30, 1809. The number of Indians present at the council when the treaty was signed was 1,390. A supplementary treaty with the Miamis was signed the same day.[50]

The cessions included a strip of land in eastern Indiana which widened

48. Secretary of war to Harrison, July 15, 1809, ibid., 356–57.
49. Harrison to the secretary of war, August 29, 1809, *Terr. Papers*, 7:671; Journal of the Proceedings at the Indian Treaty at Fort Wayne, Esarey, *Messages and Letters*, 1:365, 372.
50. Journal of the Proceedings, ibid., 362–78.

the narrow triangle in the territory ceded at the Treaty of Greenville, a sizable area north of the Vincennes tract, and (subject to Kickapoo concurrence) two smaller tracts west of the Wabash along the border of Indiana and Illinois. Money and goods were presented at the treaty grounds, and the permanent annuities of the tribes were increased. Harrison rejoiced that the cessions would contain "upwards of two millions and a half of acres and will cost less than two cents per acre."[51] Then, in order to complete the negotiations and get approval from Indians who were not at Fort Wayne, Harrison signed separate treaties at Vincennes with the Weas on October 26 and with the Kickapoos on December 9. These were the last of Harrison's treaty making before the outbreak of the War of 1812.[52]

Harrison had had his way in arranging cessions of land from separate tribes, vindicating his opinion that joint ownership by all the tribes did not obtain. Formal treaties had proved an effective vehicle for his policies, and the governor had had full support from the president, secretary of war, and the Senate, which ratified all the treaties with little trouble. But the Treaty of Fort Wayne in 1809 severely aggravated the increasing Indian hostility to white advance in the Old Northwest. Tecumseh, seeking to build a confederacy of tribes against the whites, bitterly denounced the treaty. He claimed that the chiefs who sold the land had no right to do so and that they would be killed unless the land was restored to the Indians.[53] Harrison's encounters with Tecumseh only widened the difference between them, and Harrison's victory over The Prophet at Tippecanoe in 1811 accomplished nothing toward pacifying the Indians, who for the most part sided with the British in the war that was rapidly approaching.

Other Treaties in the North and West

While Governor Harrison carried on negotiations with Indians in his territory, other commissioners dealt with tribes outside his purview. One of these was Indian agent Charles Jouett, appointed a

51. Kappler, 2:101–3; Harrison to the secretary of war, October 1, 1809, Esarey, *Messages and Letters*, 1:358–59.

52. Kappler, 2:103–5. Harrison reported in detail on his actions at Fort Wayne to the secretary of war on November 3, 1809, in which he justified his procedures. Esarey, *Messages and Letters*, 1:387–91.

53. Tecumseh's speech to Harrison, August 20, 1810, ibid., 463–69.

treaty commissioner by Secretary of War Dearborn in the spring of 1805. Dearborn instructed him to hold a treaty with Wyandot, Ottawa, Chippewa, and other Indians at which the tribes could sell to two land companies their claims within the Western Reserve of Connecticut. Connecticut had reserved these lands lying south of Lake Erie when it transferred its western lands to the federal government, and the preemption rights to the western part of this reserve had fallen to the Connecticut Land Company and a company incorporated under the name of "the proprietors of the half million acres of land, lying south of lake Erie, called Sufferers' land."[54] Jouett's task was to call the interested Indians to a council, over which he would preside, so that they could cede the lands to the land companies at terms that would be "fair and just." Dearborn hoped to keep the cession price at from one to two cents an acre, in line with what the United States was paying at the time. He told Jouett, in addition, to attempt to purchase for the United States the tract of land lying between the forty-first parallel (the southern boundary of the Connecticut preemption rights) and the Treaty of Greenville line, at not more than two cents an acre. Dearborn estimated the tract at 1 million to 1,250,000 acres.[55]

On July 4, 1805, Jouett signed two treaties with the Wyandot, Ottawa, Chippewa, Munsee and Delaware, Shawnee, and Potawatomi Indians at Fort Industry near the mouth of the Maumee. In one, the Indians sold to the land companies the desired tract for the sum of $18,916.67. In the other the tribes ceded to the United States the land between the forty-first parallel and the Treaty of Greenville line as far west as the meridian 120 miles west of Pennsylvania, for which a perpetual annuity of $1,000 was agreed upon.[56] Jouett's presence at the agreement between the Indians and the land companies, like that of John Tayler at the Seneca treaties, fulfilled the stipulations of the trade and intercourse laws that forbade sale of lands by Indians without the concurrence of the federal government. It was a strange use of a formal treaty, but it protected the interests of the United States and of the Indians, too.

The problematic nature of treaty making on the western frontier is

54. The land in question lay between the forty-first and forty-second parallels and from the Cuyahoga River on the east to a north-south line 120 miles west of the Pennsylvania border. The Connecticut lands east of the Cuyahoga had already been relinquished by the Indians at Greenville.

55. Dearborn to Jouett, April 2, 1805, WD LS, Book B, 62–64 (M15, roll 2).

56. The two treaties appear in Ratified Treaties (M668, roll 3, nos. 44 and 45) and are printed in *ASPIA,* 1:695–96; for some reason the *Statutes at Large* and Kappler's compilation print only the second of them.

well illustrated by a treaty signed by Lieutenant Zebulon M. Pike with the Sioux at the mouth of the Minnesota (then St. Peter's) River on September 23, 1805. In the treaty the Indians relinquished, for military and trading posts, a nine-mile square at the mouth of the St. Croix River and a strip nine miles wide on each side of the Mississippi from the mouth of the Minnesota up to and including the Falls of St. Anthony. The treaty itself left blank the amount of payment, which the Senate filled in with the sum of $2,000. The treaty was slow in getting to Washington, but once received, Jefferson submitted it to the Senate on March 29, 1808, even though he said the United States had no immediate plan to establish a post in the area. The Senate approved it unanimously with the $2,000 insertion on April 16, but the treaty was never proclaimed by the president.[57]

The United States negotiated treaties also with Indians in Michigan Territory, which had been cut off from Indiana Territory in 1805. Dearborn sent a commission and instructions to Governor William Hull on July 22, 1806, directing him to negotiate with the "Chiefs of such Indian Tribes or Nations, as are actually interested" in a large section of land (some four or five million acres, Dearborn estimated) lying in southeastern Michigan, and, if possible, another tract in northwestern Ohio. Dearborn was solicitous that the number of Indians invited be kept to a minimum. "No greater number of Indians should attend the Treaty," he told Hull, "than what will be necessary to include all the Chiefs of any note of the respective nations. You will find it necessary, for you to be particularly attentive to this object, otherwise you will have such a concourse, as will be not only troublesome but verry expensive. From fifty to one hundred, is as great a number, as ought to be allowed to attend." He instructed Hull, further, not to entertain at public expense "a concourse of white people, who may have the curiosity to attend the Treaty," and very little liquor was to be furnished the Indians. As to prices for the land, Dearborn suggested that it should not be more than one cent an acre and "not on any condition to exceed two Cents per acre."[58]

On November 17, 1807, Hull signed a treaty with the chiefs and warriors of the Ottawa, Chippewa, Wyandot, and Potawatomi nations,

57. *ASPIA*, 1:753–55; *Senate Ex. Proc.*, 2:77, 78, 80. The treaty does not appear in Ratified Treaties (M668), and Kappler prints it in an appendix (2:1031), not in the chronological sequence of treaties.

58. Dearborn to Hull, July 22, 1806, *Terr. Papers*, 10:63–65. This first set of instructions was never received, so on January 27, 1807, Dearborn sent another copy, which is printed in *ASPIA*, 1:748. On the small differences between the two documents, see *Terr. Papers*, 10:63n.

in which the cession of the Michigan lands was accomplished. Hull warned the Indians of impending war with Great Britain and urged them not to join the British, and in the treaty the Indians acknowledged themselves to be under the protection of the United States and that they would "prove by their conduct that they are worthy of so great a blessing." A number of small reservations for the Indians were specified in the treaty.[59]

The next year at Brownstown, south of Detroit, Hull treated with the same tribes plus the Shawnees for the additional cession, in which the United States acquired roadways through the Indian lands in north-western Ohio.[60] President Jefferson had addressed a special message to these Indians, confirming their ownership of their lands and their freedom to sell or not sell as they chose, but he also pointed to the need of the United States to connect its settlements and made an eloquent plea for the Indians to settle down on individual family farms. He, like Hull, called attention to the increasing tension with Great Britain and warned the Indians of the disaster that would strike them if they forsook their friendship with the Americans and joined the British in war.[61]

The irregularities in making treaties with western tribes, the high-handed treatment of unfriendly Indians, and the control of tribes by withholding trade are all evident in the treaty signed in 1808 with the Great and Little Osage Indians. These Indians had a history of hostility toward other tribes and toward the Americans. Militant Osage warriors stole horses and plundered the frontier, and the chiefs could not control them. At the direction of the secretary of war, William Clark, superin-tendent of Indian affairs and brigadier general of militia in Louisiana Territory, went up the Missouri some three hundred miles from its mouth to establish a trading factory and a military post (Fort Clark). The Osages were pleased with the plans for a factory and a post and, Clark said, "expressed much anxiety to become more closely under the protection of the United States than they had been." Clark, thereupon, drew up a "conditional treaty" by which the Indians on September 14, 1808, agreed to cede their lands between the Arkansas and the Missouri east of the fort. Clark took the treaty to St. Louis and delivered it to

59. Kappler, 2:92–95. For Hull's speech to the Indians, see *ASPIA*, 1:745. Jefferson's views on the need for the cession in order to provide settlers who could furnish militia in time of war are set forth in Jefferson to Senate, January 15, 1808, when he submitted the treaty for ratification. *Senate Ex. Proc.*, 2:64–65.

60. Kappler, 2:99–100.

61. Jefferson to chiefs of the Ottawas, Chippewas, Potawatomis, Wyandots, and Senecas of Sandusky, April 22, 1808, *Writings of Thomas Jefferson*, ed. Lipscomb, 16:428–32.

Meriwether Lewis, the governor, who changed the document to satisfy some Osage objections and then sent the new treaty, in the hands of the Indian agent and trader Pierre Chouteau, to the main Osage encampment in the west.[62]

In his instructions, Lewis urged Chouteau to use "that extensive influence, which you have long possessed over those nations," and he set forth the advantages that would be gained:

> This draft of a Treaty, you will observe, contemplates something more than the restoration of peace: It gives to the great and little Osage, the most efficient security, in our power to bestow: It assures to them, for their exclusive use, the lands west of the boundary line: It separates those who sanction it, from the vicious and the profligate, whom no treaties can bind, whom no menaces can intimedate, and by whose ungovernable conduct, the peace of both nations is perpetually endangered. It enables us also, to reduce to submission, without bloodshed, those who persevere in hostility, by withholding from them the merchandize necessary for their support.
>
> By these arrangements, we shall also obtain a tract of country *west* of our present settlements, and *East* of the hunting boundary of the Osage, sufficient for the purposes of our white Hunters, and for such Indian Nations, as have long been on terms of intimate friendship with us. Thus, will our Frontier be strengthened and secured, with the least possible expence to the government.

The governor was blunt. He insisted that those Osages who wanted to be friends of the United States must sign the treaty; they would be given certificates which would allow them to trade at the factory or fort. Those who did not were not to be supplied with goods, either from the factory or from private traders, under any pretext whatever.[63]

By the treaty the Osages were received into the exclusive friendship

62. Clark to Eustis, February 20, 1810, *ASPIA*, 1:764–65. Clark had earlier written letters to Dearborn on September 23 and December 2, 1808, about the circumstances of the treaty, which are printed in *Terr. Papers*, 14:224–28, 242–44.

63. Lewis to Chouteau, October 3, 1808, *Terr. Papers*, 14:229–31. See also Lewis to the president of the United States, December 15, 1808, *ASPIA*, 1:766–67. Lewis explained the occasion of the treaty. He pointed out, also, the difficulty that arose because of a land grant (within the ceded territory) made by the Indians to Chouteau. Once the United States received the cession, he said, it could decide if it wished to confirm the lands to Chouteau, but to admit the principle of Indian grants to individuals would "introduce a policy of the most ruinous tendency for the interests of the United States; in effect it would be, the Government corrupting its own agents; for, I venture to assert, that, if the Indians are permitted to bestow lands on such individuals as they may think proper, the meanest interpreter in our employment will soon acquire a princely fortune at the expense of the United States."

and protection of the United States, and they agreed not to sell lands to any foreign power or to citizens of the United States without the approval of the federal government. The United States, in return for the cession of lands, confirmed its commitment to establish a factory and a fort, to furnish a blacksmith and a horse-mill, and to reimburse its citizens for goods stolen by the Osages. Goods worth $1,200 were delivered at the signing of the treaty, and an annuity of $1,500 was stipulated.[64]

Thus did the United States use the treaty-making power in the first decade of the century to further its interests—and to some extent those of the Indians as well. The United States got land for expanding settlement and to provide for the perceived needs for security on its frontiers. And the treaties repeatedly established the dominant position of the United States, as the tribes acknowledged the friendship and the protection of the federal government. But the tribes, too, profited. Though they parted reluctantly with their lands, they faced the hard fact that land was a commodity that could be exchanged for goods they needed and could not produce for themselves. As Thomas Jefferson observed in 1803: "While they [the Indians] are learning to do better on less land, our increasing numbers will be calling for more land, and thus a coincidence of interests will be produced between those who have lands to spare, and want other necessaries, and those who have such necessaries to spare, and want lands."[65] The Indian tribes also got something more: the treaties were a form of political recognition, the attesting by the United States government that the Indian tribes with whom they signed formal treaties were separate political entities. Even though the disparity of power between the United States and the tribes was clearly evident, none of the federal officials before the War of 1812 suggested that the treaty system was a farce or that it should be ended.

64. Kappler, 2:95–99. President Madison did not submit the treaty to the Senate until January 16, 1810, and then Senate action was delayed because of questions about Chouteau's authority to negotiate and sign the treaty on behalf of the United States. A letter from Clark and a copy of Lewis's instructions to Chouteau satisfied the Senate, and that body unanimously approved ratification of the treaty on April 28. *Senate Ex. Proc.*, 2:138, 139, 144, 148. The Clark and Lewis letters are cited above, notes 62 and 63.

65. Jefferson to Hawkins, February 18, 1803, *Writings of Thomas Jefferson*, ed. Lipscomb, 10:362.

CHAPTER SIX

A Position of Dominance

The War of 1812 and After

The War of 1812 was a watershed in the history of treaty making with the Indians. The defeat of the British and their Indian allies by William Henry Harrison at the Battle of the Thames in October 1813 and the resounding defeat of hostile Creeks by Andrew Jackson at Horseshoe Bend in March 1814 removed all serious threat of Indian military resistance east of the Mississippi River. Whereas the United States, despite its frequent display of braggadocio, previously had had to keep in mind the danger of Indian wars and was often forced to deal cautiously with the Indian tribes both north and south of the Ohio, after the War of 1812 the nation acted from a position of assured dominance. The long-held republican principles of the government prevented any crushing destruction of the Indian communities, yet, even though the treaty procedures were retained, the councils became less and less a matter of sovereign nations negotiating on terms of rough equality. Treaties simply continued to be a convenient means for carrying out the complicated and burdensome task of fulfilling the federal government's constitutional task of managing Indian affairs; they served in some measure to protect the Indians and nudge them along the path toward assimilation. But at the same time responsible men began to suggest publicly that treaties were an unrealistic and obsolete method for pursuing the goals of Indian policy.

Treaties Arising from the War of 1812

The rising tensions with Great Britain that led ultimately to the outbreak of war in 1812 had already stopped negotiations with the tribes in the Old Northwest after the Treaty of Fort Wayne in 1809, and the "elucidation" of a Cherokee treaty signed near the end of 1807 was the final prewar treaty in the South. The next treaties grew out of the war itself.

In the summer after the American victory at the Thames, Secretary of War John Armstrong appointed General Harrison, Governor Isaac Shelby of Kentucky, and Governor Lewis Cass of Michigan Territory to treat with the Wyandots, Shawnees, Delawares, and other tribes that had been loyal to the United States. His original purposes were to cement the friendship in a solemn treaty, to win active support from the Indians in the continuing war with Great Britain, and to obtain a cession of lands in northwestern Ohio. But "on more mature deliberation" Armstrong dropped the request for lands and specified only two articles: "one, stipulating peace and friendship; the other, military aid to the United States, on the part of the Indians, if required."[1]

Harrison and Cass met with three thousand Indians at Greenville between July 1 and July 22, 1814, smoked the pipe of peace, explained the purposes of the United States, and denigrated the British. Harrison told the Indians "that our people, and the red people, were the only nations on earth who were really free, and governed by men of their own choice, and that this ought to induce them to be on terms of friendship with each other." The chiefs, except for a few Miamis, whom the commissioners reported were in British pay, signed the treaty on July 22, 1814, "with great apparent willingness and satisfaction."[2] The treaty proclaimed peace between the United States and the Indians and among the tribes themselves, and the signatory Indians agreed to give aid to the United States in its war against the British and the tribes who were still hostile and to make no peace with either without the consent of the United States.[3]

1. Armstrong to Shelby and to Harrison and Cass, June 11, 1814, *ASPIA*, 1:827.
2. Journal of proceedings, ibid., 828–36. The quotation is on 836. Shelby did not take part in the negotiations.
3. Kappler, 2:105–7. After the president submitted the treaty to the Senate in November, that body voted separately on articles 2–4 (concerning military aid) after

Of considerably more importance was the Treaty of Fort Jackson signed with the Creeks in August 1814, for it exacted an immense cession of Creek land in Alabama and Georgia and marked the end of any immediate Indian resistance south of the Ohio. Andrew Jackson, who had led the forces against the Creeks as commander of the Tennessee militia, was appointed to the regular army as a brigadier general (later raised to major general) in command of the Seventh Military District (comprising Tennessee, Louisiana, and Mississippi Territory), and was directed to proceed to Fort Jackson to make peace with the Indians.[4]

He assembled the Creeks—mostly friendly ones, for the hostiles had fled into Florida—and dictated a treaty, which the Indians over strong objections were forced to sign on August 9. The treaty was a punitive one, with a long preamble referring to the "unprovoked, inhuman, and sanguinary war" waged by the Creeks despite the provisions of peace in the treaty of 1790 and the kind actions of the United States toward the nation. As "an equivalent for all expenses incurred in prosecuting the war to its termination," it demanded the cession of more than twenty million acres running through what is now central Alabama and southern Georgia, and it required the Creeks to abandon all communication with British or Spanish posts and not admit as traders any persons not licensed by the United States. The United States was given the right to establish military and trading posts and roads in Creek lands and free navigation of all their waters. "Prophets and instigators of the war" were to be surrendered. In return the United States guaranteed to the Creeks their remaining land, and provided reservations for friendly chiefs "from motives of humanity." It promised to provide the means of subsistence for the destitute Creeks until new crops could furnish an adequate supply.[5]

The friendly Creeks at Fort Jackson loudly and repeatedly complained

---

motions were made to omit them, but all were passed. In the end, the Senate approved the whole treaty twenty to seven. *Senate Ex. Proc.*, 2:585–87, 593–94.

4. There is an extensive literature on Jackson's role in the war with the Creeks. Two recent accounts are Robert V. Remini, *Andrew Jackson and the Course of American Empire, 1767–1821* (New York: Harper and Row, 1977), 187–233, and Frank Lawrence Owsley, Jr., *Struggle for the Gulf Borderlands: The Creek War and the Battle of New Orleans, 1812–1815* (Gainesville: University Presses of Florida, 1981), 6–94. Jackson's instructions are in Armstrong to Jackson, May 24, 1814, *Correspondence of Andrew Jackson*, ed. John Spencer Bassett, 7 vols. (Washington: Carnegie Institution of Washington, 1926–35), 2:4–5. Armstrong enclosed a copy of earlier instructions he had sent to Thomas Pinckney.

5. Kappler, 2:107–10; the cession is shown in Royce, *Cessions*, plates 1 and 15, area no. 75. Of the Creeks who signed the treaty only one is identified as a Red Stick; the remainder were friendly Creeks.

that they were being punished by loss of their lands for the sins of the hostiles, but Jackson paid no heed. He was determined that the Indians be crushed, that national security be assured by cessions of land along the Florida/Spanish border, and that lands be opened from Tennessee to the Gulf.[6]

The Treaty of Ghent with Great Britain, signed on December 24, 1814, provided for a return to the state of affairs before the war and in Article 9 stipulated that the United States end hostilities with the Indians and restore to the tribes "all the possessions, rights, and privileges which they may have enjoyed or been entitled to in one thousand eight hundred and eleven previous to such hostilities." This would seem to have nullified the cessions made at the Treaty of Fort Jackson, and British advisers of the Creeks assured them that the Treaty of Ghent meant the return of their lands. Jackson adamantly refused to concede the point, and the administration in Washington did not or could not shake him from that purpose, nor did the British insist on compliance with Article 9. The cession stood.[7]

In the north the Indian aspects of the war wound down in somewhat different fashion. Although the battle of the Thames had meant the end of the Tecumseh-driven confederacy and its hostility to the United States, when the Treaty of Ghent was received, a good many tribes in the upper Mississippi Valley were still hostile. It was necessary to inform them that Great Britain and the United States had signed terms of peace and that they too should cease hostilities.

Secretary of War James Monroe appointed Governor William Clark of Missouri Territory, Governor Ninian Edwards of Illinois Territory,

6. Speaker of the Upper and Lower Creeks to Hawkins, August 7 and 8, 1814, and Hawkins's report of a meeting at Tustannugga, September 18, 1815, Documents (T494), roll 1, frames 177–85, 190–92; Jackson to Armstrong, August 10, 1814, *Correspondence of Jackson*, ed. Bassett, 2:24–26. For Jackson's views of what he had accomplished for the security of the nation, see Jackson to Secretary of War William Crawford, June 10, 1816, ibid., 244. See also the discussion of the treaty in Owsley, *Struggle for the Gulf Borderlands*, 86–91; Remini, *Jackson and the Course of American Empire*, 225–32; and Michael D. Green, *The Politics of Indian Removal: Creek Government and Society in Crisis* (Lincoln: University of Nebraska Press, 1982), 43.

7. The Treaty of Ghent is printed in Hunter Miller, ed., *Treaties and Other International Acts of the United States of America*, 8 vols. (Washington: GPO, 1931–48), 2:581. See also the discussion in Remini, *Jackson and the Course of American Empire*, 301–4. Considerable time passed before the Treaty of Fort Jackson was approved by the Senate. Madison submitted it to the Senate on November 18, 1814, but it was not approved by the Senate (unanimously) until February 16, 1815, incidentally the precise day on which the Senate approved the Treaty of Ghent. If there was a conflict between the provisions of the two treaties, the Senate seemed not to notice it. *Senate Ex. Proc.*, 2:615–16, 620.

and Auguste Chouteau, the prominent St. Louis trader, to carry out the terms of the Treaty of Ghent and to invite the tribes to send delegations of chiefs to a council to sign a treaty with the United States. "It is thought proper," Monroe told them, "to confine this treaty to the sole object of peace. Other arrangements between the United States and the Indian tribes adapted to their mutual interests may be entered into hereafter." Goods worth $20,000 were purchased as presents for the Indians, and Monroe sent solid silver medals for presentation to chiefs who had delivered up their British medals to Lieutenant Pike and had been promised American medals in their stead.[8]

The commissioners set the site for the treaty at Portage des Sioux, on the west bank of the Mississippi a short distance above its confluence with the Missouri, and then pursued the difficult task of finding competent and acceptable messengers to send to the various tribes whose hostility or friendship was largely unknown. Some of the tribes were slow to respond; the Sacs and Foxes especially remained hostile, and regular army troops, augmented by two large gunboats on the river, were stationed at the council site. Little by little in early July, however, representative delegations came in, turning the council grounds into a colorful and interesting spectacle.[9]

Between July 18 and September 16 the commissioners signed thirteen separate peace treaties with the following tribes or bands: Potawatomi residing on the Illinois River, Piankashaw, Teton Sioux, Sioux of the Lakes, Sioux of St. Peter's River, Yankton Sioux, Maha (Omaha), Kickapoo, Osage, Sac of the Missouri, Fox, Iowa, and Kansa. These treaties were short and for the most part identical. They asserted "perpetual peace and friendship" and a mutual forgiving of injuries. For tribes with whom the United States was already tied by treaty, the previous commitments were acknowledged and confirmed. For tribes with whom the United States had not yet made treaties, the Indians, using the traditional formula, acknowledged themselves "to be under

---

8. Monroe to Clark, Edwards, and Chouteau, March 11, 1815, and Monroe to Clark, March 25, 1815, *ASPIA*, 2:6. Monroe directed the superintendent of Indian trade to send "blankets, strouds, cloths, calicoes, handkerchiefs, cotton stuffs, ribands, gartering, frock coats, flags, silver ornaments, paints, wampum, looking-glasses, knives, fire-steels, rifles, fusils, flints, powder, tobacco, pipes, needles, &c." He specified that "these articles should be equal in quality to those which the Indians have been accustomed to receive from the British agents." Monroe to John Mason, March 27, 1815, ibid., 7.

9. This process is well described in Robert L. Fisher, "The Treaties of Portage des Sioux," *Mississippi Valley Historical Review* 19 (March 1933), 495–99. See also the account of the commissioners, October 18, 1815, *ASPIA*, 2:9–11.

the protection of the United States, and of no other nation, power, or sovereign, whatsoever."[10]

While Clark, Edwards, and Chouteau were dealing with the tribes of the upper Mississippi Valley, three other commissioners—William Henry Harrison, Duncan McArthur, and John Graham—were treating with the Indians of Ohio and Indiana and Michigan territories. "The objects of the proposed treaty," Acting Secretary of War A. J. Dallas wrote,

> are, to remind the tribes of their existing relations with the United States; to explain to them the nature of the reciprocal stipulations in the treaty of peace and amity lately concluded between the United States and Great Britain, so far as they concern the Indians; to inform them of the measures that have been taken to carry the treaty of peace into effect, by a mutual surrender of the military posts which the American and the British forces had taken from each other during the war; to warn them against any improper practices that might involve them in hostilities with the United States; to promise a punctual performance of all our engagements with them; and to insist upon the observance of good faith on their part.

The United States expected no new cessions of land but only to manifest its "disposition to cultivate peace and good-will, and to secure . . . the advantages of the treaties which already exist."[11]

The commissioners met with the tribes at Spring Wells, near Detroit, dealing not only with the Chippewa, Ottawa, and Potawatomi Indians, who had been hostile to the United States during the war and thus fell under the prescriptions of Article 9 of the Treaty of Ghent, but also with Wyandot, Delaware, Shawnee, Seneca, and Miami Indians, most of whom had been friendly; as the commissioners explained, many

10. Kappler, 2:110–17, 119–24. The treaties were approved by the Senate on December 21, 1815, and ratified together on December 26. *Senate Ex. Proc.*, 3:3, 7, 9–14. A separate treaty was made on May 13, 1816, with the Sac Indians of Rock River, who were finally persuaded to end their hostility. Kappler, 2:126–28. For instructions to the treaty commissioners for the Sac treaty, see William H. Crawford to Clark, Edwards, and Chouteau, November 24, 1815, *ASPIA*, 2:12. The same commissioners signed ten more peace treaties—with Sioux, Winnebago, Ottawa-Chippewa-Potawatomi, Menominee, Oto, Ponca, and Pawnee Indians—between June 1, 1816, and June 22, 1818. Kappler, 2:128–31, 132–33, 138–40, 156–59; Crawford to Clark, Edwards and Chouteau, May 7, 1816, *ASPIA*, 2:97. The formal language of the treaties themselves does not convey the tension and drama that sometimes accompanied the negotiations. See, for example, Clark's and Chouteau's account of their encounter with the Pawnees in a letter to Calhoun, July 9, 1818, ibid., 176.

11. Dallas to Harrison, McArthur, and Graham, June 9, 1815, *ASPIA*, 2:13.

individual Indians belonging to the friendly tribes had taken up arms in support of Great Britain, and the friendly tribes wished and expected to be included in the treaty. There was no difficulty in getting the tribes to sign on September 8, 1814, confirming previous treaties and acknowledging that they were under the protection of the United States.[12]

A Multiplicity of Treaties

Very quickly the pressure on the Indian landholdings was renewed with a vengeance. That the extinguishment of so many parcels of the Indians' landed estate proceeded so inexorably was due to the inordinate demand for lands that came after the defeat of the Indians in the War of 1812, fueled by an explosive spirit of nationalism that marked the period. And the subjugated Indians were in no position to forcefully resist the new onslaught. Treaties poured into Washington and were sent in batches to the Senate for what was almost always unanimous approval of their ratification.

After the treaties of peace, numerous new treaties were made with varied groups of Indians north of the Ohio and in the trans-Mississippi regions (some singly, some jointly with associated Indians). Between the end of the War of 1812 and the inauguration of President Andrew Jackson in 1829 (excluding a special series of treaties made with Indians along the Missouri River in 1825), there were thirty-nine treaties with twenty-four tribes in these regions; some of the treaties were signed by more than one tribe, so that there were sixty-seven separate signatory groups.[13]

Many of these treaties were negotiated by Lewis Cass, governor of Michigan Territory from 1813 to 1831, and William Clark, who was governor of Missouri Territory and then appointed superintendent of Indian affairs at St. Louis when Missouri became a state in 1821. They were the two officials most knowledgeable about northern and western Indian affairs, and together, individually, or with other commissioners,

12. Kappler, 2:117–19; Harrison and Graham to Crawford, September 9, 1815, *ASPIA,* 2:16–17. The journal of proceedings of the treaty, August 25 to September 8, 1815, is printed ibid., 17–25. The Senate approved the treaty along with the treaties signed at Portage des Sioux.

13. I am counting treaties numbered 71, 80, 87–94, 97–104, 107–9, 111–13, 116–17, 127–29, 133, 135–39, 141, 143–44 in appendix B, which shows dates, tribes involved, United States commissioners, and place of treaty making.

they had a hand in twenty-six of the thirty-nine treaties. Their views and policies were as important as those of War Department officials in Washington, for these men were generally given wide discretion in dealing with the tribes. As Secretary of War Calhoun wrote to Cass and his fellow commissioners in May 1818, "The terms to be offered [for land] depend so much on the whims and tempers of the tribes interested in the land, that no particular instructions can be given to you; but the President, reposing full confidence in your judgment and discretion, expects that you will acquire it on terms as advantageous to the United States as practicable."[14]

Although most of these treaties dealt with determination of boundaries and cessions to the United States, a number of special elements in them can be noted, some of them new to the treaty-making process.

Of singular importance was the matter of reserves or reservations retained by the tribe or by individuals when tribal lands were ceded. The United States wanted to consolidate white settlement in Ohio, Indiana, and Illinois, and the War Department informed Cass in 1818 that the "great object" was "to remove, altogether, these tribes beyond the Mississippi."[15] But generally the tribes were unwilling to remove entirely. Cass noted of his negotiations with the Chippewa Indians: "Although I am firmly persuaded that it would be better for us and for these Indians that they should migrate to the country west of the Mississippi, or, at any rate, west of Lake Michigan, yet it was impossible to give effect to that part of your instructions which relates to this subject, without hazarding the success of the negotiation."[16] It was necessary to allow reduced tracts of land to be retained by the tribes and in addition to set aside reserves for special individuals. Cass and McArthur, who negotiated a treaty with Wyandots and other Indians at the Rapids of the Miami on September 29, 1817, justified the practice:

> The treaty exhibits the result of mutual demands and of mutual compromises. We considered our instructions as rather advisory than imperative; rather intending that we should comply with the

14. Calhoun to Jonathan Jennings, Lewis Cass, and Benjamin Parke, May 3, 1818, *ASPIA*, 2:174. A similar letter was sent to Clark and Chouteau on May 8, 1818, ibid. For the mature and considered views of Cass and Clark on Indian affairs, see their report of 1829 in *Senate Doc.* no. 72, 20-2, serial 181, pp. 10–52.

15. C. Vanderventer to Cass, June 29, 1818, *ASPIA*, 2:175. See this whole letter for an amplification of this view.

16. Cass to Calhoun, September 30, 1819, ibid., 199.

general principles than with the minuter details. Any other course would have been fatal to our exertions and to the expectations of the Government. We have been compelled to admit the claims of a number of individuals, and to stipulate that patents shall be granted to them. . . .

In every case, it was the urgent wish of the Indians that land should be granted to these persons. To have refused these requests would have embodied against us an interest, and created obstacles, which no efforts of ours would have defeated or surmounted.[17]

A difficulty arose, however, because this treaty with the Wyandots specified that the reserves were to be granted "by patent, in fee simple" and that the owners could convey them to anyone they chose. Although the Senate approved most Indian treaties routinely, in this case it objected to what it considered a violation of the preemptive right of the United States government to Indian lands. The Senate Committee on the Public Lands, to whom the treaty had been referred, asserted that the provision was "unprecedented by any former treaty, and at variance with the general principles on which intercourse with the Indians tribes has been conducted." It feared that the treaty would set a bad precedent and would encourage the spread of the practice, to the detriment of both the Indians and the United States. The Senate attempted to amend the treaty, but in the end it decided to postpone action and requested the president to reopen negotiations with the tribes so that the fee-simple grants could be omitted and the reserves held "in like manner as has been practiced in other and similar cases."[18]

Calhoun, accordingly, sent Cass and McArthur the Senate's resolution and directed them to renegotiate the treaty with the Indians, but he added: "I am fearful that the change of tenure proposed by the Senate will indispose the Indians to renew the negotiations, and that they will expect not only a great increase of their annuity, but a great increase of lands to be reserved for their use." He left it up to the commissioners to accomplish whatever they could. The commissioners signed a supplementary treaty with the Indians on September 17, 1818, which specified that the reserved tracts would be held "in the same manner as Indian reservations have been heretofore held." Enlarged tracts of land were reserved for the Wyandots and Senecas (which their delegation to

17. Cass and McArthur to George Graham, September 30, 1817, ibid., 139.
18. Report of Committee on the Public Lands, December 29, 1817, ibid., 148–49; *Senate Ex. Proc.*, 3:94–121 passim.

Washington had requested and which the Senate had included as amendments to the original treaty), and additional perpetual annuities ranging from $500 to $1,000 were provided for the Wyandots, Shawnees, Senecas, and Ottawas.[19]

The War Department had learned its lesson, and Calhoun wrote to Clark and Chouteau as he sent them a commission to treat with the Quapaws: "The lands reserved for the Quapaws must be held by the tenure by which the Indians usually hold their lands, as the Senate would probably ratify no treaty which recognises in the Indians the right of acquiring individual property, with the power of selling, except to the United States." Subsequent treaties allowing reservations within the cessions provided that the reserves could not be conveyed without the consent of the president of the United States or that the Indians would hold title in the accustomed manner.[20]

An important part of the treaty negotiations and treaty stipulations were presents and annuities. Treaties in the years immediately following the War of 1812 (with only a few exceptions) were made in the West, not in Washington, and the large groups of Indians that customarily attended the councils taxed the government's ability to dispense sufficient provisions and rations to satisfy the assembled throngs at the treaty grounds. At the treaty with the Potawatomis in 1826, for example, the commissioners distributed goods worth $30,547.71 and promised an additional $900 worth. "Without this provision," they reported, "no treaty could have been formed. The Indians always arrive at our treaty grounds poor and naked. They expect to receive some part of the consideration at the moment of signing the treaty. This expectation, in fact, furnishes the only motive for their attendance, and much the most powerful motive for their assent to the measures proposed to them." The Chippewas of Lake Superior were especially destitute when Cass and Thomas L. McKenney met with them for the Treaty of Fond du Lac in 1826, and the commissioners wrote into the treaty special provisions for goods that were not authorized by their instructions. The

19. Calhoun to Cass and McArthur, May 11, 1818, *ASPIA,* 2:175; Kappler, 2:162–63. This action satisfied the Senate, and the two treaties, taken as one, were approved unanimously on December 23, 1818, and proclaimed by the president on January 4, 1819. *Senate Ex. Proc.,* 3:161. The Chippewas, Delawares, and Potawatomis, who were not affected by the changes made in the supplementary treaty, were not parties to it.

20. Calhoun to Clark and Chouteau, May 8, 1818, *ASPIA,* 2:174. For a brief discussion of the issue of tenure of Indian lands, see Robert W. McCluggage, "The Senate and Indian Land Titles, 1800–1825," *Western Historical Quarterly* 1 (October 1970): 415–25.

presents, too, they believed, would afford some control over these northern Indians and draw them away from British influence.[21]

Many of the treaties, at the urgent request of the Indians, stipulated that annuities and other payments be made in silver. There were some advantages to this practice, for silver could easily be divided and distributed to tribal members, and the United States saved the heavy costs of transportation of bulky merchandise. Although Cass worried that "with the habitual improvidence of savages, they were anxious to receive what they could speedily dissipate in childish and useless purchases, at the expense of stipulations that would be permanently useful to them," he thought the advantages outweighed the disadvantages. The payments had to be in specie, not in paper money. "Paper is almost valueless to the Indians," Cass thought, "—it is a representation of wealth, with which they are little acquainted; they require something whose amount is more palpable and obvious."[22]

There was a movement away from *perpetual* annuities, although they were by no means eliminated altogether. William Clark was especially strong on this point. After dealing with the Osages and the Kansa Indians in 1825, he wrote: "An annuity forever . . . [does] more harm than good. . . . In the treaties concluded with the Kanzas and Osages, the annuities are limited to twenty years; in the course of which time, the humane experiment now making by Government, to teach them to subsist themselves by the arts of civilized life, will have had a fair trial, and, if it succeeds, they will need no further aid from the Federal Government."[23]

Promotion of white civilization remained a strong force in treaty negotiations. Clark's treaty with the Osages in 1825, for example, stipulated:

> The United States shall, immediately, upon the ratification of this convention, or as soon thereafter as may be, cause to be furnished to the tribes or nations, aforesaid, six hundred head of cattle, six hundred hogs, one thousand domestic fowls, ten yoke of oxen, and six carts, with such farming utensils as the Superintendent of Indian Affairs may think necessary, and shall employ such persons, to aid them in their agricultural pursuits, as to the President of the United States

---

21. Cass, J. B. Ray, and John Tipton to James Barbour, October 23, 1826, *ASPIA*, 2:683; Cass and McKenney to Barbour, September 11, 1826, ibid., 682.

22. Cass to Calhoun, September 30, 1819, ibid., 199; Cass and McArthur to Graham, September 30, 1817, ibid., 139; see also Cass to Graham, July 3, 1817, ibid., 137.

23. Clark to Barbour, June 11, 1815, ibid., 592.

may seem expedient, and shall, also, provide, furnish, and support for them, one blacksmith, that their farming utensils, tools, and arms, may be seasonably repaired; and shall build, for each of the four principal chiefs, at their respective villages, a comfortable and commodious dwelling house.[24]

Money for education of Indian youth was another element in some of the treaties. A typical provision in the 1826 treaty with the Potawatomis read: "to appropriate, for the purposes of education, the annual sum of two thousand dollars, as long as the Congress of the United States may think proper, to be expended as the President may direct." In some treaties the education article (and also articles about other reforming efforts) could be struck out without affecting the rest of the treaty.[25]

The treaties in this period often stipulated that the United States would pay claims against the tribes by United States citizens for loss of property or other damage, and in 1825 the government began a practice among the northern and western tribes that was to cause trouble and concern later: providing in the treaty for the payment of specific debts owed by the tribe or by individual tribal members. Clark argued for the practice on the grounds that "a treaty with Indians should always be a complete settlement, and leave no cause for future complaint or negotiation, nor any difference unadjusted." In the Osage treaty of 1825, therefore, he paid a debt of $4,500 of "sundry individuals of the Osage tribes or nations" due to the then defunct government factory at Fort Clark, in return for which the Osages freed the United States from the obligation to maintain a military post there as promised in an earlier treaty. The treaty, as well, provided payment to United States citizens for horses and other property stolen by the Indians, a $1,000 debt owed the Delawares by the Osages, and Osage debts owed to three individuals, including Chouteau.[26]

One of the serious problems facing the United States on the northwest frontiers was the almost continuous intertribal warfare, especially between the Sioux and the Chippewas and between the Sioux and the Sacs and Foxes. It had been the federal government's practice not to be involved in conflicts between tribes, but maintenance of peace on the

24. Kappler, 2:218.
25. Ibid., 274, 275. See also treaties with the Miamis, Chippewas and others, Eel River Miamis, and Potawatomis, ibid., 279, 282, 287, 295.
26. Clark to Barbour, June 11, 1825, *ASPIA*, 2:592; Kappler, 2:219–20. See also the treaty with Sacs and Foxes, 1824, ibid., 208.

frontiers soon demanded some attention to the problem. Accordingly, the government invited Chippewas, Sacs and Foxes, Menominees, Iowas, Sioux, Winnebagos, and a portion of Ottawa, Chippewa, and Potawatomi tribes on the Illinois River to meet with Cass and Clark at Prairie du Chien, at the mouth of the Wisconsin River, "in a spirit of mutual conciliation." Besides attestations of peace and friendship among the various tribes, the treaty specified the territorial boundaries of each tribe in order "to remove all causes of future difficulty." At a spectacular gathering of some one thousand members of the different tribes, the experienced commissioners drew what boundary lines they could and postponed for future negotiations problems that could not be solved on the spot; the treaty was signed on August 19, 1825.[27]

The treaty specified that because the Chippewas were widely dispersed, the government in the following year should convene them on Lake Superior in order to explain fully to them the objects and advantages of the treaty, with the hope that it might be observed by the warriors. Thus, in July and August 1826, Cass and McKenney met with the Chippewas at Fond du Lac and signed a treaty with them on August 5, which confirmed the Treaty of Prairie du Chien.[28] A similar extension of the Treaty of Prairie du Chien was contained in a treaty with Chippewas, Menominees, and Winnebagos signed by the same commissioners on August 11, 1827, at Butte des Morts, near Green Bay. Boundaries between the tribes were drawn, but special problems concerning boundaries with the New York Indians who had recently emigrated to the region were referred to the president for decision.[29]

27. Kappler, 2:250–55. For a full discussion of the treaty council, see Charles A. Abele, "The Grand Indian Council and Treaty of Prairie du Chien, 1825" (Ph.D. diss., Loyola University of Chicago, 1969). The theory (widely disseminated, for example, by Ray Allen Billington in his textbook on the western frontier) that the real purpose of the treaty was to define tribal boundaries in order to facilitate cessions of the land by the Indians is effectively refuted in Abele's dissertation. See Ray Allen Billington and Martin Ridge, *Westward Expansion: A History of the American Frontier*, 5th ed. (New York: Macmillan Publishing Company, 1982), 296.

28. Kappler, 2:268–73. The work of the commissioners is described in Cass and McKenney to Barbour, September 11, 1826, *ASPIA*, 2:682–83; McKenney left a detailed description of the meeting in his *Sketches of a Tour to the Lakes, of the Character and Customs of the Chippeway Indians, and of Incidents Connected with the Treaty of Fond du Lac* (Baltimore: Fielding Lucas, Jr., 1827). For a discussion of the presentation of medals to the Indians at this treaty, as the American commissioners sought to ween the Indians from adherence to the British, see Francis Paul Prucha, *Indian Peace Medals in American History* (Madison: State Historical Society of Wisconsin, 1971), 44–48.

29. Kappler, 2:281–83. The treaty journal is in Documents (T494), roll 2, frames 4–33.

The negotiations at Butte des Morts highlighted a problem faced by the federal commissioners at treaties with the Indians in the northwestern regions: who were the tribal chiefs with whom the negotiations should be conducted? The tribes did not have governments as formally organized as the commissioners wanted, and the federal officers sought to remedy the situation by designating or "making" chiefs. At Butte des Morts, on the first day of the council, Cass told the Menominees that they were in "a bad situation with respect to their chiefs. There is no one to whom we can talk as head of the nation. If any thing happens, we want some person who has authority in the nation to whom we can look." He said the tribe looked "like a flock of geese without a leader," and he indicated that the commissioners would make inquiries and select a proper person to be chief. The next day McKenney reiterated the point, even more forcefully.[30] The highest dignity fell on Oshkosh, the second highest on Caron, and these two chiefs' names appear first on the list of signers for the Menominees.

Most of the treaties of cession, sometimes following explicitly the Treaty of Greenville of 1795, permitted the tribes to continue to hunt (and according to some treaties, to make maple sugar) on the ceded lands, often with the notation "as long as the [lands] shall remain the property of the United States." In the treaty with the Chippewas at Sault Ste. Marie in 1820, the United States promised the Indians "a perpetual right of fishing at the falls of St. Mary's, and also a place of encampment upon the tract hereby ceded, convenient to the fishing ground."[31]

A few treaties dealt with very specific single issues. Thus treaties with the Osages and with the Sacs and Foxes in 1822 absolved the United States from maintaining trading houses promised in earlier treaties with the tribes. Treaties with the Osage and Kansa Indians in August 1825 gave tribal consent for the president to mark out a road between Missouri and New Mexico, with the road considered to extend "to a reasonable

30. Treaty journal, Documents (T494), roll 2, frames 7–8. The "making of chiefs" did not go unnoticed, and McKenney answered criticisms that arose. He denied that the commissioners had undertaken to "constitute and appoint an Indian Chief," and he insisted that they had merely followed the British and French practice of recognizing as chiefs those who were reported by their bands as their acknowledged leaders. McKenney to Barbour, March 24, 1828, OIA LS, 4:362–63 (M21, roll 4).

31. See treaties with Chippewas (1819), Ottawas, Chippewas, and Potawatomis (1821), Quapaws (1824), and Potawatomis (1826), Kappler, 2:186, 200, 210, 275. The Sault Ste. Marie treaty appears ibid., 188. On Indian rights to produce maple sugar, see Robert H. Keller, "America's Native Sweet: Chippewa Treaties and the Right to Harvest Maple Sugar," *American Indian Quarterly* 13 (Spring 1989): 117–35.

distance on either side, so that travellers thereon may, at any time, leave the marked tract, for the purpose of finding subsistence and proper camping places."[32]

A separate series of treaties—this time merely of trade and friendship—were signed with the tribes along the Missouri River in 1825. The fur traders' expanding operations out of St. Louis aroused Indian hostility, and death and destruction soon occurred. An attempt in 1823 to punish the Indians, using United States troops from Fort Atkinson at Council Bluffs, was not vigorously pursued, and the fur traders demanded stronger military action to prevent continued Indian outrages. Congress balked at a proposal to establish a military post on the upper Missouri, in order to prevent the rich Rocky Mountain fur trade from falling into British hands, but it did authorize the president to appoint commissioners to treat with the Indians along the Missouri and authorized $10,000 for a competent military escort to the commissioners.[33]

President Adams appointed General Henry Atkinson and the Indian agent Benjamin O'Fallon as commissioners, and the two men left Council Bluffs on May 16, 1825, with a military escort of 476 men. As they moved by stages up the river, the commissioners met in council with the Indians and between June 9 and August 4 concluded nine treaties—with Poncas, Teton, Yankton and Yanktonai bands of Sioux, Oglala Sioux, Cheyennes, Hunkpapa Sioux, Arikaras, Minitarees, Mandans, and Crows. The various councils were much alike. First came a review of the troops drawn up in parade, intended to awe the Indians. There followed a formal council at which the treaty was approved and presents distributed. In the evening, shells were fired from a howitzer to further impress the Indians.[34]

The tribes asserted perpetual friendship, acknowledged that they lived within the territorial limits of the United States, recognized its

32. Kappler, 2:201–3, 246–50. The treaties with the Osage and Kansa Indians had been authorized by an act of Congress of March 3, 1825, which directed the president to mark out such a road. 4 Stat. 100–101. The treaties were negotiated by the commissioners appointed to mark out the road.

33. See the discussion of the episode in Francis Paul Prucha, *The Sword of the Republic: The United States Army on the Frontier, 1783–1846* (New York: Macmillan Company, 1969), 153–59. The authorizing legislation is in 4 Stat. 35–36 (1824).

34. Kappler, 2:225–46; Report of Atkinson and O'Fallon, November 7, 1825, *ASPIA,* 2:605–8; Russell Reid and Clell G. Gannon, eds., "Journal of the Atkinson-O'Fallon Expedition," *North Dakota Historical Quarterly* 4 (October 1919): 5–56. There is a summary account of the expedition in Roger L. Nichols, *General Henry Atkinson: A Western Military Career* (Norman: University of Oklahoma Press, 1965), 90–108.

supremacy, claimed its protection, and admitted its right to regulate trade. The United States for its part agreed to receive the Indians "into their friendship, and under their protection and to extend to them, from time to time, such benefits and acts of kindness as may be convenient, and seem just and proper to the President of the United States." The United States would license traders to supply the Indians, and the Indians in turn promised to seize and turn over to the federal authorities any unlicensed persons who sought to trade with them. The treaties prohibited private retaliation for injuries done to individuals and stipulated the return of or indemnification for stolen horses and other property.

After an unsuccessful attempt to make contact with the Blackfeet and the Assiniboins, Atkinson and O'Fallon headed downriver and arrived at Council Bluffs in mid-September. They sent messages to the Otos, Pawnees, and Omahas, and when these tribes arrived at Fort Atkinson, councils were held and treaties signed between September 26 and October 6.[35]

These treaties were a straightforward use of the treaty-making power to regularize relations with frontier tribes, to bring them formally into the political orbit of the United States, and thus force them to cut ties with the British and turn their trade to American, not British, traders.

Conventions with New York Indians

Quite different were the two conventions signed at the same time by the Seneca Indians of New York, in which they sold land to individuals who had preemption rights. In the first of these, signed on September 3, 1823, the Senecas conveyed to John Greig and Henry B. Gibson a parcel of land known as the Gordeau reservation. The "treaty" was concluded "under the authority of the United States," represented by Charles Carroll, who had been appointed commissioner, and in the presence of Nathaniel Gorham, who represented the state of Massachusetts; both these men attested to the treaty. The treaty, however, was not submitted to the Senate. According to Thomas L. Mc-

35. Kappler, 2:256–62. Kappler's title for the Omaha treaty reads "Makah Tribe," an obvious misprint for "Mahah," and the text of the treaty itself uses "Maha." The twelve treaties were submitted to the Senate on January 9, 1826; they were approved unanimously February 2 and proclaimed February 6. *Senate Ex. Proc.*, 3:471–72, 496–500.

By the PRESIDENT of the *United States of America*,
A PROCLAMATION.

WHEREAS a Treaty of peace and friendship between the United States and the Creek nation, was made and concluded on the seventh day of the present month of August: And whereas I have, by and with the advice and consent of the Senate, in due form ratified the said Treaty, Now therefore to the end that the same may be observed and performed with good faith on the part of the United States, I have ordered the said Treaty to be herewith published; and I do hereby enjoin and require all officers of the United States, civil and military, and all other citizens and inhabitants thereof, faithfully to observe and fulfil the same.

GIVEN under my hand and the seal of the United States, in the city of New-York, the fourteenth day of August, in the year of our Lord one thousand seven hundred and ninety, and in the fifteenth year of the sovereignty and independence of the United States.

By the PRESIDENT,
THOS. JEFFERSON.

G. WASHINGTON.

GEORGE WASHINGTON, President of the United States of America, To all to whom these Presents shall come, Greeting:

WHEREAS a Treaty of peace and friendship between the United States of America, and the Creek nation of Indians, was made and concluded on the seventh day of the present month of August, by HENRY KNOX, secretary for the department of war, who was duly authorized thereto by the President of the United States, with the advice and consent of the Senate, on the one part, and the Kings, Chiefs and Warriors of the said Creek nation, whose names are hereunto signed, on the other part; which Treaty is in the form and words following:

A TREATY of peace and friendship, made and concluded between the President of the United States of America, on the part and behalf of the said States, and the undersigned Kings, Chiefs and Warriors of the Creek nation of Indians, on the part and behalf of the said nation.

THE parties being desirous of establishing permanent peace and friendship between the United States and the said Creek nation, and the citizens and members thereof, and to remove the causes of war, by ascertaining their limits, and making other necessary, just and friendly arrangements: The President of the United States, by Henry Knox, secretary for the department of war, whom he hath constituted with full powers for these purposes, by and with the advice and consent of the Senate of the United States: And the Creek nation by the undersigned Kings, Chiefs and Warriors representing the said nation, have agreed to the following articles, viz.

ARTICLE I.

THERE shall be perpetual peace and friendship between all the citizens of the United States of America, and all the individuals, towns and tribes of the Upper, Middle and Lower Creeks, and Semanolies composing the Creek nation of Indians.

ARTICLE II.

THE undersigned Kings, Chiefs and Warriors, for themselves, and all parts of the Creek nation within the limits of the United States, do acknowledge themselves, and the said parts of the Creek nation, to be under the protection of the United States of America, and of no other sovereign whosoever; and they also stipulate that the said Creek nation will not hold any treaty with an individual State, or with individuals of any State.

ARTICLE III.

THE Creek nation shall deliver as soon as practicable, to the commanding officer of the troops of the United States stationed at the Rock-landing, on the Oconee river, all citizens of the United States, white inhabitants or negroes, who are now prisoners in any part of the said nation: And if any such prisoners or negroes should not be so delivered, on or before the first day of June ensuing, the Governor of Georgia may empower three persons to repair to the said nation, in order to claim and receive such prisoners and negroes.

ARTICLE IV.

THE boundary between the citizens of the Unites States and the Creek nation, is, and shall be, from where the old lines strikes the river Savannah—thence up the said river to a place on the most northern branch of the same, commonly called the Keowee, where a North East line to be drawn from the top of the Occunna mountain shall intersect—thence along the said line in a South West direction to Tugelo river—thence to the top of the Currahee mountain—thence to the head or source of the main south branch of the Oconee river, called the Appalachee—thence down the middle of the said main south branch and river Oconee, to its confluence with the Oakmulgee, which form the river Altamaha—and thence down the middle of the said Altamaha, to the old line on the said river, and thence along the said old line to the river St. Marys.

AND in order to preclude forever all disputes relatively to the head or source of the main south branch of the river Oconee, at the place where it shall be intersected by the line aforesaid from the Currahee mountain, the same shall be ascertained by an able surveyor on the part of the United States, who shall be assisted by three old citizens of Georgia, who may be appointed by the Governor of the said State, and three old Creek Chiefs to be appointed by the said nation; and the said surveyor, citizens and chiefs shall assemble for this purpose on the first day of October, one thousand seven hundred and ninety-one, at the Rock-landing on the said river Oconee, and thence proceed to ascertain the said head, or source of the main south branch of the said river, at the place where it shall be intersected by the line aforesaid, to be drawn from the Currahee mountain. And in order that the said boundary shall be rendered distinct and well known, it shall be marked by a line of felled trees at least twenty feet wide, and the trees chopped on each side from the said Currahee mountain to the head or source of the said main south branch of the Oconee river, and thence down the margin of the said main south branch and river Oconee, for the distance of twenty miles, or as much further as may be necessary to mark distinctly the said boundary. And in order to extinguish forever all claims of the Creek nation, or any part thereof, to any of the land lying to the northward and eastward of the boundary herein described, it is hereby agreed in addition to the considerations heretofore made for the said land, that the United States will cause certain valuable Indian goods, now in the State of Georgia, to be delivered to the said Creek nation; and the said United States will also cause the sum of one thousand and five hundred dollars to be paid annually to the said Creek nation. And the undersigned Kings, Chiefs and Warriors, do hereby for themselves and the whole Creek nation, their heirs and descendants, for the considerations above mentioned, RELEASE, QUIT-CLAIM, RELINQUISH AND CEDE all the land to the northward and eastward of the boundary herein described.

ARTICLE V.

THE United States solemnly guarantee to the Creek nation, all their lands within the limits of the United States to the westward and southward of the boundary described in the preceding article.

ARTICLE VI.

IF any citizen of the United States, or other person not being an Indian, shall attempt to settle on any of the Creek's lands, such person shall forfeit the protection of the United States, and the Creeks may punish him or not, as they please.

ARTICLE VII.

No citizen or inhabitant of the United States, shall attempt to hunt or destroy the game on the Creek lands; nor shall any such citizen or inhabitant go into the Creek country, without a passport first obtained from the Governor of some one of the United States, or the officer of the troops of the United States commanding at the nearest military post on the frontiers—or such other person as the President of the United States may from time to time authorize to grant the same.

ARTICLE VIII.

IF any Creek Indian or Indians, or person residing among them, or who shall take refuge in their nation, shall commit a robbery or murder, or other capital crime, on any of the citizens or inhabitants of the United States, the Creek nation, or town, or tribe to which such offender or offenders may belong, shall be bound to deliver him or them up to be punished according to the laws of the United States.

ARTICLE IX.

IF any citizen or inhabitant of the United States, or of either of the territorial districts of the United States, shall go into any town, settlement, or territory belonging to the Creek nation of Indians, and shall there commit any crime upon, or trespass against the person or property of any peaceable and friendly Indian or Indians, which if committed within the jurisdiction of any State, or within the jurisdiction of either of the said districts, against a citizen or white inhabitant thereof, would be punishable by the laws of such State or District, such offender or offenders shall be subject to the same punishment, and shall be proceeded against in the same manner as if the offence had been committed within the jurisdiction of the State or District to which he or they may belong, against a citizen or white inhabitant thereof.

ARTICLE X.

IN cases of violence on the persons or property of the individuals of either party, neither retaliation or reprisal shall be committed by the other, until satisfaction shall have been demanded of the party of which the aggressor is, and shall have been refused.

ARTICLE XI.

THE Creeks shall give notice to the citizens of the United States, of any designs which they may know, or suspect to be formed in any neighbouring tribe, or by any person whatever, against the peace and interests of the United States.

ARTICLE XII.

THAT the Creek nation may be led to a greater degree of civilization, and to become herdsmen and cultivators, instead of remaining in a state of hunters, the United States will from time to time furnish gratuitously the said nation with useful domestic animals and implements of husbandry. And further to assist the said nation in so desirable a pursuit, and at the same time to establish a certain mode of communication, the United States will send such and so many persons to reside in said nation as they may judge proper, and not exceeding four in number, who shall qualify themselves to act as interpreters. These persons shall have lands assigned them by the Creeks, for cultivation for themselves and their successors in office; but they shall be precludedexercising any kind of traffic.

ARTICLE XIII.

ALL animosities for past grievances shall henceforth cease, and the contracting parties will carry the foregoing Treaty into full execution, with all good faith and sincerity.

ARTICLE XIV.

THIS Treaty shall take effect and be obligatory on the contracting parties, as soon as the same shall have been ratified by the President of the United States, with the advice and consent of the Senate of the United States.

IN WITNESS of all and every thing herein determined between the United States of America, and the whole Creek nations, the parties have hereunto set their hands and seals, in the city of New-York, within the United States, this seventh day of August, one thousand seven hundred and ninety.

In behalf of the UNITED STATES,

HENRY KNOX,
Secretary of War, and sole Commissioner for treating with the Creek nation of Indians. (L. S.)

In behalf of themselves, and the whole Creek nation of Indians,—signed and sealed by

ALEXANDER M'GILLIVRAY,
And the Kings, Chiefs and Warriors of the Cusetahs, Little Tallisee, Big Tallisee, Tuckabatchy, Natchez, Cowetas. Of the broken Arrow, Coosades, Alabama Oaksoys.

Done in the presence of
RICHARD MORRIS, Chief Justice of the State of New-York,
RICHARD VARICK, Mayor of the City of New-York,
MARINUS WILLETT,
THOMAS LEE SHIPPEN, of Pennsylvania,
JOHN RUTLEDGE, Junior. }
JOSEPH ALLEN SMITH, } of South-Carolina.
HENRY IZARD, }
His
JOSEPH + CORNELL, Interpreter.
Mark.

(L. S. U.S.) NOW know Ye, That I having seen and considered the said Treaty, do, and with the advice and consent of the Senate of the United States, ACCEPT, RATIFY AND CONFIRM the same, and every article and clause thereof: In testimony whereof, I have cused the Seal of the United States to be hereunto affixed, and signed the same with my hand.

GIVEN at the city of New-York, the thirteenth day of August, in the year of our Lord one thousand seven hundred and ninety, and in the fifteenth year of the sovereignty and independence of the United States.

G. WASHINGTON.

By the PRESIDENT,
THOMAS JEFFERSON.

By Command of the President of the United States of America,
HENRY KNOX, Secretary for the department of War.

ALEXANDER M'GILLIVRAY, (L. S.)
Cusetahs. { Fuskatche Mico × or Bird Tail King, Neathlock × or second Man, Halletemalthle × or Blue Giver,
Little Tallisee. { Opay Mico × or the Singer, Totkeshajou × or Samouiac,
Big Tallisee. { Hopothe Mico + or Tallisee King, Opototaché × or Long Side,
Tuckabatchy. { Soholessee × or young second Man, Ochee Hajou × or Aleck Cornel,
Natchez. { Chinabee × or the great Natchez Warrior, Natzowatchehe × or the great Natchez Warrior's Brother, Thakotechee + or the Mole, Oquakobee +
Cowetas. { Tukenaih × or big Lieutenant, Homatah + or Leader, Chinnabie + or Matthews, Juleetaulemathee + or dry Pine,
Of the broken Arrow. { Chawockly Mico ×
Coosades. { Coosades Hopoy × or the Measurer, Muthee × the Miser, Stimafutchkee × or good Humour,
Alabama Chief. { Stimalejee × or Disputer,
Oaksoys. Mumagechee + David Francis,

1. Treaty of New York with the Creeks, August 7, 1790

When the Creeks under Alexander McGillivray agreed to a treaty with the United States, they signed the document with Secretary of War Henry Knox in New York, the capital. The treaty was publicly proclaimed by this printed broadside.

2. Hopothle Mico

John Trumbull, the famous American patriot and artist, made this sketch of one of the Creek chiefs who signed the Treaty of New York in 1790. The artist wrote: "I had been desirous of obtaining portraits of some of these principal men, who possessed a dignity of manner, form, countenance and expression, worthy of Roman senators."

Henry Knox, who negotiated with the Creeks on behalf of the United States, had a humanitarian view of the Indians and worked energetically for just and honorable relationships between the two cultures.

3. Henry Knox

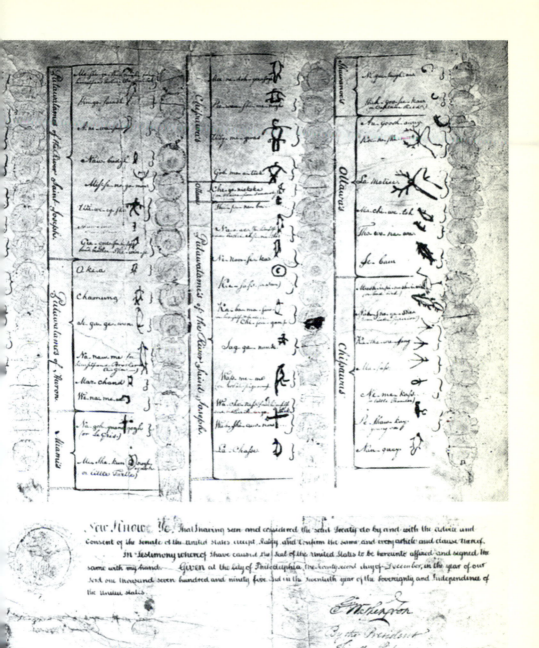

4. Treaty of Greenville, August 3, 1795

After their defeat by General Anthony Wayne at Fallen Timbers, the northwestern tribes assembled at Greenville for a peace treaty largely dictated by Wayne. This section of the original treaty shows some of the Indian names with symbols or totems attached. At the bottom is President Washington's ratification/proclamation.

Following British practice, the United States presented silver medals to Indian chiefs as a sign of peace and of the Indians' adherence to the United States. This large medal (more than 4 × 6 inches in size) was engraved by the noted Philadelphia silversmith Joseph Richardson, Jr., whose mark appears on the reverse. The medal was given at the Greenville council to one of the signatory chiefs.

GEORGE WASHINGTON PRESIDENT 1795.

General Wayne, in presenting the medals, said in part: "The medals which I shall have the honor to deliver you, you will consider as presented by the hands of your father, the Fifteen Fires of America. These you will hand down to your children's children, in commemoration of this day—a day in which the United States of America gives peace to you and all your nations, and receives you and them under the protecting wings of the eagle."

5. Washington Indian Peace Medal, 1795

6. William Clark

7. Lewis Cass

William Clark at St. Louis and Lewis Cass at Detroit were the two most experienced federal officials in Indian affairs in the early republic. They participated in many treaty councils, and their views strongly influenced government Indian policy. John C. Calhoun, secretary of war from 1817 to 1825, and Andrew Jackson, as United States military commander in the south after the War of 1812, both talked about the unsuitability of treaties with Indian tribes but continued to negotiate them in considerable numbers.

8. John C. Calhoun

9. Andrew Jackson

10. Treaty with the Quapaws, August 24, 1818

This original manuscript treaty is typical of the treaties of the period in its form, but it is highly unusual in its inclusion of a decorative map of the land cession specified in the treaty.

11. Council at Prairie du Chien, 1825

The artist James Otto Lewis attended the treaty councils at Prairie du Chien, Fond du Lac, and Butte des Morts in the mid-1820s. There he sketched portraits of the Indians and scenes of the treaty councils. Most of these were later turned into finished paintings in Detroit and then published as folios of lithographs, from which these two scenes are taken.

12. Commissioners Approaching Council at Butte des Morts, 1827

13. Sequoyah (George Guess)   14. Thomas L. McKenney

The treaty with the Western Cherokees, signed in Washington, D.C., was witnessed by Thomas L. McKenney, then head of the Indian Office in the War Department and a potent force in early Indian policy. It was signed by Sequoyah and other Cherokees in the syllabary invented by Sequoyah and widely used among the Cherokees.

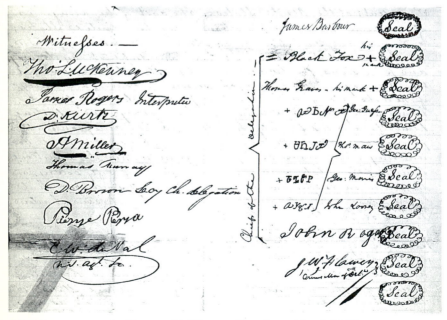

15. Signatures on the Treaty with Western Cherokees, May 6, 1828

Kenney, head of the Indian Office, "It was esteemed to be a useless ceremony; the President approving it only."[36]

The second Seneca treaty was signed at Buffalo Creek, New York, on August 31, 1826. In it the Senecas sold several tracts of land to Robert Troup, Thomas L. Ogden, and Benjamin W. Rogers, in the presence of Oliver Forward, commissioner of the United States, and Nathaniel Gorham, agent for Massachusetts. The treaty was submitted to the Senate for its approval by President John Quincy Adams on February 24, 1827. The Senate formally considered the treaty but on February 29, by a vote of twenty to twenty, failed to agree to its ratification. On April 4, by formal resolution, it stated its reasons: "That by the refusal of the Senate to ratify the treaty with the Seneca Indians, it is not intended to express any disapprobation of the terms of the contract entered into by the individuals who are parties to that contract, but merely to disclaim the necessity of an interference by the Senate with the subject matter" (the original motion read, "disclaim any power over the subject matter").[37]

The federal government in these cases was torn between two provisions of the Trade and Intercourse Act of 1802; one stipulated (following the act of 1790) that no purchase of Indian land was valid "unless the same be made by treaty or convention, entered into pursuant to the constitution," while the other authorized state agents, with the approval of the United States commissioners, to be present at an Indian treaty council and to deal with the Indians regarding compensation for claims to land extinguished by the treaty.[38]

The Southern Tribes

The southern tribes in the period after the War of 1812 differed markedly from those in the north. As Cass and Clark astutely remarked in their report on Indian affairs in 1829, "Their [the southern tribes'] political organization differs materially from that of the Northern

36. McKenney to Barbour, February 16, 1827, *ASPIA*, 2:868. The treaty is not in the State Department file of treaties, but it was printed in *Treaties between the United States of America, and the Several Indian Tribes, from 1778 to 1837* (Washington: Langtree and O'Sullivan, 1837), 305–7. Kappler prints it as an unratified treaty, 2:1033–34.

37. *ASPIA*, 2:866–68; *Senate Ex. Proc.*, 3:601, 602, 603.

38. 2 Stat. 143.

and Western tribes. With the former, power is in the hands of few, with the latter, of many."[39] This difference was manifested in treaty making. While some of the treaties with the Cherokees, Creeks, Choctaws, Chickasaws, and Seminoles were negotiated with large assemblies of tribesmen, others were conducted by a few leaders of each tribe, delegated for the purpose, and a third of the treaties were signed not in the Indian country but in Washington, D.C., where the secretary of war dealt with selected chiefs. Following the practice of the United States in appointing commissioners to negotiate and sign a treaty, with later ratification by the nation, some of the tribes specified that the treaty had to be approved by the whole tribe in council.[40] But most of the treaties obviated any tribal ratification by specifying that the contract was concluded by kings, chiefs, headmen, and warriors of the Indian nation, in council assembled, on behalf of the nation.

Between 1816 and 1828, seventeen treaties were signed with the five southern tribes dealing with cessions of land or adjustment of boundaries. The United States was concerned in the south as it was in the north about the orderly advance of white settlement. It wanted to open lands adjacent to the established settlements and to discourage wide scattering of the whites to areas far distant, and the extinguishment of Indian titles by treaty proceeded pretty much in this fashion.[41]

Significant, too, was the development of the idea of Indian removal with an *exchange* of lands; the Indians would relinquish their traditional eastern holdings and accept instead equal or comparable lands west of the Mississippi. President Jefferson had broached the idea as early as 1803, and the policy was urged upon the Cherokees in 1808–9. Not until after the War of 1812, however, were there treaty provisions for such action. In a treaty of July 8, 1817, the Cherokees agreed to give up two sizable tracts in Georgia and North Carolina for one of equal size on the Arkansas and White rivers. The treaty authorized the proportional division of annuities between the eastern Cherokees and those who chose to migrate westward and provided 640 acres to individual Indians who chose to remain where they were and become citizens. A large part of the Cherokee Nation adamantly opposed removal, but the treaty was signed by a considerable number of chiefs

39. *Senate Doc.* no. 72, 20-2, serial 181, p. 22.
40. See Kappler, 2:125, 134.
41. The seventeen treaties are given in appendix B as nos. 66–67, 73–75, 79, 81, 95–96, 105–6, 110, 114–15, 134, 140, 142.

and headmen sympathetic to such removal. The War Department feared that there would be opposition to the treaty in the Senate by members who disliked the policy of removing the Indians to west of the Mississippi and those who felt that too few chiefs had signed the treaty, but in the end the Senate approved the treaty with no dissenting votes.[42]

This Cherokee removal treaty of 1817 severely divided the Indians, and those who decided to emigrate charged persecution from the other faction, but large numbers of Cherokees, nevertheless, moved west. In 1819, in Washington, D.C., Secretary of War John C. Calhoun and a delegation of Cherokees made adjustments in the 1817 treaty, and set the division of the annuities at two-thirds for the eastern Indians and one-third for the western.[43] The Western Cherokees eventually came to deal with the federal government as a separate unit, and by a treaty of May 6, 1828, Western Cherokees and Secretary of War James Barbour agreed to a new grant of land, which moved the Cherokees beyond a newly declared western boundary of Arkansas Territory. This treaty provided to the Cherokees, in addition, "a perpetual outlet, West," as far as the sovereignty of the United States extended, and it was notable for the strong statement on the political autonomy of the tribe:

it being the anxious desire of the Government of the United States to secure to the Cherokee nation of Indians . . . *a permanent* home, and which shall, under the most solemn guarantee of the United States, be, and remain, theirs forever—a home that shall never, in all future time, be embarrassed by having extended around it the lines, or placed over it the jurisdiction of a Territory or State, nor be pressed upon by the extension, in any way, of any of the limits of any existing Territory or State.[44]

42. Kappler, 2:140–44. A long preamble to the treaty sets forth the history of the agreement in 1808–9 for exchange of lands. For Senate views, see Acting Secretary of War George Graham to Jackson, McMinn, and Meriwether, August 1, 1817, *ASPIA,* 2:143. For ratification, see *Senate Ex. Proc.,* 3:108. There is a detailed discussion of the treaty, as of all Cherokee treaties, in Charles C. Royce, "The Cherokee Nation of Indians: A Narrative of Their Official Relations with the Colonial and Federal Governments," *Fifth Annual Report of the Bureau of Ethnology,* 1883–1884 (Washington: GPO, 1887), 212–19; the report is reprinted as Charles C. Royce, *The Cherokee Nation of Indians* (Chicago: Aldine Publishing Company, 1975), with different pagination.

43. Kappler, 2:177–81; Royce, "Cherokee Nation of Indians," 219–28.

44. Kappler, 2:288–92; Royce, "Cherokee Nation of Indians," 229–49. It is interesting to note that the *treaty* was used as the vehicle for establishing a new western boundary for Arkansas. There are numerous documents concerning the Cherokees and

Choctaws, too, made progressive cessions of land, and they, like the Cherokees, moved in considerable numbers across the Mississippi into Arkansas Territory, where land was granted them in a treaty of October 18, 1820. This Treaty of Doak's Stand, negotiated by Andrew Jackson and Thomas Hinds, was an indication of the government's growing determination to remove the Indians from the states east of the Mississippi to lands west of the river. Jackson reluctantly accepted the appointment as commissioner, but then, by skillful use of subsistence supplies, bribes, and threats, got the agreement of the Indians to exchange five million acres of their lands in Mississippi for some thirteen million acres in Arkansas Territory. As was the case with the Cherokees, the citizens of Arkansas raised a great fuss over the movement of eastern Indians into lands coveted by whites and to a large extent already settled by them. In answer to these problems, Choctaw delegates met with Calhoun in Washington in 1825, and the Indians' land in Arkansas was reduced in exchange for annuities and more money for the education of Choctaw youth.[45]

With the Creek Indians, treaty negotiations ran into special difficulties when the federal negotiators attempted to bring that tribe, too, under the removal-policy umbrella. When the majority of the Creeks and their leaders adamantly resisted a removal agreement, the United States commissioners, Duncan Campbell and James Meriwether, began a series of scandalous maneuvers that involved a removal-minded faction of the nation led by William McIntosh (a chief of the Lower Towns), the Indian agent, and officials of the state of Georgia, which desperately sought to remove the remaining Creeks from within its territorial boundaries. The National Council (especially the chiefs of the Upper

---

the Choctaws and the treaties by which they moved into Arkansas in *Terr. Papers*, vols. 19–21.

45. Kappler, 2:191–95, 211–14. There is a well-documented and detailed picture of the negotiations and of Jackson's procedures in Arthur H. DeRosier, Jr., *The Removal of the Choctaw Indians* (Knoxville: University of Tennessee Press, 1970), 53–69. For documents, see *Correspondence of Jackson*, ed. Bassett, and *ASPIA*, 2:229–44, 547–58. The agitation about the Treaty of Doak's Stand, both in Mississippi and in Arkansas Territory, is described in DeRosier, *Removal of the Choctaw Indians*, 70–84. DeRosier praises Calhoun's moderation and fairness in dealing with the Indians and concludes that "the Treaty of 1825 was a favorable one for the Choctaw Indians" (p. 82). The complicated story of relations between the Cherokees and Choctaws and the citizens of Arkansas is told in some detail in Francis Paul Prucha, *American Indian Policy in the Formative Years: The Indian Trade and Intercourse Acts, 1790–1834* (Cambridge: Harvard University Press, 1962), 171–78.

Towns) firmly insisted that no more land be ceded, and it relied on an earlier law declaring death to any leader who agreed to sell land to give weight to its decision.[46]

At a meeting with the National Council in December 1824 Campbell and Meriwether tried vainly to convince the Creek leaders, but the Indians rebutted them at every turn of their argument and ended with a firm rejection of the federal proposals. Then the commissioners began to confer secretly with McIntosh. At Indian Springs on February 12, 1825, they signed a treaty of cession and removal with McIntosh and his faction, which cleared Georgia of Creeks and gave up Creek lands in Alabama. Two hundred thousand dollars were provided for the removal expenses of the McIntosh group. To the National Council and the majority of the Creek people, the treaty was "an iniquitous document grounded in fraud and chicanery and acted out in treason," but the United States commissioners rushed to Washington with the treaty, declaring it had been made with the Creek Nation.[47]

President Monroe laid the document before the Senate, and although the Creek agent and Chief Big Warrior, as representative of the National Council, followed the commissioners to the capital and argued against the validity of the treaty, the Senate on March 3, 1825, at the very end of the Monroe administration, approved the treaty without having had time to study it. John Quincy Adams, in one of his first acts as president, proclaimed the treaty on March 7.[48]

William McIntosh soon received his reward. The Creek National Council voted his execution as a traitor who had violated the laws of the nation, and on the night of April 30 McIntosh was killed at his plantation by a force of Creek warriors.

While Governor Troup of Georgia moved to support the McIntosh faction, President Adams hoped to persuade the Creek Nation to accept the treaty, and he sent General Edmund P. Gaines to press for peace and adjustment between the factions. Adams authorized Gaines to use force to prevent an early survey of the ceded grounds by Georgia, but the general could not get the Creek Council to accept the Treaty of Indian Springs. In the end, a Creek delegation went to Washington to confer

---

46. A detailed account of the complicated history of this treaty appears in Green, *Politics of Indian Removal*, 69–97.

47. *ASPIA*, 2:563–84. See also the extensive documentation submitted by the Georgia legislature to the House of Representatives, ibid., 727–862. The quotation is from Green, *Politics of Indian Removal*, 88.

48. See Adams to the Senate, January 31, 1826, *ASPIA*, 2:611–12.

with Secretary of War James Barbour about correcting the evils of the McIntosh treaty. After much argument and disagreement, a new treaty was signed on January 24, 1826.[49]

When President Adams submitted the new treaty to the Senate he explained how he had hoped to reconcile the two sides, prevent civil war among the Creeks, and protect the interests of the McIntosh faction. But his expectations had been disappointed. "In this state of things," he told the Senate,

> the question is not whether the treaty of the 12th of February last shall or shall not be executed. So far as the United States were or could be bound by it, I have been anxiously desirous of carrying it into execution; but, like other treaties, its fulfilment depends upon the will not of one, but of both the parties to it. The parties on the face of the treaty are the United States and the Creek nation; and however desirous one of them may be to give it effect, this wish must prove abortive while the other party refuses to perform its stipulations, and disavows its obligations. By the refusal of the Creek nation to perform their part of the treaty, the United States are absolved from all its engagements on their part, and the alternative left them is, either to resort to measures of war, to secure by force the advantages stipulated to them in the treaty, or to attempt the adjustment of the interest by a new compact.[50]

Adams, of course, had chosen the latter course, and he urged the Senate to accept the revised compact. In an unprecedented move, the new treaty in its first article declared the Treaty of Indian Springs "to be null and void, to every interest and purpose whatsoever." The Creek delegates, faced with no real alternative, now agreed to part with most of the lands in Georgia; the treaty provided a sum of $217,600 to be divided among the chiefs and warriors and an additional perpetual annuity of $20,000. The treaty protected the interests of the McIntosh group, restoring them to good standing within the Creek Nation and authorizing funds for those of them who wished to remove to the West.[51]

49. Kappler, 2:264–67.

50. *ASPIA*, 2:611–12. Barbour's account of the negotiations, dated January 25, 1826, appears ibid., 612–13.

51. An agreement made with the Creek Council by General Gaines at Broken Arrow, which pardoned McIntosh's followers, was referred to in the treaty but not formally incorporated in it. It is printed in Kappler, 2:1034–35. For a full discussion of the new treaty, see Richard J. Hryniewicki, "The Creek Treaty of Washington, 1826," *Georgia Historical Quarterly* 48 (December 1964): 425–41. A study that deals with Creek treaties

The Senate refused to accede to the new treaty as it was submitted because the Georgians insisted that *all* the Creek lands in Georgia be given up, and a supplementary article was signed by the Creek delegates on March 31 to extinguish their title to Georgia lands. With this in hand, the Senate ratified the treaty by a vote of thirty to seven on April 21.[52]

The Chickasaw Indians in treaties of 1816 and 1818 were similarly pressured to cede lands wanted by advancing white settlers, although the exchange of lands and removal to west of the Mississippi was not part of the negotiations. The tribe parted with lands in Alabama and Tennessee in return for cash annuities for specified terms of years. In both treaties provisions of land and money were made for particular individuals.[53]

The last of the Five Civilized Tribes, the Seminoles in Florida, underwent a similar reduction of lands, but their condition was considerably different from that of the better-established southern tribes already considered. Made up of descendants of aboriginal peoples and of Creeks migrating from Georgia and Alabama, they lacked the cohesion or the power to deal forcefully with the United States government. The United States, for its part, after the acquisition of Florida in 1821 sought to move the Indians from the territory or concentrate them in some restricted spot, opening lands for white settlers and removing the Indians from contact with the coast (thus eliminating immediate aid to foreign invaders).

At Moultrie Creek, south of St. Augustine, United States commis-

---

through 1826 is Grace M. Schwartzman and Susan K. Barnard, "A Trail of Broken Promises: Georgians and the Muscogee/Creek Treaties, 1796–1826," *Georgia Historical Quarterly* 75 (Winter 1991): 697–718.

52. *Senate Ex. Proc.*, 3:521, 525, 531–33. Complications that arose because of payment provisions proposed by the two Cherokees—John Ridge and David Vann—who served as secretaries for the Creek delegation are discussed in Hryniewicki, "Creek Treaty of Washington, 1826," 437. See also *ASPIA*, 2:665–67. The boundary line between Georgia and Alabama, however, was still in doubt, and when it was finally determined, a portion of Creek land was found to be within Georgia. By a new treaty in November 1827 the Creeks sold this territory to the United States. Kappler, 2:285–86. The story of this treaty is told in Richard J. Hryniewicki, "The Creek Treaty of November 15, 1827," *Georgia Historical Quarterly* 52 (March 1968): 1–15. For Thomas L. McKenney's part in the negotiations, see Herman J. Viola, *Thomas L. McKenney: Architect of America's Early Indian Policy, 1816–1830* (Chicago: Swallow Press, 1974), 208–10.

53. Kappler, 2:135–37, 174–77. A long report on the 1816 treaty by Indian Agent William Cocke to William H. Crawford, September 22, 1816, appears in *ASPIA*, 2:106–7. The journal of the 1818 treaty is in Documents (T494), roll 1, frames 337–50.

sioners met with the Indians (some 425 of whom appeared at the treaty grounds), and the treaty signed there concentrated the Indians in central Florida and paid them $6,000 worth of goods and an annuity of $5,000 for twenty years. In addition the United States provided rations for twelve months, paid for improvements that had to be abandoned, supplied funds for removal costs, and established separate reservations of land for six of the chiefs.[54]

Although the Indians succeeded in changing the boundaries of the reservation to include better land, they were in no position to challenge the general thrust of United States policy in their regard. The treaty declared that the chiefs and their tribes "have appealed to the humanity, and thrown themselves on, and have promised to continue under, the protection of the United States." James Gadsden, one of the negotiators, later wrote privately to Calhoun, "It is not necessary to disguise the fact to you, that the treaty effected was in a degree a treaty of imposition—The Indians would never have voluntarily assented to the terms had they not believed that we had both the power & disposition to compel obedience."[55]

Criticism of Treaty Making

The treaty-making process went forward without a great deal of reflection, for it served the expansionist purposes of the United States. The pattern was set and the constitutional provisions were adhered to. But ultimately—perhaps inevitably—a question arose about the propriety of considering the Indian tribes, no matter what their power, political organization, and sophistication, as sovereign nations, with whom the only means of dealing was by formal treaty.

54. Kappler, 2:203–7. A report on February 1, 1826, set the total cost at $87,068.21, of which $65,700 was for rations. *ASPIA*, 2:614.

55. Gadsden to the secretary of war, September 29, 1823, *Terr. Papers*, 22:752. The official report of the commissioners, September 26, 1823, is printed ibid., 747–51. Much of the story of the treaty can be followed in *Terr. Papers*, vol. 22. See also the documents, including a brief journal, in *ASPIA*, 2:429–42, 614–44. For ratification of the treaty on December 23, 1823, see *Senate Ex. Proc.*, 3:352. The Senate struck out the tenth article, which had provided grants of land as presents for Gad Humphreys, Indian agent, and Stephen Richards, interpreter. A full study of the treaty, with extensive documentation, is John K. Mahon, "The Treaty of Moultrie Creek, 1823," *Florida Historical Quarterly* 40 (April 1962): 350–72.

Not surprisingly, Andrew Jackson was the first national figure to bring the matter up. In March 1817, while military commander in the southern states, he told President Monroe that he had "long viewed treaties with the Indians an absurdity not to be reconciled with the principles of our Government." By that time he had served as official commissioner in signing treaties with Creeks, Cherokees, and Chickasaws, and he was about to resume that role; his long frontier experience, moreover, led him to consider himself an expert on Indian affairs. Jackson considered the Indians subjects of the United States, "inhabiting its territory and acknowledging its sovereignty," and he considered it absurd for a sovereign to negotiate by treaty with subjects. Congress, he maintained, had as much right to legislate for the Indians as for the citizens of the territories, and he urged that Congress make use of this right "to prescribe their bounds at pleasure, and provide for their wants and whenever the safety, interest or defence of the country should render it necessary for the Government of the United States to occupy and possess any part of the Territory, used by them for hunting, that they have the right to take it and dispose of it." Due compensation was to be given, or course, just as in any exercise of eminent domain.[56]

The Indians, in Jackson's view, had been thrown on the liberality and humanity of the government after the Revolution and after their defeat in subsequent Indian wars. Treaties would be all very well if the Indians were in fact independent nations, possessing the rights of sovereignty, but Jackson flatly denied that this was the case. The Indians, he said, "have only a possessory right to the soil, for the purpose of hunting and not the right of domain, hence I conclude that Congress has full power, by law, to regulate all the concerns of the Indians."

Jackson rejected the argument that the United States, following the example of Great Britain, had always treated the Indians as independent nations. To his mind, the policy of making treaties with the Indians grew up out of necessity at a time when the government was not strong enough to enforce its regulations among the Indians or to keep peace in any other way. Now, under changed circumstances, a more just procedure would be the forceful reduction of the Indian lands, so that the natives, confined to closer limits, would adopt the civilized existence of the whites.

Jackson condemned "the farce which has been introduced of holding

---

56. Jackson's views in this and succeeding paragraphs are in Jackson to Monroe, March 4, 1817, *Correspondence of Jackson,* ed. Bassett, 2:279–81.

treaties with them," and he spoke of the susceptibility of the chiefs to bribery. "Money," he said, "is the weapon, in the hand of the commissioner, wielded to corrupt a few of their leaders, and induce them to adopt the plans embraced by the views of the Government, when the poor of the Nation receive but little, and are, by the influence of their Chiefs, (thus managed by corruption) induced to assent to their wills. Honor [,] justice and humanity," he concluded, "certainly require that a change of Policy should take place."

Monroe replied, "The view which you have taken of the Indian title to lands is new but very deserving of attention." He asserted that the "hunter or savage state, requires, a greater extent of territory to sustain it, than is compatible with the progress and just claims of civilized life, and must yield to it." But he noted that, where the Indian title had not been extinguished, the United States title to land was good only against European nations, that it was by treaties that American limits were determined, and that it was customary to purchase title from the Indians. Yet he admitted that if the Indians did not voluntarily submit to the civilizing programs, compulsion would have to be resorted to.[57]

Jackson did not let up. When asked in June 1820 to serve again as a treaty commissioner, he wrote to Secretary of War Calhoun that he had "determined never to have any thing to do again in Indian Treaties" but that he would accept simply to please the president. On September 2 of that year he repeated to Calhoun what he had written earlier to Monroe, and on September 17 he amplified his statement:

> I do think it [making treaties with Indians] not only useless but absurd. When Congress has the power to regulate all Indian concerns, by act of Congress, and the arm of the government is sufficiently strong to carry such regulations into effect. More general justice can be done to the Indians, in this way than by treaty. When the policy of treating with the indians was first adopted it was at a time when we found them thrown upon our hands by the treaty of 1783, without any provision being made for them, and at that time they were numerous and hostile, while the arm of the government was too weak to enforce such regulations as justice and good policy required, hence the necessity of managing them by treaties. But this has passed away, the arm of government is sufficient to protect them and to carry into execution any measures called for by justice to them, or by the Safety of our borders. Hence the absurdity of holding treaties with indian tribes within our territorial limits, subject to our

57. Monroe to Jackson, October 5, 1817, ibid., 331–32.

sovregnty and municipal regulations, and to whom, by legislation, every justice can be done, and the safety of our Southern frontier perfectly secured.[58]

The secretary of war, even more than the president, received Jackson's opinions favorably. He replied that Jackson's views "appear very correct." "I entirely concur with you," he wrote, "that it is perfectly absurd to hold treaties with those within our limits, as they neither are or can be independent of our government. This opinion has been frequently communicated to Congress, and altho' they have not yet adopted it, I still hope that they will ultimately. By its adoption both ours and their interest would be advanced, and all of the objections, which may be urged against almost every Indian treaty which has been made, be thereby avoided."[59]

Yet neither Jackson nor Calhoun at the time could change the traditional procedures. During the seven and one-half years that Calhoun conducted Indian affairs as secretary of war, forty treaties were signed with the Indians. While Jackson was president, sixty-seven Indian treaties were ratified. Tradition was hard to overcome, and treaties were a convenient and generally effective way to carry out American Indian policy. The ideas that Jackson expressed, however, would not die. They surfaced again and again, without full effect, until some fifty years later Congress finally ended treaty making with the Indians.

58. Jackson to Calhoun, June 19, 1820, ibid., 3:27; Jackson to Calhoun, September 2, 1820, ibid., 32. Jackson to Calhoun, September 17, 1821, *Terr. Papers*, 22:207.

59. Calhoun to Jackson, November 16, 1821, ibid., 278. See also Calhoun report of January 15, 1820, *ASPIA*, 2:200–201.

CHAPTER SEVEN

Indian Removal and the Debate about Treaty Making

In the late 1820s and the 1830s a full-scale debate on Indian treaties renewed the criticisms of treaty making that Andrew Jackson had brought forth a decade earlier. There was a powerful onslaught against the treaties and the Indian nationhood on which they rested and an equally vigorous and eloquent defense of both, set in a framework of preservation of national faith and honor. The debate centered on the Cherokees in Georgia, but it had broader applicability.

The Georgia-Cherokee Controversy

The initial focus of debate was Georgia's demand that the United States remove the Cherokees within the state; if that were not done, Georgia threatened to extend its jurisdiction over the Cherokee lands. There were deep historical roots for the controversy, for in 1802 the state and the federal government had signed a compact by which Georgia relinquished her western lands (ultimately to be the states of Mississippi and Alabama) in return for a promise by the United States that it would extinguish the Indian title to lands in Georgia "as early as the same can be peaceably obtained on reasonable terms."[1]

As the demand for the Indian lands increased, Georgia accused the

1. The compact is printed in *Terr. Papers*, 5:142–46. The quotation is from 144.

federal government of bad faith in failing to live up to its part of the bargain. Although Monroe and John Quincy Adams listened to the complaints of Georgia and urged the Indians to leave the state, the presidents would not budge from their position that the Indians would have to act voluntarily and that the federal government would not force them. The fire was further fueled by the Cherokee adoption of a formal constitution in 1827, which declared the tribe to be a sovereign nation under the protection of the United States and in no way subject to Georgia's jurisdiction. The Georgians cried that this unconstitutionally established an *imperium in imperio*, a separate nation *within* the boundaries of the sovereign state. The federal government refused to act, and the state took the law into its own hands. Its line of action was to extend the authority of the state and its laws over the Cherokee lands, in effect withdrawing the Cherokee territory from the status of Indian country, bringing the lands under Georgia's control and, by overt as well as subtle pressure, forcing the Indians out.[2]

To justify such action Georgia struck at the heart of the treaty system, for it denied the Indians' title to the land, their sovereign jurisdiction over the territory they claimed, and the validity of the treaties with the Indians (which recognized Indian title and Indian political autonomy). From 1827 until the final removal of the Cherokees in 1838, the arguments echoed through the halls of Congress and the public press.

The Georgia legislature asserted an absolute title of Georgia to the Indian lands. Before the Revolutionary War, it argued, Great Britain had had full sovereignty over the lands, and with American independence Georgia had succeeded to that sovereignty. "The possession of the Indians was permissive. . . . they were mere tenants at will," the legislature said, and that tenancy could be ended at any time by Georgia.[3]

In 1827, to be sure, the Georgia legislature had urged the people of the state to accept any treaty that the United States might make providing for Cherokee removal, but when supporters of Cherokee rights pointed to the Cherokee treaties to support the Indians against Georgia, the argument moved beyond the question of land title to the more fundamental ones of Indian sovereignty and the consequent power to enter

<hr />

2. There is a summary discussion of these matters in Francis Paul Prucha, *The Great Father: The United States Government and the American Indians*, 2 vols. (Lincoln: University of Nebraska Press, 1984), 1:183–91. See the sources cited there.

3. *Acts of the General Assembly of the State of Georgia, 1827* (Milledgeville, Ga., 1827), 249–50. The statement was quoted by William L. Storrs in the House of Representatives on May 15, 1830, *Register of Debates in Congress*, 6:996.

into formal treaties with the United States. Georgia and its friends denied both.

Andrew Jackson was in accord with Georgia's position on Indian titles and Indian sovereignty, and his election to the presidency emboldened Georgia. In 1828 the state added Cherokee lands to certain northwestern counties of Georgia and in 1829 extended its laws over these lands, effective June 1, 1830, after which date Cherokee laws and customs would be null and void.[4] Jackson, through Secretary of War John Eaton, replied to Cherokee complaints on April 18, 1829; he told the Indians flatly that he could not support them against Georgia's claim to sovereignty and urged them to move west of the Mississippi.[5]

To the Cherokees and their friends the action of Georgia and the president's support of the state's position were a call to battle. Unable to conceive that historical practice with its promises and guarantees could be forgotten and the honor and good faith of the United States disregarded by its elected officials, these men began a concerted attack on the anti-Cherokee forces. In so doing, they brought forth all possible legal and moral arguments to uphold the rights of the Cherokees to their ancestral lands, the sovereignty of the nation within those lands, and the sanctity of the treaties in which the sovereignty and landed rights had been guaranteed. It was a full-dress discussion of Indian treaties and the treaty-making power that was unequalled in American history.

The leader in the campaign was Jeremiah Evarts, a New England lawyer who served in Boston as secretary of the American Board of Commissioners for Foreign Missions, a Congregational/Presbyterian missionary society with active missions and schools among the southern Indians. Touched by the plight of the Cherokees, many of whose leaders he knew personally through mission contacts, Evarts set to work to awaken the conscience of the nation and warn Jackson and his friends of the divine retribution they could expect if they did not turn from their evil path.[6]

---

4. William C. Dawson, comp., *A Compilation of the Laws of the State of Georgia* (Milledgeville, Ga.: Grantland and Orme, 1831), 198–99.

5. Eaton to Cherokee delegation, April 18, 1829, OIA LS, 5:408–12 (M21, roll 5); it is printed in Francis Paul Prucha, ed., *Documents of United States Indian Policy*, 2d ed. (Lincoln: University of Nebraska Press, 1990), 44–47. This document was considered at the time—by both friends and foes of Jackson—to epitomize the president's position.

6. On Evarts, see the introduction in Jeremiah Evarts, *Cherokee Removal: The "William Penn" Essays and Other Writings*, ed. Francis Paul Prucha (Knoxville: University of Tennessee Press, 1981); J. Orin Oliphant, ed., *Through the South and West with Jeremiah*

Evarts's most important work was a series of twenty-four essays that he published in the *National Intelligencer* between August 5 and December 19, 1829, under the pseudonym William Penn. The articles, with their detailed legal analysis of the Cherokee treaties and their recognition of the Cherokees as a nation, were the fullest and best statement of the Cherokee case. Numerous newspapers and periodicals reprinted them, and they circulated widely in pamphlet form; churchmen and congressmen alike drew their arguments from this source.[7]

After a detailed account of the Treaty of Hopewell (1785) and the Treaty of Holston (1791), Evarts asked, "What is a treaty?" His answer indicates his commitment to the Indian cause:

[A treaty] is a compact between independent communities, each party acting through the medium of its government. No instrument, which does not come within this definition, can be sent to the Senate of the United States, to be acted upon as within the scope of the treaty-making power. . . . The Indian tribes and nations have made treaties with the United States during the last forty years, till the whole number of treaties thus made far exceeds a hundred, every one of which was ratified by the Senate before it became obligatory. Every instance of this kind implies that the Indian communities had governments of their own; that the Indians, thus living in communities, were not subject to the laws of the United States; and that they had rights and interests distinct from the rights and interests of the people of the United States, and, in the fullest sense, public and national. All this is in accordance with facts; and the whole is implied in the single word *treaty*.[8]

Evarts recounted the Cherokees' relations with the United States, treaty by treaty, pointing out the provisions that clearly recognized the national sovereignty of the Indians, and he emphasized again and again

Evarts in 1826 (Lewisburg, Penn.: Bucknell University Press, 1956); and E. C. Tracy, *Memoir of the Life of Jeremiah Evarts, Esq.* (Boston: Crocker and Brewster, 1845). A recent book that offers a detailed account of Evarts's Christian republicanism and his support of the Cherokees is John A. Andrew III, *From Revivals to Removal: Jeremiah Evarts, the Cherokee Nation, and the Search for the Soul of America* (Athens: University of Georgia Press, 1992).

7. The essays from the *National Intelligencer* were published in pamphlet form as *Essays on the Present Crisis in the Condition of the American Indians: First Published in the National Intelligencer, under the Signature of William Penn* (Boston: Perkins and Marvin, 1829). They are reprinted in Evarts, *Cherokee Removal*, 45–199.

8. Evarts, *Cherokee Removal*, 72.

that these compacts were called treaties with a meaning that "no ingenuity can distort, pervert, or evade." He laughed at the argument of Georgia that treaties could not be made with Indian communities because they were not nations. "Unfortunately for this theory," he wrote, "it was notoriously invented to answer a particular purpose. It is not, and cannot be, entitled to the least degree of credit. Communities of Indians have been called nations, in every book of travels, geography, and history, in which they have been mentioned at all, from the discovery of America to the present day. Treaties have been made with them, (uniformly under the *name* of treaties,) during this whole period." The colony of Georgia, he noted, had always spoken of Creek and Cherokee *nations;* and it called the compacts that it made with them *treaties.*[9]

Evarts was answered belatedly by another benevolent spokesman, the Reverend Isaac McCoy, a Baptist missionary to the Indians, who had a long career of seeking to establish a separate Indian territory west of the Mississippi. In a series of six articles in the *United States' Telegraph* in August and early September 1830, McCoy spoke out sharply against his "opponents." He followed the Jacksonian position on the necessity and wisdom of removal of Indians from the eastern states, and he had an extremely negative position on Indian sovereignty and the treaties that rested on it. He flatly denied that the Indian had any rights in the land they occupied and asserted that no civilized nation had ever admitted any. "Whatever has been understood by the word treaty," he wrote," as employed in our intercourse with the Indian tribes, it is evident that it did *not* imply that they were the sovereign owners of the countries they inhabit." He considered the treaties made with Indians fundamentally fraudulent. "We cannot consider the Indians really a *party* to a contract in the conveyance of land," he argued, "when they are assembled at the pleasure of the whites, when the latter give the terms, and when the latter are as fully determined to have the land in question, or, rather, to *hold* the land in question, to which they already consider themselves entitled, if the terms offered to the Indians should *not* be agreed to, as if they should." It was clear to McCoy that the United States had not pretended to pay for the land at its full value. "Treaties

9. Ibid., 94, 148. See the echo of this argument in John Marshall's decision in *Worcester v. Georgia* (1832). Evarts orchestrated a campaign of petitions to Congress praying for justice to the Cherokees and upholding the nation's obligations to them. Some of the petitions are printed in Evarts, *Cherokee Removal*. See also Francis Paul Prucha, "Protest by Petition: Jeremiah Evarts and the Cherokee Indians," *Proceedings of the Massachusetts Historical Society* 97 (1985): 42–58.

with the Indian tribes are, *in fact*, merely matters of convenience to us, and of humanity towards them . . . ," he concluded. "In treaty we were merely purchasing their consent to leave the lands, or their consent to our occupying it."[10] McCoy's views on treaties, however, gained little support and did not much weaken the powerful theoretical case for the treaties advanced by Evarts.

Debate on the Indian Removal Bill

In his first state of the union address, on December 8, 1829, President Jackson discussed the issue of removal and recommended emigration beyond the Mississippi as the solution to the impasse between Georgia and the Cherokees. The Committee on Indian Affairs in the House and in the Senate, to whom this section of the message was referred, each reported a removal bill—the Senate with little discussion, the House with strong arguments in support of Georgia. The long debate on these bills gave voice to the cases of both Georgia and the Cherokee sympathizers. In April and May 1830 congressional debate centered on the issue; long harangues filled the air until no phase of the question of Cherokee rights and treaty procedures remained untouched.[11]

Senators and representatives from Georgia had their say, ridiculing the "cant and fanaticism" of the northern supporters of the Cherokee cause, with increasing insistence that treaties with the Indians had been a big mistake. A key advocate of Georgia's position was Wilson Lumpkin, who served successively as representative in Congress (1815–31), governor of Georgia (1831–35), and senator (1837–41). During this

10. *United States' Telegraph*, August 19, 1830. The six articles by McCoy, signed simply "Candour" or "Candor," appeared on August 18, 19, 23, 24, September 2, 7. McCoy's dream of an Indian territory and his support of the removal policy are discussed in detail in George A. Schultz, *An Indian Canaan: Isaac McCoy and the Vision of an Indian State* (Norman: University of Oklahoma Press, 1972); see especially chap. 7.

11. Jackson's message, in Fred L. Israel, ed., *The State of the Union Messages of the Presidents, 1790–1966*, 3 vols. (New York: Chelsea House, 1966), 1:308–10; *Senate Doc.* no. 61, 21-1, serial 193; *House Report* no. 227, 21-1, serial 200. The debates appear in *Register of Debates in Congress*, vol. 6. Antiremoval speeches were compiled by Jeremiah Evarts and published as *Speeches on the Passage of the Bill for the Removal of the Indians, Delivered in the Congress of the United States, April and May, 1830* (Boston: Perkins and Marvin, 1830). Some of the speeches on both sides were also circulated in pamphlet form.

long public career he fought for Georgia's rights against the Indians and against the federal government. To him the purchase of Indian lands by treaty was "nothing more than the substitute of humanity and benevolence" and had been resorted to "in preference to the sword, as the best means for agricultural and civilized communities entering into the enjoyment of their natural and just right to the benefits of the earth, evidently designed by Him who formed it for purposes more useful than Indian hunting grounds." He noted that all the old states had abandoned "treaty legislation" and had substituted for it "direct legislation" for the control and government of the Indians.[12]

In the Senate at the end of the decade, as he looked back over his career of dealing with Indian matters, Lumpkin exclaimed: "I have long since been disgusted, and with shame and confusion of face looked at the policy pursued by this Government towards the Indians. Look at your large volume of Indian Treaties! What do you there see? One recorded farce after another, couched in language of high official and formal mockery! One continued tissue of deception and deceit!" "How can any Senator," Lumpkin asked, "expect to put the negotiations of Indian treaties upon the principle and footing of similar transactions with civilized, foreign, enlightened nations? Are not these Indians in a state of dependence and pupilage? Are we not in the place of parents and guardians to them? Shall we, then, overlook all the facts connected with the subject under consideration? Shall we imagine a state of things which we know has no existence?"[13]

Lumpkin's Georgia colleagues in Congress echoed and reinforced his sentiments in their debates on the removal bills. Those who did not condemn outright the ancient practice of making treaties with the Indians spoke of changed circumstances, and a good deal of attention was given to the clauses in the Cherokee treaties in which the Indians admitted dependence upon the United States. Throughout, much ridicule was heaped on the northerners who upheld the Cherokee cause and on their memorials to Congress.[14]

---

12. *Register of Debates in Congress*, 6:1024. The same views were expressed by Lumpkin in Senate speeches in 1838 and 1840. See Wilson Lumpkin, *The Removal of the Cherokee Indians from Georgia*, 2 vols. (Wormsloe, Ga., 1907; New York: Dodd, Mead and Company, 1907), which prints many of his speeches.

13. Speech in the Senate, April 30, 1838, Lumpkin, *Removal of the Cherokees*, 2:193; speech in the Senate, March 19, 1840, ibid., 246. Both these speeches were made later than the debate in 1830 over Cherokee removal, but they well expressed the sentiments of Lumpkin and his colleagues at the time.

14. See, for example, the speeches of Senator John Forsyth and Representative James M. Wayne, *Register of Debates in Congress*, 6:325, 1131.

The anti-Jackson forces in Congress, feeling themselves on the defensive against the president's influence and the growing party sentiment that gave support to his and Georgia's views, occupied long hours on the floor of the Senate and the House in condemnation of what they feared the removal bill would mean. They drew their argument largely from Evarts's writings, and he corresponded with them regularly to bolster their resolve. They argued passionately for Indian title to the land, the long-recognized nationhood of the tribes, and the sanctity of treaties.

In the Senate, Theodore Frelinghuysen of New Jersey, known as the "Christian statesman" because of his adherence to Christian reform movements, was the principal advocate of Cherokee rights; on April 7, 8, and 9 he spoke for six hours on the issue.[15] He was seconded by Senator Peleg Sprague of Maine, who insisted that the treaties with the Cherokees had been made "with all the forms and solemnities which could give them force and efficacy; by commissioners, duly appointed with full power" and that they had been "ratified by the Senate; confirmed by the President; and announced to the world, by his proclamation, as the binding compact of the nation, and the supreme law of the land."[16]

More support came from Senator Asher Robbins of Rhode Island, who asserted: "The turning question, then, of this whole debate, I repeat, is whether the Indian nations within our territorial boundaries are competent to make treaties." He was surprised that the question had been raised at all, for "treaties upon treaties, and almost without number, have been made with Indians thus situated, without a doubt, in a single instance, of their competency to make them." To be competent to make a treaty, he said, a tribe must be a sovereign, but he distinguished, as his friends did, between independent sovereignty and dependent sovereignty and declared that it was immaterial which kind the Indians had.[17]

When the major debates shifted to the House in May, representatives from New York, New England, and other northern states repeated the timeworn arguments with renewed enthusiasm. Representative William L. Storrs of Connecticut, especially, discussed at length the treaty-making power, noting that the constitution made it a function, not of

15. His speech is given in condensed form in *Register of Debates in Congress*, 6:309–20; it was reprinted as a separate pamphlet and included in *Speeches on the Passage of the Bill for the Removal of the Indians*, 1–30.

16. *Register of Debates in Congress*, 6:344.

17. Ibid., 374–75.

the president alone, but of the executive and two-thirds of the Senate and that both the president and individual states were bound to support this supreme law of the land. Representative Isaac C. Bates of Massachusetts said that "it has been intimated, to get rid of the effect of our Indian treaties, that they are not treaties," but he ridiculed such a position:

> The treaties between the United States and the Cherokees were negotiated as treaties, and treaties between nations competent to make treaties. They were ratified as treaties. They were called treaties, not only by us, but by the French, Spanish and English, before our time. They were admitted to be treaties by Georgia. . . . How, then, can we say to the Indians nations, that what we called treaties, and ratified as treaties, were not in fact treaties?[18]

One fear that cropped up again and again in the speeches of the Cherokee defenders was that the removal bill would put power to arrange Indian affairs solely in the hands of the president (an eventuality that seemed especially painful to anti-Jacksonites, some of whom pictured "King Andrew I" usurping power). Thus, Representative John Test of Indiana complained about the "novelty" of the removal bill, which, he said, "throws into the hands of the President some twenty millions of dollars, to disburse exactly as he pleases; it throws into his hands the lives and liberties of four hundred thousand human beings, for such is about the number of Indians on both sides of the Mississippi, besides a hundred millions of acres of land, without check or control over him, no power to revise his acts; and his compacts are without the revising power of the Senate. It is a discretion which I can never consent to grant to any man." Test wanted the treaty system to continue. "Here," he said, "is safety. If the treaty is fraudulent, it can be set aside; if it is improvident, it can be rectified; if the President should drive the project too fast, or extend his operations too wide, he can be checked."[19]

Frelinghuysen wanted to amend the removal bill so that it would explicitly protect the independence of the tribes and their treaty-making power, but he was able to obtain no more than an innocuous statement that the bill would not be so construed as to cancel existing treaties or agreements between the United States and the Cherokees.[20]

Jeremiah Evarts and his friends in Congress and in the country at

18. Ibid., 998–1000, 1054.
19. Ibid., 1104, 1109.
20. Ibid., 309, 381, 383.

large argued at length for treaty rights from a legal and constitutional standpoint. But what drove them so passionately against Jackson and the Georgians was their deep Christian commitment to morality, to the honor and good faith of the nation. Evarts's fear that the nation was about to commit a serious sin by throwing aside its solemn commitments to the Cherokees was echoed strongly in the chambers of Congress.

Representative George Evans of Maine on May 18 called attention to one of Lumpkin's remarks, namely, that the time would come when it would be odious to be known as an advocate of Indian rights, and he rejoined: "Before that period shall arrive, you must burn all the records of the Government—destroy the history of the country—pervert the moral sense of the community—make injustice and oppression virtue—and breach of national faith honorable; and then, but not till then, will the visions of the gentleman assume the form of realities." Senator Frelinghuysen asked: "Do the obligations of justice change with the color of the skin? Is it one of the prerogatives of the white man, that he may disregard the dictates of moral principle, when an Indian shall be concerned?" He told the Senate: "The question has ceased to be—What are our duties? An inquiry much more embarrassing is forced upon us: How shall we most plausibly, and with the least possible violence, break our faith? Sir, we repel the inquiry—we reject such an issue—and point the guardians of public honor to the broad, plain path of faithful performance, to which they are equally urged by duty and by interest." Representative Test could not believe, he said, that the nation would "forfeit her solemn pledges, her sacred honor."[21]

Frelinghuysen and the other Cherokee supporters, despite their vigorous arguments, lost the battle in Congress. The House bill was dropped in favor of the Senate bill, and the Senate approved the measure on April 24, by a vote of 28 to 19, the House on May 26, by a vote of 103 to 97.[22] Jackson signed the bill on May 28.

John Marshall and the Cherokee Cases

The Cherokees, rejected by the president and Congress, turned next to the Supreme Court. With William Wirt (attorney general

21. Ibid., 312, 316, 1049, 1105.
22. Ibid., 383, 1135.

under Monroe and Adams) as their adviser, the Cherokees brought suit against Georgia, seeking an injunction against Georgia's encroachment on Indian lands in violation of the tribe's treaty rights.[23]

Chief Justice Marshall was sympathetic to the Cherokees' cause and to their reliance on treaties to uphold it. In *Cherokee Nation v. Georgia*, decided on March 18, 1831, Marshall wrote about the Cherokees as a state:

> They have been uniformly treated as a State from the settlement of our country. The numerous treaties made with them by the United States recognize them as a people capable of maintaining the relations of peace and war, of being responsible in their political character for any violation of their engagements, or for any aggression committed on the citizens of the United States by any individual of their community. Laws have been enacted in the spirit of these treaties. The acts of our government plainly recognize the Cherokee Nation as a State, and the Courts are bound by those acts.[24]

But Marshall would not accept the Cherokee Nation as a *foreign* nation, entitled to sue the state of Georgia under the Constitution, so he rejected the suit as outside the jurisdiction of the court. He asserted that the Indian tribes were, instead, "domestic dependent nations" and that their relation to the United States "resembles that of a ward to his guardian."[25] Two dissenting justices, however, believed that the Cherokees *were* a foreign state, and their opinion renewed hope for the Indian cause.

A law of Georgia that took effect on March 1, 1831, forbade whites to reside in the Cherokee country without a license. Two missionaries among the Indians, Samuel A. Worcester and Elizur Butler, refused to heed the law and were arrested and imprisoned. Wirt now brought suit against Georgia on Worcester's behalf, a case in which the Supreme Court clearly had jurisdiction. Marshall's decision in *Worcester v. Georgia*, delivered on March 3, 1832, was a forthright vindication of the Cherokee position:

23. The political implications of the Cherokee cases are discussed in Joseph C. Burke, "The Cherokee Cases: A Study in Law, Politics, and Morality," *Stanford Law Review* 21 (February 1969): 500–31, and William F. Swindler, "Politics as Law: The Cherokee Cases," *American Indian Law Review* 3, no. 1 (1975): 7–20. See also Ronald N. Satz, *American Indian Policy in the Jacksonian Era* (Lincoln: University of Nebraska Press, 1975), 44–50.

24. 5 Peters 16.

25. Ibid., 17.

The Indian nations had always been considered as distinct, independent political communities, retaining their original natural rights, as the undisputed possessors of the soil from time immemorial, with the single exception of that imposed by irresistible power, which excluded them from intercourse with any other European potentate than the first discoverer of the coast of the particular region claimed: and this was a restriction which those European potentates imposed on themselves, as well as on the Indians. The very term "nation," so generally applied to them, means "a people distinct from others." The Constitution, by declaring treaties already made, as well as those to be made, to be the supreme law of the land, has adopted and sanctioned the previous treaties with the Indian nations, and consequently admits their rank among those powers who are capable of making treaties.

Marshall argued that the nationhood of the Indians was not destroyed by treaties acknowledging the protection of the United States, for "the settled doctrine of the law of nations is that a weaker power does not surrender its independence—its right to self-government, by associating with a stronger and taking its protection." The Cherokee Nation, therefore, was a "distinct community, occupying its own territory, with boundaries accurately described, in which the laws of Georgia can have no force, and which the citizens of Georgia have no right to enter but with the assent of the Cherokees themselves or in conformity with treaties and with the acts of Congress." All intercourse with the Indian nations was vested, not in the state, but in the federal government.[26]

The Jackson administration paid no heed to Marshall's decision, and went ahead with its removal plans, but the long arguments about treaty rights and Indian sovereignty had not been in vain. They provided a reservoir of views and opinions that greatly bolstered the status of treaties and the federal handling of Indian affairs. And the dire evils predicted by Evarts and other anti-Jackson supporters of the Cherokees did not materialize. Removal was accomplished, not by unrestrained executive action, but through the traditional forms of treaties, and those treaties preserved the ideas of Indian sovereignty and inviolable land titles, even while the Indians were being forced to abandon their homelands in the southern states and seek a new destiny west of the Mississippi. The debates in Congress and the Supreme Court decisions had enough moral if not legal force to make impossible in the 1830s the abrogation of old treaties or the abandonment of the process of

26. 6 Peters 559–61.

treaty making. Appeals to good faith and national honor had not fallen on deaf ears.

Removal Treaties

The first of the southern tribes to sign a removal treaty was the Choctaw Nation, under a set of peculiar circumstances, which began while the debates and controversies over the Cherokees were being played out in Washington.[27]

Mississippi, encouraged by Jackson's state of the union address and following the lead of Georgia, on January 19, 1830, enacted legislation that extended the laws of the state over the persons and property of Indians within its limits and rejected any special rights or privileges that the Indians claimed.[28] Seeing the writing on the wall, the Choctaws began to act. Under the leadership of Greenwood LeFlore, a mixed blood who in the crisis had been elected to the unprecedented position of chief of the whole nation, the Choctaws drew up a removal treaty on their own, with very favorable recompense for exchanging their Mississippi lands for those to the west, and in early May 1830 sent the treaty to Jackson for presentation to the Senate.

Jackson, taken aback by the independent action of the Choctaws in drawing up their own treaty but pleased with the evidence that the tribe was reconciled to removal, sent the treaty to the Senate on May 6, 1830, together with a protest from certain of the Choctaws against the treaty. "These measures," Jackson told the Senate, "are the voluntary acts of the Indians themselves. The Government was not represented in the councils which adopted them; nor had it any previous intimation that such steps were in contemplation. The Indians convened on their own accord, settled and executed the propositions contained in the treaty presented to me, and agreed to be bound by them if within three months they should receive the approbation of the President and the Senate."[29]

Jackson did not want to accept the precise terms of this Choctaw treaty, and he sent the Senate some suggested amendments for their consideration. The president, however, "not being tenacious . . . on the

27. Arthur H. DeRosier, Jr., *The Removal of the Choctaw Indians* (Knoxville: University of Tennessee Press, 1970). See especially 100–128.

28. The law is printed in *Senate Doc.* no. 98, 21-1, serial 193, pp. 10–11.

29. *Senate Ex. Proc.*, 4:97–98.

subject," indicated a willingness to come to an agreement with the Senate. He thereupon reverted to the long-abandoned practice of seeking Senate advice *before* acting, rather than simply presenting an accomplished treaty to the Senate for approval, amendment, or rejection. He proposed a series of questions to the Senate, as Washington had done with the Creek treaty of 1790: would the Senate accept the terms proposed by the Choctaws, would it agree to modify the treaty according to Jackson's suggested amendments, or did it have further modifications to propose? Jackson justified his action as follows:

> I am fully aware that in thus resorting to the early practice of the Government, by asking the previous advice of the Senate in the [fulfillment] of this portion of my duties, I am departing from a long, and for many years an unbroken usage in similar cases. But being satisfied that this resort is consistent with the provisions of the Constitution; that it is strongly recommended in this instance by considerations of expediency; and that the reasons which have led to the observance of a different practice, though very cogent in negotiations with foreign nations do not apply with equal force to those made with Indian tribes, I flatter myself that it will not meet the disapprobation of the Senate.

He noted, too, that the Choctaws had asked that their propositions be submitted to the Senate and that the Senate's opinion would aid future negotiations if any should be required. "To be possessed of the views of the Senate on this important and delicate branch of our future negotiations," he said, "would enable the President to act much more effectively in the exercise of his particular functions. There is also the best reason to believe that measures in this respect emanating from the united counsel of the treaty-making power would be more satisfactory to the American people and to the Indians." Jackson did not want cost factors to override other, more important, considerations. "The great desideratum," he insisted, "is the removal of the Indians, and the settlement of the perplexing question involved in their present location."[30]

The Senate referred the treaty and accompanying documents to its Committee on Indian Affairs, which submitted a resolution on May 27 that the Senate *not* approve the treaty. It noted the protest against the treaty by one party of Choctaws and recommended that the president "withhold his sanction to it until the sense of the nation could be fairly

30. Ibid., 98–99.

taken, even if the terms proposed in the instrument were such as the United States would deem equitable and just." But the latter condition, it insisted, did not obtain; the committee called the treaty terms of the Choctaws "so unreasonable that the United States ought by no means to accede to them, even if the nation was unanimous in proposing them."[31]

The committee neatly sidestepped Jackson's request for prior advice on how further negotiations should proceed. "It would be a waste of time," the report said, "to go much into detail in specifying objections," although it did list articles that it thought should not be approved. The committee members had looked at the president's suggested amendments and found it "very difficult to satisfy themselves as to the precise stipulations which ought to be contained in any treaty to be concluded." Because of "very serious discontents" in the Choctaw Nation, the committee thought that "if the Senate should, in advance of any negotiation, attempt to fix in detail the terms and stipulations to be included in a treaty, such course might have the effect of defeating entirely an agreement with the Choctaws which might be highly advantageous to them and to the United States." The only suggestion it offered was that if any alterations were needed, they should consist in reducing payment offered for the lands of the Choctaws. On May 29 the Senate supported the resolution of the committee to reject the treaty, and it discharged the committee from further consideration of the subject.[32] So much for prior advice on treaty making in Jackson's time.

Jackson then proceeded on his own. He invited the Choctaw leaders to meet him at Franklin, Tennessee, where he was spending his summer vacation, but the Indians refused and proposed instead a September meeting. Thereupon Jackson sent Secretary of War John Eaton and his old friend John Coffee to treat with the Choctaws in their own country, at Dancing Rabbit Creek, where five to six thousand Indians gathered in the middle of September. Having sent the missionaries away from the treaty grounds lest they influence the Indians, Eaton and Coffee warned the Indians that if they did not move west, they would have to submit to state laws and thus lose their tribal existence. By providing generous land allotments and other benefits to tribal leaders, the commissioners were able to sign a treaty with the Choctaws on September 27.[33]

31. Ibid., 111.
32. Ibid., 111–12, 119.
33. Kappler, 2:310–19. A journal of the treaty negotiations is in Documents (T494),

The Choctaws ceded all their lands east of the Mississippi in exchange for a specified tract in the West. The new land, contrary to past practice regarding Indian land tenure, was granted to the Choctaw Nation "in fee simple . . . to inure to them while they shall exist as a nation and live on it." The national existence of the Choctaws, no longer possible in Mississippi, was strongly guaranteed by the United States in the fourth article of the treaty:

> The Government and people of the United States are hereby obliged to secure to the said Choctaw Nation of Red People the jurisdiction and government of all the persons and property that may be within their limits west, so that no Territory or State shall ever have a right to pass laws for the government of the Choctaw Nation of Red People and their descendants; and that no part of the land granted to them shall ever be embraced in any Territory or State; but the U.S. shall forever secure said Choctaw Nation from, and against, all laws except such as from time to time may be enacted in their own National Councils, not inconsistent with the Constitution, Treaties, and Laws of the United States; and except such as may, and which have been enacted by Congress, to the extent that Congress under the Constitution are required to exercise a legislation over Indian Affairs.[34]

The United States, moreover, agreed to protect the Choctaws from domestic strife and from foreign enemies "on the same principle that the citizens of the United States are protected." Annuities from older treaties would continue, and the treaty authorized an extra $20,000 for twenty years. In addition, the United States offered houses for chiefs, schools, mechanics, miscellaneous goods, and education for forty Choctaw youths for a period of twenty years. The United States would provide, at its own expense, for the removal and would furnish subsistence for twelve months in the new country.

The treaty showed the ambivalence of the removal policy: whereas it made every effort to clear Mississippi of tribal Indians and included all sorts of inducements to encourage emigration, it at the same time

---

roll 2, frames 306–17. The proceedings are summarized in DeRosier, *Removal of the Choctaw Indians*, 116–28. Older accounts are Henry S. Halbert, "The Story of the Treaty of Dancing Rabbit," *Publications of the Mississippi Historical Society* 6 (1902): 373–402; George Strother Gaines, "Dancing Rabbit Creek Treaty," *Historical and Patriotic Series of Alabama State Department of Archives and History* 10 (1928): 1–31.

34. Kappler, 2:311.

allotted lands to individual Indians within the ceded territory east of the Mississippi. The agent, William Ward, however, did not register all the latter claims as the treaty directed and thus seriously upset the intended operation of the system. All in all, the disposition of the Choctaw lands and the settlement of claims arising from their sale led to nearly interminable conflicts between the Indians, bona fide settlers, and land speculators that delayed removal and caused unsettled land titles for years following the treaty.[35]

When Jackson submitted the treaty to the Senate on December 9, Senator George Poindexter of Mississippi tried to sidetrack it, first asking for more information from the president and then, after the information had been received, offering a resolution that Indian tribes within the United States were not "independent foreign states" and that any compact or agreement with them for the "relinquishment of the title of occupancy" was not a "treaty" within the spirit and meaning of the Constitution. But the resolution was tabled, and Poindexter later withdrew it. Upset by the admission in the preamble to the treaty that the president could not protect the Choctaws within Mississippi, the Senate rejected that part of the document, but the rest was approved by a vote of thirty-three to twelve on February 21, 1831.[36]

The Creeks were the next tribe to sign a treaty. Alabama considered the removal of the Indians necessary for the development of the state, and in January 1829 the legislature extended state laws over the Creek territory as added pressure for removal. In these circumstances, even before the passage of the Removal Act, Jackson urged the Creeks to move west of the Mississippi. Creek delegates to Washington voiced their complaints to the president and to Congress, seeking to remain in Alabama under federal protection, but to little avail. Meanwhile the conditions of the Creeks got worse.[37]

Creek leaders, thereupon, drew up a plan for ceding their land in Alabama, but instead of removal to the west, they proposed a system of

35. The best discussion of the problems resulting from the allotments is Mary E. Young, *Redskins, Ruffleshirts, and Rednecks: Indian Allotments in Alabama and Mississippi, 1830–1860* (Norman: University of Oklahoma Press, 1961), 47–72. There are many documents in the Congressional Serial Set about the land problems; see, for example, *Senate Doc.* no. 266, 23-1, serial 240.

36. *Senate Ex. Proc.*, 4:126, 128, 141, 155, 160–62. The documents that Jackson submitted with the treaty are in Senate (RG 46), Sen 21B-C6. Kappler, 2:310–11, prints the preamble to the treaty but indicates in a footnote that it was not ratified.

37. See Michael D. Green, *The Politics of Indian Removal: Creek Government and Society in Crisis* (Lincoln: University of Nebraska Press, 1982), 141–73.

reservations for the Indians within the ceded territory with fee-simple title. Although this would mean allotment in severalty to heads of families, the Creeks hoped to locate the reserves in blocks, so that the towns would be kept intact and local customs could continue. A new delegation took these proposals to Washington in March 1832.[38] Secretary of War Lewis Cass rejected the initial proposition, for he disliked the size and number of the reservations, but he reached a compromise with the delegation and signed a treaty with Chief Opothleyaholo and seven other chiefs on March 24.[39]

The treaty was not specifically a removal treaty. Although the Creeks ceded to the United States all their lands east of the Mississippi, they were to receive allotments within the cession and could sell these allotments to other persons or remain on the lands themselves and after five years receive a fee-simple title. The United States solemnly guaranteed to the Indians the Creek territory west of the Mississippi, and recognized their right to govern themselves free from interference by any state or territory "so far as may be compatible with the general jurisdiction which Congress may think proper to exercise over them."

The Senate ratified the treaty with remarkable speed. Two days after the signing, Jackson submitted the treaty to the Senate, whose Committee on Indian Affairs reported it without amendment on March 29. Senator Theodore Frelinghuysen, perhaps influenced by the memorials to Congress from antiremoval forces praying that treaties under the Removal Act not be ratified, tried to delay the procedures by a resolution to recommit the treaty to committee until it could be ascertained that the Creeks who had signed the treaty had been duly authorized, but his motion lost thirty-three to seven. And on April 2 the Senate approved the treaty unanimously.[40]

The treaty on its face, indeed, seemed like a reasonable document, for it supported Creeks who chose to emigrate and provided for those who preferred to stay, but its actual operation was disastrous for the Creeks. Despite its promises to evict intruders, the federal government in fact was unwilling or unable to do so, and the Creek lands were quickly overrun. Moreover, the Indians, unused to handling financial matters, were victimized by speculators, who moved in to gain title to

38. A summary of the proposal is given ibid., 170.
39. Kappler, 2:341–43. Creek memorials prior to the treaty that complained of the acts of Alabama and demanded protection are printed in *Senate Doc.* no. 53, 21-1, serial 193, and *House Doc.* no. 102, 22-1, serial 218.
40. *Senate Ex. Proc.*, 4:232–34.

the allotments and force the Indians off the land. The frauds were spectacular and widespread, making a mockery of the treaty intentions, and the government seemed impotent to stem the speculators' chicanery.[41]

The Chickasaws faced a similar fate, suffering the same disabilities in relations with their white neighbors as the other southern tribes, and the tribal leaders ultimately decided that there was no alternative to emigration and sought to make the move as palatable as possible.[42] The negotiations began at Franklin, Tennessee, in the summer of 1830, with John Eaton and John Coffee; President Jackson appeared, too, and addressed the council. Since the meeting was outside the tribal country, it was attended by only a score of Indian delegates, yet the protocol of feasting the Indians and regaling them with presents was followed.[43]

A treaty was signed on August 31, 1830, by which the Chickasaws ceded their eastern lands in return for lands of equal extent beyond the Mississippi. But this treaty was contingent upon finding suitable lands in the West that were acceptable to the Chickasaws, for the treaty specified: "If, after proper examination, a country suitable to their wants can not be found; then, it is stipulated and agreed, that this treaty, and all its provisions, shall be considered null and void." Although a delegation of Chickasaws went west to seek an acceptable location, they could agree on none, and the treaty thus became inoperative. Jackson did not submit it to the Senate.[44]

The condition of the Chickasaws in Mississippi worsened, and new negotiations for a treaty of removal were undertaken in 1832 in the Chickasaw country at Pontotoc Creek, where the Indians signed a treaty with John Coffee on October 20 that was similar to the Franklin treaty. Chickasaw lands were ceded to the government; they would be surveyed immediately and placed on sale, to be sold for what the market would bring. Meanwhile, each adult Indian received a temporary homestead

41. T. Hartley Crawford to Joel R. Poinsett, May 11, 1838, *House Doc.* no. 452, 25-2, serial 331. A detailed history of the Creek frauds is given in Young, *Redskins, Ruffleshirts, and Rednecks*, 73–113. See also Grant Foreman, *Indian Removal: The Emigration of the Five Civilized Tribes of Indians* (Norman: University of Oklahoma Press, 1932), 129–39. On the military removal of the Creeks after the "Creek War" of 1836, see *American State Papers: Military Affairs*, 7:951–55, and Foreman, *Indian Removal*, 152–90.

42. See Arrell M. Gibson, *The Chickasaws* (Norman: University of Oklahoma Press, 1971), 122–62.

43. A statement of expenses showed board for twenty-one Indians for fifteen days at $1.25 per day, and listed the presents furnished. *House Doc.* no. 181, 22-1, serial 219, pp. 2–3.

44. Kappler, 2:1035–40.

(ranging from one section to four sections, depending on the size of the family). The money from the sale of these temporary reservations and of the surplus lands would be placed in a general fund of the Chickasaw Nation, and from it would come the costs of survey and removal.[45]

The problem of finding western lands for the emigrating Chickasaws was not solved until 1837. On January 17 of that year, at Doaksville in the Choctaw Nation, the Chickasaws and Choctaws signed a "convention and agreement," by which the Chickasaws bought the central and western portion of the Choctaw grant for $530,000 and received certain privileges within the Choctaw Nation. The parties to this convention, it should be noted, were the two tribes themselves, not the United States and the Indians, but the negotiations were held under the auspices of the federal government, and the agreement itself in its title stipulated that it was "subject to the approval of the President and Senate of the United States."[46] Jackson sent the document as a "convention" to the Senate in February 1837, saying that it had his approbation and re-questing favorable action. The Senate merely approved the "convention or agreement made and entered into between the Choctaw and Chickasaw Nations or tribes," without the usual constitutional formula of "advice and consent" to its ratification.[47]

Another treaty of 1832 was that signed with the Seminole Indians at Payne's Landing in northeastern Florida on May 9, 1832, the result of increasing white agitation for the removal of the Indians. The Indians were destitute, and the promise of food and clothing in the treaty eased the negotiations. The Seminoles, however, would not agree to emigrate

45. Ibid., 356–62. Supplementary articles were signed on October 22, which Kappler treats as a separate treaty. The Senate, to whom Jackson submitted the treaty on December 12, after requesting and receiving from the president and the secretary of war information about the Franklin treaty and amending the supplementary articles by eliminating a payment to Robert P. Currin, ratified the treaty, twenty-three to four, on February 28. *Senate Ex. Proc.*, 4:285, 290–91, 293–95, 317–21. In 1834, amendments were made to the Pontotoc treaty; see Kappler, 2:418–25.

46. See certified copy of the treaty in Documents (T494), roll 3, frames 520ff., and as printed in *Treaties between the United States of America, and the Several Indian Tribes, from 1778 to 1837* (Washington: Langtree and O'Sullivan, 1837), 687–99. The phrase is omitted in Kappler, 2:486–88.

47. *Senate Ex. Proc.*, 4:616. The president ratified the agreement on March 24, 1837. The Chickasaw district was more specifically defined in a convention and agreement between the two tribes on November 4, 1854, and in "articles of agreement and convention" between the United States and the two tribes on June 22, 1855. The region west of the ninety-eighth meridian was leased to the United States as a home for other Indians. Kappler, 2:652–53, 706–14.

until they had had an opportunity to examine the western land. The treaty, accordingly, provided that the government would send a party of the Indians to the West, where they could judge for themselves the quality of the land to be set aside for them. The members of the delegation arrived at Fort Gibson in November 1832 and were shown the region that was to be theirs in the Creek country, and they signed an agreement stating that they approved the land. This Treaty of Fort Gibson, March 28, 1833, was negotiated and signed by special commissioners—Montfort Stokes, Henry L. Ellsworth, and John F. Schermerhorn—who had been sent west by the secretary of war to investigate the western lands and to make sure that the lands assigned to the incoming Indians were suitable.[48]

The Seminoles later refused to acknowledge the treaties, and the parties soon arrived at an impasse. The government pointed to the treaties and insisted that they be fulfilled. The Indians denied that they had made the agreements specified and refused to move. The result was war, as the Seminoles retreated into the Everglades to escape removal. The Florida War—the Second Seminole War—began in 1835, and it dragged out unconscionably, as one commander after another failed to subdue the Indians. When General Thomas S. Jesup suggested in 1838 that a line be drawn through central Florida and the Indians be allowed to stay south of the line, Secretary of War Joel R. Poinsett refused to budge from the hard-line position of the government:

> The acts of the executive and the laws of congress evince a determination to carry out . . . [the removal policy], and it is to be regarded as the settled policy of the country. In pursuance of this policy, the treaty of Payne's Landing was made with the Seminoles, and the character of the officer employed on the part of the government is a guarantee of the perfectly fair manner in which that negotiation was conducted and concluded. . . . The treaty has been ratified, and is the

48. The two treaties are in Kappler, 2:344–45 and 394–95. They were not submitted to the Senate until December 24, 1833, where they were reported by the Committee on Indian Affairs without amendment on April 7, 1834, and unanimously approved the next day. *Senate Ex. Proc.*, 4:338, 386–87. John K. Mahon, "Two Seminole Treaties: Payne's Landing, 1832, and Ft. Gibson, 1833," *Florida Historical Quarterly* 41 (July 1962): 1–21, is a careful analysis of the treaties and the charges of fraud. Because he found the evidence "fragmentary and often contradictory," Mahon arrives at no judgment. But he concedes that the Seminoles did not regard the treaties as just and that their refusal to abide by them led to war.

law of the land; and the constitutional duty of the president requires that he should cause it to be executed.[49]

The war raged on until 1842, at which time the federal government declared the war won. By then, all but a remnant of the tribe had been killed or forcibly removed to Indian Territory.

The Cherokee Indians were the final southern tribe to be removed. As they had been the focus of the controversy over the removal bill, so they furnished the most controversial episode in the history of actual emigration to the West. Many Cherokees, it is true, had migrated voluntarily before the crisis of the 1830s. These Indians, known as the Old Settlers or Cherokees West, had developed their own government and a prosperous agricultural economy on the lands set aside for them by the treaty of 1828. In 1836 there were more than six thousand in this group. But the bulk of the tribe adamantly refused to consider removal and refused to accept the enticements and the warnings of the Jackson administration. Instead, they repeatedly petitioned the federal government to protect them where they lived.

Cherokee delegations encamped in Washington and sought to come to some kind of adjustment with federal officials.[50] In early 1834, a few selected chiefs entered into negotiations with Secretary of War Eaton and, over the protests of Chief John Ross and his followers, signed a removal treaty in Washington on June 19, 1834. Jackson with some misgivings submitted the treaty to the Senate. He told that body, "The practice of the Government has not been very strict on the subject of the authority of the persons negotiating treaties on the part of the Indians. Sometimes it has been done by persons representing the tribe and sometimes by the individuals composing it. I am not aware that a case similar in its features to the present has ever before required the action of the Government." He supported his action by alluding to provisions in the document that called for approval by the majority of

49. Poinsett to Jesup, March 1, 1838, in John T. Sprague, *The Origin, Progress, and Conclusion of the Florida War* (New York: D. Appleton and Company, 1848), 201–2. For a similar statement, see Poinsett to Jesup, July 25, 1837, *House Doc.* no. 78, 25-2, serial 323, pp. 32–33.

50. A clear and detailed account of these maneuverings is provided in Charles C. Royce, "The Cherokee Nation of Indians: A Narrative of Their Official Relations with the Colonial and Federal Governments," *Fifth Annual Report of the Bureau of Ethnology*, 1883–1884 (Washington: GPO, 1887), 253–304; this report was reprinted as Charles C. Royce, *The Cherokee Nation of Indians* (Chicago: Aldine Publishing Company, 1975), with different pagination.

the tribe. The Senate, however, would have nothing to do with this treaty and unceremoniously tabled it on June 30.[51]

Meanwhile rival groups solidified within the Cherokee Nation. Opposed to John Ross and his majority following was a "treaty party," led by Major Ridge, his educated and politically active son John Ridge, and two nephews, the brothers Elias Boudinot and Stand Watie. These men and their followers had come to realize that removal was inevitable and that it was futile any longer to oppose the demands of the state and federal authorities. The bitter opposition between these parties split the Cherokees into factions that persisted for decades.[52]

This factionalism was used by the United States in negotiating with the tribe. When a Ridge delegation in Washington let it be known that it was ready to treat with the United States for cession of the eastern lands and removal to the West, John F. Schermerhorn was appointed in February 1835 to deal with them, and the two parties arrived at a general understanding. The Ross delegation then submitted its own proposal for removal, which demanded a payment of $20 million for the cession of the Cherokee lands. On March 3, however, the Senate set the sum at the much lower figure of $5 million. Since Ross declined to accept this figure, a treaty between the Ridge party and Schermerhorn was signed on March 14, with the stipulation that it would be binding only when approved by the Cherokee Nation in council.[53]

Despite Schermerhorn's endeavors and Jackson's encouragement, the council, held at Red Clay in October, rejected the Ridge treaty. At the council, however, the Cherokees received notice to meet with United States commissioners on December 21, at New Echota, Georgia, to negotiate a new treaty. The notice told the Indians that those who did

51. *Senate Ex. Proc.*, 4:424–25, 445–46.

52. A reasonable and sympathetic account of the Ridge party and its arguments and decisions is Thurman Wilkins, *Cherokee Tragedy: The Story of the Ridge Family and the Decimation of a People* (New York: Macmillan Company, 1970; 2d ed. rev., Norman: University of Oklahoma Press, 1986). A memorial of November 28, 1834, is a good statement of the Ridge party's argument that removal was inevitable for preservation of the nation, in *House Doc.* no. 91, 23-2, serial 273, pp. 1–7. The best work on Ross is Gary E. Moulton, *John Ross, Cherokee Chief* (Athens: University of Georgia Press, 1978). See also *The Papers of Chief John Ross*, ed. Gary E. Moulton, 2 vols. (Norman: University of Oklahoma Press, 1985), which presents exhaustively the position of the Ross party. Theda Perdue, "The Conflict Within: Cherokees and Removal," in William L. Anderson, ed., *Cherokee Removal: Before and After* (Athens: University of Georgia Press, 1991), 55–74, argues that the Ridges represented a small middle class in the Cherokee Nation that hoped to promote its own interests against the ruling elite by the removal treaty.

53. Royce, "Cherokee Nation of Indians," 284–85. The Senate action is in *Senate Ex. Proc.*, 4:478–79, 482.

not attend would be considered to approve any document signed by the negotiators.[54]

Because Ross and his supporters boycotted the meeting, only some three hundred to five hundred Cherokees, led by the Ridges, met with Schermerhorn at New Echota, where they signed a treaty on December 29.[55] In an unusual preamble, the United States sought to justify its reliance on only a portion of the tribe by reciting the history of negotiations with the Cherokees and by noting the earlier warning that those who did not attend the council would be considered to have given their assent to whatever might be done at the council. On this shaky foundation the United States procured a removal treaty with the Cherokees. The Cherokee National Council vehemently condemned the action, and Ross, in a protest sent to the Senate, declared that "the instrument entered into at New Echota, purporting to be a treaty, is deceptive to the world, and a fraud upon the Cherokee people."[56]

The treaty ceded all Cherokee lands east of the Mississippi and for $5 million released the Indians' claims upon the United States. It confirmed the seven million acres of land granted the Cherokees in the treaty of 1828 plus the outlet to the west and provided additional lands. There were articles excluding the western lands from state or territorial jurisdiction and granting protection against unauthorized intruders and against domestic and foreign enemies, similar to those in the other removal treaties. Provision was made also for the emigration, for one year's subsistence, and for lands for Indians who desired to stay in the East. The treaty specified that the removal was to be accomplished within two years after ratification of the treaty.

President Jackson objected to the provision for preemption rights and reservations for those Cherokees who wished to remain in the states where they resided, "his desire being that the whole Cherokee people should remove together and establish themselves in the country provided for them west of the Mississippi river." Whereupon supplementary articles were concluded on March 1, 1836, which declared null and void

54. Royce, "Cherokee Nation of Indians," 285–86.

55. Kappler, 2:439–48. William Carroll was appointed commissioner to serve with Schermerhorn, but ill health prevented his attendance. His signature, nevertheless, appears on the treaty, with the notation: "I have examined the foregoing treaty, and although not present when it was made, I approve its provisions generally, and therefore sign it."

56. "Memorial and Protest of the Cherokee Nation," March 8, 1836, and other documents in *House Doc.* no. 286, 24-1, serial 292; memorial of December 15, 1837, *House Doc.* no. 99, 25-2, serial 325. See also the discussion of Ross's activities in Moulton, *John Ross*, 73–79.

the preemption rights and reservations and authorized an additional sum of $600,000 over and above the $5 million allowed for the cession of eastern lands.[57]

The Senate was well aware of the protests against the treaty, and at one point in the debate Henry Clay proposed a resolution "that the instrument of writing purporting to be a treaty concluded at New Echota . . . [was] not made and concluded by authority on the part of the Cherokee tribe competent to bind it" and that therefore the Senate could not approve it. The resolution advised the president to open a new negotiation. This motion lost by a vote of twenty-nine to fifteen. Then, with some minor amendments, the Senate voted thirty-one to fifteen to approve the treaty—a single vote beyond the two-thirds required for Senate ratification.[58]

The treaty party emigrated with little trouble; state officials treated them considerately, and they were, in general, economically well-off. They established their farms and plantations among the western Cherokees. The remainder, having rejected the treaty as a valid instrument, refused to move, and Ross used every opportunity to attempt to reverse the treaty's provisions. He encouraged his followers to stand firm, and few enrolled for emigration. Numerous petitions poured into Congress from religious and philanthropic supporters of the Cherokees, protesting the execution of the 1835 treaty.[59]

A strenuous denial of the validity of the treaty was submitted to Congress in early April 1838. It bore the signatures of 15,665 Cherokees and appealed to Congress once more for protection against the throngs of Georgians invading their lands as the deadline for removal approached.[60] Then, as the crisis continued, Ross sought finally to replace the New Echota Treaty with one of his own design, but government officials deemed his proposals unacceptable.[61]

As the deadline for removal, May 23, 1838, approached and the Indians were still on their old lands, the government ordered General Winfield Scott to the Cherokee country "with a view to the fulfillment

---

57. Kappler, 2:448–49.

58. *Senate Ex. Proc.*, 4:545–46.

59. For memorials against the treaty, see *House Doc.* nos. 374, 384, 385, and 404, 25-2, serial 330; *Senate Doc.* nos. 388, 389, 390, 402, 416, and 417, 25-2, serial 318.

60. Memorial of February 22, 1838, *House Doc.* no. 316, 25-2, serial 329. Ross and the treaty party also carried on a pamphlet war; see Prucha, *Great Father*, 238n, 239n.

61. Joel R. Poinsett to John Ross and others, May 18, 1838, *House Doc.* no. 376, 25-2, serial 330; report of Senate Committee on Indian Affairs, June 5, 1838, *Senate Doc.* no. 466, 25-2, serial 318.

of the treaty." Scott, on May 10, issued an address to the Cherokee chiefs. "The President of the United States," he told them bluntly, "has sent me, with a powerful army, to cause you, in obedience to the Treaty of 1835, to join that part of your people who are already established in prosperity on the other side of the Mississippi."[62] The resulting emigration, finally carried out under the direction of John Ross himself, became the well-known and tragic "Trail of Tears."[63]

The conflict among the Cherokees over the removal treaty continued beyond the Mississippi. It was severely exacerbated by the vengeance taken by the Ross party against the treaty party leaders for having ceded the eastern lands. On June 22, 1839, Major Ridge, John Ridge, and Elias Boudinot were brutally murdered; Stand Watie, also marked for death, escaped. Although it was clear that this was a planned political assassination, John Ross denied any complicity or approval of the deed; but he could not completely shake the accusations made against his party. The federal government remained critical of him and continually called for punishment of the murderers. Ross's insistence that he was chief of *all* the Cherokees, moreover, irritated the Old Settlers, and turmoil continued in the Cherokee country. All three parties—Ross's, the treaty party, and the Old Settlers—appealed to the federal government. Exasperated, President Polk in 1846 urged the division of the Cherokees into separate tribes, and the House Committee on Indian Affairs supported his proposal.[64]

Such action led Ross, who above all wanted a unified nation, to persuade Polk to approve a new treaty that would keep the Cherokees intact. The president thereupon appointed commissioners to negotiate

62. Documents on Scott's operations are in *House Doc.* no. 453, 25-2, serial 331; Scott's part in the removal is treated in Charles Winslow Elliott, *Winfield Scott: The Soldier and the Man* (New York: Macmillan Company, 1937), 345–55. Examples of reports of harsh treatment of the Cherokees appear in *Niles' National Register* 54 (August 18, 1838): 385, and in James Mooney, *Myths of the Cherokee*, Nineteenth Annual Report of the Bureau of American Ethnology, 1897–1898, pt. 1 (Washington: GPO, 1900), 127.

63. Descriptions of the emigration are given in Foreman, *Indian Removal*, 279–312. Moulton, *John Ross*, 95–106, discusses the removal under Ross and the subsequent controversy over removal expenses. For a brief discussion of the number of deaths on the Cherokee Trail of Tears, see fn. 58, in Prucha, *Great Father*, 1:241. There is a recent discussion, with somewhat different conclusions, in Russell Thornton, *The Cherokees: A Population History* (Lincoln: University of Nebraska Press, 1990), 73–77.

64. James K. Polk to Congress, April 13, 1846, *House Doc.* no. 185, 29-1, serial 485, pp. 1–2; this document also contains a long report of the commissioner of Indian affairs on the Cherokee conflict, memorials from the three factions, and several other pertinent documents submitted to Congress by the president in support of his message. Further documents are in *Senate Doc.* no. 301, 29-1, serial 474.

with the three Cherokee delegations in Washington in order to heal all dissension. With able advisers and a firm intent to settle past differences, the three factions worked out an agreement. This treaty of 1846, debated and amended by the Senate and finally ratified by a majority of one vote, was approved in its modified form by the Indian delegates on August 14. It provided for a unified Cherokee Nation and declared a general amnesty and an end to party distinctions. The treaty was a compromise measure, for Ross now agreed to the legitimacy of the 1835 treaty and the Old Settlers admitted that the Ross party had rights to the lands in the West.[65]

The southern Indians had been forced into treaties they did not want, treaties whose validity they denied but which were adamantly enforced by the federal government. The hardships of removal were extreme. Yet these Indian nations were not destroyed. The arguments of men like Jeremiah Evarts and his supporters in Congress and the decisions of John Marshall in the Cherokee cases provided a theoretical basis for the continuing political autonomy of the tribes and their rights to land. The removal was accomplished by means of formal treaties (which Jackson had earlier called farces), which in their recognition of the Indians' nationhood and the fee-simple ownership of land formed a foundation for continuing political existence that even tribal factionalism did not crush. With regard to the southern Indians, the treaty system had a new lease on life.

65. Kappler, 2:561–65; *Senate Ex. Proc.*, 7:149–52.

CHAPTER EIGHT

The Removal Period in the North

While the five southern tribes were signing formal treaties for their removal to the west, the multiplicity of small tribes north of the Ohio underwent a different sort of treaty making.[1] Instead of dealing with a few large tribes, which had well-established traditional homelands and organized tribal governments that could—up to a point—negotiate for terms that would protect their interests, in the north the federal government continued to face numerous tribes (some of which were badly fractionalized) and overlapping land claims that resulted from a long history of migration from place to place. Although formal treaties under constitutional provisions seemed a bit pretentious for dealing with some of these small remnants, they continued to be the vehicle used to accomplish what United States policy and interests demanded. The story of these treaties is essentially the story of the final dispossession of the Indians in the region.

1. See Francis Paul Prucha, *The Great Father: The United States Government and the American Indians*, 2 vols. (Lincoln: University of Nebraska Press, 1984), chap. 9, "Removal of the Northern Indians," 1:243–69, which I have drawn on here. Grant Foreman, *The Last Trek of the Indians* (Chicago: University of Chicago Press, 1946), 17–158, deals with the removal of the northern tribes, but the book as a whole is principally concerned with the actual emigrations. Useful articles on many of the individual tribes appear in *Handbook of North American Indians*, vol. 15, *Northeast*, ed. Bruce G. Trigger (Washington: Smithsonian Institution, 1978).

Treaties in the Old Northwest

Between 1829 and 1851, eighty-six ratified treaties were signed with twenty-six traditional tribes in New York, the Old Northwest, and the immediate trans-Mississippi areas. These tribes sometimes acted individually, sometimes in conjunction with other tribes. A good many of the tribes or bands signed more than one treaty; Potawatomi Indians alone were involved in nineteen.[2]

The government's treatment of these tribes was hardly a new departure, for it continued policies and actions that had been going on for three decades. Removal, in the sense of an exchange of lands occupied east of the Mississippi for lands west of the river, was only one element. Many of the treaties provided for cession of portions of a tribe's lands to the United States and the concentration of the displaced Indians on remaining lands, with the privilege of hunting on the ceded lands until they had been surveyed and sold to white settlers.[3]

Most of the Indians involved had a long history of shifting locales. The Delawares and Shawnees, who perhaps are extreme examples, moved frequently, step by step, toward the west from their original eastern locations.[4] None of the Indians north of the Ohio occupied precisely the same lands in 1830 that their ancestors had held when French traders first came in contact with them in the seventeenth century. The removal of these tribes by treaty in the Jacksonian era was part of

2. The chronological list of treaties in appendix B gives information on these treaties, indicating the groupings of the tribes in some of the treaties and the division of tribes into separate bands in others. The areas ceded are shown on the plates in Royce, *Cessions.*

3. James A. Clifton classifies the treaties with the Indians in the Old Northwest, 1830–1839, as follows: seventeen provided for a reduction of the land base without removal; three provided for permissive removal; eight provided for obligatory removal. His low total of twenty-eight results from omitting treaties that merely confirmed or supplemented earlier ones and from combining a number of treaties made with separate bands of Potawatomis, which were in fact a single action of ceding reservations established earlier. "Escape, Evasion, and Eviction: Adaptive Responses of the Indians of the Old Northwest to the Jackson Removal Policy of the 1830s," an unpublished paper furnished me by the author.

4. The endpaper maps in C. A. Weslager, *The Delaware Indians: A History* (New Brunswick: Rutgers University Press, 1972), graphically depict the Delaware migrations. An elaborate map of Shawnee locations and movements is in Charles Callender, "Shawnee," in Trigger, *Northeast,* 623.

their migration history, which continued even after their settlement west of the Mississippi. By 1830 most of Ohio, Indiana, and Illinois had already been freed of Indian title by treaties between the Indian groups and the United States government. What remained in these states were enclaves of natives, subsisting on agriculture and government annuities and surrounded by whites.

The presence of British Canada also affected the Indians in the Old Northwest, for many of the tribes in the region had had close economic and political ties with the British. For them, in times of trouble, Canada was an open haven. A large number of Potawatomis, Ottawas, and Chippewas, as well as small numbers of other tribes, in fact, moved into Canada.[5]

The treaties continued to provide reserves of land for individuals or for small groups within the ceded territories. Such reserves were a hedge against removal, but they were also a means of individual profit, because the Indians could dispose of them for a reasonable price and sometimes more.[6] The reservations, however, were an obstacle to the government's plan to clear the states of Indians altogether, yet so insistent were the Indians that it was necessary to allow the individual grants in order to obtain new cessions. In 1833 Lewis Cass, then secretary of war, instructed the commissioners dealing with the Potawatomis at Chicago:

> Decline, the first instances, to grant any reservations either to the Indians or others, and endeavor to prevail upon them all to remove. Should you find this impracticable, and that granting some reservations will be unavoidable, that course may be taken in the usual manner, and upon the usual conditions. But I am very anxious that individual reservations should be circumscribed within the narrowest possible limits. The whites and half-breeds press upon the Indians, and induce them to ask for these gratuities, to which they have no just pretensions; and for which neither the United States nor the

5. On the Potawatomis, see James A. Clifton, *The Prairie People: Continuity and Change in Potawatomi Indian Culture, 1665–1965* (Lawrence: Regents Press of Kansas, 1977), 301–9; Clifton, *A Place of Refuge for All Time: Migration of the American Potawatomi into Upper Canada, 1830 to 1850* (Ottawa: National Museums of Canada, 1975). For Ottawa movement to Canada, see Robert F. Bauman, "Kansas, Canada, or Starvation," *Michigan History* 36 (September 1952): 287–99. There is discussion of Indians moving to Canada in the reports of T. Hartley Crawford of January 15, 1839, *House Doc.* no. 107, 25-3, serial 346, and April 7, 1840, *House Doc.* no. 178, 26-1, serial 366.

6. See Paul W. Gates, "Indian Allotments Preceding the Dawes Act," in John G. Clark, ed., *The Frontier Challenge: Responses to the Trans-Mississippi West* (Lawrence: University Press of Kansas, 1971), 147–58.

Indians receive any real consideration. The practice, though it has long prevailed, is a bad one, and should be avoided as far as possible.[7]

In the Chicago treaty, cash payments were provided "to satisfy sundry individuals, in behalf of whom reservations were asked, which the Commissioners refused to grant."[8]

After passage of the Removal Act, President Jackson in 1831 appointed James B. Gardiner of Ohio to treat with the Ohio Indians and explain to them the necessity of moving beyond the Mississippi. "As caution is essential to the successful termination of such a business," Secretary of War Eaton told him, "reserve and silence, as to the object of your visit, is suggested to you as matter for your discretion, to make it known to the chiefs in conversation only as you pass amongst them, and explain the wishes of the Government, and its conviction that it is the only course which can secure to them happiness, and preserve them as a people." If the chiefs seemed properly disposed, Gardiner was to call them together to work out a treaty. In July and August 1831 Gardiner successfully negotiated removal treaties with the Shawnees and the Ottawas, who ceded all their lands in Ohio and accepted designated districts in the western Indian country beyond the state of Missouri. These lands were granted in fee simple, but the Indians could dispose of them only to the United States. The sums realized from ceded lands sold at public auction were to be used to build mills and to pay for improvements, with the residue invested for the Indians and a yearly interest of 5 percent paid as an annuity.[9]

With the Wyandots Gardiner had less success. Although pressed upon by white settlements, these Indians first demanded an investigation of the land proposed for their residence in the West. When an unfavorable report was returned, they refused to emigrate. The treaty that Gardiner signed with them on January 19, 1832, authorized the cession of sixteen thousand acres for which the Indians would be paid $1.25 an acre as the land was sold provided that the band "may, as they think proper, remove to Canada, or to the river Huron in Michigan, where

7. Cass to commissioners, April 8, 1833, *Senate Doc.* no. 512, 23-1, serial 246, p. 652.

8. Kappler, 2:402; see Schedule A, 404–6, for a list of payments to individuals "in lieu of Reservations."

9. Eaton to Gardiner, March 29, 1831, OIA LS, 7:172–76 (M21, roll 7); Kappler, 2:325–39.

they own a reservation of land, or to any place they may obtain a right or privilege from other Indians to go."[10]

Congress in 1832 authorized treaties to extinguish the title of the Kickapoos, Shawnees, and Delawares at Cape Girardeau in Missouri and of the Piankashaws, Weas, Peorias, and Kaskaskias in Illinois, as well as for dealing with other Shawnees and the Menominees. In October the Indians concerned assembled at Castor Hill, the home of Superintendent William Clark near St. Louis, where treaties were signed between October 24 and 29 by which the Indians gave up lands in Missouri and Illinois and accepted new lands west of the Missouri. The treaties with the Kickapoos and Shawnees provided large sums to pay off the Indians' debts.[11] The northern part of the Indian country west of the Mississippi was gradually taking shape as the home of the northern Indians.

Potawatomi Removal

The Potawatomi Indians were a good example of the piecemeal negotiations with Indians of the Old Northwest. The tribe, if one can so speak, was divided into bitter factions, each looking out for its own interests. Following the Black Hawk War of 1832, United States commissioners met with bands on the Tippecanoe River in Indiana, where the commissioners signed three separate treaties with different groups of Indians between October 20 and 27, 1832. In order to expedite the negotiations, the United States agreed to continue the practice of granting small reservations of land within the ceded districts for individuals and for village bands. Some 120 such reserves were stipulated in the three treaties; they satisfied the desire of the Indians to remain (even on reduced landholdings), but they seriously interfered with the government's intention of removing the Indians from the states.[12]

10. Kappler, 2:339–41; Carl G. Klopfenstein, "The Removal of the Wyandots from Ohio," *Ohio Historical Quarterly* 66 (April 1957): 119–36.

11. 4 Stat. 564, 594; Kappler, 2:365–67, 370–72, 376–77, 382–83. There is discussion of these treaties in Foreman, *Last Trek of the Indians*, 60–65.

12. I have depended on the general accounts of Potawatomi removal that appear in Clifton, *Prairie People*, 179–245, 279–346; R. David Edmunds, *The Potawatomis: Keepers of the Fire* (Norman: University of Oklahoma Press, 1978), 240–72; and Foreman, *Last*

The Indians drove a hard bargain and, relative to other treaties, were well paid in goods and money, with sizable tribal annuities, special annuities for chiefs, payment for stolen horses, and money for traders' debts. Trade goods valued at $177,000 were distributed at the treaty grounds, and more (worth $70,000) were promised for the next year. A total of $1,374,279 was transferred in the three treaties.[13]

As a result of the treaties, the Potawatomis were concentrated on the small reservations scattered through Michigan, Indiana, and Illinois. They now owned in common only a single large tract in northeastern Illinois and southeastern Wisconsin. Their condition was deteriorating, and it appeared inevitable that they would soon be pressured to remove altogether from the states and territories that had been their home. Some migrated voluntarily, joining Kickapoos who moved to Texas, settling in the Kickapoo reservation in Kansas, or establishing themselves on Manitoulin Island. For the rest, plans were soon afoot for a treaty at Chicago in the fall of 1833.

The negotiation at Chicago was a spectacular affair.[14] Large numbers of Indians appeared, and whites of all persuasions seeking personal fortunes were on hand to gain whatever they could. The forceful demands of the American commissioners, led by George B. Porter, governor of Michigan Territory, were met by the skillful tactics of the Indian negotiators, the mixed bloods Billy Caldwell and Alexander Robinson. The treaty promised five million acres in the west, including a triangle between the original western boundary of the state of Missouri and the Missouri River known as the Platte Purchase, for an equal amount of land given up. Debts to traders were covered, and there was a long list of payments totaling $100,000 to individuals in lieu of reservations (Schedule A) and an even longer list of payments for a variety of claims amounting to $175,000 (Schedule B); in addition, a

---

Trek of the Indians, 100–125. The treaties of October 1832 are in Kappler, 2:353–56, 367–70, 372–75.

13. Clifton, *Prairie People*, 234–35.

14. A general account of the treaty is Anselm J. Gerwing, "The Chicago Treaty of 1833," *Journal of the Illinois State Historical Society* 57 (Summer 1964): 117–42. An excellent portrayal of the many interests at work in the negotiations is in James A. Clifton, "Chicago, September 14, 1833: The Last Great Indian Treaty in the Old Northwest," *Chicago History* 9 (Summer 1980): 86–97. Documents pertaining to the treaty are printed in Milo M. Quaife, ed., "The Chicago Treaty of 1833," *Wisconsin Magazine of History* 1 (March 1918): 287–303.

twenty-year annuity was included. The Indians agreed to emigrate as soon as possible, the cost to be borne by the United States.[15]

This Chicago treaty was a notable example of the use of negotiations to satisfy a myriad of diverse individuals and groups, all of whom looked upon the treaty as a means of succeeding in their claims against the Indians or against the federal government. The long lists of persons in Schedule A and Schedule B attached to the treaty included these people. The modern ethnohistorian James Clifton has sorted them out in an amazing litany:

> They included aging agents grown feeble in the Indian Service looking for funds to soften their retirement years—men such as Thomas Forsyth. They included soon-to-be disemployed American appointed "chiefs" such as Billy Caldwell, Alexander Robinson, Shabbona, and Pokagun, all faced with premature retirement once the treaty was done and their services no longer needed, all seeking recompense for services rendered and a portion for severance pay. They included elderly old-time small merchants and Indian traders as well as vigorous representatives of the powerful American Fur Company (and their debtors, assigns, and heirs), all demanding that the government act as paymaster for Potawatomi debts, whether minor or immense. They included old residents such as Antoine Ouilmette and Mrs. Linai T. Helm, wanting their due for injuries or losses suffered during the Fort Dearborn Massacre, as well as more recent sufferers such as Rachel and Sylvia Hall, desiring compensation for privations experienced during the Black Hawk War.
>
> They also included the rising new traders, the Robert A. Forsyths and the William Ewings, desiring payment of recent debts. They included principals from the Choctaw Academy soliciting scholarships for future Potawatomi students, and missionaries seeking to finance their visions of an Indian Canaan. They included companies of frontier characters of obscure antecedents and marginal means who had long made their livings in the interstices between American and Potawatomi institutions.
>
> They included regiments of Joseph Napoleon Bourasses, Pierre Navarres, and Louis Grignons, the very old line French-Canadians, Métis (part Indian, part French) voyageurs—the traditional hewers-of-wood, drawers of water, teamsters, boatmen, interpreters, market gardeners—who for ages had served first French, later English, and

---

15. Kappler, 2:402–15; Kappler describes the treaty as made with Chippewa, Ottawa, and Potawatomi Indians, but the principal group was Potawatomi.

then American interests on this frontier. Many of these men would, now that the frontier was passing and their place in it evaporating, shortly become convert Potawatomi "chiefs" and rise as a new elite class in the West. They included, as well, a miscellaneous sundry of heirs, children, assigns, retainers, servants, employees and associates of all of the above. . . . Indeed, the long lists of payees appended to the Chicago Treaty excluded very few who had anything at all to do with affairs in the Chicago region in the half-century before the 1833 treaty.[16]

Clifton is right in seeing in this much more than bribery, fraud, or corruption. "Under the treaty protocols dramatized in speeches and debatings and beneath the apparent tawdry exchanges of the market place," he says, "was an arrangement. All those who had worked to make Chicago an American place, rather than a Potawatomi or a French or an English district, were being rewarded. The relative scale of compensation may not have been fully equitable, but rather than fraud it may be better seen as well-earned commission, instead of bribe hard-won pay, in place of embezzlement valid perquisite, in lieu of greed authentic reparation or indemnity, and as alternative to dishonesty legitimate reward."[17]

When President Jackson submitted the treaty and related documents to the Senate on January 10, 1834, he recommended ratification of the treaty, but he asked for a provision that the lists of payments in Schedule A and Schedule B be first investigated by a special commissioner sent to Chicago. Such payments would be subtracted from the gross sum specified in the treaty, and Jackson did not want that amount whittled down by spurious claims. "Considering the relations in which the Indians stand to the United States," he said, "it appears to me just to exercise their supervisory authority. It has been done in more than one instance, and as its object in this case is to ascertain whether any fraud exists, and if there does to correct it, I consider such a ratification within the proper scope of the treaty-making power."[18]

The Senate was aware of the objections made to the claims, but it was not sympathetic to Jackson's suggestion that all the claims be investigated. The Committee on Indian Affairs, which made its report on the treaty on April 7, did not recognize any advantage in such a general inquiry, for it saw no way to determine the legitimacy of the

16. Clifton, "Chicago, September 14, 1833," 94–95.
17. Ibid., 95.
18. *Senate Ex. Proc.*, 4:339–40.

claims, and, in any event, payments not made to the persons named would go to the Indians, who could then make the payments themselves. Besides, many of the payments were not contested. The report, however, did recommend cutting in half the payments indicated for Billy Caldwell and Alexander Robinson (from $10,000 to $5,000 each), and it prepared a short list of claims that it thought should be checked. It noted that "provisions in Indian treaties for the payment of debts to individuals is a growing evil, and if provisions of this kind have not heretofore been the cause of injustice to the Indians, the committee believe the Senate may safely conclude, unless some check is given, the time is not distant when they will be." The committee also recommended a change in the western lands granted to the Indians, moving the Indians from the Platte Purchase to a region in Iowa Territory north of it, for the state of Missouri desired the Platte Purchase for itself and at the time of the Chicago treaty was already making plans to acquire it. The Senate on May 22 agreed to the suggested amendments by a vote of thirty-three to one.[19]

It took some pains, however, to get the Potawatomis to agree to the changes, and in the end a special committee of only seven Indians signed the revision in the name of the tribe. The Senate on February 11, 1835, accepted the new document with the approved changes thirty-eight to three, but it took care to add a proviso to the effect that nothing else in the treaty as originally ratified would be affected. The Senate approved the nomination of T. A. Howard as commissioner to investigate the questionable claims.[20]

The Indians insisted on occupying the Platte Purchase temporarily, and it was only after much irritation on both sides and the threat of military force that the emigrants moved into Iowa, where a subagency was established for them at Council Bluffs.[21]

While the united bands represented at Chicago were seeking stability west of the Mississippi, the United States began to eliminate the pockets of Potawatomis that remained in the states on the reserves stipulated in the 1832 treaties. Most of the lands allotted to individual Indians soon passed into white hands. Then, in a series of minitreaties in 1834 and

19. Ibid., 382–85, 407–8.
20. Kappler, 2:414–15; *Senate Ex. Proc.*, 4:469–70, 481.
21. The Platte Purchase issue is discussed in R. David Edmunds, "Potawatomis in the Platte Country: An Indian Removal Incomplete," *Missouri Historical Review* 68 (July 1974): 375–92. See also documents in *Senate Doc.* no. 206, 24-1, serial 281, and *Senate Doc.* no. 348, 24-1, serial 283.

1836, made with individual chiefs and their bands, the enclaves held communally by bands were ceded to the United States for considerations of goods, money, payment of debts, and annuities, and their inhabitants agreed to move off the land.[22]

A number of the treaties vaguely specified removal "to a country provided for them by the United States, west of the Mississippi river." Through the years many of the Indians affected by these treaties migrated into Kansas, settling on a reserve along the Osage River. In the removal of Chief Menominee's band in 1838, military force was used against the resisting Indians, and the hardships endured in the emigration were long remembered. Other individuals and groups drifted northward in Michigan and Wisconsin, and about 2,500 (nearly a third of the total Potawatomi population) moved into Canada.[23]

The two large groups of Potawatomis in Iowa and on the Osage River reservation signed a treaty in 1846 in an attempt on the part of the United States to pull together into one unit the disparate strands of the Potawatomi people with whom it had been dealing. The Indian signatories agreed to cede to the United States their reservations in Iowa and eastern Kansas for $850,000. In return the United States sold them (for $87,000) a new reservation along the Kaw River, land recently ceded by the Kansa Indians.[24] The single national existence never materialized, however, for the bands from Iowa (designated finally as the Prairie Potawatomi) did not coalesce with the more acculturated Indians who had moved to the Kaw from the Osage River (designated ultimately as the Mission or the Citizen Band).[25]

22. In some cases the Senate struck out articles making grants to individuals or providing for payment of debts. See Kappler, 2:428–31, 450, 457–59, 462–63, 470–72, 488–89. *Treaties between the United States of America and the Indian Tribes, from 1778 to 1837* (Washington: Langtree and O'Sullivan, 1837), prints the articles that were struck out. They also appear in the ratification proceedings; see *Senate Ex. Proc.*, vol. 4.

23. There is a brief account of the removal of Menominee's band in Edmunds, *Potawatomis*, 266–68. See also Irving McKee, ed., *The Trail of Death: Letters of Benjamin Marie Petit* (Indianapolis: Indiana Historical Society, 1941). The Potawatomis were not simply shoved around by the paternal government of the United States: they investigated and took advantage of options open to them in their adaptive response to white pressures. "A fair number of Potawatomis were shopping around in these years," James A. Clifton notes, "inspecting, testing, and comparing the alternative possibilities of Iowa, Kansas, northern Wisconsin, or Canada before finally settling in somewhere. Their freedom of movement in this period was far greater than has generally been appreciated." *Prairie People*, 285.

24. Kappler, 2:557–60. The treaty at first failed to gain a two-thirds majority in the Senate, but the following day, on a reconsideration, the Senate approved the treaty without amendments, thirty-six to eight. *Senate Ex. Proc.*, 7:124–27.

25. Clifton, *Prairie People*, 347–403. The history of the Citizen Band is given in

Treaties with Other Tribes

The history of many of the tribes involved in removal from the Old Northwest fitted a general pattern: a succession of treaties of cession following the War of 1812, increasing pressure on the remaining lands by white settlers supported by the state and federal governments, new cessions with reserved lands for chiefs and other individuals or bands that refused to migrate beyond the Mississippi, degradation and deterioration of the tribes because of drunkenness and indolence (often a result of the annuities on which many of the Indians depended for existence), and finally, as conditions worsened and pressures increased, acquiescence in treaties that stipulated removal from the states to reservations laid out in the Indian country to the west.

Such was the case of the Miamis, whose cessions of land after the War of 1812 gave only temporary quiet. The stimulus of the Removal Act, the canal-building fever that hit Indiana after the great success of the Erie Canal, and anti-Indian sentiment created by the Black Hawk War all contributed to new demands for Miami removal. Government attempts to get cessions in 1833 failed, but the Indians' resistance was weakened, and on October 23, 1834, a treaty was signed at the Forks of the Wabash. For remuneration in cash, annuities, and payments of traders' debts, the Miamis ceded some of the reserves delineated in previous treaties.[26]

The execution of the treaty was greatly delayed; some three years and two months elapsed between the signing of the treaty in 1834 and its final proclamation by the president in December 1837. President Jackson disapproved of the treaty because he objected to the manner stipulated for paying debts and because reservations were allowed for certain individuals (thus negating full removal of the Indians from the state). Attempts were then made to get modifications in the treaty to answer the president's objections, but the Miamis were unwilling to forego the promised reservations. Finally, in September 1837, Commissioner of Indian Affairs C. A. Harris recommended sending the treaty with some

Joseph Francis Murphy, "Potawatomi Indians of the West: Origins of the Citizen Band" (Ph.D. diss., University of Oklahoma, 1961).

26. Kappler, 2:425–28. The removal of the Miamis is covered in Bert Anson, *The Miami Indians* (Norman: University of Oklahoma Press, 1970), 177–233.

amendments to the Senate, although he realized that the treaty would still provide for individual reservations. President Van Buren duly submitted the treaty on October 2, 1837, asking advice in regard to ratification with the amendments, with the proviso that if ratified the new document would be sent to the chiefs for their sanction or rejection.[27] The Senate rewrote the treaty in accordance with the instructions from the executive branch and on October 12, 1837, approved it thirty-two to one. On resubmission to them, the Miami chiefs on November 10 agreed to the revised treaty, and Van Buren proclaimed it on December 22.[28]

The inhabitants of Indiana strongly criticized the treaty for failing to rid their state of Indians, and it was clear that new negotiations would soon be undertaken. After a partial success for the United States in 1838, in 1840 the chiefs (who had long adamantly resisted removal) finally agreed to accept emigration. The treaty, however, was negotiated irregularly. The agent and the subagent, sensing a willingness on the part of the chiefs to negotiate, drew up with them an informal treaty favorable to the Indians in late November 1840, at the time of the annuity payments, without express authorization from the Indian Office to so act and without the necessary authorization and appropriation of funds by Congress. The document was sent to Commissioner of Indian Affairs T. Hartley Crawford, who saw the advantages to be gained from such a treaty and who urged the treaty on the secretary of war and the president. "It will be thus seen," he wrote the secretary, "that the negotiation of a treaty was not authorized, but if, in the opinion of the President and Senate, it shall be advisable to adopt and confirm it, I do not see any legal objections to such a course." Secretary Poinsett cautiously sent the treaty with Crawford's explanation to Van Buren, who equally cautiously submitted it to the Senate on January 4, 1841, with the remark: "Although the treaty was concluded without positive in-

27. Jackson's objections and the attempts to get the Miamis to agree to modifications in the treaty are recounted in Commissioner of Indian Affairs C. A. Harris to Secretary of War Joel R. Poinsett, September 25, 1837, OIA LS, 22:349–51 (M21, roll 22). See also Senator John Tipton's account in "Circular: To the People of Indiana," ca. July 1836, in *The John Tipton Papers*, comp. Glen A. Blackburn and ed. Nellie Armstrong Robertson and Dorothy Riker, 3 vols., Indiana Historical Collections, vols. 24–26 (Indianapolis: Indiana Historical Bureau, 1942), 3:297–99. Harris's, Poinsett's, and Van Buren's letters are in Senate (RG 46), Sen 25B-C2.

28. The original treaty and the revised treaty are both printed in 7 Stat. 458–66. For Senate action, see *Senate Ex. Proc.*, 5:42–47. The Indians' assent is printed with the treaty in Kappler, 2:428.

structions and the usual official preliminaries, its terms appear to be so advantageous and the acquisition of these lands are deemed so desirable, by reason of their importance to the State of Indiana and the Government as well as on account of the Indians themselves, who will be greatly benefitted by their removal west, that I have thought it advisable to submit it to the action of the Senate." The Senate did not object; on February 24 it ratified the treaty by a vote of twenty-three to five. The amendments entered by the Senate were confirmed by the chiefs on May 15.[29]

For the Sacs and Foxes, the loss of their lands in Iowa began with a treaty at the end of the Black Hawk War, signed at Fort Armstrong on September 21, 1833, by United States commissioners General Winfield Scott and Governor John Reynolds, of Illinois. The preamble spoke fancifully of the Black Hawk War as "an unprovoked war upon unsuspecting and defenceless citizens of the United States, sparing neither age nor sex," carried on by "certain lawless and desperate leaders, a formidable band, constituting a large portion of the Sac and Fox nation." Accordingly, the United States demanded of the Indians a considerable cession of land: a wide strip along the Mississippi running north and south almost the length of the future state of Iowa, "partly as indemnity for the expense incurred, and partly to secure the future safety and tranquillity of the invaded frontier."[30]

The Sacs and Foxes ceded more land by treaties in 1836, 1837, and 1842 and received a "tract of land suitable and convenient for Indian purposes . . . for a permanent and perpetual residence for them and their descendants" at some unspecified place on the Missouri River or its tributaries. They received also an annual payment of 5 percent of a sum of $800,000 and blacksmiths and gunsmiths, but they refused to agree to payment in the form of funds set aside for agricultural and educational purposes, for they consistently rejected the schools and religion of white society. They were allowed three years to move from the western half of the cession, and they eventually gathered at the headwaters of the Osage River in Kansas.[31]

29. Kappler, 2:531–34. The letters of Crawford to Poinsett, December 29, 1840, Poinsett to Van Buren, January 4, 1841, and Van Buren to the Senate, January 4, 1841, together with the action of the Senate are printed in *Senate Ex. Proc.*, 5:329–32, 343–44. The story of the treaty is told in Anson, *Miami Indians*, 204–8.

30. Kappler, 2:349–51.

31. Treaties of September 28, 1836, October 21, 1837, and October 11, 1842, ibid., 474–78, 495–96, 546–49; William T. Hagan, *The Sac and Fox Indians* (Norman: University of Oklahoma Press, 1958), 205–24; Donald J. Berthrong, "John Beach and

The Winnebago Indians were moved from place to place unconscionably. The peace provided by the adjustment of boundaries in the Treaty of Prairie du Chien in 1825 was broken by Winnebago attacks on white settlers, and American military force brought the surrender of the murderers. Then, in quick succession, the Winnebagos signed treaties in 1829 and 1832 that extinguished their title to lands south of the Wisconsin River. By the 1832 treaty, the United States, realizing that the Wisconsin lands remaining to the tribe would not support its members, granted to them the so-called Neutral Ground, a tract across the Mississippi lying between the lands of the Sacs and Foxes on the south and the Sioux on the north. Some Winnebagos moved to the new reservation, but they were insecure in the war zone between the hostile western tribes.[32]

The United States government wanted the Winnebagos to move entirely beyond the Mississippi, which the tribe refused to do. In 1837, however, a delegation of Winnebagos was induced to travel to Washington, D.C. There, in an irregular treaty (for the delegation had no authority to sell), the federal government pressured them into signing away the rest of their Wisconsin land. The treaty created a permanent division in the Winnebagos. One group of the Winnebagos decided it would be best to abide by the treaty and, in a series of subsequent treaties with the federal government, moved from one location to another until they ultimately ended in Nebraska, where a reservation was provided for them. The defiant remainder hid out in central Wisconsin, where they were periodically rounded up and moved to join the Winnebago faction in Nebraska, only to drift back to scattered enclaves in Wisconsin.[33]

The Chippewa (or Ojibway) Indians in Michigan, Wisconsin, and Minnesota did not take part in the general emigration of the northern tribes to the western Indian country. Although they felt the pressures of white advance and negotiated treaties for the cession of their once large estate to the United States, they managed to preserve reservations within their old territories.

---

the Removal of the Sauk and Fox from Iowa," *Iowa Journal of History* 54 (October 1956): 313–34.

32. Treaties of August 1, 1829, and September 15, 1832, Kappler, 2:300–303; 345–48; Louise Phelps Kellogg, "The Removal of the Winnebago," *Transactions of the Wisconsin Academy of Sciences, Arts and Letters* 21 (1924): 23–29.

33. These treaties are listed in appendix B as numbers 217, 240, 281, and 303. See also Nancy Oestreich Lurie, "Winnebago," in Trigger, *Northeast,* 697–700.

The western bands of Chippewas (referred to in treaties as those of the Mississippi and Lake Superior) signed a treaty in 1837 at Fort Snelling with Henry Dodge, governor of Wisconsin Territory. In it they parted with a large tract of timberland in eastern Minnesota and north-central Wisconsin in return for annuities, settlement of traders' claims, and cash for influential mixed bloods. Meanwhile, miners invaded the copper lands of the Indians along the southern shore of Lake Superior, and in 1842, by a treaty signed at La Pointe, the Chippewas sold their hunting grounds as far east as Marquette, Michigan, for similar consid-erations. Not until 1850 did the president order the Indians to prepare for removal from the ceded lands, but even then the Indians refused to consider moving entirely from their homelands. The outcome was a new treaty in 1854 in which the Chippewas accepted a group of small permanent reservations scattered across northeastern Minnesota, north-ern Wisconsin, and the Upper Peninsula of Michigan. As was customary in treaties made in the 1850s, the president was given authority, at his discretion, to allot the reservation lands in severalty.[34]

In all three treaties the Chippewas retained hunting and fishing rights. The 1837 treaty said: "The privilege of hunting, fishing, and gathering the wild rice, upon the lands, the rivers and the lakes included in the territory ceded, is guarantied to the Indians, during the pleasure of the President of the United States." The 1842 treaty read: "The Indians stipulate for the right of hunting on the ceded territory, with the other usual privileges of occupancy, until required to remove by the President of the United States." And the 1854 treaty said, more simply: "Such of [the Indians] as reside in the territory hereby ceded, shall have the right to hunt and fish therein, until otherwise ordered by the President."

The eastern bands of Chippewas in the state of Michigan met a fate similar to that of the western bands. Following a treaty of 1819 by which they lost a huge wedge of land extending from Lake Huron into central Michigan, the Chippewas (with the Ottawas) gave up the northwest quarter of the Lower Peninsula in 1836. But no wholesale removal was involved, for reserves were provided, and the Indians retained the right to use the land until it was settled by whites.[35]

---

34. Treaties of July 29, 1837, October 4, 1842, and September 30, 1854, Kappler, 2:491–93, 542–45, 648–52. Negotiations with the western Chippewas are treated in Edmund Jefferson Danziger, Jr., *The Chippewas of Lake Superior* (Norman: University of Oklahoma Press, 1978), 68–90, and Danziger, "They Would Not Be Moved: The Chippewa Treaty of 1854," *Minnesota History* 43 (Spring 1973): 175–85.

35. Treaties of September 24, 1819, and March 28, 1836, Kappler, 2:185–87, 450–

The eastern bands of Sioux also succumbed to treaty-making pressures. In 1830, at Prairie du Chien, in an attempt to end the long-standing conflicts between the Sioux and the Sacs and Foxes, the government negotiated a treaty with the tribes by which each ceded a twenty-mile-wide strip of territory along the dividing line to create the Neutral Ground later given to the Winnebagos. The buffer strip was ineffective. Then, at Washington in 1837, the Sioux were induced to cede their holdings east of the Mississippi (in what is now Wisconsin) in return for $300,000 to be invested at 5 percent, cash payments to relatives and friends of the tribe, $90,000 to pay debts due traders, and annuities in goods and provisions for agricultural development. The Senate was slow to ratify the treaty (and an earlier one of the same year with the Chippewas), and the Indians suffered because of the delay in receiving the provisions promised by the treaty. The experienced agent at St. Peter's, Lawrence Taliaferro, described the condition of the Indians and condemned the failure to carry out the treaty quickly:

> The Sioux parties to the treaty of September 29th 1837, on the 13th of January came into Fort Snelling in a Starveing condition from their hunts—there being *no game* to be found on the *Ceded territory* sufficient for the consumption of their families.
>
> The Lake Calhoun, and Contiguous St Peters bands of Medawa-kautons are represented as being in the most miserable condition of any—These people are *very Solicitous* on the subject of the fate of their late treaty with the United States—they say "we shall be rendered desperate, and we must See our Children Starve in our Lodges unless we soon get relief from the Government"—. . . .
>
> If we desire to bring the north western tribes into closer bonds of friendship with us (and nothing at this time is more to be desired) we must as speedily as practicable give them an interest in the Government, and the only way to Secure this is by entering into liberal treaty Stipulations faithfully executed, and rigidly fulfilled by the Government—
>
> If we deem peace, and tranquillity on our borders of any moment to the wellfare of the country—we should ratify at an early day the Sioux[,] Chippewa & other treaties recently entered into with the tribes—

56; Elizabeth Neumeyer, "Michigan Indians Battle against Removal," *Michigan History* 55 (Winter 1971): 275–88.

How much the Indians profited, even when the treaty was implemented, is questionable, for the annuities became a crutch for their subsistence and delayed the day when they could support themselves, and dependence upon the annuities created troubles if payment was late.[36]

The cession of their lands east of the Mississippi did not spare the Sioux from demands for their agricultural lands in Minnesota, especially after Minnesota Territory was established in 1849. The Indians were soon pressured into new cessions at treaties held in 1851—at Traverse des Sioux with the Sisseton and Wahpeton bands and at Mendota with the Mdewakanton and Wahpekute bands. These treaties exhibited in stark form the many forces that focused on treaty negotiations in order to serve non-Indian interests. The dominating force in the treaties was the interest of powerful traders like Henry H. Sibley in recovering the debts owed them by the Indians. There was adroit maneuvering by the conflicting groups of traders, missionaries, government agents, and the governor of Minnesota Territory, Alexander Ramsey, who (with Luke Lea, the newly appointed commissioner of Indian affairs) was United States commissioner for the treaties. While the Indians were divided into interest groups as well, many favoring treaties and seeking to honor and maintain kinship networks that had developed between them and the whites, it was the overweening interests of the traders that shaped the negotiations and the resulting treaties.[37]

The Sioux bands gave up most of their lands in Minnesota and eastern Dakota and came close to losing them altogether. At Traverse des Sioux, on July 23, the upper bands ceded their lands for $1,665,000,

36. Treaties of July 15, 1830, and September 29, 1837, Kappler, 2:305–10, 493–94; Lawrence Taliaferro to Wisconsin Delegate G. W. Jones, February 21, 1838, in John Porter Bloom, ed., *The Territorial Papers of the United States*, vol. 27, *Wisconsin* (Washington: National Archives, 1969), 931–32; Roy W. Meyer, *History of the Santee Sioux: United States Indian Policy on Trial* (Lincoln: University of Nebraska Press, 1967), 39–61. Taliaferro in a postscript to his letter to Jones said: "I say boldly—No man is a true friend either to his country or to the Indians—who objects to the ratification of the Sioux & other treaties of late formation   You may say this as from me if you choose—I fear some underhanded work by the *interested fur traders*—I know Some will be busy. . . . The Traders of *Prairie du Chien*, & St *Peters* seem by late advices from these places to *Know more about our Indian concerns* in the *Senate* than other persons properly interested."

37. Meyer, *Santee Sioux*, 78. Meyer's evaluation of the treaties exhibits a common "Indian-as-victim" syndrome, in which passive Indians are acted upon by white conspirators. A new ethnohistory approach to the same events in Gary Clayton Anderson, *Kinsmen of Another Kind: Dakota-White Relations in the Upper Mississippi Valley, 1650–1862* (Lincoln: University of Nebraska Press, 1984), sees the Indians, too, as having diverse motivations in regard to the treaty.

of which $275,000 was designated for the chiefs "to enable them to settle their affairs and comply with their present just engagements" and to aid in removal and subsistence for a year. But the financial provisions were heavy with the civilizing goals of the missionaries and the government agent, as funds were set aside for schools, mills, blacksmith shops, and farms. And the funds from investing the remaining sums were to be used not only for cash annuities but for a general agricultural improvement and civilization fund, for educational purposes, and for goods and provisions.[38] The Indians signed a "traders' paper," not part of the regular treaty, by which they acknowledged their debts to the traders.

Having obtained what they wanted at Traverse des Sioux, the commissioners moved down the Minnesota River to Mendota to treat with the lower bands. There on August 5 they signed a treaty similar to the one negotiated in July.[39]

These Sioux treaties provided for reservations roughly ten miles wide on each side of the Minnesota River, but the Senate eliminated the articles providing for the reservation of land within the ceded tract and stipulated the payment of ten cents an acre for that land. The president was authorized to provide a reservation outside the ceded lands, once the Indians gave their consent to the amendment.[40]

It proved difficult to get approval of the change, although the chiefs finally acquiesced. But the Indians were then, in actual fact, without a clear reservation; the president never got around to selecting the reservation called for in the Senate amendment, and the Indians continued to live on the lands originally reserved in the treaties. Finally, on June 19, 1858, in Washington, representatives of the upper and lower Sioux signed new treaties, which provided for allotment of land in the southern half of the reservations (with remaining land held for tribal uses). Wide discretion was given to the Senate to determine the title of the Indians to the lands and to provide payment for the northern half of the reservations now given up and to the secretary of the interior to manage all treaty funds according to his own discretion. Not until June 27, 1860, however, did the Senate finally confirm the Indian title to the southern part of the reservations and authorize payment of thirty cents per acre for the northern part. Most of this money, again, went to pay the "just debts" of the traders.[41]

38. Kappler, 2:588–90.
39. Kappler, 2:591–93.
40. *Senate Ex. Proc.*, 8:368–69, 382, 384, 398, 401, 404–5.
41. Kappler, 2:781–89. There is a detailed account of the treaties and subsequent

For the Menominees, treaty negotiations were complicated by the tribe's relations with the emigrant New York Indians. By a treaty of 1831 the Menominees ceded specific lands along the Fox River to the New York Indians and other tracts along the eastern shore of Lake Winnebago to the Stockbridge and Brotherton Indians. They also gave up their claims to lands lying east of Green Bay, the Fox River, and Lake Winnebago. When the Menominees objected to this treaty, however, a new agreement was drawn up in 1832 that somewhat modified the provisions. This was but the beginning in the decline of the Menominee estate, for by still another treaty in 1836 the tribe gave up its land along the western shore of Green Bay and west of Lake Winnebago, as well as a strip of pinelands along the Wisconsin River.[42]

When Wisconsin became a state in 1848, new attacks were made on the Menominee holdings. In October, Indian Commissioner William Medill forced a removal treaty upon the now weakened tribe. The Indians gave up their remaining lands in Wisconsin and were assigned a piece of land on the Crow Wing River in central Minnesota. But exploring parties reported unfavorably on the Crow Wing land, and President Millard Fillmore extended the right of the Menominees to remain on their old lands. With the support of white citizens, the Indians moved to new lands along the Wolf River in 1852. Two years later the United States confirmed this reservation in place of the Minnesota tract. The adamant refusal of the Menominees to move across the Mississippi had succeeded, although the new Menominee reservation amounted to but a fraction of the aboriginal holdings.[43]

---

actions in William Watts Folwell, *A History of Minnesota*, rev. ed., 4 vols. (St. Paul: Minnesota Historical Society, 1961), 2:393–400. The treaties are discussed more briefly in Anderson, *Kinsmen of Another Kind*, 229–31, and Meyer, *Santee Sioux*, 103–5. The cession of 1851 and the reservations along the Minnesota River are shown in Royce, *Cessions*, plates 11, 24, 33, area nos. 289, 413, 414, 440.

42. Treaties of February 8, 1831, October 27, 1832, and September 3, 1836, Kappler, 2:319–25, 377–82, 463–66; Patricia K. Ourada, *The Menominee Indians: A History* (Norman: University of Oklahoma Press, 1979), 71–98.

43. Treaties of October 18, 1848, and May 12, 1854, Kappler, 2:572–74, 626–27; Ourada, *Menominee Indians*, 99–126.

New York Indians

In the 1820s the Indians of New York State again entered into negotiations with the federal government, for pressures to remove them from the state had mounted. The Ogden Land Company, still holding preemption rights to the Indians' lands in New York, was eager to free the lands of Indian title, and a remarkable self-promoter named Eleazar Williams interested some of the Indians (mainly Oneidas, Stockbridges, and Brothertons) in emigrating. After making arrangements with local Indians in Wisconsin, Williams led a group of Indians west in 1822, and migration continued through the decade. The 1831 and 1832 Menominee treaties provided land for these New York Indians.[44]

The removal impulse of the 1830s affected the Indians who had remained in New York, and in 1838 a treaty was signed at Buffalo Creek with several bands of these Indians. Stimulated by the Ogden Land Company's heirs and by civic and political leaders in Buffalo, who wanted to make room for the expansion of the city onto adjacent Seneca reservation lands, a full-scale drive began to eliminate the Indians from the state and move them to lands west of Missouri. The move paralleled that against the Five Civilized Tribes, although on a smaller scale, for the New York Indian remnants numbered only about five thousand. The New York treaty negotiations, however, had a unique and complicated history, which showed once again the peculiarities and uncertainty of treaty making with the Indians. The story concentrates on the Senecas, the largest of the Indian groups involved and on their four small reservations: Buffalo Creek, Allegany, Cattaraugus, and Tonawanda. But the Oneida, Onondaga, Cayuga, Tuscarora, St. Regis, Stockbridge, Brotherton, and Munsee Indians were involved as well.[45]

44. Prucha, *Great Father*, 1:264–66. The Stockbridge Indians' later dealings with the United States were particularly complicated. See Marion Johnson Mochon, "Stockbridge-Munsee Cultural Adaptations: 'Assimilated Indians,'" *Proceedings of the American Philosophical Society* 112 (June 21, 1968): 182–219.

45. A census of the Indians appears in Schedule A of the treaty, Kappler, 2:508. A detailed history of the Treaty of Buffalo Creek, upon which I have relied, is Henry S. Manley, "Buying Buffalo from the Indians," *New York History* 28 (July 1947): 313–29. Because the treaty caused much controversy and there was repeated consideration of its terms by the president and by the Senate, voluminous documentation exists. A large

An aspiring New York Democratic politician and former congressman, Ransom H. Gillet, was appointed United States commissioner, and in January 1838 he met the Indian chiefs and headmen at Buffalo Creek. There he signed with them on January 15 a long and complicated treaty. The preamble traced the earlier history of the movement of New York Indians to Wisconsin, noted the difficulties with that arrangement, and asserted that the Indians now agreed on the wisdom and necessity of removing at once to the western Indian territory. The treaty, thereupon, provided for the giving up of the lands in Wisconsin set aside for the New York Indians (except for a specified tract on which they were actually settled). In return the United States promised to them a region west of Missouri as a permanent home. That land was to be held in fee simple by a patent from the president of the United States, with enough land to provide 320 acres for each Indian; a limit of five years was set on the removal to those new lands. Attached to the treaty was a deed of conveyance, by which the Seneca Indians sold their four New York reservations to John L. Ogden and Joseph Fellows for $202,000. The deed was witnessed by J. Trowbridge for the state of Massachusetts and by Gillet for the United States.[46]

President Van Buren submitted the treaty to the Senate on April 23, 1838. From that point on the treaty had rough sailing. Strong charges were made that it had been negotiated in a fraudulent manner, and the public outcry quickly reached the Senate.[47] Pamphlets appeared containing copies of contracts made between Ogden agents and certain Seneca chiefs, by which the Indians were promised sums of money for signing the treaty and promoting its passage. One such publication, issued by the Quakers, who took a special interest in the affair, ran to 256 pages. It turned out, too, that some of the chiefs had signed the treaty privately in Gillet's quarters, not in public council; of some eighty

---

number of documents are found in two files concerning Senate ratification in the National Archives: Sen (RG 46), Sen 25B-C-14 and Sen 26B-C2. Scores of these documents and others were printed for the confidential use of the Senate at the time; these are now available through *CIS Index to US Senate Executive Documents and Reports, Covering Documents and Reports Not Printed in the US Serial Set, 1817–1969*, 2 vols. (Washington: Congressional Information Service, 1987), and the accompanying microfiche. In addition, much of the material appears in *Sen. Ex. Proc.*, in House and Senate documents in the Congressional Serial Set, and in other places. See citations given below.

46. Kappler, 2:502–16.
47. *Senate Ex. Proc.*, 5:95, 98, 102.

or ninety Seneca chiefs (no one seemed able to provide an accurate figure), only thirty-one initially affixed their signatures to the document.[48]

The Senate, aware of these developments, amended the treaty—chiefly by striking out provisions for payments and services and substituting a general appropriation of $400,000 to cover costs of removal and improvements, to support the emigrating Indians for the first year in their new homes, to encourage the Indians in education, and to supply mills, houses, and implements for agriculture and mechanic arts—but it ratified the treaty only *conditionally*. The Senate resolved:

> *Provided always, and be it further resolved (two thirds of the Senators present concurring)*, That the treaty shall have no force or effect whatever, as it relates to any of said tribes, nations, or bands of New York Indians, nor shall it be understood that the Senate have assented to any of the contracts connected with it, until the same, with the amendments herein proposed, is submitted and fully and fairly explained by a commissioner of the United States to each of said tribes or bands, separately assembled in council, and they have given their free and voluntary assent thereto.

With the amendments and this proviso, the Senate, on June 11, 1838, approved the treaty by a vote of thirty-three to two.[49]

There then began a new round of councils with the tribes and bands, which occupied late August and the month of September. Gillet, who had been appointed to get additional Indian signatures, returned the treaty to Washington with new signatures, some of them privately obtained.[50]

48. The most comprehensive publication was the Quaker booklet, *The Case of the Seneca Indians in the State of New York, Illustrated by Facts* (Philadelphia: Merrihew and Thompson, 1840). Together with two other documents, it is reprinted in *The Case of the Seneca Indians in the State of New York* (Stanfordville, N.Y.: Earl M. Coleman, 1979). Another significant pamphlet, by a Seneca Indian, was M. B. Pierce, *Address on the Present Condition and Prospects of the Aboriginal Inhabitants of North America, with Particular Reference to the Seneca Nation* (Philadelphia: J. Richards, 1839). Memorials and petitions appear in *Senate Doc.* no. 33, 26-1, serial 355; *House Doc.* no. 66, 26-2, serial 383; *Senate Doc.* no. 210, 26-2, serial 378. The difficulty in determining which men to count as chiefs for approving the treaty is shown in studies of the Seneca chief systems. See Thomas S. Abler, "Fraud and Factionalism: The Seneca and the Buffalo Creek Treaty," and "Population, Moieties, and Tribal Chiefs: Early Nineteenth Century Political Organization of the Seneca Nation," two unpublished papers furnished me by the author.

49. *Senate Ex. Proc.*, 5:130–31.

50. See Kappler, 2:513–16. Reports on these developments are in T. Hartley Crawford to Joel R. Poinsett, January 15, 1839, and Poinsett to the president, January 19,

The president and the Senate next resorted to a set of neat maneuvers, each trying to place the responsibility on the other for deciding whether the conditions of the Senate for ratifying the treaty had been met. President Van Buren sent the treaty with the new signatures to the Senate, asking for "advice in regard of the sufficiency of the assent of the Senecas to the amendments proposed." The Senate Committee on Indian Affairs studied the long documents accompanying the treaty and decided that the additional signatures on the treaty had *not* been acquired "in open council"—a practice it inveighed against. The committee in the end, however, offered no recommendation, but merely submitted the facts to the full Senate for resolution.[51]

The Senate could not agree either to accept the treaty or to reject it. Instead, on March 2, 1839, it tossed the issue back to the president, declaring that whenever he should be satisfied that the Senecas had given proper assent to the amended treaty, he should proclaim the treaty and carry it into effect. Van Buren delayed. He sent Secretary of War Poinsett to meet once again with the Indians, only to discover new opposition to the treaty. The president then concluded: "That improper means have been employed to obtain the assent of the Seneca chiefs there is every reason to believe, and I have not been able to satisfy myself that I can, consistently with the resolution of the Senate of the 2d of March, 1839, cause the treaty to be carried into effect in respect to the Seneca tribe." On January 13, 1840, he asked the Senate again for its advice on ratification.[52]

The Senate, however, was still unwilling to make a clear decision. Resolutions to approve the treaty and counterresolutions to reject it were interspersed with long speeches for and against the document. Senator Ambrose H. Sevier of Arkansas explained why the treaty should be rejected, while Senator Wilson Lumpkin and Senator Silas Wright of New York detailed the advantages of the treaty and answered criticisms against it. Charges of bribery were brought up, and Wright and Senator John Norvell, of Michigan, sought to dispel the weight of the

---

1839, Records of the Office of Indian Affairs, National Archives Record Group 75, Report Books, 1:71–72, 77–78 (M348, roll 1). Henry A. S. Dearborn, a commissioner appointed by the governor of Massachusetts, attended these latter proceedings and reported them fully in his journals. See "Journals of Henry A. S. Dearborn: A Record of Councils with the Seneca and Tuscarora Indians at Buffalo and Cattaraugus in the Years 1838 and 1839," *Publications of the Buffalo Historical Society*, 7 (1904): 33–225.

51. *Senate Ex. Proc.*, 5:182–83, 208–11.

52. Ibid., 212, 218–19, 242–46, 265–66, 269.

charges. The latter argued, in fact, that bribery had become an established part of treaty making:

> Sir, has not your whole system of Indian relations been marked by
> the same species of fraud, bribery and corruption, if you choose to
> call them so? Have you not always had to make presents of money
> and goods to their chiefs, at every treaty, in every treaty, which you
> have ever made with them? . . .
>   What is it, but the most splendid bribes, that induced the Chero-
> kees and other southern tribes to remove west of the Mississippi?
> Sir, you had to pay John Ross one million of dollars to induce him
> to remove his part of the nation. To be sure, the money was given to
> him on the pretext of defraying his expenses in their removal. But it
> was a bribe on the largest scale. Millions have been paid to get rid of
> the Indians in the Southern States. And yet you talk of fraud, of
> bribery, and corruption, to a paltry amount, to induce the New York
> Indians to go where their nation may be preserved for ages.[53]

Motion after motion was made in the Senate, largely on the question
of whether the chiefs' signatures had been obtained in open council,
but there was no consensus. Finally, in three significant motions on
March 25, 1840, all resulting in tie votes, Vice President Richard M.
Johnson cast the deciding vote. First, an amendment to a motion on
the treaty itself asserting that the amended treaty had been approved
properly by all the tribes, including the Senecas was approved; second,
an amendment to require a two-thirds majority in the vote was rejected;
and finally, the amended motion to approve the treaty was approved.
In this narrow fashion, depending on the deciding vote of the vice
president, the Senate overturned its original rejection of the new treaty
and authorized the president to proclaim the whole treaty, the Seneca
section included.[54]

There was some complaint later that the treaty was invalid because
the final vote had not had a two-thirds majority, but the Senate had
rejected motions to add that requirement to the resolution it was
debating. That resolution was merely to affirm the assent of the tribes
to the amended treaty, not, strictly speaking, to ratify the treaty, which
had been done conditionally by a two-thirds majority in June 1838.

In spite of the proclamation of the treaty by Van Buren on April 4,

53. The speeches, although given in executive session, are printed in *Congressional
Globe*, 8: Appendix, 285–88 (Lumpkin), 289–95 (Sevier), 308–9 (Norvell), and 352–
59 (Wright).
54. *Senate Ex. Proc.*, 5:271–75.

the removal of the New York Indians to the Kansas lands specified in the treaty did not take place. Those lands remained vacant for many years and were eventually returned to the public domain, except for thirty-two allotments held in the northeast corner of the tract by the few New York Indians who had emigrated.[55] A new treaty with the Senecas on May 20, 1842, including a new indenture between the Senecas and Ogden and Fellows, returned the Allegany and Cattaraugus reservations to the Indians, who thus were enabled to stay in New York State.[56]

55. Royce, *Cessions*, 771. Royce shows this allotted fragment on plate 27, area no. 249.

56. Kappler, 2:537–42. Royce, *Cessions*, shows the New York reservations on plate 47. The Tonawanda Band split off from the rest of the Senecas and fought to retain its reservation. At length, by a treaty of November 5, 1857, the band was able to purchase parts of the reservation from Ogden and Fellows with money provided by the United States in return for the waiver of rights to its part of the Kansas tract. Kappler, 2:767–71.

CHAPTER NINE

Patterns in Treaty Making

By midcentury the treaty system was nearly three-quarters of a century old. It had been nudged in one direction after another and had been manipulated to serve the interests of the United States. Most of its complexities can be seen in the narrative account of treaty making, but general aspects, too, deserve attention. Although George Washington had fretted about just how the constitutional provisions would be carried out in regard to Indian treaties, many procedures soon became regularized. Where there were problems, pragmatic decisions held sway, with a good deal of discretion left in the hands of the treaty commissioners.

Treaty Commissioners

Negotiation of a treaty depended first of all on congressional authorization, and Congress acted under diverse influences. Presidents and their subordinates urged upon Congress the necessity of specific treaties, and senators, representatives, and territorial delegates were pressured by constituents who wanted land cessions and removal of the Indians from their midst. Advocates of Indian rights, too, knew how to bombard Congress, as they did at the time of the removal crisis. Then, when Congress decided to authorize a treaty and make appropriations to pay the commissioners' expenses and to buy the necessary provisions and presents for the Indians, the action was embodied in particular pieces of legislation or buried obscurely in appropriation bills.[1]

The executive branch of the government bore the burden of treaty making. Treaties, of course, were monitored by the Senate, through its authority to give or withhold "advice and consent," but the onerous duties of negotiations were seldom shared by the senators. The presidents themselves did not direct the treaty councils, though some of them—Washington, Jefferson, and Jackson—exerted considerable personal influence. The responsibilities fell to cabinet members, first the secretaries of war and then the secretaries of the interior, and their subordinates in the "Indian department." Other persons, too, were chosen to negotiate treaties, men prominent in military or political affairs of the young nation, who had or could expect to receive the respect of the Indians. At first the task was considered important enough that the president appointed the commissioners by and with the consent of the Senate, but this practice gradually disappeared.

Territorial governors, who were *ex officio* superintendents of Indian affairs, did much of the work—men like Arthur St. Clair of the Northwest Territory, William Blount of the Southwest Territory, William Henry Harrison of Indiana, Ninian Edwards of Illinois, Lewis Cass of Michigan, William Clark of Missouri, and Isaac I. Stevens of Washington. As the Indian agency system developed, increasingly it was the Indian agents—Benjamin Hawkins, Return J. Meigs, Silas Dinsmoor, Benjamin O'Fallon, James Gadsden, and Henry R. Schoolcraft, among many others—who negotiated for the United States with the Indians. If the treaties were signed at the seat of government, the secretaries of war—Henry Knox, Henry Dearborn, John C. Calhoun, James Barbour, John Eaton, Lewis Cass, and Joel R. Poinsett—played a direct part in the treaty making. But they were increasingly replaced by the commissioners of Indian affairs, Thomas L. McKenney (as first head of the Indian Office), Carey A. Harris, Luke Lea, George W. Manypenny, Charles E. Mix, William P. Dole, Dennis N. Cooley, Lewis Bogy, and Nathaniel G. Taylor. No secretary of the interior, strangely enough, was ever an official commissioner for an Indian treaty.

The commissioners for some treaties in the early years were military

1. For examples of congressional authorization, see 1 Stat. 333, 539–40, 618; 2 Stat. 82, 183–84; 4 Stat. 185, 188, 302; 9 Stat. 437, 556, 558, 572; 10 Stat. 238; 12 Stat. 792; 15 Stat. 17.

men such as Generals Anthony Wayne, James Wilkinson, and Andrew Jackson, and many less prominent officers, though usually high-ranking ones, served as commissioners. Thus Brigadier General Henry Atkinson negotiated the peace treaties along the upper Missouri River in 1825, and General Winfield Scott (with Governor Reynolds of Illinois) signed the treaty with the Sacs and Foxes in 1832 after the Black Hawk War. The commission headed by Governor Newton Edmunds of Dakota Territory that treated with the northern plains Indians at Fort Sully in 1865 included Major General S. R. Curtis and Brigadier General Henry H. Sibley. And the Indian Peace Commission, signing treaties in 1867 and 1868, comprised such important military men as Lieutenant General William T. Sherman and Brevet Major Generals William S. Harney, C. C. Auger, and Alfred H. Terry, as well as civilians.

The commissioners, by and large, were men of experience and integrity and sometimes of deep sympathy for the Indians, although almost universally they were convinced that the drive to move the Indians from their aboriginal culture toward the patterns of white society was proper and necessary. On a few occasions, however, men got the job of commissioner as a political reward or to promote some scheme of personal interest. In a few instances local agents or superintendents drew up agreements with Indians under their charge without having previously received instructions to do so, yet the resultant documents were duly ratified by the Senate and the president as formal treaties.

Since treaties became a means by which federal Indian policy was carried out, treaty making, naturally enough, became a regular part of the duties of the men already employed to manage Indian affairs—the commissioners of Indian affairs, superintendents, and agents. Congress, in fact, in February 1851 declared that "hereafter all Indian treaties shall be negotiated by such officers and agents of the Indian department as the President of the United States may designate for that purpose, and no officer or agent so employed shall receive any additional compensation for such service."[2]

Indian Negotiators

Who negotiated the treaties for the Indians? In many cases it was the whole tribe gathered at the council site. Lewis Cass and

2. 9 Stat. 586.

William Clark, who were directed in 1829 to draw up a set of regulations for dealing with the Indians, called attention to this aspect of the treaty-making business:

> We assemble the Indians in council, propose the subject to them, and discuss the various propositions made, modified, and acted on. The whole matter is fully considered and openly conducted in the presence of all the Indians of the tribes, who choose to attend, and the result is embodied in the form of a treaty. . . .
>
> When they assemble to deliberate upon their public affairs, they are pure democracies, in which every one claims an equal right to speak and vote. The public deliberations, however, are usually conducted by the elderly men, but the young men or warriors exercise the real controlling influence. No measure can be safely adopted, without their concurrence. . . .
>
> Experience has demonstrated the utility of permitting as many of the young men as are willing, to sign the treaty. They thus become committed, and no change of opinion, to which few people are more subject than Indians, will then lead them to upbraid others for an act in which they themselves thus openly participated. And this is the true reason why so many signatures are usually appended to our Indian treaties. He who signs first, incurs a heavy responsibility; and it requires no ordinary degree of resolution in the man, who thus, in the presence of his countrymen, leads the way in sanctioning a measure which many may regret after the presents are expended and the excitement of the moment has subsided.[3]

Cass and Clark, however, were speaking of their own experience with the northern tribes and admitted that their remarks did not extend universally to the southern tribes, where frequently chiefs were delegated to act in the name of the tribe. Even among the northern tribes, on occasion a small group of authorized delegates would come to the capital to negotiate and sign a treaty. In some treaties signed by Indian delegates a stipulation was inserted that the treaty would take effect only if approved by the tribe in full council.

"Tribe," however, was an inadequate term, for it was in large part an Anglo-American concept increasingly imposed upon Indian groups for convenience in dealing with them. Not only was there confusion and uncertainty about the proper political unit with which to deal—village, band, tribelet, or tribe—but the governmental structures within the units were imprecise. How much power or authority did a village chief

---

3. Report submitted to the Senate by the secretary of war, February 9, 1829, *Senate Doc.* no. 72, 20-2, serial 181, pp. 17–19.

have, for how long, and how was it passed on? How much power did a "tribal" chief have, and what was the difference between peace chiefs and war chiefs? Did certain clans within a tribe have special responsibilities or powers regarding land cessions or other aspects of treaty making? How fluid were the systems?[4]

The federal government tried to deal with recognized Indian leaders, but often there were no clearly discernible head chiefs, as Cass and McKenney had discovered when they dealt with the Menominees at Butte des Morts in 1827, and treaty commissioners resorted to "appointing" chiefs. Federal officials responsible for Indian affairs often were not well enough informed to appreciate the systems of chiefs and leaders in the various Indian groups and did not always negotiate with the appropriate men. At times, when treaties were signed at Washington, rival delegations appeared, and the United States had to decide which one to do business with.

There was no clear criterion—except, perhaps, expediency—for determining what Indian political unit would be used for carrying on the negotiations. The United States varied its decisions, sometimes treating with separate small divisions of a "tribe," as in many treaties with Potawatomis and with Chippewas, and at other times seeking to find (or designate) a single tribal chief to represent all the bands together (even over the objections of the Indians, who declared that a unitary chief was not their practice). In a good many instances tribes were grouped together for a single treaty. Sometimes these were quite disparate or even hostile groups, brought together to deal with some common issue; at other times the negotiators might represent a dominant tribe with fragments of other Indians traditionally attached to it. Treaty commissioners did not always know ahead of time how many of the tribes and bands invited to a council would actually appear—or when. So they dealt with those at hand or extended the time of signing to accommodate latecomers.

Government officials, eager to carry out the elements of Indian policy

4. See Raymond D. Fogelson, "The Context of American Indian Political History," in *The Struggle for Political Autonomy: The Second Newberry Library Conference on Themes in American Indian History* (Chicago: Newberry Library, 1989), 8–21. There is an excellent discussion of "tribe" in Morton H. Fried, *The Notion of Tribe* (Menlo Park, Calif.: Cummings Publishing Company, 1975). Fried asserts that "the most massive and familiar phenomena of tribalism occur as a consequence of the impinging on simple cultures of much more complexly organized societies" (p. 10). He calls the kind of tribe we know "a secondary sociopolitical phenomenon, brought about by the intercession of more complexly ordered societies, states in particular" (p. 114).

imbedded in treaties, on occasion selected chiefs who were in favor of the government's policies and dealt with them to the exclusion of less receptive tribal leaders. Chief Lawyer, considered the head chief of the Nez Perces, agreed to and signed a treaty in 1863, but chiefs of significant bands within the Nez Perces did not sign and claimed that the treaty provisions did not apply to them. Honest misunderstandings arose on the part of federal officials, who frequently were frustrated in dealing with groups whose acknowledged chiefs signed treaties but were then unable to enforce the provisions among their tribal members.

Interpreters

Key figures at the treaty councils and always among the witnesses signing Indian treaties were the interpreters. A few of them were prominent men on the frontiers, but more often they were faceless individuals, neglected by historians.[5] Their importance, nevertheless, was tremendous, for if the treaties were to make much sense as contracts, the two parties needed to understand what each was saying. The importance was amplified by the fact that the English version of the treaties alone was the standard. Nor was it only a matter of accurate translation of speeches and documents. Deep cultural differences between the Indians and the whites often made the understanding of the *meaning* of the treaty items different on each side.

The interpreters at the treaty councils, to a large extent, came from a pool of agency interpreters authorized by law.[6] And Indians often brought "their" interpreters to meetings, individuals of long acquaintance with the tribes and highly respected by the Indians they represented. Some interpreters were traders who knew Indian languages and

5. A historical article devoted to interpreters is Yasuhide Kawashima, "Forest Diplomats: The Role of Interpreters in Indian-White Relations on the Early American Frontier," *American Indian Quarterly* 13 (Winter 1989): 1–14, but it deals with the colonial period only. In that period many of the interpreters were important frontier diplomats, serving as cultural go-betweens, not simply as translators, a condition that did not obtain so fully in later times under the United States government. Another study of the colonial period is J. Frederick Fausz, "Middlemen in Peace and War: Virginia's Earliest Indian Interpreters, 1608–1632," *Virginia Magazine of History and Biography* 95 (January, 1987): 41–64.

6. See authorization of interpreters in 4 Stat. 737 (1834). Originally, in 1834, the salary was set at $300 a year; in 1851 it was raised to $400 and to $500 for the far western states. 9 Stat. 587.

customs; others were whites (men and women) who had taken up life among the Indians, sometimes originally as captives. A great many were mixed bloods, and a considerable number who witnessed treaties were illiterate and signed their names on the treaty documents with a mark. For only a few treaties was it possible to do without interpreters altogether because the Indian delegates themselves knew English.

Problems of accurate translation occurred at nearly all the treaty councils, more so, of course, when the United States commissioners met tribes who had not had sustained contact with white society. Thus Thomas Fitzpatrick, a competent and respected agent, had difficulties when he dealt with Comanches, Kiowas, and Apaches at Fort Atkinson on the Arkansas River in 1853. He wrote:

> At first, almost insurmountable difficulties presented themselves, in the distant and suspicious bearing of the chiefs, and the utter impossibility of obtaining any interpreters who understood their intricate languages. But little intercourse had ever existed between them and the white race, and that usually of the most unfriendly character. . . . There were no trappers or traders amongst them who could facilitate an interview; no one who could speak a syllable of the English tongue; none present in whom mutual confidence could be reposed; and the "sign language," that common to all the wild tribes of the west, while it might answer the purpose of barter, could not be relied upon in matters of so much importance and delicacy.

Eventually, Mexican prisoners of the Indians established some communication through use of Spanish, and different persons interpreted the same speeches, to aid in accuracy. An Arapaho Indian who had lived with the Comanches gave some help, and even sign language was resorted to. In the end the agent was satisfied that "a full understanding of what transpired was finally arrived at on both sides."[7]

Interracial communication at the treaty councils of Governor Isaac I. Stevens with the Puget Sound tribes in 1854–55 was conducted in Chinook Jargon, a lingua franca along the Pacific Northwest coast but hardly an effective tool for sensitive negotiations, for it had a vocabulary of only about five hundred words, and a single word might be used to

7. Fitzpatrick to A. Cumming, November 19, 1853, CIA AR, 1853, serial 690, p. 360. See also the discussion in LeRoy R. Hafen, *Broken Hand: The Life of Thomas Fitzpatrick, Mountain Man, Guide, and Indian Agent* (Denver: Old West Publishing Company, 1973), 309–10.

translate a number of different English words.[8] Such difficulties in communication were noted by Indian Commissioner Francis A. Walker in 1872, as he explained the government's forbearance in dealing with recalcitrant Indians. He spoke of "the extreme untrustworthiness of many of the interpreters on whom the Government is obliged to rely in bringing its intentions to the knowledge of the Indians."[9]

Critics of federal Indian policy sometimes charge that the government negotiators, through the connivance of interpreters, deceived the Indians about the terms in the treaties signed by unsuspecting and trusting chiefs. But such accusations do less than justice to the American commissioners, who, for the most part, sought earnestly to convey the treaties' terms to the Indians. It is true that often enough the Indians were displeased with the treaty provisions, but the United States had overwhelming power compared to that of the tribes and could ultimately compel agreement to its terms. It did not need to resort to deceit as a major tool of Indian diplomacy. Nor do they do justice to the Indian leaders, who were astute enough to bring along interpreters on whom they felt they could rely and who argued strongly for their own positions—even though in many cases they lost the argument. On occasion the Indians, after the fact, complained that they had not understood the treaties they had signed, but it is hard to judge whether that was due to poor or deceitful interpreters or to a change in mind on the part of the Indians after they saw the effects of the treaties or after the presents and provisions that had drawn them to the treaty grounds had been dissipated.[10]

Considering the handicaps under which they worked, the interpreters, by and large, did a respectable job, and, although the Indians may not have liked what the treaties stipulated, pains were taken to be sure

8. See the brief article "Chinook Jargon" in Howard R. Lamar, ed., *The Reader's Encyclopedia of the American West* (New York: Thomas Y. Crowell Company, 1977), 208–9.

9. CIA AR, 1872, serial 1560, p. 395.

10. See complaints of the Delaware chief John Killbuck to George Morgan, January 20, 1779, in Louise Phelps Kellogg, *Frontier Advance on the Upper Ohio, 1778–1779* (Madison: State Historical Society of Wisconsin, 1916), 203–4. The story of Osage Indians who complained in 1808 that they had not understood the treaty provisions is told in Meriwether Lewis to the president, December 15, 1808, *ASPIA*, 1:766–67.

It has been asserted that the Winnebago Indians who signed a treaty in Washington on November 1, 1837, had been intentionally deceived by the interpreter. Nancy Oestreich Lurie, "Winnebago," *Handbook of North American Indians*, vol. 15, *Northeast*, ed. Bruce G. Trigger (Washington: Smithsonian Institution, 1978), 699. But the citation Lurie gives does not substantiate this accusation.

they understood the provisions. In early councils the interpreters were sworn to translate accurately, and many of the interpreters who signed the treaties as witnesses had "sworn interpreter" entered after their names. Most councils had more than one interpreter, so that they could aid and, if need be, correct each other. When several tribes were present at a treaty council, of course, it was necessary to have interpreters who could handle the various languages.

A good example of the latter case was the treaty council at Medicine Lodge Creek in southern Kansas in 1867, when the Indian Peace Commission met with southern plains tribes, a council about which we know a good deal because of the large number of newspaper reporters on hand.[11] The Indians there spoke seven different languages, and while only three interpreters signed the treaties as witnesses, the reporters mention five in all. The most important of these was Phillip McCuster, a frontiersman married to a Comanche woman; he had been an army scout and had acted as interpreter for the army and for the Interior Department. McCuster was so valuable because Comanche, the best known of the plains Indian tongues, served as a middle stage in the translating; once a speech had been rendered into Comanche, tribal interpreters could translate for their own tribes. Another interpreter was Mrs. Margaret Adams, whose father was a French-Canadian trader and whose mother was an Arapaho. She attracted much attention. An historian of the treaty says, "When she appeared at the first Grand Councils at Medicine Lodge, wearing a red satin dress, she created a sensation—particularly among the Indians. [Reporter George C.] Brown's comment on Mrs. Adams was to the effect that she came to all the meetings drunk."[12]

The Treaty of Fort Laramie of 1851, a complex council of many tribes, depended upon the ability of the interpreters. The participation of the Crows, one of the principal tribes present, was described by the reporter for the *Missouri Republican*:

> Mr. [Robert] Meldrum, the Crow interpreter, has been many years among them, and is, in feeling and habits, almost identified with them. He is, withal, an intelligent man, understands their language perfectly, and is capable of comprehending the extent, effect

11. The work of the reporters is described and analyzed in Douglas C. Jones, *The Treaty of Medicine Lodge: The Story of the Great Treaty Council as Told by Eyewitnesses* (Norman: University of Oklahoma Press, 1966).

12. Ibid., 108. Jones gives a detailed account of the business of interpreting at the council; see especially pages 104–9.

and importance of the propositions submitted. In addition to Mr. Meldrum, the Crows have unbounded confidence in Mr. [Alexander] Culbertson, who had induced them to attend the treaty. He has long been at the head of the principal trading post on the headwaters of the Missouri, and the Indians regard him with great respect and consideration. These men were able to explain to the Crows, very fully and satisfactorily, all the various propositions.[13]

Later, at the final meeting, the same reporter noted: "When the Council was opened, Col. Mitchell explained the purpose of the assemblage to be the signing of the treaty, as it had been prepared in conformity to previous agreement. He then read it to them, sentence by sentence, and caused it to be fully explained by the different Interpreters. At the instance of some of the Chiefs, portions of it were read several times, for their better understanding. Every effort was made, and successfully, too, to give them the full and just import of each article."[14]

Indians could be insistent in getting interpreters who pleased them. The Nez Perces, for example, in the treaty of 1863, wanted as interpreter Pessior B. Whitman, rather than other men at hand, for they considered him more thoroughly acquainted with their language. "They stated," the journal of the treaty proceedings said, "that it was possible they might have some plain, some hard things to say, and the Commissioners on the other hand might have the same to reply. Whatever might thus be spoken by either party they wished to be just as plainly or sharply interpreted." They argued, too, that Whitman, who no longer lived with the tribe, would be considered impartial by all the Indian bands involved. The commissioners agreed to send for Whitman, who eventually arrived.[15]

When delegations of Indians went to Washington to negotiate treaties or merely to visit the Great Father, they were accompanied by interpreters, some of whom were tribal members and shared in the enter-

13. *Missouri Republican*, November 9, 1851, letter from the editor dated September 11, 1851, typed transcript supplied me by Raymond DeMallie. Both of the interpreters were long-time traders. See the biographical sketches by Roy H. Mattison (Culbertson) and John E. Wickman (Meldrum) in LeRoy R. Hafen, ed., *The Mountain Men and the Fur Trade of the Far West*, 10 vols. (Glendale, Calif,: Arthur H. Clark Company, 1965–72), 1:253–56; 9:279–81. The volumes of the set offer considerable information about traders as interpreters.

14. *Missouri Republican*, November 30, 1851, letter from the editor dated September 17, 1851.

15. Journal of treaty proceedings, Documents (T494), roll 6, frames 657–58; C. H. Hale to William P. Dole, June 30, 1863, ibid., frame 760.

tainment and presents that the delegates received. They, like the delegates, could succumb to the enticements of the urban environment, which may have aggravated their linguistic limitations.[16] But the government officials sought for honest communication with the Indians.

Other Witnesses

There were many persons attendant on the treaty negotiations and signatory as witnesses to the formal treaty documents. Chief among these were members of the United States army. Many of the treaties were negotiated at or in the vicinity of military posts, as the popular names of the treaties abundantly indicate—for example, Fort Pitt, Fort Stanwix, Fort McIntosh, Fort Harmar, Fort Greenville, Fort Wayne, Fort Jackson, Fort Armstrong, Fort Gibson, Fort Leavenworth, Fort Bridger, Fort Sully, and Fort Laramie. Others were signed at settlements in which an army post was a dominant feature—namely, Detroit, Vincennes, Chicago, Green Bay, Sault Ste. Marie, and Rock Island. For some councils, a detachment of troops was considered a necessary part of the American entourage, for there was a recurring fear that the Indians called to council might be hostile and that trouble might erupt without warning at the treaty grounds. In other cases, where several tribes were gathered together, there was danger that old and persisting enmity between tribes would break out in armed clashes. Military officers, if not taking an active part in the negotiations, signed many treaty documents as witnesses.

Although in some cases the army troops were considered an absolute necessity to protect the American treaty commissioners, in many others their presence served principally as a means to overawe the Indians and impress them with the power and grandeur of the United States. Parades and special military maneuvers and the firing of salutes were frequently a part of the council ceremonies. It should not be forgotten, however, that the Indians could play the same game. Western treaty councils were attended by immense numbers of Indians, among whom were many war chiefs and warriors, who presented a striking military presence of

16. See the passing discussion of interpreters in Herman J. Viola, *Diplomats in Buckskins: A History of Indian Delegations in Washington City* (Washington: Smithsonian Institution Press, 1981). Some of Viola's best stories, however, refer to the post-treaty period.

their own. And the Indians, too, delighted in astonishing the assembled Americans with their feats of horsemanship.

Besides the military officers and their troops there was a great mixture of other whites at the treaty negotiations on the frontier, which were often elaborate and spectacular affairs drawing people who were concerned about the outcome of the negotiations and others who were merely curious. Distinguished travelers affixed their names to the treaties whose councils they attended, giving, one supposes, an added touch of authority and solemnity to the documents. State and territorial officials and legislators appear on the lists—governors, territorial secretaries, attorneys general, judges and lawyers, justices of the peace, mayors, militia officers, and territorial delegates—along with federal employees such as Indian agents, subagents, factors, registers of the land office, postmasters, army paymasters, surveyors, Indian farmers, and (in the councils of the Indian Peace Commission) a phonographer. Resident or traveling clergymen and missionaries—men like Benedict Flaget, Catholic bishop of Bardstown, Kentucky, who witnessed the treaty with the Potawatomis in 1818; Methodist missionary to the Wyandots James Wheeler; Catholic missionary to the Menominees F. J. Bonduel; Presbyterian missionary to the Sioux Stephen R. Riggs; and the Jesuit Pierre-Jean De Smet and the Episcopalian Samuel D. Hinman, who attested the signing of some of the Indians to the Treaty of Fort Laramie in 1868—and newspaper editors and reporters all made their appearance from time to time, as did an array of Indian traders.

Traders and the Treaties

It is easy to think of the treaties by which the Indian title to land was extinguished as compacts between two parties, the Indian tribe and the United States government—and such, legally, they were. But in fact there was sometimes an influential and occasionally dominating third party: traders. When the fur trade flourished, traders supplied the Indians with goods in return for furs, but as the hunting lands were circumscribed and the fur-bearing animals disappeared, the Indians paid the traders from their annuities, or the government bought large quantities of goods for the Indians directly from the traders. As cessions multiplied and annuities and other payments grew, the traders became more and more involved in the treaty process. Indians were indebted to the traders for goods received on credit; the debts could be recovered only by provisions in the treaties for cash annuities, by which the Indians could pay the debts, or by direct allotment of funds in the treaties to cover specified obligations.[17]

Beginning with the Osage treaty of 1825, allowance of traders' claims became almost universal in treaties signed with the Indians in the Old Northwest. And as the pressures for removal increased and removal treaties seemed necessary at any price, the rewards for the Indians and for the traders were considerable, as table 1 makes clear.

In addition, because the treaty negotiations were usually eased by generous handouts to the attending Indians and because the treaties often specified large payments in goods as well as in cash, the traders profited by furnishing these supplies, often at inflated prices. The traders, moreover, had a deep interest in the lands allotted individual Indians in the treaties, for such lands could quickly fall into their hands. So much influence did the traders have over the Indians that in many cases the government would have been unable to procure the treaties of cession it wanted without providing adequately for the traders' interests.

The exorbitance of many traders' claims called for government investigation and adjudication lest unscrupulous merchants grow inordinately rich at the expense of the Indians and the United States Treasury. The Senate refused, from time to time, to ratify treaties until the claims against the Indians were checked, and the War Department issued regulations for the payment of claims. Sometimes special commissioners or commissions were appointed to decide on claims and adjust the payments among diverse claimants, and they were given detailed instructions. Those investigating the claims under the Winnebago treaty of 1837 were told:

17. I follow here my account in Francis Paul Prucha, *The Great Father: The United States Government and the American Indians*, 2 vols. (Lincoln: University of Nebraska Press, 1984), 1:266–69. The best general account of the role of the traders is James L. Clayton, "The Impact of Traders' Claims on the American Fur Trade," in David M. Ellis, ed., *The Frontier in American Development: Essays in Honor of Paul Wallace Gates* (Ithaca: Cornell University Press, 1969), 299–322. Other studies, which deal with more restricted areas or tribes, are Paul Wallace Gates, "Introduction," in *The John Tipton Papers*, comp. Glen A. Blackburn and ed. Nellie Armstrong Robertson and Dorothy Riker, 3 vols., Indiana Historical Collections, vols. 24–26 (Indianapolis: Indiana Historical Bureau, 1942), 1:3–53; and Robert A. Trennert, "A Trader's Role in the Potawatomi Removal from Indiana: The Case of George W. Ewing," *Old Northwest* 4 (March 1978): 3–24. Trennert has expanded his account of the traders in *Indian Traders on the Middle Border: The House of Ewing, 1827–54* (Lincoln: University of Nebraska Press, 1981).

Table 1 *Fur Traders' Debt Claims Provided for by Treaty Funds, 1825–1842.*

Year	Tribe	Amount ($)	Year	Tribe	Amount ($)
1825	Osage	1,500	1833	Quapaw	4,100
	Kansas	500		Potawatomi	175,000
1826	Potawatomi	9,573	1836	Ottawa	300,000
	Miami	7,727		Menominee	90,000
1828	Potawatomi	10,000	1837	Chippewa	70,000
1829	Chippewa	3,000		Sioux	90,000
	Winnebago	11,601		Sac and Fox	100,000
1831	Ottawa	20,000		Winnebago	200,000
1832	Sac and Fox	40,000	1838	Miami	150,000
	Potawatomi	28,700	1840	Miami	250,000
	Potawatomi	62,400	1842	Wyandot	23,800
	Shawnee	12,000		Chippewa	75,000
	Potawatomi	20,700		Sac and Fox	258,000
	Total			2,013,601	

SOURCE: Compiled from Kappler, vol. 2, and printed in James L. Clayton, "The Impact of Traders' Claims on the American Fur Trade," in David M. Ellis, ed., *The Frontier in American Development: Essays in Honor of Paul Wallace Gates* (Ithaca: Cornell University Press, 1969), 303. Copyright 1969, Cornell University; used by permission of the publisher, Cornell University Press.

> You will require the respective creditors to deposit with you tran-
> scripts of their claims, exhibiting names, dates, articles, prices, and
> the original consideration of each claim. . . . If original books or
> entries cannot be produced, their loss or destruction must be proved.
> The sale of spirituous liquors to Indians being prohibited by the laws
> of the United States, no item of charge on that account will, under
> any circumstances, be allowed. . . . If [the claim] be against an
> individual Indian, he should be called before you, and each item in
> the account be explained to him, and his assent or dissent to it
> required.

The Indian Office recognized the forces pulling in two directions and instructed the commissioners further: "The moral duty of paying every just claim should be pressed upon the Indians; and, in receiving their statements, you will bear in mind the danger arising on the one hand from the disposition to evade an obligation; and on the other, from the exercise of improper influence by any of the claimants."[18] The commis-

18. C. A. Harris to commissioners, July 26, 1838, *House Doc.* no. 229, 25-3, serial

sioners found it impossible to carry out their duties with the exactitude wanted by the commissioner of Indian affairs, but they went about their business carefully and made judgments on the validity of the claims presented. In some cases claims were scaled down or disallowed altogether.

The attitude of the traders toward removal was often ambivalent. These men shared the sentiment of other white settlers that the Indians should be moved to the west to clear the land for white exploitation, and often they had a direct interest in the ceded lands. Yet it was not easy to give up the large profits they made in supplying the Indians where they were. Even though most traders realized that removal was inevitable, they worked to delay the emigration as much as possible. Each new treaty could be another bonanza. In 1838 the commissioner of Indian affairs asserted that disturbances arising in the removal of the Indians were caused "by the large indebtedness of the Indians to their traders, and to the undue influence of the latter over them." He said he was confident "that their influence is not only prejudicial to the Indians, but has been frequently exercised to defeat negotiations with them, and to prevent the accomplishment of objects sanctioned by treaties, and others devised and calculated to promote their welfare and permanent improvement."[19]

It was the government's unwavering objective to rid the regions east of the Mississippi of Indians, and since it was often necessary to get the traders' acquiescence if not active support, measures were taken to circumvent any obstructionism. Thus in the Potawatomi removal the government threatened to pay no more claims until the Indians had emigrated. Then, on March 3, 1843, the Senate, by a two-thirds majority, resolved that in future negotiations of treaties with the Indians "no reservations of land should be made in favor of any person, nor the payment of any debts provided for," and it sent the resolution to the president.[20] But many old debts were still outstanding, and claims dragged on and on, much to the irritation of the overburdened Indian Office. In later treaties the claims of the traders against the Indians still

---

349, pp. 5–6; the undated report of two commissioners appears ibid., 14–21. For other accounts of investigation of claims, see Trennert, "Trader's Role," and Clayton, "Traders' Claims."

19. Harris to Poinsett, February 12, 1838, *Senate Doc.* no. 198, 25-2, serial 316, p. 2.

20. *Senate Ex. Proc.*, 6:170, 184.

had to be recognized if the desired cessions were to be obtained. Even though the government did not pay the traders directly, large sums were provided to enable the Indians "to settle their affairs and comply with their present just engagements."[21]

Presents and Medals for the Indians

An important element in United States policy toward the Indians was the distribution of presents to Indian chiefs as a means of winning their favor and attaching them to the United States. It was a practice that went back to colonial times, and, although presents were given outside of treaty negotiations, such gifts were an established part of treaty making and clearly distinguished Indian treaties from treaties signed with European powers.[22] The Indian chiefs expected gifts as part of treaty protocol; an abrupt stop to the practice would have imperiled success at the treaty councils. While special gifts were distributed to chiefs, where they might do the most good as a thinly veiled form of bribery, large sums were spent as well on provisions (food and clothing) for the multitudes of Indians who thronged to the councils, in large part just to receive such presents. As Cass and Clark noted in their 1829 report to the secretary of war,

> Provisions must also be regularly issued to the Indians. They are capable of great abstinence and great repletion. They come to the treaty ground expecting to be fed and clothed, and it is essential to the success of the negotiation with them, that their wants should be supplied, and themselves kept in good humor. Nothing short of the daily issue of a pound and a half of fresh beef, and a pound and a half of flour or bread, for each person, will satisfy them; and this quantity will not, unless there is a considerable proportion of children. The men are generally accompanied by their families, nor will they attend without them. All come expecting to partake of the provisions which are to be issued, and of the goods to be distributed.

21. Sioux treaties of 1851, Kappler, 2:589, 591; Lucile M. Kane, "The Sioux Treaties and the Traders," *Minnesota History* 32 (June 1951): 65–80.

22. There is a brief discussion of presents for Indians in Prucha, *Great Father*, 1:168–71. An excellent study of the use of presents in colonial times is Wilbur R. Jacobs, *Diplomacy and Indian Gifts: Anglo-French Rivalry along the Ohio and Northwest Frontier, 1748–1763* (Stanford: Stanford University Press, 1950). Jacobs provides great detail not only on the use and significance of the presents but on the kinds of goods provided.

Without the operations of these powerful motives, few cessions of land would be obtained.[23]

It is sometimes difficult to distinguish how much of the provisions expended at the council grounds were presents, strictly speaking, and how much were part of the consideration paid for land cessions. Many goods were distributed prior to the signing of a treaty, and this occurred even if the council failed to produce a formal cession agreement.

The large silver medals presented by treaty commissioners at the councils (medals in a gradation of sizes to distinguish between great chiefs and lesser ones) were very special marks of recognition for the chiefs and warriors. The medals bore pictures of the Great Father, the president, and other symbols of peace and friendship or promotion of the government's civilizing plans. While the medals were presented in large numbers on the frontiers by Indian agents and other government officials in order to gain the friendship of tribal leaders and were a indication of Indian acceptance of loyalty to the United States, they were especially important instruments of diplomacy at treaty councils, where their presentation to chiefs frequently marked the culmination of the treaty signing.[24]

Thus by the second of the secret articles of the Treaty of New York with the Creeks in 1790, the United States presented "a great medal with proper ornaments" to each of the six "great medal chiefs" named in the article—three from the upper Creeks, two from the lower Creeks, and one from the Seminoles.[25] Medals also entered into General Anthony Wayne's negotiations at Greenville in 1795. Their significance in marking a switch from the Indians' adherence to the United States rather than to the British can be seen in the speech of New Corn, a Potawatomi chief, on his arrival at the council. "I hope, after our treaty," he told Wayne, "you will exchange our old medals, and supply us with General Washington's. My young men will no longer listen to the former; they wish for the latter. They have thrown off the British, and henceforth will view the Americans as their only true friends."[26] Wayne did not

23. Report of February 9, 1829, 20.

24. A full history of the use of medals as an element of Indian policy is given in Francis Paul Prucha, *Indian Peace Medals in American History* (Madison: State Historical Society of Wisconsin, 1971).

25. The title "great medal chief" came from the usage of John Stuart, the British Indian superintendent in the south, who so designated influential tribal leaders. See Prucha, *Indian Peace Medals*, 3–5.

26. Minutes of the Treaty of Greenville, June 17, 1795, *ASPIA*, 1:564.

disappoint the chief. The treaty was signed on August 3, after long days of council meetings and passing of wampum belts, and on August 7 the general again addressed the Indians.

> Listen! all you nations present. I have hitherto addressed you as brothers. I now adopt you all, in the name of the President and Fifteen great Fires of America, as their children, and you are so accordingly. The medals which I shall have the honor to deliver you, you will consider as presented by the hands of your father, the Fifteen Fires of America. These you will hand down to your children's children, in commemoration of this day—a day in which the United States of America gives peace to you and all your nations, and receives you and them under the protecting wings of her eagle.[27]

Lewis Cass and Thomas L. McKenney, in two treaties they negotiated in 1826 and 1827, used the medals as symbols of the United States. In a formal presentation to Chippewa chiefs and warriors at the Treaty of Fond du Lac in 1826, McKenney spoke at length to the Indians: "We stand here to put medals around their [the great men's] necks—and smaller medals we will put around the necks of your first warriors, and best young men. All these medals have on one side of them your great father's face, and on the other side is his pipe, his peace hatchet, and his hand." McKenney told the Indians that a medal was a gift from their Great Father himself. "It is a new heart," he said. "Your great father has told us to come up here, and put it in the breast of his great Chippeway children."[28] Similarly, at Butte des Morts in 1827 the two commissioners gave medals and other gifts to the Indians designated as principal chiefs of the Menominees. At the end of the council the medals were presented with this admonition:

> We have hung medals around your necks & put new American hearts into you. You must now take firm hold of your American fathers hand & keep fast hold. You must give your young men good advice. You must drive away all bad words from your ears. These medals open the path to our great council fires. If at any time you want to say any thing to your great father, these medals are your passports.[29]

---

27. Ibid., 580.
28. Thomas L. McKenney, *Sketches of a Tour to the Lakes, of the Character and Customs of the Chippeway Indians, and of Incidents Connected with the Treaty of Fond du Lac* (Baltimore: Fielding Lucas, Jr., 1827), 473–74.
29. Treaty journal, Documents (T494), roll 2, frame 30.

Farther west as well Indian medals flooded the Indian country. The commissioners at the Treaties of Portage des Sioux in 1815, for example, presented medals to the chiefs (some of them in lieu of British medals surrendered to Lieutenant Zebulon Pike on his expedition to the upper Mississippi in 1805), and Atkinson and O'Fallon took medals with them when they ascended the Missouri in 1825 and gave them out at their treaty councils. The medals continued to be major instruments in Indian policy as long as treaties were made and even later.

Land Cessions and Payment for Them

Treaties were the legal instruments by which the federal government acquired full title to the great public domain stretching west of the Appalachian Mountains. Whereas the British government by the Treaty of Paris in 1783 recognized United States jurisdiction and ultimate sovereignty over the lands as far as the Mississippi, and the new nation eventually acquired the trans-Mississippi West as well, the Indian right of occupancy to much of that land was recognized by the president, Congress, and the courts. The Indian title had to be extinguished by formal treaties.

But what precisely was the title that the United States agreed to pay for in the treaties? That depended, to begin with, on the European doctrine of preemption, which divided rights to territory into two classes. There was a fee-simple right of absolute dominion over the land, a right claimed by the European "discoverers" of the area; there was, second, the right of occupancy, sometimes called right of the soil, which permitted occupants to enjoy the usufruct of the land as long as they occupied it. By preemption the white governments asserted their exclusive right to purchase or inherit the Indians' right of occupancy when the Indians decided to sell or when they no longer existed on the land.[30]

For Henry Knox the practice was dictated by common principles of human decency and the honor and dignity of the nation. Thus he wrote to President Washington on June 15, 1789: "It is presumable, that a nation solicitous of establishing its character on the broad basis of justice, would not only hesitate at, but reject every proposition to benefit

---

30. I draw here on the discussion in Prucha, *Great Father*, 1:58–60.

itself, by the injury of any neighboring community, however contempt-ible and weak it might be, either with respect to its manners or power. . . . The Indians being the prior occupants, possess the right of the soil. It cannot be taken from them unless by their free consent, or by the right of conquest in case of a just war." He wanted the Indian rights to be ascertained and declared by law, and he wrote: "Were it enacted that the Indians possess the right to all their territory which they have not fairly conveyed, and that they should not be divested thereof, but in consequence of open treaties, made under the authority of the United States, the foundation of peace and justice would be laid."[31]

Knox was seconded by Secretary of State Thomas Jefferson, who, when questioned by the British minister in 1792 about American rights to Indian lands, replied:

> 1st. A right to pre-emption of their lands; that is to say, the sole and exclusive right of purchasing from them whenever they should be willing to sell. 2d. A right of regulating the commerce between them and the whites. . . . We consider it as established by the usage of different nations into a kind of *Jus gentium* for America, that a white nation settling down and declaring that such and such are their limits, makes an invasion of those limits by any other white nation an act of war, but gives no right of soil against the native possessors.[32]

A year later, in replying to queries posed by Washington to his cabinet, Jefferson was equally clear: "I considered our right of pre-emption of the Indian lands, not as amounting to any dominion, or jurisdiction, or paramountship whatever, but merely in the nature of a remainder after the extinguishment of a present right, which gave us no present right whatever, but of preventing other nations from taking possession, and so defeating our expectancy; that the Indians had the full, undivided and independent sovereignty as long as they choose to keep it, and that this might be forever."[33] Jefferson maintained these views as president. When he proposed a constitutional amendment to

31. Knox to Washington, June 15, 1789, and January 4, 1790, *ASPIA*, 1:13, 61.

32. *The Writings of Thomas Jefferson*, ed. Andrew A. Lipscomb, 20 vols. (Washington: Thomas Jefferson Memorial Association, 1903–4), 17:328–29.

33. Ibid., 1:340–41. See also the statements in support of Indian rights in Jefferson to Knox, August 10, 1791, ibid., 8:226–27, and Jefferson to Knox, August 26, 1790, *The Papers of Thomas Jefferson*, ed. Julian P. Boyd, 24 vols. to date (Princeton: Princeton University Press, 1950—), 17:430–31.

ratify the Louisiana Purchase, he included a statement of respect for the Indians' "right of occupancy in the soil."[34]

The Supreme Court under John Marshall endorsed the doctrine of preemption. In *Fletcher v. Peck* (1810), the Court declared that the "nature of the Indian title, which is certainly to be respected by all courts, until it be legitimately extinguished, is not such as to be absolutely repugnant to seizin in fee on the part of the State," and the Court expanded this doctrine in *Johnson and Graham's Lessee v. McIntosh* (1823). With citations of colonial precedents to back up his position, Marshall maintained that the United States, or the several states, had exclusive power to extinguish the Indian right of occupancy. The Indians' right, he declared, "is no more incompatible with a seizin in fee, than a lease for years, and might as effectually bar an ejectment." He continued, "It has never been contended that the Indian title amounted to nothing. Their right of possession has never been questioned."[35]

But if the Indian right of occupancy did not amount to nothing, what precisely did it amount to in monetary terms? That was a crucial question in treaty negotiations, where payments for land cessions were determined. It would appear that the United States commissioners paid as little as they could get away with, and usually they were given discretion in setting amounts, depending upon what the Indians would accept. They certainly were not governed by any consideration of what the lands might ultimately be worth.

In 1804 Secretary of War Henry Dearborn provided an explicit model for calculating the price to be offered to Choctaws for cessions asked of them, showing clearly the limited title to hunting lands accorded the Indians by the United States. Dearborn proposed estimating as nearly as possible the actual profit the Indians annually derived from hunting on a given tract and the probable profits for the next fifty years. "For instance," he wrote in preliminary instructions to Silas Dinsmoor, one of the commissioners, "if the Choctaws derive an annual profit of $3000 from hunting on the whole of the tract proposed to be ceded . . . , and if they will probably continue to derive an equal advantage for 50 or 60 years to come, then it would be proper to allow them such a sum paid down as would bring an interest of $3000 a year, or such an annuity as would be equal to $3000. They would in such a case make an advan-

34. *The Writings of Thomas Jefferson*, ed. Paul Leicester Ford, 10 vols. (New York: G. P. Putnam's Sons, 1892–99), 8:241–43.

35. 6 Cranch 142–43; 8 Wheaton 592.

tageous bargain, as the annuity would be perpetual, and they would have permission to hunt on the land until it should be taken up by individuals and settled."[36]

North of the Ohio the same rationale prevailed, and prices for Indian land were kept very low. For example, in the spring of 1805 Dearborn appointed the Indian agent Charles Jouett a treaty commissioner to get cessions of land in the Western Reserve of Connecticut. Jouett was instructed by Dearborn to get one cession, for the benefit of land companies in the Reserve, at a "fair and just" price in line with what the United States was paying at the time, namely, one to two cents an acre. Dearborn directed the agent to purchase a second tract at not more than two cents an acre.[37] As the negotiator of a treaty with the Miamis in September 1809, Governor William Henry Harrison of Indiana Territory rejoiced that the cession would contain "upwards of two millions and a half of acres and will cost less than two cents per acre."[38] This, of course, was a far cry from the price of two dollars an acre set in the land law of 1800 for sale of the public domain in fee simple to white settlers.

As time passed and the Indians became increasingly reluctant to part with more land, the United States had to increase its offers. This was especially true in the removal period of the late 1820s and the 1830s, when the importance of the cessions to the white population and the adamant position taken by some tribes to cede no more territory combined to hike the prices. The Chickasaws did better than most tribes, for the individual homesteads assigned to the Indians sold for a minimum of $1.25 an acre (the minimum price at that time for the public domain) and some of them brought more. The unallotted lands— some 4 million acres out of the entire cession of 6,422,400 acres—was sold at public auction under a graduation principle and brought about $3.3 million to the Chickasaw general fund.[39]

Northern Indians, too, steadily asked higher prices for their land, as Cass and Clark noted in 1829.

36. Dearborn to Dinsmoor, October 25, 1804, WD LS, Book B, 19–20 (M15, roll 2).

37. Dearborn to Jouett, April 2, 1805, ibid., 62–64 (M15, roll 2).

38. Harrison to the secretary of war, October 1, 1809, Logan Esarey, ed., *Messages and Letters of William Henry Harrison*, 2 vols., Indiana Historical Collections, vols. 7, 9 (Indianapolis: Indiana Historical Commission, 1922), 1:358.

39. See the account in Arrell M. Gibson, *The Chickasaws* (Norman: University of Oklahoma Press, 1971), 160–66.

A visible increase is manifest in the value of the consideration given from time to time for cessions of land. By the earlier treaties, a few articles of goods or clothing, specially enumerated, were considered a full satisfaction for the most important purchases. But, by degrees, the system of annuities was introduced, and even the characteristic improvidence of the Indians was compelled to yield something of the present to the future. As the stock of goods in market increased, and that of land diminished, the usual effect was observed in the change of their relative value. Some of the tribes, and particularly the Miamies, now receive an amount in annuities, which bears so considerable a proportion to their numbers, as to enable them, with very little exertion, to procure a support. Probably not less than $150 annually, falls to the lot of each family of that tribe. But the difficulty of procuring cessions is every year increased. The Indians are more and more reluctant to cede, and more and more anxious to procure high prices for cessions when made. It is not difficult to foresee, that the present system must come to a close by its own operation.[40]

It is difficult to calculate the total amount paid by the United States for the Indian lands it purchased by treaty. Felix S. Cohen, a close and sympathetic student of Indian affairs, wrote in 1947 that "any such calculation would have to take account of the conjectural value of a myriad of commodities, special services, and tax exemptions, which commonly took the place of cash," and he offered a conservative estimate that placed the total price of Indian lands sold to the United States at more than $800 million. Was this a fair price? Cohen replied: "The only fair answer to that question is that except in a very few cases where military duress was present the price paid was one that satisfied the

40. Report of February 9, 1829, 17–18. Representative James M. Wayne, of Georgia, in the debates over Indian removal in 1830, stressed the increasing costs of land cessions and echoed Cass's and Clark's opinion that the heavy costs would bring down the whole system. At the end of a long speech on March 24, 1830, he listed as well the incidental expenses of treaty making: "Sir, I invite gentlemen in the opposition to look at our expenditure, year after year, for holding treaties with Indians for cessions of lands, under our present system, and they will be startled at the sums paid to commissioners, secretaries, interpreters, messengers, bakers, and butchers; for the erection of buildings, council houses, mess houses, kitchens, and cabins; for corn, beef, pork, and salt—not alone for the subsistence of the Indians and their families while the treaty is in progress, but for their support on their return home. And then come those hundreds of contingencies for horses for expresses and their riders, stationery, pipes, tobacco, paint, and ammunition, and medical expenses, with a swarm of *et ceteras*, the cost of which is never known until a demand is made for payment—and the reserve of all these abuses is a heavy item of goods for distribution to the Indians." *Register of Debates in Congress*, 6:1131.

Indians. Whether the Indians should have been satisfied and what the land would be worth now if it had never been sold are questions that lead us to ethereal realms of speculation."[41]

Without exact records or methods of determining what counted as payment, "ethereal realms of speculation" are tempting. One legal scholar recently estimated that the United States took two billion acres of land claimed by Indians, half of which was purchased by treaty or agreement for less than seventy-five cents an acre; the rest, he said, was unilaterally confiscated by the federal government without payment, or the title was simply extinguished without formal action. He asserted that in 1970 the lands thus "purchased, confiscated, or otherwise acquired by the United States had a value of over $560,000,000,000 ($300 per acre) exclusive of improvements and structures."[42]

A new study, moving beyond mere speculation, draws upon the deliberations of the Indian Claims Commission to assess what the United States paid for Indian lands. Using the central and northern Great Plains as a case study, the author concludes that the United States paid the Indians $29,977,015 for 290 million acres of land in that region, or an average compensation of about ten cents an acre.[43]

In the face of wide discrepancies in appraisals and accounting, the Indian Claims Commission decided over the years that the sums paid

41. Felix S. Cohen, "Original Indian Title," in *The Legal Conscience: Selected Papers of Felix S. Cohen*, ed. Lucy Kramer Cohen (New Haven: Yale University Press, 1960), 281–83. The article was originally published in 1947. The $800 million figure has been picked up by others. See President Truman's remarks on signing the Indian Claims Commission Act, August 13, 1946, *Public Papers of the Presidents of the United States: Harry S. Truman, 1946* (Washington: GPO, 1962), 414; H. D. Rosenthal, *Their Day in Court: A History of the Indian Claims Commission* (New York: Garland Publishing, 1990), 7.

42. Russel Lawrence Barsh, "Indian Land Claims Policy in the United States," *North Dakota Law Review* 58 (1982): 7–8. Barsh offers no careful accounting of land values at the time of purchase and no figures dealing with the varied payments made for the land. Today's value of lands, of course, is not directly pertinent to a determination of what the lands were justly worth at the time of cession.

43. David J. Wishart, "Compensation for Dispossession: Payments to the Indians for Their Lands on the Central and Northern Great Plains in the 19th Century," *National Geographic Research* 6 (Winter 1990): 94–109. The article, replete with tables, maps, and charts, is a pioneer attempt to use the data gathered by the Indian Claims Commission for a sizable area, but the complications in accounting and the legal maneuvering in the cases raise questions about the historical accuracy of the commission's findings. For a detailed account of the legal complications in the Sioux claims under the Fort Laramie Treaty of 1868 and the Manypenny Commission agreement of 1876, see Edward Lazarus, *Black Hills, White Justice: The Sioux Nation versus the United States, 1775 to the Present* (New York: HarperCollins, 1991).

the Indians, whether in cash annuities or provision of goods, supplies, and services, did not equal the fair market value of the land at date of cession. A large part of the $818 million awarded by the Indian Claims Commission on petitions from Indian groups for unpaid claims was awarded for "grossly inadequate and unconscionable" payment for the ceded lands. But Cohen was right in noting that at the treaty negotiations the Indians, after receiving the presents distributed at the council and promises for substantial annuities or other benefits (in many cases, at the insistence of the Indians, greater than the government had initially offered) generally left the council grounds without complaint about the sums.

Whatever the treaty commissions finally agreed to in the treaties was monitored carefully in many cases by the Senate, which at times refused to ratify treaties in which it thought there were extravagant costs (as in the case of the treaties with the California Indians in 1851). The Senate often amended treaties to cut down the size or duration of the payments. More damaging and unconscionable was the failure of the federal government at times to pay the full sums promised in the treaties and to make sure that the goods and services stipulated were of high quality.[44]

The question of preemption rights and the nature of Indian title to the land—either in cases of aboriginal title or in title recognized by treaty in reservations set aside for continual Indian possession—was closely attended to. The federal government feared that the absolute title to the land it claimed (subject always to Indian rights of occupancy) would be transferred to Indian tribes or to individual Indians, who might then dispose of the lands contrary to the interests of the United States. But pragmatic decisions sometimes overrode such views, notably in the removal treaties signed in the 1830s with the Five Civilized Tribes, to whom, in exchange for their land in the southeastern United States, the government conveyed other land west of the Mississippi "in fee simple to them and their descendants, to inure to them while they shall exist as a nation and live on it." The revision of the Chickasaw removal treaty assigned allotments to individual Indians in fee simple.[45]

44. The records of the Indian Claims Commission indicate, although sometimes unclearly, that the sums agreed upon did not always find their way into the hands of the Indians, and the corruption in supplying goods to the Indians, especially in the 1850s and 1860s, was one of the forces that sparked an aggressive Indian reform movement after the Civil War.

45. Kappler, 2:311.

There were a great many varieties of land transfers in the treaties beyond the simple sale or cession of lands to the United States to be added to the public domain and made available to white settlers. There were the exchanges of land that were at the heart of the Indian removal policy of the 1830s—the giving up of eastern land by Indians in return for lands assigned to them west of the Mississippi. There were sales of lands by the Indians to private land companies that claimed preemptive rights in New York State and in the Western Reserve of Connecticut in Ohio, in which transactions the United States commissioners acted merely as witnesses in order to signify the legal approval of the federal government. Many treaties reserved areas of land within the cessions for individuals and for bands of Indians who would not agree to remove from their ancestral homes. Later treaties provided for individual allotments of land when the tribal holdings were ceded, in the government's attempt to force the Indians into white landholding patterns. After the Civil War some treaties provided that the beneficiaries of the cessions would be railroad corporations, not the public domain—a practice that ran afoul of Congress.

While on the surface the treaties were contracts between two parties bargaining in good faith, in many cases the dominant power of the United States made it possible for the federal government to force its will upon the dependent Indians, in regard to both lands transferred and payments for them. But the Indians had an interest in the land cessions, too. As the fur trade declined, land was the commodity by which Indians could buy the manufactured goods of white society that had become necessities for them and by which they could obtain food and clothing needed to avoid severe suffering or starvation. Land was used to cancel debts to traders, some of which ran to high figures, but the United States, effectively vindicating its claim to preemption rights, would not allow the tribes to pay the debts *directly*. All land transfers had to be done by formal treaty, and some treaties were simply commercial documents, not diplomatic ones.

By treaty the United States acquired other land rights besides land cessions to provide for white settlement. Treaties provided land for trading posts and military posts, roads, railroad rights of way, telegraph lines, and inns and ferries, often with provisional stipulations that allowed the United States to determine the precise places at its pleasure. Thus the treaty that Indian Agent Thomas Fitzpatrick made with the Comanches, Kiowas, and Apaches at Fort Atkinson in 1853 included the expansive clause: "The aforesaid Indian tribes do also hereby fully recognize and acknowledge the right of the United States to lay off and mark out roads or highways—to make reservations of land necessary thereto—to locate depots—and to establish military and other posts within the territories inhabited by the said tribes."[46]

The land cessions and payments for them were at the heart of the treaty system, and ramifications of those transactions still abide.

46. Ibid., 600.

CHAPTER TEN

Treaties in the Expanding West

The removal treaties of the 1830s, federal officials had hoped, would for the most part end the Indian problem. By 1840, lands east of the Mississippi had been freed of Indian title, except for a few small spots, and most of the eastern tribes had been located behind what some historians have labeled the Permanent Indian Frontier. Then, suddenly, the ease and tranquility that the Indian Office had foreseen was seriously disrupted. Dramatic events in the 1840s overturned the premises upon which American Indian policy had been based; the concept of a north-south line separating white settlement from Indian country was shattered, and before long the barrier itself was physically destroyed. In three short years Texas (1845), the Oregon Country (1846), and the Mexican Cession (1848) were added to American territory, and the relationship between the United States and the Indians was radically changed.[1]

With the territorial additions the federal government accepted responsibility for new groups of Indians, and old policies were stretched to try to make them fit the new situations. Increasingly, makers of Indian policy relied on reservations, in many cases small parcels of land "reserved" out of the original holdings of the tribes or bands, which were intended as a temporary expedient to prevent clashes between resident

---

1. For a general account of the development of Indian policy in these new regions, see Francis Paul Prucha, *The Great Father: The United States Government and the American Indians*, 2 vols. (Lincoln: University of Nebraska Press, 1984), 1:315–409. I have used some sections from this work in the present chapter.

Indians and oncoming white settlers and to provide secure areas in which the humanitarian programs for acculturating Indians to white society could be carried out.

The government conceived of no way to deal with the new problems except by the traditional method of formal treaties. The decade of the 1850s rivaled the 1830s in the number of treaties concluded and would have outstripped the earlier decade if all the treaties negotiated had been ratified. At the end of 1856, Commissioner of Indian Affairs George W. Manypenny reported, "Since the 4th of March, 1853, fifty-two treaties with various Indian tribes have been entered into. . . . Thirty-two of these treaties have been ratified, and twenty are now before the Senate for its consideration and action. In no former equal period of our history have so many treaties been made, or such vast accessions of land been obtained." He provided a threefold classification of the treaties: "first, treaties of peace and friendship; second, treaties of acquisition, with a view of colonizing the Indians on reservations; and third, treaties of acquisition, and providing for the permanent settlement of the individuals of the tribes, at once or in the future, on separate tracts of lands or homesteads, and for the gradual abolition of the tribal character."[2]

Treaty making in the 1850s, however, ran into a good many snags. The Indian Office and the treaty commissioners appointed were not well acquainted with the newfound Indians and made mistakes in trying to determine tribal organization and the chiefs with whom the United States should deal. For Indians in the southwest there was no consensus about the status of their land titles under Spanish rule and what land status they carried over under American rule. And, for a variety of reasons, the Senate delayed and in some cases refused outright to ratify certain treaties, reducing to naught the efforts of commissioners to set up arrangements that would regularize the Indians' relations with the United States and protect their land rights. Despite some successes, the treaty system seriously deteriorated during the decade.

2. CIA AR, 1856, serial 875, p. 571.

Treaties with the Plains Indians

The heavy migration to Oregon and California passed directly through Indian territories, and the consequent destruction of buffalo and grazing lands forced the Indians to seek new hunting grounds and increased intertribal irritations. To meet the crisis, federal officials sought to free the middle section of the plains of its Indian inhabitants by moving them to two great "colonies," one already well established in the south as the Indian Territory and a similar one to be laid out north of the lines of travel.[3] Meanwhile, the Indians were to be kept at peace by compensation for the damage done by the whites traveling to the Pacific.

Commissioner of Indian Affairs William Medill planned a grand meeting with the plains Indians, and he sent a proposal to the secretary of the interior in June 1849. Noting the damage done by westering emigrants to the Indians' means of subsistence, he wrote, "Under these circumstances, whatever may be the nature and extent of their title to the lands, I think it would be sound policy to make them some annual compensation for the right of way through the country, and, in consideration of the destruction of the buffalo therein." He recommended payment in "goods, stock, agricultural implements, &c, which would be more useful and far better for them than money," and he urged that the Indians be encouraged "to resort to agricultural pursuits in order that they may be prepared to sustain themselves when the buffalo shall have so far disappeared as no longer to afford them a certain or adequate means of subsistence." The Indians, too, should be bound to remain in the districts claimed by each of their tribes. To accomplish all this a treaty of friendship with the tribes seemed necessary. In February 1851 Congress appropriated $100,000 "for expenses of holding treaties with the wild tribes of the prairie, and for bringing delegates to the seat of government."[4]

Building on Medill's plan, the new commissioner of Indian affairs,

3. See the statement of William Medill in CIA AR, 1848, serial 537, p. 390. Similar statements appear in the commissioners' reports for 1849, 1850, and 1851.

4. Medill to Thomas Ewing, June 15, 1849, Records of the Office of Indian Affairs, National Archives Record Group 75, Report Books, 6:193–95 (M348, roll 6); 9 Stat. 572.

Orlando Brown, sent instructions to Thomas Fitzpatrick, agent of the Upper Platte Agency and long-time trader, guide, and friend of the Indians. Together with David D. Mitchell, superintendent of Indian affairs at St. Louis, Fitzpatrick was directed to assemble the Indians and negotiate a treaty with them. As a further step, "to impress the Indians of the Prairies with some just idea of our greatness and power, and to inspire them with a proper degree of respect for the government," Brown instructed him to bring a delegation of chiefs to Washington.[5]

Out of all of this came the Treaty of Fort Laramie of 1851, drawn up at one of the most dramatic of all Indian councils. Fitzpatrick and Mitchell sent out runners to call the Indians to the council, and large delegations arrived—Sioux, Cheyennes, Arapahos, Crows, Assiniboins, Gros Ventres, Mandans, and Arikaras—some ten thousand Indians in all, who finally encamped along the Platte at Horse Creek, thirty-six miles downriver from Fort Laramie, where there was space and forage for the large assembly. Because there had been a long history of bitter hostility between some of the tribes present, there was question whether the small United States military force of some two hundred troops could maintain peace, but the Indians behaved in an orderly fashion throughout the council. The assembly of Americans was impressive, too. The army officers included Colonel Samuel Cooper, adjutant general of the army, and the secretary of the council was A. B. Chambers, editor of the *Missouri Republican*, who was assisted by B. Gratz Brown (a young lawyer who later became governor of Missouri and then vice-presidential candidate in 1872). Father Pierre-Jean De Smet, the famous Jesuit missionary (highly respected by the Indians), was on hand. In the slowly paced and formal council proceedings, Superintendent Mitchell outlined the proposals of the United States, his remarks were translated by the interpreters for the various tribes, and after counselling among themselves, the Indians replied. Despite the resistance of the Sioux, who lived in bands, each with its own chief or chiefs, Mitchell insisted on appointing a single chief over all the Sioux. Finally, on September 17 the treaty was signed, and then on September 20, the long-awaited supply train with goods for the Indians arrived. With the distribution of goods the next day, the council dispersed.[6]

5. Brown to Fitzpatrick, August 16, 1849, OIA LS, 42:294–96 (M21, roll 42).
6. There is an excellent account of the drama of the event in LeRoy R. Hafen, *Broken Hand: The Life of Thomas Fitzpatrick, Mountain Man, Guide, and Indian Agent*, rev. ed. (Denver: Old West Publishing Company, 1973), 281–301. A description of the council by A. B. Chambers is in the *Missouri Republican*, October 6, 17, 22–24, 26, 29, and

The treaty document was brief. The Indians agreed to cease hostilities among themselves and to make a lasting peace, and to that end the treaty spelled out in detail the boundaries of each of the tribes. The Indians recognized the right of the United States to establish roads and military posts in their territories, and they promised to make restitution for wrongs committed against whites lawfully passing through their lands. In return the United States agreed to protect the Indians from white depredations and to pay annuities of $50,000 a year for fifty years—the annuities to be paid in "provisions, merchandise, domestic animals, and agricultural implements, in such proportions as may be deemed best adapted to their condition by the President of the United States."[7]

Superintendent Mitchell reported optimistically on the treaty, noting that the presents distributed at the council satisfied the Indians for all past destruction of buffalo, grass, and timber by the emigrating whites. He felt a need, however, to justify the large annuity. "Fifty thousand dollars for a limited period of years is a small amount to be distributed among at least fifty thousand Indians," he wrote to the commissioner of Indian affairs, "especially when we consider that we have taken, or are rapidly taking away from them all means of support, by what may be considered a partial occupancy of their soil. On the score of economy, to say nothing of justice or humanity, I believe that amount would be well expended." Mitchell saw no alternative to providing means for the Indians to turn to agriculture and grazing, and he thought that fifty years would be enough time "to give the experiment a fair trial, and solve the great problem whether or not an Indian can be made a civilized man."[8]

President Millard Fillmore submitted the treaty to the Senate on February 17, 1852, and the Senate Committee on Indian Affairs re-

November 2, 9, 23, 30, 1851, typed transcript furnished by Raymond DeMallie. There is a perceptive account of the ritual aspects of the council proceedings in Raymond J. DeMallie, "Touching the Pen: Plains Indian Treaty Councils in Ethnohistorical Perspective," in Frederick C. Luebke, ed., *Ethnicity on the Great Plains* (Lincoln: University of Nebraska Press, 1980), 41–46. See also the accounts of the council, based largely on the *Missouri Republican* articles, in LeRoy R. Hafen and Francis Marion Young, *Fort Laramie and the Pageant of the West, 1834–1890* (Glendale, Calif.: Arthur H. Clark Company, 1938), 177–96, and Burton S. Hill, "The Great Indian Treaty Council of 1851," *Nebraska History* 47 (March 1966): 85–110.

7. Kappler, 2:594–96.

8. Mitchell to Luke Lea, November 11, 1851, CIA AR, 1851, serial 613, pp. 289–90.

ported it without amendment on April 19. But when the Senate next considered the treaty on May 24, it amended the treaty and began the process that eventually seriously clouded the status of the document. It first unanimously struck out the provision of paying the annuity for fifty years and then attempted to set a different duration. It voted down motions to substitute twenty-five years or twenty years and finally agreed on "the term of ten years with the right to continue the same at the discretion of the President of the United States for a period not exceeding five years thereafter." So amended, the treaty was approved by a vote of forty-four to seven.[9] The Senate, clearly, was not convinced by Mitchell's arguments. No doubt it felt that $2.5 million over fifty years was too much for a treaty in which no land cessions were made, and the new policy of strictly limiting the duration of annuities ran counter to a term as long as fifty years. It was hoped the civilizing provisions would have taken effect sooner than that.[10]

Following the Treaty of Fort Laramie, Agent Fitzpatrick accompanied a delegation of chiefs to see Washington and the well-developed eastern sections of the nation. The Indians were feted at St. Louis and at other places along their route, and in January 1852 they had a formal meeting with President Fillmore in one of the parlors of the White House.[11]

The next year, Fitzpatrick by himself negotiated a treaty at Fort Atkinson on the Arkansas River in Kansas with the Comanche, Kiowa, and Apache Indians living south of the Arkansas River. With considerable difficulty, he established communication with the Indians and at the end of July 1853 signed a treaty with them similar to that of Fort Laramie two years before. An annuity of $18,000 worth of goods for ten years, subject to a five-year extension, was provided. A final article stipulated that if the United States decided it would be wise to establish farms among the Indians for their benefit, the annuities could be changed into a fund for that purpose. The Indians were hesitant to allow routes and military posts within their country, and Fitzpatrick felt that the concessions finally made were "extremely fortunate," for they could obviate the need for new treaty arrangements when transportation routes through the Indian lands needed to be developed.[12]

9. *Senate Ex. Proc.*, 8:368–69, 382, 388–90.

10. For a discussion of the problems in the ratification of the treaty, see pp. 440–42 below.

11. See the account in Hafen, *Broken Hand*, 302–7.

12. Kappler, 2:600–602; Fitzpatrick to A. Cumming, November 19, 1853, CIA AR, 1853, serial 690, pp. 362–63.

The Manypenny Treaties

There still remained a need to politically organize the central plains (as a necessary condition for a central route for a Pacific railroad, the dream of promoters like Senator Stephen A. Douglas) and to provide lands for white settlers already pressing upon the eastern boundary of the Indian country beyond Missouri and Iowa. The Kansas-Nebraska Act of May 30, 1854, which set up two territorial governments (vainly hoping to ease the growing North-South conflict), however, did not of itself free the lands in those new territories of their Indian title.

That difficult task fell to Commissioner of Indian Affairs Manypenny, a man who believed that for the Indians' own sake the western territories should be organized and the Indians moved out of the way of white emigrants. Under a congressional authorization of March 3, 1853, which provided for negotiations with Indian tribes west of Missouri and Iowa, Manypenny moved ahead energetically to fit the border tribes into "the new order of things." He visited them, held councils with them, and tried to get them to agree to cede their lands and move to the southern or northern colonies, but the Indians would have none of such absolute removal. All they would grant was cession of some of their lands if they were allowed to keep small reserves in the areas where they were then situated. In a series of nine treaties made with the Indian chiefs in Washington between March 15 and July 5, 1854, Manypenny got what he could from the Otos and Missouris, Omahas, Delawares, Shawnees, Peorias, Piankashaws, Weas, and Miamis. These tribes held some fifteen million acres, all of which were ceded except for 1,342,000 acres retained as reduced reservations.[13]

The treaties were much alike, and the Oto and Missouri treaty of March 5 is a good example.[14] It provided for the cession of the tribes' holdings west of the Missouri River and designated a reduced area within the old reservation to which the Indians agreed to remove within a year. A significant characteristic of this treaty, as of all these treaties,

13. CIA AR, 1853, serial 690, p. 251; 10 Stat. 238; CIA AR, 1854, serial 746, pp. 213–14; Royce, *Cessions*, plate 41, area numbers 314–15; plate 27, area numbers 316–18, 324–30. For data on these treaties, see appendix B, nos. 257–60, 262–66.
14. Kappler, 2:608–11.

was the provision for allotting lands in the newly designated reserve in farm-sized plots to individual Indians. The president was given discretionary authority to survey the land, set it off in lots, and assign the lots in specified amounts (for example, a quarter section to a family of two, and eighty acres to a single adult) to all Indians who were "willing to avail of the privilege" and would locate on the lots as a permanent home. There were to be regulations for bequeathing the land and restrictions on its lease or sale. If the Indians left the land to "rove from place to place," their patents would be revoked and their annuities withheld until they returned and "resumed the pursuits of industry." Any residue of land after all the Indians had received an allotment was to be sold for the benefit of the Indians.

In return, the United States agreed to pay the Otos and Missouris annuities on a sliding scale from $5,000 to $20,000 over the next thirty-eight years. The president would decide what proportion, if any, was to be paid in money and what proportion expended for education and other means of acculturation. Another $20,000 was granted to help the Indians to move, subsist for a year, and establish themselves on their farms. Moreover, the government would build a grist and saw mill and a blacksmith shop and for ten years would employ a miller, a blacksmith, and a farmer. Annuities would be withheld from anyone who drank liquor or brought it into the Indian lands. Thus were these Indians, who had been subjected to the civilizing policies of the government for a number of decades, to be finally incorporated into white society. The continued Indian residence in Kansas and Nebraska, however, was not intended to impede the westward movement of the whites, for the Indians agreed to allow "all the necessary roads and highways, and railroads, which may be constructed as the country improves" to run through their lands, with just compensation to be paid in money.[15]

The policy of allotments followed in these treaties did not work out well, for aggressive settlers and speculators desired the choice lands still in the hands of the Indians and paid little attention to Indian rights. The decade of sectional conflict in Bleeding Kansas further aggravated the situation of the hapless Indians, and the federal government failed to protect them.[16]

15. Clauses in the various treaties pertained to the special conditions of each tribe; the treaties with the Delawares and the Shawnees were the most complex. Most of the treaties made land grants to missionary societies that maintained schools for the Indians. These treaties were approved by large majorities in the Senate. See *Senate Ex. Proc.*, vol. 9.

16. See Manypenny's complaints about the mistreatment of the Indians in CIA AR, 1856, serial 875, p. 572. A detailed and critical account of the conflicts over Indian lands

The California Indians

For the numerous small bands of Indians in California, the treaty system failed altogether, showing both the difficult problems that faced the treaty commissioners and the inability of the federal government to substitute any effective alternative policy to provide protection for the Indians from the onrush of miners and agricultural settlers.[17] Federal officials were especially ignorant concerning the California Indians, and the three men sent to California in 1850 to negotiate treaties with the Indians shared their ignorance. As a group, the commissioners signed a treaty in March 19, 1851, with Indians whom they took to be leaders of six tribes in the San Joaquin Valley, and on April 29 they made another treaty with sixteen more tribes. Later, in order to speed the work, the commissioners split up, each moving to a designated region to continue the treaty making. By January 7, 1852, the commissioners and the Indians had signed eighteen treaties.[18]

in Kansas after 1854 is in Paul Wallace Gates, *Fifty Million Acres: Conflicts over Kansas Land Policy, 1854–1890* (Ithaca: Cornell University Press, 1954). What happened to the Indian reserves in Kansas is described in H. Craig Miner and William E. Unrau, *The End of Indian Kansas: A Study of Cultural Revolution, 1854–1871* (Lawrence: Regents Press of Kansas, 1978). For the complicated story of the indefinite land grants (confirmed by an 1855 treaty) made to certain Wyandot Indians when they moved from Ohio, see Homer E. Socolofsky, "Wyandot Floats," *Kansas Historical Quarterly* 36 (Autumn 1970): 241–304. The pertinent Wyandot treaties are in Kappler, 2:677–81, 960, 963.

17. Indian policy in California has been well documented in two older works: William H. Ellison, "The Federal Indian Policy in California, 1846–1860," *Mississippi Valley Historical Review* 9 (June 1922): 37–67, and Alban W. Hoopes, *Indian Affairs and Their Administration: With Special Reference to the Far West, 1849–1860* (Philadelphia: University of Pennsylvania Press, 1932), 35–68. The story is told again in George E. Anderson and Robert F. Heizer, "Treaty-making by the Federal Government in California 1851–1852," in George E. Anderson, W. H. Ellison, and Robert F. Heizer, *Treaty Making and Treaty Rejection by the Federal Government in California, 1850–1852* (Socorro, N. Mex.: Ballena Press, 1978), 1–36.

18. The instructions of A. S. Loughery to Redick McKee, George W. Barbour, and O. M. Wozencraft, October 15, 1850, are in *Senate Ex. Doc.* no. 4, 33-special session, serial 688, pp. 8–9. The various reports of the three commissioners and journals of their activity appear in the same Senate document. See also Alban W. Hoopes, ed., "The Journal of George W. Barbour, May 1 to October 4, 1851," *Southwestern Historical Quarterly* 40 (October 1936): 145–53, and 40 (January 1937): 247–61; and Chad L. Hoopes, "Redick McKee and the Humboldt Bay Region, 1851–1852," *California Historical Society Quarterly* 49 (September 1970): 195–219. The treaties are printed in Kappler, 4:1081–1128. A

In the treaties the Indians recognized the United States as sole sovereign over the land ceded by Mexico in 1848, placed themselves under the protection of the United States, and agreed to keep peace. They ceded their claims in return for definite reservations specified for them. Subsistence in the form of beef cattle was to be provided while they were moving and settling on the reservations, and the government promised to pay annuities in the form of clothing, agricultural implements, and livestock and to provide farmers, blacksmiths, and school teachers for a period of years. The eighteen treaties set aside 11,700 square miles (7,488,000 acres) of land, about 7.5 percent of the state.[19]

The three commissioners did their work rapidly, and they acted without the detailed knowledge of the Indians that modern anthropologists can provide. Although 139 tribes or bands were represented in the eighteen treaties, an enumeration in 1926 indicated that more than 175 tribes were not included in the treaties. Thirty years later, a study conducted under Indian Claims Commission litigation reported that of the 139 signatory groups, 67 were identifiable as tribelets, 45 were merely village names, 14 were duplicates spelled differently without the commissioners realizing it, and 13 were either personal names or unidentifiable.[20]

In the end the irregularities did not matter, for the Senate, without considering any amendments, on July 8, 1852, unanimously rejected each of the eighteen treaties.[21] There is some question whether, even at the beginning, a majority of the Senate had intended to authorize treaties of cession rather than mere treaties of peace and friendship, for there was considerable feeling in Congress that the California Indians had no land titles and therefore that no treaties were needed to extinguish them. Other aspects of the treaties, too, militated against their ratification. There was strong opposition from Californians, who saw large

---

copy of the Senate printing of the treaties, when it lifted the injunction of secrecy on them on January 18, 1905, is in Documents (T494), roll 8, frames 410–45.

19. The calculations on areas ceded are those of Ellison, "Federal Indian Policy in California," 57, and have been generally accepted. The map of California in Royce, *Cessions*, plate 7, purports to show the lands ceded (all of California west of the Sierra Nevada) and the reservations established, but the map is based on faulty information and assumptions. Robert F. Heizer, "Treaties," in *Handbook of North American Indians*, vol. 8, *California*, ed. Robert F. Heizer (Washington: Smithsonian Institution, 1978), 703–4.

20. Heizer, "Treaties," in *Handbook*, 8:703.

21. *Senate Ex. Proc.*, 8:390–94, 409–10, 417–20. The Senate resolutions are printed without comment in "The Rejected California Treaties," *Indian Historian* 6 (Winter 1973): 23–25, and in Kappler, 4:1081–85 note.

regions to be snatched from their grasp and reserved for the Indians, whom they despised. Furthermore, the costs of the treaties had grown to nearly $1 million, far beyond the total of $50,000 that had been appropriated. The commissioners, working on the spot, had felt it necessary to contract for large numbers of cattle to feed the Indians, and they also provided for further subsistence and annuities in the treaties. The new superintendent of Indian affairs in California, Edward F. Beale, argued strongly for the treaties, and Commissioner of Indian Affairs Luke Lea agreed. But Lea was aware of peculiar circumstances with regard to the treaties; he wrote to Secretary of the Interior Alexander H. H. Stuart in transmitting the documents:

> In considering this important and perplexing question, it should not be forgotten that our Indian affairs in California, like everything else pertaining to that country, are in an extraordinary and anomalous condition. Those entrusted with their management have had to contend with manifold embarrassments and difficulties. That they have made mistakes or fallen into error is by no means a matter of surprise. It would be strange if they had not. Their conduct in some respects has been improper. I allude particularly to their making contracts for fulfilling treaties in advance of their ratification. In this they certainly acted without authority.

Secretary Stuart wanted a special investigation made about the treaties, but he was afraid that delay would be dangerous and recommended to the president that they be submitted to the Senate for its decision.[22]

The federal government attempted then to make some provision for

---

22. Beale's report to Lea, May 11, 1852, Lea's report to Stuart, May 14, 1852, and Stuart to the president, May 22, 1852, are in Senate (RG 46), Sen 32B-C2; they are printed in a note in Kappler, 4:1085–89. The question of the nonratification by the Senate is thoroughly treated in Harry Kelsey, "The California Indian Treaty Myth," *Southern California Quarterly* 55 (Fall 1973): 225–38. Kelsey considers and rejects the idea that there was a conspiracy by the Senate to keep information about the treaties secret and argues for the importance of the question of Indian land titles in the rejection of the treaties. A strong statement about California opposition to the treaties is William H. Ellison, "Rejection of California Indian Treaties: A Study in Local Influence on National Policy," *Grizzly Bear* 37 (May 1925): 4–5, 86; 37 (June 1925): 4–5, supplement 7; 37 (July 1925): 6–7, reprinted in Anderson, Ellison, and Heizer, *Treaty Making and Treaty Rejection*, 50–70. A good view of California sentiment against the treaties is provided in "Majority and Minority Reports of the Special Committee [of the California State Senate] to Inquire into the Treaties Made by the United States Commissioners with the Indians of California," and "Senate Committee Debate on Appropriation of Funds for Aid to Indians of California Provided by the Three Treaty Commissioners," printed ibid., 37–49, 71–122.

the California bands outside the treaty system, and a number of small reservations were established, but the Indians had no clear title to the land, were beset by aggressive white land seekers, and lived on a kind of government dole on the few spots saved for them. Whatever the difficulties, the United States clearly decided to forego any more treaties with these rapidly disappearing Indians. In 1864, when a purported treaty of peace and friendship between the United States and the Indians of Hoopa Valley was sent to Washington by the Indian agent Austin Wiley, the commissioner of Indian affairs replied that the government did not contemplate any more formal treaties with the California tribes. If any agreements were made with the Indians, the papers should simply be signed by the chiefs to show their commitment and then forwarded to the Indian Office.[23]

Treaties in the Oregon Country

In the Oregon Country early attempts at treaties were hardly more successful than those in California. The Territory of Oregon was not created until 1848, two years after United States title to the region south of the forty-ninth parallel was recognized by Great Britain. The territorial governor was eager to remove the Indians from the areas of settlement, and the territorial delegate in Congress pushed through a law in 1850 that called for the appointment of commissioners to negotiate treaties with the Indians of Oregon for that purpose. The law also authorized a superintendent of Indian affairs distinct from the governor, a position to which Anson Dart of Wisconsin was appointed.[24]

On October 25, 1850, three commissioners, including the new territorial governor, were appointed to negotiate treaties with the Indian tribes in Oregon Territory. The goal of the government, they were told, was to free the land west of the Cascades entirely of Indian title and to move all the Indians to some spot to the east. Their instructions made it clear that the payments stipulated for the ceded lands were to be in objects beneficial to the Indians—agricultural assistance, blacksmiths and mechanics, farmers to teach cultivation, physicians, and "ample

---

23. William P. Dole to Wiley, October 3, 1864, CIA AR, 1864, serial 1220, p. 282.
24. 9 Stat. 437; Lea to Dart, July 20, 1850, CIA AR, 1850, serial 587, pp. 148–51.

provision for the purposes of education"—and that no part should be paid in money.[25]

The Indians, however, were adamant in refusing to accept removal from their homelands, and the commissioners were forced to outline an alternative:

> It will be impossible to remove the Indians of Willamette and lower Columbia valleys, without a resort to force, nor do we think it very desirable to do so. As before stated they are friendly and well disposed, they live almost entirely by fishing, and the wages they receive from the whites for their labor. They possess little or no skill as hunters or warriors. And to remove them from their fisheries and means of procuring labor from the whites would in our opinion insure their annihilation in a short time either from want or by the hands of their more warlike neighbors. General satisfaction we believe would be felt by the Indians and the citizens to allow them small reservations of a few sections and a portion of their fishing grounds.[26]

This is what the commissioners provided in the six treaties they signed with the Indians in April and May 1851. Then, when Congress directed that all treaty making be carried on by regular officers of the Indian department, not by special commissioners, Dart continued the negotiations by himself. During the summer and fall of 1851 he signed thirteen treaties with Indian bands.[27]

None of the nineteen treaties signed by the commissioners and by Dart were ever ratified. When President Fillmore submitted the treaties to the Senate on July 31, 1852, he transmitted as well a letter from Secretary of the Interior Stuart, in which Stuart noted the objection of the commissioner of Indian affairs to the provisions that allowed reservations near the white settlers. But Stuart wrote, "I have carefully examined the correspondence of the commissioners, & the treaties, &

25. A. S. Loughery to J. P. Gaines, Alonzo H. Skinner, and Beverly S. Allen, October 25, 1850, ibid., 145–47.

26. Commissioners to Luke Lea, February 8, 1851, quoted in Hoopes, *Indian Affairs and Their Administration*, 78–79. The commissioners made the same point when they submitted the treaties containing provisions for reserved lands, contrary to the directions they had received. See commissioners to Lea, April 19 and May 14, 1851, CIA AR, 1851, pp. 467–72.

27. The treaty making is discussed in detail in C. F. Coan, "The First Stage of the Federal Indian Policy in the Pacific Northwest, 1849–1852," *Oregon Historical Society Quarterly* 22 (March 1921): 46–65. In an appendix, pp. 65–89, Coan reprints the report of Dart to Lea, November 7, 1851, transmitting the treaties; also reprinted there are the few treaties that are extant. Some of these treaties appear in Documents (T494), roll 8.

have come to the conclusion that if some of their provisions are objectionable, they are greatly over-balanced by the positive benefits to be derived from others. By these treaties the Indian title to a very large and valuable territory is extinguished on terms beneficial to the Indians & advantageous to the United States." Moreover, he argued, the Indians would not sign a treaty that demanded their removal to another area.[28]

The treaties were reported by the Senate Committee on Indian Affairs without amendment on August 31 and then were simply tabled, never to be considered again.[29] The failure to eliminate the Indians completely from west of the Cascades by providing residual reservations for the tribes, of course, played an important part, for in this sense the treaties failed to accomplish what the congressional directive had stipulated. Some of the treaties, too, were negotiated with mere remnants of once more populous tribes. The Wheelappa Band of Chinooks, with whom Dart signed a treaty on August 9, 1851, for example, had only two male survivors and a few women and children. And the cost of the annuities may have been another point of objection.[30] But without treaties, there was no firm settlement of the Indian problems facing the government in Oregon; meanwhile, increasing numbers of whites moved into the territory, seeking the rich lands.

In the summer of 1853, Joel Palmer, an Oregon pioneer, replaced Dart as superintendent of Indian affairs, and he initiated a new series of treaties. He began with a treaty of cession with Rogue River Indians at Table Rock on September 10, 1853, which was ratified on April 12, 1854.[31] With this success behind him, Palmer proceeded to negotiate a series of treaties between September 19, 1853, and December 21, 1855, with other tribes along the coast and with tribes in central Oregon that eliminated Indian title over much of the area between the Cascades and the coast, as well as a sizable section of the interior.[32]

28. Stuart to the president, July 30, 1852, Senate (RG 46), Sen 32B-C4.

29. *Senate Ex. Proc.*, 8:430–32, 452.

30. Coan, "First Stage," 59, 65.

31. Kappler, 2:603–5; *Senate Ex. Proc.*, 9:236, 287–88. The Indians agreed to a Senate amendment on November 11, 1854. Palmer had not been instructed by the Indian Office to negotiate treaties, but the commissioner of Indian affairs, nevertheless, approved the treaty, and President Franklin Pierce submitted it to the Senate. See Charles E. Mix to R. McClelland, January 24, 1854, in Senate (RG 46), Sen 33B-C4.

32. See treaties nos. 255–56, 270–72, 275, 286, and 293 in appendix B. The areas ceded are shown in Royce, *Cessions*, plates 8 and 51, area nos. 312, 313, 343, 344, 352, 369, 401. C. F. Coan, "The Adoption of the Reservation Policy in the Pacific Northwest, 1853–1855," *Oregon Historical Society Quarterly* 23 (March 1922): 2–27, deals with the treaty making in Oregon and Washington. See also Terence O'Donnell, *An Arrow in the*

The Palmer treaties fitted well into the pattern established in the 1850s. There was little indication in them that two sovereign equals were negotiating. For lack of other acceptable and established procedures, the treaties were the vehicle chosen to accomplish what the United States government wanted as it reacted to cries from western settlers and to the philosophical principles dominant in government circles. The Indians were to be moved out of the way of the whites, not, as in the case of the removal of the eastern tribes, to open spaces in the west, but to limited reserves within their old, more extensive territorial claims or to other specified locations within the territory. Most of the treaties were made with "confederated tribes and bands," an often more or less arbitrary grouping for convenience. In all of them the chiefs and headmen of these bands acknowledged their dependence on the United States and promised to stay on friendly terms with the citizens, sometimes consenting "to submit to, and observe all laws, rules, and regulations which may be prescribed by the United States for the government of said Indians." They agreed, moreover, to grant rights of way through their lands for roads and railroads. All claims of the Indians to lands were given up in return for small reservations within their old limits, but most of the Palmer treaties included a blanket agreement to move from these reserves to other locations selected by the government "should the President at any time believe it demanded by the public good and promotive of the best interests of said Indians."

All the treaties spoke specifically of "civilization" and had the usual provisions for annuity payments in goods conducive to that end, for land in severalty for those Indians "willing to avail themselves of the privilege and who will locate thereon as a permanent home," and for blacksmith shops, hospitals, schools, and prohibition of liquor. Although government officials no doubt rejoiced in the framework of existence for the Indians envisaged in the treaties, the negotiations were in fact a nearly complete capitulation of the tribes to superior power.

The treaties signed by Palmer with the Indians in 1853, 1854, and early 1855 were ratified and proclaimed in good time. When war broke out in 1855, ratification of the later treaties was delayed. President Pierce submitted them to the Senate on August 9, 1856, where they were referred to the Committee on Indian Affairs. On January 12, 1858,

Earth: General Joel Palmer and the Indians of Oregon (Portland: Oregon Historical Society Press, 1991).

the new Congress reassigned them to the committee, and in early June the committee reported them without amendment, but not until March 8, 1859, did the Senate finally approve them, by a vote of thirty-nine to eight.[33] The delay caused incalculable problems in dealing with the Indians, who did not understand why the benefits promised them in the treaties were not forthcoming.

Treaties Negotiated by Governor Stevens

The treaties in newly created Washington Territory, which was broken off from Oregon Territory in 1853, were the work of Isaac Ingalls Stevens, the first territorial governor.[34] Stevens, a bright young West Point graduate with service in the Mexican War, was placed in charge of the party surveying the northern route for a Pacific railroad, and when he arrived in Washington Territory he quickly wrote to the commissioner of Indian affairs of the "urgent necessity" to sign treaties with the Indians west of the Cascades. He was astute enough to realize, however, that it would be impossible to remove the Indians completely because of their attachment to their homelands and their reliance on fishing as a livelihood, so he intended to provide small reserves for them in their present locations. He was interested as well in the eastern tribes of his large territory, and on a trip to Washington, D.C., in 1854, he pushed the idea of treaties with both groups. Congress appropriated $45,000 for negotiating treaties with the Indians of Washington Territory and another $80,000 for a council with "the Blackfeet, Gros Ven-

33. *Senate Ex. Proc.*, 9:287–89, 436–37, 442–43; 10:132, 135–36, 287, 438–39; 11:83, 87–88.

34. A scholarly biography of Stevens that pays close attention to his handling of Indian affairs is Kent D. Richards, *Isaac I. Stevens: Young Man in a Hurry* (Provo, Utah: Brigham Young University Press, 1979). Hazard Stevens, *The Life of Isaac Ingalls Stevens*, 2 vols. (Boston: Houghton, Mifflin and Company, 1900), is by his son and must be used with caution because of its favorable bias, but it contains detailed accounts of the Indian councils. There are accounts of Stevens's treaties in Clifford E. Trafzer, ed., *Indians, Superintendents, and Councils: Northwestern Indian Policy, 1850–1855* (Lanham, Md.: University Press of America, 1986); the chapters, written by different individuals, are in general very critical of Stevens.

tres, and other wild tribes of Indians immediately within or adjacent to the eastern boundary of Washington Territory."[35]

In preparation for treating with the Puget Sound Indians, Stevens organized a commission, which met first on December 7, 1854. The application of a pattern common to the whole nation can be seen in the report of the meeting, for the commission read and discussed the recent treaties that Commissioner Manypenny had signed with the Otos and Missouris and with the Omahas. After considerable discussion of reservations, fishing stations, schools, and farms, George Gibbs, a talented Harvard graduate who was a member of the group, was delegated to prepare a "programme of a Treaty" in accordance with the views of the commission.[36]

When the commission met again three days later, a draft of a treaty was ready. Thus prepared, Stevens and his assistants met on Christmas Day with a number of tribes at Medicine Creek at the mouth of the Nisqually River. This was not to be a "negotiation" but an imposition on the Indians of the treaty provisions Stevens brought with him, for he was highly paternalistic. He spoke to the assembled Indians in a flowery and patronizing manner that expressed his view of relations between the government and the tribes.

> This is a great day for you and for us. A day of Peace and Friendship between you and the Whites for all time to come. You are about to be paid for your lands, and the Great Father has sent me to-day to treat with you concerning the payment. The Great Father lives far off. He has many children: some of them came here when he knew but little of them or the Indians, and he has sent me to inquire into these things. We went through the Country last year, learned your numbers and saw your wants. We felt much for you and went to the Great Father to tell him what we had seen. The Great Father felt for his children—he pitied them, and he has sent me here to-day to express those feelings, and to make a Treaty for your benefit.[37]

The prepared treaty was explained to the Indians point by point through an interpreter who used the Chinook Jargon, which was then

35. Stevens to George W. Manypenny, December 26 and December 29, 1853, *Senate Ex. Doc.* no. 34, 33-1, serial 698, pp. 6–7, 13–14; Manypenny to Robert McClelland, February 6, 1854, ibid., 1–4; 10 Stat. 330. A valuable study on the treaties with the Puget Sound Indians is Barbara Lane, "Background of Treaty Making in Western Washington," *American Indian Journal* 3 (April 1977): 2–11.

36. Documents (T494), roll 5, frames 205–6.

37. Ibid., frames 206–10.

translated for the Indians in their own language. And without objections the Indians signed the treaty on December 26. The provisions were very much like those made by Palmer with the Oregon Indians, but in addition the following special stipulations were made to protect fishing and gathering rights: "The right of taking fish, at all usual and accustomed grounds and stations, is further secured to said Indians in common with all citizens of the Territory, and of erecting temporary houses for the purpose of curing, together with the privilege of hunting, gathering roots and berries, and pasturing their horses on open and unclaimed lands." Beyond the graduated annuity payments and payments of removal costs, the United States agreed to maintain for twenty years an agricultural and industrial school for the children of the signatory bands and for those of other tribes and bands, at a general agency to be set up for the Puget Sound region. One article of the treaty authorized the president to move the Indians to other reserves or to consolidate them with other friendly tribes into a single reserve and to provide for homesteading on individual lots within the reservation limits.[38]

Stevens sent the treaty to the commissioner of Indian affairs at the end of the month, noting that he was "highly gratified at the result, as in the first instance they [the Indians] desired more reserves and larger reserves." The reserves that were set up had been selected so as not to interfere with existing white claims or the progress of settlement, yet to enable the Indians to continue their traditional subsistence patterns. The provision for later consolidation, Stevens said, would obviate any objection to the number of reserves he had created. The treaty was ratified by unanimous vote of the Senate on March 3, 1855.[39]

Stevens then proceeded quickly to sign similar treaties with other bands in the Puget Sound area: at Point Elliott on January 22, 1855, at Point No Point on January 26, and at Neah Bay on January 31.[40] The governor delivered his prepared message to the Indians, and the chiefs replied, sometimes with strong objections to giving up their lands. But what resistance there was quickly disappeared, and Stevens's paternalism was evident throughout. He told the Indians at Point No Point:

38. Kappler, 2:661–64.

39. Stevens to Manypenny, December 30, 1854, Documents (T494), roll 5, frames 193–200; *Senate Ex. Proc.*, 9:415, 416, 436.

40. Kappler, 2:669–77, 682–85. Extracts from the proceedings at Point No Point are printed in Charles M. Gates, ed., "The Indian Treaty of Point No Point," *Pacific Northwest Quarterly* 46 (April 1955): 52–58.

This paper [the treaty] is such as a man would give to his children and I will tell you why. This paper gives you a home. Does not a father give his children a home? This paper gives you a school. Does not a father send his children to school? It gives you Mechanics and a Doctor to teach and cure you. Is not that fatherly? This paper secures your fish. Does not a father give food to his children? Besides fish you can hunt, gather roots and berries. Besides it says you shall not drink whiskey, and does not a father prevent his children from drinking the *"fire" water*? Besides all this, the paper says you shall be paid for your lands as has been explained to you.[41]

These treaties, with that of Medicine Creek, cleared a wide area of land around Puget Sound.[42] But the treaties after Medicine Creek, unfortunately, got caught in the ratification delays that affected the later treaties of Palmer with the Oregon bands, and they were not approved by the Senate until March 1859.[43]

In the summer and fall of 1855 Stevens held three great councils with the Indians of the interior. The first was at Walla Walla in late May and early June, attended by Joel Palmer as well as Stevens and made up of delegations of Walla Walla, Cayuse, Umatilla, Yakima, and Nez Perce Indians. The Indians, aside from the generally friendly Nez Perces, were hostile, and concessions, including special cash annuities for the chiefs, had to be made to get signatures on the treaties. Two treaties were signed on June 9, one with the Walla Wallas, Cayuses, and Umatillas and a second with the Yakimas. Another on June 11 was signed with the Nez Perces. They contained the usual provisions for cessions, reservations, annuity payments, employment of mechanics, articles for agricultural development, and means for moral improvement and education.[44] But the treaties were not the successes that Stevens assumed, for the chiefs were offended by the terms that the whites proposed and could see their crushing effect. The Jesuit missionary Joseph Joset commented: "The chiefs agreed to a mock treaty in order to gain time and prepare for war."[45]

41. Documents (T494), roll 5, frame 294.

42. The ceded land and the reservations are shown in Royce *Cessions*, plates 60 and 63, area nos. 345–56.

43. *Senate Ex. Proc.*, 11:84–85.

44. Kappler, 2:694–706. There is an excellent account of the council and its background in Alvin M. Josephy, Jr., *The Nez Perce Indians and the Opening of the Northwest* (New Haven: Yale University Press, 1965), 285–332; a shortened version is Josephy, "A Most Satisfactory Council," *American Heritage* 16 (October 1965): 26–31, 70–76.

45. Quoted in Robert Ignatius Burns, *The Jesuits and the Indian Wars of the Northwest*

While Palmer went down the Columbia to The Dalles for a treaty with the Indians of that area, Stevens in mid-July moved on to Hell Gate on the Clark Fork just beyond the northern end of the Bitterroot Valley in what is now western Montana for a council with the Flathead, Kutenai, and Pend d'Oreille Indians. Here, too, there was much agitation among the Indians as they argued about a proper location for the reduced reservation the government expected them to accept. The deep Indian attachment to traditional homelands was not appreciated by the whites, who looked chiefly at the economic potentialities of a reservation for sustaining the Indians in a peaceful agricultural existence. The Indians signed the treaty on July 16, 1855, with the understanding that the president would survey the region and designate an acceptable spot.[46]

The final grand council was held in October with the Blackfeet, Flatheads, and Nez Perces at the mouth of the Judith River in present-day Montana. It fulfilled a need, observed by Stevens when he crossed the continent with the railroad survey expedition in 1853, for a treaty of peace between the often warring tribes of the northern Rockies, and the $80,000 appropriated by Congress in 1854 had been for this purpose. Joel Palmer and Alfred Cumming, superintendent of the Central Superintendency, were named with Stevens as commissioners for the treaty. After some false starts occasioned by a delay in the arrival of goods to be distributed as presents, the council was opened on October 16 by Stevens and Cumming with 3,500 Indians in attendance; Joel Palmer did not come. The treaty, signed the next day, began with a formal statement of perpetual peace between the United States and the Indians, and the signatory tribes agreed to maintain peaceful rela-

---

(New Haven: Yale University Press, 1966), 79. Hazard Stevens drew the same conclusion, asserting that with one exception the chiefs "all signed the treaties as a deliberate act of treachery, in order to lull the whites into fancied security, give time for Governor Stevens to depart to the distant Blackfoot country, where he would probably be 'wiped out' by those truculent savages, and for the Nez Perces to return home, and also for completing their preparations for a widespread and simultaneous onslaught on all settlements." *Isaac Ingalls Stevens*, 2:61.

46. Kappler, 2:722–25. Palmer's treaty of June 25 appears ibid., 714–19. A thorough critical account of the Hell Gate council is in Burns, *Jesuits and the Indian Wars*, 96–114. An incomplete version of the official minutes is in Albert J. Partoll, ed., "The Flathead Indian Treaty Council of 1855," *Pacific Northwest Quarterly* 29 (July 1938): 283–314. See also Burns, "A Jesuit at the Hell Gate Treaty of 1855," *Mid-America* 34 (April 1952): 87–114.

tions among themselves and with other tribes. Boundaries were specified for common hunting grounds for the Indians for a period of ninety-nine years, and the lands belonging exclusively to the Blackfeet were described. The United States agreed to provide the Blackfeet with certain annuities and to instruct them in agricultural and mechanical pursuits, to educate their children, and in other aspects to promote their "civilization and Christianization." This treaty was ratified by the Senate on April 15, 1856.[47]

The earlier treaties at Walla Walla and Hell Gate had to wait for ratification until March 1859, when they were handled with those signed with the western Washington tribes and Palmer's Oregon treaties. The delay in treaty ratification, which seriously complicated Indian relations, was due primarily to the wars that broke out in 1855, as increasing penetration of their country by whites stirred up both the Rogue River Indians in Oregon and the Yakimas and their allies in central Washington. This military action in Oregon and Washington decisively defeated the Indians, and the movement to the reservations and the change toward white ways of life that the treaties specified became the lot of the Indians in the Pacific Northwest.

Texas, New Mexico, and Utah

In the other areas of the new West—Texas, New Mexico, and Utah—treaty making was problematic, for the regular operation of the set principles in United States Indian policy was interrupted by special circumstances. In Texas, state autonomy, in New Mexico, the long tradition of Indian raiding into Mexican settlements, and in Utah, the overriding presence of the Mormons were significant obstacles.

With the annexation of Texas in 1845, the United States took on responsibility for Indian affairs, but Texas retained control of its public domain; the federal government had no lands from which to provide

47. Manypenny to Cumming, Stevens, and Palmer, May 3, 1855, CIA AR, 1855, serial 810, pp. 530–31; Kappler, 2:736–40; *Senate Ex. Proc.*, 10:75. For accounts of the council, see Burns, *Jesuits and the Indian Wars*, 117–23; John C. Ewers, *The Blackfeet: Raiders on the Northwestern Plains* (Norman: University of Oklahoma Press, 1958), 214–22; and Alfred J. Partoll, ed., "The Blackfoot Indian Peace Council," *Frontier and Midland: A Magazine of the West* 17 (Spring 1937): 199–207.

reservations for the Indians, and it was unable to extend over them the restrictions and protections of the trade and intercourse laws. The string of small military posts established in the new state did little to control the Indians. Then in September 1845, two peace commissioners, Pierce M. Butler and M. G. Lewis, were sent to conciliate the Indians. They called a council of the tribes in Texas for January 1846, but it was not until May that the Indians—Comanches, Anadarkos, Caddos, Lipan Apaches, and others—assembled at Council Springs on the Brazos River. By that time the war with Mexico had begun, and it was important for the United States to keep the restive Indians peaceful.[48] On May 15 the tribes signed a treaty that included the traditional provisions: the Indians acknowledged themselves to be under the exclusive protection of the United States and agreed to keep peace with the Americans and with other Indians; the United States assumed sole right to regulate trade and intercourse with the signatory tribes; the Indians agreed to give up all captives; punishment for crimes between Indians and whites was provided for (there was a separate article on horse stealing); the United States promised to erect trading houses and agencies on the border of the tribes; a special provision prohibited liquor traffic; and there was, finally, the usual stipulation, at the discretion of the president, for blacksmiths, schoolteachers, and "preachers of the gospel."[49]

Robert S. Neighbors, the agent appointed for Texas, called a great council of the tribes at the end of September 1847 to explain the treaty and to allay their fears, but the continued advance of surveyors and settlers caused new raids and hostility along the frontier. Eventually the state of Texas provided lands for the Indians. The two reservations that were set up in 1854–55, however, failed to provide a solution to the problems in Texas, and in 1859 the reservations were abandoned and the Indians moved north of the Red River into Indian Territory. All this was done without treaties.

In New Mexico the Pueblo Indians were considered to be "civilized Indians," living in organized communities and dependent upon agriculture for their subsistence. Aside from an uprising at Taos in January

48. Details of the negotiations are given in Butler and Lewis to William Medill, August 8, 1848, *Senate Report* no. 171, 30-1, serial 512, pp. 29–37. For the record kept by a Cherokee Indian who accompanied Butler and Lewis, see Grant Foreman, ed., "The Journal of Elijah Hicks," *Chronicles of Oklahoma* 13 (March 1935): 68–99.

49. Kappler, 2:554–57; Grant Foreman, "The Texas Comanche Treaty of 1846," *Southwestern Historical Quarterly* 51 (April 1948): 313–32. Senate amendments and ratification are in *Senate Ex. Proc.*, 7:194–95.

1847 that killed Charles Bent, the head of a provisional territorial government, the Indians were peaceful, and the United States never entered into treaty arrangements with them. Attention was turned instead to the Apaches and Navajos, whose warlike existence and continual raiding of Mexican settlements kept the area in turmoil.

The military governor of New Mexico appointed in October 1848, Lieutenant Colonel John M. Washington, intended to follow the conventional Indian policy of the day. "The period has arrived," he wrote to the War Department in February 1849, "when they [the Indians] must restrain themselves within prescribed limits and cultivate the earth for an honest livelyhood, or, be destroyed."[50] Together with James S. Calhoun, who had been appointed Indian agent early in 1849, Washington coerced one group of Navajos into a treaty on September 9, 1849, in which the chiefs agreed to recognize United States jurisdiction and to submit to the trade and intercourse laws, to return captives and stolen property and remain at peace, and to allow the federal government to determine their boundaries.[51] Before the end of the year, Calhoun had negotiated a similar treaty with the Utes, in which these Indians promised "to build up pueblos, or to settle in such other manner as will enable them most successfully to cultivate the soil, and pursue such other industrial pursuits as will best promote their happiness and prosperity," to cease their "roving and rambling habits," and to support themselves "by their own industry, aided and directed as it may be by the wisdom, justice, and humanity of the American people."[52] The treaties did not bring the peace they promised. Although Calhoun planned to end depredations by a display of military force and then to settle the various tribes on reservations separated from each other, hostilities continued.

On July 1, 1852, a treaty was negotiated with the Mescalero Apaches

50. Washington to Roger Jones, February 3, 1849, quoted in Robert A. Trennert, Jr., *Alternative to Extinction: Federal Indian Policy and the Beginnings of the Reservation System, 1846–51* (Philadelphia: Temple University Press, 1975), 113.

51. Kappler, 2:583–85. Documents regarding Washington's Navajo expedition are in *House Ex. Doc.* no. 5, 31-1, serial 569, pp. 104–15. Calhoun's early reports to the secretary of the interior and the commissioner of Indian affairs are in *House Ex. Doc.* no. 17, 31-1, serial 573, pp. 198–229. The standard work on Calhoun is Annie Heloise Abel, ed., *The Official Correspondence of James S. Calhoun While Indian Agent at Santa Fe and Superintendent of Indian Affairs in New Mexico* (Washington: GPO, 1915).

52. Kappler, 2:585–87. The two treaties were quickly ratified by heavy majorities in the Senate without amendment. *Senate Ex. Proc.*, 8:229–30.

by Colonel Edwin V. Sumner and Indian Agent John Greiner. The commissioner of Indian affairs and the secretary of the interior both admitted that the two men had never been "duly authorized to negotiate a treaty on the part of the United States," but they recommended the treaty's approval as sound policy, and the president and the Senate agreed. The treaty provisions followed those of the earlier treaties with the Navajos and with the Utes.[53] However inappropriate such an idealistic treaty may have been in the circumstances, peace was maintained in New Mexico for two years. Then the old trouble of raids and attacks and army retaliation broke the peace.

The next move came from Congress, which in the summer of 1854 appropriated $30,000 for the negotiation of treaties with the Apaches, Navajos, and Utes in New Mexico. The money provided the opportunity to apply the policy that was maturing in the mind of Indian Commissioner Manypenny, who believed that the only solution was to extend to New Mexico (and to its sister territory, Utah) the system of reservations that was being developed elsewhere.[54]

Accordingly, David Meriwether, who had become governor of New Mexico Territory in 1853, negotiated six treaties in the summer of 1855—with the Mimbres Band of Gila Apaches, Mescalero Apaches, Navajos, Capote Band of Utes, Muache Band of Utes, and Jicarilla Apaches. These treaties were much alike and embodied Manypenny's principles. In return for cession of all their claims to land, the bands were given defined reservations, and they agreed to settle on them and to "cultivate the soil and raise flocks and herds for a subsistence." In turn the United States promised gradually reduced annuities for a set period of years, but the payments were to be made at the direction of the president, who could determine what proportion, if any, would be paid in money and what proportion might be expended for moral improvement and civilization. Furthermore, the president, at his discretion, could survey the reservations and allot parcels of land to individual Indian families. Additional articles prohibited the making, selling, or using of spirituous liquors on the reservations and provided that the trade and intercourse laws would remain in force over the Indian lands.[55]

Here was a clear indication of the theoretical policy of the government

---

53. Kappler, 2:598–600. Letters of Luke Lea and A. H. H. Stuart in support of the treaty are in Senate (RG 46), Sen 33B-C1.

54. 10 Stat. 330; CIA AR, 1854, serial 746, p. 222.

55. Two of the treaties—with the Capote Utes and the Muache Utes—are printed in Kappler, 5:686–92.

to turn the Indians of the newly acquired territories into settled agri-culturalists, no matter what the Indians' traditions and inclinations might be or what the capabilities of the land for farming. Meriwether reported that the Utes "very reluctantly consented to commence the cultivation of the soil for a subsistence"; but he had strong hopes that success with this relatively amicable band would have "a powerful effect upon all the other bands of this savage tribe." Meriwether's chief goal in the treaties can be seen in his exultant report to Manypenny when he forwarded them: "Each treaty contains a stipulation requiring the Indians to *cultivate* the land assigned to them." Although the governor urged speedy approval of the treaties, the Senate unanimously rejected all of them on March 13, 1857. Yet the negotiations appear to have had some effect, for Manypenny reported at the end of 1856 that depredations in New Mexico had been less serious than in any of the previous years.[56]

In Utah, the continual conflict between federal agents and Mormon officials clouded Indian relations.[57] Both sides, however, saw the need for treaties. John Wilson, who temporarily served as Indian agent at Salt Lake City, proposed in 1849 that the Indian title to lands near the Great Salt Lake be extinguished "by treaty," and his successor John H. Holeman asserted that a treaty with the various tribes in Utah "would have the effect of preventing depredations on their lands, quieting their excitement against the whites, and ultimately save the Government from much trouble and expense." The Mormon leader Brigham Young was of the same mind. He wanted the government to promote schools and other measures to civilize the Indians, and he declared: "If previous to any such arrangements being made for their benefit it becomes necessary to enter into Treaty stipulations with them, then we should not delay that operation any longer, but go about it as speedily as possible."[58] The movement for a treaty in Utah was abortive. Young's estimates of goods

56. Meriwether to Manypenny, August 14, 1855, ibid., 689; Meriwether to Many-penny, September 1855, CIA AR, 1855, serial 810, p. 507; CIA AR, 1856, serial 875, p. 566; *Senate Ex. Proc.*, 10:254–55.

57. For useful discussion of this matter, see Dale L. Morgan, "The Administration of Indian Affairs in Utah, 1851–1858," *Pacific Historical Review* 17 (November 1948): 383–409, and Hoopes, *Administration of Indian Affairs*, 131–59.

58. Wilson to Thomas Ewing, September 4, 1849, *House Ex. Doc.* no. 17, 31-1, serial 573, p. 105; Holeman to Luke Lea, September 21, 1851, CIA AR, 1851, serial 613, p. 446; Young to Lea, November 30, 1851, Records of the Office of Indian Affairs, National Archives Record Group 75, Letters Received, Utah Superintendency, U/1-1852 (M234, roll 897, frame 217).

needed for treating with the Indians were merely filed away because the similar arrangements suggested for the Indians in New Mexico had been turned down by the Senate.[59]

The stretching of the treaty system to encompass the new American empire in the West was thus only partially effective. The policy of the government toward these Indians was embodied in the treaties signed, but the Senate frequently balked at ratifying the treaties, and in other cases simple administrative measures replaced formal treaties. Few, if any, officials at the seat of government seemed to worry about these discrepancies.

59. Morgan, "Indian Affairs in Utah," 396.

CHAPTER ELEVEN

The Civil War Decade

The 1860s were the final decade of formal treaty making. The period was a significant one, for the Civil War disrupted the treaty relations between the United States and the tribes in the Indian Territory, and wars between Indians and whites on the plains and in the mountains during and after the Civil War ended with new attempts to return to a peaceful reservation status by means of treaty negotiations. Treaty making seemed to have a new lease on life, and there were few indications that it would soon end.[1]

Southern Tribes and the Civil War

The Five Civilized Tribes, which had received strong guarantees of their national status in the removal treaties of the 1830s, exerted their sovereign powers at the beginning of the Civil War by overthrowing their loyalty to the Union and aligning themselves—by means of new treaties—with the Confederate States of America. Some of these tribes, with slaveholding leaders, sympathized with the Confederacy, and the inability of Lincoln's government to provide protection

1. For the general context of Indian policy in the period, see Francis Paul Prucha, *The Great Father: The United States Government and the American Indians*, 2 vols. (Lincoln: University of Nebraska Press, 1984), 1: 411–78. I have used some sections from that account here.

against Confederate troops who invaded the territory made the switch of alliance seem desirable. The Choctaws and Chickasaws, the first and strongest adherents to the Southern cause, were bordered by the aggressive Confederate states of Arkansas and Texas, and the other tribes, too, despite large Unionist factions (especially among the Creeks and Cherokees), with a sense of desperation joined the movement.[2]

To foster the transition and negotiate the new treaties, the Confederate government sent the able Albert Pike to woo the southern Indian leaders with persuasive arguments and enticing promises. Although unsuccessful at first with Chief John Ross of the Cherokees, who stoutly maintained a position of neutrality, Pike quickly won over the other tribes. The Creeks signed a treaty with him on July 10, 1861, the Choctaws and Chickasaws on July 12, and the Seminoles on August 1. All these treaties began with a preamble that indicated the Confederacy's offer "to assume and accept the protectorate of the several nations and tribes of Indians occupying the country west of Arkansas and Missouri, and to recognize them as their wards, subject to all the rights, privileges and immunities, titles and guaranties, with each of said nations and tribes under treaties made with them by the United States of America" and the Indians' agreement thereto. Despite the treaties' reference to the Indians as "wards," the documents marked a formal transfer of political allegiance and loyalty of the tribes from the Union to the Confederacy. The tribes, moreover, agreed to offensive and defensive military alliances with the South.[3]

The treaties recognized the existing territorial limits of the tribes and guaranteed fee-simple ownership of the lands within the boundaries. They contained the stipulation that the Indian lands were to be held in common and (unlike any treaty between the United States and Indian

2. The most complete and thoroughly documented study of these Indians in the war is the series of three volumes by Annie Heloise Abel under the general title *The Slaveholding Indians* (Cleveland: Arthur H. Clark Company), vol. 1 (1915): *The American Indian as Slaveholder and Secessionist: An Omitted Chapter in the Diplomatic History of the Southern Confederacy*; vol. 2 (1919): *The American Indian as Participant in the Civil War*; and vol. 3 (1925): *The American Indian under Reconstruction*. A shorter general article is Annie Heloise Abel, "The Indians in the Civil War," *American Historical Review* 15 (January 1910): 281–96.

3. The treaties are printed in *The War of the Rebellion: A Compilation of the Official Records of the Union and Confederate Armies*, 70 vols. (Washington: GPO, 1880–1901), series 4, 1:426–43, 445–66, 513–27; henceforth cited as *Official Records*. They are exhaustively analyzed in Abel, *American Indian as Slaveholder*, 157–80. See also Kenny A. Franks, "An Analysis of the Confederate Treaties with the Five Civilized Tribes," *Chronicles of Oklahoma* 50 (Winter 1972–73): 458–73.

tribes) added "so long as grass shall grow and water run." The lands were never to be included in any state or territory, nor would a tribe, without its own consent, be organized as a territory or state. In many respects the treaties were the same as the earlier treaties with the United States, but the new treaties were more generous to the tribes, and the tone was one of conciliation rather than dictation, for Pike promised the Indians many things that they had been contending for with the United States. The treaties allowed the Indians more control of their trade, guaranteed property rights in slaves, and promised financial benefits. Of course, it was understandable that the rights of the Indians would be clearly recognized by the Confederacy, which desperately needed the Indian alliances.

The treaties, as Pike negotiated them, contained a provision for Indian delegates in the Confederate Congress, and the Choctaw-Chickasaw treaty provided for ultimate statehood (to which the Creeks, Seminoles, and Cherokees could be joined). President Jefferson Davis objected to both these provisions as impolitic and unconstitutional, and the treaties were amended to leave the decision on delegates and admission of states to the House of Representatives and to Congress.[4]

At length Ross's resistance was worn down, and on October 7 he, too, threw in his lot with the Confederacy, hoping to prevent the widening gap between Cherokee factions and no doubt enticed by the attractive terms offered by Pike: Cherokee Nation control over its lands, the right to incorporate other tribes into the nation, rights of self-government, control over the appointment of agents, a Cherokee court, a delegate in the House of Representatives, and provision for sale of the Neutral Lands that the Cherokees owned in Kansas.[5]

Meanwhile Pike had signed treaties with the Wichita and Comanche Indians on August 12, which were primarily treaties of peace and of promoting civilization and which were intended to satisfy the citizens

4. Davis message of December 12, 1861, James D. Richardson, comp., *The Messages and Papers of Jefferson Davis and the Confederacy, Including the Diplomatic Correspondence, 1861–1865*, new ed., 2 vols. (New York: Chelsea House–Robert Hector, 1966), 1:149–51. The ratification action of the Confederate Congress is printed with each treaty in *Official Records*.

5. *Official Records*, series 4, 1:669–87. A summary of the treaty is in Morris L. Wardell, *A Political History of the Cherokee Nation, 1838–1907* (Norman: University of Oklahoma Press, 1935), 139–41. A "Declaration of the people of the Cherokee Nation of the causes which have impelled them to unite their fortunes with those of the Confederate States of America," October 28, 1861, is in *Official Records*, series 1, 13:503–5.

of Texas, who were ravaged by Indian raids. They contained little to distinguish them from treaties made by the United States with the western tribes, except, of course, that the Indians placed themselves under the laws and protection of the Confederacy. They were full of paternalistic rhetoric and asked the tribes to "settle upon their reserves, become industrious, and prepare to support themselves, and live in peace and quietness."[6] Pike negotiated treaties, as well, with the small Indian groups in the northeastern section of the Indian Territory— Osages, Shawnees, Senecas, and Quapaws. By these treaties, signed on October 2 and 4, 1861, the tribes submitted to the Confederacy and agreed to join in the war against the Union.[7]

The Confederacy used strong arguments in dealing with the Indians, not the least of which was that the expansionist forces of the United States threatened the Indians' autonomy if not their very existence. But the South, too, was interested in the Indian lands. In transmitting the treaties to President Davis, Pike extolled the beauty and fertility of the country. "The concessions made the Indians are really far more for *our* benefit than for *theirs*," he wrote; "and that it is *we*, a thousand times more than they, who are interested to have this country, the finest, in my opinion, on the continent, opened to settlement and formed into a State."[8]

In the end, of course, the fine promises made to the Indians by Pike came to nothing because under the pressures of the war the Confederacy was unable to live up to its treaties and to furnish the tribes adequate protection from the ultimate invasion of Union forces.[9] The last years of the war were disastrous for the Indian Territory. Guerrilla warfare caused widespread destruction, and political disorganization resulted in corruption and exploitation. Refugee Indians with Union sentiments who had fled into Kansas were in an especially serious plight.

When the Civil War ended, the Indians, who had disowned their treaty obligations with the United States, concluded formal alliances

6. *Official Records*, series 4, 1:542–54. See also Arrell M. Gibson, "Confederates on the Plains: The Pike Mission to Wichita Agency," *Great Plains Journal* 4 (Fall 1964): 7–16.

7. *Official Records*, series 4, 1:636–66.

8. Pike, "Report of the Commissioner of the Confederate States to the Indian Nations West of Arkansas," quoted in Gibson, "Confederates on the Plains," 15–16.

9. Kenny A. Franks, "The Implementation of the Confederate Treaties with the Five Civilized Tribes," *Chronicles of Oklahoma* 51 (Spring 1973): 21–33, and "The Confederate States and the Five Civilized Tribes: A Breakdown in Relations," *Journal of the West* 12 (July 1973): 439–54.

with the South, and furnished many men who fought tenaciously for the Confederate cause, faced a United States intent on dealing strongly with such wayward tribes. There was considerable sentiment for direct action by Congress to consolidate the Indian tribes and establish a regular territorial government for the Indian Territory. Such a move would have bypassed the treaty system, shattered the unique Indian proprietorship of the lands provided by the removal treaties of the 1830s, and opened the riches of the area to all comers. Lincoln's commissioner of Indian affairs, William P. Dole, to his credit, fought to prevent a territorial government that would destroy the treaty guarantees made by the federal government. He saw no advantages in changing the government of the Indian Territory and noted that such action would be "at variance with our long established Indian policy." Although he admitted that there was question about the force of treaty obligations toward Indians who had joined the Confederacy, Dole insisted that the obligations were intact toward Indians who had remained loyal and that to violate them would mean "a gross breach of national faith."[10]

Dole was not alone. When Senator James Harlan drew up a bill to establish a regular territory with set boundaries and a government similar to that of other federal territories, an amendment offered by Senator James R. Doolittle provided that the bill would go into effect by means of *treaties* with the tribes. And Senator Lafayette S. Foster of Connecticut spoke strongly against the bill, arguing in terms reminiscent of the debate against removal in 1830 that the measure would be "a stain upon the national honor, a breach of the national faith." The bill passed the Senate on March 2, 1865, just before the adjournment of the Thirty-eighth Congress, but it was never debated or voted upon in the House.[11]

Harlan's bill, nevertheless, became the basis for negotiations with the southern Indians, who were called to meet with federal commissioners at Fort Smith in September 1865. The conference was under the direction of the new commissioner of Indian affairs, Dennis N. Cooley, a friend and associate of Harlan, who was now secretary of the interior. He was assisted by Elijah Sells, head of the Southern Superintendency; Thomas Wister, a well-known Quaker from Pennsylvania; General W. S. Harney; and Colonel Ely S. Parker, a Seneca Indian and General Grant's

10. Dole to Caleb Smith, March 17, 1862, quoted in Abel, *American Indian under Reconstruction*, 235–36n.

11. Abel, *American Indian under Reconstruction*, 244–66, quotes extensively from the Senate debates of February 23, 24, and March 2, 1866, and discusses the matter fully, 219–67.

aide-de-camp, who later became commissioner of Indian affairs. The goal of the commission was well summarized in a telegraph from Harlan to Cooley en route to Fort Smith: "The President is willing to grant them peace; but wants land for other Indians, and a civil government for the whole Territory." Cooley also carried to Fort Smith a copy of the Harlan bill and a long letter of instructions from Secretary Harlan.[12]

When the conference opened on September 8, only the loyal factions of the tribes were on hand, but Cooley proceeded anyway to address the gathering as though he were talking to Confederate Indians, telling them they had forfeited their annuities and rights to land in the Indian Territory but that the president was willing to make new treaties with them. The delegates were startled by what they heard, for none of them had come with authority from their tribes to make treaties, but the next day Cooley continued in his course and outlined for the Indians the stipulations that were to be included in the treaties.

The tribes must declare peace among themselves and with the United States and assist the United States in compelling the Indians of the plains to maintain peaceful relations. They must abolish slavery forever and incorporate former slaves into their tribes or otherwise provide for them, and a portion of the lands of the tribes must be set apart for friendly tribes from Kansas and elsewhere. It was the policy of the government, Cooley told the Indians, to consolidate all the tribes in the Indian Territory into a single government. Finally, no white persons, except officers, agents, and employees of the government or of companies building internal improvements, would be allowed to reside in the Indian Territory unless formally incorporated into a tribe.[13]

The Indian delegates, aside from their insistence that they were not authorized to negotiate new treaties with the United States, were strongly opposed to some of the points Cooley proposed. They were hesitant about incorporating the freed slaves into their nations, and they were especially hostile to the scheme of a territorial government that had been the heart of the Harlan bill. The best that Cooley's commission could accomplish at Fort Smith was an agreement of amity between the tribes and the United States, dated September 13, 1865. In it the Indians

12. Harlan to Cooley, August 24, 1865, quoted in Gary L. Roberts, "Dennis Nelson Cooley, 1865–66," in Robert M. Kvasnicka and Herman J. Viola, eds., *The Commissioners of Indian Affairs, 1824–1937* (Lincoln: University of Nebraska Press, 1979), 103; Harlan to commissioners, August 16, 1865, quoted in full in Abel, *American Indian under Reconstruction*, 219–26.

13. CIA AR, 1865, serial 1248, pp. 482–83.

acknowledged once more that they were under the exclusive jurisdiction of the United States, and they canceled and repudiated the treaties they had made with the Confederacy. In turn, the United States promised peace and friendship and renewed protection of the tribes.[14]

Formal treaties were signed the next year in Washington by Cooley, Sells, and Parker with the Seminoles (March 21), Choctaws and Chickasaws (April 28), Creeks (June 14), and Cherokees (July 19). The treaties had common provisions and built upon the points laid out by Cooley at Fort Smith, but considerable modifications were made to meet the protestations of the Indians. The tribes gave up sections of their land to make homes for other Indians, emancipated their slaves, prohibited slavery, and provided for the men and women who had been freed. The treaties stipulated a general council of all the tribes in the Indian Territory (looking toward territorial government but for the present stopping short of it); and rights of way for railroads were authorized. The Seminoles gave up their entire territory and accepted a new region to the east. The Choctaws and Chickasaws sold to the United States their lands west of the ninety-eighth meridian; the Creek land was cut in two. But the Cherokees, although they sold the parcels of land they owned in Kansas and gave the United States an option on their outlet to the west that lay beyond the ninety-sixth meridian, lost none of their lands; they agreed to admit other Indians to their territories west of the ninety-eighth meridian, however. The Choctaw-Chickasaw treaty and that of the Cherokees included provisions for survey of their lands and allotment of them in severalty whenever approved by the tribal councils.[15]

The treaties were signed with reunited tribes, although the divisions were by no means all healed. Among the Choctaws and Chickasaws there was little trouble, for there had been no fundamental split into loyal and secessionist parties. The Creeks and Seminoles patched up their divisions and sent national delegations to Washington to negotiate with the government. But among the Cherokees hostile factions per-

14. The agreement is printed in the minutes of the council, ibid., 514–15. It is printed among unratified treaties in Kappler, 2:1050–52.

15. Kappler, 2:910–15, 918–37, 942–50. There is detailed coverage in Abel, *American Indian under Reconstruction*, 301–63. See also the following articles on the separate treaties: Harry Henslick, "The Seminole Treaty of 1866," *Chronicles of Oklahoma* 48 (Autumn 1970): 280–94; Gail Balman, "The Creek Treaty of 1866," ibid. (Summer 1970): 184–96; Marion Ray McCullar, "The Choctaw-Chickasaw Reconstruction Treaty of 1866," *Journal of the West* 12 (July 1973): 462–70; Paul F. Lambert, "The Cherokee Reconstruction Treaty of 1866," ibid., 471–89.

sisted, and both groups were on hand in Washington. The northern Cherokees, acting through the National Council, sent a delegation led by John Ross, who was in ill health and close to the end of his life. A southern delegation, led by Elias C. Boudinot and William P. Adair, sought its own ends. Cooley dealt with both delegations, but he was favorably inclined toward the southern group, for it was sympathetic with his proposals for a territorial government and his encouragement of railroad development in the Indian Territory. He was not averse, however, to considering a division of the Cherokee Nation into northern and southern parts. Cooley sent a treaty made with the southern delegates to the president in May, justifying his action at great length in an anti-Ross pamphlet he published at the same time entitled *The Cherokee Question*. But President Andrew Johnson refused to forward the treaty to the Senate. The commissioner of Indian affairs was then forced to come to terms with the northern delegation, with whom he finally signed a treaty that was ratified by the Senate on July 27. The treaty represented compromises on both sides. The southern faction was offered a degree of autonomy in the Canadian District, lying between the Arkansas and Canadian rivers, but the unity of the nation was preserved. John Ross died on August 1, 1866, ten days before the proclamation of the treaty, and new leadership was found for the distracted nation.[16]

Indians in the North and West

While action with the tribes in the Indian Territory held center stage in the federal government's Indian affairs during the Civil

16. Extended accounts of the treaty negotiations and the relations of the factions appear in Wardell, *Cherokee Nation*, 194–207, and in Abel, *American Indian under Reconstruction*, 345–63. Cooley's pamphlet is *The Cherokee Question: Report of the Commissioner of Indian Affairs to the President of the United States, June 15, 1866, Being Supplementary to the Report of the Commissioners Appointed by the President to Treat with the Indians South of Kansas, and Which Assembled at Fort Smith, Ark., in September, 1865* (Washington: GPO, 1866). The pamphlet is reprinted, with introduction and notes to refute its anti-Ross position, in Joseph B. Thoburn, ed., "The Cherokee Question," *Chronicles of Oklahoma* 2 (June 1924): 141–242. The heated nature of the conflict between the two Cherokee parties can be seen in the small pamphlet war they conducted in the summer of 1866; the pamphlets are conveniently listed in Lester Hargrett, *The Gilcrease-Hargrett Catalogue of Imprints* (Norman: University of Oklahoma Press, 1972), 55–56. Ross's last days are treated in Gary E. Moulton, *John Ross, Cherokee Chief* (Athens: University of Georgia Press, 1978), 184–96.

War, the war also brought military engagements with Indians that had little to do directly with the sectional conflict. Whites continued to move into Indian lands, almost unmindful of the great war being waged, and many regular troops were withdrawn from the frontier, to be replaced by less able and poorly disciplined volunteers.

The violent outbreak of Santee Sioux in Minnesota in 1862 resulted in a mass execution of Indians deemed guilty and the removal of the Sioux from the state. Even the Winnebagos in Minnesota, who had played no part in the uprising, were forced out—first to Dakota and then to Nebraska—all without the benefit of negotiations or treaties.

In an unprecedented move, under pressure from the white citizens of Minnesota, Congress cancelled certain provisions of earlier treaties with the Sioux. On February 16, 1863, Congress declared that all treaties with the Sisseton, Wahpeton, Mdewakanton, and Wahpekute bands of Sioux were "abrogated and annulled, so far as said treaties or any of them purport to impose any future obligation on the United States, and all lands and rights of occupancy within the State of Minnesota, and all annuities and claims heretofore accorded to said Indians, or any of them, to be forfeited to the United States." The money thus saved was to be used to compensate whites for their losses; individual Indians who had aided whites, however, would receive eighty acres from the public lands in severalty.[17]

When the Indians in Minnesota rose up against the white settlers in 1862, there had been general consternation, for whites feared a widespread conspiracy among the Indians to attack all along the frontier while the nation was engaged in the Civil War. Although these fears proved groundless, the restlessness among the Sioux, Cheyennes, and Arapahos worried the Indian Office and the War Department and unnerved territorial officials in the West.

In February 1861, by a treaty signed at Fort Wise on the upper Arkansas, peaceful chiefs, including Black Kettle and White Antelope of the Cheyennes and Little Raven of the Arapahos, had agreed to give up the lands assigned them in the Treaty of Fort Laramie of 1851 and accept a reservation along the Arkansas. The land of the reservation would be allotted in severalty to individual members of the tribes in order to promote "settled habits of industry and enterprise." The treaty provided annuities for fifteen years, totaling $450,000, to be spent at the discretion of the secretary of the interior for agricultural development among the tribes, and land for the support of schools. The Indians who

17. 12A Stat. 652–54.

signed the treaty agreed to induce the portions of the tribes not represented to join them in this great step toward civilization.[18] This treaty is another example of the government's sincere but unreasonable expectations of inducing the nomadic plains Indians to settle down on individual lots as agriculturalists.

The chiefs who agreed to the Fort Wise treaty had no success in drawing others to a radical change of life. Meanwhile the great westward migration of whites continued. Stage and freight lines moved across Kansas, and the burgeoning traffic cut sharply into the hunting grounds of the Indians, who reacted with sporadic raids on stations and settlements.

It was enough to alarm Colorado Territory to the point of panic, and on November 29, 1864, Colonel John M. Chivington, military commander of the District of Colorado, with volunteer troops attacked a group of peaceful Cheyennes and Arapahos at Sand Creek. The resulting massacre became a never-to-be-forgotten symbol of what was wrong with United States treatment of the Indians.[19]

Sand Creek intensified Indian hostilities on the plains. Black Kettle and others who escaped were aided by Northern Cheyennes, Sioux, and Arapahos and by the Comanches and Kiowas, and the Indians fought off the troops sent out to quiet them. The army planned an extensive campaign, but humanitarian outcries over Sand Creek and the desire of the Indians themselves for peace led to treaty negotiations instead.

A special United States treaty commission met with the Cheyennes and Arapahos, Comanches, Kiowas, and Kiowa-Apaches on the Little Arkansas River in October 1865, the month following the Fort Smith council. The commission was guided by instructions drawn up by Secretary Harlan, which emphasized that the Indians, to obviate violent collisions with the advancing tide of white migration, must give up their "wandering life" and settle on reservations. The western Indians were to be assigned tracts of land as remote as possible from the whites. Although Harlan admitted that "a sudden transition from a savage and nomadic life to the more quiet and confining pursuits of civilization is not to be expected," the lands were to be suitable for the ultimate adoption of pastoral and agricultural life. He insisted that the govern-

18. Kappler, 2:807–11.
19. The literature on Sand Creek is extensive. Useful accounts are Stan Hoig, *The Sand Creek Massacre* (Norman: University of Oklahoma Press, 1961), and Michael A. Sievers, "Sands of Sand Creek Historiography," *Colorado Magazine* 49 (Spring 1972): 116–42.

ment would have to furnish the assistance necessary for a transition to a new way of life and improvement of the Indians' moral and intellectual condition. "The nation cannot adopt the policy of exterminating them," he said. "Our self-respect, our Christian faith, and a common dependence on an all-wise Creator and benefactor forbid it. Other nations will judge our character by our treatment of the feeble tribes to whom we sustain the relation of guardian. Morally and legally there is no distinction between destroying them and rendering it impossible for them to escape annihilation by withholding from them adequate means of support."[20]

On October 14, 1865, the commission signed a treaty with the Cheyennes and Arapahos present, in which the Indians agreed to give up their lands in Colorado and accept a reservation which lay partly in Kansas and partly in the Indian Territory. Three days later a similar agreement was concluded with the Kiowa-Apaches, and on the following day one was signed with the Comanches and Kiowas, who were to get a reservation in the Indian Territory and in the panhandle of Texas. The treaties included the stipulations Harlan had outlined in his instructions. Although the Indians were permitted to range over their old lands, they agreed not to disturb the roads, military posts, and towns of the whites, and the government agreed to pay annuities for forty years, "in such manner and for such purposes as, in the judgment of the Secretary of the Interior . . . will best subserve their wants and interests as a people." Although the treaties brought a temporary peace, they did not solve the problem because the reservations to be established never materialized. The control of Texas over its lands nullified the agreement with the Comanches and Kiowas, and Kansas refused to allow a reservation within its boundaries.[21]

For the northern plains, Governor Newton Edmunds of Dakota Territory arranged a commission of civilians and military officers to negotiate with the Sioux in the hope of ending Indian raids. The commission met the peace chiefs of the various bands at Fort Sully in

20. Harlan to commissioners, August 16, 1865, in Abel, *American Indian under Reconstruction*, 224–5. These instructions were actually drawn up for Cooley and the commissioners who went to Fort Smith, in case they would have an opportunity to deal with the southern plains tribes, which they did not.

21. Kappler, 2:887–95; Donald J. Berthrong, *The Southern Cheyennes* (Norman: University of Oklahoma Press, 1963), 224–44; William H. Leckie, *The Military Conquest of the Southern Plains* (Norman: University of Oklahoma Press, 1963), 23–26. Council proceedings are in CIA AR, 1865, serial 1248, pp. 699–720. See also *Senate Ex. Proc.*, 14:485, 755, 827–29.

October 1865 and between October 10 and 28 signed nine treaties with the Minneconjou, Lower Brulé, Two Kettle, Blackfeet, Sans Arc, Hunkpapa, and Oglala bands of Teton Sioux and with two bands of Yanktonai.[22] These were treaties of peace in which the Indians agreed to "obligate and bind themselves individually and collectively, not only to cease all hostilities against the persons and property of . . . [United States] citizens, but to use their influence, and, if requisite, physical force, to prevent other bands of the Dakota or Sioux, or other adjacent tribes, from making hostile demonstrations against the Government or people of the United States." The Indians promised to discontinue attacks on other tribes, to promote peace in the whole region, and to submit controversies with other tribes to the arbitration of the president of the United States. They promised to stay clear of overland transportation routes, for which action each band was to receive sums varying from $6,000 to $10,000 or $30 per lodge annually. Provisions were made for those Indians who wanted to settle down on individual parcels of land for agricultural or similar pursuits. Although the treaties gave the Senate carte blanche to amend the stipulations without Indian approval, the Senate used the power sparingly. Only slightly amended, the nine treaties were unanimously approved on March 5, 1866.[23]

Commissioner Dole's Defense of the Treaty System

The open hostility of many Indians during the Civil War brought to the fore the question of military control of Indian affairs. One challenge to civilian management, which was aimed directly at the treaty policy, came from General John Pope. Pope had been sent by Lincoln to put down the Sioux uprising in Minnesota in 1862, where he headed the newly created Department of the Northwest, and his encounter with the Indians there made him an instant Indian specialist. While engaged with hostile Indians, Pope's military commanders dealt with the Indians (including prisoners and captives) without much concern for the Indian Office, but Pope wanted a general overhaul of

22. Kappler, 2:883–87, 896–908.
23. *Senate Ex. Proc.*, 14:581–83. Correspondence from various official sources relating to the origins and activities of the Edmunds Commission is printed in *South Dakota Historical Collections* 9 (1918): 409–65.

16. Potawatomi Indian Council, 1837

Agent Abel Pepper held numerous councils in the mid-1830s with Potawatomi Indians, who ceded small reserves of land they still held in Indiana. An 1837 council, depicted by the artist George Winter, who attended it, concerned removal to the west, not a treaty, but it was typical of the treaty councils. The first and second pages of the treaty of September 23, 1836, show crossed-out sections and interlinear changes, such as were found on a number of treaties.

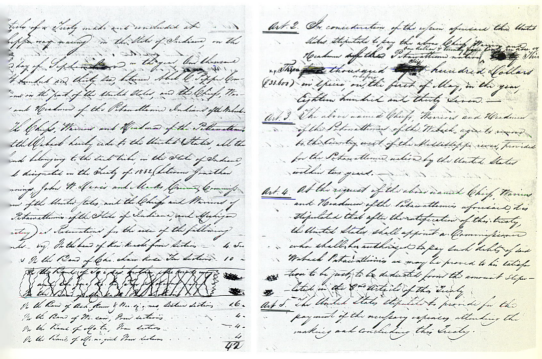

17. Treaty with the Potawatomis, September 23, 1836

18. Treaty of Traverse des Sioux, July 23, 1851

Frank B. Mayer, a young Baltimore artist, was present at the Traverse des Sioux treaty council and made sketches of the Indians and of the council grounds. Mayer hoped to use the drawings as sources for a large oil painting, which would be his masterpiece. In 1885 he produced an oil "sketch" of his proposed painting, which is reproduced here, but he got no further. A later artist, Frank D. Millet, used this oil painting as the basis for a more detailed and finished work that now hangs in the Minnesota State Capitol, but it does not have the historical authenticity of Mayer's "sketch."

Mayer's painting incorporates many common features of treaty councils held in the Indian country: an arbor or canopy to offer shade and give an air of formality to the proceedings, the American flag flying over the assembly, the face-off of United States commissioners and the Indian chiefs, the table with the secretary taking the signatures of the Indians, the gathering of white witnesses (some of whom were interpreters) behind the commissioners, and the large number of Indians (with families) in attendance.

Meldrum was an interpreter for the Crows at the large multitribal council held on the Platte below Fort Laramie in 1851. Of Scottish ancestry, he entered the Upper Missouri fur trade and dealt especially with the Crows. He married into the tribe, knew their language well, and was accepted by the Indians as one of themselves.

19. Robert Meldrum

When Culbertson, a native Pennsylvanian, acted as interpreter for the Assiniboins and Gros Ventres at the Fort Laramie Treaty of 1851, he had been for many years a trader on the Upper Missouri and head of Fort Union for a decade. He had an Indian wife, and the Indians knew him well and respected him. This drawing is by Gustav Sohon.

20. Alexander Culbertson

21. Arrival of Nez Perce Indians at the Walla Walla Council, 1855

When Isaac I. Stevens negotiated treaties with the Indians in what are now Washington and Montana, he had the services of an enlisted man in the army, a German immigrant named Gustav Sohon, who had considerable artistic ability. Sohon's portraits of Indian chiefs and others and his rendering of the treaty councils that Stevens held with the Indians form a valuable pictorial record of treaty making. Here are two of Sohon's scenes.

22. Blackfeet Treaty Council, 1855

Stevens was thirty-five years old, a graduate of West Point who had served in the Mexican War, when he was appointed the first governor of Washington Territory in 1853. One biographer called him a "young man in a hurry," and he had strong paternalistic ideas about forcing the tribes into the white man's pattern. Two of the many Indian leaders he dealt with are shown here in sketches by Gustav Sohon: Peo-Peo-Mox-Mox of the Walla Wallas and Lawyer of the Nez Perces.

23. Isaac I. Stevens

24. Peo-Peo-Mox-Mox   25. Chief Lawyer

Now, therefore, be it known that I, James Buchanan, President of the United States of America, do, in pursuance of the advice and consent of the Senate, as expressed in their resolution of the eighth of March, eighteen hundred and fifty-nine, accept, ratify and confirm the said Treaty.

In Testimony Whereof, I have caused the Seal of the United States to be hereto affixed and have signed the same with my hand.

Done at the City of Washington, this twenty-ninth day of April, in the year of Our Lord, one thousand eight hundred and fifty-nine and of the Independence of the United States, the eighty-third.

James Buchanan

By the President.

Lewis Cass
Secretary of State.

26. Presidential Signature and Seal, Treaty with the Nez Perces, June 11, 1855

Once the Senate had given its advice and consent to a treaty, the State Department prepared a ratification formula for the president to sign, which was attached to the treaty and included the seal of the United States. The forms used during President Buchanan's administration were elegantly prepared. Note that the president's signature on this treaty is attested by Lewis Cass, then secretary of state.

27. Sac and Fox Delegation in Washington, D.C., February 1867

Of the 367 Indian treaties that were negotiated and signed in Washington, D.C. Tribal delegates, together with interpreters and agents, came to the capital to speak with the Great Father and to negotiate agreements with the government. On such occasions they usually had pictures taken in their best attire. In this staged photograph, Commissioner of Indian Affairs Lewis V. Bogy (center, standing) is reading a paper to the Sac and Fox delegation. Bogy signed the treaty as principal commissioner for the United States, but the Senate, in March 1867, refused to approve his appointment to the office of commissioner of Indian affairs.

federal Indian policy. In a letter to General Henry W. Halleck, general-in-chief of the army, in 1863, Pope strongly criticized existing policy and called for agreements with the hostile Indians that would be treaties of peace only, with no purchase of lands and no annuities of any kind.[24]

Pope's most ambitious statement was the plan he drew up and forwarded to Secretary of War Edwin M. Stanton in February 1864. His plan was twofold. The "reserve and annuity Indians" along the frontier he proposed to move, with or without their consent, to some reservation within the settled portions of the country, take away their arms, stop the payment of their annuities, and spend any money due or appropriated for them in building villages and supplying them with food and clothing. "So long as Indians retain their tribal organization and are treated in their corporate and not their individual capacity," he said, "the change of habits and of ideas necessary to effect this result cannot be accomplished, nor can these results ever be obtained under any circumstances until the Indian is no longer an object of cupidity to the white man." For the "wild Indians" of the West with whom treaties had not yet been made, Pope proposed military control. All these Indians should be gathered at some point beyond the "western limit of the great fertile region between the Mississippi River and the Rocky Mountains," where the army could be left to deal with them without treaties and without the use of Indian agents. Pope saw no reason to treat the Indians as sovereign nations with territorial rights. Treat them completely as wards of the government, he insisted, with the western tribes under complete military control and the partially civilized ones cared for far away from the disruptive forces they were encountering on the frontiers.[25]

Indian Commissioner Dole refused to consider such a radical departure from accepted practice, and at first he simply ignored it. But when General Halleck arranged for the publication of Pope's plan in the *Army and Navy Journal* and sent his cousin Bishop Henry B. Whipple, the Episcopal missionary in Minnesota, to promote the plan with Dole and with President Lincoln, the commissioner felt obliged to reply. In so doing, he provided one of the clearest statements in support of the treaty system that ever came from the Indian Office. He ridiculed the idea of easily removing Indians from their homelands without their

24. Pope to Halleck, September 23, 1863, *Official Records*, series 1, vol. 22, pt. 2: 569–70.
25. Pope to Stanton, February 6, 1864, ibid., vol. 34, pt. 2: 259–64; the document is printed also in CIA AR, 1864, serial 1220, pp. 568–73.

consent, challenged Pope's assumption that there were free lands forever out of the way of white expansion, and forthrightly denied that military control would remove fraud and corruption in the Indian service. Dole favored retention of the present reservation policy, which he said had been "gradually improving by experience."[26]

Dole's eloquent plea for continuing the treaty system was an outright rejection of Pope's contention that the military should be given arbitrary control of the Indians. Dole's position was that there should be a mutual understanding between the Indians and whites about the boundaries of the Indian territory, the laws that were to be applied to Indians, and "the reciprocal duties and obligations resting upon each race, whether regarded as individuals or distinct communities." And he compared two methods by which that mutual understanding could be arrived at:

> First, by availing ourselves of our overwhelming numerical, physical, and intellectual superiority, we may set apart a country for the use of the Indians, prescribe the laws by which they shall be governed, and the rules to be observed in the intercourse of the two races, and compel a conformity on the part of the Indians; or, secondly, we may, as has been the almost universal practice of the government, after resorting to military force only so far as may be necessary in order to induce the Indians to consent to negotiate, bring about this understanding through the instrumentality of treaties to which they are parties, and as such have yielded their assent.[27]

Dole recognized that the overwhelming power of the United States enabled the government to adopt either of these methods, and the use of that power in imposing treaty agreements upon tribes who were not really free to give or withhold assent may have blurred any practical difference between the two methods. Yet the distinction that Dole saw was based on significant theoretical principles. The military plan advanced by Pope, he argued, entirely ignored the independence of the Indians and reduced them to absolute subjection, whereas the treaty system did not altogether deprive them of "their sense of nationality and independence as a people." Moreover, arbitrary military control would lead the Indian to regard the whites as "merciless despots and tyrants, who have deprived them of their homes and liberties," whereas treaties, although they rested on a recognition that the Indians as belligerents could not cope with the United States, might lead the In-

26. Dole to J. P. Usher, April 6, 1864, ibid., 573–75.
27. CIA AR, 1864, 150.

dians toward friendship and a gradual appreciation of the advantages and blessings of civilization. Dole asserted that the military plan was put forward for economic rather than humanitarian reasons, and he disputed even the economic benefits of it. He concluded that the advantages of the second method "seem so apparent that I can hardly realize that the former is seriously advocated." He remained firmly convinced that no better system could be found "for the management of the Indians" than the system then followed: "the fixing of the rights, duties, and obligations of each race towards the other through the instrumentality of treaties."[28]

In thus taking an adamant stand against turning the Indians over to the War Department, Dole maintained an essential principle of Indian policy at a time when it might have been easy to gain substantial public as well as official support for a transfer. More significantly, Dole refused to consider Pope's recommendation to end the treaty system, cancel annuity payments, and manage the Indians without in any way seeking their consent or legally establishing Indian rights and the government's responsibilities.[29]

An Array of Treaties

A great many other treaties in the 1860s continued to carry out the government's varied Indian policies. They cannot all be discussed here in detail; a number of examples will suffice.

That the treaty process could be manipulated to serve white political and economic interests is well illustrated by the series of treaties made with Indian tribes and bands in Kansas. There the pressure to develop railroads through Indian reservations and to dispose of Indian lands for the benefit of railroad corporations influenced the Indians as well as the white citizens. The Delawares made treaties in 1860, 1861, and 1866 in which they accepted allotments (reserving some lands to be held in common) and sold the surplus lands, not to the government but to railroad interests, and then finally withdrew from Kansas altogether to

28. Ibid.
29. Pope's plan and Dole's rejection of it are discussed in Richard N. Ellis, *General Pope and U. S. Indian Policy* (Albuquerque: University of New Mexico Press, 1979), 31–51. I do not agree with Ellis's strong charge that Dole "completely distorted Pope's proposals" (p. 47).

settle in the Indian Territory to the south. Other deals were made with the Potawatomis in 1861, 1866, and 1867, with the Kickapoos in 1862, and with a group of small tribes in 1867. It was part of the continuing drive to free Kansas of Indian lands, but it was not simply a white scheme to defraud the Indians, for in the beginning at least the Indian leaders, too, saw advantages in railroad development that would bring economic benefits to the state, in which the tribes would share. The Potawatomis in 1861, for example, accepted the railroad so that the value of their retained lands would be increased and a means would be provided for getting their surplus products to market.[30]

Meanwhile the federal government dealt with bands of Chippewas in seven treaties signed in 1863, 1864, 1866, and 1867, all but two of which were negotiated in Washington by the commissioners of Indian affairs and chiefs of the bands. The treaties concerned land cessions, establishment of reduced reservations, payment of annuities, and a variety of civilizing elements.[31] The eastern Sioux, too, were affected, as the government established reservations for groups of Minnesota Sioux who had not taken part in the uprising in 1862, some of whom had in fact aided the whites. In a treaty of February 19, 1867, the government laid out the Sisseton (Lake Traverse) Reservation and the Devils Lake Reservation for these members of the Sisseton and Wahpeton bands. The Indians were received back into the good graces of the United States, and the treaty made provisions for an agricultural life.[32]

Farther to the west, the government, pressured by the expanding white population in Colorado Territory, entered into formal treaty

30. Kappler, 2:826. For data on the treaties, see appendix B, nos. 307, 310, 350 (Delaware); 311, 346, 355 (Potawatomi); 314 (Kickapoo); 354 (mixed bands). The Delaware treaties are discussed at length in C. A. Weslager, *The Delaware Indians: A History* (New Brunswick: Rutgers University Press, 1972), chap. 16. A critical account of the fleecing of the Indians by scheming whites is in Paul Wallace Gates, *Fifty Million Acres: Conflicts over Kansas Land Policy, 1854–1890* (Ithaca: Cornell University Press, 1954), chap. 7. A more balanced account, which understands the advantages that the Indians originally saw in the railroad deals, is in H. Craig Miner and William E. Unrau, *The End of Indian Kansas: A Study of Cultural Revolution, 1854–1871* (Lawrence: Regents Press of Kansas, 1978), chap. 2. A particularly sordid case of treaty use to defraud the Indians is told in extraordinary detail in William E. Unrau and H. Craig Miner, *Tribal Dispossession and the Ottawa Indian University Fraud* (Norman: University of Oklahoma Press, 1985).

31. See appendix B, nos. 315, 320, 323, 324, 326, 347, and 356 for data on these treaties.

32. Kappler, 2:956–59. See Roy W. Meyer, *History of the Santee Sioux: United States Indian Policy on Trial* (Lincoln: University of Nebraska Press, 1967), 198–201.

relations with the Ute Indians, following the pattern well set in earlier years with other tribes. The Tabeguache Band of Utes, in a treaty of October 7, 1863, acknowledged the supremacy of the United States and claimed its protection, while ceding their land claims and accepting a specified reservation. The Indians allowed roads through their lands and permitted United States citizens to mine minerals within the reservation. The government provided annuities for ten years in goods and provisions. And, "in case the chiefs . . . shall announce to the agent a willingness and determination on their part, and on the part of their people, to begin and follow agricultural or pastoral pursuits by farming or raising stock, and growing wool," sheep and cattle would be added and the annuity goods changed to "a character suited to such change of life." Though ratified by the Senate on March 25, 1864, and ultimately proclaimed by Lincoln in December, the treaty was not implemented.[33] Then on June 8, 1865, the Colorado Utes, together with bands in Utah, ceded all their claims except to the Uintah reservation in Utah, but the agreement was not ratified. Finally, on March 2, 1868, in Washington, a new treaty extended the treaty of 1863 to other bands and created new reservation boundaries. The treaty made provision for two agencies, for individual allotments to those who wanted them, and for schools and other incentives toward farming and the adoption of white culture.[34]

In 1863 negotiations were made with various groups of Shoshones. The resulting treaties provided for military posts and settlements, for lines of communication through the lands claimed by the Indians, and, in return for destruction of game caused by the inroads, small annuities for twenty years. Some of the treaties authorized the president to set aside reservations within the Indians' traditional lands whenever he should "deem it expedient for them to abandon the roaming life, which they now lead, and become herdsmen or agriculturalists." Mindful of the undetermined status of Indian land claims in the region acquired from Mexico in 1848, the commissioners included a cautionary clause to the effect that the Indians' rights to land were only those that they had had under the laws of Mexico.[35]

The Nez Perce Indians furnished a striking example of Indians

33. Kappler, 2:856–59; *Senate Ex. Proc.*, 13:461–63.
34. Royce, *Cessions*, 849; Kappler, 2:990–96.
35. See appendix B, nos. 317–19 and 322, for data on these treaties. There is a table of "Treaties and Agreements, 1846–1906" made with Indians in the Great Basin (Utes, Shoshones, Bannocks, and Paiutes) in *Handbook of North American Indians*, vol. 11, *Great Basin*, ed. Warren L. D'Azevedo (Washington: Smithsonian Institution, 1986), 526–27.

overrun by the mining frontier, which continued its advance during the Civil War years. In June 1863 Calvin H. Hale, superintendent of Indian affairs for Washington Territory, and two Indian agents signed a treaty with these Indians, supplementary to and amending the Stevens treaty of 1855. In the new treaty the signatory Indians ceded lands reserved in the earlier treaty and accepted a reduced reservation. They were encouraged to take individual allotments in the new reservation, and the government promised an array of agricultural implements, mills, schools, churches, and other tools of civilization. When the Senate ratified the treaty on June 26, 1866, it made some amendments, which were appropriately sent to the Indians for their approval.[36]

The Indians, hoping to recover their old lands if the 1863 treaty were not approved, refused to agree to the amendments. Finally, in April 1867, the Indian Office sought to have the Senate recede from its amendments so that the treaty could go into effect, and the Senate agreed, ratifying the treaty in its original form on April 17.[37]

Here is a good example of how time ran its course despite the initial failure of the Senate to ratify the treaty. The settlers presented the government with a fait accompli, and the Senate acquiesced and belatedly ratified the treaty. The treaty is also an example of the government's insistence that it deal with an entire tribe, not with separate bands, and that a ratified treaty bound the entire tribe. The nontreaty chiefs (among them Joseph and his son, young Joseph) did not sign the treaty, which had been negotiated by Lawyer and other treaty chiefs, and did not consider themselves bound by its provisions, a circumstance that laid the foundation for the dramatic encounter between Chief Joseph's band and the United States army in 1877.[38]

By the time the treaty was finally ratified and proclaimed, new complaints of white encroachments induced Lawyer and his followers to seek a new council, this time in Washington, where they could meet

36. For a detailed account of this treaty and the conditions under which it was signed, see Alvin M. Josephy, Jr., *The Nez Perce Indians and the Opening of the Northwest* (New Haven: Yale University Press, 1965), 386–442. The old and new reservations are clearly delineated in Royce, *Cessions*, plates 16, 51, and 60, area nos. 441 (old) and 442 (new). Senate ratification is in *Senate Ex. Proc.*, vol. 14, pt. 2: 872–73.

37. *Senate Ex. Proc.*, vol. 15, pt. 2: 662, 748–49.

38. Josephy makes a good deal of this point, asserting, "The treaty was a fraudulant act on the part of both Lawyer and the commissioners. On the one hand, Lawyer and his followers had no right to sign away the lands of the other bands, and they knew it. . . . On the other hand the commissioners followed a time-worn and deceitful procedure of extinguishing title to Indian land when the rightful owners refused to sell." *Nez Perce Indians*, 430.

directly with the president. At length such a meeting was authorized, and Lawyer and a small party reached the capital in May 1868. Amidst enjoying the sights and pleasures of Washington, the Indians signed a new treaty on August 13, 1868, with Commissioner of Indian Affairs Nathaniel G. Taylor. The document preserved lands for a United States military post, provided for extra allotment lands, protected the timber resources of the Indians, and guaranteed money for teachers.[39]

The United States Indian Peace Commission

The treaties of 1867 and 1868 signed by the United States Indian Peace Commission were the most important of the final Indian treaties, and they epitomized the radical reformist Indian policy that emerged in the years immediately following the Civil War.

The treaties of 1865 on the southern and northern plains had proved ineffective, and new reports on the deteriorating condition of Indian tribes and their hostility sparked an intense determination by the federal government to correct these problems once and for all. The report of a Joint Special Committee of Congress headed by Senator James R. Doolittle, submitted in January 1867, described in detail the degradation of the Indians' condition and the causes of Indian hostility; and the Powder River War along the Bozeman Trail, with the startling ambush and destruction of Lieutenant William Fetterman's command on December 21, 1866, had led to a special investigating committee, whose report reinforced the conclusions of the Doolittle Committee.[40] The central plains, too, were on fire, and hostile Indians terrorized the regions on both sides of the Platte River.

The reports and statements of 1867 crystallized in a firm recommendation for a reservation scheme by which the plains Indians would be moved out of the way of the whites. Although this was by no means a novel idea, officials now asserted the urgency and absolute necessity of such an arrangement in order to save the Indians. The Indians should be made to move to the reservations, where they would be given

39. Kappler, 2:1024–25. See Josephy, *Nez Perce Indians*, 438–40, for an account of the delegation's trip and work.

40. The Doolittle Committee report was published as *Condition of the Indian Tribes* (Washington: GPO, 1867), and as *Senate Report* no. 156, 39-2, serial 1279. The reports on the Fetterman disaster are in *Senate Ex. Doc.* no. 13, 40-1, serial 1308.

livestock, agricultural implements, and spinning and weaving equipment to enable them to move toward self-support; schooling in letters and industry; and missionary instruction in Christianity. There they could be isolated from all whites except government employees and others permitted on the reservations.

By an act of June 20, 1867, Congress created the United States Indian Peace Commission, intending to take the business of negotiating with the Indians out of the hands of the executive and the regular Indian Office officials and give it instead to a special group of civilians and military leaders with interest and competence in Indian affairs. The body had authority to call together the chiefs of the warring tribes, find the causes of hostility, and negotiate treaties that would "remove all just causes of complaint on their part, and at the same time establish security for person and property along the lines of railroad now being constructed to the Pacific and other thoroughfares of travel to the western Territories, and such as will most likely insure civilization for the Indians and peace and safety for the whites." For Indians who did not then occupy reservations under treaty agreements, the commissioners would select reservations for their permanent homes.[41]

The act itself named Commissioner of Indian Affairs Taylor as chairman and Senator John B. Henderson of Missouri, Samuel F. Tappan, and John B. Sanborn as civilian members. The president appointed three high-ranking army officers: General William Tecumseh Sherman, Major General Alfred H. Terry, and retired general William S. Harney. An extra member, Major General Christopher C. Augur, at first substituted for Sherman and then became a regular member of the commission.

The Peace Commission, after an abortive attempt to deal with the Indians on the northern plains, negotiated first with the Kiowas, Comanches, Apaches, Cheyennes, and Arapahos at Medicine Lodge Creek in southern Kansas. On October 21 and 28, three treaties were signed with different groups; they assigned the Indians to two reservations in the western part of the Indian Territory, where the United States would furnish rations and other goods needed to turn them into happy farmers. It is clear that the Indians did not want to settle down and live in houses but adamantly wanted to continue their nomadic life as buffalo hunters. The commissioners insisted that the old way of life was at an end, for the buffalo were fast disappearing. The chiefs seemed not to hear the

41. 15 Stat. 17.

warnings, and they signed the treaty when the commissioners agreed to allow them "to hunt on any lands south of the Arkansas River so long as the buffalo may range thereon in such numbers as to justify the chase."[42]

One needs only to read the treaties—with their extensive provision for arable land for farming; construction of warehouses, mechanics shops, and other buildings; a "land book" to record individual allotments; compulsory education; agricultural seeds and implements; and a farmer, blacksmith, and physician—to see the strong thrust toward civilization that dominated the documents. The treaties, annually for thirty years, provided "for each male person over fourteen years of age, a suit of good substantial woolen clothing, consisting of coat, pantaloons, flannel shirt, hat, and a pair of home-made socks, [and] for each female over twelve years of age, a flannel skirt, or goods necessary to make it, a pair of woolen hose, *and* twelve yards of calico, and twelve yards of 'domestic,'" plus lesser provisions of the same kind for boys and girls. The Indians promised to make the reservations their permanent home, and agreed that the "United States may pass such laws, on the subject of alienation and descent of property and on all subjects connected with the government of the said Indians on said reservations, and the internal policy thereof, as may be thought proper." The treaties stipulated that the land of the reservations should be held in common and that no cession of the lands should be valid "unless executed and signed by at least three-fourths of all the adult male Indians occupying the same." The philosophical basis for these treaties and others made by the Peace Commission appears in its first report of January 7, 1868. Written by Taylor, the report is a denunciatory tirade against the evils of the Indian system, and it is suffused with evangelical sentiments favoring the civilization of the Indians, their mingling with white citizens, and their ultimate absorption into white society.[43]

---

42. Kappler, 2:977–89. The work of the Peace Commission, including the treaty negotiations, was extensively reported in the public press, for a large corps of newspaper reporters was at Medicine Lodge. The reports of the journalists are examined in detail in Douglas C. Jones, *The Treaty of Medicine Lodge: The Story of the Great Treaty Council As Told by Eyewitnesses* (Norman: University of Oklahoma Press, 1966). The book is a good place to get the feel of a treaty negotiation with the plains Indians, for it provides an almost day-by-day (sometimes hour-by-hour) account. Some of the proceedings of the council at Medicine Lodge Creek are printed in *Papers Relating to Talks and Councils Held with the Indians in Dakota and Montana Territories in the Years 1866–1869* (Washington: GPO, 1910), 56–66.

43. "Report to the President by the Indian Peace Commission," January 17, 1868,

In the spring of 1868 the Peace Commission met the northern tribes at Fort Laramie. It signed treaties with the Sioux, beginning with the Brulé, on April 29, with the Crows on May 7, and with the Northern Cheyennes and Northern Arapahos on May 10. Other Sioux signed the treaty at the end of May at Fort Laramie. Red Cloud of the Oglala Sioux, however, refused to treat until the forts along the Bozeman Trail were demolished. The government gave in, largely because the extension of the Union Pacific made possible a new supply route to Montana west of the Big Horn Mountains; the forts were dismantled and burned in the summer, and Red Cloud finally signed the treaty in November.[44]

Meanwhile, attention turned to hostile bands of Sioux along the upper Missouri, chiefly Hunkpapas under Sitting Bull, who had little understanding or interest in what was taking place at Fort Laramie. They wanted the whites and the government posts (Fort Buford and Fort Stephenson) out of their country, and they continued warring to achieve this objective. To deal with these Indians, the government enlisted the aid of the Jesuit missionary Pierre-Jean De Smet, who in June 1868 led an Indian peace delegation from Fort Rice to Sitting Bull's camp on the Powder River. De Smet spoke of peace to the Indian leaders, and Sitting Bull, in turn, urged peace as well (although thinking in terms of his demands for white withdrawal). Some of Sitting Bull's associates, led by Gall, accompanied the peace mission back to Fort Rice, where on July 2 they signed the Fort Laramie Treaty. That Gall and the other Indian signers understood the import of the treaty with its assimilative terms is difficult to believe.[45]

CIA AR, 1868, serial 1366, pp. 496–510. The report is also printed in *House Ex. Doc.* no. 97, 40-2, serial 1337.

44. Kappler, 2:998–1015; because the signing of the treaty took place at various times, the printed lists of signatures and witnesses are not completely accurate. A useful compilation of journals and other documents of the Indian Peace Commission is published in Vine Deloria, Jr., and Raymond DeMallie, eds., *Proceedings of the Great Peace Commission of 1867–1868* (Washington: Institute for the Development of Indian Law, 1975). The volume is intended as study material for students, however, and the texts have been edited for that purpose. See also *Papers Relating to Talks and Councils Held with the Indians*, passim.

45. There are accounts of the peace mission by De Smet in *Life, Letters, and Travels of Father Pierre-Jean De Smet, S.J., 1801–1873*, ed. Hiram Martin Chittenden and Alfred Talbot Richardson, 4 vols. (New York: Francis P. Harper, 1905), 3:899–922, and in *Papers Relating to Talks and Councils Held with the Indians*, 108–13. A journal kept by Charles Galpin, the interpreter, is printed in Louis Pfaller, ed., "The Galpin Journal: Dramatic Record of an Odyssey of Peace," *Montana, the Magazine of Western History* 18

The treaty set aside the Great Sioux Reserve west of the Missouri River in Dakota, and the chiefs agreed to settle at the agencies and accept reservation life. Much has been made of the land provisions of the Fort Laramie Treaty because of modern concern of Indians to protect a community land base, but the treaty, like those at Medicine Lodge Creek, was a reformist document aimed at attaining the humanitarian civilizing goals of the Peace Commission, namely, to turn the nomadic warriors into peaceful farmers.

The treaties of the Peace Commission were a triumph of theory and faith over hard reality. Aside from the fact that cultivation of the soil in quarter- or half-section lots was infeasible in most of the area covered by the reservations and that successful enterprise tended to be in grazing rather than in agriculture, the tribes that signed the treaties were not prepared to conform suddenly to the philanthropists' views of the good life of English education and neat farms.

Members of the Peace Commission also negotiated with the Navajos. General Sherman and Samuel Tappan in May 1868 met with these Indians at the Bosque Redondo in eastern New Mexico, where they had been forcibly moved in 1864 to prevent their raiding in New Mexico and to train them in agricultural pursuits. The commissioners could see for themselves the tragedy of the Indians' enforced exile at Fort Sumner and the impossibility of moving them to the alien lands of the Indian Territory. Heeding the Indians' plea to be allowed to return to their homeland, the commissioners signed a treaty with them on June 1, which set reservation boundaries and provided for the return of the Navajos. All the customary stipulations for advancing the Indians toward civilization were included.[46] The pervasiveness of the civilization policy of the government can be seen here. Although the situation of the Navajos in New Mexico was quite different from that of the northern

---

(April 1968): 2–23. A recent account, which discusses the sources, is Robert M. Utley, *The Lance and the Shield: The Life and Times of Sitting Bull* (New York: Henry Holt and Company, 1993), chap. 7.

46. Kappler, 2:1015–20; John L. Kessell, "General Sherman and the Navajo Treaty of 1868: A Basic and Expedient Misunderstanding," *Western Historical Quarterly* 12 (July 1981): 251–72; Gerald Thompson, *The Army and the Navajo* (Tucson: University of Arizona Press, 1976), 151–57. A brief account is David Lanehart, "Regaining Dinetah: The Navajo and the Indian Peace Commission at Fort Sumner," in John R. Wunder, ed., *Working the Range: Essays on the History of Western Land Management and the Environment* (Westport, Conn.: Greenwood Press, 1985), 25–38.

plains tribes who signed the Treaty of Fort Laramie, the provisions for selecting homesteads, for school attendance, and the like were almost identical.

Another treaty, similar in its stipulations to the others, was signed with the eastern band of Shoshones and the Bannocks at Fort Bridger on July 3, 1868. This and the Nez Perce treaty signed in Washington on August 13, 1868, were the last of the formal treaties between the United States government and the Indian tribes.[47]

The agitation that arose in Congress in the late 1860s about whether or not treaty making with the Indian tribes should continue had an effect upon treaty-making activities even before treaty making was finally ended in 1871.[48] There was delay in the Senate in acting upon treaties submitted by the president, many were rejected outright by the Senate when a vote on ratification was finally taken, and some were withdrawn by the president after they had been submitted but before final Senate action.

Thus, for example, on December 18, 1868, shortly after the opening of the third session of the Fortieth Congress, sixteen treaties, dating from February 3, 1863, to May 27, 1868, some of which had been delayed by the president and others which had languished in the Senate, were recommitted to the Committee on Indian Affairs; a good number of these had been signed at Washington. A group of them were rejected by the Senate on February 16, 1869, and others were rejected on March 15 of the same year.[49] A year later, on February 8, 1870, President Grant, on the advice of Secretary of the Interior Jacob D. Cox, withdrew from the Senate the 1868 treaty with the Great and Little Osages (which had created a great stir in the House) and similar treaties of early 1869 with the Kaws, Sacs and Foxes of the Missouri, and Iowas, all of which had provided for sale of ceded Indian lands to railroad companies. Cox spoke strongly against such sales:

> The possessory rights of the Indians should only be extinguished in favor of the United States, and the land to which such rights had attached should, thenceforth, be subject to the laws regulating the disposal of the public domain, including those which provide for homestead settlements and pre-emption entries. . . . The policy of

47. Kappler, 2:1020–25.
48. See the discussion in the following chapter on the end of treaty making with the Indians.
49. *Senate Ex. Proc.*, 16:413, 477–78; 17:7, 361.

selling, by virtue of an Indian treaty stipulation, immense bodies of land to a corporation, is of comparatively recent origin. It seriously retards their settlement and cultivation, and should not, I submit, be hereafter sanctioned by that branch of the Government, which is clothed with the power of making treaties.

Cox objected to the low price per acre provided in the treaties, and for that reason also recommended the withdrawal of a treaty with the Oto and Missouri Indians. The Senate on February 14 returned the treaties to the president.[50]

The stage was now set for the dramatic debate in Congress about whether or not treaty making was, after all, the proper means for doing business with the Indians.

50. Cox to the president, February 4, 1870, and Grant to Senate, February 4, 1870, Senate (RG46), Sen 41B-C3; *Senate Ex. Proc.*, 17:365. On April 22, 1869, the Senate had returned, at the president's request, a treaty of March 4, 1867, with the Shawnee Indians. Ibid., 243.

PART THREE

Deterioration

The treaties made by the United States Indian Peace Commission were among the most important of the hundreds signed with Indian tribes. They were also almost the last. The growing feeling among white Americans that it did not make sense to treat with the Indian tribes as though they were independent sovereign nations—when the Indians seemed in fact to be wards of the government—finally reached its culmination. Aided by the pique of the House of Representatives that it was left out of the treaty-making process and thus had less say in Indian matters than it wanted, the attack on treaty making came to a head in 1871. In that year Congress attached to an Indian appropriation bill a proviso that henceforth no treaties would be made with Indian tribes, although it reaffirmed the validity of those already ratified.

The tasks in managing Indian relations for which treaties had been essential were then accomplished by other means. A strong movement developed both within and outside the federal government to weaken if not completely abrogate the old treaties, which were thought to inhibit the full assimilation of Indians into white society. The increasing attacks on tribalism became, of necessity, attacks upon the treaties as well. There was no sudden or complete abrogation of the treaties and their stipulations, however, for continuing reliance on treaty rights came from Indians and some of their white advocates. This was especially the case among the Five Civilized Tribes in the Indian Territory, whose astute leaders knew how to cite their treaties effectively and how to appeal to the sense of justice of the American people and the honor of the nation in living up to its commitments.

Yet at the end of the nineteenth century and early in the twentieth, special commissions, new laws, and Supreme Court decisions made clear that treaty provisions, once considered sacred, need no longer be adhered to. The Indians were to be individualized as yeoman farmers on their allotted lands, brought under the sway of American law, and treated as individual citizens not tribal members. The treaty system had deteriorated to the point of collapse.

CHAPTER TWELVE

The End of Treaty Making

After the flurry of treaty making in the decades of the 1850s and 1860s—the many treaties of Commissioner of Indian Affairs George W. Manypenny, the Pacific Northwest treaties of Joel Palmer and Isaac I. Stevens, the Reconstruction treaties with the Five Civilized Tribes, and the treaties of the Indian Peace Commission—it might seem strange that the United States suddenly and unilaterally decreed the end of treaty making on March 3, 1871.

Antitreaty Sentiment

As a matter of fact, however, sentiment against treaty making had been steadily growing in the United States. There was a deepening appreciation of the anomaly, a conviction that the Indian tribes no longer possessed the attributes of sovereign nations necessary to make new treaties between themselves and the United States reasonable and acceptable contracts. Even professed friends of the Indians were loud in their condemnation of the treaty system and insisted that no more Indian treaties be negotiated. One of the earliest and most outspoken of these critics was Henry B. Whipple, Episcopal Bishop of Minnesota, who kept in close contact with the Sioux and Chippewa Indians. His sincere concern for their rights and interests was displayed in his courageous defense of the Sioux in the aftermath of the uprising in 1862, when his voice of reason and moderation sounded strange among the settlers' demands for vengeance. Yet Whipple had given up on treaties as the proper way to deal with the tribes.

After his first visit to the Indian country, he wrote to President Buchanan on April 9, 1860, "frankly as a Christian bishop may write to the Chief Magistrate of a Christian Nation," pleading for reform in the Indian system. The first of the evils he enumerated was that the government policy had been "to treat the red man as an equal," and the first of his eight recommendations was to treat the Indians as wards. When Lincoln became president, the bishop directed his campaign to him, asserting that it was "impolitic for our Government to treat a heathen community living within our borders as an independent nation, instead of regarding them as our wards."[1]

Whipple saved his strongest blast for an article in the *North American Review* in October 1864, on the "Indian system." "Our first dealing with these savages," he wrote, "is one of those blunders which is worse than a crime. We recognize a wandering tribe as an independent and sovereign nation. We send ambassadors to make a treaty as with our equals, knowing that every provision of that treaty will be our own, that those with whom we make it cannot compel us to observe it, that they are to live within our territory, yet not subject to our laws, that they have no government of their own, and are to receive none from us." Whipple asserted that treaties were "usually conceived and executed in fraud." The real parties to the treaties, in his mind, were Indian agents, traders, and politicians, not the United States and the Indians; the real purpose, to pay the worthless debts of the Indian traders and to create jobs for political favorites, not to buy the Indian lands at a fair price and help the Indians spend the purchase money wisely to further their civilization.[2]

Such opinions were strongly reflected in the views of the United States Board of Indian Commissioners, the body of religiously oriented philanthropists authorized by Congress in April 1869 to exercise joint control with the secretary of the interior over the disbursement of funds

1. Henry Benjamin Whipple, *Lights and Shadows of a Long Episcopate* (New York: Macmillan Company, 1899), 50–53, 124, 138–40.

2. Henry B. Whipple, "The Indian System," *North American Review* 99 (October 1864): 450–51. See also the criticism of treaties by a Presbyterian clergyman from Minnesota, Edward D. Neill, in a pamphlet published by the government, *Effort and Failure to Civilize the Aborigines: Letter to Hon. N. G. Taylor, Commissioner of Indian Affairs, from Edward D. Neill* (Washington: GPO, 1868).

appropriated for the Indians and to provide a lay committee to oversee Indian policy in general.[3] In its first annual report, written by the chairman, Felix R. Brunot, a Pittsburgh industrialist, the board was forthright in its condemnation of existing Indian policy and its recommendations for reform. It flatly declared: "The treaty system should be abandoned, and as soon as any just method can be devised to accomplish it, existing treaties should be abrogated," and "the legal status of the uncivilized Indians should be that of wards of the government."[4]

The reasons for such a decision and the depth of the feeling that treaties were wrong were expressed in a statement of Brunot:

> The United States first creates the fiction that a few thousand savages stand in the position of equality in capacity, power, and right of negotiation with a civilised nation. They next proceed to impress upon the savages, with all the form of treaty and the solemnity of parchment, signatures and seals, the preposterous idea that they are the owners in fee of the fabulous tracts of country over which their nomadic habits have led them or their ancestors to roam. The title being thus settled, they purchase and promise payment for a portion of the territory, and further bind themselves in the most solemn manner to protect and defend the Indians in the possession of some immense remainder defined by boundary in the treaty, thus becoming, as it were, *particeps criminis* with the savages in resisting the "encroachments" of civilisation and the progressive movement of the age. Having entered into this last-named impracticable obligation, the fact of its non-performance becomes the occasion of disgraceful and expensive war to subdue their victims to the point of submission to another treaty. And so the tragedy of war and the farce of treaty have been enacted again and again, each time with increasing shame to the nation.[5]

The recurring word in condemnations of the treaty system was "farce." President Grant's first commissioner of Indian affairs, the Seneca Indian leader Ely S. Parker, opposed further treaties with the Indians. "Because treaties have been made with them . . . ," he wrote, "they have become falsely impressed with the notion of national independence. It

3. For the formation of the board and its activities, see Francis Paul Prucha, *American Indian Policy in Crisis: Christian Reformers and the Indians, 1865–1900* (Norman: University of Oklahoma Press, 1976), 33–46.

4. *Report of the Board of Indian Commissioners*, 1869, p. 10.

5. Charles Lewis Slattery, *Felix Reville Brunot, 1820–1898: A Civilian in the War for the Union, President of the First Board of Indian Commissioners* (New York: Longmans, Green, and Company, 1901), 156.

is time that this idea should be dispelled, and the government cease the cruel farce of thus dealing with its helpless and ignorant wards." Parker asserted that the tribes were not sovereign nations—for "none of them have an organized government of such inherent strength as would secure a faithful obedience of its people to the observance of compacts of this character." Like other reformers, he called the Indians wards of the government and noted that "the only title the law concedes to them to the lands they occupy or claim is a mere possessory one."[6] Grant, too, when he first met with the Board of Indian Commissioners, remarked that the treaty system had been a mistake and ought to be abandoned.[7]

Such criticism of Indian treaties, arising in the general ferment over Indian affairs that developed during the Civil War and in the immediate post–Civil War years, was nothing new. Again and again, similar arguments had been made by responsible persons, who saw the anomaly of dealing with the Indians as dependent wards of the United States while at the same time signing formal treaties with them as though they were independent foreign nations, and by self-interested citizens, who hoped to acquire Indian lands for their own well-being and prosperity. But these arguments had been repeatedly turned aside because treaty making, together with the regulation of Indian trade under the commerce clause of the Constitution, had become the principal means for conducting Indian affairs.

What was new in the 1860s, the added force that finally brought the treaty house tumbling to the ground, was the resentment of the House of Representatives over its exclusion from dealing with the Indians. If Indian affairs could be handled solely by the president and the Senate under their constitutional treaty-making power, then the popularly elected House was left out in the cold.

6. CIA AR, 1869, serial 1414, p. 448. Parker made a strong personal statement about the "absurdity of the United States Government making treaties with the Indian tribes" in his autobiography published in *Proceedings of the Buffalo Historical Society* 8 (1905): 532–33.

7. Minutes of May 27, 1869, Records of the Board of Indian Commissioners, Minutes of Meetings, vol. 1, pp. 6–7, National Archives Record Group 75. Grant, as interim secretary of war, had written in his report of November 1867, "Indians have no principal chiefs, but roam in small bands, and fight independently; hence the impossibility to make treaties with them." *House Ex. Doc.* no. 1, 40-2, serial 1324, p. 30.

Distribution of Indian Lands by Treaty

The first reason for House anger and recalcitrance was the disposition of Indian lands to railroads or speculators by treaty provisions. The immediate issue was a treaty signed in May 1868 with the Great and Little Osage Indians. According to its terms some eight million acres of land owned by the Indians along the southern boundary of Kansas were to be ceded to the government, not to become part of the public domain and subject to disposal under the public land laws of the United States, but instead transferred to the Leavenworth, Lawrence, and Galveston Railroad. The company would pay twenty cents an acre for the land and use the proceeds from the sale of the tract for railroad construction.[8]

The opposition of the House of Representatives to such a measure came to a head in the second session of the Fortieth Congress on June 18, 1868, in a report from the Committee on Indian Affairs. The discussion was directed largely by Representative Sidney Clarke of Kansas, chairman of the committee; it was not a debate, strictly speaking, for no one spoke against the report.[9]

The arguments were pointed and strongly expressed. Clarke called the treaty "one of the most remarkable transactions that has ever occurred in the whole history of this Government. . . . It is neither more nor less than the transfer of eight million acres of land, which properly belong to the public domain of the United States, which belong to the landless millions in all parts of the country, into the hands of a railroad corporation, to be subjected to their supreme and unlimited control." He asserted that the details of the treaty had been all worked out in Washington by the president of the railroad company before the commissioners were sent out to negotiate with the Indians. "It was not made by the commission at all," he said, "but by the parties in interest." Representative George Washington Julian of Indiana, chairman of the

8. A thorough discussion of this abortive treaty and House opposition to it is in Paul Wallace Gates, *Fifty Million Acres: Conflicts over Kansas Land Policy, 1854–1890* (Ithaca: Cornell University Press, 1954), chap. 6. The treaty is printed in *Congressional Globe*, 40th Cong., 2d sess. (June 18, 1868), 3259–61.

9. The report, together with related documents, is in *House Report* no. 63, 40-2, serial 1358. It appears also in *Congressional Globe*, 40th Cong., 2d sess. (June 18, 1868), 3256–57.

Committee on Public Lands, declared that the commission was "a thieving commission, organized to cheat the Indians, and aid and abet the cold-blooded rapacity of railroad monopolists," a commission "for swindling, spoliation, and plunder." His patience was at an end. "In 1861," he asserted, "we began this policy of special treaty stipulations by which the jurisdiction of Congress over the public domain has been to a very great extent overthrown in the interest of monopolists and thieves; and, sir, this Osage Indian treaty is the crowning flower and fruit, the rich culmination of the system. It has grown worse and worse, and more and more defiant, because it has been unchecked in its course."[10]

Since the Osage lands were not to be made part of the public domain, the opponents of the treaty pointed out that the granting of sections of land in each township for support of schools would not obtain, that squatters on those Indian lands could not be provided for under homestead or preemption laws, and that the settlement of the southern sixth of the state of Kansas would thus be seriously obstructed. Some were upset, too, that offers for the Osage lands made by other railroad companies had simply been ignored by the treaty commission.[11]

There is no doubt that the House represented the citizens of the United States, for whom the increasingly liberal land laws for disposition of the public domain had been enacted. Now there was shock because vast Indian lands were being disposed of by treaty outside the public land policies that the House thought were firmly in place. The move of the House, therefore, was to deny that the treaty-making power of the president and Senate extended to the disposition of Indian lands by treaty "otherwise than by absolute cession to the United States, and for purposes for which Congress alone is competent to provide."[12] In the end, the House on July 18, 1868, resolved unanimously:

> That the objects, terms, conditions, and stipulations of the aforesaid pretended treaty are not within the treaty-making power, nor are they authorized either by the Constitution or laws of the United States; and therefore this House does solemnly condemn the same,

10. *Congressional Globe,* ibid., 3261, 3264.
11. See *House Report* no. 63. A strong protest against the treaty was made by the Kansas legislature on January 20, 1869; see *Senate Misc. Doc.* no. 34, 40-3, serial 1361, or *House Misc. Doc.* no. 49, 40-3, serial 1385.
12. *Congressional Globe,* 40th Cong., 2d sess., 3257.

and does also earnestly but respectfully express the hope and expectation that the Senate will not ratify the said pretended treaty.[13]

This was strong language, yet the remedy called for by the House at this point was simply nonratification by the Senate, not abolition of the treaty-making power itself in regard to Indian tribes. The Senate heard the cries and did not ratify the Osage treaty. The lands were disposed of by other provisions, which the House had a hand in making.[14]

Attack on the Treaty-Making Power

The House did not forget the issue of disposition of Indian lands by treaty, but it soon turned to another and more explosive question: Did the House have a positive role in ratification of Indian treaties because of its power to appropriate money from the Treasury to fulfill treaty provisions? Here was a constitutional question that went to the very heart of the treaty system, and the debate on the question and its outcome profoundly affected the course of American Indian policy.

At issue was the series of treaties negotiated in 1867 and 1868 by the United States Indian Peace Commission. When the Indian appropriation bill for 1870 passed the House on February 4, 1869, it authorized the payment of $2,312,260, without making specific provision for all of the stipulations in the Peace Commission's treaties (with the southern plains Indians at Medicine Lodge Creek, the northern plains tribes at Fort Laramie, the Navajos, and the Shoshones and Bannocks), not all of which had yet been ratified by the Senate. The Senate Committee on Appropriations added a modest $540,963 to the bill, but the Senate Committee on Indian Affairs added the huge sum of $3,800,734, in order to pay for the annuities and other goods and

13. Ibid., 3265–66. More than a week earlier President Andrew Johnson had sent to the House a letter of Secretary of the Interior O. H. Browning, dated June 9, 1868, in support of the negotiations of the Osage treaty. See *House ex. Doc.* no. 310, 40-2, serial 1345, pp. 1–3. This document, in three parts, contains papers relative to the treaty and its negotiation.

14. Gates, *Fifty Million Acres*, 210–25.

services promised the Indians in the treaties. The Senate additions made the total appropriation under the bill $6,653,957.[15]

When the Senate amendments reached the House on February 27, 1869, during the third session of the Fortieth Congress, a violent debate exploded, which continued off and on until March 1, 1871, at the end of the third session of the Forty-first Congress. Not only did the members of the House refuse to accede to the appropriations added by the Senate, but they undertook a fundamental analysis and criticism of the treaty-making power of the president and the Senate under the Constitution, to which was added the question of whether the Indian tribes were apt groups for signing treaties with the United States. The Senate strongly asserted its rights, and the issue was joined. It was an extended and important congressional debate about treaty making, and it is worth following in some detail.[16]

The debate began as an outburst of indignation over the Senate amendments because they added so much money to the appropriations under the 1867 and 1868 treaties, much of it for items that House members thought highly inappropriate. Representative Benjamin Franklin Butler of Massachusetts, chairman of the Committee on Appropriations, went immediately to the heart of matter: "The first question to be settled by us is this: whether the House by appropriations to carry out the provisions of these treaties will sanction this method of dealing with the Indians? If these treaties are to be sanctioned and appropriated for[,] gentlemen will see that it takes from the House the power substantially of legislating on Indian affairs. . . . The whole matter resolves itself into this: are we in future to deal with these Indians by treaties and carry out this policy [of civilization] or are we to deal with them in a different manner?" The whole committee was decidedly hostile

15. *Congressional Globe*, 40th Cong., 3d sess. (February 27, 1869), 1700. The treaties were ratified between July 25, 1868, and February 26, 1869; they are printed in chronological order in Kappler, 2: 982ff.

16. Only brief accounts of the debate appear in secondary sources. See, for example, Loring Benson Priest, *Uncle Sam's Stepchildren: The Reformation of United States Indian Policy, 1865–1887* (New Brunswick: Rutgers University Press, 1942), 96–99; Laurence F. Schmeckebier, *The Office of Indian Affairs: Its History, Activities, and Organization* (Baltimore: Johns Hopkins Press, 1927), 55–58. There is an account of the final part of the debate, that in the third session of the Forty-first Congress, in John R. Wunder, "No More Treaties: The Resolution of 1871 and the Alteration of Indian Rights to Their Homelands," in John R. Wunder, ed., *Working the Range: Essays on the History of Western Land Management and the Environment* (Westport, Conn.: Greenwood Press, 1985), 39–56.

to the Senate action, and one member called it "the deepest villainy of anything that has been before this House for a great many years."[17]

The treaties and the policy they represented, however, were not without eloquent support in the House. Three members, especially, stood behind the treaties as a matter of public honor. Walter A. Burleigh, delegate from the Territory of Dakota, where he had at one time been an Indian agent, spoke at great length of the responsibility owed the Indians. Representative William Windom of Minnesota insisted on honoring the treaties, confining his remarks to what he called "the great question, namely, shall we comply with our treaty stipulations with these Indians or not?" He noted that the House could discuss the constitutional issues involved but that "the Sioux Indians and the other wild Indians on the plains are not very good constitutional lawyers, and that however we may decide this question of constitutional law it will not obviate the results of a breach of faith on our part." He pointed to the high quality of the members of the Peace Commission who had negotiated the treaties and made the promises to the Indians, and he feared an expensive Indian war, far more expensive than the Senate amendments, if the treaty promises were unfulfilled. He proposed that the House go along with the Senate as "a matter of the wisest economy, to say nothing about the public faith and the public honor." Carrying out the treaty stipulations, he insisted, was "alike due to the public faith which has been pledged and to the spirit of humanity which ought to actuate the dealings of a powerful republican Government." To Burleigh and Windom was added William Higby of California, who pointed out that the very law of Congress that authorized the Peace Commission had directed the commission to make treaties under the direction of the president, subject to the action of the Senate.[18] (All three of these men, it was noted, had not been reelected to Congress.)

The sympathetic views of these men toward the provisions in the treaties did not seem to arouse much immediate support in the House. Instead, they were challenged by Representative John A. Logan of

17. *Congressional Globe*, 40th Cong., 3d sess. (February 27, 1869), 1699, 1701.

18. Ibid., 1701–5. The law authorized the Peace Commission "in their discretion, under the direction of the President, to make and conclude with said bands or tribes such treaty stipulations, subject to the action of the Senate, as may remove all just causes of complaint on their part, and at the same time establish security for person and property along the lines of railroad now being constructed to the Pacific and other thoroughfares of travel in the western Territories, and such as will most likely insure civilization for the Indians and peace and safety for the whites." 15 Stat. 17 (1867).

Illinois, who declared that "the idea of this Government making treaties with bands of wild and roving Indians is simply preposterous and ridiculous. It is not good judgment or statesmanship; it is child's play, nothing more and nothing less." Logan especially ridiculed the terms of the treaties that provided clothes for the Indians for a period of thirty years ("for each male person over fourteen years of age, a suit of good substantial woolen clothing, consisting of coat, pantaloons, flannel shirt, hat, and a pair of home-made socks") and a yoke of oxen to each Indian family settled on the reservation ("one good well-broken pair of American oxen"). And amid great laughter he lampooned the three men who had spoken in favor of the treaties.[19]

The House refused to concur in the Senate amendments, and the Senate would not back down. A conference committee failed to resolve the deadlock, so the Fortieth Congress ended on March 3, 1869, without having passed an Indian appropriation bill.

Action of the Forty-First Congress

The Forty-first Congress, which opened the following day, March 4, was faced with resolving the pressing issue. How could the management of Indian affairs be continued if no appropriation bill were passed, and how could the Indians be kept peaceful if there was no authorization for funds to meet treaty stipulations and other Indian needs?

Intense and vehement debate in the House continued in March and April 1869. Representative Clarke considered the whole matter "a fraud from the beginning to end, manipulated, directed, and controlled by Indian agents and superintendents, who made these treaties in Washington, took them out to the Indian country, and went through the farce of having them signed by these Indians." On March 19 he offered this amendment to the bill:

> *Provided,* That from and after the passage of this act the Indian tribes in the States and Territories of the United States shall be held to be incapable of making treaties with the United States, and no such treaty shall hereafter be made.

19. *Congressional Globe*, 40th Cong., 3d sess. (February 27, 1869), 1707.

And he reinforced this proviso with another that declared no agreement or contract made hereafter with Indian tribes would be valid unless approved by act of Congress.[20] The motion, however, was ruled out of order as "independent legislation." Then the appropriation bill, without funds to fulfill all the stipulations of the treaties of 1867 and 1868, was once more passed by the House and sent to the Senate.[21]

As might have been expected, the Senate, like the House, held to its previous actions; it passed various appropriations for carrying out the treaties that were so hated by the House. It also considered in some detail the question of treaty making and of fulfilling treaties made and ratified. Senator James Harlan of Iowa spoke eloquently about the history of treaty making and about maintaining the good faith of the nation. He was seconded by Senator William P. Fessenden of Maine, who said of the Peace Commission treaties: "I do not know whether the treaties are wise; my impression is that they may be so now. They have been negotiated. The Senate has recognized them and ratified them. They are, therefore, to that extent the law of the land." While admitting the authority of the House to make or refuse to make appropriations to carry out the treaties, Fessenden insisted that good faith required fulfillment of any treaty already made with the Indians, for the Indians, not understanding the intricacies of congressional politics, would look upon the rejection of treaties by the House simply as broken faith. When he looked to the future, however, he was less sure that treaties were proper. "I am for putting an end to the idea," he said, "that these roving bands of Indians, which have now become so comparatively weak, are to be recognized longer as independent nations. I am for dealing with them kindly and wisely as well as we can, and I am opposed to the further multiplication of these treaties. I say this because I am in favor of executing in good faith those we have already made."[22] It was an accurate foreshadowing of the position that both the Senate and the House would ultimately take two years later.

Senator Richard Yates of Illinois represented those who took a harsher view of the treaty system, for he held adamantly that the Indian tribes were not civilized nations, that they never had owned the lands they ceded in treaties, and that making treaties with them had been an egregious mistake. His extreme views were rebutted by Harlan and

20. Ibid., 41st Cong., 1st sess. (March 19, 1869), 170.
21. Ibid., 173.
22. Ibid. (April 1, 1869), 417–18.

others and seemed to have little impact in the Senate as a whole.[23] The Senate, as in the previous session, passed the appropriation bill with its own amendments and returned it, as a challenge, to the House.[24]

It was a challenge that the House eagerly accepted. Representative Henry L. Dawes, who, as chairman of the Appropriations Committee, directed the debate, was careful not to impugn the character of the members of the Peace Commission, but he charged them with extravagance in their provisions for Indian civilization and argued that if these provisions were approved (they were to run, he noted, for thirty years), the United States would enter upon "a policy in reference to the tribes of Indians from which it will then be too late to depart, however we may be convinced hereafter that another and a different one would be more economical and equally just in keeping faith toward them and hastening on that day when they shall be self-reliant or semi-civilized and merge with the people of this common country under common laws."[25]

Dawes's colleague from Massachusetts, Benjamin Butler, was one of the most vociferous in upholding the prerogatives of the House. He admitted that the House had no power in treaty *making,* but he insisted that it did in treaty *ratifying.* Furthermore, he challenged the power of the United States any longer to make treaties with Indians, who, he argued, had all been made citizens by the Fourteenth Amendment. "Can we make valid treaties," he asked rhetorically, "with a portion of the people within our own jurisdiction?" He ended with a dramatic appeal to the House: "Upon the question whether we will or will not stand up against these treaties I hope the House will stand as firmly as the rock of ages; that we will never agree to them. Let war come; let anything come that may come, before we will agree to them, and begin again to perpetuate this vicious system of treaties with the Indians."[26]

23. Ibid., 421–22.
24. Ibid. (April 2, 1869), 442–51.
25. Ibid. (April 6, 1869), 557. For a discussion of Dawes's role in the Indian treaty question as chairman of the Committee on Appropriations, see Fred H. Nicklason, "The Early Career of Henry L. Dawes, 1816–1871" (Ph.D. diss., Yale University, 1967), 366–72.
26. Ibid., 560, 561. Butler's interpretation of the effect of the Fourteenth Amendment on Indian citizenship did not prove correct, and the Senate Committee on the Judiciary on December 14, 1870, reported its opinion that, because Indians were not under the jurisdiction of the United States, the amendment did not make them citizens and that "it follows that the treaties heretofore made between the United States and the Indian tribes are not annulled by the amendment." *Senate Report* no. 268, 41-3, serial 1443. See the

Meanwhile the Indians who had signed the treaties were waiting for the goods promised them. Without an appropriation bill they would receive nothing. How could the impasse between the House and the Senate be broken—or at least skirted for the time being?

A compromise was offered by Dawes; he proposed a special appropriation of $2 million to allow the president to fulfill the new treaty obligations. Clarke strongly protested, for such a stopgap measure did not end treaty making entirely, as he had proposed in his earlier amendment on March 19. When he urged correcting the evil once and for all by his amendment, Dawes countered that the Senate might reject the whole appropriation bill, leaving the Indian Office in an impossible situation.[27] The compromise was accepted, and the bill as enacted said:

> That there be appropriated the further sum of two millions of dollars, or so much thereof as may be necessary, to enable the President to maintain the peace among and with the various tribes, bands, and parties of Indians, and to promote civilization among said Indians, bring them, where practicable, upon reservations, relieve their necessities, and encourage their efforts at self-support.

But a proviso was added by the House and accepted by the Senate that nothing in the bill could be construed to ratify or approve the 1867–68 treaties. Added, too, was the provision for the Board of Indian Commissioners to aid the president in carrying out the act.[28] The temporary relief, however, merely postponed settlement of the issue that so violently divided the House and the Senate.

In February 1870 the House turned to the new Indian appropriation bill, this one for the year ending June 30, 1871, and the whole drama was played out again. By then President Grant had become worried about the lack of appropriations to carry out ratified treaties, and he sent to the Senate a forceful report by Secretary of the Interior Jacob D. Cox, dated March 7, 1870, which pointed to problems on the

---

discussion in Francis Paul Prucha, *The Great Father: The United States Government and the Indians*, 2 vols. (Lincoln: University of Nebraska Press, 1984), 2:682–84.

27. *Congressional Globe*, 41st Cong., 1st sess. (April 6, 1869), 559, 563–64. Clarke was explicit, however, in supporting *old* treaty obligations: "The amendment I propose does not in any way interfere with any treaty which has been made and ratified up to the present time. It proposes that hereafter no treaty shall be made."

28. 16 Stat. 40 (1869). Dawes strongly defended the conference committee report. *Congressional Globe*, 41st Cong., 1st sess. (April 8, 1869), 647–49.

frontiers caused by congressional debate and action that called into question the validity of the treaties of the Indian Peace Commission and by extension of all treaties with the Indians. The resulting uncertainty, Cox said, "has produced a general disorganization—the white frontiersmen and the settlers denying the rights of Indians under treaties, on the one hand, and the Indians themselves upbraiding us with our breach of faith, and becoming dangerously unquiet, on the other." He pleaded for action that would uphold the provisions of the treaties and enable the Indian Office "to inspire the Indian tribes with the belief that the strictest good faith would be kept with them." Cox did note, however, that no new treaties had been negotiated during the past year except those previously ordered by Congress and that "every effort has been made to prepare the Indians for a policy in which government of the tribes by law and in accordance with contracts to be made under a system of general legislation by Congress, shall be substituted for the existing condition of things, in which treaties have been made with them as if with foreign powers." But he worried that such a change in policy would not succeed with the Indians unless all existing agreements were faithfully kept.[29]

House opposition to the treaty system as a whole was reinforced by the first report of the Board of Indian Commissioners, which urged the end of treaty making and the abrogation of existing treaties if a "just method" could be devised. Representative Clarke referred explicitly to the report and declared that whereas he had previously held the sanctity of existing treaties, he was now beginning to see that "the time will come in the progress of our Indian affairs, under the carrying out of an improved and liberal and just policy, when it will be necessary, not only in the interest of this Government, not only for financial considerations, but in the interest of the Indians themselves, to abrogate, to a certain extent at least, the Indian treaties already existing." Then he offered again his amendment to end further treaty making and was again ruled out of order. In the same debate Representative Aaron A. Sargent of California spoke strongly about the evil of repudiating treaties already ratified, but he suggested prorating annuities downward for tribes that had declined in numbers since the treaties were made. Representative William Lawrence of Ohio argued that with or without Clarke's declaration prohibiting future treaties, in fact conditions were such that no more Indian treaties would be made, and he was gratified, he said that

29. *Senate Ex. Doc.* no. 57, 41-2, serial 1406.

the president had recently withdrawn treaties pending before the Senate. The only strong voice speaking out in favor of treaties was that of Representative Eugene M. Wilson of Minnesota, who protested "against the disposition which seems to be manifested here, to overturn our whole policy for eighty years past in relation to Indian treaties." If Indians were treated like other citizens, he feared that they would be overwhelmed by unscrupulous white settlers and speculators, and he cited *Worcester v. Georgia* in support of the sanctity of Indian treaties.[30]

The House enacted an appropriation bill, again without providing for funds specifically to fulfill the treaties at issue but substituting this typical statement (from the Crow appropriation) for the various tribes:

> For this amount to be expended in such goods, provisions, and other articles as the President may from time to time determine, including insurance and transportation thereof, in instructing in agricultural and mechanical pursuits, in providing employees, educating children, procuring medicine and medical attendance, care for and support of the aged, sick, and infirm, for the helpless orphans of said Indians, and in any other respect to promote their civilization, comfort, and improvement, one hundred thousand dollars.[31]

It included its regular provision about not ratifying treaties still at issue. The Senate took out the general phrases and inserted specific provisions to carry out the treaties.

The lower house responded to this action on June 29, 1870, by a long disquisition from Sargent, in which he reiterated the policy of the House regarding the Peace Commission's treaties. "My judgment," he said, "is that it is not wise, so far as the Government is concerned, or for the Indians themselves, for us to yield our assent to the practice by which treaties are made and carried out. They open the door to frauds and corruptions without number. We must hereafter deal with the Indians by legislation and not by negotiations. It is a question, not of money, but of principle. I am prepared to recommend any reasonable appropriation to secure the peace with the Indians and save them from misery." He, in fact, urged larger appropriations than the House had made, for he realized that with the westward expansion of railroads and white settlement the Indians' hunting patterns had been inevitably disrupted. "We must restrain the Indians upon smaller reservations and

30. *Congressional Globe*, 41st Cong. 2d sess. (February 25, 1870), 1579, 1580.
31. H.R. 1169, 41st Cong., microfilm publication of bills and resolutions, Library of Congress Photoduplication Service, 1964.

within smaller limits, [and] we need to increase the amount of the appropriations which we make to feed the Indians and induce them to resort to agriculture as a means of livelihood." He reasserted his opinion that "we cannot in any well-considered policy recognize the Indians as independent nations within our own midst."[32]

It was clear that little by little the position of each house was hardening. There was less emphasis on Indian affairs and Indian policy in general and increasing weight given to the *rights* of the House and of the Senate in Indian treaty matters. Punctilio, in the minds of some of the members, seemed to outweigh all else. Garrett Davis of Kentucky was the most outspoken in the Senate as the debates resumed on July 14. "Why, sir," he cried, "the claim of the House is monstrous. What do the House propose to do? To expunge the treaty-making power as it is organized and vested by our Constitution, so far as it relates to all the Indian tribes. Shall they be countenanced or tolerated in this position of usurpation? . . . Will the Senate submit to such an atrocious aggression upon their constitutional rights?" Senator Charles D. Drake of Missouri argued (with little support) that a treaty ratified by the Senate was equivalent to an appropriation and needed no action from the House for the money to be withdrawn from the Treasury. That was his interpretation of a treaty as the "supreme law of the land," and he did not propose, he said, "to yield to the extraordinary, unprecedented, new-fangled, and utterly indefensible position taken by the House of Representatives."[33] A conference committee was called, since neither house would agree to the other's amendments. But the conference committee, too, failed to reach agreement.

At this point Dawes offered and the House passed a substitute for the appropriation bill, which would authorize a blanket grant of $5 million to enable the president "to maintain the peace among the several tribes, bands, and parties of Indians, to pay the annuities of some, and to provide civilization among said Indians, and bring them where practicable upon reservations, relieve their necessities, and encourage their efforts at self-support." The Senate inserted its original appropriation bill for Dawes's bill. The House would not concur, so still another conference committee was appointed.[34]

The time set for adjournment was now pressing upon Congress, and

32. *Congressional Globe*, 41st Cong., 2d sess. (June 29, 1870), 4971–72.

33. Ibid. (July 14, 1870), 5586, 5588–89. Drake's views, of course, were repudiated by the House. Ibid. (July 15, 1870), 5638.

34. Ibid. (July 14, 1870), 5589, 5607, 5609–10.

President Grant on the last day of the session personally urged the two houses to pass an Indian appropriation bill before adjourning, postponing the time of adjournment if need be. "Without such appropriation," the president said, "Indian hostilities are sure to ensue, and with them suffering, loss of life, and expenditures vast as compared with the amount asked for."[35]

In the confusion of the last day, the House agreed to recede from disagreement with Senate amendments and to accept a proviso that read: "That nothing in this act contained, or in any of the provisions thereof, shall be so construed as to ratify, approve, or disaffirm any treaty made with said tribes, bands, or parties of Indians since the 20th of July, 1867, or affirm or disaffirm any of the powers of the Executive and Senate over the subject." In this form the bill was passed and signed.[36] Representative Sargent, at the beginning of the next session, explained apologetically to the House that the conference committee, of which he had been a member, had accepted the form that was "less emphatic in expressing the opinion of the House," in that it said the law would neither affirm *nor disaffirm* the validity of the treaties instead of insisting that it would not affirm, ratify, or countenance them. The slip, he said, was due to the "weary closing hours of the last session" and the committee had not wanted another impasse that would necessitate the extension of the session or the calling of a special session in order to provide funds for the Indians.[37]

Final Action

On January 4, 1871, Sargent reported a new bill for Indian appropriations and for "fulfilling so-called treaty stipulation" for the year ending June 30, 1872.[38] The debate in the House moved along smoothly enough in consideration of particular items in the bill, with some consideration of the nature of the government's Indian policy. Dawes spoke ardently for a change in that policy, one that would ensure

35. *Senate Ex. Doc.* no. 115, 41-2, serial 1407.

36. *Congressional Globe*, 41st Cong., 2d sess. (July 15, 1870), 5625, 5663. Through clerical error, the disclaimer was omitted from the act; to correct the mistake, the clause was added to the appropriation act for 1872. See 16 Stat. 570 (1871).

37. *Congressional Globe*, 41st Cong., 3d sess. (January 26, 1871), 763.

38. Ibid. (January 4, 1871), 307.

peace. In a foreshadowing of his later role as the proponent in the Senate of allotment of Indian lands in severalty, he declared that the policy for the future should be "one of planting the Indian upon the soil in severalty, giving him an idea of the rights of property, of *meum et tuum*, and all the associations which gather around the few acres that are his and all that is associated with the name of home." There was no specific reference to the question of treaty making until January 26. Then, when the last particular tribal item, that for the Yankton Indians, was read, Representative Lawrence immediately moved to add what was becoming the standard proviso: "That nothing in this act contained shall be construed to ratify any of the so-called treaties entered into with any tribe, band, or party of Indians since the 20th July, 1867." This at once triggered new discussion of the treaty-making issue. Some, like Dawes, thought such an amendment, similar to past disclaimers, would merely postpone a solution. Others debated again the two sides of the question, and Sargent had another opportunity to express his views. "Now, I admit the treaty-making power with foreign nations," he said. "But I deny that there can be such nations on our own soil. . . . [The Indians] are simply the wards of the Government, to whom we furnish means of existence, and not independent nations with whom we are to treat as our equals. Ought not that fact to be admitted? Has not the comedy of 'treaties,' 'potentates,' 'nations,' been played long enough? Is it not played out?"[39]

Defenders of the Indians and their treaties were not yet ready to admit defeat, but they weakened on the question of making future treaties. Wilson of Minnesota renewed his support for existing treaties. "When we have treated with some poor, weak, miserable tribe, shall we refuse to make good our promises because they were incompetent to make a better bargain? We, at least," he said, "were of full age. Will gentlemen tell us to repudiate our contract because we were dealing with minors?" His position was firm: "I believe the Indians have a vested right under the treaties which have been made with them, and I do not think we can interfere with those rights." But his concern was for treaties already ratified. "I should like to see a future policy adopted in which no treaties should be made," he said. "I think it would be better. But this propriety for the future does not authorize us to repudiate the past." Representative Joseph S. Smith of Oregon also defended the present

39. Ibid. (January 25, 1871), 733–37; (January 26, 1871), 763, 765. In the same debate Representative Thomas Fitch of Nevada presented an extreme anti-Indian view that was not widely held. Ibid. (January 25, 1871), 732.

treaty system and moved (unsuccessfully) to strike out the words *so-called* before *treaties* in the amendment. "A treaty made by the Government of the United States," he argued, "is just what a treaty is made by any other Government; and when it is made in pursuance of our Constitution it binds every department of the Government and the House of Representatives. The Supreme Court of the United States has sustained the treaties made by our treaty-making power with the Indian tribes ever since our Government has had an existence. And it is too late to question their validity now."[40]

But Lawrence's amendment to the Yankton appropriation was in the end agreed to, and the bill with amendments passed the House on January 27.[41] The bill was considered by the Senate in early February. When an amendment was offered to strike out *so-called,* Senator William M. Stewart, of Nevada, objected with a vigorous statement against treaties:

> I regard all these Indian treaties as a sham, and I want them to be spoken of as "so-called treaties." . . . The whole Indian policy of feeding drunken, worthless, vagabond Indians, giving them money to squander between them and their Indian agents, has been a growing disgrace to this country for years. Many of these treaties are made with irresponsible tribes or with no tribes at all. Many of the treaties continue to exist long after the Indians have ceased to exist, and continue for the sole benefit of speculators and peculators. I think if we dignify them by calling them "so-called treaties" that is going far enough. That phrase pleases the House. They are getting ashamed of these treaties; the country is getting ashamed of them.[42]

But he gained no support for his diatribe against the treaties, and the words *so-called* were eliminated. After long debate over various provisions in the bill, an amended bill was passed thirty-eight to two on February 23, with the offending words *so-called* removed from the title of the bill as well as the text.[43] The bill went back to the House, which refused to concur in the changes made by the Senate. Once more a conference committee was established.

Both sides by this time must have been thoroughly tired of the issue, and the debates in both the House and the Senate indicated that a rough

40. Ibid. (January 26, 1871), 766.
41. Ibid., 767; (January 27, 1871), 790.
42. Ibid. (February 10, 1871), 1112.
43. Ibid. (February 22, 1871), 1480; (February 23, 1871), 1600.

consensus had been reached. The validity of past treaties was so strongly supported that it would have been impossible to pass a measure abrogating them in any way (distasteful as they remained to some members). The long history of treaty making, the decisions of the Supreme Court (especially the Marshall cases), and a strongly held conviction by many members that the faith and honor of the nation could be preserved only by upholding the stipulations and promises made in the treaties all contributed to this position. But the consensus, in the Senate as well as in the House, included the belief that no more treaties should be made with the Indians. This decision rested as much on the opinion that the tribes then existing did not constitute independent nations as on the adamant position the House took that treaty making eliminated it from essential participation in the regulation of Indian affairs.

The conference committee worked successfully to a position that both sides would accept. The Senate in its consideration of the appropriation bill had eliminated Lawrence's amendment to the Yankton clause concerning nonratification of recent treaties. The House refused to concur in that change. As a compromise, the conference committee struck out Lawrence's words and substituted the final solution to the quarrel, the great compromise on treaty making—still clinging to the Yankton appropriation:

> *Provided,* That hereafter no Indian nation or tribe within the territory of the United States shall be acknowledged or recognized as an independent nation, tribe, or power with whom the United States may contract by treaty; *Provided further,* That nothing herein contained shall be construed to invalidate or impair the obligation of any treaty heretofore lawfully made and ratified with any such Indian nation or tribe.[44]

The members of the conference committee then had to sell their decision to the two houses, and the reception of their report tells us something of the mood of each house. The House of Representatives rejoiced. Representative Sargent, reporting on March 1 the action of the conference committee, noted that "the contest which has now proceeded for some five or six years over the question whether the

44. Ibid. (March 1, 1871), 1810. The wording of this clause was taken from a separate resolution, offered in the House on February 11, 1871, by William H. Armstrong of Pennsylvania, on which no action had been taken at the time. *Congressional Globe*, 41st Cong., 3d sess., 1154. Sargent, as a member of the conference committee, acknowledged the debt of the committee to Armstrong's earlier resolution. Ibid. (March 1, 1871), 1811.

Senate had the right, or should continue to exercise the power, to make treaties with scattered bands of Indians within our own territory has been yielded by the Senate." The report was a "matter of congratulation for the House," he said. "It will save millions of money to the Treasury. It breaks up a most improvident system, and admits the right of the House of Representatives to deal with these questions by legislation." Some members questioned Sargent about whether the final version of the bill ratified any treaties, and Sargent insisted that "there is not a word of ratification of any treaty in the bill." But he also declared that appropriations were made to fulfill stipulations of ratified treaties (including the Peace Commission treaties, although he did not openly say so). "It would be bad taste," he remarked, "and I think bad faith to refuse to appropriate under treaties heretofore made, and the House will never take that position." Representative James B. Beck of Kentucky, who had also been a member of the conference committee, said that the House had "gained almost everything that it had a right to expect." Representative Lawrence regarded the action "as the grandest triumph, for the past ten years, in the interest of the people, and in the interest of the power of the popular branch of the Congress over this subject." He adverted to the fact that Indian lands could no longer be disposed of by treaties contrary to the public land laws and pointed to the economy in the management of Indian tribes that would result once the "extravagant demands" made by treaties were no longer possible.[45]

Representative William H. Armstrong of Pennsylvania who had provided the wording for the clause in an independent resolution he had introduced on February 11, however, stressed the point that the constitutional treaty-making authority of the President and the Senate had been left intact. What had been done had been to determine that Indian tribes were no longer fit subjects for the exercise of that power. In the future, he said, "our dealings with them will be as mere domestic communities, with whom we may contract, but only with the approval of Congress. They will be contracts, not treaties." But he noted that this did not affect past treaties, and he spoke of the "propriety in the distinct reaffirmation of our adherence to all our treaty obligations." Thereupon the House approved the conference committee report.[46]

The reaction of the Senate, of course, was considerably less enthusiastic than that of the House of Representatives. Senator Davis contin-

45. Ibid., 1811–12.
46. Ibid., 1812.

ued to object to ending treaty making with Indian tribes, pointing to the well-organized tribes in Indian Territory to refute the derogatory statements made by the House about the character of existing tribes, and he objected strongly to the "vicious and . . . most reprehensible practice" of engrafting substantive legislation onto an appropriation bill. Senator Samuel C. Pomeroy of Kansas objected to the "sort of toadyism to the House of Representatives" that he viewed the conference report as representing.[47]

But supporters of the report, chiefly Senators Harlan of Iowa and John P. Stockton of New Jersey, both of whom had been members of the conference committee, managed to quiet whatever objections the majority of senators might have had. They insisted that the bill did not limit the prerogative of the president and Senate to make treaties with foreign nations, but simply declared that Indians tribes were not to be treated as foreigners. And they emphasized the proviso that nothing in the act was to be so construed as to invalidate any Indian treaty already ratified. So the Senate, on March 1, following the pattern of the House, approved the conference committee report without a roll call. The bill was enrolled, and President Grant signed it on March 3, 1871, as the Forty-first Congress expired.[48]

It was a momentous act—but the change in Indian policy that it brought was neither as sudden nor as complete as its advocates had hoped for at the time and as many historians and other students of Indian affairs have assumed in our own day. The anomaly simply took a new twist: tribes were no longer to be considered sovereign political entities with whom the federal government would make treaties, but at the same time the old treaties that recognized such sovereignty were still to be in effect. The history of Indian treaties, therefore, did not end in 1871.

47. Ibid., 1821, 1822.
48. Ibid., 1823–25. The proviso appears in 16 Stat. 567. There was little public attention paid to the measure. The *New York Times* reported briefly on the Senate debate over the conference report and noted its acceptance without a roll call vote. March 2, 1871, 5.

CHAPTER THIRTEEN

Treaty Substitutes

Congress finally ended the making of formal treaties with Indian tribes, but it did not thereby solve "the Indian problem." Rather, the legislative action of 1871 created new difficulties, which were clearly seen by Francis A. Walker, the gifted and perceptive statistician who, nine months later, became commissioner of Indian affairs. Writing in the *North American Review* in April 1873, he excoriated Congress for removing the main vehicle for dealing with the Indian tribes. "In abruptly terminating thus the long series of Indian treaties," he wrote, "and forever closing the only course of procedures known for the adjustment of difficulties, and even for the administration of ordinary business, with Indian tribes, Congress provided no substitute, and up to the present time has neglected to prescribe the methods by which, after the abrogation of the national character of the Indians, either their internal matters or their relations with the general government are to be regulated." He noted that the Indian trade and intercourse law of 1834 was largely predicated upon tribal organization and asserted that "all the life and virtue" of the act had been taken away. And he spoke of the "unpardonable negligence of the national legislature in failing to provide a substitute for the time-honored policy which was destroyed by the Act of 1871."[1]

Congress in declaring that Indian tribes should no longer be acknowl-

1. Francis A. Walker, *The Indian Question* (Boston: James R. Osgood and Company, 1874), 12–13; the book reprinted the *North American Review* article as chapter 1.

edged as independent political entities with whom the United States might contract by treaty, did not thereby end the tribal organization of the Indian communities. Some of the Indian treaties, notably the ones negotiated and ratified in 1867–68, stipulated that any new cession of lands guaranteed to the tribes in the treaties would be valid only if approved by a specified majority of the adult males of the tribe, thereby necessitating new negotiations with the tribal authorities when additional cessions were desired by the United States. Although Indian-policy reformers wanted to deal only with individual Indians as wards of the government, it proved impossible to destroy the tribes all at once or to avoid treating with the Indians on a tribal basis. The proviso in the act of 1871 that honored previously ratified treaties, a clear example of the strong force of national honor and the obligations of past promises, gave the treaties—and thereby the tribes—a long-time and, in our own day, an increasingly vital role.

The solution to the awkward situation created by the anomaly in the law of 1871 was the use (never formally proclaimed) of "treaty substitutes."[2] By means of bilateral agreements, negotiated with the tribes in the manner of treaties but ratified or confirmed by both houses of Congress; by unilateral statutes, which on occasion required formal consent of the tribes; and by executive orders, which became the dominant means of establishing and modifying the Indian reservations (once done by treaty), the federal government carried on its dealings with the tribes to the end of the nineteenth century and well into the twentieth. As time passed, in fact, the reservations upon which tribal existence depended, came to rest less on treaties than on the treaty substitutes. The 162 Indian reservations of 1890, for example, had been established in the following ways:

By executive order	56
By executive order under authority of act of Congress	6
By act of Congress	28
By treaty, with boundaries defined or enlarged by executive order	15
By treaty or agreement and act of Congress	5

2. I first became aware of the usefulness of this phrase in Charles F. Wilkinson, *American Indians, Time, and the Law: Native Societies in a Modern Constitutional Democracy* (New Haven: Yale University Press, 1987), which discusses these substitutes briefly on pages 8, 63–68, 100–103.

By unratified treaty   1
By treaty or agreement   51

A report in 1952 from the commissioner of Indian affairs indicated that
out of a total of 42,785,935 acres of tribal trust land, only 9,471,081
acres had been established by treaty, while 23,043,439 acres had been
set up by executive order.[3]

Agreements

Agreements, at first the chief treaty substitutes, were a
direct continuation of the treaty process, despite the constitutional
differences. They began in 1872 with the Shoshones and continued
until 1911, when the final agreement was made with a band of Southern
Utes. Some of them were specifically directed and authorized by Congress; others were negotiated by the Indian Office to solve particular
needs; still others resulted from Indian initiative. Most of the agreements
concerned cession of land or other modifications of reservation boundaries, but other purposes (such as allotment of lands, grants of rights of
way to railroads, or commutation of perpetual annuity payments) were
also operative. The precise nature and processes of the agreements can
be seen in the examples discussed below.[4]

The system of agreements began, ironically, with a series of councils
held with western tribes by Felix R. Brunot, president of the Board of
Indian Commissioners, who had been appointed to that task by the
secretary of the interior. Brunot apparently set aside the principles he
had enunciated so vehemently in the first report of the board in 1869—
that the treaty system was an egregious mistake and that the Indians
should be dealt with simply as wards of the nation—and, with Thomas
Cree, secretary of the Board of Indian Commissioners, went first to the
eastern band of Shoshones in Wyoming. There, in September 1872 he
negotiated with them what he (searching for acceptable terminology to

3. Cyrus Thomas, "Introduction," in Royce, *Cessions*, 641; "Report with Respect to
the House Resolution Authorizing the Committee on Interior and Insular Affairs to
Conduct an Investigation of the Bureau of Indian Affairs," *House Report* no. 2503, 82-2,
serial 11582, p. 60. An excellent overview of the post-1871 use of agreements, statutes,
and executive orders in establishing and modifying Indian reservations is presented in
Royce, *Cessions*, 856–948.
4. Appendix C contains a list of ratified agreements, 1872–1911.

replace "treaty") called "articles of convention."[5] Because the treaty with the Shoshones and Bannocks at Fort Bridger, concluded by the United States Indian Peace Commission in 1868, had stipulated that any cession be approved by at least a majority of the adult male Indians, the convention was careful to note that Brunot had dealt with the "chief, headmen, and men of the eastern band of Shoshone Indians, constituting a majority of all the adult male Indians of said band or tribe of Indians, and duly authorized to act in the premises."

The Brunot agreement specified that "this convention or agreement is made subject to the approval of the President and the ratification or rejection by the Congress of the United States." It had elements of a real treaty negotiation and was not simply a convention imposed upon the Indians by the government. Brunot's instructions were to effect an exchange of lands, but the Shoshones considered the lands to be received in exchange as worthless and subject to the incursions of other tribes. In the end, they agreed instead to sell outright the land that the government sought. To free the part of the reservation into which miners had moved and made improvements, Brunot convinced the Indians to part with the land in return for $25,000, to be spent ($5,000 for each of five years) for stock cattle, plus a salary of $500 a year for five years to Chief Washakie. Brunot, however, was embarrassed by the Indians' acceptance of his first offer for the land. "Acting upon my experience of the general habit of Indians," he reported to the secretary of the interior, "the Shoshones were offered a sum as the basis of further negotiation, and which I supposed would have to be increased to meet the demands of the Indians. When the terms first offered were promptly accepted, I did not feel at liberty to make an addition." Instead he asked that Congress appropriate an extra $10,000 to build houses for the Indians, an action Congress failed to take.[6]

Next, in August 1873, joined now by Eliphalet Whittlesey of the Board of Indian Commissioners, and James Wright, the Crow agent, Brunot signed articles of convention with the Crow Indians at the Crow Agency in Montana. The men, appointed by the secretary of the interior as commissioners under congressional authorization of March 3, 1873, persuaded the Crows to agree to give up their reservation along the

5. Kappler, 1:153–55..

6. 18 Stat. pt. 3, 291–92 (1874); Kappler, 1:153–55; Brunot to Columbus Delano, October 18, 1872, in CIA AR, 1872, serial 1560, pp. 509–11. The agreement was ratified on December 15, 1874.

Yellowstone River in southern Montana and accept in its place a new reservation in the Judith Basin to the north. Brunot justified the removal on the grounds that the Crows would be moving away from the railroad and to a place better suited to their needs. But the people of Montana were delighted that one of the finest valleys in the West would be opened to white settlement. The Crows, however, ultimately refused to move and Congress did not ratify the agreement.[7]

Finally, Brunot signed an agreement in September 1873 with the Utes under Chief Ouray. Congress on April 23, 1872, had authorized the secretary of the interior to negotiate with the Utes for cession of part of the reservation set up for them in 1868, and commissioners had unsuccessfully tried to make a deal with the Indians in 1872. Brunot, who attended that council as an observer, not as an official commissioner, learned that the chief's son had been captured by Cheyennes and Arapahos some fifteen years earlier, and he and Thomas Cree were able to locate the boy and reunite him with his father in the offices of the Board of Indian Commissioners in Washington, D.C. The next year, when Brunot and another member of the Board of Indian Commissioners, Nathan Bishop, were appointed to try again to negotiate with the Utes, the kindness to Ouray paid handsome dividends. The chief's gratitude, Brunot's biographer wrote, "did what a special commission could not do, and when Mr. Brunot told him he thought it right for him to sell a portion of his reservation, Ouray threw all his strong influence in favour of the sale, though a year before he intended opposition to the bitter end." The Utes ceded the southern half of their reservation in southwestern Colorado for a sum of money that would produce $25,000 a year—plus a lifetime annual salary of $1,000 for Ouray.[8] There was little or nothing in the Brunot articles of convention to distinguish them from earlier treaties except the provision in the

---

7. The agreement is printed in Kappler, 4:1142–45. It is discussed in Charles Lewis Slattery, *Felix Reville Brunot, 1820–1898: A Civilian in the War for the Union, President of the First Board of Indian Commissioners* (New York: Longmans, Green, and Company, 1901), 207–13, and in CIA AR, 1873, serial 1601, pp. 481–86, which also includes a narrative of the proceedings and a report of the council, August 11–16, 1873. The authorization of the agreement is in 17 Stat. 626.

8. Slattery, *Brunot,* 191–92, 214–15. The story of Ouray's lost son is told in Ann Woodbury Hafen, "Efforts to Recover the Stolen Son of Chief Ouray," *Colorado Magazine* 16 (January 1939): 53–62. The agreement was ratified on April 29, 1874. 18 Stat. pt. 3, 36–41; Kappler, 1:151–52. See also Brunot's report and the council proceedings in CIA AR, 1873, serial 1601, pp. 451–81. Bishop did not appear for the negotiations, which were handled by Brunot and Cree.

agreements that they were subject to ratification or rejection by Congress, and perhaps the reputation Brunot had for humanitarian interest in Indian welfare.

Brunot's term, "articles of convention," did not take hold, nor was the word "contract" used, even though it had been clear in the minds of the congressmen who debated the issue of treaties that they were talking about contracts between the federal government and the tribal authorities. It became official usage to refer to the results of the post-1871 negotiations as "agreements." Yet, just as it was impossible to eliminate the procedures and substance that had marked the earlier treaties, so it seemed impossible to end the use of the word "treaty." In the minds of many Indians and government officials alike, the new agreements were still treaties.

The House document that printed a letter from Secretary of the Interior Columbus Delano in 1874 urging ratification of Brunot's convention with the Shoshones was entitled "Treaty with the Shoshone and Bannock Indians." In 1876, responding to agitation for cession of the Black Hills, the legislature of Minnesota asked Congress to "provide for a treaty with the Indians" occupying the Black Hills. An 1888 House document requesting an investigation of the Pratt Commission (which had been sent out to get Indian signatures to an agreement for cession of part of their reserve) was called "Sioux Indian Treaty"; and in 1891 the report of the House Committee on Indian Affairs relative to new negotiations with the Crow Indians used the word "treaty" throughout. A final example is the agreement negotiated with the Yankton Sioux on December 31, 1892. When ratification was delayed, the chiefs and headmen who had "signed the treaty of December 31, 1892," petitioned the government for ratification. The title of the pertinent House document consistently called the agreement a treaty.[9]

A number of the agreements were negotiated as a result of the government's desire—under pressure from advancing white settlers and miners—to reduce the reservations set up by the Indian Peace Commission's treaties of 1867 and 1868. Of special concern was the Great Sioux Reserve, stretching from the Missouri River to the western boundary of Dakota, established by the Treaty of Fort Laramie. Since Article 12 of that treaty stipulated that any cession required approval of at least three-fourths of all the adult male Indians, it was necessary to begin a

---

9. *House Ex. Doc.* no. 61, 43-1, serial 1607; *House Misc. Doc.* no. 95, 44-1, serial 1701; 19 Stat. 45 (1876); *House Misc. Doc.* no. 576, 50-1, serial 2570; *House Report* no. 3700, 51-2, serial 2887; *House Ex. Doc.* no. 80, 53-2, serial 3223.

process of formal negotiations with the tribes. The first attempt was a full-scale negotiation between a council of the interested tribes and a commission headed by Senator William B. Allison of Iowa. Held near the Red Cloud Agency, the council was a failure. The commission was not clear about whether it was seeking a leasing of the Black Hills for use of miners or an outright cession, and the Indians demanded more for a sale than the commission would agree to. The commission ended its report with the recommendation that Congress should simply fix a fair price for the Black Hills and present the matter to the Indians "as a finality."[10]

After the Indians defeated Custer in June 1876 and while the army was still pursuing the hostiles, Congress decided on an ultimatum to the Sioux. It ruled that the Indians would receive no more subsistence unless they relinquished the lands wanted by the whites, including the Black Hills; a new commission, headed by a former commissioner of Indian affairs, George W. Manypenny, was appointed to take the message to the Indians and get their signatures on the agreement. Meeting at the Red Cloud Agency and at other agencies in September and October 1876, Manypenny got the Indians' Xs, but he ignored the requirement of approval by three-fourths of the adult males. The agreement, like the Indian Peace Commission treaties of a decade earlier, was replete with provisions for artisans to aid the Indians move toward civilization and with pledges by the Indians "to observe each and all of the stipulations herein contained, to select allotments of land as soon as possible after their removal to their permanent home, and to use their best efforts to learn to cultivate the same."[11]

Similarly, commissions were sent out to treat with the Crows in 1880 for a cession of land and allotments in severalty, to replace in part the unratified agreement made by Felix Brunot seven years earlier, again in 1881 to obtain a right of way for the Northern Pacific Railroad, and

10. See "Report of the Commission Appointed to Treat with the Sioux Indians for the Relinquishment of the Black Hills," in CIA AR, 1875, serial 1680, pp. 686–702. A full account of the Allison Commission's work is given in James C. Olson, *Red Cloud and the Sioux Problem* (Lincoln: University of Nebraska Press, 1965), chap. 11.

11. The report of the commission, December 18, 1876, is in *Senate Ex. Doc.* no. 9, 44-2, serial 1718, which also includes the journal of proceedings. There is an account in Olson, *Red Cloud*, 224–30. The agreement was ratified by Congress on February 28, 1877. 19 Stat. 154–64; Kappler, 1:168–73. There is extended discussion of this agreement in relation to Sioux claims to the Black Hills in Edward Lazarus, *Black Hills, White Justice: The Sioux Nation versus the United States, 1775 to the Present* (New York: HarperCollins, 1991); see index under "Treaty of 1876."

still again in 1890 for a further reduction of the reservation and the opening of surplus lands to white settlement.[12] The 1890 agreement was modified by an agreement in August 1892; and seven years later still another agreement for reduction of the Crow reserve was signed.[13] The negotiations were authorized in general or in particular by Congress, and the documents specified that they would take effect only when ratified by Congress. The agreements were careful to state that a majority of adult male Indians had participated in the signing of the agreements. They were, for all practical purposes, except in method of ratification, treaties changing the provisions of the Treaty of Fort Laramie made with the Crows in 1868.

For the tribes in the Indian Territory, who required special attention, two blue-ribbon commissions were appointed late in the nineteenth century to negotiate agreements. The first of these, originally called the Cherokee Commission, was appointed "to negotiate with the Cherokee Indians and with all other Indians owning or claiming lands lying west of the ninety-sixth degree of longitude in the Indian Territory for the cession to the United States of all their title, claim, or interest of every kind or character in and to such lands." Lands ceded would become part of the public domain and be open to homesteading or other disposition under the public land laws.[14]

After an initial failure to negotiate successfully with the Cherokees for the Cherokee Outlet, the commission was reconstituted in January 1890 with David H. Jerome, former governor of Michigan, as chairman. The new commission, henceforth known generally as the Jerome Commission, began its work in May 1890 and by November 23, 1892, had signed eleven agreements—with Iowas; Sacs and Foxes; the Citizen Band of Potawatomi; Absentee Shawnees; Cheyennes and Arapahos; Wichitas and affiliated bands; Kickapoos; Tonkawas; Cherokees (who relinquished the Outlet); Comanches, Kiowas, and Apaches; and Pawnees. These Indians, by and large, opposed land cessions, but the commission persisted, sometimes threatening that if the Indians did not

12. See appendix C, agreements nos. 9, 11, 29.
13. The agreements appear in Kappler, 1:450–53n, and 3:87–97. For comparable agreements with Shoshone and Bannock Indians, see appendix C, agreements nos. 8, 10, 19, 49, 54, 69.
14. 25 Stat. 1005–6 (1889). The history of the Cherokee Commission is told in Berlin B. Chapman, "The Cherokee Commission, 1889–1893," *Indiana Magazine of History* 42 (June 1946): 177–90, and in a series by the same author in *Chronicles of Oklahoma*, September 1937, June 1938, March 1939, December 1941, and Winter 1948–49.

accept the terms, they would ultimately get less. In the end the Indians parted with more than 15 million acres. The agreements commonly provided a 160-acre allotment in severalty for each Indian on the tribal rolls, and the surplus land was bought by the government for white homesteading. The sale of the Cherokee Outlet for more than $8.5 million was the largest transaction; when the Outlet was opened to settlement on September 16, 1893, a hundred thousand persons rushed in to locate homesteads.[15]

The second group sent to Indian Territory was the Commission to the Five Civilized Tribes (called, after its chairman Henry L. Dawes, the Dawes Commission). The main thrust of American Indian policy at the end of the nineteenth century was the allotment of the reservations in severalty, an intensified drive to individualize the land holdings of the Indians as a means of assimilation into white society. The General Allotment Act (Dawes Act) of 1887 was the culmination of this drive, but the Five Civilized Tribes were specifically excluded from the law, and humanitarian reformers and government officials persisted in their attempts to bring those Indians, too, under the allotment policy. The legislation of March 3, 1893, that authorized the Dawes Commission directed the commission, first, to procure the allotment of lands for each of the tribes and, second, to arrange the cession to the United States of any lands not needed for allotments. But the commission was given broad powers to negotiate the agreements, with the final goal of enabling "the ultimate creation of a Territory of the United States with a view to the admission of the same as a state in the Union."[16] The Indians at first refused to negotiate concerning any of the proposals made to them, but after heavy pressure from Indian reformers and government officials, they succumbed.

In April 1897 the Dawes Commission signed the Atoka Agreement with the Choctaws and Chickasaws. Agreements were made with the

15. The agreements were ratified by Congress at different times between February 13, 1891, and June 6, 1900. See appendix C, agreements nos. 24–28, 31–34, 36, 39. Details on each of the agreements are given in Grant Foreman, *A History of Oklahoma* (Norman: University of Oklahoma Press, 1942), 244–53. A discussion of the Jerome Commission agreements in the perspective of their effect on the collapse of the treaty system is given below, pp. 350–52.

16. 27 Stat. 645–46. The work of the Dawes Commission can be followed in two articles by Loren N. Brown: "The Dawes Commission," *Chronicles of Oklahoma* 9 (March 1931): 70–105, and "The Establishment of the Dawes Commission for Indian Territory," ibid. 18 (June 1940): 171–81. Official reports and related documents are in the *Annual Report of the Commission to the Five Civilized Tribes*, 1894–1905 (issued under varying titles).

Creeks in September of that year, with the Seminoles in October 1899, and finally with the Cherokees in April 1900. Congress ratified and approved them at various dates between June 1898 and June 1902.[17]

The agreements of the Jerome and Dawes commissions were used to carry out the increasingly strong commitment of the United States to its policy of allotment and tribal dissolution. The tribes "agreed" in the end because they realized that they had no other choice, even though in form an agreement looked like a treaty negotiated between competent political entities with a quid pro quo, signatures of the agreeing parties, and ratification by Congress.

Other agreements of less national moment, but significant enough for the tribes involved, were negotiated not by specially appointed commissions but by Indian inspectors. The office of inspector had been established by Congress in 1873 to provide experienced men (usually successful agents or others knowledgeable in Indian affairs) to act as troubleshooters for the commissioner of Indian affairs and the secretary of the interior. In dealing with tribes to settle some past difficulty, to arrange for removals, or to obtain land cessions, the government regularly used the inspectors as the official federal commissioners authorized to draw up a formal agreement. The task of these men was not so much to negotiate—although that term was commonly used—as to convince the Indians to accept the government's proposals and also to make sure that the Indians got as good a deal as possible given the political and economic pressures that arose. There were from three to five inspectors at any one time, and beginning in 1880 special agents were appointed who acted much like inspectors.[18] Thus Inspector Robert S. Gardner negotiated an agreement with the Yakimas in 1885 and one with the Shoshones and Bannocks in 1887. In 1896 Inspector Province McCormick negotiated with the Indians of the San Carlos Reservation. And Special Agent John Lane signed agreements with the Yakimas and with the Coeur d'Alenes in 1894.[19]

The work of these men, however, was greatly overshadowed by that of James McLaughlin, a long-time agent highly respected by the Indians,

17. See appendix C, agreements nos. 51–53, 58–60, 67–68. The part played by these agreements in the collapse of the treaty system is discussed below, pp. 353–55.

18. A brief account of the inspectors appears in Francis Paul Prucha, *The Great Father: The United States Government and the American Indians*, 2 vols. (Lincoln: University of Nebraska Press, 1984), 1:589–93. See also Paul Stuart, *The Indian Office: Growth and Development of an American Institution, 1865–1900* (Ann Arbor: UMI Research Press, 1979), chaps. 6–8.

19. See appendix C, agreements nos. 14, 19, 44–45, 48.

who was appointed Indian inspector in 1895.[20] McLaughlin was a realist who unabashedly argued that the Indians should be forced to stand on their own in American society, but he strove to get justice for them and was able to convince the tribes he dealt with that he was getting them the best bargain possible. He spoke in his autobiography, first published in 1910, about his work in "modern treaty-making" and declared: "Treaty-making with the Indians has been my business very generally since my appointment as inspector. I have made all the treaties,—or agreements, as they are designated now, legally,—with two exceptions, that have been entered into in the past thirteen years."[21]

Ten of McLaughlin's "treaties" were formally ratified, with the text of the agreements printed in the *Statutes at Large*. But they were only a portion of his work with the tribes, with whom he often made agreements that did not go through the formal agreement procedures. McLaughlin found the Indians "shrewder in diplomacy than might be expected by those who judge of their capacity from the manner in which they have been deprived of their native riches," but he admitted that the proposals all came from the government and that his work was to convince the Indians to accept them—a work in which he was eminently successful, by his own account, a fact that he attributed to "merely a matter of being familiar with the Indian character."[22]

Although most of the post-1871 agreements dealt with land cession, allotment, or opening up surplus lands for white settlement, other ends also were sought. Agreements were made for railroad rights of way or

20. It is possible to follow McLaughlin's work in some detail because of the existence of published sources. He himself published an autobiography, *My Friend the Indian*, new ed. (Boston: Houghton Mifflin Company, 1926), and there is a useful, although uncritical, biography by Louis L. Pfaller, *James McLaughlin: The Man with an Indian Heart* (New York: Vantage Press, 1978). Pfaller has edited a thirty-six-reel microfilm edition of McLaughlin's papers, *Major James McLaughlin Papers* (Richardton, N.D.: Assumption College, 1968), which includes papers of McLaughlin deposited at Assumption College and selected documents from the National Archives. The papers include council proceedings with some of the tribes.

21. *My Friend the Indian*, 291. McLaughlin wrote: "There was a treaty-making commission that was organized in President Cleveland's last term, but the commission made only two treaties in the several years of its existence,—one known as the Fort Hall treaty, and the other with the Crows" (p. 292). See appendix C, agreements nos. 54 and 57 for this commission's work.

22. *My Friend the Indian*, 293, 312, and chap. 17 passim. See appendix C for McLaughlin's agreements printed in the *Statutes at Large*. His own list is in *My Friend the Indian*, 295. McLaughlin's work was highly praised by George Bird Grinnell in his introduction to the 1926 edition of *My Friend the Indian* and by Pfaller in *James McLaughlin*. It is clear that the government placed great confidence in him and in his role as "treaty-maker."

for leasing of lands (with agreements made between the tribe and the corporation and then formally approved or confirmed by act of Congress).[23] In other cases agreements called for the commutation of perpetual annuity payments.[24] The formally ratified agreement with the Kansa Indians in 1902 was drawn up by the tribe and then presented to the government for approval.[25] On occasion Congress gave what amounted to prior ratification. Thus a specially appointed commission of 1889 was directed to make agreements with Chippewas in Minnesota to consolidate on the White Earth and Red Lake reservations, with the provision that they must be assented to in writing by two-thirds of the male Indians over eighteen years of age, and that they would take effect when approved by the president of the United States.[26]

The procedures in agreement making followed a more or less standard form. Usually there was specific or general authorization by Congress for the secretary of the interior to negotiate with specified Indian tribes. The secretary (or the commissioner of Indian affairs in his name) appointed a commissioner or commissioners to carry on the negotiations. What the United States hoped to gain from the agreement was set forth in instructions to the commissioners, together with the limits that the government placed on payments or other benefits to the Indians, although the federal negotiators were given a relatively free hand, and they sometimes had to depart from the strict letter of their instructions in order to get the Indians to agree. The commissioners in sending the signed agreement to the Indian Office or the secretary (with the long list of Indian signatories) also sent certificates that the agreement had been properly interpreted to the Indians and understood by them and that the requisite percentage of adult Indians had signed (if previous treaties with the tribe included a specific requirement). Included also was a report by the commissioners explaining in detail the important elements in the negotiations and justifying their action. Often the minutes of the councils with the tribes were submitted as well.

With this material in hand, the commissioner of Indian affairs reported at length to the secretary (including in his report a general narrative of the case) with his recommendations for acceptance, rejection, or amendment; the secretary in turn added his comments. In some

23. See, for example, appendix C, agreements nos. 6, 41, 50.
24. Ibid., agreements nos. 71–72.
25. Ibid., agreement no. 65.
26. 25 Stat. 642–46 (1889); the agreements and the statements of presidential approval are printed in *House Ex. Doc.* no. 247, 51-1, serial 2747, pp. 27–66.

cases the executive officers requested a statement from the Attorney General's Office about acceptability of the legal provisions and sometimes from the commissioner of the General Land Office, who might set forth specific provisions for the cession and disposition of the land involved. Finally, there was a draft of a bill, which included the agreement (usually without the Indian signatures), plus recommendations for implementing the agreement. When all this material was ready, the secretary either sent the whole docket to the president to transmit to Congress, or he himself sent it directly to the House and the Senate.

When received in the House or the Senate, the material was immediately referred to the Committee on Indian Affairs, which would report the bill (sometimes with amendments), and then the agreement was ready for consideration by the full house. Whereas the action in the executive branch usually moved ahead expeditiously, that was not the case in Congress. Often there was considerable delay because of more pressing business or because conflicts of interest surfaced that made it difficult if not impossible to get congressional approval. Such delays were embarrassing to the executive branch, which in some cases repeatedly resubmitted the agreement, hoping for speedy action. It was difficult to explain to tribes who had granted rights of way to railroads, for example, why the railroads had already been built but the payments promised in the agreements had not been forthcoming. A number of agreements, in the end, were never ratified. Those that were ratified carried the statement that the agreement in question had been "accepted, ratified, and confirmed" and were printed in appropriate sequence in the *Statutes at Large*. Some were made part of the current Indian appropriation act; others were separate laws. In most cases the statutes included the full text of the agreement, but in others the actual agreement was only referred to and not printed.[27]

The procedures, however, were not cut and dried, and irregularities sometimes made it difficult to determine whether an agreement had in fact been ratified by Congress. An illustrative instance is the agreement with the Indians of the Colville Reservation signed on May 9, 1891.

A bill to ratify the agreement passed the House, but the Senate, arguing against Indian title because the lands being ceded had been established as a reservation by executive order, refused to approve it. A drastically amended bill dropped the text of the 1891 agreement and

---

27. In the latter cases the text of the agreements is entered in a footnote in Kappler. See appendix C for the location of ratified agreements in the *Statutes at Large* and in Kappler.

restored the pertinent lands to the public domain without mention of payment to the Indians. The Indians repeatedly claimed compensation for the lands given up, and the commissioners of Indian affairs and the secretaries of the interior supported their claim, insisting that the Indians had title to the land under aboriginal rights. Ultimately, in 1906, Congress provided $1.5 million "to carry into effect the agreement" of May 9, 1891. Actual payment was made to the tribes over a five-year period; each of the appropriation acts referred to ratification of the agreement by the law of 1906. Finally, in 1975, the Supreme Court in *Antoine v. Washington* declared that there was no doubt that these statements ratified the 1891 agreement, but even if there were doubt, the "canon of construction applied over a century and a half by this Court is that the wording of treaties and statutes ratifying agreements with the Indians is not to be construed to their prejudice." It had been a long and roundabout road to the ratification of the Colville agreement.[28]

A glance at the list of ratified agreements (see appendix C) will show that the agreement-making process died out shortly after the turn of the century. A large number of the agreements, as we have seen, concerned cession of lands that were in some sense protected by treaties, and after the passage of the General Allotment Act (Dawes Act) of 1887 agreements were used for the cession of the "surplus lands" that remained in a reservation after all the Indians there had received allotments. When the Supreme Court in *Lone Wolf v. Hitchcock,* January 5, 1903, declared that Congress had "plenary authority" over Indian affairs, that consent of the Indians was not always necessary to obtain cessions of land, and that Congress had the power to abrogate treaty provisions, the need of formal treaty-like agreements for the cession of Indian lands seemed to be obviated.[29]

Only five ratified agreements were signed after *Lone Wolf.* Two of these (with the Shoshones/Arapahos and with the Indians of the Port Madison Reservation) were a continuation of the old procedures. Two others (with the Sacs and Foxes and with the Potawatomis) concerned commutation of annuities, not land cessions. And the final agreement (with the Wiminuche Band of Southern Utes on May 10, 1911) com-

28. Agreement and related documents in *Senate Ex. Doc.* no. 15, 52-1, serial 2892; 27 Stat. 62–64; 420 U.S. 194–207. *Senate Report* no. 2561, 59-1, serial 4905, pp. 134–40, provides a historical account of the affair and strong support of the Indians' claims.

29. *Lone Wolf v. Hitchcock,* 187 U.S. 553. Discussion of the *Lone Wolf* decision appears below, pp. 355–56, 367–68.

pleted a process of negotiation that had begun in 1903 for the addition of ancient Indian ruins to Mesa Verde National Park.[30]

The sanctity of the stipulations in the agreements came ultimately to equal that of stipulations in the treaties. In determining the rights of Indians and their protection within "Indian country," the means of establishing the Indian country—by treaty or by agreement—has been largely considered immaterial.[31] Similarly, the preemption of state law can rest on agreements and statutes as well as on treaties. Thus, for example, in *Dick v. United States* (1908) the Supreme Court upheld the validity of an article in the 1893 agreement with the Nez Perce Indians that prohibited the introduction of intoxicating liquor for twenty-five years into lands ceded by the agreement, even though those lands were now part of the state of Idaho. It compared the case with *United States v. Forty-three Gallons of Whiskey* (1876), in which a provision in the treaty of 1863 with Chippewa Indians had made a similar prohibition. The Court, in upholding the Nez Perce agreement, declared that it was "a valid regulation based upon the treaty-making power of the United States and upon the power of Congress to regulate commerce with those Indians."[32]

The clearest and most direct recognition of the force of agreements, however, came on February 19, 1975, in *Antoine v. Washington*.[33] The case involved the taking of deer by Indians during the closed season in the state of Washington, and the Washington Supreme Court decided against the Indians on the basis that the land on which they had hunted had been set aside, not by treaty, but by the *agreement* of May 9, 1891. It argued, further, that the supremacy clause of the Constitution did not require state acquiescence in the 1891 agreement, which was merely a contract between the tribe and the federal government to which the state was not a party.

The United States Supreme Court put both of these contentions to rest, as it overturned the state court's decision. It said that the end of treaty making in 1871 meant only that henceforth Indian relations would be governed by acts of Congress, not by treaty. "The change," the decision declared, "in no way affected Congress' plenary powers to

30. See appendix C, agreements nos. 69–73.
31. See *Felix S. Cohen's Handbook of Federal Indian Law*, 1982 ed. (Charlottesville, Va.: Michie Bobbs-Merrill, 1982), 127–28.
32. *Dick v. United States*, 208 U.S. 340–59.
33. 420 U.S. 194–207. The case is discussed in Wilkinson, *American Indians, Time, and the Law*, 64–65.

legislate on problems of Indians, including legislating the ratification of contracts of the Executive Branch with Indian tribes to which affected States were not parties. . . . Once ratified by Act of Congress, the provisions of the agreements become law, and like treaties, the supreme law of the land."[34]

Statutes

It is difficult to draw an accurate line between agreements and other legislation by which Congress handled Indian affairs. After 1871 many statutes accomplished what before had been the subject matter of formal treaties. Indians were moved, lands changed hands, allotments were prescribed and implemented, provisions for civilization programs were enacted, and the list goes on and on. In a sense, Congress was *both* continuing the treaty system by means of negotiated agreements *and* dealing with the Indians by direct legislation as it did with white citizens of the United States.

But there was a middle ground, as well, in laws that required Indian consent before they took effect, statutes lying between negotiated agreements and unilateral congressional action. Thus in 1881, Congress authorized the secretary of the interior, "with the consent of the Otoe and Missouria Tribes of Indians, expressed in open council," to sell the remainder of the tribes' reservation in Kansas. With similar consent the secretary could secure other reservation lands for the Indians, remove them to the new reservation, and spend a limited amount of money for their "comfort and advancement in civilization." In 1889 it provided for the appraisal of certain lands within the Pipestone Indian Reservation in southwestern Minnesota and their sale at auction by the secretary of the interior. The act would take effect "so soon as, and not until, a majority of the adult male Indians of the Yankton tribe of Sioux Indians consent." At the same time Congress directed that the allotment provisions of the Dawes Act be extended to the lands of the United Peoria and Miami Indians of the Indian Territory. Taking language from

34. 420 U.S. 203–4. The Court quoted with approval *Choate v. Trapp* (1912), which declared that in the government's dealings with Indians, the "construction, instead of being strict, is liberal; doubtful expressions, instead of being resolved in favor of the United States, are to be resolved in favor of a weak and defenseless people, who are wards of the nation, and dependent wholly upon its protection and good faith" (p. 200).

treaties, the statute declared that its provisions would not take effect "until the consent thereto of each of said tribes separately shall have been signified by three-fourths of the adult male members thereof." The next year Congress authorized sale of timber on the Menominee Reservation, but it declared that the act would remain inoperative "until full and satisfactory evidence shall have been placed on the files of the office of the Commissioner of Indian Affairs that the sales of timber and the manner of disposing of the proceeds of same herein authorized have the sanction of the tribe, evidenced by orders of agreement taken in full council." And in 1899 a law provided for the sale of the surplus lands on the Potawatomi and Kickapoo reservations in Kansas, with the stipulation that there be obtained "the consent of a majority of the chiefs, headmen and male adults . . . expressed in open council by each tribe."[35]

A major case was the reduction of the Great Sioux Reserve in Dakota. The agreement of 1876 by which the United States acquired the Black Hills did not end the land hunger of the whites for Sioux land. In August 1882, at the urging of the Dakota delegate, Congress authorized further negotiations with the Sioux in order to change the existing treaties, and Secretary of the Interior Henry M. Teller appointed a committee headed by Newton Edmunds to deal with the Indians.[36] With an agreement prepared beforehand, the Edmunds Commission sought signatures from the various bands of Sioux, but the Indians were strongly opposed to any land cession and the commission got very few signatures. When Edmunds nevertheless submitted the agreement to Teller and Teller forwarded it to Congress for ratification, strong opposition developed among the Indians and the newly formed Indian reform organizations, notably the Indian Rights Association. Their complaint was that the agreement did not have the approval of three-fourths of the adult male Indians, as required by the Treaty of Fort Laramie of 1868. Senator Dawes was able to block the measure, and an attempt to get more signatures failed.

Dawes and other reformers objected to the illegal procedures of the Edmunds Commission, not to the idea of reducing the Great Sioux Reserve. Dawes himself submitted a bill, known as Dawes's Sioux Bill, to bring about the changes that were desired. The bill proposed to

35. 21 Stat. 380–81 (1881); 25 Stat. 1012–15 (1889); 26 Stat. 146–47 (1890); 30 Stat. 909 (1899).

36. Documents on the Edmunds Commission are in *Senate Ex. Doc.* no. 70, 48-1, serial 2165.

divide the large reservation into five separate reservations, with considerable surplus land to be made available for whites, and to set up a fund from the proceeds of the sale of land to promote Indian self-support and assimilation. After much delay, Congress finally passed the measure, and the president approved it on April 30, 1888. The bill, as was expected after the strong criticism of the work of Edmunds, stipulated that the act should take effect only after consent had been given by the different bands of Sioux as prescribed by the Treaty of Fort Laramie of 1868.[37]

A new commission headed by Richard Henry Pratt failed to get the Indians' acceptance, for the Indians were leery of signing anything and insisted, if land was to be sold, on a substantially higher price than Dawes's bill allowed. To break the impasse, Congress on March 2, 1889, passed a new bill that provided a more generous financial arrangement, and it authorized a new commission to deal with the Sioux. This commission, of which Major General George Crook was the most influential member, by working behind the scenes got 4,463 signatures out of the 5,678 eligible to vote.[38]

Indian consent, however, gradually disappeared as a major element. Of key significance was the General Allotment Act (Dawes Act) of February 8, 1887, the most important law affecting Indian affairs after the ban on treaty making in 1871. It was the culmination of a long drive on the part of reformers and of the federal government to individualize Indian land tenure by allotting the tribally held reservation lands in small parcels to Indian families and individuals. The allotment provisions of the treaties negotiated by Commissioner of Indian Affairs Manypenny in the 1850s clearly foreshadowed the Dawes Act, but those provisions applied only to the specific tribes with whom the treaties were made. What the reformers wanted was a *general* allotment law that would give the government authority to divide up reservations into allotments and dispose of the "surplus" land without resorting to a new piece of legislation for each case. That is what the Dawes Act, at long last, provided. The House of Representatives wanted the law to require consent of a majority of the tribe before the law's provisions were applied, but in the struggle in Congress to get approval of the bill that

37. 25 Stat. 94–104. The story of the Sioux affair and of Dawes's measure is told in Francis Paul Prucha, *American Indian Policy in Crisis: Christian Reformers and the Indian, 1865–1900* (Norman: University of Oklahoma Press, 1976), 172–87.

38. 25 Stat. 888–99, 1002. For details on the commission's work, see *Senate Ex. Doc.* no. 51, 51-1, serial 2682. There is a good account in Olson, *Red Cloud*, 306–19.

provision was discarded, and the president was authorized, at his discretion, to survey reservations and allot the lands in severalty to the Indians residing on them. Here was clearly a treaty function (a radical disposition of Indian reservation lands) effected by unilateral congressional legislation.[39]

In the first decade of the twentieth century voluminous legislation increasingly affected all aspects of the Indians' lives.[40]

Executive Orders

The third class of treaty substitutes was executive orders issued by the president of the United States. Whereas Indian reservations had once been established by treaty or statute, new ones were now formed and old ones modified by executive order.[41]

The status of such reservations was not as clear as that for reservations established by treaty or by statute, which had a constitutional basis or came from specific congressional authority. The authority allowing the president alone to reserve land from the public domain for exclusive Indian occupancy and use is difficult to pin down, for there was no general law authorizing the president to so act. The federal courts simply sustained the executive in these actions on the basis of a long-standing acquiescence on the part of Congress and the public.[42]

39. For information on early allotment provisions in treaties, see Paul W. Gates, "Indian Allotments Preceding the Dawes Act," in *The Frontier Challenge: Responses to the Trans-Mississippi West*, ed. John G. Clark (Lawrence: University Press of Kansas, 1971), 141–70; and *Cohen's Handbook of Federal Indian Law*, 1982 ed., 98–102. There are sixty-seven treaties, laws, and agreements prior to the Dawes Act (beginning in 1830) listed in "Schedule of Treaties and Acts of Congress Authorizing Allotments of Land in Severalty," in Royce, *Cessions*, 645–47. The Dawes Act is in 24 Stat. 388–91. For discussion of the law, see D. S. Otis, *The Dawes Act and the Allotment of Indian Lands*, edited and with an introduction by Francis Paul Prucha (Norman: University of Oklahoma Press, 1973), and Prucha, *Great Father*, 2:659–73.

40. See part 7, "The Nation's Wards," in Prucha, *Great Father*, 2:759–916.

41. The executive orders are printed in Kappler, 1:801–936; 3:667–91; 4:1001–53. They are available also in *Executive Orders Relating to Indian Reservations, 1855–1922* (Wilmington, Del.: Scholarly Resources, 1975), which reprints two earlier government publications. The orders are arranged by states and then by reservations; it is difficult to follow them in chronological sequence.

42. See "Memorandum regarding the power of the president to set aside by proclamation or executive order public lands for Indian reservations and other public purposes, and the right of the president to revoke such order," in Kappler, 3:692–95. Kappler prints opinions of the attorney general, May 27, 1924, and of the solicitor of the

Thus the Supreme Court in 1868 rejected a contention that lands could be reserved from sale and set apart for public purposes only by a specific act of Congress. The Court ruled: "From an early period in the history of the government it has been the practice of the President to order, from time to time, as the exigencies of the public service required, parcels of land belonging to the United States to be reserved from sale and set apart for public uses." Moreover, acts of Congress often presumed that the authority existed. The preemption acts of 1830 and 1841, for example, declared that the right of preemption did not extend to "any land, which is reserved from sale by act of Congress, or *by order of the President*" or to "lands included in any reservation, by any treaty, law, or *proclamation of the President of the United States.*" And the Dawes Act of 1887 similarly implied presidential authority when it specified that the allotment process would apply to Indians "located upon any reservation created for their use, either by treaty stipulation or by virtue of an act of Congress or *executive order setting apart the same for their use.*"[43]

The use of executive orders to establish Indian reservations began even before the end of treaty making in 1871, but at first many such orders had a connection of some kind with a treaty or with an act of Congress. The first use of executive order to establish a reservation was in May 1855, when the president, in anticipation of a treaty with the Ottawa and Chippewa Indians (later signed at Detroit, July 31, 1855), withdrew from the market certain townships in Isabella and Emmett counties, Michigan, for Indian use. Only part of these lands were reserved by the treaty, and the remainder were returned to the public domain in 1860.[44] An executive order of September 25, 1855, formally withdrew lands for the use of the Ontonagon Band of Chippewas, as provided for by a treaty of the previous year.[45] In November of the

Department of the Interior, March 6, 1926, on the matter. Ibid., 4:1056–64. See also Wilkinson, *American Indians, Time, and the Law*, 65–67.

43. "Memorandum," Kappler, 3:693; 4 Stat. 421, 5 Stat. 456, 24 Stat. 388 (emphasis added in the quotations).

44. Order of May 14, 1855, Kappler, 1:846–47. See details on the arrangement given in Royce, *Cessions*, 810–11, under treaty of July 31, 1855.

45. Order of September 25, 1855, Kappler, 1:848–49. The treaty specified, "The Ontonagon band and that subdivision of the La Pointe band of which Buffalo is chief, may each select, on or near the lake shore, four sections of land, under the direction of the President, the boundaries of which shall be defined hereafter." Treaty of September 30, 1854, ibid., 2:649.

same year the president by executive order set aside a reservation for Klamath Indians along the Klamath River in California, a tract selected by the Indian superintendent as one of two additional reserves authorized by act of Congress.[46] On June 30, 1857, the president established the Grand Ronde Reservation for Indians of the Willamette Valley, in accordance with the treaty of January 22, 1855, which allowed the Indians "to remain within the limits of the country ceded, and on such temporary reserves as may be made for them by the superintendent of Indian affairs, until a suitable district of country shall be designated for their permanent home."[47]

But the executive also acted independently of treaty or statute. Thus in 1864, President Lincoln established a reservation at the Bosque Redondo in New Mexico for Apache Indians, and in 1867 President Johnson established the Fort Hall Reservation for the Shoshone and Bannock Indians in Idaho.[48] After 1871, the use of executive orders to establish and modify Indian reservations increased tremendously; an order was the chief vehicle for the purpose, although agreements ratified by Congress and other acts of Congress continued to play a part.

The executive order was a convenient instrument to use. An order could be easily changed and a new one substituted as occasion demanded; many Indian reservation boundaries were frequently changed, and some seemed to be continually in flux. An example was the Mescalero Apache Reservation. After the futile attempt to settle these Indians at the Bosque Redondo in 1864, a new reservation at Fort Stanton was established in 1873. The commissioner of Indian affairs drew up the specifications and sent them through the secretary of the interior to the president. President Grant on May 29 issued the following order:

It is hereby ordered that the tract of country above described [by the commissioner of Indian affairs] be withheld from entry and settlement as public lands, and that the same be set apart as a

46. Order of November 16, 1855, Kappler, 1:816–17; 10 Stat. 699 (1855).
47. Kappler, 1:886; 2:665.
48. Orders of January 15, 1864, and June 14, 1867, Kappler, 1:835–37, 870. Of the Fort Hall Reservation, Royce notes: "This reserve was set apart in general terms for the Indians of southern Idaho, and many of the Shoshoni and Bannocks established themselves thereon. Subsequently, by treaty of July 3, 1868, with the Shoshoni and Bannock, the President was authorized to set apart a reserve for the Bannock whenever they desired. It was therefore decided to accept the Fort Hall reserve as the one contemplated by the treaty, and it was so done by Executive order of July 30, 1869." See treaty of July 3, 1868, in Kappler, 2:1020–24; executive order of July 30, 1869, ibid., 1:838–39.

reservation for the Mescalero Apache Indians, as recommended by the Secretary of the Interior and Commissioner of Indian Affairs.[49]

But this was just the beginning. In February 1874 Grant cancelled the order and substituted a new one with a new boundary specification, and the same action was repeated in 1875, 1882, and 1883. The 1882 and 1883 orders set the described land aside for the Mescaleros and "such other Indians as the Department may see fit to locate thereon." And in 1910 small holdings within the reservation were restored to the public domain.[50]

Executive orders were not uniform in terminology or in scope. The commonest form set aside a designated area for a particular tribe for its "use," or "use and occupancy," or as a "reservation." Some set land aside as an addition to an existing reservation (sometimes by simply reciting the new boundaries). On the other hand, many orders restored previously reserved lands to the public domain, in some cases substituting new lands for a reservation or as an addition to an established reservation. In other cases land was withdrawn from the public domain for an indefinite period, to extend until some specified event occurred, or it was set aside vaguely "for Indian purposes." Some orders designated the reservation for a specified tribe and for other Indians at the discretion of the secretary of the interior, as was the case with the Mescaleros. On occasion an Indian agent or superintendent, on his own authority, set land aside for a group of Indians and then sought confirmation of his action from his superiors; if the superiors concurred, the president issued an executive order. A reservation could also be created by administrative action prior to the issuance of an order, in which case the executive order simply gave formal sanction to the action.[51]

At length, after the great use of orders reaching back to pre–Civil War days, Congress prohibited further executive orders for establishing or changing Indian reservations. First a law of May 25, 1918, provided that no additional reservations should be created or existing reservations enlarged in Arizona or New Mexico; and in the following year Congress declared that "hereafter no public lands of the United States shall be

49. Kappler, 1:870–71; the recommendations of the secretary and the commissioner are attached.

50. Kappler, 1:871–73; 3:685. The changes in the reservation boundaries are shown in Royce, *Cessions*, plate 45, area nos. 643, 644; the original executive order reservation of 1873 is shown by a blue line.

51. Any reading of the executive orders will turn up such an array of examples. I follow here the list given in *Cohen's Handbook of Federal Indian Law*, 1982 ed., 497–99, which includes citations of orders exemplifying each category.

withdrawn by Executive Order, proclamation, or otherwise, for or as an Indian reservation except by act of Congress." In 1927 Congress prohibited the changing of boundaries on executive order reservations except by statute.[52]

From time to time a question arose about the legal status of the executive order reservations. How secure was the Indian title to such land? In a series of cases the Supreme Court decided emphatically that such reservations were to be equated with reservations created by treaty or by statute. Thus in *Spalding v. Chandler* (1896) the Court decided: "When Indian reservations were created, either by treaty or executive order, the Indians held the land by the same character of title, to wit, the right to possess and occupy the lands for the uses and purposes designated." Over the years the Supreme Court knocked down attempts to deny or weaken Indian control of the lands in executive order reservations. In 1913 it decided that the Hoopa Valley Reservation, set aside by executive order, was Indian country for the purposes of criminal prosecutions. In 1963 it confirmed the reservation of water as well as of land by declaring that the executive order reservations concerned had been "uniformly and universally treated as reservations by map makers, surveyors, and the public." The Court said, "We can give but short shrift at this late date to the argument that the reservations either of land or water are invalid because they were originally set apart by the Executive." And in 1982 the Court ruled: "The fact that the Jicarilla Apache Reservation was established by Executive Order rather than by treaty or statute does not affect our analysis; the Tribe's sovereign power is not affected by the manner in which its reservation was created."[53]

The treaty substitutes at first retained the idea of negotiation with the Indians or made other provision for Indian consent, actions clearly in accord with the long-standing principles upholding the faith and honor of the United States in dealing with Indians. But that position, especially as times changed after the turn of the century, was severely eroded. Meanwhile, paralleling the use of treaty substitutes and their decline was agitation against the principle of any negotiating with Indians that filled the decades following the prohibition of treaty making in 1871.

52. 40 Stat. 570; 41 Stat. 34; 44 Stat. pt. 2, 1347. See the debate on the first law in *Congressional Record*, 58:738–40. Executive orders continued to be used, primarily to extend the trust status of Indian lands.

53. 160 U.S. 403; *Donnelly v. United States*, 228 U.S. 243–78 (1913); *Arizona v. California I*, 373 U.S. 598 (1963); *Merrion v. Jicarilla Apache Tribe*, 455 U.S. 134n (1982).

CHAPTER FOURTEEN

The Collapse of
the Treaty System

The debate in Congress over treaties and their appropriateness in the prevailing conditions of the United States following the Civil War was carried forward on a broad scale in the decades after 1871, even as the treaty substitutes came into play. The condemnation of the old treaties as anachronistic was met by firm and often emotional support of these treaties as sacred contracts that no honorable government could break. At first the supporters of the inviolability of treaties held their own against the treaties' critics, but little by little they were broken down, until by the closing years of the nineteenth century and the opening years of the twentieth, reliance on existing treaties all but disappeared.

It was not, however, a simple story of honest and faithful men and women fighting against the forces of selfishness and evil, for many righteous Christian reformers came to see in the treaties a hindrance and a block to the advancement of the Indians that they so zealously promoted. The dream of the reformers and their government allies was the destruction of everything that held the Indians distinct from the rest of American citizens, and the chief obstacle was tribalism in all its manifestations. Unless tribalism and its remnants were destroyed, they believed, there was little chance that the Indians as individuals could be completely absorbed into mainstream America.[1]

1. In this chapter I have drawn to some extent on Francis Paul Prucha, *The Great Father: The United States Government and the American Indians*, 2 vols. (Lincoln: University of Nebraska Press, 1984), especially chap. 29, "Liquidating the Indian Territory." A

There had long been agitation, of course, against treating with the Indians as independent nations. Criticism of treaty making from distinguished Americans had been an important force in the decision of Congress to end the process in 1871, and it seemed that the compromise reached—no more treaties but confirmation of the inviolability of treaties already ratified—would quiet the issue. But the anomaly of that situation almost immediately led to a new attack upon the treaties already in existence.

Opposition to treaties at the end of the Civil War can be read not only as a cry to stop making new treaties but also as a condemnation of the past system and a proposal to abrogate existing treaties. These sentiments came to the fore again after 1871. Humanitarians concerned with the rights of the Indians were forced at first to insist that treaty rights be respected at all costs, and an emphasis on the faith and honor of the government in dealing with Indians never completely disappeared. A radical hindrance to the civilization of the Indians, Commissioner of Indian Affairs Edward P. Smith pointed out in 1873, was "the anomalous relation of many of the Indian tribes to the Government, which requires them to be treated as sovereign powers and wards at one and the same time." Smith proposed that "so far, and as rapidly as possible, all recognition of Indians in any other relation than strictly as subjects of the Government should cease." Smith was honest enough to admit, however, that to carry out his proposal would require "radical legislation." Three years later, his successor as commissioner, John Q. Smith, noted: "There is a very general and growing opinion that observance of the strict letter of treaties with Indians is in many cases at variance both with their own best interests and with sound public policy."[2]

The economic expansion after the Civil War also brought new pressures against the landholdings of the Indians. To land-hungry whites and their representatives in Congress it appeared that Indians owned more land than they could profitably use, and railroad corporations, intent on crossing Indian reservations and seeking lands along their routes, added another powerful force to cut down or break up Indian reservations. What stood in the way of these promoters were the treaties

---

valuable and provocative account of the deterioration of sovereignty after the Civil War in one of the tribes in the Indian Territory appears in William G. McLoughlin, *After the Trail of Tears: The Cherokees' Struggle for Sovereignty, 1839-1880* (Chapel Hill: University of North Carolina Press, 1993), chaps. 10–13 and Epilogue.

2. CIA AR, 1873, serial 1601, p. 371; ibid., 1876, serial 1749, p. 389.

that guaranteed ownership of the soil to the Indians and a measure of self-government on those lands.

Attempts to Organize the Indian Territory

Much of the attention focused on the Indian Territory, where there was both a growing problem with treaties in the minds of whites and a firm defense of treaty rights by an articulate group of tribal leaders. Tension arose because of the drive to create a regular territorial government for the Indian Territory.

After the Civil War, both Commissioner Dennis N. Cooley's stipulations to the defeated Indians of the Five Civilized Tribes at Fort Smith in 1865 and the treaties signed with the tribes the next year in Washington, D.C., referred to a consolidated, confederated government in the Indian Territory, although the treaties of 1866 also reaffirmed and declared to be in full force the provisions of the earlier treaties entered into before the Indians joined the Confederacy.[3] Ely S. Parker, President Grant's first commissioner of Indian affairs, in 1869 urged that the general council spoken of in the Reconstruction treaties be organized. "The accomplishment of this much-desired object," he said, "will give the Indians a feeling of security in the permanent possession of their homes, and tend greatly to advance them in all respects that constitute the character of an enlightened and civilized people. The next progressive step would be a territorial form of government, followed by their admission into the Union as a State."[4]

Congress, in July 1866, had provided conditional land grants to railroad corporations building lines through the Indian Territory. Ten or twenty alternate sections of land along the right of way were granted to the companies "whenever the Indian title shall be extinguished by treaty or otherwise" and the lands became part of the public domain.[5] The Indians were mortally afraid that any change in their governmental status or system of land tenure, by undercutting treaty protection of the lands, would be interpreted as fulfilling the conditions for these grants.

There had been some proposals for legislation to provide territorial

3. For Cooley's demands, see CIA AR, 1865, serial 1248, pp. 482–83. For treaty stipulations see, for example, the treaty with the Creeks, in Kappler, 2:934–36.
4. CIA AR, 1869, serial 1414, pp. 450–51.
5. 14 Stat. 238, 291, 294.

organization for the Indian Territory in the late 1860s, but the concerted drive began with a resolution of Representative James R. McCormick of Missouri, from the Committee on the Territories, on January 13, 1870. The resolution sought an inquiry "into the expediency of establishing a territorial government over the civilized Indians inhabiting that portion of the country known as the 'Indian Territory.'" The need adduced in the resolution for such territorial government was couched in reasonable and seemingly innocuous language—but each phrase cut deep into the cherished treaty rights of the Indians to communal land ownership and tribal self-government and brought consternation if not panic to tribal leaders in the Indian Territory. The resolution read in part:

> Whereas the Cherokee and Choctaw Indians are a civilized people, following agricultural and manufacturing pursuits, governed by written laws and evincing other characteristics of capacity for self-government; and whereas in their tribal relations they hold their lands in common and not by individuals in fee simple, which circumstance leaves their land at any time subject to be disposed of by treaty, rendering uncertain their permanence, prosperity, and perpetuity; and whereas it is desirable to give to these people a government republican in form, to secure them individually in their right to lands, and to incorporate them with the citizens of the United States under a territorial form of government, thereby securing to them full protection as citizens of the United States and securing to them a more rapid development of their civilization and country . . .[6]

In subsequent years numerous bills were introduced into both houses of Congress to establish a regular territorial government.[7] The tone of these measures can be seen in the support for a bill introduced on March 17, 1870, by Senator Benjamin F. Rice of Arkansas, for the organization of a "Territory of Ok-la-homa." The Committee on the Territories, in reporting favorably on the bill, indicated the desire to destroy the separateness of the Indians: "It is in consonance with the new policy of the government, born of the war and matured by the fifteenth amendment, that no alien race shall exist upon our soil; all shall be citizens irrespective of race, color, or previous condition of servitude. It is a part

6. *House Misc. Doc.* no. 21, 41-2, serial 1431.

7. A list of the principal bills between 1865 and 1879 to organize the Indian Territory or otherwise extend federal jurisdiction over the area appears in Roy Gittinger, *The Formation of the State of Oklahoma, 1803–1906* (Norman: University of Oklahoma Press, 1939), 267–70.

of the inexorable logic of the times that the Indian must adapt himself to the rights and duties of citizenship."[8] At the heart of the matter was the conviction that there were too few Indians on too much land, that if the Indians could be forced to work homesteads of their own, they would find their salvation and the rest of the land could be put into profitable production by white settlers.[9]

Aside from the purported advantages to the Indians from territorial government, United States citizenship, and land in severalty, the advocates of territorial organization made much of what they considered the lawlessness of the Indian Territory. The Indian governments were criticized as ineffective, the courts as inadequate, the protection of the rights of whites and former slaves as almost completely lacking. What severely complicated the matter was the growing number of whites within the Five Civilized Tribes, a great majority of whom were farmers and other laborers who had been invited in by the Indians to work. Since the tribal governments pertained to the Indians alone, the demand arose for an adequate means to protect the personal and property rights of these whites.[10]

As the years passed and the white population continued to increase, the complaints grew. Secretary of the Interior Zachariah Chandler declared in 1876 that the necessity of devising some simple and satisfactory form of government for the Indian Territory was growing more and more urgent and soon had to be met. His commissioner of Indian affairs, John Q. Smith, was more outspoken. "The anomalous form of government, if government it can be called, at present existing in the Indian Territory must soon be changed . . . ," he wrote. "The idea that that Territory is to consist forever of a collection of little independent or semi-independent nationalities is preposterous."[11]

Congressional pressures did not subside. The Senate, in February 1878, instructed its Committee on the Territories to ascertain whether a civil form of government could not be organized over the Indian Territory for the better protection of life and property and whether the lands held in common could not be divided in severalty without con-

8. *Senate Report* no. 131, 41-2, serial 1409, p. 4.

9. See statements of this view, for example, in *Senate Report* no. 336, 41-3, serial 1443; Report of the Secretary of the Interior, 1871, in *House Ex. Doc.* no. 1, pt. 5, 42-2, serial 1505, pp. 7–8.

10. Report of the Secretary of the Interior, 1873, in *House Ex. Doc.* no. 1, pt. 5, 43-1, serial 1601, p. x; ibid., 1874, *House Ex. Doc.* no. 1, pt. 5, 43-2, serial 1639, p. xiv.

11. Report of the Secretary of the Interior, 1876, in *House Ex. Doc.* no. 1, pt. 5, 44-2, serial 1749, pp. vii-viii; CIA AR, 1876, serial 1749, p. 390.

firming the conditional grants of lands made to railroads. The committee took its charge seriously, sending members to the Indian Territory to interview inhabitants and collecting extensive historical documentation. It recommended the establishment within the territory of a United States court having criminal and civil jurisdiction, that the Indians should become citizens of the United States, and that they should have representation in Congress similar to that of other territories. It asserted that the lands could be divided in severalty without confirming the railroad grants, but it did not press the matter of individual allotment.[12]

Use of Treaty Rights to Oppose Territorial Organization

Despite the widespread feeling that changes in the Indian Territory were necessary and in the face of powerful economic interests, all the legislative measures introduced in the late 1860s and the 1870s failed. The opponents of territorial organization in those years were able to forestall radical change.

Foremost among these opponents were the Indians themselves, who spoke through their chiefs, their councils, and most especially through the special agents or delegates maintained in the national capital by each of the Five Civilized Tribes to look after tribal interests and to lobby for the protection of Indian rights.[13] These astute spokesmen, countering each move toward territorial organization with forceful memorials to Congress protesting the action, had two lines of defense. First, they pointed to the protection of their lands and of their autonomy in their treaties with the United States, and, concomitantly, they relied upon the sense of fairness and honor of the legislators to prevent any violation of the stipulations of the treaties.[14]

12. Resolution of February 25, 1878, *Senate Misc. Doc.* no. 77, 45-2, serial 1786; *Senate Report* no. 744, 45-3, serial 1839.

13. The work of the delegates can be seen in Francis Paul Prucha, "The Board of Indian Commissioners and the Delegates of the Five Tribes," *Chronicles of Oklahoma* 56 (Fall 1978): 247–64; and Thomas M. Holm, "The Cherokee Delegates and the Opposition to the Allotment of Indian Lands" (M.A. thesis, University of Oklahoma, 1974). See also W. David Baird, *Peter Pitchlynn: Chief of the Choctaws* (Norman: University of Oklahoma Press, 1972), a biography of an important Choctaw delegate.

14. A convenient listing of memorials, together with other pertinent documents, is in Grant Foreman, *A History of Oklahoma* (Norman: University of Oklahoma Press, 1942),

The agitation began after McCormick's resolution. Thoroughly alarmed, the delegates of the Five Civilized Tribes began their campaign of memorials and protests to the president and to Congress. The Creek delegates wrote to President Grant on February 26, 1870:

> It is with painful anxiety we have witnessed the introduction into Congress and the discussion of measures which, if matured and acted upon, would unavoidably result ultimately in the ruin and extinction of our people. We are jealous of the smallest infraction of our treaties, knowing it would be taken advantage of and held as a precedent by those who are anxious to get our lands; that the breach would rapidly widen, till soon our treaties would be held sacred no longer. . . . We cling to our treaties and hope for safety in the strength and good faith of the government.

With the letter went an earlier statement from the principal chief of the Creeks, which made the same point. Creeks meeting in a convention at Ocmulgee on February 10, 1870, sent along their own resolutions, insisting that their national character had been recognized and confirmed again and again "by the highest laws known to political societies, namely, treaties."[15]

The Cherokee chief Lewis Downey, in a like appeal that he and the Cherokee delegates submitted in March 1870, spoke out against the establishment of territorial government, the abrogation of treaties, and the forcing of United States citizenship upon the Indians, and he charged that "all these various movements spring from a common source and look to a common end—the extinguishment of our land titles." He cited specific treaties made with the Cherokees, which not only guaranteed the right of the soil but that the lands would be for the Indians "a permanent home—a home that shall never in all future time, be embarrassed by having extended around it or placed over it the jurisdiction of a Territory or State, nor be pressed upon by the extension in any way of any of the limits of any existing Territory or State."[16]

The Choctaw delegate Peter Pitchlynn similarly sent a protest from his nation, dated March 17, 1870; it was a long and eloquent recitation

---

363–66. See also Steven L. Johnson, *Guide to American Indian Documents in the Congressional Serial Set: 1817–1899* (New York: Clearwater Publishing Company, 1977).

15. The documents are in *Senate Misc. Doc.* no. 76, 41-2, serial 1408.

16. *Senate Misc. Doc.* no. 83, 41-2, serial 1408. The quotation, not quite exact, is from the Cherokee treaty of May 6, 1828, in Kappler, 2:288.

of treaty rights and a charge that railroad interests were seeking the Indians' lands at the expense of the broken faith on the part of the United States. He concluded: "The said Choctaw nation doth solemnly appeal to the sense of justice and honor of the Congress of the United States, sacredly to observe the faith of treaties and to guard and to preserve their guarantees and that of the Constitution which makes them the supreme law of the land."[17]

When Senator Rice's bill was introduced and when the Senate Committee on the Territories reported favorably on it, asserting that it was "in all material respects in conformity to the treaties [of 1866] with the Choctaw and Chickasaw, Creek, Seminole, and Cherokee Indian tribes," the Indian leaders renewed and stepped up their opposition. A memorial from Cherokee, Creek, and Choctaw delegates took issue with the Senate committee's report and raised three legal questions:

> First. Whether Congress has the constitutional right, in view of our status, treaties, and existing laws, to establish a territorial government over us.
> Second. Whether we are citizens under the fourteenth amendment to the Constitution.
> Third. Whether the bill does not contain provisions violative of our treaty stipulations.

"We believe it to be wrong in principle on all these questions, and various others," the Indians said. The memorial detailed the provisions of specific treaties and how the bill would change or violate them.[18]

In June 1870 the Ocmulgee Council, the representative body organized in response to the treaties of 1866, added its voice of protest: "We ask nothing from the people and authorities of the United States aside from their respect and good fellowship, but what they have promised—*an observance of their treaties.*"[19] Bills for territorial organization continued to be introduced through the 1870s, and the Indians repeated their well-argued protests, pointing to the treaty provisions protecting their land and their government and relying on "the honor and integrity of the American Congress and Government."[20]

17. *Senate Misc. Doc.* no. 90, 41-2, serial 1408, quotation on p. 12.
18. *Senate Report* no. 131, 41-2, serial 1409; *Senate Misc. Doc.* no. 143, 41-2, serial 1408.
19. Address of the Ocmulgee Council, June 4, 1870, in *Senate Misc. Doc.* no. 154, 41-2, serial 1408.
20. The quotation is from a protest of December 6, 1873, from the Ocmulgee Council, in *House Misc. Doc.* no. 88, 43-1, serial 1618. See also protest of January 20,

The congressional committees that favorably reported territorial bills were not unaware of the treaty argument made by the Indians. Nor were they prepared to argue for an out-and-out abrogation of the treaties. But they were convinced of the need for change in the Indian Territory and did not think treaties should hamper the government in doing what was needed. Thus Senator James W. Nye of Nevada, in reporting for the Committee on the Territories in February 1871, argued for the power of Congress to legislate for Indians, saying that Indians should not be treated differently from other citizens. He admitted that the Indians opposed the bill, but he did not think that fact should be given much weight.[21] More bills were introduced in the late 1870s, and the same arguments were advanced against them by the Indian delegates.[22]

The Indians were not without support, for many persons agreed with their analysis of their existing treaty rights. Initially such support came from the Board of Indian Commissioners, when that body was established in 1869 as a watchdog for Indian rights and an aid in the formulation of a just Indian policy. It was at the board's annual winter meetings with representatives of missionary groups participating in Grant's "peace policy" that the Indians found a forum for presentation of their views on self-government and treaty rights. Beginning with the first meeting in January 1872 and extending into the early 1880s, Indian delegates were in attendance.[23]

The pleas for protection of their rights made by the Indian delegates in 1872 were well received by the Board of Indian Commissioners. In its official report to the president of the United States in November 1872 the board declared: "The convictions of the Board that it is the imperative duty of the Government to adhere to its treaty stipulations with the civilized tribes of the Indian Territory, and to protect them

---

1874, in *House Misc. Doc.* no. 87, 43-1, serial 1618; Chickasaw memorial of January 6, 1875, *Senate Misc. Doc.* no. 34, 43-2, serial 1630; Cherokee memorial of January 20, 1875, *Senate Misc. Doc.* no. 66, 43-2, serial 1630; and Creek memorial of January 26, 1875, *Senate Misc. Doc.* no. 71, 43-2, serial 1630.

21. *Senate Report* no. 336, 41-3, serial 1443.

22. See *Senate Misc. Doc.* no. 82, 45-2, serial 1786; *House Misc. Doc.* no. 32, 45-2, serial 1815; *Senate Misc. Doc.* no. 73, 45-3, serial 1833; *House Misc. Doc.* no. 13, 46-1, serial 1876; and *Senate Misc. Doc.* no. 41, 46-2, serial 1890.

23. For a detailed account of the relations of the Indian delegates with the Board of Indian Commissioners, see Prucha, "Board of Indian Commissioners and the Delegates of the Five Tribes."

against the attempts being made upon their country for the settlement of the whites, have undergone no change." Its supporting voice was strong: "If national honor requires the observance of national obligations entered into with the strong, how much more with the weak. To repudiate, either directly or by any indirection, our solemn treaty obligations with this feeble people, would be dishonor, meriting the scorn of the civilized world." Again at the 1874 conference the Indian spokesmen boldly set forth their claims, emphasizing their treaty rights of self-government, and the board in its report for that year reconfirmed the position it had taken earlier.[24]

When the personnel of the board changed with the en masse resignation of the members in 1874, however, the Indians lost support. The new membership on the board moved increasingly to a position (firmly held by the humanitarian reformers interested in Indian affairs) that the Indian ways of government and land tenure should be ended and the detribalized individual Indians absorbed into American society. So they paid scant attention to the repeated representations made at their meetings by the delegates of the Five Tribes. They sided with those who sought to impose a regular territorial government on the Indian Territory, although they initially included the disclaimer "not inconsistent with existing treaties."[25]

The Position of Congress

The Indians from the Indian Territory fared better in Congress than they did with the Board of Indian Commissioners. Although bills for territorial organization were introduced and received some vocal support (to a large extent from representatives and senators from Missouri and other states close to the Indian Territory), the measures did not, in fact, advance very far in Congress. Some bills were reported back from the committees to which they had been referred, but even these were eventually postponed or tabled, and many others never came out of committee. Not a single one of the many bills was ever passed by either house, and the few debates on the measures in the House of Representatives (there were none in the Senate) indicated

24. *Report of the Board of Indian Commissioners*, 1872, p. 11; ibid., 1873, pp. 4–5, 211–15.
25. Ibid., 1875, p. 14.

strong support for the Indians' position. The Indian protests and memorials found their mark, and in the 1870s the Five Tribes won their battle.

The initial sentiment in Congress for territorial organization faded away as committee reports upheld the Indians' rights. Thus a House bill of 1872 for a new government in the Indian Territory elicited a strong minority report from the Committee on the Territories, which was a scorching condemnation of the measure:

> They do not think any such Territory should be organized, because they do not believe such action would be nationally just or honorable, wise or expedient. It is neither just or honorable because the faith of the nation has been pledged many times over against the legislation contemplated by these bills. Fifty solemn treaties made with these Indian tribes guarantee them their rights over and over again.

The report cited the treaty of May 6, 1828, with the Cherokees and the treaty of August 7, 1856, with the Creeks and Seminoles. "These and similar treaties of like import," it said, "are in force and binding today. If there is any binding force in solemn guarantee and written covenant, in plighted faith and national honor, then we cannot, must not, establish this Territory." The agitation from the measure, it insisted, came from railroad companies intent of gaining the land grants that were contingent on extinction of Indian titles.[26]

Later bills in the 1870s made little or no headway. In February 1875 a bill was adversely reported by the House Committee on Indian Affairs. The committee asked Congress to disapprove the bill and kindred bills, which would destroy or impair the nation's obligations to the Indians. "The people of this great nation ought to know, and those of the Indian Territory ought to be re-assured," the report said, "that the Congress of the United States cannot and will not lend its sanction to any measure tarnishing the nation's honor, especially where its faith has been plighted by solemn guarantee and written covenant. . . . No amount of sophistry should be permitted to mystify or divert the mind from this important feature of these bills, called by whatever name. Their operation will be the subversion of the Indian nationalities in the Territory." The bill was tabled.[27]

When the House Committee on the Territories in March 3, 1879,

26. *House Report* no. 89, 42-2, serial 1543. See also the debate in *Congressional Globe*, 42d Cong., 3d sess., 613–16, 652–54.
27. *House Report* no. 151, 43-2, serial 1659, p. 1; *Congressional Record*, 3:1313.

reported on one of the final bills introduced for territorial organization, it recommended against passage. After a very long discussion of all sorts of historical materials and citation of treaties and laws, often on a tribe-by-tribe basis, the committee finally reached its conclusions:

1. That the bill under consideration conflicts with existing treaty stipulations.

2. That while the right to decide in the last resort that a treaty is no longer binding is undoubtedly lodged in Congress, the exercise of that right is a judicial act affecting the honor and dignity of the nation, requiring for its justification reasons which commend themselves to the principles of equity and good conscience, particularly where the parties to the compacts with the United States are weak and powerless and depend solely on the good faith of the government.

3. That no such reasons exist for violating the treaty stipulations which reserve the Indian Territory exclusively for Indians and which secure . . . [to the Indians] the right of self-government under the restrictions of the United States Constitution.[28]

Thus ended the long attempt to find a solution to perceived problems among the Five Civilized Tribes in the Indian Territory and to open up their lands for white settlement and development by organizing a regular territory. The argument of the tribes had won out, as the House Committee on the Territories candidly admitted in February 1890, when it reported a new kind of bill for a "Territory of Oklahoma" that excluded the Five Tribes. The committee said that it would have recommended a measure which would have embraced within the boundaries of the Territory of Oklahoma the whole of the Indian Territory had it not been for the fact that the Five Civilized Tribes objected and cited treaty stipulations to sustain their objection.[29]

Attacks on Treaties in the 1880s and 1890s

The victory for treaty rights was short-lived, for the decades of the 1880s and 1890s brought new forces that undermined

28. *House Report* no. 188, 45-3, serial 1867. The quotation is on p. 37.
29. *House Report* no. 66, 51-1, serial 2807.

the nation status of the Indian tribes, their communal landholding, and other elements of tribal status that gave treaties their significance.

A key element in the changed situation was the appearance in the early 1880s of new groups of reform-minded Christian men and women who took a special interest in Indians. The most important of these was the Indian Rights Association, founded by Herbert Welsh and friends in 1882, which was supported by groups such as the National Women's Indian Association and the Boston Indian Citizenship Committee. Members of these groups, beginning in 1883, met each year in conjunction with a meeting of the Board of Indian Commissioners at Lake Mohonk, New York, hosted by the owner of a resort hotel, who was a member of the board. These annual Lake Mohonk Conferences of Friends of the Indian were a focal point of agitation for a new drive to finally detribalize the Indians and absorb individual Indians into social and political life as patriotic American citizens.[30]

The tribalism of the Indians, with communal land ownership and treaty rights that perpetuated a separation from the rest of American society, was anathema to these reformers. To be sure, they were high-minded Christians, and their initial posture toward Indian policy called for a firm adherence to the rights guaranteed to the Indians by treaties. The constitution of the Indian Rights Association, for example, said, "The object of this Association shall be to secure to the Indians of the United States the political and civil rights already guaranteed to them by treaty and statutes of the United States, and such as their civilization and circumstances may justify." And there was always a strong current of opinion in their meetings that treaty rights were sacred and could not be abrogated without Indian consent. Yet it became increasingly clear that treaty stipulations perpetuated tribalism and thus stood in the way of the full implementation of the reformers' program. Little by little the weight of the reform groups' influence was shifted against upholding treaty rights.

The most outspoken critic was the noted clergyman and reformer Lyman Abbott, editor of the *Christian Union* (later *Outlook*), who was a regular participant at the Lake Mohonk Conference and frequently a member of its platform committee. Abbott thought that the solution to

---

30. The work of these groups is recounted in Francis Paul Prucha, *American Indian Policy in Crisis: Christian Reformers and the Indian, 1865–1900* (Norman: University of Oklahoma Press, 1976); their writings are collected in Francis Paul Prucha, ed., *Americanizing the American Indians: Writings by the "Friends of the Indian" 1880–1900* (Cambridge: Harvard University Press, 1973).

the Indian problem lay in the complete annihilation of the reservation system, and he did not care if that meant violating treaties. In a passionate outburst at Lake Mohonk in 1885, he noted that he was speaking to Christian men and women, friends of humanity and friends of equal rights, and that not one of them would

> change, or alter, or break a treaty that he may be benefited by the breaking of it. But if we have made a bad contract it is better broken than kept. . . . It is not right to do a wrong thing, and if you have agreed to do a wrong thing, that agreement does not make it right. If we have made contracts the result of which, as shown by later experience, is inhumanity and degradation, we are not bound to go on with them—we are bound to stop. . . . We have no right to do a wrong because we have covenanted to. . . .
>
> When our fathers landed on these shores, there was no alternative but to make treaties with the Indians; it was necessary. We have now passed beyond the epoch in which it is right or necessary to make treaties, and have so officially declared. We can no longer be bound by our forefathers; we must adapt our policy to the change of circumstances.

"We evangelical ministers," he concluded, "believe in immediate repentance. I hold to immediate repentance as a national duty. Cease to do evil, cease instantly, abruptly, immediately."[31]

Most of Abbott's listeners, however, were not quite ready for *immediate* repentance, for they were committed to maintaining formal treaty rights. Even though Abbott served on the resolutions committee, he was unable to swing it to his way of thinking. The platform adopted was a compromise. It agreed to the principle of allotting the lands of the reservations in severalty, and it urged that negotiations be undertaken to modify existing treaties and that "these negotiations should be pressed in every honorable way until the consent of the Indians be obtained." For the present the conference rejected the proposal to abrogate the treaties or to force land in severalty upon the Indians.[32]

Yet the tide of opinion was flowing in Abbott's direction. In 1886 at Lake Mohonk, Philip C. Garrett, a Philadelphia lawyer and a member of the executive committee of the Indian Rights Association, spoke dramatically about destroying the distinctions between Indians and whites. "But the treaties," he exclaimed; "we are stopped again by the

31. *Lake Mohonk Conference Proceedings*, 1885, 50–54.
32. Ibid., 49.

existence of hundreds of alleged treaties, which imply the perpetual existence of the tribes, or contain some obligation unfulfilled." He did not, of course, want to "commend the infraction of any treaty really contracted between two powers," but he questioned whether "so-called treaties" were really treaties and thus solemnly binding. If they were not real contracts between two consenting parties—and he presented examples that suggested they were not—then, for the sake of the Indians, they should be cast aside. He concluded:

> If an act of emancipation will buy them life, manhood, civilization, and Christianity, at the sacrifice of a few chieftain's feathers, a few worthless bits of parchment, the cohesion of the tribal relation, and the traditions of their race; then, in the name of all that is really worth having, let us shed the few tears necessary to embalm these relics of the past, and have done with them; and, with fraternal cordiality, let us welcome to the bosom of the nation this brother whom we have wronged long enough.[33]

At the same meeting, Charles C. Painter, who served as the Indian Rights Association's agent in Washington, painted a grim history of a treaty system based on the self-interests of the whites, and he concluded, "These treaties in many of their provisions constitute one of the greatest obstacles in the way of Indian civilization."[34]

The chief wedges to break apart the old system were, in the minds of the reformers, the allotment of reservation land in severalty and the granting of citizenship to the Indians. By this breaking up of tribal landholding and of tribal political authority over the individual, the system perpetuated by the treaties could be destroyed. In the early years of the Indian Rights Association and the Lake Mohonk Conference, allotment was foremost in the mind of the reformers, until at last they got what they wanted in the Dawes Act of 1887, a general allotment law, which authorized the president to break up the reservations without the consent of the Indians and which declared the allotted Indians to be citizens of the United States.[35]

The sentiments of the reformers were well represented in Congress.

33. Ibid., 1886, pp. 10–11.
34. Ibid., 19.
35. There is a discussion of agitation for allotment and of the Dawes Act in Prucha, *American Indian Policy in Crisis*, chap. 8. See also D. S. Otis, *The Dawes Act and the Allotment of Indian Lands*, ed. Francis Paul Prucha (Norman: University of Oklahoma Press, 1973), and Wilcomb E. Washburn, *The Assault on Indian Tribalism: The General Allotment Law (Dawes Act) of 1887* (Philadelphia: J. B. Lippincott Company, 1975).

Perhaps the most outspoken critic of treaties there was Senator Henry M. Teller of Colorado, who had served as secretary of the interior from 1882 to 1885 and was considered especially knowledgeable on Indian affairs. During debate in January 1886 on a bill to divide the Great Sioux Reserve in Dakota, he said he "would abrogate every Indian treaty we have ever made" and simply legislate for the best interests of the Indians. He argued that many treaties were impossible to execute and had to be continually violated; it would be better to abrogate them altogether, and he did not doubt that Congress had the power to do so.[36]

American Law for the Indians

While debate continued on the sanctity of treaties, the United States moved to bring the Indians, to some extent at least, within the web of American law. Indian police, as an extension of the Indian agent's authority, were appointed on the reservations to keep order, and so-called courts of Indian offenses, with Indian judges, augmented the policemen's work. These institutions worked within the tribal/reservation system.[37] Not so the extension of federal criminal jurisdiction over Indians by the Major Crimes Act of 1885. The law was the reformers' answer to the Supreme Court decision in *ex parte Crow Dog*, in which the Court overturned the murder conviction of Crow Dog, a Sioux Indian who had killed Spotted Tail, because federal criminal laws did not apply to crimes of Indian against Indian on the reservations. By the act, seven crimes were made federal offenses, a heavy blow against the Indians' autonomy in their internal affairs. In 1886 the Supreme Court, in *United States v. Kagama*, upheld the act as within the competency of Congress. "These Indian tribes *are* the wards of the nation. They are communities *dependent* on the United States. Dependent largely for their daily food. Dependent for their political rights. . . . From their very weakness and helplessness, so largely due to the course of dealing of the Federal Government with them and the treaties in which it has

36. *Congressional Record*, 17:812–13, 947.
37. The fullest account of these institutions is William T. Hagan, *Indian Police and Judges: Experiments in Acculturation and Control* (New Haven: Yale University Press, 1966).

been promised, there arises the duty of protection, and with it the power."[38]

Some persons, most notably Professor James Bradley Thayer of the Harvard Law School, wanted a full-blown system of courts for the Indians to bring them as individuals under American law. It mattered little to Thayer whether or not the Indians wanted to abandon tribal relations; the United States could simply ignore the tribes and deal directly with the individuals. Thayer had support from the law committee of the Indian Rights Association and from the American Bar Association, but in the end he failed to get congressional authorization for his campaign, in large part because Senator Henry L. Dawes, relying on the citizenship provisions of the Dawes Act, fought the measure as unnecessary.[39]

The Jerome Commission

As might be expected, affairs in the Indian Territory caught the attention of the new reformers. Whites who sought an inroad into the Indian lands, having failed to open them through establishment of a regular territorial government, now sought to open particular sections that were free of Indian settlement. The first focus was on the Oklahoma District, a central area of two million acres, purchased from the Five Civilized Tribes but never assigned to other Indians. So-called "boomers" moved into the area unbidden, only to be removed by federal troops; the action was repeated over and over again until at last in 1889 President Benjamin Harrison proclaimed the region open to homesteading and whites poured in in the first of the Oklahoma "land runs." Congress, a year later, in the Oklahoma Organic Act, provided territorial government for the region and joined to it the largely uninhabited public lands in the Oklahoma panhandle (called No Man's Land). This Oklahoma Territory did not touch the Five Civilized Tribes.[40]

The acquisition of surplus Indian lands for white homesteading was accomplished by the Jerome and Dawes commissions. Although these specially appointed groups played a prominent role in signing formal

38. 23 Stat. 385; 118 U.S. 383–84.

39. For a discussion of Thayer's work, see Prucha, *American Indian Policy in Crisis*, 335–41.

40. Ibid., 384–86, and the references cited there.

agreements with the Indians as a continuation, in a sense, of treaty making, they were also key elements in the steady weakening of Indian tribal governments and therefore the influence of treaties in Indian life. They were instruments in the movement to end tribalism that so strongly marked the last years of the nineteenth century.

The Jerome Commission turned its attention to the Cherokee Outlet and to the surplus lands of the Cheyenne and Arapaho, Comanche, Kiowa, Apache, and other Indian tribes in the western part of the Indian Territory. These lands were acquired with little trouble, for most of the Indians were convinced that change was inevitable. The Iowa Tribe, with whom the commission signed its first agreement on May 20, 1890, comprised only eighty-six members, and the commissioners found no well-organized government. They spoke of the "very limited extent of the Iowas' real title and interest in and to said tract of country," which had been set aside for them by an executive order in 1883. The Sac and Fox Indians were described as "progressive" and prepared for allotment, and they made no appeal to treaty rights. For the Cheyenne and Arapaho Indians, who held their land under the Treaty of Medicine Lodge Creek of 1867, the commissioners managed to get signatures of three-fourths of the adult males as prescribed by that treaty. The Tonkawas, who had moved in 1885 from the Iowa Reservation to land in the Cherokee Outlet vacated by the Nez Perces, in the opinion of the commission did not have any rights at all to the surplus lands remaining after the tribal members were allotted. The sum to be paid them was to be "fixed on the basis of the necessities of the situation and the destitute condition of the Indians." For most of these Indians, allotments had already been made, which were merely confirmed by the agreement. The Wichita Indians and affiliated tribes at first objected to taking lands in severalty and having whites move in among them, but they ultimately capitulated to the commission. "Their title is possessory only," the commission reported, "[and] they do not have a treaty or even an agreement with the United States, that it shall be their country."[41]

There were complications arising from treaties in which the Choctaws and Chickasaws had reversion claims if the lands assigned to certain of the tribes were given up as surplus after allotments had been made, and there were possible treaty rights of Iowas and Sacs and Foxes not living in the Indian Territory to funds that might be paid for the surplus acres.

41. *Senate Ex. Doc.* no. 171, 51-1, serial 2688 (Iowa); ibid. no. 172, 51-1, serial 2688 (Sac and Fox); ibid. no. 1, 51-2, serial 2818 (Cheyenne and Arapaho); ibid. no. 13, 52-1, serial 2892 (Tonkawa); ibid. no. 14, 52-1, serial 2892 (Wichita).

The commissioners and the Department of Interior officials urged Congress to consider the claims, and various adjustments were made. But in the case of Indians who had not been assigned their reservations by treaty, with clear stipulations about alienation of the land, the power of Congress to dispose of Indian lands was strongly argued. Cited to back up these arguments were *United States v. Kagama* (1886) and the *Cherokee Tobacco Case*, a decision of the Supreme Court in 1870, in which an 1868 tobacco and liquor excise law was upheld against Cherokees despite a provision in the Cherokees' treaty of 1866 that said the Cherokees should have the right to market their products within their territory without restraint. In the Cherokee case the Court held:

> A treaty may supersede a prior act of Congress, and an act of Congress may supersede a prior treaty. In the cases referred to, these principles were applied to treaties with foreign nations. Treaties with Indian nations within the jurisdiction of the United States, whatever considerations of humanity and good faith may be involved and require their faithful observance, cannot be more obligatory. They have no higher sanctity; and no greater inviolability or immunity from legislative invasion can be claimed for them.[42]

The most significant of the Jerome Commission agreements was signed October 21, 1892, with the Kiowas, Comanches, and Apaches. It tested the power of the federal government to dispose of Indian lands without appropriate consent of the tribe, and it was the basis for the *Lone Wolf* case of 1903, discussed below.

All eleven agreements were signed and ratified by Congress. Where applicable, the commissioners had made an attempt to recognize treaty rights and the nationhood of the negotiating Indians. Yet the result was the individualization of the Indian lands through allotment and thus the effective destruction of the tribal base. As areas were opened, they were organized as counties and incorporated into Oklahoma Territory.[43]

42. 11 Wallace 621. For examples of the arguments, see letter of Secretary of the Interior John W. Noble to the president, June 27, 1890, in *Senate Ex. Doc.* no. 171, 51-1, serial 2688, p. 5; letter of Assistant Attorney General George H. Shields to secretary of the interior, June 23, 1890, in *Senate Ex. Doc.* no. 172, 51-1, serial 2688, p. 13.

43. Details on each of the agreements are provided in Foreman, *History of Oklahoma*, 144–53. References to the published agreements are in appendix C, agreements nos. 24–28, 31–34, 36, 39.

The Dawes Commission and the Curtis Act

The problems of the Five Civilized Tribes pointed to in the 1870s were much on the minds of government officials and of the Lake Mohonk Indian reformers. Commissioner of Indian Affairs John D. C. Atkins in 1885 inveighed against the political status of the Indian Territory. "The idea of maintaining permanently an *imperium in imperio*, such as now exists, must, in some respects be abandoned," he wrote in his annual report. "The idea of Indian nationality is fast melting away, and the more intelligent Indians are themselves awaking to that fact. In a word, the Indians in the Indian Territory must sooner or later break up their tribal relations, take their lands in severalty, and to all intents and purposes become citizens of the United States, and be amenable to its laws, as well as enjoy all of its high and distinguished privileges." And the next year he called attention to what he considered unconscionable land monopolies held by a few Indians. Of one landholding he exclaimed, "What a baronial estate! In theory the lands are held in common under the tribal relation, and are equally owned by each member of the tribe, but in point of fact they are simply held in the grasping hand of moneyed monopolists and powerful and influential leaders and politicians, who pay no rental to the other members of the tribe." And he asked, "Are these the sacred rights secured by treaty, which the United States are pledged to respect and defend?"[44]

The Dawes Commission was supposed to address and solve these problems. But, because the Indians of the Five Tribes were not receptive to the work of the commission, its attempts at negotiations in the first year came to nothing. The conditions that the Dawes Commission faced were those that had long agitated the reformers, and they were emphasized anew in the report of a special Senate committee under Senator Teller, sent to investigate the situation. The reports of both groups depicted a crisis resulting from the great influx of whites into the territory and from the monopolization of land by a few individuals. The reformers at Lake Mohonk, in response to criticism that the Dawes Commission

44. CIA AR, 1885, serial 2379, p. 13; ibid., 1886, serial 2467, pp. 81–84. The commissioner's arguments in 1886 were supported by Secretary of the Interior L. Q. C. Lamar, ibid., 19–21.

aimed to violate the treaty rights of the tribes, sent a special agent of their own, Charles F. Meserve, to study the conditions, and Meserve agreed wholeheartedly with Dawes and Teller.[45]

These men and their supporters set the argument about violation of treaties on its head. They insisted that the government must act without consent of the Indians, for the tribes themselves had destroyed the force of the treaties by admitting whites to tribal citizenship under their laws and by inviting white people to come within their jurisdiction. The Indian lands were to have been held in trust for *all* Indians, but monopolists had broken the trust. After a second year of ineffective negotiations the Dawes Committee asserted that the tribal governments were "wholly corrupt, irresponsible, and unworthy to be longer trusted," and that the promises of self-government made in the treaties were no longer binding.[46]

At Lake Mohonk, where he appeared regularly to report on his work in the Indian Territory, Dawes asserted that his commission "asked for the violation of no treaty obligations, however questionable might have been the power to enter by treaty into any such relation. They ask that these treaty stipulations be enforced." The old reformer Bishop Whipple wanted it known that the Indians had forfeited their old treaty rights by taking the side of the Confederacy during the Civil War and that after the war they had been received back into friendship under quite different conditions. "Familiar as I am with Indian wrongs," he concluded, "I have never had my heart more deeply stirred than in listening to Senator Dawes and to Mr. Meserve; and from my heart I can only say, God be praised for raising up such men to do his work."[47]

Congress heeded the messages proclaimed by Dawes, Teller, and the other reformers. In June 1896 it directed the Dawes Commission to make out rolls of Indian citizens in preparation for allotment and declared it to be the duty of the United States "to establish a government in the Indian Territory which will rectify the many inequalities and discriminations now existing."[48] Under this mandate the Dawes Commission moved rapidly toward the dissolution of the Five Civilized Tribes, concluding agreements with all the tribes between 1897 and

45. *Annual Report of the Commission to the Five Civilized Tribes*, 1894; Report of Select Committee on the Five Civilized Tribes, May 7, 1894, *Senate Report* no. 377, 53-2, serial 3183; *Report of the Indian Rights Association*, 1896, p. 9; Charles F. Meserve, *The Dawes Commission and the Five Civilized Tribes of Indian Territory* (Philadelphia, 1896).

46. *Senate Report* no. 377, 53-2, serial 3183; *Annual Report of the Commission to the Five Civilized Tribes*, 1894, 17, 20; ibid., 1895, 20.

47. *Lake Mohonk Conference Proceedings*, 1896, 54, 57.

48. 29 Stat. 339–40.

1902. The Curtis Act of June 28, 1898, abolished tribal laws and tribal courts and brought all persons in the Indian Territory, regardless of race, under United States authority. The act, entitled "an act for the protection of the people of the Indian Territory, and for other purposes," was unilateral action by the United States that signaled the end of the tribal governments; it was practically an organic act for the establishment of the long-sought territorial government.[49]

The *Lone Wolf* Case

Treaty rights came into full play during the negotiations and in the long subsequent history of the 1892 agreement with the Kiowas, Comanches, and Apaches that ended only with a Supreme Court decision in 1903. These tribes held their lands under the Treaty of Medicine Lodge Creek, and the Indians pointedly presented a copy of the treaty to the commissioners at the beginning of the negotiations. They noted that the benefits promised by the treaty still had four more years to run, and they adamantly opposed negotiating before then. They pointed, also, to the desperate conditions of the Cheyennes and Arapahos, who had recently accepted allotments. Nevertheless, the commissioners persisted, and at least superficially adhered to the three-fourths approval stipulations of the 1867 treaty (of the 562 male adult Indians certified by the Indian agent, 456 signed the agreement).[50]

Almost immediately, however, protests from the Indian leaders arose. They claimed that the provisions of the agreement had been misrepresented to them by the interpreters, that they had been subjected to threats, and that in fact three-fourths of the adult males had not signed (the total number of such Indians had been miscalculated by the agent, and some of the signers were whites, not tribal members). Such key federal officials as Secretary of the Interior C. N. Bliss, Secretary of the Interior Ethan Allen Hitchcock, and Commissioner of Indian Affairs William A. Jones agreed with the Indians and urged Congress not to ratify the agreement as presented. The Indian Office, in response to a

49. 30 Stat. 495–519. A system of federal courts had already been gradually extended over the Indian Territory; see discussion in Prucha, *American Indian Policy in Crisis*, 390–91.

50. A recent and full account of the agreement and its subsequent history is given in Ann Laquer Estin, "Lone Wolf v. Hitchcock: The Long Shadow," in *The Aggressions of Civilization: Federal Indian Policy since the 1880s*, ed. Sandra L. Cadwalader and Vine Deloria, Jr. (Philadelphia: Temple University Press, 1984), 215–45.

Senate resolution, presented evidence in January 1899 that the actual number of male Indians in the tribes in 1892 had been 639 who were twenty-one years of age or over and 725 who were eighteen years of age and over, and that the number signing thus actually fell below the required three-fourths. Congress, nevertheless, ratified the agreement on June 6, 1900, influenced no doubt by the insistence of whites in the region that the reservation be opened.[51]

The Kiowa chief Lone Wolf and other Kiowas then resorted to the courts. With legal help from William M. Springer, former representative from Illinois and federal judge in the Indian Territory, and from the Indian Rights Association, the Indians took their case to the Supreme Court. On January 5, 1903, the Court in the landmark decision, *Lone Wolf v. Hitchcock,* decided against the Indians and asserted the plenary authority of Congress over Indian relations and its power to pass laws abrogating treaty stipulations.

> The contention in effect ignores the status of the contracting Indians and the relation of dependency they bore and continue to bear towards the government of the United States. To uphold the claim would be to adjudge that the indirect operation of the treaty was to materially limit and qualify the controlling authority of Congress in respect to the care and protection of the Indians. . . .
>
> The power exists to abrogate the provisions of an Indian treaty, though presumably such power will be exercised only when circumstances arise which will not only justify the government in disregarding the stipulations of the treaty, but may demand, in the interest of the country and the Indians themselves, that it should do so.

The Court said that it must "presume that Congress acted in perfect good faith in the dealings with the Indians of which complaint is made," and it denied that the Indians had been deprived of their property; there had been "a mere change in the form of investment of Indian tribal property," from land to money.[52]

After the *Lone Wolf* decision the idea of requiring Indian consent for the disposition of their lands was largely discarded in regard to statutes

---

51. The Indians' protests of October 20, 1893, and January 15, 1900, are in *Senate Misc. Doc.* no. 102, 53-2, serial 3167, and *Senate Doc.* no. 76, 56-1, serial 3850. For support from federal officials, see *Senate Doc.* no. 77, 55-3, serial 3731, pp. 1–2, and *Senate Doc.* no. 76, 56-1, serial 3850. The calculation of numbers of adult male Indians is in *Senate Doc.* no. 84, 55-3, serial 3731.

52. 187 U.S. 563–68. The case is discussed in *Report of the Indian Rights Association,* 1903, 20–24.

as well as to agreements, and Congress unilaterally provided for the sale of surplus lands remaining after allotments had been completed.

An early and notable example was the disposition in 1904 of a portion of the Rosebud Sioux Reservation in South Dakota (Gregory County). On September 14, 1901, the Sioux had signed a formal agreement with Indian Inspector James McLaughlin for sale of the unallotted lands for $1,040,000, and McLaughlin acquired signatures of the required three-fourths of the adult male Indians. But between the signing of the agreement in 1901 and its amendment and ratification in 1904, a new situation had developed, and the bill submitted for ratification of the agreement eliminated the direct payment by the government for ceded lands and substituted a new procedure whereby the lands were paid for by settlers at specified prices, which were reduced as time passed, with the money received deposited in the Treasury for the benefit of the Indians. There was no provision for getting Indian approval of the new arrangements.[53]

This elimination of Indian consent was consciously done. The House Committee on Indian Affairs, in its report on the bill, admitted that the legislation presented "a new idea in acquiring Indian lands," and it raised the question whether Congress had the right to dispose of Indian lands without the consent of the Indians and whether it would be proper to pass the bill "without providing for submitting it to the Indians for their ratification and approval, in accordance with existing treaty stipulations." The committee, however, argued that the new bill provided as much money for the Indians as the original agreement had (which it noted had received approval by more than three-fourths of the adult males), and in the end it decided, in any case, that Indian approval was not needed. Its justification was the *Lone Wolf* decision (which, in fact, it printed in its report). The committee relied heavily, too, on the testimony of Commissioner of Indian Affairs William A. Jones before the committee.[54]

Both the committee and the commissioner, in accepting the authority to act without Indian consent, asserted the responsibility of the government to act in good faith in the Indians' best interests, but these statements did not satisfy the watchdogs of Indian rights. Soon harsh criticism of the Rosebud bill arose from the Indian Rights Association and other Indian advocates. The association, forced to accept the

53. Both McLaughlin's original agreement and the amended agreement are printed in 33 Stat. 254–58 (1904).

54. *House Report* no. 443, 58-2, serial 4578, pp. 1–5. See the discussion of Jones's strong opinion that the Indians' consent was unnecessary, below pp. 363–64.

principle of plenary legislative power asserted in the *Lone Wolf* case, now turned its attention to the fairness of the proposed legislation and argued for a higher price to be set on the lands taken. Although it broadcast its plea through newspaper articles and a special pamphlet, the association was unable to prevent the passage of the measure and could not persuade the president to veto it.[55] Congress, with the continued support of Commissioner Jones, similarly revised an earlier agreement with the Crow Indians and provided for opening their lands in the pattern of the Rosebud legislation, and other measures followed suit.[56]

Thus the treaty system, upon which the tribes in the Indian Territory had so long depended for protection, collapsed. And there were few outside of the Indians themselves who mourned its passing. The Indian Rights Association in 1896 opted for a middle course, it said, between "land-grabbing and spoliation on the one side; a sentimentalism which takes no account of facts on the other." But ultimately the Indian Rights Association was "quite content to let the tribe go." It noted that all recent Indian legislation had contemplated the extinction of the tribes and that the great majority of Indian reformers were agreed on that policy. The association wanted to do all that could be done wisely "to save and guard the individual Indian."[57]

Tribes outside the Indian Territory had already largely fallen under the domination of the United States—wards confined on Indian reservations, with the power and dignity of independent nations supported by treaty guarantees all but forgotten. Step by step the treaty system had faded away as the United States sought conformity and rejected alien enclaves within the boundaries of its sovereignty. Congress asserted its plenary power over Indian affairs, and that power was upheld by the courts.

55. "Memorial of the Indian Rights Association on Behalf of the Rosebud Indians," February 15, 1904, *Senate Doc.* no. 158, 58-2, serial 4590; *Another "Century of Dishonor"?* (Philadelphia: Indian Rights Association, 1904).

56. The Crow agreement in question was that of August 14, 1899; the amended ratification is dated April 27, 1904. *House Report* no. 890, 58-2, serial 4579; 33 Stat. 352–62. See the discussion in Frederick E. Hoxie, *A Final Promise: The Campaign to Assimilate the Indians, 1880–1920* (Lincoln: University of Nebraska Press, 1984), 154–58. It might be noted that when a new cession of land on the Rosebud Reservation was arranged in 1907, there was no formal agreement similar to the one of 1901; Congress simply legislated the opening of the lands, following the procedures established in 1904 (although the initial price per acre was set at six dollars).

57. *Report of the Indian Rights Association*, 1896, 12.

PART FOUR

Renewal:
The Twentieth Century

The antitribalism that undercut the force of Indian treaties at the end of the nineteenth century carried into the twentieth century. Government officials and reformers alike assumed that the assimilation of the Indians signaled by the allotment and citizenship provisions of the Dawes Act and the fulfillment of that policy by an enhanced and aggressive national Indian school system was to be the destiny of the Indians. Treaties were indeed only relics of the past. Nor did the *Lone Wolf* decision in 1903 bode well for the fate of the treaties in the new century.

The old treaties, nevertheless, still had life in them, and as the century advanced, there was a resurgence of tribal spirit and a reawakening of tribal sovereignty, in which treaty rights came to play a vital role once again. John Collier's Indian New Deal of the 1930s rehabilitated tribal governments and tribal cultures without much regard for treaties. But in subsequent decades the sparks kept alive by traditionalist Indians once more broke into flame, and "treaty rights" became a rallying cry in the 1960s and beyond.

An important element in the renewal was agitation about Indian claims against the federal government for payments or other benefits arising out of the old ratified treaties. At first the claims came before the United States Court of Claims, with which the tribes had little success. Then, with the establishment of the Indian Claims Commission in 1946, a new forum appeared, and all the tribes entered cases. A great many of the dockets concerned claims for land or additional payments for land, and treaty stipulations became the foundation for most of the cases.

Moreover, the late twentieth century saw a Red Power movement modeled on Black Power that sought to restore recognition of tribal sovereignty and to revitalize or re-create the status of Indian tribes, enabling them to deal once more with the United States by means of treaties. These hopes, at least in their extreme form, may never be realized, but the existence of the old treaties and the rights they stipulate is a political reality, which the anomaly embodied in their circumstances cannot destroy.

CHAPTER FIFTEEN

Treaties in the New Century

Judgments about Indian treaties during the early decades of the twentieth century, like judgments about other elements of Indian affairs in that period, are difficult to make. It was the time in which Edward S. Curtis produced his monumental *The North American Indian* (29 volumes, 1907–30) with its photographs of the "vanishing race," and in which the Philadelphia dry goods magnate Rodman Wanamaker sent expeditions into the West to photograph the final gatherings of the tribes but also to applaud the assimilation of the passing race into American society. The theme was powerfully presented in the book of Wanamaker's protege Joseph K. Dixon, *The Vanishing Race* (1913). And at the Panama-Pacific International Exposition in San Francisco in 1915 the sculptor James Earle Fraser exhibited his famed portrayal of a pathetic head-bowed Indian on a wornout pony, *The End of the Trail*. It was the period, as well, in which the positive assimilationist legislative program of the late-nineteenth-century reformers was carried out in administrative detail.[1]

---

1. A full account of Indian affairs in these decades is given in Francis Paul Prucha, *The Great Father: The United States Government and the American Indians*, 2 vols. (Lincoln: University of Nebraska Press, 1984), pt. 7. For other approaches to the period, see Frederick E. Hoxie, *A Final Promise: The Campaign to Assimilate the Indians, 1880–1920* (Lincoln: University of Nebraska Press, 1984), and Thomas M. Holm, "Indians and Progressives: From Vanishing Policy to the Indian New Deal" (Ph.D. diss., University of Oklahoma, 1978). The place of Curtis, Wanamaker, Dixon, and Fraser in the enduring American myth of the disappearing Indians is well described in Brian W. Dippie, *The*

On the level of government officialdom there was little question that tribalism (which was the foundation on which the treaty system rested) was a thing of the past and that whatever remnants might still remain should be quickly and efficiently stamped out. In this respect these decades were a continuation—in fact, a culmination—of the movement that had been gathering force in the last decades of the previous century. The Indian reform organizations, which had sparked the changing views toward the proper place of Indians in American society, did not break out of the old mold.

But the policies of the federal officials and humanitarian groups were not easily implemented among the reservation Indians, many of whom held conservatively to their traditions and looked upon the treaties as the guarantee of the old ways. In addition, unsatisfied Indian claims against the United States, based chiefly on treaty stipulations, maintained the treaties as still-living documents that could not be ignored.

Continuing Antitribalism

Official Indian policy turned away from dealing with Indians as tribes and dealt with individual Indians about their allotments, schooling, and health. It was a situation in which treaties and subsequent agreements were not important, and little attention was paid to them. Most federal officials considered the treaty system nearly if not totally defunct. The early twentieth century was marked by strong-minded commissioners of Indian affairs, who held office for long terms, and they had a common goal of assimilating the individual Indians into white society, with little regard for tribal holdovers and the treaties once made with the tribes.

William Jones (commissioner from 1897 to 1905), in his obsession with moving the Indians toward self-support, hit hard at the rations delivered to Indians, often in pursuance of treaty stipulations, and he fought against per capita payment of annuities based on treaty provisions. He declared in 1901 "that the indiscriminate issue of rations was an effectual barrier to civilization; that the periodical distribution of

---

Vanishing American: White Attitudes and U.S. Indian Policy (Middletown, Conn.: Wesleyan University Press, 1982), 208–15, 218–20.

large sums of money was demoralizing in the extreme." He set about to put all able-bodied Indian men to work despite what treaties or agreements might have promised them, and he adopted a policy of reducing rations for such Indians.[2]

Jones felt it was time for a change. "Heretofore the dealing had been with the tribe," he wrote; "it would now be with the individual. He would no longer be looked upon simply as one of a dependent community to be dealt with as a whole, but would be considered independently and treated as one capable of developing those qualities which would lift him above the level of a pauper and fit him to become a useful member of society." Jones noted that there was criticism of this move, but in the end the results were "favorable even beyond expectation."[3]

It might be argued that Jones's policy on rations was a reasonable one, but he had a cavalier approach to treaty rights that might obstruct the sale of surplus reservation land. His advice to Congress in the reduction of the Rosebud Reservation in 1904 was unequivocal. In an interchange with Representative Charles H. Burke of South Dakota, Jones spoke bluntly:

> If you depend upon the consent of the Indians as to the disposition of the lands where they have the fee to the land, you will have difficulty in getting it, and I think the decision in the Lone Wolf case, that Congress can do as it sees fit with the property of the Indians will enable you to dispose of that land without the consent of the Indians. If you wait for their consent in these matters, it will be fifty years before you can do away with the reservations. . . .
>
> Mr. BURKE: Would you make that statement general or would you except reservations where there may be in existence treaty relations that provide directly to the contrary? For instance, do you know there is in existence among the Sioux—I think in the treaty of 1868— a provision that the Indians will not be deprived of their lands without the consent of three-fourths, and that provision was reenacted, I think, in the treaty of 1889.
>
> Commissioner JONES: I will go to the extreme. I do not think I would ask the consent of the Indians in that case. Supposing you were the guardian or ward [*sic*] of a child 8 or 10 years of age, would

---

2. CIA AR, 1901, serial 4290, p. 1. For Jones's views on of the matter of rations and annuities, see ibid., 1900, serial 4101, pp. 5–12; ibid., 1902, serial 4458, pp. 2–8. In the next year Jones provided lists of treaties and of agreements, as if he were in a sense making a final accounting of a now obsolete policy. Ibid., 1903, serial 4645, pp. 32–34, 469–79.

3. Ibid., 1902, serial 4458, pp. 7–8.

you ask the consent of the child as to the investment of its funds? No; you would not, and I do not think it is a good business principle in this case.[4]

Jones's successor, Francis E. Leupp (1905–9), was firm in his conviction that Indians should be individualized and assimilated.[5] After he left office, he set forth his candid views about Indian affairs in a book called *The Indian and His Problem* (1910). He had no use for "so-called 'treaties,'" which assumed that the reservation belonged absolutely to the Indians. "Although not a few of the treaties contained figurative language designed to convey to the tribes concerned the idea of perpetuity of physical possession," he wrote, "every allotment law, and every moral argument made in behalf of allotment as a remedy for some of the more crying evils of the reservation system, plainly recognized that system as but a passing phase in the history of Indian development, and to such extent discredited the notion of a permanent tribal title." Leupp thus welcomed the decision in the *Lone Wolf* case and saw benefits in the disposal of surplus reservation lands without the hindrance of seeking Indian consent. He made fun, too, of "petty items" in treaties, which were "now outgrown and absurd, and all of them annoying." His proposed solution was to obtain Indian consent to capitalize the various annuities provided for by their treaties.[6]

Robert G. Valentine, who acted as Leupp's assistant commissioner and then followed him in office (1909–13), held the same view about proper policy in dealing with Indians: to do everything possible to educate them for citizenship. One bar to success in his efforts came in the "perpetual annuities provided for in the treaties of various groups of Indians," moneys that kept the Indians in a state of dependence and assured them of income without labor. Valentine, with some success, worked for the commutation of these annuities into a one-time payment to be distributed to the individual Indians. Well into his term of office, he rejoiced at the outcome:

> Tribal organization is breaking up and the office, in its administrative activities, has its work greatly increased through the necessity of dealing separately with many individuals where formerly it dealt with groups; the point of evolution thus reached in transacting

4. *House Report* no. 443, 58-2, serial 4578, p. 4.
5. See CIA AR, 1905, serial 4959, p. 3; ibid., 1908, serial 5453, pp. 11–12.
6. Francis E. Leupp, *The Indian and His Problem* (New York: Charles Scribner's Sons, 1910), 81, 176–78; see chap. 5, "Disposing of the Surplus," 79–95.

business is almost epochal, for it marks the time when each Indian begins to stand forward as his own business man, and, in a measure, reaches the status of white citizens.[7]

With Cato Sells (commissioner 1913–21) the detribalization of the Indians moved forward rapidly. Under the provisions of the Burke Act of 1906, which allowed granting of fee patents for allotments to Indians who were competent to handle their own affairs before the end of the twenty-five-year trust period set by the Dawes Act, large numbers of Indians were severed from government supervision and thrown out into the white world. "It is my fixed purpose to bring about the speedy individualizing of the Indians," Sells said in his first year in office, "and to this end I shall continue to devote my best efforts." In 1917 he issued his famous Declaration of Policy in the Administration of Indian Affairs, in which he noted that the solution to the Indian problem was "individual and not collective" and in which he pushed aggressively to separate "competent" Indians from government concern by setting up categories of such Indians on the basis of blood quantum and English education.[8] Sells's program was disastrous for many Indians, who quickly lost or disposed of their individual lands as soon as they were declared competent and received patents in fee, but Sells seems not to have noticed.

His successor, Charles H. Burke (1921–29), slowed down the patenting process, but he was as much an assimilationist as his predecessors. He supported the "aim of inducing by this transfer of tribal to individual holdings a departure from old communal traits and customs to self-dependent conditions and to a democratic conception of the civilization with which the Indian must be assimilated if he is to survive."[9]

Indian reform groups, likewise, paid little attention to treaties and protection of the Indians' treaty rights as they moved into the twentieth century. The Lake Mohonk Conference of Friends of the Indian, the

---

7. CIA AR, 1910, serial 5976, p. 27; ibid., 1911, serial 6223, pp. 3, 45. See also his laudatory evaluation of the Indians' new status in "A Decade of Indian Affairs," ibid., 1912, serial 6409, pp. 3–4.

8. Ibid., 1913, serial 6634, p. 45; ibid., 1917, serial 7358, pp. 3–4. For Sells's policy on speeding up the declarations of Indian competency, see Janet McDonnell, "Competency Commissions and Indian Land Policy, 1913–1920," *South Dakota History* 11 (Winter 1980): 21–34.

9. *Report of the Commissioner of Indian Affairs*, 1921 (Washington: GPO, 1921), 25. See Sean J. Flynn, "Western Assimilationist: Charles H. Burke and the Burke Act," *Midwest Review*, 2d ser., 11 (Spring 1989): 1–15, which emphasizes Burke's assimilationist views both as representative and as commissioner of Indian affairs.

Board of Indian Commissioners, and the Indian Rights Association, which had carried on a drive for assimilation in the closing decades of the nineteenth century, saw their main goals fulfilled in legislation and thought the remaining problems were simply those of efficient administration.

The Lake Mohonk Conference, which continued its annual meetings until 1916, replayed over and over its old record from the previous century—detribalization, individualization, and assimilation of the Indians. If treaties were noted at all, it was as an obstacle to progress of the Indians toward the goal of complete citizenship. In 1901 the conference listened to an address by James M. Taylor, president of Vassar College, who posed a rhetorical question: "If there are treaties with Indian tribes which are standing absolutely in the way of the interests of the Indian, then is it fair, because of the mere abstract love of truth, that we continue to pauperize the Indian, to make less and less of a man of him, to threaten him, indeed, with effacement, simply that we may keep a treaty that our fathers made with him?" The audience seemed to approve.[10] Protection of treaty rights was not a part of the Lake Mohonk agenda.

The Board of Indian Commissioners, still tightly associated with the Lake Mohonk Conference, independently echoed these views in its annual reports, and it pushed a number of policies toward detribalization. It hammered on the idea of breaking up the tribal trust funds, as the Dawes Act allotments had broken up the tribal land. "There is an essential difference between the old method of dealing with Indians and the new method," the Board declared in 1900. "The old method dealt with them in the mass and as tribes. The new method proposes to deal with them as individuals." It saw the tribal funds as *the rallying point and the shelter for the spirit of conservatism* which seeks to keep the Indians out of the life-giving current of American civilization, American public school life, and citizenship."[11] Yet the Board of Indian Commissioners, as might be expected of Christian philanthropists, was not unaware of the obligation of justice toward the Indians. It saw in the *Lone Wolf* decision the danger of greedy whites moving into Indian lands, and it demanded that Congress make every effort to secure the best price for the Indians in the disposal of the surplus reservation lands. "The tendency to tamper with ethical standards of trusteeship in such legis-

10. *Lake Mohonk Conference Proceedings*, 1901, 126, 128.
11. *Report of the Board of Indian Commissioners*, 1900, 6, 9–10; ibid., 1901, 8; emphasis in original.

lation," it warned, "while it is unjust to the Indians, entails upon the whites in Congress and throughout the country an infinitely heavier loss in the degradation of moral standards and of the sense of public honor."[12]

Limited Concern for Treaty Rights

Of the Indian reform groups from the nineteenth century that carried over into the twentieth, only the Indian Rights Association was still concerned about treaty rights. That is understandable, for one of the main purposes of the association at its founding in 1882 had been "to secure to the Indians of the United States the political and civil rights already guaranteed to them by treaty and statute." And in the early years of the new century this devotion to treaty rights was still in evidence. In 1901 the association supported claims of Indians on Puget Sound to tidelands under the treaty made with Governor Stevens in 1855, and in 1902 it warned: "The present tendency of Congress to disregard the solemn rights guaranteed to the Indian by treaty is alarming." The association's Washington agent, in the same year, asserted: "That the legislative and executive branches of our Government are seeking to enter upon a new policy in the treatment of our Indian wards there can be no doubt. The tendency seems to favor the abrogation and violation of solemn treaty obligations."[13]

The confirmation of congressional abrogation of Indian treaties by the Supreme Court in *Lone Wolf v. Hitchcock* was an especially sore point with the Indian Rights Association, which had actively supported the Indians in the case. It called the preliminary decision by the Court of Appeals of the District of Columbia a "doctrine of a very disquieting nature," and, while admitting a defective title to executive order reservations, it stoutly maintained that the treaty reservations were quite different. "To their maintenance as an inviolate home for Indians, the United States has always been pledged, as everybody has considered and supposed, in the most solemn manner possible." In a tone of pique, it asserted:

12. Ibid., 1906, 16.
13. *Report of the Indian Rights Association*, 1901, 65–66; ibid., 1902, 3, 5; S. M. Brosius, *A New Indian Policy—The Red Man's Rights in Jeopardy* (Philadelphia: Indian Rights Association, 1902), 1.

It is now distinctly understood that Congress has a right to do as it pleases; that it is under no obligation to respect any treaty, for the Indians have no rights which command respect. What is to be hoped for by an appeal to Congress can readily be anticipated from the history of the legislation by which Lone Wolf and his tribe have been deprived of that which had by express treaty stipulations apparently been secured to them.[14]

Although the Indian Rights Association was forced to acquiesce, albeit reluctantly, in the *Lone Wolf* decision, it continued to support Indian rights in other ways, relying on treaties when the occasion arose. Thus it fought for Yakima Indian fishing rights and water rights under the treaty of 1855.[15] And it demanded that Congress appropriate money for Navajo schools under the provision of the treaty of 1868. "It would seem," it said in 1912, "that Congress cannot in good faith longer delay in providing liberally for schools in view of its solemn obligations of treaty to this neglected people."[16]

Yet the thrust of the Indian Rights Association's program in the twentieth century did not differ greatly from the movement toward assimilation advocated by the Lake Mohonk "Friends" and the Board of Indian Commissioners, and though it fought with Commissioner Leupp, it in general publicly supported the programs of the government to cut the Indians loose from government supervision as self-supporting citizens. "We are convinced," the executive committee said in 1914, "that there will be no substantial or satisfactory solution of the Indian question until the red man is set free."[17]

The white reform groups were joined in the second decade of the century by the Society of American Indians, a group of educated Indians, mostly professionals, who sought to promote the Indian heritage and Indians' pride in their race, while at the same time taking part fully in white society. They sought to free the Indians from the restraining hold of the Indian Bureau. Beginning in 1911 and stretching into the 1920s, the society held annual meetings and published a quarterly (eventually called *American Indian Magazine*), and the members appeared to be a useful complement to the white reformers. They were not concerned

14. *Report of the Indian Rights Association*, 1902, 17; ibid., 1903, 24; see also ibid., 1910, 19–20.
15. Ibid., 1905, 39–41; 1912, 49–52; 1913, 72–75.
16. Ibid., 1912, 65–66; see also the report of the association's Washington agent, ibid., 1913, 54.
17. Ibid., 1914, 18–19.

about tribal treaty rights, for they were a pan-Indian group, with little focus on tribal communities on reservations.[18]

Treaty provisions were upheld, however, in two significant Supreme Court cases in the first decade of the century. In 1908, in the case of *Quick Bear v. Leupp,* the Court approved the use of "treaty funds" (money appropriated annually for Indians according to stipulations in treaties) for Indian schools run by Catholic missionaries. Against the arguments of the Indian Rights Association, which acted in the name of Reuben Quick Bear, a Rosebud Sioux, claiming that such use of the funds was contrary to congressional prohibitions on the use of federal funds for sectarian schools, the Court said that the treaty funds were not public money but rather Indian money and that the Indians could determine if they wanted to use some of it for Catholic schools.[19]

Earlier in the same year, in *Winters v. United States*, the Supreme Court—in a landmark case with many ramifications for Indian water rights—decreed that where land was reserved to an Indian tribe, there was an implied reservation of water necessary for the irrigation of the lands. The Indians of the Fort Belknap Reservation, the Court decided, in giving up some land did not thereby relinquish the right to appropriate the waters of the Milk River necessary for agricultural and other purposes upon the reservation. Although the particular case rested on a treaty substitute, an agreement with the Indians in 1888, the principle was later applied to all reservations, whether established by treaty, agreement, act of Congress, or executive order.[20]

Even federal officials intent on destroying tribalism called upon the treaties when it served their purposes, notably in their continuing campaign against the liquor traffic. The obsession of many Indians with intoxicating liquors and their ability to satisfy their thirst in areas

18. For a full discussion of the Society of American Indians, see Hazel W. Hertzberg, *The Search for an American Indian Identity: Modern Pan-Indian Movements* (Syracuse: Syracuse University Press, 1971), pt. 1. For a biography of one notable member of the Society of American Indians, see Peter Iverson, *Carlos Montezuma and the Changing World of American Indians* (Albuquerque: University of New Mexico Press, 1982).

19. 210 U.S. 77–82. The Court also approved the use of "trust funds" (money set aside in trust for the Sioux by the agreement of 1889) for the same purpose. There is a full discussion of the matter in Francis Paul Prucha, *The Churches and the Indian Schools, 1888–1912* (Lincoln: University of Nebraska Press, 1979).

20. 207 U.S. 564–78. See also *Arizona v. California,* 373 U.S. 546–602 (1963). *Winters* and its implications are fully examined in two articles by Norris Hundley, Jr.: "The Dark and Bloody Ground of Indian Water Rights: Confusion Elevated to Principle," *Western Historical Quarterly* 9 (October 1978): 455–82, and "The 'Winters' Decision and Indian Water Rights: A Mystery Reexamined," ibid. 13 (January 1982): 17–42.

surrounding the reservations (where the prohibitions legislated for Indian country did not hold) frustrated the best efforts of the Indian Office. One particular point of infection appeared at the Chippewa reservations in the state of Minnesota.

In 1909 Commissioner Valentine noted that when lands had been ceded by the Indians, the treaties had prohibited the manufacture and sale of intoxicating liquors *within the ceded areas* until Congress or the president removed the prohibition, and he asserted that neither Congress nor the president had so acted.[21] Valentine declared that the Indian Office was "acting upon the policy that these treaty provisions were made for the protection of the Indians, and their aid will be invoked to whatever extent is necessary." And he acted forcefully. Circulars were issued warning liquor distributors in the affected counties of Minnesota that the stipulations of the treaties of 1855 and 1863 would be enforced, and he reported that about 125 saloons had been closed, much whiskey destroyed, and many convictions secured. "This vigorous action," he noted, "has had great deterrent effect."[22]

This early success soon suffered a setback, for the whiskey sellers got an injunction against the enforcement of the treaty of 1855 from the United States Circuit Court, Minnesota District, Fourth Division, which argued in 1911 that when Minnesota entered the union in 1858, it did so on an equal footing with other states, including the power to regulate the liquor traffic, and that thus the treaty provisions had been repealed by implication. Enforcement was held in abeyance, and the problem fell to Valentine's successor, Cato Sells. Finally, on June 8, 1914, the Supreme Court of the United States upheld the enforcement of the treaties prohibiting liquor and denied a rehearing of the case, and Sells successfully renewed enforcement activities. Neither Valentine nor Sells seemed to be disturbed by their eager and energetic reliance on old treaties, which in general they opposed.[23]

21. Valentine cited six treaties, 1851–63, with Sioux, Chippewa, and Winnebago Indians and two agreements with Yankton Sioux and Nez Perces of 1894. See CIA AR, 1909, serial 5747, pp. 13–15.

22. CIA AR, 1909, serial 5747, p. 15; ibid., 1910, serial 5976, p. 12.

23. The circuit court decision is in 183 F. 611–26; the Supreme Court case is *Johnson v. Gearlds,* 234 U.S. 422–48. See also CIA AR, 1911, serial 6223, pp. 35–36; ibid., 1914, serial 6815, p. 45; ibid., 1915, serial 6992, pp. 11–12; and ibid., 1916, serial 7160, pp. 61–62.

Residual Tribalism and Reliance on Treaties

On some reservations (which persisted as legal and administrative entities despite the best antireservation efforts of the Indian reformers) tribalism and interest in treaties had by no means disappeared. While Indians like those in the Society of American Indians wanted to maintain their heritage without regard for tribal reservation boundaries, most Indians in the period were not yet inclined or prepared to pull away completely from the past, even though they lost much of their customary way of life under the bombardment of land allotment, fee patents, white education, division of tribal funds, and citizenship— all aimed at assimilating the Indians into white society. Indian ways were forced to change, and although some Indians—"progressive" they were called—accepted the changes as inevitable and even desirable, for many the old life was still what they wanted.

The diversity of views was well demonstrated among the Five Civilized Tribes in the Indian Territory as the area moved toward statehood. A Senate select committee was appointed in 1906 to investigate conditions in the territory; between November 11, 1906, and January 9, 1907, the five-member committee held public hearings in the Indian Territory. "These meetings were open and free . . . ," the committee's report said. "Special effort, and with marked success, was made to have the Indians, both those of the full and those of the mixed bloods, fully represented." Educated Indians, often mixed bloods, were willing if not eager to accept allotments and have restriction on their land removed, but the traditional full bloods resisted change. The committee members tried to convince them that it was no longer possible to maintain tribal communal land tenure and that they should accept allotments and make the best of the new conditions, but some Indians were adamant.[24]

24. "Report of the Select Committee to Investigate Matters Connected with Affairs in the Indian Territory, with Hearings, November 11, 1906—January 9, 1907," *Senate Report* no. 5013, 59-2, serials 5062–63. The committee held public hearings in the Indian Territory at Vinita, Muskogee, McAlester, Ardmore, Tulsa, and Bartlesville. The formal report covers eight pages, to which are appended 2,132 pages of hearings. A summary of conservative testimony is given in Angie Debo, *And Still the Waters Run* (Princeton: Princeton University Press, 1940), chap. 5, "The Voice of the Indian Territory." I have followed Debo's lead, perhaps unwisely. W. David Baird has used the same Senate report to show effectively that Oklahoma Indians favored modernization and acceptance of

At the committee's hearing at Vinita on November 13, Eufala Harjo, a fullblood Creek, reported:

> I am here asking for the treaty [of 1832], and the treaty that I am here asking for—I will never stop asking for this treaty, the old treaty that our fathers made with the Government which gave us this land forever, as long as the grass grew and water ran. I will keep on asking for it, for my old fathers and your old fathers made that treaty with us away back there on the other side of the Mississippi, and they said that this land out here was to be ours as a nation for ever, and that is the treaty I want, for we are to have it as long as the grass grows, water runs, and the sun rises, we should have this land, and we are still asking for this land just as the treaty says.[25]

Similarly, Redbird Smith, a fullblood Cherokee, asked for adherence to the old treaties. "I live under these respective treaties that have been made between the Government of the United States and the Indians," he said, "and I am resting now under these treaties, and I am suffering from the infraction of them."[26]

The committee members explained that subsequent agreements had been made by the Indians which changed conditions, but they could not convince these men and those they represented that allotment was there to stay nor weaken the hope of the Indians that the Great Father would be the guarantor of their old treaty rights. Outside the Five Civilized Tribes, there was less organized or articulate reliance on treaty rights. Allotment and assimilation policies were resisted, but to a large extent the old ways were suppressed, even though the new did not take hold quickly or completely.

Nevertheless, when Indian policy changed in the 1930s, there was a strong tribal persistence that was amenable to restoration and revitalization. One force that made this possible was the continuing life of the old treaties. When Congress in 1871, conscious of the good faith and honor of the nation, added to its prohibition of further treaty making the proviso that nothing in the new law should be construed to "invalidate or impair the obligation of any treaty heretofore lawfully made

---

industrial society—without becoming any less *Indian*. See his article "Are the Five Tribes of Oklahoma 'Real' Indians?" *Western Historical Quarterly* 21 (February 1990): 10–11. All one can conclude is that *some* Indians in Oklahoma held firmly to reliance on their treaty rights.

25. "Report of the Select Committee," 93.

26. Ibid., 97.

and ratified," it set the course for a perpetuation of Indian tribalism that at the time it could hardly have foreseen. Treaties (and subsequent agreements) were still on the books. They had not been abrogated across the board, as some reformers had suggested. They presupposed some sort of tribal organization, and they provided a minimal sort of tribal identity inherited from the Indians by whom the treaties had been signed. Such groups still looked for the fulfillment of the promises made in the treaties by the United States government. The treaties were there to be called into play as occasions demanded.

John Collier

A new Indian reform figure, John Collier, emerged in the early 1920s. Collier was a New York social worker who became interested in Indian culture and Indian rights after a visit to Taos Pueblo in 1920, and he devoted the rest of his career to Indian affairs. He found in the communal life of the Pueblos an antidote to the individualism of industrial life in the United States and thought he had found a solution to the ills of the nation. He thus rejected the drive for individualization and Americanization of the Indians represented by the Dawes Act and carried on by the traditional Indian reform organizations and the government officials of the Progressive Era. His goal, instead, was the protection and restoration of Indian cultural ways, with an emphasis on communal tribal practices. Working with like-minded friends, especially through the American Indian Defense Association, of which he was the directing force, Collier sought to hold back and reverse the tide that was moving the Indians willy-nilly into white civilization.[27]

Treaties, however, were not on Collier's mind. He was interested in human rights not treaty rights, perhaps because the Pueblo Indians, who were his primary contact with the Indian world, had not had a treaty relationship with the federal government. In the dozen years before he became commissioner of Indian affairs in 1933, Collier was an aggressive and articulate critic of all the Indian Bureau stood for, leading campaigns to protect the lands of the Pueblos from white

27. Collier's activities are thoroughly treated in Kenneth R. Philp, *John Collier's Crusade for Indian Reform, 1920–1954* (Tucson: University of Arizona Press, 1977), and Lawrence C. Kelly, *The Assault on Assimilation: John Collier and the Origins of Indian Policy Reform* (Albuquerque: University of New Mexico Press, 1983).

encroachment, to support and glorify the traditional religious ceremonies of the Indians against critics who wanted to stamp them out as pagan and immoral, and to prevent white exploitation of Indian resources, but one searches in vain for explicit reliance on treaties in his efforts.

Collier's campaign against the Indian Bureau could not be ignored, and Secretary of the Interior Hubert Work instituted discussions and investigations into the bureau's Indian policy. Thus in December 1923 Work called together the Advisory Council on Indian Affairs (often called the Committee of One Hundred) to advise him on Indian matters. The hundred people invited (of whom about sixty showed up) were a broad cross section of people interested in the Indians. Collier was there, mixing with representatives of the Board of Indian Commissioners, the Indian Rights Association, the Society of American Indians, missionary groups, and a miscellaneous array of other notables. The resolutions of the committee dealt with such topics as Indian art and music, health, education, Pueblo lands, and the evils of Indian dances and of peyote, but, except indirectly in a discussion of Indian claims against the government, there was no interest shown in Indian treaties.[28]

The Committee of One Hundred did little if anything to correct the evils perceived in the management of Indian affairs, and later in the decade Secretary Work instigated, through the Brookings Institution, a more thorough study, conducted by Lewis Meriam and a staff of experts. The result was *The Problem of Indian Administration* (usually known as the Meriam Report), submitted in February 1928. It was a forthright indictment of the administration of Indian affairs, which, rather than attacking the traditional policies themselves, demanded a more efficient carrying out of the Indian Bureau's functions. Like the Committee of One Hundred, it ignored the treaties, aside from their basis for unsettled claims of Indian groups against the United States.[29] Treaties had all but disappeared from public consciousness.

As commissioner of Indian affairs, John Collier aggressively promoted a new policy in Indian affairs that revived tribalism and Indian

---

28. "The Indian Problem: Resolution of the Committee of One Hundred Appointed by the Secretary of the Interior and a Review of the Indian Problem," *House Doc.* no. 149, 68-1, serial 8273; Hubert Work, *Indian Policies: Comments on the Resolutions of the Advisory Council on Indian Affairs* (Washington: GPO, 1924).

29. Lewis Meriam and others, *The Problem of Indian Administration* (Baltimore: Johns Hopkins Press, 1928).

cultures. In the Indian Reorganization (Wheeler-Howard) Act of 1934, Congress adopted much of his program, for the law authorized the renewal or strengthening of Indian tribal governments (with formal constitutions and bylaws) and provided, as well, for tribal corporate economic organization. Not all Indians, however, were eager to accept Collier's vision of their future, which included in its original form a return of allotted lands to communal ownership, and Collier ran into considerable opposition from Indians who had adjusted to the allotment policy and from others who were afraid of the new ways.

Hearings in 1934 before the House and Senate committees considering the original Wheeler-Howard bill included considerable testimony of Indians against the measure; very little was said about treaty rights, although in a couple of instances treaties were referred to. The Yakima tribal council in opposing the bill submitted a statement that said in part: "We feel that the best interests of the Indians can be preserved by the continuance of treaty laws and carried out in conformity with the treaty of 1855, entered into between the fathers of some of the undersigned chiefs and Governor Stevens of the Territory of Washington." And the Quapaw Indians in a memorandum of objections to the bill listed the treaties upon which their rights to their land rested and quoted from their treaty of 1833.[30]

In the hearings and in the regional congresses of Indians called by Collier to explain his proposals, Collier perceived substantial support (except perhaps among the Indians of Oklahoma), and he made amendments in his original proposal to eliminate strands of opposition among the Indians and the lawmakers. In the end, the law created a new structure of tribal councils and elected officials. Although the new forms were not without their faults and traditionalists among some of the tribes would come to ridicule these tribal governments as puppets of the Bureau of Indian Affairs, the councils and their elected heads became a continuing and powerful force in Indian affairs. The emphasis of Collier and his Indian New Deal on tribal government made possible

30. "To Grant to Indians Living under Federal Tutelage the Freedom to Organize for Purposes of Local Self-Government and Economic Enterprise," *Hearings before the Committee on Indian Affairs, United States Senate, Seventy-third Congress, Second Session, on S. 2755 and S. 3645* (1934), 354–55 (Quapaw) and 408 (Yakima). Rupert Costo cited such evidence in 1983 and left the impression that reliance on treaties was more widespread in the Indians' opposition than it actually was. See Kenneth R. Philp, ed., *Indian Self-Rule: First-Hand Accounts of Indian-White Relations from Roosevelt to Reagan* (Salt Lake City: Howe Brothers, 1986), 49.

the perpetuation of the concept of tribal sovereignty that came to play a dominant role in relations between the Indians and white society.[31]

It is hard to tell how deeply ingrained Collier's views on Indian self-government were in the minds of legislators and the general public. Long before Collier resigned his office in 1945, there had been growing opposition to his policies and programs in Congress, and support for treaties was weak or missing. In the late 1940s, a statement by a white "friend" of the Indians from the 1920s provided a broad account of Indian treaty making in the *Chronicles of Oklahoma*, which ridiculed the treaties as outmoded and largely responsible for "the peculiar wardship status of the American Indian." It condemned the "segregation" of the Indians and asserted: "To hold them in the grip of a treaty made generations ago is indeed a dead hand laid upon their future."[32]

Indian Claims

Despite the general lack of interest in the old treaties on the part of government officials and Indian reformers, there nevertheless remained among the Indians a strong undercurrent of reliance on them and the rights they guaranteed. This arose from the continuing claims that Indian tribes had against the United States, claims that were based largely on the treaties signed in the past. Many Indians expected to receive an economic windfall if their claims were resolved in their favor, and reservation tribal groups continued to see in the treaties a basis for autonomy and sovereignty. The treaties gave a boost to tribal persistence, which many persons of the period were denigrating; the government had to face *tribal* action from Indians whose tribalism it thought had

31. See "The Legacy of the Indian New Deal," in Prucha, *Great Father*, 2: 1009–12. This view is not universally accepted. Rupert Costo, a Cahuilla Indian from California and a violent opponent of the Indian Reorganization Act, said in 1983: "The IRA did not allow the Indians their independence, which was guaranteed in treaties and agreements and confirmed in court decisions. It did not protect their sovereignty. Collier did not invent self-government: the right of Indians to make their own decisions, to make their own mistakes, to control their own destiny. The IRA had within it, in its wording and in its instruments, such as the tribal constitutions, the destruction of the treaties and of Indian self-government." Philp, *Indian Self-Rule*, 48.

32. G. E. E. Lindquist, "Indian Treaty Making," *Chronicles of Oklahoma* 26 (Winter 1948–49): 416, 438. The article was written in collaboration with Flora Warren Seymour. Both authors had been members of the Board of Indian Commissioners.

been pretty well quashed. For Indians—and their lawyers—the treaties were still vital documents. The claims kept tribal consciousness alive during a dark period when detribalization and total assimilation were in vogue. Various Indian groups insisted that land guaranteed them by treaty had been taken from them illegally, that land ceded by treaties had not been adequately paid for, that promises of services and benefits made in treaties had not been kept, and that in other ways formal treaty stipulations had been violated.

Such Indian claims had a long and convoluted history. Although the sovereignty of the United States protected the government from suits, Congress from time to time specifically authorized such suits. A law of 1855 created a Court of Claims with authority to render judgments, but an amendment in 1863 excepted from the court's jurisdiction "any claim against the government . . . growing out of or dependent on any treaty stipulation entered into with foreign nations or with the Indian tribes."[33] Tribes with claims against the government had to seek a remedy directly from Congress, and they had trouble persuading Congress to pass the necessary legislation. Then, beginning in 1881 with a petition of the Choctaws, Congress passed special jurisdictional acts authorizing the Court of Claims to accept Indian cases. From that time until the establishment of the Indian Claims Commission in 1946, more than two hundred Indian claims were handled by the court.[34]

The vast majority of suits instituted by the Indians dealt with the construction of treaties and with questions about their fulfillment, but the failure of the government to live up to its trust responsibilities was also a subject of the litigation, and there were some personal claims for services rendered Indians. The Court of Claims, like other federal courts, construed the Indian treaties and agreements liberally in favor of the Indians, but the court interpreted strictly the authorization given in the pertinent jurisdictional acts.

33. 10 Stat. 612–14; 12 Stat. 767.
34. See "Indian Tribal Claims Filed in U.S. Court of Claims Arranged by Dates When Petitions Were Filed (1881–1946)," in *House Report* no. 2503, 82-2, serial 11582, pp. 1563–71. A compilation of the claims, made in 1947 by E. B. Smith, chief of the Indian Tribal Claims Section, U.S. General Accounting Office, was published as *Indian Tribal Claims Decided in the Court of Claims of the United States, Briefed and Compiled to June 30, 1947*, 2 vols. (Washington: University Publications of America, 1976). House and Senate hearings on Indian Claims Commission bills in 1935 and 1945 also furnish useful information. For a brief historical account, see Glen A. Wilkinson, "Indian Tribal Claims before the Court of Claims," *Georgetown Law Journal* 55 (December 1966): 511–28.

The Indian cases before the Court of Claims between 1881 and 1920 were relatively few (thirty-four petitions entered in that forty-year period); they proceeded without extreme delay, and in many cases the Indians received a favorable judgment, although not always what they had claimed. From 1920 on the whole business tremendously expanded. In the decade of the 1920s (1920–29), sixty-five new dockets were entered, in the 1930s (1930–39), eighty-three dockets, and in the 1940s (1940–46), twenty-one more, some of which had not been decided by the time the Indian Claims Commission was established. With the increased case load, delays in adjudication mounted, and a large proportion of the claims were dismissed because of lack of prosecution or because offsets equaled or exceeded the established claim.[35]

Agitation thus arose for some better and more expeditious way to handle the Indian claims. The motivation came not from a devotion to treaties and an intention to preserve or reinstate their validity but from a desire to end what the Board of Indian Commissioners in 1930 called the "lethargy of expectancy," the unwillingness of the Indians to work for self-support because they kept hoping for some large windfall from successful claims. As early as 1910 ex-commissioner Leupp saw the problem. The claims, whether good, bad, or indifferent, all had a common flaw. "Morally," he argued, "it would be a happy day for the dependent race if Congress were to obligate itself irrevocably never to entertain any more of them. They only serve to keep a multitude of Indians in a state of feverish expectancy of getting something for nothing, which is fatal to their steady industry and peace of mind." Leupp recommended creation of a special court or the addition of a branch to the Court of Claims to handle Indian claims exclusively, and he wanted a time limit set for the final adjudication of all claims.[36]

Then, in 1913, the Board of Indian Commissioners, "in view of the numerous claims asserted by Indian tribes or attorneys interested in their behalf, in connection with alleged breach of treaty obligations," recommended the appointment of a proficient group to study the treaties and how they had been administered, so that the secretary of the interior, "where prima facie grounds for claims are found to exist," might push for the necessary jurisdictional legislation. The goal was not only to determine promptly the just claims of Indian tribes against the govern-

---

35. These figures are taken from *House Report* no. 2503, serial 11582, 153–71. For an extended discussion of the matter, see H. D. Rosenthal, *Their Day in Court: A History of the Indian Claims Commission* (New York: Garland Publishing, 1990), 3–46.

36. Leupp, *The Indian and His Problem*, 194–96.

ment, but to make sure that the Indians did not employ attorneys "under unconscionable contracts" to handle their claims.[37]

Secretary Work's Committee of One Hundred in 1923, noting the denial of easy access to the Court of Claims to Indians tribes, recommended legislation to "enable every group or tribe of Indians to obtain through the Court of Claims a judicial and final accounting with their guardian, the United States." The increase in the number of jurisdictional acts and cases filed with the Court of Claims in the 1920s, with delays and negative judgments, made the problem more visible. In the Meriam Report of 1928 an urgent plea was made for new procedures to speed up the cumbersome and unsatisfactory process of handling the Indians' claims. What the Meriam staff wanted was creation of a special group to study the outstanding claims and then to submit its recommendations to the secretary of the interior, who in turn would draft a suitable jurisdictional bill to forward to Congress.[38]

The Board of Indian Commissioners at the same time echoed the concern expressed by the Meriam Report. It noted that the "honor of the Nation" was involved as well as the rights of the tribes, and it repeated its earlier warning that "great expectations are injuriously affecting the industrial and social progress of the Indians."[39] The board was encouraged by the initial stand taken by the new commissioner of Indian affairs, Charles J. Rhoads, appointed by President Hoover on April 18, 1929. Rhoads came into office pledging to follow the Meriam Report, and he was greeted enthusiastically, even by John Collier and his American Indian Defense Association. Rhoads recommended a special Indian claims commission and noted that unless something like this were done, the claims might well run on for another century. "There can be no liquidation of the Government's guardianship over Indians," he declared, "until this inheritance of treaties and alleged broken treaties and governmental laches of the past is absorbed."[40]

The movement to speed up the Indian claims action gathered momentum, not out of concern for treaties and the Indian rights stipulated in them as a basis for continuing or strengthening tribal status (perhaps

37. *Report of the Board of Indian Commissioners*, 1912–13, 14; the board repeated its recommendation in its report for 1913–14, 10.

38. "The Indian Problem," in serial 8273, pp. 3–4; Work, *Indian Policies*, 11; Meriam, *Problem of Indian Administration*, 19, 468, 748, 805–11.

39. *Report of the Board of Indian Commissioners*, 1928, 10–13; 1930, 18–19; 1931, 21.

40. See discussion of Rhoads's proposals in Prucha, *Great Father*, 2:925–26. The proposals, in the form of four letters, are printed in *Congressional Record*, 72:1051–53.

leading again to tribal autonomy and sovereignty), but rather, in a sense, to wipe out remaining remnants of tribal authority. Congress, however, refused to act. An Indian claims commission remained high on Collier's agenda, but even he, as commissioner of Indian affairs, was unable to push a measure through Congress. Although a number of bills were introduced between 1935 and 1945, none was able to overcome the strong opposition of members of Congress, some of whom looked upon the measure as a raid upon the Treasury intended to benefit not the Indians but their lawyers.[41]

Finally, after a long and bitter legislative battle, the Indian Claims Commission Act became law on August 13, 1946. It provided for a commission of three persons (enlarged to five in 1967), with appropriate staff, to hear claims against the United States on behalf of any Indian tribe or other identifiable group of Indians. The commission could deal with a broad variety of claims arising under laws, treaties, or executive orders, including those that would result "if the treaties, contracts, and agreements between the claimant and the United States were revised on the grounds of fraud, duress, unconscionable consideration, mutual or unilateral mistake, whether of law or fact, or any other ground cognizable by a court of equity." No statute of limitations or laches would have effect, but the United States could use all other defenses, and in the determination of relief, deductions were to be made for payments made on the claims and for other offsets, including "all money or property given to or funds expended gratuitously for the benefit of the claimant."[42]

Nearly all of the 176 tribes or bands that were notified of the act filed one or more claims on old grievances; in the end there were 370 petitions, which were broken down into 617 dockets. The commission was nearly overwhelmed, for the adversarial proceedings that developed between the tribal lawyers and the Justice Department (which defended the United States) greatly slowed down the process. The life of the commission had to be extended in 1956, 1961, 1967, 1972, and 1976; the body finally went out of existence on September 30, 1978.[43]

41. The struggle to enact a measure is well described in Rosenthal, *Their Day in Court*, 47–109.

42. 60 Stat. 1049–56.

43. An alphabetical list of cases and an index by docket number are given in *United States Indian Claims Commission, August 13, 1946—September 30, 1978: Final Report* (Washington: GPO, 1979), 23–123. An administrative history of the working of the commission is in Rosenthal, *Their Day in Court*, chaps. 3–7, and in a shorter piece by Rosenthal: "Indian Claims and the American Conscience: A Brief History of the Indian

By that time hardly a treaty existed that had not come into play in determination of Indian claims. Arthur V. Watkins, then chief commissioner on the Indian Claims Commission, was queried in 1965 by the House Committee on Interior and Insular Affairs about the need for a comprehensive study of Indian treaties. He replied negatively and said:

> This Commission has been in existence now for 18 years and most of the major treaties have been before us and have been studied, interpreted, and argued to great lengths. The attorneys for the Indians and for the Department of Justice have had to make comprehensive studies of every treaty in every treaty case that has been filed with us. They have spent years on these matters and we have the benefit of their work. There is no doubt that if a study had been made before the Indian Claims Commission came into being then it might have been of some help, but it is doubtful that any study made now could take the place of the intensive work already done by the lawyers, anthropologists, historians, and others who have had to prepare themselves on these treaty matters. . . . Most of the 852 causes of action filed with us involve treaties of one kind or another.[44]

With such a large number of dockets, of course, it is impossible here to cover the full use of treaties in the arguments of the cases, but two brief examples will give some insight into the reliance on the treaties in adjudicating the tribal claims.

One example is Docket 18-S, the claim made by a group of Chippewa Indians identified as Chippewas of Lake Superior and Chippewas of the Mississippi, for lands ceded by the treaty of October 4, 1842, an area designated as Royce Area 261.[45] The Indians claimed "recognized" title to this land under the Treaty of Prairie du Chien, August 19, 1825, confirmed by subsequent treaties of 1826 and 1827. The commission in August 1968 considered this question, and after noting similar Indian Claims Commission and Court of Claims judgments made earlier, it declared that the Chippewas did indeed hold the land in Royce Area

Claims Commission," in Imre Sutton, ed., *Irredeemable America: The Indians' Estate and Land Claims* (Albuquerque: University of New Mexico Press, 1985), 35–70. See also *Decisions of the Indian Claims Commission*, microfiche ed. (New York: Clearwater Publishing Company, 1973–78).

44. "Federal Opinion on the Need for an Indian Treaty Study," *House Report* no. 1044, 89-1, serial 12667-2, pp. 106–7.

45. In land cases, the Indian Claims Commission relied on the area designations employed in Royce, *Cessions*.

261 by recognized title and could now present proof that they had received inadequate payment for its cession.[46]

But not until January 1976 did the Indian Claims Commission again take action on Docket 18-S. Then it found that Royce Area 261 contained 10,538,000 acres, divided roughly equally between the present states of Michigan (Upper Peninsula) and Wisconsin. The commission, as was usual in these cases, heard detailed—and conflicting— testimony from the Indians and from the United States about the value of this land as of March 28, 1843, which the commission selected as the date of proclamation of the treaty. The appraisers for the Chippewas set the surface value of this land at $14,500,000 and the mineral value at $12,784,000, a total of $27,284,000. The Justice Department countered these figures with greatly reduced values from their own appraisers, leaving the commissioners the difficult task of arriving at a decision about the cession's "fair market value" in 1843. In the end, the commission decided that the surface value had been $7,262,818 and the mineral value, $1,600,000, a total of only $8,862,818. This was a far cry from the more than $27 million claimed by the Indians, but considerably above what the Justice Department had argued for.[47]

It was necessary, next, to decide how much the United States had paid to these Indians, following the stipulations of the treaty for cash annuities, goods, and services. The commission, after deciding what the promised goods and services had been worth, determined that the United States, in the treaty, had agreed to a consideration of $875,000 for the cession. Then it asked how much of this sum had actually been paid to the Indians over the years. The Justice Department lawyers were hard pressed to produce accurate figures, for vouchers were missing and it was often difficult to separate the moneys due under the 1842 treaty from lump sums paid under more than one treaty, and the commission repeatedly disallowed considerations claimed. In the end offsets amounting to $346,689.68 were authorized—payments for cash annuities, blacksmithing, tribal debts, pay of farmers and carpenters, and education. With the concurrence of the defendant, the commission on April 28, 1976, had dismissed any claims for gratuitous offsets. The final award, made on November 23, 1977, was $8,516,128.32, divided

---

46. "Recognized" title required a particular act of Congress—a treaty or a statute— that declared that the tribe had a permanent legal interest in the land, not merely a title resulting from exclusive aboriginal occupancy. The early deliberations of the commission are in *Decisions of the Indian Claims Commission*, 19:319–40.

47. Ibid., 37:146–92.

(according to a two-thirds/one-third formula in Article 8 of the Chippewa treaty of 1854) as follows: $5,677,418.88 to the Chippewas of Lake Superior and $2,838,709.44 to the Chippewas of the Mississippi.[48]

A second example is the suit brought by the Nez Perce Tribe for additional payment for lands ceded in the treaty of June 9, 1863, which it claimed had been paid for at far below the market value of the lands at time of cession (Docket 175-A). It was accepted that the tribe had recognized title to these lands arising from the treaty of June 11, 1855. The commission, from an examination of articles in the treaty with an appraisal of what the nonmonetary payments were worth, found that the consideration paid by the United States to the Nez Perce Indians under the treaty amounted to $352,394.94. For this amount the Nez Perces ceded 6,932,270 acres, which the commission, after breaking down the land into various categories—grazing land, mineral land, timber land, farming land, and the like—determined had had a fair market value of $4,650,000 as of April 17, 1867, the date of the proclamation of the treaty. The payment of the government to the tribe for the land was thus found to have been "grossly inadequate and unconscionable." The tribe was entitled to recover the difference between the consideration paid and the value of the lands, or $4,297,605.06. From this sum, according to the rules of the commission, were to be deducted gratuitous payments made to the tribe from the United States Treasury. The attorneys on the two sides reached an out-of-court compromise on the amount of these offsets, namely, $140,000. When this was subtracted, the final judgment on June 17, 1960, allowed the tribe $4,157,605.06. Indian attorneys' fees of $415,760.50 (a strict 10 percent of the award) were authorized on April 30, 1962.[49]

The Indian Claims Commission never achieved the finality in dealing with the claims that its proponents envisaged. The idea was to wipe the slate clean, end the Indians' expectations of large sums of moneys due them, and make possible the new initiatives of the Indian Office without the dead hand of past treaty provisions as a hindrance. Senator Watkins wrote in 1957 that "a basic purpose of Congress in setting up the Indian

48. Ibid., 41:102–29.

49. Ibid., 8:269–70, 298–99, 778, 780. Other Nez Perce claims were settled in other dockets: that concerning the 1855 reservation in Docket 175 and that concerning the amount of gold extracted from Nez Perce lands by white intruders in Docket 180. An article by an expert witness in the cases is Francis Haines, "The Nez Perce Tribe versus the United States," *Idaho Yesterdays* 8 (Spring 1964): 18–25.

Claims Commission was to clear the way toward complete freedom of the Indians by assuring a final settlement of all obligations—real or purported—of the federal government to the Indian tribes and other groups."[50]

This vision was never fulfilled. Instead of satisfying the Indians, the adversarial proceedings and the limited awards created new Indian dissatisfaction, and the sole remedy of money payments precluded the return of land that the Indians desired. The moneys—total awards of $818 million—were distributed largely in per capita payments and were quickly dissipated. The treaties and their stipulations were not eliminated; they remained as a vital and increasingly important source for a variety of Indian rights.

50. Arthur V. Watkins, "Termination of Federal Supervision: The Removal of Restrictions over Indian Property and Persons," *Annals of the American Academy of Political and Social Science* 311 (May 1957): 50.

CHAPTER SIXTEEN

Treaties before the Supreme Court

The United States Supreme Court, like the Court of Claims and the Indian Claims Commission, relied heavily on treaties in deciding Indian-related cases. "The most important single element in the Supreme Court's thought about Indian affairs," one thoughtful historian has concluded, "is the crucial importance of treaties, with the result that Indian rights, immunities, and special privileges have been upheld with some consistency."[1] Although conditions in the United States in the 1960s, 1970s, and 1980s in many ways were radically different from conditions in the days when the treaties were negotiated and ratified and although the Indian tribes themselves were hardly the same communities that signed the treaties, the Supreme Court, by and large, has gone out of its way to protect rights that were either explicitly or implicitly promised in the treaties. The treaties, which reformers at the end of the nineteenth century considered an obstacle to the progress of the Indians, have turned out, in the late twentieth century, to be one of the principal bastions of protection for the lands, the political autonomy, and the hunting and fishing rights of present-day reservation Indians.[2]

1. Robert H. Keller, Jr., "William O. Douglas, the Supreme Court, and American Indians," *American Indian Law Review* 3, no. 2 (1975): 333–34.
2. The use of treaties by the Supreme Court has been extensively discussed by Charles F. Wilkinson in *American Indians, Time, and the Law: Native Societies in a Modern Constitutional Democracy* (New Haven: Yale University Press, 1987), and our conclusions are generally in agreement. Wilkinson is more concerned than I, however, to see how the

Construing Indian Treaties

The principles followed by the Supreme Court and the criteria adopted for construing Indian treaties have again and again been expressly stated by the Court in its decisions. The Court, to be sure, has adamantly upheld the *power* of Congress to abrogate Indian treaties unilaterally, relying on *Lone Wolf v. Hitchcock,* but the modern stance of the Court has been to insist that Congress's intention to abrogate the provisions of a treaty must be beyond doubt. "Absent explicit statutory language," the justices said in 1979, "we have been extremely reluctant to find congressional abrogation of treaty rights." Congressional intention to abrogate or modify a treaty must be "clear and plain"; it "is not to be lightly imputed to the Congress"; statutes cannot be construed "as abrogating treaty rights in 'a backhanded way.'" In sum, the Court declared: "Indian treaty rights are too fundamental to be easily cast aside." Thus the Court, while realizing that the treaties were contracts between two parties, has understood their uniqueness.[3]

In 1973 the Court quoted with approval an earlier decision that asserted, "Doubtful expressions are to be resolved in favor of the weak and defenseless people who are the wards of the nation, dependent upon its protection and good faith." And treaties were "not to be read as an ordinary contract agreed upon by parties dealing at arm's length with equal bargaining positions." When it was a question of grants of land, the treaties were "not to be considered as exercises in ordinary conveyancing." Treaties, moreover, were to be interpreted as the Indians would have understood them.[4]

Court handled the problem of interpreting old and to some extent time-bound treaties and statutes so that they would apply reasonably to the changed circumstances of the tribes and of American society in general in the last half of the twentieth century—a major theme of his study. See also the valuable material in Keller, "William O. Douglas," 333–45, 353–55, which focuses on a single justice but which nevertheless has much to say about the Court's treatment of Indians between 1939 and 1975. For an extended discussion of Supreme Court action on Indian matters that is unduly harsh in its judgment of the Court, see Milner S. Ball, "Constitution, Court, Indian Tribes," *American Bar Foundation Research Journal,* 1987 (Winter): 1–140.

3. *United States v. Dion,* 476 U.S. 738–40, with citations of pertinent cases on which the Court relied and from which it quoted.

4. *McClanahan v. Arizona State Tax Commission,* 411 U.S. 173–75 (1973); *Choctaw*

The standards for determining how a clear and plain intent can be demonstrated have varied from case to case, as the Court admitted in 1986 in *United States v. Dion*. In some cases the Court looked for an express declaration of intent to abrogate treaty rights. In others it relied not only on the face of the law but also on the statute's legislative history and surrounding circumstances. Thus, while the Court considered explicit statements by Congress preferable, it did not rigidly hold to that preference if other evidence was sufficiently compelling. "What is essential," the Court declared, "is clear evidence that Congress actually considered the conflict between its intended action on the one hand and Indian treaty rights on the other, and chose to resolve that conflict by abrogating the treaty."[5]

The result was a series of decisions about land claims, tribal sovereignty and jurisdiction, and hunting and fishing rights that greatly benefited Indian tribes and helped tremendously to reestablish and revitalize Indian reservation communities. It should not be assumed, however, that all this was accomplished without controversy or that the treaty provisions were so "clear and plain" that unanimity in the courts came as a matter of course. In fact, the provisions in the treaties pertinent to the issues in the cases were frequently vague and seldom spoke precisely to the points that the Court needed to decide. Treaties negotiated in the eighteenth and nineteenth centuries were usually explicit enough on the issues they were drawn up to provide for. Precise boundaries of cessions were noted, explicit payments to be made were set down, and criminal jurisdictional lines were drawn. But the federal commissioners and the Indian signers of a treaty could not be expected

---

Nation v. Oklahoma, 397 U.S. 631 (1970). The Supreme Court in recent cases has relied on a rich arsenal of previous decisions to show that treaties should be interpreted in favor of the Indians. The question of court action relative to abrogation of treaties is studied thoroughly and competently from a legal standpoint in Charles F. Wilkinson and John M. Volkman, "Judicial Review of Indian Treaty Abrogation: 'As Long as Water Flows, or Grass Grows upon the Earth'—How Long a Time Is That?" *California Law Review* 63 (May 1975): 601–61. Some of the key decisions on which a liberal interpretation of treaties in favor of the Indians is based are discussed in Russel Lawrence Barsh and James Youngblood Henderson, "Contrary Jurisprudence: Tribal Interests in Navigable Waterways before and after *Montana v. United States*," *Washington Law Review* 56 (1981): 651–54. These authors, however, see "a judicial assault on liberal construction of Indian laws and treaties that began in 1978" (p. 654). See also Craig A. Decker, "The Construction of Indian Treaties, Agreements, and Statutes," *American Indian Law Review* 5, no. 2 (1977): 299–302.

5. 476 U.S. 739–40. The Court provides references to cases upholding these principles.

to have foreseen the radically changed circumstances brought about by the final military subjugation of the tribes, the successful attacks of reformers on tribalism and tribal reservations, and the later commitments to protect and reinstitute Indian rights. And it is within these new circumstances that the justices of the Supreme Court have had to read and construe the treaty provisions. It is no wonder that no incontrovertible rule of law has been established with regard to Indian rights based on Indian treaties. Instead, there have been frequent reversals of lower court decisions and numerous strong dissenting opinions in the Supreme Court itself.

Of the twenty-five Supreme Court cases between 1959 and 1986 that turned in some way upon treaty provisions, nineteen reversed lower court decisions. Only twelve of the decisions were unanimous; six cases had three dissenting justices; five had two dissenters; and two had a single dissenter. The outcomes thus rested often enough upon a somewhat shaky base.

Land Questions

Because the Indian Claims Commission had been set up in part to adjudicate Indian land issues, few Indian cases dealing specifically with land reached the Supreme Court. But those that did were of considerable importance. The most important, at least in terms of the size of the compensation awarded for loss of lands, was the case dealing with Sioux claims to the Black Hills, *United States v. Sioux Nation of Indians*, decided on June 30, 1980.[6] The issue was whether the Sioux Tribe was due compensation with interest for the "taking" of the Black Hills by the agreement of 1876 (confirmed by statute on February 28, 1877) in violation of the three-fourths-vote provision of the Fort Laramie Treaty of 1868. The Black Hills was a region of special value to the Sioux because it was considered a religious site.[7]

6. 448 U.S. 371–437.
7. The Court treats the history at considerable length, ibid., 374–84, and there is a brief account in Francis Paul Prucha, *The Great Father: The United States Government and the American Indians*, 2 vols. (Lincoln: University of Nebraska Press, 1984), 2:632–33, which I follow here. See also Stephen Cosby Hanson, "*United States v. Sioux Nation*: Political Questions, Moral Imperative, and the National Honor," *American Indian Law Review* 8, no. 2 (1980): 459–84. A recent study, which treats the complex legal maneuverings and the varying Indian views in the long history of the case, is Edward Lazarus,

The Sioux carried on a long struggle to get just compensation for this loss of land. In 1920 Congress passed a special jurisdictional act allowing adjudication of the claim, but the Court of Claims dismissed the case. After a good deal of legal sparring, involving the Indian Claims Commission and the Court of Claims, Congress authorized the Court of Claims to review the merits of the case, and that court held in 1979 that the Sioux were entitled to an award of interest at an annual rate of 5 percent on a principal sum of $17.5 million, dating from 1877. In the same year, the Supreme Court agreed to accept the case "in order to review the important constitutional questions presented by this case, questions not only of longstanding concern to the Sioux, but also of significant economic import to the Government."[8]

Much of the Court's opinion concerned questions of court jurisdiction and procedure, but the substantive issue was at last decided. *Sioux Nation*, the Court recognized, closely paralleled *Lone Wolf v. Hitchcock*, which had been decided against the Indians. Now it was at pains to show why the Sioux case differed from *Lone Wolf*. In the earlier case, the Court had found that Congress had purported to give adequate compensation and that it had merely changed the form of investment of Indian tribal property. The Court had then relied on the principle that Congress had full power and had acted in good faith, and it said that the Indians should seek relief from Congress not the courts. In the three-quarters of a century between the two cases, a new atmosphere had developed that made impossible a repetition of such findings. By an eight to one majority, the justices in 1980 accepted the Indians' plea and supported the earlier conclusion of the Court of Claims by declaring:

> The terms of the 1877 Act did not effect "a mere change in the form of investment of Indian tribal property." . . . Rather, the 1877 Act effected a taking of tribal property, property which had been set aside for the exclusive occupation of the Sioux by the Fort Laramie Treaty of 1868. That taking implied an obligation on the part of the Government to make just compensation to the Sioux Nation, and that obligation, including an award of interest, must now, at last, be paid.[9]

Black Hills, White Justice: The Sioux Nation versus the United States, 1775 to the Present (New York: HarperCollins, 1991).

8. 448 U.S. 390. There is a discussion of the jurisdictional questions, 384–90. Lazarus, *Black Hills, White Justice*, is especially good on this matter.

9. 448 U.S. 423–24.

The determination that United States acquisition of the Black Hills, to the value of $17.5 million, was a taking under the terms of the Fifth Amendment and required interest as well as the principal meant that the Sioux were awarded $105 million. Ironically, after the decades of complicated and frustrating struggle by the tribes' lawyers, who had finally won out against the lawyers of the Justice Department, the Oglala Sioux refused to accept the award. They demanded the return of their sacred land and would not give up that claim in return for money.[10]

A quite different land issue from that in *Sioux Nation* was at stake in *Choctaw Nation v. Oklahoma,* decided a decade earlier, on April 27, 1970.[11] Here the Court had to analyze early treaties to see what the intent of the United States government had been in granting lands to the Choctaws and the Cherokees in what is now Oklahoma. Did the treaties and subsequent patents based on the treaties convey ownership of the riverbed of the Arkansas River to the tribes, or did that ownership remain with the federal government for conveyance to Oklahoma when it became a state in 1907? Oklahoma argued that by accepted standards of ordinary conveyancing "the land descriptions in the treaties, standing alone, actually exclude the river beds." The Court, after a long discussion on the provisions of the Treaty of Dancing Rabbit Creek with the Choctaws (1830), the Treaty of New Echota with the Cherokees (1835), and the nature of the grants of land to these tribes, retorted that these treaties were "not to be considered as exercises in ordinary conveyancing." "The Indian Nations," the Court said, "did not seek out the United States and agree upon an exchange of lands in an arm's-length transaction. Rather, treaties were imposed upon them and they had no choice but to consent." Because of such circumstances, the justices insisted that the treaties had to be interpreted as the *Indians* would have understood them and that "any doubtful expression in them should be resolved in the Indians' favor." It noted, moreover, that the Treaty of Dancing Rabbit Creek itself had provided that "in the construction of this Treaty wherever well founded doubt shall arise, it shall be construed most favourably towards the Choctaws."[12] Much of the opinion was devoted to an examination of the historical record to determine how the Indians would have interpreted the treaties.

To counter the claim of Oklahoma that the United States had reserved

10. See Lazarus, *Black Hills, White Justice*, chap. 17, for a discussion of the postdecision history and the Oglala refusal to give up their claims to the Black Hills.

11. 397 U.S. 620–54.

12. Ibid., 628, 630–31. The Court cited earlier opinions on this same point.

the riverbeds of navigable rivers to itself so that it could convey them to a future state, the Court relied on a provision in the Choctaw treaty that no part of the land granted them should ever be embraced in a territory or state. "In the light of this promise," the Court asserted, "it is only by the purest of legal fictions that there can be found even the semblance of an understanding (on which Oklahoma necessarily places its principal reliance), that the United States retained title in order to grant it to some future State."[13]

The Court was split four to three, however, and a vigorous dissenting opinion argued that numerous precedents supported the principle that navigable rivers and their beds were under the sovereignty of the federal government and that for the Indians to prevail in the case "there must be found in their grant a 'very plain' basis for concluding that the United States intended to convey an interest in the river bed." The dissenting justices declared that neither the patents nor the treaties satisfied that standard.[14] The difficulties in interpreting *intent* arose because the treaties and other documents are silent about the precise point at issue; neither the treaties nor the patents mentioned the riverbed of the Arkansas River.

The problem arose again in a similar case, *Montana v. United States*, which was decided on March 24, 1981, *against* the Indians. Here the question was whether the Crow Indians owned the riverbed of the Big Horn River. The majority of the Court argued that title to land under navigable rivers could be presumed to rest in the United States, which held it in order to give it to future states.[15] The Treaty of Fort Laramie of 1868, which had initially set up the Crow Reservation astride the Big Horn River, did not expressly refer to the riverbed, and the Court this time found that "whatever property rights the language of the 1868 treaty created, . . . its language is not strong enough to overcome the presumption" of federal ownership. The Court held that because a riverbed was within the reservation boundaries did not automatically mean tribal ownership of it. Nor did the treaty provision granting "absolute and undisturbed use and occupation" of the reservation give the Indians exclusive right to occupy all the territory within the described boundaries.[16]

---

13. Ibid., 635. The Choctaw treaty provision is in Kappler, 2:311; a similar phrase was included in the Cherokee treaty, ibid., 442.
14. 397 U.S. 648. The full dissent covers pp. 643–54.
15. 450 U.S. 544–81.
16. Ibid., 554–55.

The majority of the Court, of course, could not avoid considering the opposite conclusion reached a decade earlier, and in a footnote to the opinion argued that *Montana* differed from *Choctaw Nation v. Oklahoma*. "Neither the special historical origins of the Choctaw and Cherokee treaties nor the crucial provisions granting Indian lands in fee simple and promising freedom from state jurisdiction in those treaties," the justices said, "have any counterparts in the terms and circumstances of the Crow treaties of 1851 and 1868."[17] Those differences did not convince the three justices who entered a dissenting opinion. The dissenters restated the principle that treaties were to be construed as the Indians understood them and argued that the Crows certainly thought that they controlled the rivers that lay entirely within the reservation set up in 1868.[18]

Other land cases considered whether or not Indian reservations established by treaties had subsequently been reduced or entirely given up. Here was a question of continuing reservation status, which demanded a careful study of the treaties that had established or guaranteed Indian ownership of land and of later acts that might have diminished the Indian lands and consequently jurisdiction over them. In four cases, the Supreme Court decided that reservation rights claimed by the Indians no longer existed.

The first of these was *Federal Power Commission v. Tuscarora Indian Nation*, of March 7, 1960.[19] It was a sticky case early in the new era and was decided by a six to three majority. The question was whether the United States under amendments to the Federal Power Act of 1935 could take Tuscarora lands for a reservoir. The argument turned on whether the Treaty of Fort Stanwix (1784), the Treaty of Fort Harmar (1789), and the Treaty of Canandaigua (1794), all of which protected rights in land, applied to the Tuscaroras in this case, as the Indians argued. The Court decided in favor of the Federal Power Commission against the Indians on the basis that the Tuscaroras' lands were not a "reservation" in the sense that Indian reservations were excluded under the Federal Power Act.[20]

17. Ibid., 555–56n.
18. Ibid., 569–81. Indians have retained riverbeds to navigable rivers by decisions of lower federal courts not considered by the Supreme Court; see Wilkinson, *American Indians, Time, and the Law*, 51 and 170, n. 90. *Montana v. United States* also concerned tribal jurisdiction over non-Indians and aroused strong criticism; see references below in note 49.
19. 362 U.S. 99–142.
20. The treaties are in Kappler, 2:5–6, 23–25, 34–37.

In a somewhat involved argument, tucked away in a footnote, the Supreme Court declared that the first two treaties related to other lands and principally to other Indian tribes and that the third treaty, though covering the lands in question, had been made with the Seneca Indians. These Indians in a contract of 1797 and with the approval of the United States, had sold their interest in the lands to Robert Morris, thus freeing them from the effects of the Treaty of Canandaigua. Morris in turn had sold the lands to the Holland Land Company, which conveyed the area in question to the Tuscarora Nation in fee simple. The Indians' title, then, rested upon the conveyance from Morris, not on any treaty. So the Court decided that the Federal Power Commission was authorized to take the lands with a just compensation because "the lands in question are not subject to any treaty between the United States and the Tuscaroras."[21]

The majority opinion called forth a strong dissent, which foreshadowed later, more liberal interpretations of treaty rights. The minority, led by Justice Hugo L. Black, held that the lands of the Tuscaroras *were* a reservation and therefore protected, and it argued that the Treaty of Canandaigua *did* apply to the Tuscaroras. In an eloquent statement, Black wrote: "The solemn pledge of the United States to its wards is not to be construed like a money-lender's mortgage. Up to this time it has always been the established rule that this Court would give treaties with the Indians an enlarged interpretation; one that would assure them beyond all doubt that this Government does not engage in sharp practices with its wards." At the end Black said, "I regret that this Court is to be the governmental agency that breaks faith with this dependent people. Great nations, like great men, should keep their word."[22]

In later cases, less emotionally charged but still matters of controversy among the justices, the Court again decided that reservation or tribal status had been ended and that consequently the treaty rights originally enjoyed by the Indians in question no longer applied. In *DeCoteau v. District County Court for the Tenth Judicial District*, March 3, 1975, the Court decided that part of the Lake Traverse Indian Reservation had lost its Indian country status by an agreement of 1889 ratified by Congress in 1891.[23] A treaty of 1867 between the United States and the Sisseton and Wahpeton bands of the Sioux had set up the original reservation. Although the majority opinion declared that "this Court

21. 362 U.S. 121–23n, 123.
22. Ibid., 137–38, 142.
23. 420 U.S. 425–68.

does not lightly conclude that an Indian reservation has been terminated," it nevertheless decided that the law of 1891, providing for the sale of unallotted lands, had thereby reduced the reservation. (In an unusual move, the Court appended to its decision the full texts of the treaty and the 1891 law.) The dissenting opinion of Justice William O. Douglas, in which he was joined by two other justices, insisted that the sale of lands had in no way altered the boundaries of the original reservation and that the tribes still had jurisdictional rights within those boundaries.[24]

Delaware Tribal Business Committee v. Weeks, of February 23, 1977, involved a group of Delaware Indians who had remained in Kansas when other groups of the tribe moved to Oklahoma in 1866.[25] These Kansas Delawares wanted to share in an award made by the Indian Claims Commission for violation of a treaty of 1854 with the Delawares, but the Court declared that by the removal treaty of 1866 these Indians had lost their status as tribal members and become simply individual citizens. The opinion analyzed the 1866 treaty in some detail, and only one justice dissented.[26]

In *Rosebud Sioux Tribe v. Kneip, Governor of South Dakota,* April 4, 1977, the document in question was not strictly a treaty but rather an agreement that postdated the end of treaty making in 1871.[27] The agreement of 1889, which reduced the Great Sioux Reserve and set up six separate reservations including Rosebud, was considered by the Court as though it had been a treaty, and in fact twice in the the opinion the agreement is called the "1889 Treaty." The Court asked whether Congress in laws of 1904, 1907, and 1910 intended to reduce the Rosebud Reservation as set up in 1889. Relying on the precedent of *Lone Wolf v. Hitchcock,* the Court declared: "We conclude that, although the Acts of 1904, 1907, and 1910 were unilateral Acts of Congress without the consent of three-quarters of the members of the tribe required by the original Treaty, that fact does not have a bearing." What was compelling to the justices was the clear intent of Congress to exercise its plenary power in abrogating treaty provisions. As might be expected, in a decision that appeared to go against Indian treaty rights, three justices joined in a dissenting opinion. They maintained that the Court had obliterated distinctions made in *DeCoteau* and by holding against the tribe "when the evidence concerning congressional intent is

24. Ibid., 444, 449–60, 460–61.
25. 430 U.S. 73–98.
26. The treaties in question are in Kappler, 2:614–18, 937–42.
27. 430 U.S. 584–633.

palpably ambiguous" had eroded the generally accepted principles of interpreting Indian statutes. They could find no "express provision disestablishing the Reservation."[28]

Treaty rights entered only indirectly, as a sort of fundamental basis for Indian land claims, in cases involving the Oneida Indians, who claimed land that allegedly had been ceded invalidly to the state of New York. The cessions went against the Indian Trade and Intercourse Law of 1790, which prohibited sale of Indian lands to any state, unless the contract had been made at a public treaty held under the authority of the United States.[29] Treaties were relevant to the Oneida claims in confirming the original rights of the Indians to the lands in question.

In *Oneida Indian Nation of New York v. County of Oneida, New York*, decided on January 21, 1974, the Court discussed the importance of treaties at great length.[30] "The Federal Government," it said, "took early steps to deal with the Indians through treaty, the principal purpose often being to recognize and guarantee the rights of Indians to specified areas of land." This was the case with the Oneidas and other New York Indians, and the applicable treaties are listed in a footnote. In further historical analysis, the Court noted that "the possessory and treaty rights of Indian tribes to their lands have been the recurring theme of many other cases."[31] Yet the crux of the case was not treaty rights but whether the transfer of lands to New York had been validly made, and litigation on that point continued during the next decade. When the Supreme Court considered the matter again in *County of Oneida v. Oneida Indian Nation*, March 4, 1985, it upheld by a five to four majority the tribe's federal common-law right of action for unlawful possession of the lands, which was not barred by any statute of limitations, so the tribal position that it could sue in federal courts was upheld.[32]

Jurisdictional Questions

The question of diminution or termination of reservation status was not always essentially one of land ownership. At stake as well was tribal jurisdiction over the lands in question, perhaps a more

28. Ibid., 587, 618.
29. 1 Stat. 138.
30. 414 U.S. 661–84.
31. Ibid., 667, 669. A footnote cites earlier cases.
32. 470 U.S. 226–73.

important question than that of property rights. Treaties had provided not only land rights but political autonomy for the tribes—a kind of semisovereignty at least—within the boundaries of their reservations. The Supreme Court has clearly recognized the importance of this second aspect of the treaties in its decisions.

Problems arose when states extended their jurisdiction over the Indian reservations. Wanting their sovereignty to extend over *all* the lands within their boundaries, states taxed and regulated activities within the Indian lands. The Supreme Court from time to time was called upon to decide whether such state action was proper. In its consideration about how and to what extent state laws were excluded from reservations, two lines of thought were evident. State jurisdiction was excluded if jurisdiction had been preempted by the federal government, which had a special responsibility toward the Indians and the Indian reservations. But another question also was asked: Did the state action interfere with the legitimate exercise of authority by tribal governments? In revitalizing tribal governmental authority over reservations and their inhabitants, the Court's decisions played a significant role. And interpretation of treaties was a vital part of its decision making.

The treaty between the United States and the Navajo Nation signed in 1868 was the basis for a number of significant decisions upholding Indian tribal jurisdiction. This treaty had ended the Indians' exile at the Bosque Redondo on the Pecos River in eastern New Mexico and, in return for a promise of peace, had provided a reservation for the Navajos in their old homeland. In Article 2, the treaty specified in some detail the exclusiveness of the reservation:

> [The reservation is] set apart for the use and occupation of the Navajo tribe of Indians, and for such other friendly tribes or individual Indians as from time to time they may be willing, with the consent of the United States, to admit among them; and the United States agrees that no persons except those herein so authorized to do, and except such officers, soldiers, agents, and employés of the Government, or of the Indians, as may be authorized to enter upon Indian reservations in discharge of duties imposed by law, or the orders of the President, shall ever be permitted to pass over, settle upon, or reside in, the territory described in this article.[33]

The first important case to rely upon the protection of tribal autonomy expressed in this treaty article was *Williams v. Lee,* decided on

33. Kappler, 2:1016.

January 12, 1959, a case that "opened the modern era of federal Indian law."[34] The case concerned a suit by a non-Indian to enforce a debt incurred by Indians on the Navajo Reservation, entered in the Apache County Superior Court of Arizona. The Supreme Court decided that the case, instead, fell exclusively within the tribal courts, so that tribal self-government could be protected and promoted.

From a reading of Article 2 of the 1868 treaty, the Court found implicit in the treaty terms "the understanding that the internal affairs of the Indians remained exclusively within the jurisdiction of whatever tribal government existed." It compared the treaty with the Cherokee treaties involved in *Worcester v. Georgia* (1832), and it noted that Congress and the Bureau of Indian Affairs had "assisted in strengthening the Navajo tribal government and its courts." The Court expressly remarked that the 1871 law ending treaty making did not impair the obligations in existing ratified treaties and that "thus the 1868 treaty with the Navajos survived this Act."[35]

In reversing the decision of the Supreme Court of Arizona, which had upheld the jurisdiction of the Apache County Superior Court, the unanimous opinion of the United States Supreme Court concluded: "The cases in this Court have consistently guarded the authority of Indian governments over their reservations. Congress recognized this authority in the Navajos in the Treaty of 1868, and has done so ever since. If this power is to be taken away from them, it is for Congress to do it."[36] It was a bold and auspicious beginning of the "modern era."

Williams was followed in April 1965 by *Warren Trading Post Co. v. Arizona Tax Commission*, which again, in a unanimous decision, reversed the Supreme Court of Arizona on an issue of tribal versus state jurisdiction on the Navajo Reservation.[37] The Court denied the authority of the state of Arizona to tax the Warren Trading Post, a business run by non-Indians on the reservation; it did so on the basis that the federal government, not states, controlled Indian trade. As in *Williams,* the Court relied on the Navajo treaty of 1868:

> The Navajo Reservation was set apart as a "permanent home" for the Navajos in a treaty made with the "Navajo nation or tribe of Indians" on June 1, 1868. Long before that, in fact from the very

34. 358 U.S. 217–23; the quotation is from Wilkinson, *American Indians, Time, and the Law*, 1. Wilkinson gives reasons for considering the case "a watershed" on 1–3.

35. 358 U.S. 221–22, 221n.

36. Ibid., 223.

37. 380 U.S. 685–92.

first days of our Government, the Federal Government had been permitting the Indians largely to govern themselves, free from state interference, and had exercised through statutes and treaties a sweeping and dominant control over persons who wished to trade with Indians and Indian tribes.[38]

Similarly, in *McClanahan v. Arizona State Tax Commission*, of March 27, 1973, the Court ruled that the Arizona income tax did not apply to an Indian whose income was wholly derived from reservation sources.[39] The argument was based chiefly on the self-governing powers of the Navajo Indians as set forth in the treaty of 1868, and there was heavy reliance on *Williams v. Lee*. The Court refused to place principal reliance simply on the sovereignty of the tribe however. "The trend," it said, "has been away from the idea of inherent Indian sovereignty as a bar to state jurisdiction and toward reliance on federal pre-emption. . . . The modern cases thus tend to avoid reliance on platonic notions of Indian sovereignty and to look instead to the applicable treaties and statutes which define the limits of state power." In *McClanahan* the Indian sovereignty doctrine did not provide a "definitive resolution" of the case but rather "a backdrop" against which to read applicable treaties and federal statutes.[40]

Following this principle, the Court ruled that Arizona had exceeded its lawful authority in taxing the appellant. Turning at once to the 1868 treaty, the justices stated: "The treaty nowhere explicitly states that the Navajos were to be free from state law or exempt from state taxes. But the document is not to be read as an ordinary contract agreed upon by parties dealing at arm's length with equal bargaining positions." In such circumstances, the Court adopted the rule from *Carpenter v. Shaw* (1930) that "doubtful expressions are to be resolved in favor of the weak and defenseless people who are the wards of the nation, dependent upon its protection and good faith."[41]

---

38. Ibid., 686–87. The opinion cites the treaty with the Delawares in 1778 and notes similar provisions in other early treaties; it again declared that the law of 1871 "left the obligations of existing treaties unimpaired."

39. 411 U.S. 164–81.

40. Ibid., 172.

41. Ibid., 174. The question of limiting state jurisdiction over tribes was faced also in *Metlakatla Indian Community v. Egan, Governor of Alaska*, March 5, 1962 (369 U.S. 45–59), which upheld the power of the secretary of the interior to protect Indian fishing rights against state authority. The decision of the Court was based on a law of 1891, not on treaties, but it cited at length treaties that had expressly excluded state laws, using them as an analogy in the present case.

More remarkable, because of the boost it gave to the doctrine of retained inherent sovereignty of Indian tribes, was *United States v. Wheeler,* decided on March 22, 1978.[42] The question before the Court was whether the double jeopardy clause of the Fifth Amendment barred prosecution of a Navajo Indian in a federal court because he had been convicted earlier in a tribal court of a lesser included offense arising from the same incident. Accepting the doctrine of inherent tribal sovereignty set forth by Felix S. Cohen, a sovereignty antedating the United States government and not resting on a grant of authority from Congress, the Supreme Court ruled that there was no double jeopardy because the two courts were arms of separate and distinct sovereigns. It admitted that by treaties and by statutes some elements of Indian sovereignty had been taken away, but until Congress acts, it said, "tribes retain their existing sovereign powers." An examination of the treaties made with the Navajos in 1849 and in 1868 showed that neither of them "deprived the Tribe of its *own* jurisdiction to charge, try, and punish members of the Tribe for violations of tribal law." The Court reinforced its decision by quoting from *Williams v. Lee:* "Implicit in these treaty terms . . . was the understanding that the internal affairs of the Indians remained exclusively within the jurisdiction of whatever tribal government existed."[43] The Court also cited *Warren Trading Post* and laws and other previous cases that showed the same retention of tribal powers.

If tribal criminal jurisdiction extended to tribal members on a reservation as a part of inherent sovereignty, however, it did not extend to nonmembers. In a case decided two weeks before Wheeler, the Supreme Court placed a sharp restriction on tribal criminal authority over non-Indians living on a reservation. The case of *Oliphant v. Suquamish Indian Tribe,* March 6, 1978, concerned Mark Oliphant, a non-Indian residing on the Port Madison Reservation in the state of Washington, who had been arrested by tribal authorities, charged with assaulting a tribal officer and resisting arrest.[44] Oliphant claimed he was not subject to tribal authority. The Supreme Court, overturning the decision of the United States Court of Appeals for the Ninth Circuit, voted against the

---

42. 435 U.S. 313–32. The question of Indian sovereignty is expertly discussed in Arthur Lazarus, Jr., "Tribal Sovereignty under United States Law," in William R. Swagerty, ed., *Indian Sovereignty: Proceedings of the Second Annual Conference on Problems concerning American Indians Today* (Chicago: Newberry Library, 1979), 28–46.

43. 435 U.S. 323–24.

44. 435 U.S. 191–212.

tribe's contentions that its jurisdiction flowed automatically from its "retained inherent powers of government" over the reservation. The justices in the majority opinion in the six to two decision discussed at length the history of Indian courts and of laws and cases that showed a common understanding that non-Indians were not to be tried in Indian courts, taking the Choctaw treaty of 1830 as an example of nonjurisdiction. Then they turned to the Treaty of Point Elliot (1853), which had set up the reservation in question. Noting the Indians' acknowledgment of their "dependence on the government of the United States" and their agreement "not to shelter or conceal offenders against the laws of the United States, but to deliver them up to the authorities for trial," the justices declared, somewhat lamely:

> By themselves, these treaty provisions would probably not be sufficient to remove criminal jurisdiction over non-Indians if the Tribe otherwise retained such jurisdiction. But an examination of our earlier precedents satisfies us that, even ignoring treaty provisions and congressional policy, Indians do not have criminal jurisdiction over non-Indians absent affirmative delegation of such power by Congress.[45]

Indian tribes considered *Oliphant* a damaging blow to their sovereign revival, and it showed the problems of relying on the provisions of ancient treaties to determine issues arising in very changed modern circumstances.[46] Two justices, too, dissented from the Court's opinion. Justice Thurgood Marshall, who wrote the dissent, agreed with the Court of Appeals that the "power to preserve order on the reservation . . . is a sine qua non of the sovereignty that the Suquamish originally possessed." Without an affirmative withdrawal of that power in a treaty or statute, he asserted, "Indian tribes enjoy as a necessary aspect of their retained sovereignty the right to try and punish all persons who commit offenses against tribal law within the reservation."[47]

But the Court did not relent. In *Montana v. United States* (1981), it extended the ruling of *Oliphant* to strike down tribal authority to

45. Ibid., 206–8. The Court may well have been influenced by the circumstances of the Port Madison Reservation noted in a footnote to the opinion (p. 193n). Sixty-three percent of the land on the reservation was owned in fee simple by non-Indians, and there were nearly 3,000 non-Indians living within the reservation boundaries, compared with approximately 50 Indians.

46. References to opposition to the opinion are noted in Prucha, *Great Father*, 2:1189n.

47. 435 U.S. 212.

28. United States Indian Peace Commission, 1868

To ease the crisis of wars and unrest on the Indian frontiers, Congress in 1867 established an Indian Peace Commission, made up of important civilians and high-ranking military officers, which was empowered to sign treaties with the tribes. This photograph of members of the commission was taken at Fort Laramie in 1868. Left to right, it shows General Alfred H. Terry, General William S. Harney, General William T. Sherman, Commissioner of Indian Affairs Nathaniel G. Taylor, Samuel F. Tappan, and General C. C. Auger posing with an unidentified Indian woman. The commission dealt with southern plains tribes at Medicine Lodge Creek, with northern plains tribes at Fort Laramie, with the Navajos at Fort Sumner, and with the Shoshones and Bannocks at Fort Bridger.

The Indian Peace Commission met with the Kiowas, Comanches, Apaches, and southern Cheyennes and Arapahos at Medicine Lodge Creek in southern Kansas and procured treaties of peace and advancement in civilization. Satank and Satanta, two Kiowa chiefs, signed the treaties, but they would not stay confined to the reservations assigned to them at Medicine Lodge Creek.

29. Medicine Lodge Creek Council, October 1867

30. Satank

31. Satanta

The Peace Commission traveled with a large retinue, and it was joined at
Medicine Lodge Creek by a corps of journalists, who covered the events
in great detail for their readers. This scene of the commissioners' camp
was painted by Hermann Stieffel, a private of the Fifth Infantry.

32. Peace Commissioners' Camp, Medicine Lodge Creek

33. Fort Laramie Treaty Council, 1868

The photographer Alexander Gardner took numerous pictures at the Fort Laramie council. This one shows the full commission talking with Indians under a rough canopy or "council lodge" made of buffalo skins.

The Sioux leader Red Cloud refused to sign the Fort Laramie Treaty until the United States military posts along the Bozeman Trail in the Powder River Valley were abandoned, as the treaty promised. He ultimately signed the treaty at the fort long after the commission had departed. This fine portrait of the chief was taken by Gardner in Washington, D.C. in 1872.

34. Red Cloud

Members of the Indian Peace Commission, after signing the Fort Laramie treaties in 1868, also made treaties in the summer of that year with the Navajos at Fort Sumner and with the Shoshones and Bannocks at Fort Bridger. Barboncito was the first to sign the Navajo treaty, Washakie the first to sign for the Shoshones.

35. Barboncito

36. Washakie

37. Shoshone Delegation in Washington, D.C., 1880

Delegates from the Lemhi and Fort Hall agencies signed an agreement on May 14, 1880. With them in this formal photograph by C. M. Bell are the Indian agent and an interpreter.

38. Henry L. Dawes

Henry L. Dawes, after he retired from the Senate, headed the Dawes Commission, which signed agreements with the Five Civilized Tribes in the Indian Territory for the allotment of their lands.

39. James McLaughlin

James McLaughlin, a long-time Indian agent who was respected by the Indians, was appointed Indian inspector in 1895. In that office he concluded numerous agreements with western tribes.

40. Muckleshoot Treaty Rights March, 1966

41. Anti-Boldt Demonstration, 1974

On the basis of treaties signed with
Isaac I. Stevens in the mid-1850s,
Indians in Washington State more
than a century later began to assert
their fishing rights with "fish-ins"
and protest marches. When Federal
District Judge George Boldt upheld
their rights and authorized them to
take up to 50 percent of the harvestable fish, angry white protesters
condemned Boldt and his decision.

42. Treaty Beer

In Wisconsin, federal court decisions in favor of Chippewa spearfishing in areas ceded by nineteenth-century treaties produced a tremendous white backlash, for people objected to Indians' receiving "special treatment." To raise money to fight the Indians' protected rights one group sold Treaty Beer, with anti-Indian messages on the cans. Sometimes violent crowds gathered to protest and obstruct the spearfishing.

43. Protest against Chippewa Spearfishing, 1991

regulate hunting and fishing of non-Indians on reservation lands owned in fee simple by nonmembers of the Crow Tribe.[48] It looked at the Treaty of Fort Laramie of 1851, which "nowhere suggested that Congress intended to grant authority to the Crow Tribe to regulate hunting and fishing by nonmembers on nonmember lands," and at the Treaty of Fort Laramie of 1868, which "arguably conferred upon the Tribe the authority to control fishing and hunting" on the reservation. But it concluded: "That authority could only extend to land on which the Tribe exercises 'absolute and undisturbed use and occupation.' . . . If the 1868 treaty created tribal power to restrict or prohibit non-Indian hunting and fishing on the reservation, that power cannot apply to lands held in fee by non-Indians." The Court noted the Indians' argument that it had inherent sovereignty, but turned it aside with the remark that inherent sovereignty is not so broad as to apply to non-Indian lands.[49]

While these decisions cut back broad extensions of tribal jurisdiction over non-Indians, an earlier case, *Morton v. Mancari*, decided unanimously on June 17, 1974, had extended the principle of special treatment of Indians by the United States government.[50] The case was brought against the secretary of the interior by non-Indian employees of the Bureau of Indian Affairs who claimed that preferential hiring of Indians (initiated in the Indian Reorganization Act of 1934 and extended by the secretary of the interior in 1972) was contrary to the Equal Employment Opportunity Act of 1972 and that such preference deprived them of property rights without due process of law. In reversing the decision of the United States District Court for the District of New Mexico, the Supreme Court rejected the idea of "racial" preference and declared that the preference was granted to the Indians "not as a discrete racial group, but, rather, as members of quasi-sovereign tribal entities whose lives and activities are governed by the BIA in a unique fashion." The resolution of the case turned on "the unique legal status of Indian

48. 450 U.S. 544–81.

49. Ibid., 558–59, 563. There has been strong negative reaction to *Montana* because of the restrictions it put upon tribal jurisdiction (as it upheld *Oliphant*) and because the Court seemed to ignore the principle that treaties were to be construed as they would have been understood by the Indians. See, for example, the bitter attack on the decision that appeared in Barsh and Henderson, "Contrary Jurisprudence," 684–85; and Sarah Arnott, "In the Aftermath of the Bighorn River Decision: Montana Has Title, Indian Law Doctrines Are Clouded, and Trust Questions Remain," *Public Land Law Review* 2 (Spring 1981): 1–56.

50. 417 U.S. 535–55. See Brian Douglas Baird, "*Morton v. Mancari:* New Vitality for the Indian Preference Statutes," *Tulsa Law Journal* 10, no. 3 (1975): 454–62.

tribes under federal law and upon the plenary power of Congress, based on *a history of treaties* and the assumption of a 'guardian-ward' status, to legislate in behalf of federally recognized Indian tribes."[51]

Hunting and Fishing Rights

A liberal interpretation of treaty rights was nowhere more evident than in the vindication of tribal hunting and fishing rights. The most remarkable developments came in the state of Washington, where state action to limit or prohibit Indian fishing for salmon and steelhead trout brought an outbreak of protests—the famous "fish-ins" of 1964, in which groups of Indians determined to continue fishing in opposition to state laws. This widely publicized agitation was soon followed by a series of court decisions.[52]

The basis for the Indians' claims was the series of treaties negotiated with the Pacific Coast Indians by Isaac I. Stevens, governor of Washington Territory, in the 1850s. The one principally relied upon was the Treaty of Medicine Creek, signed on December 26, 1854, with "chiefs, head-men, and delegates" of the Nisqually, Puyallup, Steilacoom, and other tribes, which for the purposes of the treaty were regarded as one nation. The important statement for the courts more than a century later was Article 3, which said in part: "The right of taking fish, at all usual and accustomed grounds and stations, is further secured to said Indians in common with all citizens of the Territory."[53] When the treaties were signed, there was a great abundance of fish and few whites for the Indians to contend with, but by the middle of the twentieth century, as the resources were threatened with depletion, the rights enunciated so vaguely in the treaties assumed new and vital importance.

51. 417 U.S. 551, 553–54; emphasis added. The Court based this plenary power on constitutional provisions—the commerce clause and the power of the president, by and with the advice and consent of the Senate, to make treaties.

52. Useful studies of the fishing rights issue in the state of Washington are two reports prepared for the American Friends Service Committee: *Uncommon Controversy: Fishing Rights of the Muckleshoot, Puyallup, and Nisqually Indians* (Seattle: University of Washington Press, 1970), and Fay G. Cohen, *Treaties on Trial: The Continuing Controversy over Northwest Indian Fishing Rights* (Seattle: University of Washington Press, 1986).

53. Kappler, 2:662. Similar provisions appeared in the Treaty of Point Elliot, January 22, 1855, the Treaty of Point No Point, January 26, 1855, and the Treaty of Neah Bay, January 31, 1855. Ibid., 670, 674, 682.

Two earlier decisions of the Supreme Court had pointed the way. In 1904 the Court had ruled that Indians could not be barred from their usual fishing sites and that they had easements over both public and private lands to get there. And in 1942, the Court had declared that the state could not regulate off-reservation Indian fishing.[54] It was a series of cases extending for a little more than a decade (1968–79), however, that newly examined the treaties in great detail and in the end, by a remarkably elastic reading of the provisions, came down firmly on the side of existing Indian rights. There was continual sparring with the state of Washington, which (influenced no doubt by the pleas of commercial fishing interests and those who fished for sport) insisted on its right to regulate Indian fishing in the interests of conservation.

The first case to reach the United States Supreme Court (which affirmed a decision of the Supreme Court of Washington) was *Puyallup Tribe v. Department of Game of Washington* (known as *Puyallup I*), decided on May 27, 1968.[55] Citing the Treaty of Medicine Creek, the Court renewed its vindication of the right of the Indians to fish off-reservation at accustomed sites. It quoted *United States v. Winans* (1904): "To construe the treaty as giving the Indians 'no rights but such as they would have without the treaty' . . . would be 'an impotent outcome to negotiations and a convention, which seemed to promise more and give the word of the Nation for more.'" But the Court accepted the authority of Washington to restrict the *type* of fishing done by the Indians. It assumed that nets were used by the Indians at the time the treaty was signed and that there were commercial aspects to the fishing. "But the *manner* in which fishing may be done and its purpose. . . ," the opinion said, "are not mentioned in the Treaty. We would have quite a different case if the Treaty had preserved the right to fish at the 'usual and accustomed places' *in the 'usual and accustomed' manner*. But the Treaty is silent as to the mode or modes of fishing that are guaranteed."[56]

In 1973 the issue again reached the Supreme Court in *Department of Game of Washington v. Puyallup Tribe* (*Puyallup II*), November 19, 1973.[57] The state of Washington had barred all Indian net fishing of steelhead trout because those who engaged in sport fishing, with hook and line, caught all the steelhead that could be taken under conservation

---

54. *United States v. Winans*, 198 U.S. 371–84 (1904); *Tulee v. State of Washington*, 315 U.S. 681–85 (1942).
55. 391 U.S. 392–403.
56. Ibid., 397, 398; emphasis is in the original.
57. 414 U.S. 44–50.

measures. On the basis of the Treaty of Medicine Creek, the United States Supreme Court reversed the decision of the Supreme Court of Washington, which it ruled had discriminated against the Indians. It did not deny, however, that conservation measures might be necessary to prevent the extinction of the species. "We do not imply," it said, "that these fishing rights persist down to the very last steelhead in the river. . . . The police power of the State is adequate to prevent the steelhead from following the fate of the passenger pigeon; and the Treaty does not give the Indians a federal right to pursue the last living steelhead until it enters their nets."[58]

The conservation issue was faced once more in *Puyallup Tribe, Inc. v. Department of Game of Washington* (*Puyallup III*), decided on June 23, 1977, which repeated much about Indian treaty rights that had been worked over in *Puyallup I* and *Puyallup II*.[59] The new issue was the authority of the state to regulate the tribe's on-reservation fishing rights. Although the Court vacated the decision of the Supreme Court of Washington that the state could regulate the tribe's fishing on the reservation, it upheld the regulatory authority of the state when regulations were reasonable and necessary for the conservation of fish.

Thus the rights of Indians to fish "at all usual and accustomed grounds and stations," subject to reasonable conservation regulations of the state, were well established. What was still in question, however, was the precise meaning of the treaty phrases "the right of taking fish" and "in common with all citizens of the Territory." Did they mean that the Indians were entitled to a definite amount or percentage of the catch? In 1970 a group of Indian tribes filed suit in the Federal District Court for the Western District seeking a determination of their rights to a fair share of the fish. After three and a half years of intensive study, Judge George Boldt wrote a long opinion that thoroughly analyzed the treaties, the migratory patterns of the fish, Indian fishing patterns, and the history of state regulation. Because his findings showed a reduction of Indian rights over the years by state regulation and non-Indian encroachment, Boldt enunciated a set of principles to govern Indian fishing: the treaties reserved fishing rights for Indians that differed from those of other citizens; off-reservation fishing rights extended to all places that a tribe had customarily fished; and the state could regulate Indian fishing only to the extent needed to conserve fish resources.[60]

58. Ibid., 49.
59. 433 U.S. 165–85.
60. *United States v. State of Washington*, 384 F. Supp. 312–423. I have relied here on

All of that seemed reasonable enough and was in accord with previous judicial decisions. But Boldt took a further step. The Indians' right to take fish "in common with the citizens of the Territory," he determined, meant not only access to fishing sites but a fair share of the fish, which he ruled was up to 50 percent of the harvestable number of fish, exclusive of catches used for subsistence or for ceremonial purposes. Non-Indian reaction to this bombshell was violent and much of the outcry was aimed personally against Boldt, who was accused of racial discrimination.[61] Boldt's decision was confirmed by the United States Court of Appeals, Ninth Circuit, but the United States Supreme Court at the time refused to accept the case for review.

The problems of enforcing the decision of the district court, which the state of Washington refused to do, led to demands for further litigation, and in 1979 the Supreme Court at last agreed to hear the case. In *Washington v. Washington State Commercial Passenger Fishing Vessel Association*, decided on July 2, 1979, the Court in a six to three decision upheld the Boldt decision.[62] It reviewed once more the provisions of the Treaty of Medicine Creek to determine what they meant in the light of the expectations at the time the treaty was signed. The tribes did lose, however, by the Court's inclusion of fish caught for subsistence and ceremonial uses as well as fish taken within reservation boundaries in the 50 percent figure. The Court also considered the percentage as a maximum, which might be reduced under changing circumstances.

That the imprecise terms of the treaty might be construed in different ways was clear from the dissent of Justice Lewis F. Powell and the two other justices who joined him. Powell's interpretation of the treaties gave the Indians *access* to fishing sites but not a guaranteed percentage of the fish. "I would hold," he wrote, "that the treaties give to the Indians several significant rights that should be respected. . . . These

---

Prucha, *Great Father*, 2:1184–85, which is based largely on *Indian Tribes, a Continuing Quest for Survival*, a Report of the United States Commission on Civil Rights (Washington: GPO, 1981), 70–71.

61. For references to non-Indian views, see Prucha, *Great Father*, 2:1185, n. 34.

62. 443 U.S. 658–708. One can see the detailed reliance on the treaties and the documents relating to their negotiation in the briefs submitted in this case. The case occasioned considerable literature, of which the following might be noted: Joe Ryan, "Indian Treaties, Indian Fish: The Controversy of Fishing in Common," *American Indian Journal* 5 (April 1979): 2–10; Rod Vessels, "Treaties: Fishing Rights in the Pacific Northwest—The Supreme Court 'Legislates' an Equitable Solution," *American Indian Law Review* 8, no. 1 (1980): 117–37.

rights, privileges, and exemptions—possessed only by Indians—are quite substantial. I find no basis for according them additional advantages."[63]

The heavy weight of treaty terms protecting hunting and fishing rights appeared in other cases, although less dramatically than in the long-drawn controversy of the Puyallups with the state of Washington. One was *Menominee Tribe of Indians v. United States*, May 27, 1968, which rested upon the Treaty of Wolf River in 1854 with the Menominee Indians.[64] The treaty, by which the Menominees were provided a new reservation on the Wolf River, did not explicitly mention hunting and fishing rights, saying only that the new reservation was "to be held as Indian lands are held." The Court insisted that this must be interpreted to include hunting and fishing rights, for "the essence of the Treaty of Wolf River was that the Indians were authorized to maintain on the new lands ceded to them as a reservation their way of life which included hunting and fishing."[65] The question at issue was whether the termination of the Menominees as a federally recognized tribe by a law of 1954 had deprived the Indians of those rights. When the Indians, who thought they had lost the rights, applied to the Court of Claims for compensation, the court found that no compensation was due because in fact the rights had never been taken away.

The Supreme Court accepted that argument. It looked at the termination act of the Menominees and at the contemporaneous Public Law 280 (which gave the state criminal jurisdiction over all Indian country in Wisconsin, but which also explicitly said that the law did not deprive the Indians of treaty rights to hunting, trapping, and fishing) and declined "to construe the Termination Act as a back-handed way of abrogating the hunting and fishing rights of these Indians." While admitting again the power of Congress to abrogate those rights, it ruled that Congress had not done so, for "the intention to abrogate or modify a treaty is not to be lightly imputed to the Congress." The majority opinion went further. "We find it difficult to believe," it read, "that Congress, without explicit statement, would subject the United States to a claim for compensation by destroying property rights conferred by treaty, particularly when Congress was purporting by the Termination Act to settle the Government's financial obligations toward the Indians." A dissenting opinion argued the opposite—that the Indians *had* lost

63. 443 U.S. 707–8.
64. 391 U.S. 404–17.
65. Ibid., 406.

their hunting and fishing rights and were due just compensation for them.[66]

Other cases based on a reading of treaties have turned out less favorably for the Indians. *Oregon Department of Fish and Wildlife v. Klamath Indian Tribe*, decided on July 2, 1985, denied the right of Klamath Indians to hunt and fish free of state regulation on lands ceded in a 1901 agreement.[67] The decision was based chiefly on the treaty signed in 1864 with the Klamaths, by which the Indians ceded "all their right, title and claim to all the country claimed by them" and moved to a new reservation. Although the treaty gave them an "exclusive right of taking fish in the streams and lakes, included in said reservation, and of gathering edible roots, seeds, and berries within its limits," the Court found that "no right to hunt or fish outside the reservation was preserved." A search of the historical record of the negotiations for the treaty disclosed "no reference to continuation of any special hunting or fishing rights for members of the Tribe." The Court thus concluded:

> The language of the 1864 Treaty indicates that the Tribe's rights to hunt and fish were restricted to the reservation. The broad language used in the 1901 Agreement, virtually identical to that used to extinguish off-reservation rights in the 1864 Treaty, accomplished a diminution of the reservation boundaries, and no language in the 1901 Agreement evidences any intent to preserve special off-reservation hunting or fishing rights for the Tribe.[68]

In *United States v. Dion*, June 11, 1986, the Court found clear congressional intent to abrogate admitted treaty rights.[69] The case concerned a Yankton Indian convicted of hunting eagles protected by the Eagle Protection Act (1940) and the Endangered Species Act (1973). The treaty with the Yanktons of April 19, 1858, had placed no restrictions on the Indians' hunting rights within their reservation, but that was not at issue here. What the Court asked was whether Congress had clearly abrogated those rights, and it answered yes. The Eagle Protection Act permitted the taking of eagles under permit for religious purposes, and the Court argued that Congress thereby had indicated its recognition that the hunting prohibition would have an effect on the

---

66. Ibid., 412–17. Another case of Indian hunting rights was *Antoine v. Washington* (1975), which said hunting on ceded lands was not subject to state regulation. 420 U.S. 194–222.

67. 473 U.S. 753–87.

68. Ibid., 755, 770. Two justices dissented.

69. 476 U.S. 734–46.

tribe but had met it, not by exempting the Indians from the statutes, but by authorizing permits where appropriate. It concluded: "Congress' 1962 action . . . reflected an unmistakable and explicit legislative policy choice that Indian hunting of the bald or golden eagle, except pursuant to permit, is inconsistent with the need to preserve those species. We therefore read the statute as having abrogated that treaty right."[70] The decision included a long statement of principles to be followed in finding an abrogation of a treaty, as though the justices felt a bit uneasy about their action and were determined to justify it fully and show that they were not lightly agreeing to the taking away of Indian treaty rights.

These Supreme Court readings of Indian treaties and of Congress's intent in regard to the rights they stipulated, while not uniformly favorable to the Indians, nevertheless helped significantly to provide an atmosphere in which claims for protection of Indian rights of whatever kind could flourish.

70. Ibid., 745.

CHAPTER SEVENTEEN

Treaty-Rights Activism

The stirring up of interest in Indian treaties that came with the cases before the Indian Claims Commission and the Supreme Court had wide ramifications in the 1960s, 1970s, and 1980s. While the lawyers for the tribes drew upon the treaty stipulations in presenting their clients' cases, often picking and choosing whatever seemed to have the best chances of success without much reliance on tribal wishes, Indians across the nation and their non-Indian supporters developed an increasingly active "treaty rights" position, which drew disparate groups together in protest against treaty violations (real or perceived) and which furnished a vehicle for making Indian rights and the Indians' plight visible to a broad public. The Red Power movement, of course, was multifaceted and demanded aboriginal rights and general human rights that transcended the treaties, but much of the argumentation rested upon the ratified treaties, which for many acquired a new importance.

There was a widespread use of Indian treaty rhetoric. While the court cases rested on detailed analysis of historical and legal documents pertinent to the issues, many Indians and their supporters continued an often unthinking and ill-informed reliance on treaties for almost anything they thought Indians were entitled to. The word *treaty* was bandied about by many Indians as though the word had only one connotation: a diplomatic contract between two fully sovereign nations. There was little or no understanding of the many actions of Indians and of the United States that over time had legally restricted tribal sovereignty. Anything an Indian group wanted could be said to be provided "in the treaties." And, conversely, every evil encountered could be blamed on the "broken treaties." Such treaty fantasies may have raised ungrounded expectations among Indians and hindered the effective work that needed to be done to improve the social and economic conditions of Indians living today, but the rhetoric was pervasive enough to keep non-Indians aware that the anomaly of Indian treaties was not simply a thing of the past.[1]

Early Activism

The first major sign of organized Indian activism was the gathering in June 1961 of the American Indian Chicago Conference. The idea of the anthropologist Sol Tax of the University of Chicago and endorsed by the National Congress of American Indians, the conference was attended by some 460 Indians of ninety tribes. The Indians voiced their concerns about their welfare and their place in American society and offered a series of recommendations. Although set in a context of working for progress on specific needs within the governmental system of the United States, the conference did call attention, but only briefly, to treaty rights. "It is a universal desire among all Indians that their treaties and trust-protected lands remain intact and beyond the reach of predatory men . . . ," the conference's *Declaration of Indian Purpose* said. "The right of self-government, a right which the Indians possessed before the coming of the white man, has never been extinguished. . . . A treaty, in the minds of our people, is an eternal word. Events often make it seem expedient to depart from the pledged word, but we are conscious that the first departure creates a logic for the second departure, until there is nothing left of the word."[2]

Many who attended the Chicago conference were young Indians, and in August 1961 they organized an activist group called the National

1. Interesting examples of what some have called a "treaty psychosis" can be found in Stephen E. Feraca, *Why Don't They Give Them Guns?: The Great American Indian Myth* (Lanham, Md.: University Press of America, 1990), 73–105.

2. *Declaration of Indian Purpose* (Chicago: American Indian Chicago Conference, 1961), 15–16. See also Nancy Oestreich Lurie, "The Voice of the American Indian: Report on the American Indian Chicago Conference," *Current Anthropology* 2 (December 1961): 478–500.

Indian Youth Council (NIYC). The group was prominent in the fish-ins in Washington State in the mid-1960s, protesting state fishing regulations to call attention to the Indians' treaty rights to fish, which had been repeatedly ignored or violated by state officials.[3]

The next major protest was the seizure of Alcatraz Island, the abandoned federal prison in San Francisco Bay. The Indians called themselves "Indians of All Tribes," and they justified their occupation on an erroneous reading of the Fort Laramie Treaty of 1868, which they claimed gave Indians the right to federal property no longer in use. Other takeovers of unoccupied federal sites followed, such as Fort Lawton in Seattle and the Coast Guard station in Milwaukee. Although the Indians were eventually evacuated from Alcatraz and failed also in their other occupations, the idea of Indian rights received a tremendous boost, for the news media gave much attention to the events, and Alcatraz became an important symbol for the tribes.[4]

Renewal of Treaty Status

There developed a strong, recurring movement to restore the tribes' treaty-status relationship with the United States government, which went beyond protests about specific rights. Ignoring or consciously rejecting the anomalous situation in regard to treaties that a detailed historical account depicts, advocates of renewed treaty status proposed an idealistic return to the past or some new construct that fitted a particular theory. For some Indians it was merely an exercise in nostalgia; for others, a handle with which to pressure the government for attention to the Indians' troubles; for a few, a hoped-for theoretical status looking back to some idea of absolute sovereignty.

A striking example of this movement was the Trail of Broken Treaties in the fall of 1972. This was a caravan of Indian people originating in cities on the West Coast, gathering adherents as it proceeded toward

3. There is a discussion of the fish-ins, in the context of the larger fishing-rights controversy, in Alvin M. Josephy, Jr., *Now That the Buffalo's Gone: A Study of Today's American Indians* (New York: Alfred A. Knopf, 1982), 177–211. See also Stan Steiner, *The New Indians* (New York: Harper and Row, 1968), 48–64.

4. Peter Blue Cloud, ed., *Alcatraz Is Not an Island* (Berkeley: Wingbow Press, 1972); Richard Oakes, "Alcatraz Is Not an Island," *Ramparts* 11 (December 1972): 35–41, 62; Jeff Sklansky, "Rock, Reservation, and Prison: The Native American Occupation of Alcatraz Island," *American Indian Culture and Research Journal* 13, no. 2 (1989): 29–68.

Washington, D.C. Its purpose was to draw Indians together in their protests, to make known in this public, eye-catching way the Indians' grievances, and to demand from federal officials a righting of wrongs. The caravan brought to the capital a paper containing Twenty Points, a list of demands drawn up in Minneapolis by leaders of the militant American Indian Movement (AIM), who intended the demands to serve as a focus for negotiating with the federal government at the highest levels.[5]

Seven of the first eight demands dealt with treaties. The first one forthrightly called for the president and Congress to repeal the provision in the 1871 law that had ended treaty making with Indian tribes—"in order that Indian Nations may represent their own interests in the manner and method envisioned and provided in the Federal Constitution." It was a naive assumption—if, indeed, it was meant to be a serious proposal—that a century of developing relations between the Indian groups and the United States outside a treaty system could be wiped out by legislative fiat.

The second point asked for the establishment by Congress of a Treaty Commission to sign new treaties with Indian peoples. "Authority should be granted," it read, "to allow Tribes to contract by separate and individual treaty, multi-tribal or regional groupings, or national collective, respecting general or limited subject matter." Point three departed from the concern about treaties, but the fourth point demanded a special presidential commission "to review domestic treaty commitments and complaints of chronic violations and to recommend or act for corrective action," in the hope that such a body could reduce the Indians' reliance on litigation to protect their rights and thus reduce the heavy costs of attorneys.

Point five demanded that the president submit to the Senate in the next Congress the treaties that were at one time signed with Indian tribes but never ratified by the Senate, the purpose to be "restoring the rule of law to the relationships between such Indians and the United States, and resuming a recognition of rights controlled by treaty relations." Next came a general statement that Congress should pass a joint resolution declaring that "as a matter of public policy and good faith, all Indian people in the United States shall be considered to be in treaty relations with the Federal Government and governed by doctrines of

5. The Twenty Points are printed in "Seizure of Bureau of Indian Affairs Headquarters," *Hearings before the Subcommittee on Indian Affairs of the Committee on Interior and Insular Affairs, House of Representatives, 92d Congress, 2d Session* (1972), 162–71.

such relationship." The seventh point demanded mandatory relief against treaty-rights violations, on petition of a tribe, by means of federal district court enjoinders or injunctions against non-Indian parties engaged in injurious actions until the court could determine that there was in fact no treaty violation and that the Indians' interests and rights were protected and secure from harm. Finally, the eighth point asked for a law that would give the Indians a right to issue a declaration concerning the interpretation of treaty or other rights that would be binding on the courts unless successfully challenged in the Supreme Court. The remaining points dealt with a variety of issues that were beyond or outside the scope of treaties, including restoration of an Indian land base, consolidation of Indian natural resources, jurisdiction over non-Indians within reservations, replacement of the Bureau of Indian Affairs by an Office of Federal Indian Relations and Community Reconstruction within the president's office, and provisions for health, housing, education, employment, and economic development. The tribes' dependence upon the federal government exhibited in these demands was clearly at odds with the demands for treaty-status sovereignty.

Vine Deloria, Jr., then riding high as a spokesman for Indian activists, gave a contemporary and very favorable evaluation of the treaty-related proposals:

> First, they were extremely accurate in their assessment of the feelings of Indians around the nation. . . . Second, the points outlined a fairly sophisticated understanding of a type of relationship with the federal government that could best be defined as a quasi-protectorate status. It would have severely limited the arbitrary exercise of power by the federal government over the rights of the tribes. Most of all, the acceptance of the Twenty Points would have meant that the treaties which the United States had signed with the respective tribes a century earlier would have the rightful, legal status which they deserved, equal to the legal status accorded foreign treaties.[6]

Unfortunately, there was no serious discussion of these proposals by high federal officials. Rebuffed by the officials and frustrated because of lack of provisions for food and housing, the caravan members in early November seized the Bureau of Indian Affairs building, and when they heard of threats to remove them forcibly, the Indians trashed the interior

---

6. Vine Deloria, Jr., *Behind the Trail of Broken Treaties: An Indian Declaration of Independence* (New York: Delacorte Press, 1974), 53. The whole book is an argument for a kind of independent status for the Indian tribes.

of the building, fortified their positions as well as they could, and prepared to give their lives in repulsing any attack by riot police. Cooler heads ultimately prevailed. The Indians, getting a face-saving commitment that their complaints would be investigated and supplied with travel funds to return home, left the building. The destruction of the building, and the carrying away of BIA records, however, made any serious consideration of the Twenty Points unlikely.[7]

The cursory reply to them in mid-January 1973 by Frank Carlucci, deputy director of the Office of Management and Budget, pretty much brushed them aside. The idea that the Indians should again become sovereign political entities with whom the United States would sign new treaties was rejected out of hand:

> Over one hundred years ago the Congress decided that it was no longer appropriate for the United States to make treaties with Indian tribes. By 1924, all Indians were citizens of the United States and of the states in which they resided. The citizenship relationship with one's government and the treaty relationship are mutually exclusive; a government makes treaties with foreign nations, not with its own citizens. If renunciation of citizenship is implied here, or secession, these are wholly backward steps, inappropriate for a nation which is a Union.[8]

"To call for new treaties," he said in regard to point six, "is to raise a false issue, unconstitutional in concept, misleading to Indian people, and diversionary from the real problems that do need our continued energies." He noted that the Nixon administration was sympathetic to the Indians' need to represent their own interests and that means were already at hand or had been proposed. He pointed to the Indian Claims Commission, Nixon's proposed Indian Trust Council Authority, and federal action to protect Indian rights, which obviated any need for the review commission demanded in point four. He denied a need for the judicial changes called for in points seven and eight, for what he called "the skewing of America's judicial principles or the creation of any new built-in preferences for or against specific groups or institutions."[9]

The militant activists who had led the Trail of Broken Treaties, of

---

7. See references on this affair given in Francis Paul Prucha, *The Great Father: The United States Government and the American Indians*, 2 vols. (Lincoln: University of Nebraska Press, 1984), 2:1118n. There is a brief account in Josephy, *Now That the Buffalo's Gone*, 237–43.

8. "Seizure of Bureau of Indian Affairs Headquarters," 171.

9. Ibid., 173–74.

course, were not satisfied by the reply, and the desperation that had lain behind the Twenty Points soon erupted in the seizure of the village of Wounded Knee on the Pine Ridge Reservation in South Dakota and in armed confrontation there between Indians and the federal government.

The Wounded Knee occupation, however, had an additional dimension: the conflict between two groups of Indians on the Pine Ridge Reservation. One was led by Richard Wilson, the elected chairman of the tribal council under the governmental setup that originated with the Indian Reorganization Act in 1934, whom the federal government supported as head of the legitimate tribal government. The other was composed of opponents of Wilson—AIM leaders, who despised him and his autocratic methods, and "traditional" leaders, who objected to the "BIA government" of Wilson and wanted to return to earlier days. The cry was for a return to the conditions at the time of the 1868 Fort Laramie Treaty, which the Sioux had signed as a sovereign nation and which guaranteed to the Indians a large reservation and hunting grounds to the west. It was the traditionalists' claim, echoing the Twenty Points, that the treaty was still in effect and that changes in land ownership and tribal government since then had been illegal.[10]

This position was seen most dramatically in the proclamation on March 11, 1973, in the middle of the Wounded Knee occupation and confrontation, of the Independent Oglala Sioux Nation, whose relationship with the federal government would rest on the Fort Laramie Treaty. A provisional government was planned, and the nation announced its intention to send a delegation to the United Nations and to ask for support and recognition from the Iroquois Indians. The Oglala Nation got nowhere, for the federal government stiffened its resistance to the occupiers. When United States negotiators finally met with the Wounded Knee leaders and agreed to consider their demands, the Oglala Sioux Nation faded away.

The impasse, however, continued after the occupation of Wounded Knee ended, as traditionalists, under the aegis of a Teton Sioux Treaty Council, conferred in person and by letter with presidential negotiators, who had agreed to listen to Sioux complaints. The Indians harped on the establishment of a presidential treaty commission (an echo of the Twenty Points), which would negotiate new treaties and investigate existing treaties and the rights they guaranteed the Indians and recom-

---

10. There is an extensive literature on Wounded Knee, and the news media gave the event full coverage. See, for example, the citations in Prucha, *Great Father*, 2:1119n.

mend to Congress the repeal or amendment of statutes "enacted since 1871 which conflict with and take away original sovereignty in every area." Near the end of 1973, these men set forth anew a "bill of particulars" regarding the Fort Laramie Treaty of 1868 and asked for the government's understanding of the legal effect of the treaty. Pointing to what they considered violations of that treaty, they asked the presidential task force for specific documented answers to the violations set forth.[11]

The government spokesmen again rejected the Indians' position. Leonard Garment, President Nixon's special assistant, provided the federal government's answer in a letter addressed to "the traditional chiefs and headmen of the Teton Sioux," an answer that the repeated recommendations of the Indians failed to shake. Garment quoted the law of 1871 that forbade further treaty making with the Indian tribes and said: "What this means is that the days of treaty-making with the American Indians ended in 1871, 102 years ago. Any changes made in the terms of treaties or laws relating to Indians have since been made by agreements ratified for both Houses of Congress, or by statutes of Congress. Only Congress can rescind or change in any way statutes enacted since 1871, such as the Indian Reorganization Act." He noted that committees in Congress spent much time on Indian affairs, and he urged the Indians to use that forum. "Insofar as you wish to propose any specific changes in existing treaties or statutes," he said, "the Congress is, in effect, a Treaty Commission and you should make sure that your spokesmen appear before the Senate Subcommittee and present their views as to which treaties or statutes should be amended and in precisely what way."[12]

The failure of confrontational tactics and the rejection of the treaty-related items in the Twenty Points, the impotence of the Independent Oglala Sioux Nation, and the failure of the Oglala Sioux Treaty Council to have their demands met were setbacks for Indians who dreamed of a revival of the treaty system and dealing with the federal government on the basis of newly negotiated treaties.

The next general Indian policy reform movement, the American

11. Frank Fools Crow and Matthew King to Leonard Garment, June 9, 1973, and to Richard M. Nixon, November 19, 1973, in "Occupation of Wounded Knee," *Hearings before the Subcommittee on Indian Affairs of the Committee on Interior and Insular Affairs, United States Senate, 93d Congress, 1st Session, on the Causes and Aftermath of the Wounded Knee Takeover* (1973), 150–54, 315–22.

12. Leonard Garment to the Traditional Chiefs and Headmen of the Teton Sioux, May 29, 1973, ibid., 302–3.

Indian Policy Review Commission (AIPRC) of 1975–77 emphasized Indian sovereignty and the trust responsibility of the federal government for Indian welfare and did not make treaty status a key issue. When it referred to treaties at all, it was as a vague basis for sovereignty and as a foundation for some aspects of the government's trust responsibility. Thus Task Force One of the AIPRC, devoted to trust responsibilities and the federal-Indian relationship, wrote in its report:

> The treaties of protection and dependence did not divest the Tribes of their national character, nor diminish the paramount obligations for health care and educational opportunities entitled to the Indian people. However, to the extent that the Indian Tribes' capacities were diminished for meeting these obligations, either immediately or subsequently, the basic responsibility in some measure would necessarily shift to, or be shared by, the United States.[13]

The AIPRC was generally of limited impact because of its failure to provide an expert analysis of the historical and legal status of the Indian tribes and because its strong advocacy position on the questions of sovereignty and trust responsibility lost it support among moderate groups. The idea of independent sovereign tribes and a renewal of the old treaty relationship, however, was not dead, and from time to time it surfaced again in particular cases.

Some Mohawks kept alive an insistence that their independence as a sovereign nation should be recognized. Thus in May 1974 Mohawks from Caughnawaga and St. Regis (Akwasasne) occupied a 612-acre site near Moss Lake, New York, in the center of the Adirondack Mountains, which the Indians spoke of as the "repossession" of lands within boundaries of land they claimed in New York State and Vermont. The Indians issued a manifesto proclaiming the reestablishment of the Independent North American Indian State of Ganienkeh on lands that had been part of their ancient homeland. They denied the validity of the eighteenth-century treaties by which their land had been ceded. Confrontation of the Indians with state forces led ultimately to a negotiated settlement, by which the Indians moved to a new location, on land provided by the state, in the northeast corner of New York,

13. Task Force One of the American Indian Policy Review Commission, *Report on Trust Responsibilities and the Federal-Indian Relationship; Including Treaty Review* (Washington: GPO, 1976), 27.

near the town of Altona. There Ganienkeh continued its uneasy existence.[14]

Another earnest but unsuccessful push for international status for American Indian tribes came in 1974 with the establishment of an International Indian Treaty Council at a meeting of Indian peoples at the Standing Rock Reservation. In a Declaration of Principles, the council asserted: "Indigenous nations or groups should be accorded such degree of independence as they may desire in accordance with international law" and "treaties and other agreements entered into by indigenous nations or groups with other states, whether denominated as treaties or otherwise, shall be recognized and applied in the same manner and according to the same international laws and principles as the treaties and agreements entered into by other states." The council's goals were to focus international attention on the conditions of Indian people and to gain some kind of recognition from the United Nations, and in 1977 the United Nations gave the Treaty Council status as a Non-Governmental Organization (NGO). With the aid of the Institute for the Development of Indian Law, a Washington-based public interest law firm dedicated to support of Indian peoples, the International Treaty Council organized an International NGO Conference on Discrimination against Indigenous Populations in the Americas, which met at the Geneva headquarters of the United Nations on September 20–23, 1977. Some 250 delegates attended, including representatives of more than fifty international nongovernmental organizations and Indian delegates or observers from Canada, the United States, and Central and South America.[15]

Three commissions (on legal affairs, economic affairs, and social and cultural affairs) summarized the discussions in formal reports. The "Legal Commission Report" noted that "delegates from several indigenous nations, in particular the Six Nations Confederacy and the Lakota Nation, demanded immediate recognition as states under international

14. Gail H. Landsman, *Sovereignty and Symbol: Indian-White Conflict at Ganienkeh* (Albuquerque: University of New Mexico Press, 1988), especially chap. 2. The book is primarily a study of symbols in the dispute, but it nevertheless provides an extensive discussion of the issues. A "Ganienkeh Manifesto" issued by the Indians is printed in the book's appendix A, 195–204. See also "Trouble in the Land of the Flint," *Time,* December 23, 1974, 16.

15. See "Declaration of Principles for the Defense of the Indigenous Nations and Peoples of the Western Hemisphere," printed in *Congressional Record,* 124:23139–40. Reports about the Geneva Conference are in *American Indian Journal,* September 1977 and November 1977.

law based upon treaties which clearly recognized their status as sovereign nations." A "Final Resolution" pulled together material from the commissions into a series of recommendations for recognition of the concerns of indigenous peoples and ways to meet them.[16]

It was a glorious time for Russell Means, the Sioux AIM leader, and for Oren Lyons, his counterpart among the Six Nations, and their associates. The City of Geneva, before the opening of the conference, held a reception for the delegates of the Six Nations in honor of Deskaheh, who was remembered in Geneva for his attempts to bring Indian issues to the attention of the League of Nations in 1923, and the Iroquois delegation triumphantly used their own passports going and returning.[17] But aside from the extensive media coverage, which without doubt alerted many people to the grievances and concerns of indigenous peoples in the hemisphere, few results came from the conference for Indians in the United States.

The demands of Indian activists for international recognition of sovereign nationhood were unheeded, and the conference had no effect on the legal status of the Indian tribes in the United States or on their treaties. This, however, has not stopped unthinking people from continuing to presume that American Indian tribes have an international status.[18]

Treaty Fishing Rights

The emphasis on treaties that accompanied the fish-ins in Washington State in the mid-1960s and the Boldt decision in the mid-1970s was renewed with other fishing rights cases that did not reach the Supreme Court but that nevertheless got wide attention and gen-

16. "Legal Commission Report" and "Final Resolution" in *American Indian Journal*, November 1977, 4–5, 9.

17. Ibid., 6.

18. Two recent examples: In arguing that the president should implement the domestic programs needed by the Indians, one religious spokesman said, "Of course, it is not a domestic problem at all; it is an international problem because two sovereign nations are involved, Indian Tribes and the United States of America." Theodore Zuern, in *Bureau of Catholic Indian Missions Newsletter*, August/September 1991, 3. An account of a symposium of American Indian writers in 1991 referred to the event as "international in that it involved Indians representing tribes from the Abenaki in New York to the Oglala Sioux in South Dakota." Faith B. Miracle, "Editor's Notes," *Wisconsin Academy Review* 38 (Winter 1991–92): 2.

erated considerable white protest, some of it violent. The cases kept the Indian treaties and the rights they guaranteed the tribes much in the public mind. Two sets of cases were of special importance.

One set concerned the Indians of Michigan and the rights they claimed to fish in Lake Michigan without observing the restrictions enacted by the state. Over the years the Indians had not pressed their rights, and Michigan eventually enacted hunting and fishing regulations. But, alert to the actions in Washington State, beginning in the 1960s Michigan Indians brought isolated cases before local courts for recognition of their rights under treaty provisions. On the other side, Michigan asserted sovereignty over the fisheries and charged the Chippewa and Ottawa fishers with destroying fish resources by use of gill nets. Local non-Indians and vociferous advocates of sport fishing (the latter supported by the state, which did not want to lose the lucrative tourist trade) increasingly challenged the Indians' actions and their rights.[19]

The case of *United States v. Michigan,* which was heard before Judge Noel P. Fox of the United States District Court for the Western District of Michigan, became the legal focus of the conflict. It sought to decide whether the twentieth-century descendants of nineteenth-century treaty signatories had retained fishing rights under the treaties, and if those rights were present, what kind and how many fish the Indians could take. After long testimony by expert witnesses, Fox, on May 7, 1979, strongly affirmed the Indians' rights under their treaties of 1836 and 1855, the first of which had provided "the right of hunting on the lands ceded, with the other usual privileges of occupancy, until the land is required for settlement."[20] His decision was wide-ranging:

> The mere passage of time has not eroded, and cannot erode the rights guaranteed by solemn treaties that both sides pledged on their honor to uphold. The Indians have a right to fish today wherever fish are to be found within the area of cession—as they had at the time of cession—a right established by aboriginal right and confirmed by the Treaty of Ghent, and the Treaty of 1836. The right is not a static right today any more than it was during treaty times. The right is not limited as to the species of fish, origin of fish, the purpose of use or the time or manner of taking. It may be exercised utilizing improvements in fishing techniques, methods and gear.

19. The Michigan events are recounted in Robert Doherty, *Disputed Waters: Native Americans and the Great Lakes Fishery* (Lexington: University Press of Kentucky, 1990).
    20. Kappler, 2:454.

Fox emphasized the treaty basis of these rights. "Because the right of the . . . tribes to fish in ceded waters of the Great Lakes is protected by treaties . . . , that right is preserved and protected under the supreme law of the land, does not depend on State law, is distinct from the rights and privileges held by non-Indians and may not be qualified by any action of the state . . . except as authorized by Congress." Although the state appealed the decision, the United States Court of Appeals, Sixth Circuit, refused to revise the decision, and the United States Supreme Court would not review it.[21]

A second set of cases concerned Chippewa spearfishing in Wisconsin, which generated a tremendous amount of white backlash from persons devoted to sport fishing and from resort owners. The public controversy arose with *Lac Courte Oreilles Band of Lake Superior Chippewa Indians v. Voigt,* which dealt with the arrest of two Indians of the band for spearfishing in ceded territory. The band sued Lester P. Voigt, secretary of the Wisconsin Department of Natural Resources, and other individuals for interfering with off-reservation fishing rights of the Indians under their treaties of 1837 and 1842. Judge James Doyle of the United States District Court for the Western District of Wisconsin on September 20, 1978, ruled against the Indians on the basis that the 1854 treaty had extinguished the rights granted in the earlier treaties. But on appeal, the United States Court of Appeals, Seventh Circuit, in 1983, reversed the Voigt decision of Judge Doyle and restored the treaty rights, and the United States Supreme Court refused to review the case.[22]

After a complicated series of legal maneuverings involving the district court (under Judge Doyle and his successor, Judge Barbara Crabb), the six Chippewa tribes of Wisconsin, and the state of Wisconsin—all carried on in the midst of violent and abusive protests from non-Indians, covered extensively by the media—the Indians' rights were vindicated. On March 19, 1991, Judge Crabb issued a Final Judgment, which

21. 471 F. Supp. 280–81. There is a long discussion of the case and the arguments on the two sides in Doherty, *Disputed Waters*, chap. 6; note also Doherty's treatment of subsequent negotiated settlements in regard to management of the fisheries. The actions of the Court of Appeals are in 623 F.2d 448–50 (May 28, 1980) and 653 F.2d 277–80 (July 10, 1981).

22. 464 F. Supp. 1316–76, under the name of *United States v. Bouchard;* 700 F.2d 341–65; 464 U.S. 805. The whole affair and its historical background are treated in Ronald N. Satz, *Chippewa Treaty Rights: The Reserved Rights of Wisconsin's Chippewa Indians in Historical Perspective*, Transactions of the Wisconsin Academy of Sciences, Arts and Letters, vol. 79, no. 1 (Madison: Wisconsin Academy of Sciences, Arts and Letters, 1991).

summarized and clarified the complicated litigation. The usufructory rights of the tribes arising from the treaties of 1837 and 1842, Crabb said, included "rights to those forms of animal life, fish, vegetation, and so on that they utilized at treaty time" and the "right to use all of the methods of harvesting employed at treaty times and those developed since." The Indians were denied the right to harvest commercial lumber on ceded lands, but they could gather "miscellaneous forest products, namely, such items as firewood, tree bark, maple sap, lodge poles, boughs, and marsh hay." The fruits of the exercise of these rights could be traded or sold to non-Indians. The Indians were granted the right to regulate their own off-reservation harvesting of walleyes and muskellunges. The tribal harvestable natural resources to which the Indians retained a usufructory right were to be apportioned equally between the Indians and all other persons. These rights, however, did not apply to sections of the ceded territory that were privately owned.[23]

The six Chippewa tribes in Wisconsin and the state of Wisconsin formally accepted the final order on May 20, 1991. Both sides agreed to restrictions on some rights for which they had originally contended, but they did this in the interests of peace. The long legal struggle was over.[24] By that time there were few citizens of Wisconsin or of the nation who did not know of the continuing treaty rights of the Wisconsin Indians and that the federal courts would stand firm against great pressures in vindicating those rights juridically.[25]

Backlash

The growing strength of tribal governments after 1960 and the recognition by the courts of their still-existing, though partial, sovereign powers caused a backlash, which some observers friendly to the Indians have seen as an anti-Indian movement. The opposition rested on two principal grounds. One was the fear of non-Indians who

23. The Final Judgment is printed in Satz, *Chippewa Treaty Rights*, 187–91.

24. Ibid., 193, 195–97.

25. All opposition to the Indians' rights, of course, did not disappear, and an organized protest movement continued. See, for example, an article in the *Milwaukee Journal*, April 6, 1992, about plans for "peaceful demonstrations" against spearfishing. The anthropologist James A. Clifton has argued at some length that the court decisions were flawed. See Clifton, "Information Concerning the Lake Superior Chippewa, Their Treaties with the United States, and the Voigt Case," prepublication draft supplied me by the author.

lived within reservation boundaries on land owned by them in fee that tribal jurisdiction would be extended over them and their property. A second was opposition to treaty-grounded rights held by Indian tribes to fish (and hunt and gather) on off-reservation sites or lands ceded in the treaties. The arguments were couched in terms of "equal rights" and "equal opportunities" for all American citizens, and Indians were denounced as "super citizens" because the courts recognized rights for them that were not accorded non-Indians.

There was a great deal of heat generated in the attack on Indian rights and often little clear understanding of the historical and legal basis for special tribal rights. As non-Indians attacked these rights, many Indians reacted, naturally enough, by strongly exercising their rights and by campaigning to win support for themselves in Congress and in the courts. As the anti-Indian groups organized to support their own positions, so too did groups form to counteract them and to proclaim support for treaty rights. Each side saw its position clearly, and there was little appreciation of the anomalies that underlay the conflict of views. It was difficult for the white protesters to grasp and accept the fact that tribal governments exercised jurisdiction over reservations whose boundaries now included non-Indians and non-Indian land (with some cases in which the Indians were only a small minority), to admit that Indian citizens had legal fishing rights that non-Indian citizens did not have, and to live with the fact that a state's jurisdiction did not fully extend over Indian lands within the state.

The backlash reached an early peak in the Ninety-fifth Congress in 1977 and 1978, as bills were introduced that were intended to destroy or weaken Indian treaty rights. The most damaging bill was deceptively entitled the Native American Equal Opportunity Act; it would have unilaterally abrogated all Indian treaties, broken up Indian communal assets, and terminated the special services guaranteed to Indians. It was introduced in 1977 by Representative John E. (Jack) Cunningham, a freshman member of Congress from Washington State, who had run on a platform that called for abrogation of treaties, especially those that guaranteed Indian fishing rights. After his initial measure made no progress in the House, Cunningham introduced a similar bill in 1978, which was more detailed on how the bill would be implemented and which called for the abolition of the Bureau of Indian Affairs. He declared: "While we encourage diversity in this country, we must not have two classes of citizens, whether black or white, immigrant American or Native American. It is for this reason that Congress must act to end the confusion caused by judicial interpretations of treaties and Executive Orders." Two other bills were introduced by a longtime representative from Washington, Lloyd Meeds, who once had been an active advocate of Indian rights but who drew the line on extending tribal sovereignty. His bills would have weakened tribal powers by extending state and local jurisdiction over tribal lands and other resources and would have severely limited Indian rights to water. Other bills sought to extinguish land titles of Indians in Maine and New York, change traditional hunting and fishing rights, and increase state criminal jurisdiction on reservations.[26]

The Indians' response to this proposed legislation was a public march of Indians from the West Coast to Washington, D.C., dubbed the Longest Walk. It was led by traditionalists (who opposed the elected tribal governments), AIM members, and a group who declared themselves to be spiritual elders. While the old motivation of calling public attention to the injustices suffered by Indians was still evident, the immediate rationale was to unify protest against the impending legislation, which would have weakened the Indians' status in American society. The congressional initiatives against Indian treaty rights were enough to frighten tribal heads and councils into giving hesitant support to the Longest Walk, even though it was managed by their traditionalist and AIM rivals.[27]

The movement sputtered and failed, but it was the occasion of a public debate about the nature and status of the tribal governments. Some alert observers of the Indian scene who were sympathetic to Indian needs in modern American society denounced the Longest Walk, considering its demands a futile attempt to turn back the clock. They argued that the democratically elected tribal governments (under constitutions going back to the Indian Reorganization Act) were a fact of life and here to stay, that the future welfare of the Indians and their

26. Cunningham's bills are printed in *Congressional Record*, 123:29777, and 124:20848–49, together with his remarks about the measures. For introduction of Meeds's bills, see *Congressional Record*, 123:37033; Meeds justified his position in an opinion piece in the *Washington Post*, October 22, 1977. See also Emma R. Gross, *Contemporary Federal Indian Policy toward American Indians* (Westport, Conn.: Greenwood Press, 1989), 87–91, and the articles cited in the next footnote.

27. Peter Monkres, "The Longest Walk: An Indian Pilgrimage," *Christian Century* 95 (April 5, 1978): 350–52; Phil Shenk, "The Longest Walk: Marching for Indian Self-Preservation," *Sojourners* 7 (July 1978): 10–12; "Tepees on the Mall," *Newsweek*, July 31, 1978, 27. A manifesto and other statements from the leaders of the Longest Walk are printed in *Congressional Record*, 124:23134–40.

push for a degree of political autonomy depended on strengthening, not weakening, those governments. Traditionalists countered that the elected councils had capitulated to white mainstream pressures and neglected or repudiated traditional Indian cultures (including religious ways).[28] While treaties and treaty rights did not always get explicit attention, it was return to a treaty-status relationship with white society that the traditionalists wanted and, at the least, protection against congressional action that would abrogate all treaties or in lesser ways eat into the recognition of tribal sovereignty (however limited) that had been gained in recent years.

The legislation proposed by Cunningham, Meeds, and other like-minded persons did not get enough backing to be enacted into law, but groups of citizens opposed to special rights for Indians continued their campaign. Although these "equal rights" groups sought to appear as national organizations with broad countrywide support, they in fact were generated by local issues, and their broader appeal and action seemed to come chiefly from the fact that the same few leaders appeared on the boards or advisory committees of the several groups. The strong focal points were the states of Washington, Montana, and Wisconsin.

The drive had begun with the organization by white protesters in 1976 of the Interstate Congress for Equal Rights and Responsibilities (ICERR), which had been sparked by nontribal landowners and by non-Indian sport and commercial fishing interests in Washington State, who fought the extension of tribal sovereignty on such reservations as Quinault and Port Madison, who condemned the Boldt decision of 1974, which they felt exalted Indian treaty fishing rights out of all proportion, and who influenced the congressional backlash in 1977 and 1978. New organizations with the same agenda appeared from time to time; as some faded away, others took their places. Thus the issues in the state of Washington were agitated by Steelhead and Salmon Protection Action Washington Now (S/SPAWN), organized in 1983 with a slight name change in 1985 to widen its appeal and by the new 1989 group called United Property Owners of Washington (UPOW). In Montana, beginning in the late 1970s, Montanans Against Discrimination (MAD) opposed assertion of tribal powers within reservation boundaries, to be succeeded later by All Citizens Equal (ACE). Mean-

28. See the exchange of views between Wilcolm E. Washburn, who attacked the Longest Walk and its arguments, and Joseph De La Cruz, head of the National Tribal Chairmen's Association, who condemned Washburn's views, in the op-ed pages of the *New York Times*, July 20 and August 2, 1978.

while the successes of the Wisconsin Chippewa Indians in protecting their rights to off-reservation spearfishing brought to life Protect Americans' Rights and Resources (PARR) and a more violently confrontational group, Stop Treaty Abuse (STA). In 1988 a new umbrella organization, Citizens' Equal Rights Alliance (CERA), appeared, which assumed much of the leadership for anti-treaty-rights activity, with a concentration on court cases. There was also a limited attempt by the Wisconsin Counties Association (WCA) to organize a National Coalition on Federal Indian Policy (NCFIP), but its organizational meeting in Salt Lake City in 1990 came to nothing, and most responsible county and state officials ignored or condemned the attempt.[29]

The continuing proclamations and actions of these groups spawned coalitions of organizations that support Indian treaty rights and spend a good deal of time monitoring the activities of the protesters. Churches have been especially busy and have issued pastoral letters and other statements in support of Indian treaty rights and Indian sovereignty. Although misunderstanding about the history of Indian sovereignty weakens the force of their appeals, they emphasize the importance of morality and justice in the issues and appeal to the latent guilt complex among liberal Americans in regard to the Indians. For example, the Washington State Indian fishing question occasioned the formation in Seattle of a National Coalition to Support Indian Treaties, with the following institutions among its membership:

American Friends Service Committee
Lutheran Church of America
Jesuit Conference, Office of Social Ministries
United Methodist Church, Office of Emerging Issues
United Church of Christ, Minnesota Conference
Washington State Catholic Conference
Seattle Fellowship of Reconciliation
Seattle Unitarians for Social Justice
Church Council of Greater Seattle
National Lawyers Guild, Seattle and Portland

29. A comprehensive account from a pro-Indian perspective is Rudolph C. Rÿser, *Anti-Indian Movement on the Tribal Frontier* (Kenmore, Wash.: Center for World Indigenous Studies, 1991). Rÿser sees a linkage of the anti-Indian organizations with extreme right-wing groups. See also "Paleface Uprising," *Newsweek,* April 10, 1978, 39–40, and, for the Wisconsin story, Satz, *Chippewa Treaty Rights,* 101–24.

Tacoma Dominican Sisters
National Ministries of American Baptist Churches[30]

A more recent coalition, with headquarters in Milwaukee, Wisconsin, is HONOR (Honor Our Neighbors' Origins and Rights), which seeks "to promote justice through affirmation of treaty rights, respect for tribal sovereignty, and recognition of government-to-government relationship." Its initiative comes from the Evangelical Lutheran Church of America, and it has institutional membership similar to that of the Seattle coalition.[31]

From the Past to the Future

The treaties came out of very mixed sentiments on the part of whites. The avarice of whites for rich Indian lands was reflected to a large degree in their representatives in Congress and in the executive branch of the federal government, although it was frequently expressed in terms of "promoting the spirit of enterprise" and the proper utilization or exploitation of the resources of the earth. The Indians had no right, it was asserted, to hold in sterile embrace the vast lands that they used only casually or not at all. But on the other side, there was strong support—in the federal government and outside—for the aboriginal rights of the Indians to the land (limited as these might be to rights of occupancy or of the soil) and even stronger support for property rights embodied in the treaties. The treaties were seen as contracts which no nation could violate without losing its honor and its good name among the other nations of the world. This was an especially sensitive point among those who considered the United States *the* great experiment in republican government and an example or beacon for the rest of the

30. See *Questions and Answers on Treaty Rights* (Seattle: National Coalition to Support Indian Treaties, n.d.).

31. Sharon Metz, *The Anti-Indian Movement* (n.p., Episcopal Council of Indian Ministries, 1991), and HONOR brochures. See also the statement issued by the National Conference of Catholic Bishops, "1992: A Time for Remembering, Reconciling and Recommitting Ourselves as a People: Pastoral Reflections on the Fifth Centenary and Native American Peoples," which among other things, renewed "a commitment to press for justice in the prompt and fair adjudication of treaty rights." *Origins* 21 (January 9, 1992): 493–99.

world. And the sanctity of property and of contracts that supported it was a principle of faith that dominated American legal history.

The history of the treaty system contains a debate between those who pointed to "the plighted faith and national honor" that permeated the treaties and those who argued that treaties with the Indian tribes were a fraud and a delusion because the Indian communities were not political entities of such nature as to warrant consideration as sovereign nations. There were high-minded and honorable men and women on both sides of the question. Many felt deeply that Indians should be treated as wards of the nation until they were acculturated enough to be fully assimilated into white society. But only a few argued for breaking the contracts made in officially ratified documents and abrogating the treaties without the proper consent of the tribes (which was generally not forthcoming). The varying sentiments are intermixed and provide a rich context in which the treaties and their history must be viewed.

The failure of either extreme to win out perpetuates the anomaly. Elements of sovereignty survive in the tribal governments, *and* the federal government accepts a trust responsibility to protect and otherwise care for the Indians. To add to the confusion, Indian leaders claim that one of the main obligations of the federal government under its trust responsibility is precisely to protect and strengthen Indian sovereignty and the rights that come with it. This is the real world, the world resting on historical decisions and historical accidents. It is clearly a world in flux as new decisions are made and new unexpected events occur. Indian sovereignty and treaty rights, in practice, extend only as far as they are recognized—by the federal and state governments and the people they represent. It is not impossible, though at the present highly improbable, that the demands made by advocates for a return to full sovereignty and the old treaty status might some day be recognized. One thing, however, seems sure: Indian treaties and the rights they guarantee will remain, whatever the makeup of the various components of the anomalous whole.

APPENDIX A

Treaty Documents and Their Promulgation

The original treaties were manuscript documents hand drafted by the secretaries of the treaty commissions.[1] Written in black ink on heavy paper, they spelled out in final form the agreements reached during the often drawn-out negotiations between the United States commissioners and the Indian chiefs and warriors present. Although most of the treaties have headings indicating a "treaty of peace and friendship" or "articles of a treaty," from time to time other terminology was used, such as "articles of agreement and convention," "articles of treaty and agreement," or, more simply, "a convention." The treaty with the Senecas in 1802 by which the Indians sold land to private individuals was called an "indenture."

There was some attempt, on occasion, to ornament the document with bold headings or subheadings, but in general the treaties are plain but legible documents. There was no effort to have the treaties engrossed by a skilled scribe, and in some cases two or three different hands are distinguishable in the writing of the treaty.[2] Occasionally a treaty was turned out in poor physical shape, with items crudely blacked out, corrections inserted, and writing showing through the sheets from the reverse side. To the Wyandot treaty of January 19, 1832, an "explana-

1. These documents, which formed the State Department Ratified Indian Treaties file, are now in General Records of the United States Government, National Archives Group 11 (M668).

2. See, for example, Choctaw and Chickasaw treaty of April 28, 1866, and Cherokee treaty of July 19, 1866 (M668, roll 15, treaty nos. 355 and 358).

tion" was appended noting that an article in the first draft of the treaty was rejected by the Indians and therefore eliminated, but that "circumstances did not admit of time to remodel and copy the whole treaty." And a note was added before the signatures on the Osage treaty of September 29, 1865, indicating that "the interlineations and erasures on the seventh and tenth pages were made before signing."[3] The proclamation forms drawn up for the president's signature were generally better prepared, and a large seal with ribbons was prominently attached. The forms for James Buchanan's administration are notable for their fine calligraphy.

Although the Indian treaties had the same legal force as treaties made with European nations, they were in general prepared with much less attention to elegance and decoration. The European nations and the United States exchanged ratification copies of the treaties that had bindings of cloth or leather, with gold or silver skippets containing large wax impressions of the official seals.[4]

Treaties with foreign nations other than Great Britain had official versions in both languages, while Indian treaties were issued only in English, for the preliterate status of the tribes precluded an Indian language version. The Cherokees, however, since they had developed a written language using their syllabary, did attempt to have their 1866 treaty issued in their language. The State Department was agreeable, provided the Cherokee version was issued with a statement that would "preclude the inference that the United States are committed to, or bound by any thing except the original English of the Treaty." The Interior Department agreed to pay for translation and publication in the Cherokee language and characters, but it is not clear whether, in fact, such a version of the treaty was published.[5]

Signatures

At the end of a treaty document, the signatures of the United States commissioners appear first, followed by the names of the

---

3. Ratified Treaties (M668, roll 6, frame 426; roll 13, treaty no. 338).

4. See photographs of the seals and skippets in *The "Art" of Diplomacy* (Washington: National Archives, 1971).

5. Henry Stanbery to O. H. Browning, August 4, 1866, and James Harlan to William H. Seward, August 4, 1866, typed copies in Ratified Treaties (M668, roll 15, treaty no. 358).

Indian signatories, to which are appended "his X mark," unless, as on rare occasions, the Indian signer was literate and could sign his own name. The marking of the X, whether done by the Indian himself or by the secretary, with the Indian "touching the pen," was usually a solemn affair.[6]

On some of the treaties, each signature had a seal attached, but if materials for seals were not on hand, a seal was crudely drawn in. Often ribbons were attached in order to add a note of importance and formality. The treaty with the Western Cherokees of May 6, 1828, was signed by the Cherokees using the Cherokee syllabary, each name marked with a small cross geared to a note below that read, "Written by the signers in their language, & in the characters now in use among them, as discovered by Geo: Guess."[7] In some early treaties with western tribes, the Indians' names and marks are followed by roughly drawn symbols or totems— an animal, a bird, or a turtle.[8]

The treaties were also signed by the witnesses, sometimes in parallel columns with the Indian signatures, sometimes at the very end. These witnesses included the commission secretary, the interpreters, army officers, and a variety of other personages.

There was no set practice about the number of copies of a given treaty that were formally signed. While it seems reasonable that the Indians as well as the United States would want an official copy of the documents, the written document, for the Indians, was of less importance than the exchange of speeches at the council. In fact, there are few recorded cases in which multiple copies were signed at the treaty ceremonies. This was done, however, even in some early treaties. The first of the treaties—that with the Delawares in 1778—was signed in three copies, with one copy sent to the Continental Congress, one given to the chiefs, and a third left with General Lachlan McIntosh, commandant at Fort Pitt. The treaty negotiated with the Cherokees at Hopewell

6. See Raymond J. DeMallie, "Touching the Pen: Plains Indian Treaty Councils in Ethnohistorical Perspective," in Frederick C. Luebke, ed., *Ethnicity on the Great Plains* (Lincoln: University of Nebraska Press, 1980), 40, 42. There is a dramatic account of an Indian signing a treaty in George A. McCall, *Letters from the Frontiers, Written during a Period of Thirty Years' Service in the Army of the United States* (Philadelphia: J. B. Lippincott and Company, 1868), 241.

7. Ratified Treaties (M668, roll 6, treaty no. 152).

8. See treaty with the Chippewas and other tribes, November 18, 1808; treaty with Wyandots and other tribes, September 8, 1815, Ratified Treaties (M668, roll 3, frames 348, 430; roll 4, frame 65). Similar signatures on the Treaty of Greenville, August 3, 1795, are shown in Herman J. Viola, *The National Archives of the United States* (New York: Harry N. Abrams, 1984), frontispiece and 131; the original is in Ratified Treaties (M668, roll 2, frame 296–97).

in 1785 was signed in duplicate so that each of the negotiating parties had a copy.[9] The sale of Seneca lands to Oliver Phelps and others in 1802 was done in triplicate—both the treaty and the attached indenture—so that the United States, the Indians, and the private purchasers would each have a copy. And the Choctaw treaty of 1803 was also signed in triplicate. Similar multiple signing and distribution was done in two treaties of 1854 and 1855, in which the United States witnessed land deals between the Choctaws and the Chickasaws, and one in 1856 between the Creeks and the Seminoles. In these cases, the treaty text itself indicates the signing in triplicate. The United States commissioner of the Ute treaty of 1849, James S. Calhoun, wrote at the bottom of the original treaty document "Signed in duplicate."[10]

Even though treaties were not *signed* in duplicate or triplicate (creating in effect multiple "original" copies), copies of the treaties were written out—how often cannot be determined. One clear case was the Cherokee treaty of 1804, in which the government mislaid the original treaty and a copy of the treaty in the possession of the Cherokees was used for ratification, finally, in 1824. Other manuscript copies are extant in government archives.

Ratification and Proclamation

The United States in its dealing with the Indians by treaty quickly developed a set format for "perfecting" the treaties according to constitutional requirements after they had been negotiated and formally signed. The treaty commissioners sent the treaty to the secretary of war or the secretary of the interior, usually through the commissioner of Indian affairs, following the creation of that office in 1832. There was a letter of transmittal and often a report on how the negotiations had been conducted and an explanation of the terms in the treaty. Frequently a journal of proceedings was included, in some cases very brief summaries of each day's proceedings, in others a long and detailed account with nearly verbatim transcriptions of the speeches of the commissioners and of the Indians. The commissioner of Indian affairs sent the treaty

---

9. Council minutes published in David I. Bushnell, Jr., "The Virginia Frontier in History—1778," part 5, "The Treaty of Fort Pitt," *Virginia Magazine of History and Biography* 24 (April 1916): 176; *ASPIA*, 1:43.

10. Kappler, 2:61, 62, 653, 711, 763; Ratified Treaties (M688, roll 10, frame 80).

to the secretary with recommendations about ratification; the secretary in turn sent the treaty, with the commissioner of Indian affair's report and sometimes a report of his own, to the president. The president, at his discretion, submitted the treaty with the reports and other pertinent documents to the Senate for its constitutional action of advising and consenting to its ratification.[11]

Now it was the senators' turn to put their stamp upon the treaty, and the treaties themselves contained explicit notations about such ratification, most of them specifying that the articles would be binding on both parties "as soon as they shall have been ratified by the President of the United States of America, by and with the advice and consent of the Senate of the said United States."[12] But there were a number of variations. The peace treaty of May 13, 1816, with the Sacs of Rock River put the stipulation negatively: "This treaty shall take effect and be obligatory on the contracting parties, unless the same shall be disapproved by the president and senate of the United States, or by the president only; and in the mean time all hostilities shall cease from this date." The Treaty of Prairie du Chien of 1825 specified that the treaty became obligatory on the tribes at the date of signing and on the United States only after its ratification. The Apaches in 1852 signed a treaty that was to be binding on both parties from the date of signing, "subject only to such modifications and amendments as may be adopted by the government of the United States."[13] The treaties with the Potawatomis and with the Miamis in 1826 had the unusual notation, "This treaty, after the same shall be ratified by the President and Senate, shall be binding on the United States," a reflection, no doubt, of the principle that the Indians were represented at the negotiations by their chiefs, the United States only by appointed commissioners, whose work was subject to ratification.[14]

Unexpectedly, for a body that under the Constitution had joint responsibility with the president for treaty making, the Senate, except in a few instances, acted perfunctorily. Following a run-in with George Washington about what "advice and consent" meant, the Senate backed

11. These documents for a good many of the treaties are assembled in Senate (RG 46). Some appear among the documents indexed in CIS *Index to US Senate Executive Documents and Reports, Covering Documents and Reports Not Printed in the US Serial Set, 1817–1969*, 2 vols. (Washington: Congressional Information Service, 1987).

12. This precise formula is from the treaty with the Chickasaws, July 23, 1805, Kappler, 2:80.

13. Ibid., 128, 254, 599.

14. Ibid., 275, 280.

away from taking an active part and regularly approved treaties with a unanimous or nearly unanimous vote after receiving the treaties in completed form. Not counting the 7 treaties completed under the Continental Congress and 7 more for which there was no division of votes into yeas and nays, the action can be followed on 354 treaties. Of these, the Senate unanimously approved 191 without amendment and 25 more with one or two negative votes. In addition, it unanimously approved 57 treaties to which it had added amendments and 12 amended treaties with one or two negative votes. This makes 285 treaties ratified by the Senate almost unanimously. There were 69 others that were approved with three or more negative votes, but close decisions were exceptional.[15]

At times, to be sure, the Senate stopped the treaties altogether. It tabled some of those it received from the president, and sometimes it voted to reject them outright (the case of 18 treaties with the California tribes in 1851 is a notorious example).[16]

The formal action of the Senate (approval, approval with amendments, or rejection) was sent to the president in the form of an attested copy of the Senate's resolution, with the original treaty attached. The president returned the treaty with the Senate's resolution to the executive department from which he had received it.

There was a further anomalous procedure, for, although responsibility for Indian affairs, including treaty negotiations, fell to the War or Interior Department, the filing and safekeeping of the treaties and their promulgation were duties of the Department of State. Eventually, then, the original treaty with the Senate's attested resolution of advice and consent was forwarded to the secretary of state, who had a formal ratification/proclamation document drawn up for the president to sign. A set form was adopted at the very beginning of the national government, which was used with slight variations until treaty making ended in 1871.[17] The document of ratification was then printed for distribution. Occasionally a special proclamation by the president urging proper

15. This compilation is based upon a careful scrutiny of *Senate Ex. Proc.* done by Marc Ferrara, who aided me as a graduate research assistant at Boston College in 1983–84. Senate action on treaties was done in executive session and recorded in *Senate Ex. Proc.* From time to time, in individual cases, the Senate lifted the secrecy from the treaty ratification proceedings at the time of its action, and ultimately, after a lapse of time, it authorized publication of the executive proceedings.

16. See appendix D, "Unratified Treaties."

17. See, for example, the Cherokee treaty at Holston in 1791, Ratified Treaties (M668, roll 2, frames 232ff.).

enforcement of the treaty was used also at the beginning of the document, as in the case of the Creek treaty of 1790, which was then issued as a broadside.[18]

The treaties antedating 1790 in the State Department file do not have a presidential ratification attached to them, but there has been little question of the validity of these treaties on that account.[19] From the Creek treaty of 1790 on, with few exceptions, all treaties have a clear ratification/proclamation by the president.[20]

As the practice developed, the presidential statements at the beginning and the end were on separate pages of paper, but in some cases the statements were pasted onto the treaty proper. George Washington also entered his ratification statement for some treaties on the treaty paper itself when there was room at the end.[21] Beginning with the 1820s, the Ratified Indian Treaties file generally has printed copies of the treaties, which include the ratification by the president. There are printed copies of some earlier treaties, but not all of them found their way into the file.

Senate Amendments

The ratification process was more complicated when the Senate amended a treaty and advised and consented to its ratification only with the amendments. The amendments were sometimes made on the initiative of individual senators or by the Committee on Indian Affairs, to which the treaties and accompanying documents were routinely referred, but often the amendments had actually been suggested

18. Ibid., frame 222.

19. The *Statutes at Large* indicates ratification on September 27, 1789, of the Fort Harmar treaty of January 9, 1789, with the Wyandots and other western tribes. Clarence E. Carter argues that the treaty of Fort Harmar with the Six Nations of the same date was never completed by Senate ratification and presidential proclamation and was, therefore, not a valid treaty, even though high government officials later assumed its validity and acted accordingly. The treaty was sent to the State Department in 1797, however, and it appears as number 16 in the Ratified Treaties. See *Terr. Papers*, 2:183n, 186n; John Stagg to George Taylor, May 9, 1797, Ratified Treaties (M668, roll 2, frame 210).

20. For some reason the *Statutes at Large* (followed by Kappler) indicates "ratified" rather than "proclaimed" for the treaties at Portage des Sioux in 1815 and some others of the same period, but the form of the president's action is the same as that for other treaties.

21. See treaty with the Sacs and Foxes, September 3, 1822, Ratified Treaties (M668, roll 5, frames 204ff.); Treaty of Greenville, August 3, 1795, ibid. (M668, roll 2, frame 298).

by the commissioner of Indian affairs or the department secretary and sent to the Senate in their reports accompanying the treaty. The president and the executive department officials did not consider themselves authorized to change a treaty once it had been signed by the treaty commissioners and the Indians. When they decided, on receiving the treaty, that changes were in order, they suggested amendments with the hope that they would be incorporated by the Senate. The Senate regularly acceded to the suggested changes and approved the treaty only with such amendments.[22]

Considerable difficulty arose in resubmitting an amended treaty to the Indians for their assent to the changes. A number of treaties were ratified and carried into effect without any attempt to get the Indians' approval. But the injustice of such unilateral changes was apparent, and the government regularly sought assent to the amendments by tribal leaders (for it was usually impossible to assemble the whole tribe again). In some cases, the Senate specifically required it. Thus the Senate on February 25, 1841, in amending a treaty with the Miami Indians of November 28, 1840, included in its resolution the proviso: "that the assent of said Indians shall be properly obtained to the same." The Indian assent was obtained on May 15, 1841, and President Tyler ratified the amended treaty on June 7, 1841.[23] And in the treaty with the Delaware Indians of July 2, 1861, the Senate added to its resolution of amendment: "And provided, that this Treaty shall not go into operation and be binding on them until accepted by the Indians thus amended." President Lincoln specifically designated Commissioner of Indian Affairs William P. Dole to present the amended treaty to the Indians and to record their acceptance.[24]

Congress, too, in making appropriations for carrying out treaties, could protect the right of the Indians to approve Senate amendments, as it did in 1836 by adding this provision to the section of the Indian appropriation act dealing with the Ottawa and Chippewa treaty of

22. This action can be followed best in the Senate's treaty ratification files. See, for example, actions of the Twenty-fourth and Twenty-fifth Congresses, Senate (RG 46), Sen 24B and Sen 25B. I at first misunderstood the Senate's action in amending so many treaties. The considerable number of such cases led me to believe that the Senate played a major part in the final form of the treaties, but after studying the Senate's treaty ratification files (containing many letters from the executive officers recommending amendments, which the Senate accepted), I had to revise my judgment.

23. Ratified Treaties (M668, roll 9, treaty no. 239). The Senate resolution and the Indians' assent are printed in 7 Stat. 585–86.

24. Ratified Treaties (M668, roll 12, treaty no. 317).

March 28, 1836: "That no part of the above appropriations for carrying into effect the treaty with the Chippewas and Ottawas, shall be drawn from the Treasury except what may be necessary for the expenses of collecting and subsisting the Indians, and for the expenses of concluding the treaty, heretofore incurred . . . until the assent of the said Indians shall be given to the changes proposed by the resolution of the Senate."[25]

As the Senate made amendments with increasing frequency, considerable care was taken to get Indian approval. Sometimes, when the treaty and Senate resolution with amendments were sent to the State Department for promulgation, the secretary of state returned the documents to the Department of the Interior with such a notation as "to the end that the Senate's amendments to said treaties may be duly submitted to the respective tribes of Indians for their ratification." When the form for the president's ratification of amended treaties was drawn up, it included a copy of the Senate's amendments and the Indians' assent thereto.

In the case of the treaty with the Western Band of Shoshones of October 1, 1863, the Indian Office neglected to fill a blank in the treaty concerning the number of thousands of dollars worth of provisions and clothing to be given as presents at the conclusion of the treaty. When the Senate got the treaty with the blank not filled in, it formally amended the treaty to insert the word "five." The acting secretary of the interior sent the treaty to the secretary of state for promulgation, with the note: "I would respectfully suggest in connection with the amendment, that the blank in the 8th article was an oversight;—intended to have been filled by this Department, and therefore it is not necessary to send it to the Indians for the assent to the insertion of the word five. Should you concur with me in this view, I will thank you to insert the word five in the blank of the 8th article and promulgate the treaty."[26]

The State Department was not prepared to change a treaty so casually; Secretary of State Seward replied:

In my view, this Department is not invested with the power of making the correction suggested, more especially as the Senate has formally required the reference of the Treaty again to the Indians by its resolution advising the ratification thereof with a proposed amendment. If, therefore, in consideration of the clerical omission before

25. 5 Stat. 75.
26. W. T. Otto to William H. Seward, June 29, 1866, typed copy in Ratified Treaties (M668, roll 13, treaty no. 326).

the Treaty was submitted to the Senate it is now by you deemed inadvisable to send the instrument back to the Indians for their assent, the next best course would seem to be for the Department of the Interior, through the Executive to remit it, with the accompanying resolution back to the Senate filling in the wanting word and making explanation of the facts, when the Senate could modify its resolution accordingly. The Treaty with the resolution, is herewith enclosed.[27]

The Department of the Interior chose to seek the assent of the Indians, which was given on June 17, 1869, and the treaty was proclaimed on October 21, with the document of assent included.[28]

A treaty with the Great and Little Osage Indians of September 29, 1865, contained a provision that "should the Senate reject or amend any of the above articles, such rejection or amendment shall not affect the other provisions of the treaty, but the same shall go into effect when ratified by the Senate and approved by the President." The Senate on June 26, 1866, approved the treaty but with certain amendments, and Secretary of State Seward saw problems in spite of the proviso. He told Secretary Harlan, "It will be perceived, however, that if, under these circumstances, the treaty were promulgated at this time, it would be in a very incomplete and indeterminate state until the consent of the Indians concerned should have been given to the Senate's amendments." He suggested that the assent of the Osages be obtained before the promulgation of the treaty, and that was done.[29]

When the United States dealt with the northern plains Indians at Fort Sully in the fall of 1865, it removed the need for Indian assent to Senate amendments by adding at the end of each of the treaties the remarkable provision: "Any amendment or modification of this treaty by the Senate of the United States shall be considered final and binding upon the said band, represented in council, as part of this treaty, in the same manner as if it had been subsequently presented and agreed to by the chiefs and head-men of said band."[30] Secretary Harlan declared that the clause had been inserted "in pursuance of the direction of the

27. Seward to James Harlan, July 3, 1866, typed copy, ibid.

28. Ratified Treaties (M668, roll 13, treaty no. 326).

29. See documents in Ratified Treaties (M668, roll 13, treaty 338). A typed copy of Seward to Harlan, June 28, 1866, is filed with the treaty.

30. See, for example, treaty of October 10, 1865, with the Miniconjou Sioux, Kappler, 2:884.

President, with the concurrence of his cabinet, and delivered by this Department to the Commissioners who negotiated with the Indian tribes respectively, for the purpose of obviating the necessity of re-submitting them, should the Senate ratify them with amendments."[31] The Senate used this authority sparingly.

On rare occasions, the Indians refused assent to amendments. Then the Senate was asked to withdraw from its amendments and approve the treaty as originally submitted. One important case was the treaty with the Nez Perces in 1863. The Indians hoped that by refusing to accept the amended treaty they might regain the lands ceded in the treaty, but Commissioner of Indian Affairs Nathaniel G. Taylor realized the impossibility of getting back the ceded lands already in the hands of white miners and settlers. He argued in 1867:

> In view of the long agitation induced among the Indians by the delay in ratification of this treaty, the constant encroachment by the whites upon their lands, the time necessarily occupied in communi-cating with that distant region, and the fact that Congress had already appropriated the amounts stipulated under the treaty in question, both for the current and next fiscal years, I am induced to recommend that the Senate be requested to reconsider its amendments, and allow the treaty to go into effect without alteration or amendments. . . .
>
> The amendments proposed were doubtless in the interest of the Indians, but they do not appear to be of such an important character as to outweigh the good to be gained by putting the treaty into immediate operation, and closing all agitation upon the subject.[32]

The secretary of the interior sent the treaty to the Senate on April 8, 1867, with the request for ratification without the amendments, but there was still another obstacle. The Senate, as a matter of protocol, sent it back to him with the notation that the treaty might be "trans-mitted to the Senate, if deemed necessary, by the President of the United States." Accordingly, President Johnson sent the treaty to the Senate on April 11, and the Senate promptly ratified it in its original form on April 17.[33]

31. Typed copy of Harlan to Seward, March 8, 1866, in Ratified Treaties (M668, roll 14, treaty no. 339); *Senate Ex. Proc.* 14, pt. 2: 581–83. Kappler failed to pick up the amendment in his printing of the treaty with the Upper Yanktonai, where the phrase eliminated by the Senate still appears. Kappler, 2:905.

32. Taylor to Orville H. Browning, April 5, 1867, Senate (RG 46), Sen 40B-C10.

33. *Senate Ex. Proc.* 15, pt. 2: 662, 748–49.

The Case of the Fort Laramie Treaty of 1851

The most notorious and complicated case of seeking Indian assent to a substantial change made in a treaty by the Senate was that of the Treaty of Fort Laramie of 1851. It shows how haphazard the treatment of a treaty could be and how convoluted the process of formal promulgation. After the Senate reduced the annuity payments promised in the treaty from *fifty* years to *ten* years (with an additional five years at the discretion of the president), the process of getting the Indians to approve the drastic change began. A suggestion that it was unnecessary to obtain such Indian consent was strongly rejected by Commissioner of Indian Affairs Luke Lea:

> A treaty is a contract. The word has a definite and well understood meaning. Ex vi termini it imports the idea of an agreement, and necessarily implies mutuality of assent. . . . How then can that be considered a contract, a treaty which contains provisions prescribed arbitrarily by one of the parties without even the knowledge of the other? . . .
>
> I am aware that there are several instances in which Indian treaties have been amended and promulgated as duly ratified without submitting them to the Indians for approval, but how such a proceeding, in view of the legal principles involved, can be considered anything but a mockery of the highest and most solemn form of contract it is difficult to perceive.[34]

Directions were sent to the agents to obtain tribal approval, and three agreements were eventually made, two by Thomas Fitzpatrick in 1853 and one by Alfred J. Vaughn, agent of the Upper Missouri Agency, in 1854. Then, no doubt because of the delay, confusion arose about whether such approval had indeed been attained, and the treaty was never proclaimed by the president, even though the annuities were duly paid for fifteen years.[35]

The confusion is well documented. One of the copies of the treaty in the Indian Office file has an endorsement that reads: "This [amend-

34. Lea to A. H. H. Stuart, May 29, 1852, printed in Kappler, 4:1078.
35. The documents of assent to the amendment are in Documents (T494), roll 4, frame 796.

ment] was to be submitted to the Indians, but they were never got together for the purpose. The . . . amount has, however, been appropriated and distributed annually in goods—this year 1865 being the last of the fifteen." This view obtained for many years. When treaties from the 1850s were printed in the *United States Statutes at Large* in 1867, the Fort Laramie Treaty was omitted, with an explanatory note that said in part: "This assent of all the Tribes [to the amendment] has not been obtained, and consequently, although Congress appropriates money for the fulfilment of its stipulations, it is not yet in a proper form for publication." Charles J. Kappler in his 1904 compilation of Indian treaties printed the amended treaty in its proper chronological order, with a footnote: "This treaty as signed was ratified by the Senate with an amendment changing the annuity in Article 7 from fifty years to ten years, subject to its acceptance by the tribes. Assent of all tribes except the Crows was procured . . . , and in subsequent agreements this treaty has been recognized as in force." In 1929 Kappler admitted his error and printed an array of documents about the treaty ratification, including a copy of the Crow approval of the amendment. He included a long undated Indian Office memorandum from the mid-1920s about the matter, which gives a detailed account and which concludes: "Through oversight or inadvertence the Indian Service and the Department of the Interior neglected to formally advise the Secretary of State of the assent of the Indians to the ratification of article 7 of the 1851 treaty, and for that reason it would seem the treaty was never formally promulgated by the President of the United States."[36]

Did the "oversight or inadvertence" invalidate the treaty? Some persons thought it did, because the treaty had not been "perfected," and as a result the treaty was never added to the State Department Ratified Indian Treaties file. Then in the 1920s the Interior Department made a new attempt to get the treaty proclaimed; it sent its copy of the treaty with the three amendment agreements to the State Department, with a request that the treaty be laid before the president, at long last, for formal ratification. In reply, Secretary of State Francis B. Kellogg rejected the proposal on the basis that the act of 1871 had prohibited further treaty making. And he questioned whether, "as a matter of law, the treaty has been duly ratified by all the signatory bands and tribes of

36. Ibid., frame 756; 11 Stat. 749; Kappler, 2:594; 4:1065–81; quotation on 1073. A detailed account of the approval of the amendment (especially in regard to the Sioux) is given in Harry Anderson, "The Controversial Sioux Amendment to the Fort Laramie Treaty of 1851," *Nebraska History* 37 (September 1956): 201–20.

Indians so as to warrant ratification by the President, if that action were otherwise unobjectionable." He returned the documents to the Interior Department.[37] The Interior Department on its side argued: "There is no question as to the lack of ratification by the President of the United States, nor is there any question as to the ratification *by all the signatory bands and tribes of Indians*. However, the provisions of the treaty have all been fulfilled, and the only purpose in obtaining a ratification by the President at this time was to obtain its publication in the Statutes at Large." In the end, no action was taken. Thus did the treaty remain in limbo.[38]

Printing the Treaties

Printed copies exist for a number of the earliest treaties, but whether they were printed by order of the government or issued by private printers cannot easily be determined. Some of them furnish simply the text of the treaty, while others, often in the form of a broadside, contain the president's proclamation and were intended to promulgate the treaty to the public. The Ratified Indian Treaties file has

37. Kellogg to secretary of the interior, May 11, 1928, Documents (T494), roll 4, frames 805–6.

38. There was considerable argument about whether or not a formal proclamation by the president was necessary for the validity of the treaty. Secretary of the interior to secretary of state, May 11, 1928; memorandum of John R. Reeves, May 15, 1928; memorandum of E. B. Merritt to Assistant Secretary of the Interior John H. Edwards, May 17, 1928, ibid., frames 807, 813–14. A legal opinion cited the Supreme Court decision of April 11, 1898, in *New York Indians v. United States*, 170 U.S. 23, in which the Court decided that a proviso added to the Treaty of Buffalo Creek of 1838 was not present in the treaty as proclaimed by the president and was therefore unratified and not operative. The Indian Office in 1928 was apparently unaware of two decisions of the United States Court of Claims that had declared that ratification by the president was not necessary for the validity of the Fort Laramie Treaty. In *Roy v. United States and Ogallala Indians* (1910), the court affirmed the validity of the treaty. It could find no provision in the Constitution or in subsequent laws that required proclamation by the president. "Certainly," the court said, "as to Indian treaties the contention that proclamation is necessary to give them binding force as between the parties is without reason. The Indians were our wards, and we thus occupied a fiduciary relation to them. The Sioux signed the treaty in the first instance, and when ratified and amended by the Senate they agreed to it as amended. They afterward received annuities under it, and their rights to the lands described in it were repeatedly recognized. . . . To now hold that the treaty never had any binding force on the United States or its citizens would be contrary to good faith and common honesty." 45 Ct. Cl. 183. A somewhat similar decision but of less general applicability was *Moore v. United States and the Sioux and Cheyennes* (1897), ibid., 32: 593–98.

printed copies of some early treaties (Fort Stanwix, Fort McIntosh, Greater Miami, and Hopewell) and a broadside of the Creek treaty of 1790.[39] Beginning with the Sac and Fox treaty of August 4, 1824, the file generally includes a printed copy of the president's proclamation of the treaty, including the Senate resolution with amendments and the Indians' assent to the amendments. In the 1850s and 1860s, the State Department printed multiple copies of the treaty proclamations, regularly sending a batch (often 250 copies) to the Indian Office for its use.[40]

Congress, in a law of April 20, 1818, directed the State Department to cause the laws and treaties of the United States to be published in newspapers in the District of Columbia and in the states and territories. That this was meant to include Indian treaties was clear from an amendment to the act in 1820, which specified that Indian treaties "shall be published only in one newspaper and that to be within the limits of the state, or territory, to which the subject matter of such treaty shall belong." In 1842 such publication of laws and treaties was limited to newspapers in the District of Columbia only, but in 1846 the publication in state and territorial newspapers was reinstated.[41] Indian treaties were especially designated in the appropriation act for fiscal year 1856, section 14: "That the treaties made during the present Congress, with the Indian tribes, and those to be made in future, shall be published as the laws and other treaties in the newspapers of such States and Territories as the Secretary of the Interior may think expedient."[42] In the 1850s and 1860s the secretary of state frequently wrote to the Indian Office asking for the state or territory in which given treaties should be published in newspapers and then got the names of particular papers from the clerk of the House of Representatives or from the secretary of the interior. Whereupon he sent the editors of the designated papers printed copies of the proclaimed treaty.[43]

In more permanent form the treaties ultimately found their way into

39. Ratified Treaties (M668, roll 2). A good many other early prints, some of them broadsides, appear in the microform publication *Early American Imprints*. See Clifford K. Shipton and James E. Mooney, *National Index of American Imprints through 1800: The Short-Title Evans* (Worcester, Mass.: American Antiquarian Society, 1969), under "U.S. President" and "U.S. Treaties."

40. Ratified Treaties (M668, roll 5, frames 235ff.); John Appleton to Charles E. Mix, April 14, 1859, typed copy, ibid. (M668, roll 12, treaty no. 305).

41. 3 Stat. 439, 576; 9 Stat. 77.

42. 10 Stat. 671.

43. See numerous typed copies of letters on this matter in Ratified Treaties (M668, rolls 13, 14, and 15).

print in published volumes of collected treaties. As early as June 14, 1790, Congress resolved "that all treaties made, or which shall be made and promulg[at]ed, under the authority of the United States, shall, from time to time, be published and annexed to their code of laws, by the Secretary of State."[44] In 1826 a preliminary volume of Indian treaties was prepared under the direction of the War Department, followed by an extended revision in 1837, whose title page indicated that it was "compiled and printed by the direction, and under the supervision, of the commissioner of Indian affairs." In 1846, treaties through 1842 were issued in volume 7 of the *Statutes at Large*, a volume devoted only to the Indian treaties. Subsequent treaties—and a few earlier ones not included in volume 7—were printed at the back of appropriate volumes of the *Statutes,* although not always in correct chronological order.

The irregularity in the chronological order was due in part to delays in ratification of the treaties by the Senate and proclamation by the president. Thus the treaties with Indians in the Pacific Northwest that were signed in 1855 and should have appeared in volume 10 of the *Statutes* were not proclaimed until 1859 and thus published out of proper order in volume 12. In part, also, the delays resulted from inadvertence or clerical neglect. In early 1859 the Indian Office notified the Senate that three treaties of 1837, 1839, and 1842 had never appeared in the *Statutes at Large*, and the Senate, after referring the matter to the Committee on Printing, which was charged with determining the authenticity of the treaties, ordered that they be printed. They thus finally appeared in volume 11.[45] And as late as April 1870, the Indian Office told the State Department that the supplementary treaty with the Cherokees of April 27, 1868, "upon which this office has based and will continue to base its action in its relations with the tribe," had not appeared in its proper place in the *Statutes.* The secretary of state replied that the omission had already been called to his attention and that it would be corrected in the next edition of the laws, as it was.[46]

Finally, in 1904, a full compilation of the treaties, carefully prepared and edited by Charles J. Kappler, clerk to the Senate Committee on Indian Affairs, was published by the Government Printing Office; it reproduced the texts from the *Statutes* and has become the standard

44. 1 Stat. 187.
45. *Senate Journal*, 35-2, serial 973, pp. 189–90, 285; *Congressional Globe*, 35th Cong., 2d sess., 602, 877.
46. E. S. Parker to J. D. Cox, April 5, 1870; Hamilton Fish to W. T. Otto, April 8, 1870, typed copies in Ratified Treaties (M668, roll 16, frames 168–70).

reference work for treaty texts. Whereas the earlier printing, including the *Statutes at Large*, generally printed the original treaty and then appended a notation of the amendments made by the Senate and ratified by the president (thus following the form used in the official presidential proclamations of the treaties), Kappler usually, but not always, prints the treaty *as amended*.[47]

The various published versions do not display great uniformity in their handling of the treaties or in their concordance with the original manuscript in matters of spelling, capitalization, and punctuation. Standards for exact reproduction in printed form of manuscript originals, which modern editors follow, were unknown in earlier times, and each editor or publisher tended to follow the spelling and punctuation rules of his own time. Thus the editor of the 1837 *Treaties between the United States of America and the Several Indian Tribes, from 1778 to 1837* noted in the preface, "It was originally intended to have collated each Treaty with the original manuscript in the Department of State; but upon making the trial it was found that the differences were altogether unimportant, and were occasioned, principally, by the punctuation, which was generally incorrect." The volume followed the printed copies of the treaties that came after Senate ratification.

Clarence E. Carter, the meticulous editor of *The Territorial Papers of the United States*, collated the original copy of the 1789 Treaty of Fort Harmar with the printed text in the *Statutes at Large* and in Kappler's *Treaties*. Although he found no important differences in words, he found more than 170 punctuation discrepancies. He wrote: "In these two versions more than 60 marks of punctuation found in the original treaty were omitted, more than 60 new points were inserted, and over 40 original punctuation marks were altered, many of which changes tend to obscure the sense." In the 1795 Treaty of Greenville, Carter found more than one hundred changes in punctuation between the original manuscript and the *Statutes*.[48]

One element of inconsistency in spelling was Indian tribal names, for which no standardized spelling was established in the nineteenth century. Thus in Kappler's printing of treaties with the Potawatomis, the tribal name is entered in twenty-seven different ways, none of which agrees with the standardized form used by Kappler in his titles to the treaties and by later editors.

47. Citations to both Kappler and to the *Statutes at Large* for each treaty are given in appendix B.
48. *Terr. Papers*, 2:174n, 525n.

Ratified Indian Treaties

Formal and solemn as treaties are, those made by the United States with American Indian tribes are not free of irregularities that make it difficult to prepare a definitive list of them. The original ratified treaties in the State Department's Ratified Indian Treaties file are arranged chronologically, with a serial number assigned to each. These serial numbers are given in the list below in square brackets.

This list follows largely the compilation of ratified treaties printed in Charles J. Kappler, compiler, *Indian Affairs: Laws and Treaties*, vol. 2, *Treaties* (Washington: Government Printing Office, 1904), which takes its text from the official publication in the *United States Statutes at Large*. Although the list depends heavily on Kappler's *Treaties*, other compilations and lists of treaties, discussed below in "Sources for the Study of American Indian Treaties," have been used, as well as an unpublished "List of Ratified Indian Treaties," prepared by Robert M. Kvasnicka for volume 4 of the Smithsonian Institution's *Handbook of North American Indians* but not published in the *Handbook*.

The date of proclamation is the date when the president formally confirmed the treaty, signed it, and affixed the great seal of the United States. This date, sometimes called date of "ratification," is provided in most cases by Kappler. Where there is a question, the original document in the Ratified Indian Treaties file, Record Group 11 (M668), has been followed. Six treaty documents not included in the list are considered at the end.

A bar graph (p. 503) displays the concentration of treaty making in chronological order, but it shows only the number of treaties each year and does not distinguish between important treaties and minor ones.

A map (pp. 504–5) shows the council sites for the treaties. Sources for the map: Each ratified treaty, usually in the title and sometimes also at the end of the treaty, indicates the place at which the treaty was signed. Some of the locations—for example, established cities and well-known military posts, were easy to pinpoint. But many—like shifting Indian villages, Indian agencies, or temporary encampments in the Indian country—were more difficult to determine. Modern commercial atlases and state maps were useful if the old place names continued. Especially helpful were the maps in Charles Royce, *Indian Land Cessions*, and the maps in James Truslow Adams, *Atlas of American History*. Edward E. Hill's *The Office of Indian Affairs, 1824–1880: Historical Sketches* helped to trace the location of Indian agencies at which treaty councils were held. I have also used the files of old maps of the American Geographical Society, now located at the University of Wisconsin-Milwaukee, and was helped in some especially difficult cases by Ralph E. Ehrenberg, chief of the Geography and Map Division of the Library of Congress, and his staff.

Ratified Indian Treaties

Number and Date	Tribes	Place	Commissioners	Citations
1 [8]. Sept. 17, 1778	Delaware	Fort Pitt	Andrew Lewis; Thomas Lewis	Kappler, 3–5; 7 Stat. 13–15
2 [9]. Oct. 22, 1784	Six Nations	Fort Stanwix	Oliver Walcott; Richard Butler; Arthur Lee	Kappler, 5–6; 7 Stat. 15–16
3 [10]. Jan. 21, 1785	Wyandot; Delaware; Chippewa; Ottawa	Fort McIntosh	George R. Clark; Richard Butler; Arthur Lee	Kappler, 6–8; 7 Stat. 16–18
4 [11]. Nov. 28, 1785	Cherokee	Hopewell	Benjamin Hawkins; Andrew Pickens; Joseph Martin; Lachlan McIntosh	Kappler, 8–11; 7 Stat. 18–21
5 [12]. Jan. 3, 1786	Choctaw	Hopewell	Benjamin Hawkins; Andrew Pickens; Joseph Martin	Kappler, 11–14; 7 Stat. 21–23
6 [13]. Jan. 10, 1786	Chickasaw	Hopewell	Benjamin Hawkins; Andrew Pickens; Joseph Martin	Kappler, 14–16; 7 Stat. 24–26
7 [14]. Jan. 31, 1786	Shawnee	Mouth of the Great Miami	George R. Clark; Richard Butler; Samuel H. Parsons	Kappler, 16–18; 7 Stat. 26–27

8 [15].	Jan. 9, 1789; ratified Sept. 29, 1789	Wyandot; Delaware; Ottawa; Chippewa; Potawatomi; Sac	Fort Harmar	Arthur St. Clair	Kappler, 18–23; 7 Stat. 28–32
9 [16].	Jan. 9, 1789	Six Nations	Fort Harmar	Arthur St. Clair	Kappler, 23–25; 7 Stat. 33–35
10 [17].	Aug. 7, 1790; proclaimed Aug. 13, 1790	Creek	New York	Henry Knox	Kappler, 25–29; 7 Stat. 35–38
11 [18].	July 2, 1791; proclaimed Nov. 11, 1791	Cherokee	Holston River	William Blount	Kappler, 29–32; 7 Stat. 39–42
	Additional article: Feb. 17, 1792				
12 [20].	June 26, 1794; proclaimed Jan. 21, 1795	Cherokee	Philadelphia	Henry Knox	Kappler, 32–33; 7 Stat. 42–43
			Philadelphia	Henry Knox	Kappler, 33–34; 7 Stat. 43–44
13 [21].	Nov. 11, 1794; proclaimed Jan. 21, 1795	Six Nations	Canandaigua	Timothy Pickering	Kappler, 34–37; 7 Stat. 44–47
14 [22].	Dec. 2, 1794; proclaimed Jan. 21, 1795	Oneida; Tuscarora; Stockbridge	Oneida	Timothy Pickering	Kappler, 37–39; 7 Stat. 47–48

Ratified Indian Treaties

Number and Date	Tribes	Place	Commissioners	Citations
15 [23]. Aug. 3, 1795; proclaimed Dec. 22, 1795	Wyandot; Delaware; Shawnee; Ottawa; Chippewa; Potawatomi; Miami; Eel River; Wea; Kickapoo; Piankashaw; Kaskaskia	Greenville	Anthony Wayne	Kappler, 39–45; 7 Stat. 49–54
16 [24]. May 31, 1796; proclaimed Jan. 31, 1797	Seven Nations of Canada	New York	Abraham Ogden	Kappler, 45–46; 7 Stat. 55–56
17 [25]. June 29, 1796; proclaimed Mar. 24, 1797	Creek	Colerain	Benjamin Hawkins; George Clymer; Andrew Pickens	Kappler, 46–50; 7 Stat. 56–60
18 [26]. Mar. 29, 1797; proclaimed Apr. 27, 1798	Mohawk	Albany	Isaac Smith	Kappler, 50–51; 7 Stat. 61
19 [29]. Oct. 2, 1798; proclaimed Jan. 30, 1799	Cherokee	Tellico	Thomas Butler; George Walton	Kappler, 51–55; 7 Stat. 62–65
20 [30]. Oct. 24, 1801; proclaimed May 4, 1802	Chickasaw	Chickasaw Bluffs	James Wilkinson; Benjamin Hawkins; Andrew Pickens	Kappler, 55–56; 7 Stat. 65–66

	Date	Tribe	Place	Commissioners	Reference
21 [31].	Dec. 17, 1801; proclaimed May 4, 1802	Choctaw	Fort Adams	James Wilkinson; Benjamin Hawkins; Andrew Pickens	Kappler, 56–58; 7 Stat. 66–68
22 [32].	June 16, 1802; proclaimed Jan. 11, 1803	Creek	near Fort Wilkinson	James Wilkinson; Benjamin Hawkins	Kappler, 58–59; 7 Stat. 68–70
23 [33].	June 30, 1802; proclaimed Jan. 12, 1803	Seneca	Buffalo Creek	John Tayler	Kappler, 60–62; 7 Stat. 70–72
24 [34].	June 30, 1802; proclaimed Feb. 7, 1803	Seneca	Buffalo Creek	John Tayler	Kappler, 62; 7 Stat. 72–73
25 [35].	Oct. 17, 1802; proclaimed Jan. 20, 1803	Choctaw	Fort Confederation	James Wilkinson	Kappler, 63–64; 7 Stat. 73–74
26 [36].	June 7, 1803; proclaimed Dec. 26, 1803	Delaware; Shawnee; Potawatomi; Miami; Eel River; Wea; Kickapoo; Piankashaw; Kaskaskia	Fort Wayne	William Henry Harrison	Kappler, 64–65; 7 Stat. 74–76

Ratified Indian Treaties

Number and Date	Tribes	Place	Commissioners	Citations
27 [37]. Aug. 7, 1803; proclaimed Dec. 23, 1803	Eel River; Wyandot; Piankashaw; Kaskaskia; Kickapoo	Vincennes	William Henry Harrison	Kappler, 66; 7 Stat. 77
28 [38]. Aug. 13, 1803; proclaimed Dec. 23, 1803	Kaskaskia	Vincennes	William Henry Harrison	Kappler, 67–68; 7 Stat. 78–79
29 [39]. Aug. 31, 1803; proclaimed Dec. 26, 1803	Choctaw	Hoe-Buckin-too-pa	James Wilkinson	Kappler, 69–70; 7 Stat. 80–81
30 [40]. Aug. 18, 1804; proclaimed Feb. 14, 1805	Delaware	Vincennes	William Henry Harrison	Kappler, 70–72; 7 Stat. 81–83
31 [41]. Aug. 27, 1804; proclaimed Feb. 6, 1805	Piankashaw	Vincennes	William Henry Harrison	Kappler, 72–73; 7 Stat. 83–84
32 [42]. Oct. 24, 1804; proclaimed May 17, 1824	Cherokee	Tellico	Daniel Smith; Return J. Meigs	Kappler, 73–74; 7 Stat. 228–29
33 [43]. Nov. 3, 1804; proclaimed Feb. 21, 1805	Sac and Fox	St. Louis	William Henry Harrison	Kappler, 74–77; 7 Stat. 84–87

				American State Papers: Indian Affairs 1:696
34 [44]. July 4, 1805; proclaimed Jan. 25, 1806	Wyandot; Ottawa; Chippewa; Munsee; Delaware; Shawnee; Potawatomi	Fort Industry	Charles Jouett	*American State Papers: Indian Affairs* 1:696
35 [45]. July 4, 1805; proclaimed Apr. 24, 1806	Wyandot; Ottawa; Chippewa; Munsee; Delaware; Shawnee; Potawatomi	Fort Industry	Charles Jouett	Kappler, 77–78; 7 Stat. 87–89
36 [46]. July 23, 1805; proclaimed May 23, 1807	Chickasaw	Chickasaw country	James Robertson; Silas Dinsmoor	Kappler, 79–80; 7 Stat. 89–90
37 [47]. Aug. 21, 1805; proclaimed Apr. 24, 1806	Delaware; Potawatomi; Miami; Eel River; Wea	Grouseland, near Vincennes	William Henry Harrison	Kappler, 80–82; 7 Stat. 91–93
38 [48]. Oct. 25, 1805; proclaimed Apr. 24, 1806	Cherokee	Tellico	Return J. Meigs; Daniel Smith	Kappler, 82–83; 7 Stat. 93–94

Ratified Indian Treaties

Number and Date	Tribes	Place	Commissioners	Citations
39 [49]. Oct. 27, 1805; proclaimed June 10, 1806	Cherokee	Tellico	Return J. Meigs; Daniel Smith	Kappler, 84; 7 Stat. 95–96
40 [50]. Nov. 14, 1805; proclaimed June 2, 1806	Creek	Washington	Henry Dearborn	Kappler, 85–86; 7 Stat. 96–98
41 [51]. Nov. 16, 1805; proclaimed Feb. 25, 1808	Choctaw	Mount Dexter	James Robertson; Silas Dinsmoor	Kappler, 87–88; 7 Stat. 98–100
42 [52]. Dec. 30, 1805; proclaimed May 23, 1807	Piankashaw	Vincennes	William Henry Harrison	Kappler, 89–90; 7 Stat. 100–101
43 [53]. Jan. 7, 1806; proclaimed May 22, 1807	Cherokee	Washington	Henry Dearborn	Kappler, 90–91; 7 Stat. 101–3
Elucidation Sept. 11, 1807			James Robertson; Return J. Meigs	Kappler, 91–92; 7 Stat. 103–4
44 [54]. Nov. 17, 1807; proclaimed Jan. 27, 1808	Ottawa; Chippewa; Wyandot; Potawatomi	Detroit	William Hull	Kappler, 92–94; 7 Stat. 105–7
45 [55]. Nov. 10, 1808; proclaimed Apr. 28, 1810	Osage	Fort Clark	Peter Chouteau	Kappler, 95–99; 7 Stat. 107–11

No.		Date	Tribes	Place	Commissioners	Citation
46	[56].	Nov. 25, 1808; proclaimed Mar. 3, 1809	Chippewa; Ottawa; Potawatomi; Wyandot; Shawnee	Brownstown	William Hull	Kappler, 99–100; 7 Stat. 112–13
47	[57].	Sept. 30, 1809; proclaimed Jan. 16, 1810	Delaware; Potawatomi; Miami; Eel River	Fort Wayne	William Henry Harrison	Kappler, 101–3; 7 Stat. 113–16
48	[58].	Oct. 26, 1809; proclaimed Jan. 25, 1810	Wea	Vincennes	William Henry Harrison	Kappler, 103–4; 7 Stat. 116–17
49	[59].	Dec. 9, 1809; proclaimed Mar. 8, 1810	Kickapoo	Vincennes	William Henry Harrison	Kappler, 104–5; 7 Stat. 117
50	[60].	July 22, 1814; proclaimed Dec. 21, 1814	Wyandot; Delaware; Shawnee; Seneca; Miami	Greenville	William Henry Harrison; Lewis Cass	Kappler, 105–7; 7 Stat. 118–20
51	[61].	Aug. 9, 1814; proclaimed Feb. 16, 1815	Creek	Fort Jackson	Andrew Jackson	Kappler, 107–10; 7 Stat. 120–22
52	[62].	July 18, 1815; proclaimed Dec. 26, 1815	Potawatomi	Portage des Sioux	William Clark; Ninian Edwards; Auguste Chouteau	Kappler, 110–11; 7 Stat. 123

Ratified Indian Treaties

Number and Date	Tribes	Place	Commissioners	Citations
53 [63]. July 18, 1815; proclaimed Dec. 26, 1815	Piankashaw	Portage des Sioux	William Clark; Ninian Edwards; Auguste Chouteau	Kappler, 111–12; 7 Stat. 124
54 [64]. July 19, 1815; proclaimed Dec. 26, 1815	Teton	Portage des Sioux	William Clark; Ninian Edwards; Auguste Chouteau	Kappler, 112–13; 7 Stat. 125
55 [65]. July 19, 1815; proclaimed Dec. 26, 1815	Sioux of the Lakes	Portage des Sioux	William Clark; Ninian Edwards; Auguste Chouteau	Kappler, 113; 7 Stat. 126
56 [66]. July 19, 1815; proclaimed Dec. 26, 1815	Sioux of St. Peter's River	Portage des Sioux	William Clark; Ninian Edwards; Auguste Chouteau	Kappler, 114; 7 Stat. 127
57 [67]. July 19, 1815; proclaimed Dec. 26, 1815	Yankton Sioux	Portage des Sioux	William Clark; Ninian Edwards; Auguste Chouteau	Kappler, 115; 7 Stat. 128
58 [68]. July 20, 1815; proclaimed Dec. 26, 1815	Omaha	Portage des Sioux	William Clark; Ninian Edwards; Auguste Chouteau	Kappler, 115–16; 7 Stat. 129
59 [69]. Sept. 2, 1815; proclaimed Dec. 26, 1815	Kickapoo	Portage des Sioux	William Clark; Ninian Edwards; Auguste Chouteau	Kappler, 116–17; 7 Stat. 130

60	[70].	Sept. 8, 1815; proclaimed Dec. 26, 1815	Wyandot; Delaware; Seneca; Shawnee; Miami; Chippewa; Ottawa; Potawatomi	Spring Wells	William Henry Harrison; Duncan McArthur; John Graham	Kappler, 117–18; 7 Stat. 131–33
61	[71].	Sept. 12, 1815; proclaimed Dec. 26, 1815	Osage	Portage des Sioux	William Clark; Ninian Edwards; Auguste Chouteau	Kappler, 119–20; 7 Stat. 133–34
62	[72].	Sept. 13, 1815; proclaimed Dec. 26, 1815	Sac	Portage des Sioux	William Clark; Ninian Edwards; Auguste Chouteau	Kappler, 120–21; 7 Stat. 134–35
63	[73].	Sept. 14, 1815; proclaimed Dec. 26, 1815	Fox	Portage des Sioux	William Clark; Ninian Edwards; Auguste Chouteau	Kappler, 121–22; 7 Stat. 135–36
64	[74].	Sept. 16, 1815; proclaimed Dec. 26, 1815	Iowa	Portage des Sioux	William Clark; Ninian Edwards; Auguste Chouteau	Kappler, 122–23; 7 Stat. 136–37
65	[75].	Oct. 28, 1815; proclaimed Dec. 26, 1815	Kansa	St. Louis	Ninian Edwards; Auguste Chouteau	Kappler, 123–24; 7 Stat. 137–38
66	[76].	Mar. 22, 1816; proclaimed Apr. 8, 1816	Cherokee	Washington	George Graham	Kappler, 124–25; 7 Stat. 138–39

Ratified Indian Treaties

Number and Date	Tribes	Place	Commissioners	Citations
67 [77]. Mar. 22, 1816; proclaimed Apr. 8, 1816	Cherokee	Washington	George Graham	Kappler, 125–26; 7 Stat. 139–40
68 [78]. May 13, 1816; proclaimed Dec. 30, 1816	Sac of Rock River	St. Louis	William Clark; Ninian Edwards; Auguste Chouteau	Kappler, 126–28; 7 Stat. 141–42
69 [79]. June 1, 1816; proclaimed Dec. 30, 1816	Sioux	St. Louis	William Clark; Ninian Edwards; Auguste Chouteau	Kappler, 128–30; 7 Stat. 143–44
70 [80]. June 3, 1816; proclaimed Dec. 30, 1816	Winnebago	St. Louis	William Clark; Ninian Edwards; Auguste Chouteau	Kappler, 130–31; 7 Stat. 144–45
71 [81]. June 4, 1816; proclaimed Dec. 30, 1816	Wea; Kickapoo	Fort Harrison	Benjamin Parke	Kappler, 131–32; 7 Stat. 145–46
72 [82]. Aug. 24, 1816; proclaimed Dec. 30, 1816	Ottawa; Chippewa; Potawatomi	St. Louis	Ninian Edwards; William Clark; Auguste Chouteau	Kappler, 132–33; 7 Stat. 146–48
73 [83]. Sept. 14, 1816; proclaimed Dec. 30, 1816	Cherokee	Chickasaw council house	Andrew Jackson; David Meriwether; Jesse Franklin	Kappler, 133–34; 7 Stat. 148–49
74 [84]. Sept. 20, 1816; proclaimed Dec. 30, 1816	Chickasaw	Chickasaw council house	Andrew Jackson; David Meriwether; Jesse Franklin	Kappler, 135–37; 7 Stat. 150–52

		Date; proclaimed	Nation	Place	Commissioners	Citation
75	[85].	Oct. 24, 1816; proclaimed Dec. 30, 1816	Choctaw	Choctaw trading house	John Coffee; John Rhea; John McKee	Kappler, 137; 7 Stat. 152–53
76	[86].	Mar. 30, 1817; proclaimed Dec. 26, 1817	Menominee	St. Louis	William Clark; Ninian Edwards; Auguste Chouteau	Kappler, 138; 7 Stat. 153–54
77	[87].	June 24, 1817; proclaimed Dec. 26, 1817	Oto	St. Louis	William Clark; Auguste Chouteau	Kappler, 139; 7 Stat. 154–55
78	[88].	June 25, 1817; proclaimed Dec. 26, 1817	Ponca	St. Louis	William Clark; Auguste Chouteau	Kappler, 140; 7 Stat. 155–56
79	[89].	July 8, 1817; proclaimed Dec. 26, 1817	Cherokee	Cherokee Agency	Andrew Jackson; Joseph McMinn; David Meriwether	Kappler, 140–44; 7 Stat. 156–60
80	[90].	Sept. 29, 1817; proclaimed Jan. 4, 1819	Wyandot; Seneca; Delaware; Shawnee; Potawatomi; Ottawa; Chippewa	Rapids of the Miami	Lewis Cass; Duncan McArthur	Kappler, 145–55; 7 Stat. 160–70
81	[91].	Jan. 22, 1818; proclaimed Mar. 28, 1818	Creek	Creek Agency	David Brydie Mitchell	Kappler, 155–56; 7 Stat. 171–72

Ratified Indian Treaties

Number and Date	Tribes	Place	Commissioners	Citations
82 [92]. June 18, 1818; proclaimed Jan. 7, 1819	Grand Pawnee	St. Louis	William Clark; Auguste Chouteau	Kappler, 156–57; 7 Stat. 172–73
83 [93]. June 19, 1818; proclaimed Jan. 7, 1819	Noisy Pawnee	St. Louis	William Clark; Auguste Chouteau	Kappler, 157–58; 7 Stat. 173–74
84 [94]. June 20, 1818; proclaimed Jan. 7, 1819	Pawnee Republic	St. Louis	William Clark; Auguste Chouteau	Kappler, 158–59; 7 Stat. 174–75
85 [95]. June 22, 1818; proclaimed Jan. 5, 1819	Pawnee Marhar	St. Louis	William Clark; Auguste Chouteau	Kappler, 159; 7 Stat. 175–76
86 [96]. Aug. 24, 1818; proclaimed Jan. 5, 1819	Quapaw	St. Louis	William Clark; Auguste Chouteau	Kappler, 160–61; 7 Stat. 176–78
87 [97]. Sept. 17, 1818; proclaimed Jan. 4, 1819	Wyandot; Seneca; Shawnee; Ottawa	St. Mary's	Lewis Cass; Duncan McArthur	Kappler, 162–63; 7 Stat. 178–80
88 [98]. Sept. 20, 1818; proclaimed Jan. 7, 1819	Wyandot	St. Mary's	Lewis Cass	Kappler, 164; 7 Stat. 180–81

No.	Date	Tribe	Place	Commissioners	Reference
89 [99].	Sept. 25, 1818; proclaimed Jan. 5, 1819	Peoria; Kaskaskia; Michigamea; Cahokia; Tamaroa	Edwardsville	Ninian Edwards; Auguste Chouteau	Kappler, 165–66; 7 Stat. 181–83
90 [100].	Sept. 25, 1818; proclaimed Jan. 7, 1819	Osage	St. Louis	William Clark	Kappler, 167–68; 7 Stat. 183–84
91 [101]	Oct. 2, 1818; proclaimed Jan. 15, 1819	Potawatomi	St. Mary's	Jonathan Jennings; Lewis Cass; Benjamin Parke	Kappler, 168–69; 7 Stat. 185–86
92 [102].	Oct. 2, 1818; proclaimed Jan. 7, 1819	Wea	St. Mary's	Jonathan Jennings; Lewis Cass; Benjamin Parke	Kappler, 169–70; 7 Stat. 186–87
93 [103].	Oct. 3, 1818; proclaimed Jan. 15, 1819	Delaware	St. Mary's	Jonathan Jennings; Lewis Cass; Benjamin Parke	Kappler, 170–71; 7 Stat. 188–89
94 [104].	Oct. 6, 1818; proclaimed Jan. 15, 1819	Miami	St. Mary's	Jonathan Jennings; Lewis Cass; Benjamin Parke	Kappler, 171–74; 7 Stat. 189–92
95 [105].	Oct. 19, 1818; proclaimed Jan. 15, 1819	Chickasaw	Old Town	Isaac Shelby; Andrew Jackson	Kappler, 174–77; 7 Stat. 192–95
96 [106].	Feb. 27, 1819; proclaimed Mar. 10, 1819	Cherokee	Washington	John C. Calhoun	Kappler, 177–81; 7 Stat. 195–200

Ratified Indian Treaties

Number and Date	Tribes	Place	Commissioners	Citations
97 [107]. July 30, 1819; proclaimed Jan. 13, 1821	Kickapoo	Edwardsville	Auguste Chouteau; Benjamin Stephenson	Kappler, 182–83; 7 Stat. 200–202
98 [108]. Aug. 30, 1819; proclaimed May 10, 1820	Kickapoo of the Vermilion	Fort Harrison	Benjamin Parke	Kappler, 184; 7 Stat. 202–3
99 [109]. Sept. 24, 1819; proclaimed Mar. 25, 1820	Chippewa	Saginaw	Lewis Cass	Kappler, 185–87; 7 Stat. 203–6
100 [110]. June 16, 1820; proclaimed Mar. 2, 1821	Chippewa	Sault Ste. Marie	Lewis Cass	Kappler, 187–88; 7 Stat. 206–7
101 [111]. July 6, 1820; proclaimed Mar. 8, 1821	Ottawa; Chippewa	L'Arbre Croche and Michilimackinac	Lewis Cass	Kappler, 188–89; 7 Stat. 207
102 [112]. July 19, 1820; proclaimed Jan. 13, 1821	Kickapoo	St. Louis	Auguste Chouteau; Benjamin Stephenson	Kappler, 189–90; 7 Stat. 208–9
103 [113]. Aug. 11, 1820; proclaimed Jan. 8, 1821	Wea	Vincennes	Benjamin Parke	Kappler, 190; 7 Stat. 209
104 [114]. Sept. 5, 1820; proclaimed Jan. 8, 1821	Kickapoo of the Vermilion	Vincennes	Benjamin Parke	Kappler, 191; 7 Stat. 210

No.	Date	Tribe	Place	Commissioners	Citation
105 [115].	Oct. 18, 1820; proclaimed Jan. 8, 1821	Choctaw	Doak's Stand	Andrew Jackson; Thomas Hinds	Kappler, 191–95; 7 Stat. 210–14
106 [116].	Jan. 8, 1821; proclaimed Mar. 2, 1821	Creek	Indian Springs	Daniel M. Forney; David Meriwether	Kappler, 195–97; 7 Stat. 215–16
	Articles of agreement with Georgia: Jan. 8, 1821				Kappler, 197–98; 7 Stat. 217–18
107 [117].	Aug. 29, 1821; proclaimed Mar. 25, 1822	Ottawa; Chippewa; Potawatomi	Chicago	Lewis Cass; Solomon Sibley	Kappler, 198–201; 7 Stat. 218–21
108 [118].	Aug. 31, 1822; proclaimed Feb. 13, 1823	Osage	Marais des Cygnes Factory	Richard Graham	Kappler, 201–2; 7 Stat. 222
109 [119].	Sept. 3, 1822; proclaimed Feb. 13, 1823	Sac and Fox	Fort Armstrong	Thomas Forsyth	Kappler, 202–3; 7 Stat. 223
110 [120].	Sept. 18, 1823; proclaimed Jan. 2, 1824	Florida tribes	Moultrie Creek	William P. Duval; James Gadsden; Bernard Segui	Kappler, 203–7; 7 Stat. 224–28
111 [121].	Aug. 4, 1824; proclaimed Jan. 18, 1825	Sac and Fox	Washington	William Clark	Kappler, 207–8; 7 Stat. 229–30

Ratified Indian Treaties

Number and Date	Tribes	Place	Commissioners	Citations
112 [122]. Aug. 4, 1824; proclaimed Jan. 18, 1825	Iowa	Washington	William Clark	Kappler, 208–9; 7 Stat. 231–32
113 [123]. Nov. 15, 1824; proclaimed Feb. 19, 1825	Quapaw	Harrington's	Robert Crittenden	Kappler, 210–11; 7 Stat. 232–34
114 [124]. Jan. 20, 1825; proclaimed Feb. 19, 1825	Choctaw	Washington	John C. Calhoun	Kappler, 211–14; 7 Stat. 234–36
115 [125]. Feb. 12, 1825; proclaimed Mar. 7, 1825	Creek	Indian Springs	Duncan G. Campbell; James Meriwether	Kappler, 214–17; 7 Stat. 237–40
116 [126]. June 2, 1825; proclaimed Dec. 30, 1825	Osage	St. Louis	William Clark	Kappler, 217–21; 7 Stat. 240–44
117 [127]. June 3, 1825; proclaimed Dec. 30, 1825	Kansa	St. Louis	William Clark	Kappler, 222–25; 7 Stat. 244–47
118 [128]. June 9, 1825; proclaimed Feb. 6, 1826	Ponca	Ponca Village	Henry Atkinson; Benjamin O'Fallon	Kappler, 225–27; 7 Stat. 247–49
119 [129]. June 22, 1825; proclaimed Feb. 6, 1826	Sioux: Teton, Yankton, Yanktonai	Fort Lookout	Henry Atkinson; Benjamin O'Fallon	Kappler, 227–30; 7 Stat. 250–52

No.	Date; proclaimed	Tribe	Location	Commissioners	Citation
120 [130].	July 5, 1825; proclaimed Feb. 6, 1826	Sioux: Sioune, Oglala	Teton River	Henry Atkinson; Benjamin O'Fallon	Kappler, 230–32; 7 Stat. 252–54
121 [131].	July 6, 1825; proclaimed Feb. 6, 1826	Cheyenne	Teton River	Henry Atkinson; Benjamin O'Fallon	Kappler, 232–34; 7 Stat. 255–57
122 [132].	July 16, 1825; proclaimed Feb. 6, 1826	Hunkpapa Sioux	Arikara Village	Henry Atkinson; Benjamin O'Fallon	Kappler, 235–36; 7 Stat. 257–59
123 [133].	July 18, 1825; proclaimed Feb. 6, 1826	Arikara	Arikara Village	Henry Atkinson; Benjamin O'Fallon	Kappler, 237–39; 7 Stat. 259–61
124 [134].	July 30, 1825; proclaimed Feb. 6, 1826	Minitari	Lower Mandan Village	Henry Atkinson; Benjamin O'Fallon	Kappler, 239–41; 7 Stat. 261–63
125 [135].	July 30, 1825; proclaimed Feb. 6, 1826	Mandan	Mandan Village	Henry Atkinson; Benjamin O'Fallon	Kappler, 242–44; 7 Stat. 264–66
126 [136].	Aug. 4, 1825; proclaimed Feb. 6, 1826	Crow	Mandan Village	Henry Atkinson; Benjamin O'Fallon	Kappler, 244–46; 7 Stat. 266–68
127 [137].	Aug. 10, 1825; proclaimed May 3, 1826	Osage	Council Grove	Benjamin H. Reeves; George C. Sibley; Thomas Mather	Kappler, 246–48; 7 Stat. 268–70

Ratified Indian Treaties

Number and Date	Tribes	Place	Commissioners	Citations
128 [138]. Aug. 16, 1825; proclaimed May 3, 1826	Kansa	Sora Kansas Creek	Benjamin H. Reeves; George C. Sibley; Thomas Mather	Kappler, 248–50; 7 Stat. 270–72
129 [139]. Aug. 19, 1825; proclaimed Feb. 6, 1826	Sioux; Chippewa; Sac and Fox; Menominee; Iowa; Winnebago; Ottawa; Potawatomi	Prairie du Chien	William Clark; Lewis Cass	Kappler, 250–55; 7 Stat. 272–77
130 [140]. Sept. 26, 1825; proclaimed Feb. 6, 1826	Oto and Missouri	Fort Atkinson	Henry Atkinson; Benjamin O'Fallon	Kappler, 256–58; 7 Stat. 277–79
131 [141]. Sept. 30. 1825; proclaimed Feb. 6, 1826	Pawnee	Fort Atkinson	Henry Atkinson; Benjamin O'Fallon	Kappler, 258–60; 7 Stat. 279–81
132 [142]. Oct. 6, 1825; proclaimed Feb. 6, 1826	Maha (Omaha)	Fort Atkinson	Henry Atkinson; Benjamin O'Fallon	Kappler, 260–62; 7 Stat. 282–84
133 [143]. Nov. 7, 1825; proclaimed Dec. 30, 1825	Shawnee	St. Louis	William Clark	Kappler, 262–64; 7 Stat. 284–86
134 [144]. Jan. 24, 1826; proclaimed Apr. 22, 1826	Creek	Washington	James Barbour	Kappler, 264–68; 7 Stat. 286–90

No.	Date	Tribe	Where concluded	Commissioners	Citation
135 [145].	Aug. 5, 1826; proclaimed Feb. 7, 1827	Chippewa	Fond du Lac	Lewis Cass; Thomas L. McKenney	Kappler, 268–73; 7 Stat. 290–95
136 [146].	Oct. 16, 1826; proclaimed Feb. 7, 1827	Potawatomi	Wabash River	Lewis Cass; James Brown Ray; John Tipton	Kappler, 273–77; 7 Stat. 295–99
137 [147].	Oct. 23, 1826; proclaimed Jan. 24, 1827	Miami	Wabash River	Lewis Cass; James Brown Ray; John Tipton	Kappler, 278–81; 7 Stat. 300–303
138 [148].	Aug. 11, 1827; proclaimed Feb. 23, 1829	Chippewa; Menominee; Winnebago	Butte des Morts	Lewis Cass; Thomas L. McKenney	Kappler, 281–83; 7 Stat. 303–5
139 [149].	Sept. 19, 1827; proclaimed Feb. 23, 1829	Potawatomi	St. Joseph	Lewis Cass	Kappler, 283–84; 7 Stat. 305–6
140 [150].	Nov. 15, 1827; proclaimed Mar. 4, 1828	Creek	Creek Agency	Thomas L. McKenney; John Crowell	Kappler, 284–86; 7 Stat. 307–9
141 [151].	Feb. 11, 1828; proclaimed May 7, 1828	Miami (Eel River)	Wyandot Village	John Tipton	Kappler, 286–87; 7 Stat. 309–10
142 [152].	May 6, 1828; proclaimed May 28, 1828	Western Cherokee	Washington	James Barbour	Kappler, 288–92; 7 Stat. 311–15

Ratified Indian Treaties

Number and Date	Tribes	Place	Commissioners	Citations
143 [153]. Aug. 25, 1828; proclaimed Jan. 7, 1829	Winnebago; United tribes: Potawatomi, Chippewa, Ottawa	Green Bay	Lewis Cass; Pierre Menard	Kappler, 292–94; 7 Stat. 315–17
144 [154]. Sept. 20, 1828; proclaimed Jan. 7, 1829	Potawatomi	St. Joseph River	Lewis Cass; Pierre Menard	Kappler, 294–97; 7 Stat. 317–20
145 [155]. July 29, 1829; proclaimed Jan. 2, 1830	United tribes: Potawatomi, Ottawa, Chippewa	Prairie du Chien	John McNeil; Pierre Menard; Caleb Atwater	Kappler, 297–300; 7 Stat. 320–22
146 [156]. Aug. 1, 1829; proclaimed Jan. 2, 1830	Winnebago	Prairie du Chien	John McNeil; Pierre Menard; Caleb Atwater	Kappler, 300–303; 7 Stat. 323–25
147 [157]. Aug. 3, 1829; proclaimed Jan. 2, 1830	Delaware	Little Sandusky	John McElvain	Kappler, 303–4; 7 Stat. 326
148 [158]. Sept. 24, 1829; proclaimed Mar. 24, 1831	Delaware	James Fork of White River	George Vashon	Kappler, 304–5; 7 Stat. 327–28

No. & Date	Tribe	Place	Commissioners	Citation
149 [159]. July 15, 1830; proclaimed Feb. 24, 1831 / Assent to treaty by Yankton and Santee Sioux at St. Louis, Oct. 13, 1830	Sac and Fox; Sioux: Mdewakanton, Wahpeton, Wahpekute, Sisseton; Omaha; Iowa; Oto and Missouri	Prairie du Chien	William Clark; Willoughby Morgan	Kappler, 305–10; 7 Stat. 328–32
150 [160]. Sept. 27, 1830; proclaimed Feb. 24, 1831	Choctaw	Dancing Rabbit Creek	John H. Eaton; John Coffee	Kappler, 310–19; 7 Stat. 333–42
151 [161]. Feb. 8, 1831; proclaimed July 9, 1832 / Supplementary articles, Feb. 17, 1831	Menominee	Washington	John H. Eaton; Samuel C. Stambaugh	Kappler, 319–23; 7 Stat. 342–46 / Kappler, 323–25; 7 Stat. 346–48
152 [162]. Feb. 28, 1831; proclaimed Mar. 24, 1831	Seneca	Washington	James B. Gardiner	Kappler, 325–27; 7 Stat. 348–50
153 [163]. July 20, 1831; proclaimed Apr. 6, 1832	Seneca; Shawnee	Lewistown	James B. Gardiner; John McElvain	Kappler, 327–31; 7 Stat. 351–54
154 [164]. Aug. 8, 1831; proclaimed Apr. 6, 1832	Shawnee	Wapakoneta	James B. Gardiner; John McElvain	Kappler, 331–34; 7 Stat. 355–58

Ratified Indian Treaties

Number and Date	Tribes	Place	Commissioners	Citations
155 [165]. Aug. 30, 1831; proclaimed Apr. 6, 1832	Ottawa	Miami Bay	James B. Gardiner	Kappler, 335–39; 7 Stat. 359–64
156 [166]. Jan. 19, 1832; proclaimed Apr. 6, 1832	Wyandot	McCutcheonville	James B. Gardiner	Kappler, 339–41; 7 Stat. 364–65
157 [167]. Mar. 24, 1832; proclaimed Apr. 4, 1832	Creek	Washington	Lewis Cass	Kappler, 341–43; 7 Stat. 366–68
158 [168]. May 9, 1832; proclaimed Apr. 12, 1834	Seminole	Payne's Landing	James Gadsden	Kappler, 344–45; 7 Stat. 368–70
159 [169]. Sept. 15, 1832; proclaimed Feb. 13, 1833	Winnebago	Fort Armstrong	Winfield Scott; John Reynolds	Kappler, 345–48; 7 Stat. 370–73
160 [170]. Sept. 21, 1832; proclaimed Feb. 13, 1833	Sac and Fox	Fort Armstrong	Winfield Scott; John Reynolds	Kappler, 349–51; 7 Stat. 374–76
161 [171]. Oct. 11, 1832; proclaimed Feb. 13, 1833	Apalachicola	Tallahassee	James Gadsden	Kappler, 352; 7 Stat. 377–78
162 [172]. Oct. 20, 1832; proclaimed Jan. 21, 1833	Potawatomi	Camp Tippecanoe	Jonathan Jennings; John W. Davis; Marks Crume	Kappler, 353–56; 7 Stat. 378–81

No.	Date	Tribe	Place	Commissioners	Reference
163 [173].	Oct. 20, 1832; proclaimed Mar. 1, 1833	Chickasaw	Pontotoc Creek	John Coffee	Kappler, 356–62; 7 Stat. 381–87
	Supplementary articles, Oct. 22, 1832				Kappler, 362–64; 7 Stat. 388–91
164 [174].	Oct. 24, 1832; proclaimed Feb. 13, 1833	Kickapoo	Castor Hill	William Clark; Frank J. Allen; Nathan Kouns	Kappler, 365–67; 7 Stat. 391–93
	Supplementary article at Fort Leavenworth, Nov. 26, 1832				Kappler, 367; 7 Stat. 393–94
165 [175].	Oct. 26, 1832; proclaimed Jan. 21, 1833	Potawatomi	Tippecanoe River	Jonathan Jennings; John W. Davis; Marks Crume	Kappler, 367–70; 7 Stat. 394–97
166 [176].	Oct. 26, 1832; proclaimed Feb. 12, 1833	Shawnee; Delaware	Castor Hill	William Clark; Frank J. Allen; Nathan Kouns	Kappler, 370–72; 7 Stat. 397–99
167 [177].	Oct. 27, 1832; proclaimed Jan. 21, 1833	Potawatomi	Tippecanoe River	Jonathan Jennings; John W. Davis; Marks Crume	Kappler, 372–75; 7 Stat. 399–403
168 [178].	Oct. 27, 1832; proclaimed Feb. 12, 1833	Kaskaskia; Peoria; Michigamea; Cahokia; Tamaroa	Castor Hill	William Clark; Frank J. Allen; Nathan Kouns	Kappler, 376–77; 7 Stat. 403–5

Ratified Indian Treaties

Number and Date	Tribes	Place	Commissioners	Citations
169 [179]. Oct. 27, 1832; proclaimed Mar. 13, 1833	Menominee	Green Bay	George B. Porter	Kappler, 377–81; 7 Stat. 405–8
Appendix with New York Indians, Oct. 27, 1832				Kappler, 381–82; 7 Stat. 409–10
170 [180]. Oct. 29, 1832; proclaimed Feb. 12, 1833	Piankashaw; Wea	Castor Hill	William Clark; Frank J. Allen; Nathan Kouns	Kappler, 382–83; 7 Stat. 410–11
171 [181]. Dec. 29, 1832; proclaimed Mar. 22, 1833	Seneca; Shawnee	Seneca Agency	Henry L. Ellsworth; John F. Schermerhorn	Kappler, 383–85; 7 Stat. 411–13
172 [182]. Feb. 14, 1833; proclaimed Apr. 12, 1834	Western Cherokee	Fort Gibson	Montfort Stokes; Henry L. Ellsworth; John F. Schermerhorn	Kappler, 385–88; 7 Stat. 414–16
173 [183]. Feb. 14, 1833; proclaimed Apr. 12, 1834	Creek	Fort Gibson	Montfort Stokes; Henry L. Ellsworth; John F. Schermerhorn	Kappler, 388–91; 7 Stat. 417–20
174 [184]. Feb. 18, 1833; proclaimed Mar. 22, 1833	Ottawa	Maumee	George B. Porter	Kappler, 392–94; 7 Stat. 420–23
175 [185]. Mar. 28, 1833; proclaimed Apr. 12, 1834	Seminole	Fort Gibson	Montfort Stokes; Henry L. Ellsworth; John F. Schermerhorn	Kappler, 394–95; 7 Stat. 423–24

No.	Date	Tribe	Place	Commissioner(s)	Citation
176 [186].	May 13, 1833; proclaimed Apr. 12, 1834	Quapaw	New Gascony	John F. Schermerhorn	Kappler, 395–97; 7 Stat. 424–26
177 [187].	June 18, 1833; proclaimed Apr. 12, 1834	Apalachicola	Pope's	James Gadsden	Kappler, 398–400; 7 Stat. 427–29
178 [188].	Sept. 21, 1833; proclaimed Apr. 12, 1834	Oto and Missouri	Oto Village	Henry L. Ellsworth	Kappler, 400–401; 7 Stat. 429–31
179 [189].	Sept. 26, 1833; proclaimed Feb. 21, 1835	United tribes: Potawatomi, Ottawa, Chippewa	Chicago	George B. Porter; Thomas J. V. Owen; William Weatherford	Kappler, 402–10; 7 Stat. 431–41
	Supplementary articles, Sept. 27, 1833				Kappler, 410–15; 7 Stat. 442–48
180 [190].	Oct. 9, 1833; proclaimed Apr. 12, 1834	Pawnee	Grand Pawnee Village	Henry L. Ellsworth	Kappler, 416–18; 7 Stat. 448–50
181 [191].	May 24, 1834; proclaimed July 1, 1834	Chickasaw	Washington	John H. Eaton	Kappler, 418–25; 7 Stat. 450–57
182 [192].	Oct. 23, 1834; proclaimed Dec. 22, 1837	Miami	Forks of the Wabash	William Marshall	Kappler, 425–28; 7 Stat. 458–66
183 [193].	Dec. 4, 1834; proclaimed Mar. 16, 1835	Potawatomi	Lake Maxinkukee	William Marshall	Kappler, 428–29; 7 Stat. 467

Ratified Indian Treaties

Number and Date	Tribes	Place	Commissioners	Citations
184 [194]. Dec. 10, 1834; proclaimed Mar. 16, 1835	Potawatomi	Tippecanoe River	William Marshall	Kappler, 429; 7 Stat. 467–68
185 [195]. Dec. 16, 1834; proclaimed Mar. 16, 1835	Potawatomi	Potawatomi Mills	William Marshall	Kappler, 430; 7 Stat. 468–69
186 [196]. Dec. 17, 1834; proclaimed Mar. 16, 1835	Potawatomi	Indian Agency, Logansport	William Marshall	Kappler, 431; 7 Stat. 469–70
187 [197]. July 1, 1835; proclaimed Feb. 2, 1836	Caddo	Agency House, Caddo Nation	Jehiel Brooks	Kappler, 432–34; 7 Stat. 470–73
188 [198]. Aug. 24, 1835; proclaimed May 19, 1836	Comanche and Wichita; Cherokee, Muskogee, Choctaw, Osage, Seneca, and Quapaw	Camp Holmes	Montfort Stokes; Matthew Arbuckle	Kappler, 435–39; 7 Stat. 474–77
189 [199]. Dec. 29, 1835; proclaimed May 23, 1836 Supplementary articles, Mar. 1, 1836	Cherokee	New Echota	William Carroll; John F. Schermerhorn	Kappler, 439–48; 7 Stat. 478–88 Kappler, 448–49; 7 Stat. 488–89
190 [200]. Mar. 26, 1836; proclaimed June 4, 1836	Potawatomi	Turkey Creek Prairie	Abel C. Pepper	Kappler, 450; 7 Stat. 490–91

No.	Date; proclaimed	Tribe	Place	Commissioner	Reference
191 [201].	Mar. 28, 1836; proclaimed May 27, 1836 Supplementary article, Mar. 31, 1836	Ottawa; Chippewa	Washington	Henry R. Schoolcraft	Kappler, 450–56; 7 Stat. 491–96 Kappler, 456; 7 Stat. 496–97
192 [202].	Mar. 29, 1836; proclaimed June 4, 1836	Potawatomi	Tippecanoe River	Abel C. Pepper	Kappler, 457; 7 Stat. 498
193 [203].	Apr. 11, 1836; proclaimed May 25, 1836	Potawatomi	Tippecanoe River	Abel C. Pepper	Kappler, 457–58; 7 Stat. 499
194 [204].	Apr. 22, 1836; proclaimed May 25, 1836	Potawatomi	Indian Agency	Abel C. Pepper	Kappler, 458–59; 7 Stat. 500
195 [205].	Apr. 22, 1836; proclaimed May 25, 1836	Potawatomi	Indian Agency	Abel C. Pepper	Kappler, 459; 7 Stat. 501
196 [206].	Apr. 23, 1836; proclaimed May 16, 1836	Wyandot	Washington	John A. Bryan	Kappler, 460–61; 7 Stat. 502–3
197 [207].	May 9, 1836; proclaimed May 25, 1836	Chippewa	Washington	Henry R. Schoolcraft	Kappler, 461–62; 7 Stat. 503–4
198 [208].	Aug. 5, 1836; proclaimed Feb. 18, 1837	Potawatomi	Yellow River	Abel C. Pepper	Kappler, 462–63; 7 Stat. 505–6

Ratified Indian Treaties

Number and Date	Tribes	Place	Commissioners	Citations
199 [209]. Sept. 3, 1836; proclaimed Feb. 15, 1837	Menominee	Cedar Point	Henry Dodge	Kappler, 463–66; 7 Stat. 506–9
200 [210]. Sept. 10 1836; proclaimed Feb. 15, 1837	Sioux (Wabasha Band)	—	Zachary Taylor	Kappler, 466–67; 7 Stat. 510–11
201 [211]. Sept. 17, 1836; proclaimed Feb. 15, 1837	Iowa; Sac and Fox of the Missouri	Fort Leavenworth	William Clark	Kappler, 468–70; 7 Stat. 511–13
202 [212]. Sept. 20, 1836; proclaimed Feb. 18, 1837	Potawatomi	Chippewanaung	Abel C. Pepper	Kappler, 470; 7 Stat. 513–14
203 [213]. Sept. 22, 1836; proclaimed Feb. 16, 1837	Potawatomi	Chippewanaung	Abel C. Pepper	Kappler, 471; 7 Stat. 514
204 [214]. Sept. 23, 1836; proclaimed Feb. 18, 1837	Potawatomi	Chippewanaung	Abel C. Pepper	Kappler, 471–72; 7 Stat. 515–16
205 [215]. Sept. 27, 1836; proclaimed Feb. 15, 1837	Sac and Fox	opposite Rock Island	Henry Dodge	Kappler, 473; 7 Stat. 516–17
206 [216]. Sept. 28, 1836; proclaimed Feb. 27, 1837	Sac and Fox	opposite Rock Island	Henry Dodge	Kappler, 474–75; 7 Stat. 517–19
Alternate version proclaimed Dec. 13, 1837				Kappler, 476–78; 7 Stat. 520–23

No.	Date	Tribe	Location	Signers/Witnesses	Reference
207 [217].	Oct. 15, 1836; proclaimed Feb. 15, 1837	Oto; Missouri; Omaha; Sioux: Yankton, Santee	Bellevue	John Dougherty; Joshua Pilcher	Kappler, 479–81; 7 Stat. 524–26
208 [218].	Nov. 30, 1836; proclaimed Feb. 18, 1837	Sioux: Wahpekute, Sisseton, Mdewakanton	St. Peter's	Lawrence Taliaferro	Kappler, 481–82; 7 Stat. 527–28
209 [219].	Jan. 14, 1837; proclaimed July 2, 1838	Chippewa (Saginaw Band)	Detroit	Henry R. Schoolcraft	Kappler, 482–86; 7 Stat. 528–32
210 [220].	Jan. 17, 1837; proclaimed Mar. 24, 1837	Choctaw; Chickasaw	Doaksville	William Armstrong and Henry R. Carter (witnesses)	Kappler, 486–88; 11 Stat. 573–75
211 [221].	Feb. 11, 1837; proclaimed Feb. 18, 1837	Potawatomi	Washington	John T. Douglass	Kappler, 488–89; 7 Stat. 532–33
212 [222].	May 26, 1837; proclaimed Feb. 21, 1838	Kiowa; Kataka; Tawakoni	Fort Gibson	Montfort Stokes; A. P. Chouteau	Kappler, 489–91; 7 Stat. 533–36
213 [223].	July 29, 1837; proclaimed June 15, 1838	Chippewa	St. Peter's	Henry Dodge	Kappler, 491–93; 7 Stat. 536–38

Ratified Indian Treaties

Number and Date	Tribes	Place	Commissioners	Citations
214 [224]. Sept. 29, 1837; proclaimed June 15, 1838	Sioux	Washington	Joel R. Poinsett	Kappler, 493–94; 7 Stat. 538–40
215 [225]. Oct. 21, 1837; proclaimed Feb. 21, 1838	Sac and Fox	Washington	Carey A. Harris	Kappler, 495–96; 7 Stat. 540–42
216 [226]. Oct. 21, 1837; proclaimed Feb. 21, 1838	Yankton Sioux	Washington	Carey A. Harris	Kappler, 496–97; 7 Stat. 542–43
217 [227]. Oct. 21, 1837; proclaimed Feb. 21, 1838	Sac and Fox of the Missouri	Washington	Carey A. Harris	Kappler, 497–98; 7 Stat. 543–44
218 [228]. Nov. 1, 1837; proclaimed June 15, 1838	Winnebago	Washington	Carey A. Harris	Kappler, 498–500; 7 Stat. 544–46
219 [229]. Nov. 23, 1837; proclaimed Feb. 21, 1838	Iowa	St. Louis	Joshua Pilcher	Kappler, 500–501; 7 Stat. 547
220 [see 219]. Dec. 20, 1837; proclaimed July 2, 1838	Chippewa (Saginaw Band)	Flint River	Henry R. Schoolcraft	Kappler, 501–2; 7 Stat. 547–49

No. / Date	Tribe	Location	Commissioner	Citation
221 [230]. Jan. 15, 1838; proclaimed Apr. 4, 1840	New York Indians	Buffalo Creek	Ransom H. Gillet	Kappler, 502–12; 7 Stat. 550–61
Supplementary article with St. Regis Indians, Feb. 13, 1838				Kappler, 512–16; 7 Stat. 561–64
222 [231]. Jan. 23, 1838; proclaimed July 2, 1838	Chippewa (Saginaw bands)	Saginaw	Henry R. Schoolcraft	Kappler, 516–17; 7 Stat. 565–66
223 [232]. Feb. 3, 1838; proclaimed May 17, 1838	Oneida (First Christian, Orchard)	Washington	Carey A. Harris	Kappler, 517–18; 7 Stat. 566–67
224 [233]. Oct. 19, 1838; proclaimed Mar 2, 1839	Iowa	Great Nemaha Subagency	John Dougherty	Kappler, 518–19; 7 Stat. 568–69
225 [234]. Nov. 6, 1838; proclaimed Feb. 8, 1839	Miami	Forks of the Wabash	Abel C. Pepper	Kappler, 519–24; 7 Stat. 569–74
226 [235]. Nov. 23, 1838; proclaimed Mar. 2, 1839	Creek	Fort Gibson	William Armstrong; Matthew Arbuckle	Kappler, 524–25; 7 Stat. 574–75
227 [236]. Jan. 11, 1839; proclaimed Mar. 2, 1839	Osage	Fort Gibson	Matthew Arbuckle	Kappler, 525–27; 7 Stat. 576–78

Ratified Indian Treaties

Number and Date	Tribes	Place	Commissioners	Citations
228 [237]. Feb. 7, 1839; proclaimed Mar. 2, 1839	Chippewa (Saginaw bands)	Lower Saginaw	John Hulbert	Kappler, 528–29; 7 Stat. 578–79
229 [238]. Sept. 3, 1839; proclaimed May 16, 1840	Stockbridge; Munsee	Stockbridge	Albert Gallup	Kappler, 529–31; 7 Stat. 580–82; 11 Stat. 577–79
230 [239]. Nov. 28, 1840; proclaimed June 7, 1841	Miami	Forks of the Wabash	Samuel Milroy; Allen Hamilton	Kappler, 531–34; 7 Stat. 582–86
231 [240]. Mar. 17, 1842; proclaimed Oct. 5, 1842	Wyandot	Upper Sandusky	John Johnston	Kappler, 534–37; 11 Stat. 581–85
232 [241]. May 20, 1842; proclaimed Aug. 26, 1842	Seneca	Buffalo Creek	Ambrose Spencer	Kappler, 537–42; 7 Stat. 586–91
233 [242]. Oct. 4, 1842; proclaimed Mar. 23, 1843	Chippewa of Mississippi and Lake Superior	La Pointe	Robert Stuart	Kappler, 542–45; 7 Stat. 591–95
234 [243]. Oct. 11, 1842; proclaimed Mar. 23, 1843	Sac and Fox	Sac and Fox Agency	John Chambers	Kappler, 546–49; 7 Stat. 596–600
235 [244]. Jan. 4, 1845; proclaimed July 18, 1845	Creek; Seminole	Creek Agency	William Armstrong; P. M. Butler; James Logan; Thomas L. Judge	Kappler, 550–52; 9 Stat. 821–25

No. / Date	Tribe	Commissioners	Place	Citation
236 [245]. Jan. 14, 1846; proclaimed Apr. 15, 1846	Kansa	Thomas H. Harvey; Richard W. Cummins	Methodist Mission	Kappler, 552–54; 9 Stat. 842–44
237 [246]. May 15, 1846; proclaimed Mar. 8, 1847	Comanche; Ioni (Hainai); Anadarko; Caddo; Lipan; Longwha (Tonkawa); Kichai; Tawakoni; Wichita; Waco	P. M. Butler; M. G. Lewis	Council Springs	Kappler, 554–57; 9 Stat. 844–48
238 [247]. June 5 and 17, 1846; proclaimed July 23, 1846	Potawatomi; Chippewa; Ottawa	T. P. Andrews; Thomas H. Harvey; Gideon C. Matlock	Council Bluffs and Potawatomi Creek	Kappler, 557–60; 9 Stat. 853–56
239 [248]. Aug. 6, 1846; proclaimed Aug. 17, 1846	Cherokee	Edmund Burke; William Armstrong; Albion K. Parris	Washington	Kappler, 561–65; 9 Stat. 871–77
240 [249]. Oct. 13, 1846; proclaimed Feb. 4, 1847	Winnebago	Albion K. Parris; John J. Abert; T. P. Andrews	Washington	Kappler, 565–67; 9 Stat. 878–80
241 [250]. Aug. 2, 1847; proclaimed Apr. 7, 1848	Chippewa of Mississippi and Lake Superior	Isaac A. Verplank; Henry M. Rice	Fond du Lac	Kappler, 567–69; 9 Stat. 904–7

Ratified Indian Treaties

Number and Date	Tribes	Place	Commissioners	Citations
242 [251]. Aug. 21, 1847; proclaimed Apr. 7, 1848	Chippewa (Pillager Band)	Leech Lake	Isaac A. Verplank; Henry M. Rice	Kappler, 569–70; 9 Stat. 908–9
243 [252]. Aug. 6, 1848; proclaimed Jan. 8, 1849	Pawnee: Grand, Loup, Republican, Tappage	Fort Childs	Ludwell E. Powell	Kappler, 571–72; 9 Stat. 949–51
244 [253]. Oct. 18, 1848; proclaimed Jan. 23, 1849	Menominee	Lake Powawhaykonnay	William Medill	Kappler, 572–74; 9 Stat. 952–54
245 [254]. Nov. 24, 1848; proclaimed Mar. 2, 1849	Stockbridge	Stockbridge	Morgan L. Martin; Albert G. Ellis	Kappler, 574–82; 9 Stat. 955–64
246 [255]. Sept. 9, 1849; proclaimed Sept. 24, 1850	Navajo	Canyon de Chelly	John M. Washington; James S. Calhoun	Kappler, 583–85; 9 Stat. 974–76
247 [256]. Dec. 30, 1849; proclaimed Sept. 24, 1850	Ute	Abiquiu	James S. Calhoun	Kappler, 585–87; 9 Stat. 984–86
248 [257]. Apr. 1, 1850; proclaimed Sept. 30, 1850	Wyandot	Washington	Ardavan S. Loughery	Kappler, 587–88; 9 Stat. 987–94
249 [258]. July 23, 1851; proclaimed Feb. 24, 1853	Sioux: Sisseton, Wahpeton	Traverse des Sioux	Luke Lea; Alexander Ramsey	Kappler, 588–90; 10 Stat. 949–53

No.	Date	Tribe	Place	Commissioners	Citation
250 [259].	Aug. 5, 1851; proclaimed Feb. 24, 1853	Sioux: Mdewakanton, Wahpekute	Mendota	Luke Lea; Alexander Ramsey	Kappler, 591–93; 10 Stat. 954–59
251 [—].	Sept. 17, 1851	Sioux; Cheyenne; Arapaho; Crow; Assiniboin; Gros Ventre; Mandan; Arikara	Fort Laramie	D. D. Mitchell; Thomas Fitzpatrick	Kappler, 594–96; 11 Stat. 749n.

Note: The treaty was not perfected, but subsequent agreements recognized the treaty as in force. It is not in the Ratified Indian Treaties file (RG 11) nor in *Statutes at Large.*

No.	Date	Tribe	Place	Commissioners	Citation
252 [260].	June 22, 1852; proclaimed Feb. 24, 1853	Chickasaw	Washington	Kenton Harper	Kappler, 596–98; 10 Stat. 974–77
253 [261].	July 1, 1852; proclaimed Mar. 25, 1853	Apache	Santa Fe	E. V. Sumner; John Greiner	Kappler, 598–600; 10 Stat. 974–77
254 [262].	July 27, 1853; proclaimed Feb. 12, 1854	Comanche; Kiowa; Apache	Fort Atkinson	Thomas Fitzpatrick	Kappler, 600–602; 10 Stat. 1013–17
255 [263].	Sept. 10, 1853; proclaimed Feb. 5, 1855	Rogue River	Table Rock	Joel Palmer; Samuel H. Culver	Kappler, 603–5; 10 Stat. 1018–21

Ratified Indian Treaties

Number and Date	Tribes	Place	Commissioners	Citations
256 [264]. Sept. 19, 1853; proclaimed Feb. 5, 1855	Umpqua (Cow Creek Band)	Cow Creek	Joel Palmer	Kappler, 606–7; 10 Stat. 1027–30
257 [265]. Mar. 15, 1854; proclaimed June 21, 1854	Oto and Missouri	Washington	George W. Manypenny	Kappler, 608–11; 10 Stat. 1038–42
258 [266]. Mar. 16, 1854; proclaimed June 21, 1854	Omaha	Washington	George W. Manypenny	Kappler, 611–14; 10 Stat. 1043–47
259 [267]. May 6, 1854; proclaimed July 17, 1854	Delaware	Washington	George W. Manypenny	Kappler, 614–18; 10 Stat. 1048–52
260 [268]. May 10, 1854; proclaimed Nov. 2, 1854	Shawnee	Washington	George W. Manypenny	Kappler, 618–26; 10 Stat. 1053–63
261 [269]. May 12, 1854; proclaimed Aug. 2, 1854	Menominee	Falls of Wolf River	Francis Huebschmann	Kappler, 626–27; 10 Stat. 1064–68
262 [270]. May 17, 1854; proclaimed July 17, 1854	Iowa	Washington	George W. Manypenny	Kappler, 628–31; 10 Stat. 1069–73
263 [271]. May 18, 1854; proclaimed July 17, 1854	Sac and Fox of the Missouri	Washington	George W. Manypenny	Kappler, 631–33; 10 Stat. 1074–77

No.	Date	Nation	Place	Commissioner	Citation
264 [272].	May 18, 1854; proclaimed July 17, 1854	Kickapoo	Washington	George W. Manypenny	Kappler, 634–36; 10 Stat. 1078–81
265 [273].	May 30, 1854; proclaimed Aug. 10, 1854	Kaskaskia; Peoria; Piankashaw; Wea	Washington	George W. Manypenny	Kappler, 636–41; 10 Stat. 1082–87
266 [274].	June 5, 1854; proclaimed Aug. 4, 1854	Miami	Washington	George W. Manypenny	Kappler, 641–46; 10 Stat. 1093–1100
267 [—].	June 13, 1854; ratified July 21, 1854	Creek	Washington	W. H. Garret	Kappler, 647; 11 Stat. 599–600.

Note: Supplement to treaty of Nov. 23, 1838, no. [235], and filed with it in Ratified Indian Treaties file (RG 11).

No.	Date	Nation	Place	Commissioner	Citation
268 [275].	Sept. 30, 1854; proclaimed Jan. 29, 1855	Chippewa of Mississippi and Lake Superior	La Pointe	Henry C. Gilbert; David B. Herriman	Kappler, 648–52; 10 Stat. 1109–15
269 [276].	Nov. 4, 1854; proclaimed Apr. 10, 1855	Choctaw; Chickasaw	Doaksville	Douglas H. Cooper (witness)	Kappler, 652–53; 10 Stat. 1116–18
270 [277].	Nov. 15, 1854; proclaimed Apr. 7, 1855	Rogue River	Table Rock	Joel Palmer	Kappler, 654–55; 10 Stat. 1119–21
271 [278].	Nov. 18, 1854; proclaimed Apr. 10, 1855	Chasta; Scoton; Umpqua	Applegate Creek	Joel Palmer	Kappler, 655–57; 10 Stat. 1122–24

Ratified Indian Treaties

Number and Date	Tribes	Place	Commissioners	Citations
272 [279]. Nov. 29, 1854; proclaimed Mar. 30, 1855	Umpqua; Kalapuya	Calapooia Creek	Joel Palmer	Kappler, 657–60; 10 Stat. 1125–29
273 [280]. Dec. 9, 1854; proclaimed Apr. 10, 1855	Oto and Missouri	Nebraska City	George Hepner	Kappler, 660–61; 10 Stat. 1130–31; 11 Stat. 605–6
274 [281]. Dec. 26, 1854; proclaimed Apr. 10, 1855	Nisqually; Puyallup; Steilacoom; Squaxin; and others	Medicine Creek	Isaac I. Stevens	Kappler, 661–64; 10 Stat. 1132–37
275 [282]. Jan. 22, 1855; proclaimed Apr. 10, 1855	Kalapuya; Molala; Tumwater; Clackamas	Dayton	Joel Palmer	Kappler, 665–69; 10 Stat. 1143–49
276 [283]. Jan. 22, 1855; proclaimed Apr. 11, 1859	Duwamish; Suquamish; Snoqualmie; Stillaguamish; Snohomish; Skagit; Swinomish; Lummi; and others	Point Elliott	Isaac I. Stevens	Kappler, 669–73; 12 Stat. 927–32
277 [284]. Jan. 26, 1855; proclaimed Apr. 29, 1859	Clallam; Twana; Chemakum	Point No Point	Isaac I. Stevens	Kappler, 674–77; 12 Stat. 933–37

No.	Date	Tribe	Location	Commissioner	Citation
278 [285].	Jan. 31, 1855; proclaimed Mar. 1, 1855	Wyandot	Washington	George W. Manypenny	Kappler, 677–81; 10 Stat. 1159–64
279 [286].	Jan. 31, 1855; proclaimed Apr. 18, 1859	Makah	Neah Bay	Isaac I. Stevens	Kappler, 682–85; 12 Stat. 939–43
280 [287].	Feb. 22, 1855; proclaimed Apr. 7, 1855	Chippewa: Mississippi, Pillager, Lake Winnibigoshish	Washington	George W. Manypenny	Kappler, 685–90; 10 Stat. 1165–71
281 [288].	Feb. 27, 1855; proclaimed Mar. 23, 1855	Winnebago	Washington	George W. Manypenny	Kappler, 690–93; 10 Stat. 1172–76
282 [289].	June 9, 1855; proclaimed Apr. 11, 1859	Walla Walla; Cayuse; Umatilla	Camp Stevens	Isaac I. Stevens; Joel Palmer	Kappler, 694–98; 12 Stat. 945–50
283 [290].	June 9, 1855; proclaimed Apr. 18, 1859	Yakima and confederated bands	Camp Stevens	Isaac I. Stevens	Kappler, 698–702; 12 Stat. 951–56
284 [291].	June 11, 1855; proclaimed Apr. 29, 1859	Nez Perce	Camp Stevens	Isaac I. Stevens; Joel Palmer	Kappler, 702–6; 12 Stat. 957–62
285 [292].	June 22, 1855; proclaimed Mar. 4, 1856	Choctaw; Chickasaw	Washington	George W. Manypenny	Kappler, 706–14; 11 Stat. 611–19

Ratified Indian Treaties

Number and Date	Tribes	Place	Commissioners	Citations
286 [293]. June 25, 1855; proclaimed Apr. 18, 1859	Walla Walla; Wasco	The Dalles	Joel Palmer	Kappler, 714–19; 12 Stat. 963–70
287 [294]. July 1, 1855, and Jan. 25, 1856; proclaimed Apr. 11, 1859	Quinault; Quileute	Quinault River and Olympia	Isaac I. Stevens	Kappler, 719–21; 12 Stat. 971–74
288 [295]. July 16, 1855; proclaimed Apr. 18, 1859	Flathead; Kutenai; Upper Pend d'Oreille	Hell Gate	Isaac I. Stevens	Kappler, 722–25; 12 Stat. 975–79
289 [296]. July 31, 1855; proclaimed Sept. 10, 1856	Ottawa; Chippewa	Detroit	George W. Manypenny; Henry C. Gilbert	Kappler, 725–31; 11 Stat. 621–29
290 [297]. Aug. 2, 1855; proclaimed Apr. 24, 1856	Chippewa of Sault Ste. Marie	Detroit	George W. Manypenny; Henry C. Gilbert	Kappler, 732; 11 Stat. 631–32
291 [298]. Aug. 2, 1855; proclaimed June 21, 1856	Chippewa of Saginaw and other bands	Detroit	George W. Manypenny; Henry C. Gilbert	Kappler, 733–35; 11 Stat. 633–37
292 [299]. Oct. 17, 1855; proclaimed Apr. 25, 1856	Blackfeet: Piegan, Blood, Blackfeet, Gros Ventre; Flathead: Flathead, Upper Pend d'Oreille, Kutenai; Nez Perce	Judith River	Alfred Cumming; Isaac I. Stevens	Kappler, 736–40; 11 Stat. 657–62

No.	Date; proclaimed	Tribe	Place	Commissioner	Citation
293 [300].	Dec. 21, 1855; proclaimed Apr. 27, 1859	Molala	Dayton	Joel Palmer	Kappler, 740–42; 12 Stat. 981–83
294 [301].	Feb. 5, 1856; proclaimed Sept. 8, 1856	Stockbridge; Munsee	Stockbridge	Francis Huebschmann	Kappler, 742–55; 11 Stat. 663–78
295 [302].	Feb. 11, 1856; proclaimed Apr. 24, 1856	Menominee	Keshena	Francis Huebschmann	Kappler, 755–56; 11 Stat. 679–81
296 [303].	Aug. 7, 1856; proclaimed Aug. 28, 1856	Creek; Seminole	Washington	George W. Manypenny	Kappler, 756–63; 11 Stat. 699–707
297 [304].	Sept. 24, 1857; proclaimed May 26, 1858	Pawnee	Table Creek	James W. Denver	Kappler, 764–67; 11 Stat. 729–34
298 [305].	Nov. 5, 1857; proclaimed Mar. 31, 1859	Seneca (Tonawanda Band)	Tonawanda Reservation	Charles E. Mix	Kappler, 767–71; 11 Stat. 735–40; 12 Stat. 991–96
299 [306].	May 12, 1858; proclaimed Apr. 11, 1859	Ponca	Washington	Charles E. Mix	Kappler, 772–75; 12 Stat. 997–1001
300 [307].	Apr. 19, 1858; proclaimed Feb. 26, 1859	Yankton Sioux	Washington	Charles E. Mix	Kappler, 776–81; 11 Stat. 743–49

Ratified Indian Treaties

Number and Date	Tribes	Place	Commissioners	Citations
301 [308]. June 19, 1858; proclaimed Mar. 31, 1859	Sioux: Mdewakanton, Wahpekute	Washington	Charles E. Mix	Kappler, 781–85; 12 Stat. 1031–36
302 [309]. June 19, 1858; proclaimed Mar. 31, 1859	Sioux: Sisseton, Wahpeton	Washington	Charles E. Mix	Kappler, 785–89; 12 Stat. 1037–41
Resolution of the Senate concerning this treaty and the previous treaty, June 27, 1860				Kappler, 789; 12 Stat. 1042
303 [310]. Apr. 15, 1859; proclaimed Mar. 23, 1861	Winnebago	Washington	Charles E. Mix	Kappler, 790–92; 12 Stat. 1101–4
304 [311]. July 16, 1859; proclaimed July 9, 1860	Chippewa: Swan Creek, Black River; Munsee	Sac and Fox Agency	David Crawford	Kappler, 792–96; 12 Stat. 1105–9
305 [312]. Oct. 1, 1859; proclaimed July 9, 1860	Sac and Fox	Sac and Fox Agency	Alfred B. Greenwood	Kappler, 796–99; 15 Stat. 467–71
306 [313]. Oct. 5, 1859; proclaimed Nov. 17, 1860	Kansa	Kansas Agency	Alfred B. Greenwood	Kappler, 800–803; 12 Stat. 1111–16
307 [314]. May 30, 1860; proclaimed Aug. 22, 1860	Delaware	Sarcoxieville	Thomas B. Sykes	Kappler, 803–7; 12 Stat. 1129–34

No.	Tribe	Place	Commissioner	Citation	Date
308 [315].	Arapaho; Cheyenne	Fort Wise	Albert G. Boone; F. B. Culver	Kappler, 807–11; 12 Stat. 1163–69	Feb. 18, 1861; proclaimed Dec. 5, 1961
309 [316].	Sac and Fox of Missouri; Iowa	Great Nemaha Agency	David Vanderslice	Kappler, 811–14; 12 Stat. 1171–75	Mar. 6, 1861; proclaimed Mar. 26, 1863
310 [317].	Delaware	Leavenworth City	William P. Dole	Kappler, 814–24; 12 Stat. 1177–85	July 2, 1861; proclaimed Oct. 4, 1861
311 [318].	Potawatomi	Agency on Kansas River	William W. Ross	Kappler, 824–28; 12 Stat. 1191–97	Nov. 15, 1861; proclaimed Apr. 19, 1862
312 [319].	Kansa	Kansas Agency	H. W. Farnsworth	Kappler, 829–30; 12 Stat. 1221–24	Mar. 13, 1862; proclaimed Mar. 16, 1863
313 [320].	Ottawa of Blanchard's Fork and Roche de Boeuf	Washington	William P. Dole	Kappler, 830–34; 12 Stat. 1237–43	June 24, 1862; proclaimed July 28, 1862
314 [321].	Kickapoo	Kickapoo Agency	Charles B. Keith	Kappler, 835–39; 13 Stat. 623–30	June 28, 1862; proclaimed May 28, 1863
315 [322].	Chippewa: Mississippi, Pillager, Lake Winnibigoshish	Washington	William P. Dole; Clark W. Thompson	Kappler, 839–42; 12 Stat. 1249–55	Mar. 11, 1863; proclaimed Mar. 19, 1863

Ratified Indian Treaties

Number and Date	Tribes	Place	Commissioners	Citations
316 [323]. June 9, 1863; proclaimed Apr. 20, 1867	Nez Perce	Lapwai	Calvin H. Hale; Charles Hutchins; S. D. Howe	Kappler, 843–48; 14 Stat. 647–54
317 [324]. July 2, 1863; proclaimed June 7, 1869	Eastern Shoshone	Fort Bridger	James Duane Doty; Luther Mann, Jr.	Kappler, 848–50; 18 Stat. pt. 3, 685–88
318 [325]. July 30, 1863; proclaimed Jan. 17, 1865	Northern Shoshone; Western Shoshone	Box Elder	P. Edward Connor; James Duane Doty	Kappler, 850–51; 13 Stat. 663–65
319 [326]. Oct. 1, 1863; proclaimed Oct. 21, 1869	Western Shoshone	Ruby Valley	James W. Nye; James Duane Doty	Kappler, 851–53; 18 Stat. pt. 3, 689–92
320 [327]. Oct. 2, 1863; proclaimed May 5, 1864	Chippewa: Red Lake, Pembina	Old Crossing of Red Lake River	Alexander Ramsey; Ashley C. Morrill	Kappler, 853–55; 13 Stat. 667–71
321 [328]. Oct. 7, 1863; proclaimed Dec. 14, 1864	Ute (Tabeguache)	Tabeguache Agency, Conejos	John Evans; Michael Steck; Simeon Whiteley; Lafayette Head	Kappler, 856–59; 13 Stat. 673–79
322 [329]. Oct. 12, 1863; proclaimed Jan. 17, 1865	Shoshone-Gosiute	Tuilla Valley	James Duane Doty; P. Edward Connor	Kappler, 859–60; 13 Stat. 681–84
323 [330]. Apr. 12, 1864; proclaimed Apr. 25, 1864	Chippewa: Red Lake, Pembina	Washington	Clark W. Thompson; Ashley C. Morrill	Kappler, 861–62; 13 Stat. 689–92

No.	Date	Tribe	Place	Negotiators	Citation
324 [331].	May 7, 1864; proclaimed Mar. 20, 1865	Chippewa: Mississippi, Pillager, Lake Winnibigoshish	Washington	William P. Dole; Clark W. Thompson	Kappler, 862–65; 13 Stat. 693–97
325 [332].	Oct. 14, 1864; proclaimed Feb. 17, 1870	Klamath; Modoc; Northern Paiute or Snake (Yakuskin)	Klamath Lake	J. W. Perit Huntington; William Logan	Kappler, 865–68; 16 Stat. 707–12
326 [333].	Oct. 18, 1864; proclaimed Aug. 16, 1866	Chippewa: Saginaw, Swan Creek, Black River	Isabella Reservation	H. J. Alford; D. C. Leach	Kappler, 868–71; 14 Stat. 657–63
327 [334].	Mar. 6, 1865; proclaimed Feb. 15, 1866	Omaha	Washington	Clark W. Thompson; Robert W. Furness	Kappler, 872–73; 14 Stat. 667–69
328 [335].	Mar. 8, 1865; proclaimed Mar. 28, 1866	Winnebago	Washington	William P. Dole; Clark W. Thompson; St. A. D. Balcombe	Kappler, 874–75; 14 Stat. 671–73
329 [336].	Mar. 10, 1865; proclaimed Mar. 28, 1867	Ponca	Washington	William P. Dole	Kappler, 875–76; 14 Stat. 675–77
330 [337].	Aug. 12, 1865; proclaimed July 10, 1866	Northern Paiute or Snake (Walpapi)	Sprague River Valley	J. W. Perit Huntington	Kappler, 876–78; 14 Stat. 683–85
331 [338].	Sept. 29, 1865; proclaimed Jan. 21, 1867	Osage	Canville Trading Post	Dennis N. Cooley; Elijah Sells	Kappler, 878–83; 14 Stat. 687–93

Ratified Indian Treaties

Number and Date	Tribes	Place	Commissioners	Citations
332 [339]. Oct. 10, 1865; proclaimed Mar. 17, 1866	Sioux (Minneconjou)	Fort Sully	Newton Edmunds; Edward B. Taylor; S. R. Curtis; H. H. Sibley; Henry W. Reed; Orrin Guernsey	Kappler, 883–84; 14 Stat. 695–97
333 [340]. Oct. 14, 1865; proclaimed Mar. 17, 1866	Sioux (Lower Brulé)	Fort Sully	As for no. 332	Kappler, 885–87; 14 Stat. 699–702
334 [341] Oct. 14, 1865; proclaimed Feb. 2, 1867	Cheyenne; Arapaho	Little Arkansas River	John B. Sanborn; William S. Harney; Thomas Murphy; Kit Carson; William W. Bent; Jesse H. Leavenworth; James Steele	Kappler, 887–91; 14 Stat. 703–11
335 [342]. Oct. 17, 1865; proclaimed May 26, 1866	Apache; Cheyenne; Arapaho	Little Arkansas River	John B. Sanborn; William S. Harney; James Steele; William W. Bent; Kit Carson; Thomas Murphy; Jesse H. Leavenworth	Kappler, 891–92; 14 Stat. 713–15

No.	Date	Tribe	Location	Commissioners	Citation
336 [343].	Oct. 18, 1865; proclaimed May 26, 1866	Comanche; Kiowa	Little Arkansas River	John B. Sanborn; William S. Harney; Thomas Murphy; Kit Carson; William W. Bent; Jesse H. Leavenworth; James Steele	Kappler, 892–95; 14 Stat. 717–21
337 [344].	Oct. 19, 1865; proclaimed Mar. 17, 1866	Sioux (Two Kettle)	Fort Sully	Newton Edmunds; Edward B. Taylor; S. R. Curtis; H. H. Sibley; Henry W. Reed; Orrin Guernsey	Kappler, 896–97; 14 Stat. 723–26
338 [345].	Oct. 19, 1865; proclaimed Mar. 17, 1866	Sioux (Blackfoot)	Fort Sully	As for no. 337	Kappler, 898–99; 14 Stat. 727–29
339 [346].	Oct. 20, 1865; proclaimed Mar. 17, 1866	Sioux (Sans Arc)	Fort Sully	As for no. 337	Kappler, 899–901; 14 Stat. 731–33
340 [347].	Oct. 20, 1865; proclaimed Mar. 17, 1866	Sioux (Hunkpapa)	Fort Sully	As for no. 337	Kappler, 901–3; 14 Stat. 739–41
341 [348].	Oct. 20, 1865; proclaimed Mar. 17, 1866	Sioux (Yanktonai)	Fort Sully	As for no. 337	Kappler, 903–4; 14 Stat. 735–37

Ratified Indian Treaties

Number and Date	Tribes	Place	Commissioners	Citations
342 [349]. Oct. 28, 1865; proclaimed Mar. 17, 1866	Sioux (Upper Yanktonai)	Fort Sully	As for no. 337	Kappler, 905–6; 14 Stat. 743–45
343 [350]. Oct. 28, 1865; proclaimed Mar. 17, 1866	Sioux (Oglala)	Fort Sully	As for no. 337	Kappler, 906–8; 14 Stat. 747–49
344 [351]. Nov. 15, 1865; proclaimed Mar. 28, 1867	Middle Oregon tribes	Warm Springs Agency	J. W. Perit Huntington	Kappler, 908–9; 14 Stat. 751–53
345 [352]. Mar. 21, 1866; proclaimed Aug. 16, 1866	Seminole	Washington	Dennis N. Cooley; Elijah Sells; Ely S. Parker	Kappler, 910–15; 14 Stat. 755–61
346 [353]. Mar. 29, 1866; proclaimed May 5, 1866	Potawatomi	Washington	Dennis N. Cooley	Kappler, 916; 14 Stat. 763–64
347 [354]. Apr. 7, 1866; proclaimed May 5, 1866	Chippewa (Bois Forte Band)	Washington	Dennis N. Cooley; E. E. L. Taylor	Kappler, 916–18; 14 Stat. 765–68
348 [355]. Apr. 28, 1866; proclaimed July 10, 1866	Choctaw; Chickasaw	Washington	Dennis N. Cooley; Elijah Sells; Ely S. Parker	Kappler, 918–31; 14 Stat. 769–84
349 [356]. June 14, 1866; proclaimed Aug. 11, 1866	Creek	Washington	Dennis N. Cooley; Elijah Sells; Ely S. Parker	Kappler, 931–37; 14 Stat. 785–92

	Date	Tribe	Place	Commissioners	Reference
350 [357].	July 4, 1866; proclaimed Aug. 10, 1866	Delaware	Delaware Agency	Thomas Murphy; John G. Pratt; William H. Watson	Kappler, 937–42; 14 Stat. 793–98
351 [358].	July 19, 1866; proclaimed Aug. 11, 1866	Cherokee	Washington	Dennis N. Cooley; Elijah Sells	Kappler, 942–50; 14 Stat. 799–809
352 [359].	Feb. 18, 1867; proclaimed Oct. 14, 1868	Sac and Fox of the Mississippi	Washington	Lewis V. Bogy; William H. Watson; Thomas Murphy; Henry W. Martin	Kappler, 951–56; 15 Stat. 495–504
353 [360].	Feb. 19, 1867; proclaimed May 2, 1867	Sioux: Sisseton, Wahpeton	Washington	Lewis V. Bogy; William H. Watson	Kappler, 956–59; 15 Stat. 505–11
354 [361].	Feb. 23, 1867; proclaimed Oct. 14, 1868	Seneca; Mixed Seneca and Shawnee; Quapaw; Confederated tribes: Peoria, Kaskaskia, Wea, Piankashaw; Miami; Ottawa (Blanchard's Fork and Roche de Boeuf); Wyandot	Washington	Lewis V. Bogy; William H. Watson; Thomas Murphy; George C. Snow; G. A. Colton	Kappler, 960–69; 15 Stat. 513–29

Ratified Indian Treaties

Number and Date	Tribes	Place	Commissioners	Citations
355 [362]. Feb. 27, 1867; proclaimed Aug. 7, 1868	Potawatomi	Washington	Lewis V. Bogy; William H. Watson; Thomas Murphy; Luther R. Palmer	Kappler, 970–74; 15 Stat. 531–38
356 [363]. Mar. 19, 1867; proclaimed Apr. 18, 1867	Chippewa of the Mississippi	Washington	Lewis V. Bogy; William H. Watson; Joel B. Bassett	Kappler, 974–76; 16 Stat. 719–23
357 [364]. Oct. 21, 1867; proclaimed Aug. 25, 1868	Kiowa; Comanche	Medicine Lodge Creek	Nathaniel G. Taylor; William S. Harney; C. C. Augur; Alfred H. Terry; John B. Sanborn; Samuel F. Tappan; J. B. Henderson	Kappler, 977–82; 15 Stat. 581–87
358 [365]. Oct. 21, 1867; proclaimed Aug. 25, 1868	Kiowa; Comanche; Apache	Medicine Lodge Creek	As for no. 357	Kappler, 982–84; 15 Stat. 589–92
359 [366]. Oct. 28, 1867; proclaimed Aug. 19, 1868	Cheyenne; Arapaho	Medicine Lodge Creek	As for no. 357	Kappler, 984–89; 15 Stat. 593–99
360 [367]. Mar. 2, 1868; proclaimed Nov. 6, 1868	Ute: Tabeguache, Muache, Capote, Wiminuche, Yampa, Grand River, Uintah	Washington	Nathaniel G. Taylor; Alexander C. Hunt; Kit Carson	Kappler, 990–96; 15 Stat. 619–27

No.	Date	Tribe	Place	Commissioners	Citation
361 [368].	Apr. 27, 1868; proclaimed June 10, 1868	Cherokee	Washington	Nathaniel G. Taylor	Kappler, 996–97; 16 Stat. 727–29
362 [369].	Apr. 29, 1868, and later; proclaimed Feb. 24, 1869	Sioux: Brulé, Oglala, Minneconjou, Yanktonai, Hunkpapa, Blackfoot, Cuthead, Two Kettle, Sans Arc, Santee; Arapaho	Fort Laramie	William T. Sherman; William S. Harney; Alfred H. Terry; C. C. Augur; J. B. Henderson; Nathaniel G. Taylor; John B. Sanborn; Samuel F. Tappan	Kappler, 998–1007; 15 Stat. 635–47
363 [370].	May 7, 1868; proclaimed Aug. 12, 1868	Crow	Fort Laramie	William T. Sherman; William S. Harney; Alfred H. Terry; C. C. Augur; John B. Sanborn; Samuel F. Tappan	Kappler, 1008–11; 15 Stat. 649–53
364 [371].	May 10, 1868; proclaimed Aug. 25, 1868	Northern Cheyenne; Northern Arapaho	Fort Laramie	As for no. 363	Kappler, 1012–15; 15 Stat. 655–59
365 [372].	June 1, 1868; proclaimed Aug. 12, 1868	Navajo	Fort Sumner	William T. Sherman; Samuel F. Tappan	Kappler, 1015–20; 15 Stat. 667–72

Ratified Indian Treaties

Number and Date	Tribes	Place	Commissioners	Citations
366 [373]. July 3, 1868; proclaimed Feb. 24, 1869	Eastern Shoshone; Bannock	Fort Bridger	Nathaniel G. Taylor; William T. Sherman; William S. Harney; John B. Sanborn; Samuel F. Tappan; C. C. Augur	Kappler, 1020–24; 15 Stat. 673–78
367 [374]. Aug. 13, 1868; proclaimed Feb. 24, 1869	Nez Perce	Washington	Nathaniel G. Taylor	Kappler, 1024–25; 15 Stat. 693–95

Omitted Treaties

The following "treaties" are omitted from the foregoing table, although arguments can be made for their inclusion.

1. Agreement with the Five Nations, approved by the Senate, March 26, 1792, and proclaimed by the president, April 23, 1792. This single article provided an annuity of $1,500 for "clothing, domestic animals, and implements of husbandry, and for encouraging useful artificers to reside in their villages." The proclamation appears in the State Department Ratified Indian Treaties file as no. 19 (M668, roll 2, frames 249ff.). It is printed in *American State Papers: Indian Affairs*, 1:232, and in Kappler, *Treaties*, Appendix, 1027. The Senate action is in *Journal of the Executive Proceedings of the Senate*, 1:116. The annuity is incorporated in the seventh article of the treaty with the Six Nations, November 11, 1794, Kappler, *Treaties*, 36, where Kappler erroneously notes, "It appears that this treaty was never ratified by the Senate."

2. Contract between the Seneca nation and Robert Morris, September 15, 1797. This document appears in the State Department Ratified Indian Treaties file as no. 27 (M668, roll 2, frames 328ff.). It is printed in Appendix I, *Statutes at Large*, 7:601–3, and in Kappler, *Treaties*, Appendix, 1027–30. The treaty was approved by the Senate on December 12, 1797, with the condition, "as soon as the President shall be satisfied that the investment of the money has been made conformably to the intention of the said treaty." *Journal of the Executive Proceedings of the Senate*, 1:254–55. President John Adams proclaimed the treaty on April 11, 1798 (see M668, roll 2).

3. Convention between the Oneida Indians and the State of New York, June 1, 1798. This document appears in the State Department Ratified Indian Treaties file as no. 28 (M668, roll 2, frames 334ff.). The Senate unanimously approved the treaty on February 13, 1799. *Journal of the Executive Proceedings of the Senate*, 1:312. President John Adams proclaimed it on February 21, 1799 (see M668, roll 2). It is not printed in the *Statutes at Large* or in Kappler, *Treaties*.

4. Treaty between the State of New York and the Oneida Indians, June 4, 1802, and treaty between the State of New York and the Seneca Indians, August 20, 1802. These treaties (with two others) were submitted to the Senate by President Thomas Jefferson on December 27, 1802. They are printed in *American State Papers: Indian Affairs*, 1:664–66. The Senate approved them unanimously on December 31. *Journal of the Executive Proceedings of the Senate*, 1:428. They were never proclaimed by the president and do not appear in the State Department Ratified Indian Treaties file; they are not printed in the *Statutes at Large* or in Kappler, *Treaties*.

5. Treaty with the Sioux, September 23, 1805, concluded at the mouth of St. Peter's River by Zebulon Montgomery Pike. This treaty is not in the State Department Ratified Indian Treaties file, but it was approved by the Senate on April 16, 1808, with an amendment specifying payment of $2,000. *Journal of the Executive Proceedings of the Senate*, 2:77, 78, 80. It seems, however, never to have been proclaimed by the president. It is printed in *American State Papers: Indian Affairs*, 1:753–54, and in Kappler, *Treaties*, Appendix, 1031.

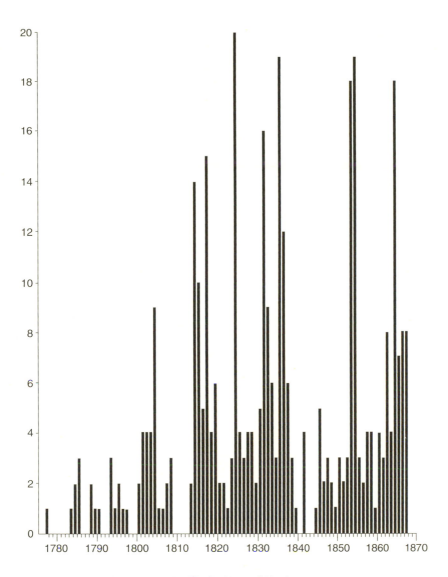

Number of Ratified Indian Treaties by Year of Signing

Ratified Indian Treaty Council Sites

The purpose of this map is simply to provide a general picture of the widespread locations at which Indian treaties were signed. Some of the sites indicated are approximations, for the exact sites could not be determined. A few places are omitted altogether. Comments about the sources for the map are given in the introduction to appendix B.

Lake River
Leech Lake
nd du Lac(2) • • La Pointe(2) • Sault Ste. Marie
Michilmackinac

Falls of Wolf River
(Keshena)(2)
rse des • Butte des • Green Bay(2)
ioux • St. Peter's Morts Cedar Point
(Mendota)(3) Isabella • • Saginaw(3)
Stockbridge(3) • Flint River
• Prairie du Chien(4) Detroit(5) •
Spring Wells
St. Joseph(2) • Brownstown
Chicago(2) •
ncil Bluffs •
kinson)(4) Rock Island(5) • 1 2 • 5
vue (Ft. Armstrong) 3 • 4 5 • 6
6 • 9 10 • 8
raska City • Sac and Fox 7 8-9 11
reat Nemaha Agency Wyandot Village 7 10
Agency(2) Ft. Harrison(2) Greenville(2)
• Ft. Leavenworth (2) • Mouth of Great Miami
Portage des • Vincennes(10)
5 Sioux(12)
Ft. Clark Edwardsville(2)
• St. Louis(24)
8
• Marais des Cygnes Factory
ek •James Fork of White River Holston River
ncy
• Ft. Gibson(6) Tellico(4)
Chickasaw Cherokee Agency • Hopewell(3)
Bluffs
Holmes New Gascony New Echota
• Pontotoc Creek
• Doaksville(2) Chickasaw Council Indian
Harrington's House(2) Springs(2) • Ft. Wilkinson
Mt. Dexter •
• Ft. Jackson
Dancing
Caddo Agency Doak's Stand Rabbit Creek • Creek Agency(2)
Old Town • Ft. Confederation
Choctaw Trading House
Hoe Buckintoopa Colerain
• Ft. Adams Moultrie Creek
il Springs Tallahassee •
Payne's Landing •

KEY TO NUMBERED SITES

Ratified Agreements with Indian Tribes, 1872–1911

The agreements are listed here chronologically by date of signing, with the names of the Indian tribes affected and the commissioners for the United States. For each agreement the date of ratification and the location in the *Statutes at Large* and in Kappler, *Indian Affairs: Laws and Treaties* are given. Although in most cases the full agreement is printed in the *Statutes at Large*, in a few cases only the ratification is indicated. In these instances Kappler usually supplies the text of the agreement in a footnote.

Many agreements were negotiated by specially appointed commissioners. Some were made by the Jerome Commission or the Dawes Commission; others were negotiated by Indian Inspector James McLaughlin. In a few cases no commissioner is named in the document.

It will be noted that some of the agreements (as was the case also with treaties) were ratified or confirmed by Congress a considerable time after they were negotiated. Many of the agreements were ratified by special acts of Congress. For others the ratification was included in an Indian appropriation act. Some (which do not appear in this table) were never ratified.

I have been helped by an unpublished "List of Documents Concerning the Negotiation of Ratified Indian Agreements," prepared by John H. Martin, which is used as a finding aid in the National Archives. I have also used two lists, kindly furnished me by Robert M. Kvasnicka, who prepared them for the Smithsonian Institution's *Handbook of North*

American Indians, though they were never used in that publication. One of the lists shows chronologically the ratified agreements, the other the unratified agreements. Differences in the various lists come from different judgments about what constituted a separate agreement and about which agreements were in fact ratified.

There is no segregated file of agreements in the records of the National Archives, and material on the agreements is dispersed throughout larger collections. This is not critical for research (aside from the lack of an authorized list of such agreements) because official documentation is readily available in published form.

When the Senate considered *treaties,* under the formal constitutional provision of giving advice and consent, it did so in executive session, and only the treaties, when finally ratified, were published in the *Statutes at Large*. Other material such as instructions to the commissioners, reports of the commissioners, council proceedings, and recommendations of the president, the secretary of war or secretary of the interior, and the commissioner of Indian affairs must be sought in manuscript form in the National Archives or in disparate published sources. Since the ratified *agreements,* on the other hand, were regular statutes of Congress, all the documentation sent to Congress by the president or the secretary of the interior when ratification of an agreement was sought is usually found attached to the letter of transmittal from the executive branch and published by Congress. In addition, the agreements can be traced in the *Congressional Record* as they made their way through Congress, and often, too, in printed reports of the Committee on Indian Affairs in the House and the Senate. A good place to track down such material is in the various chronological sections of the *CIS US Serial Set Index*, under "agreements."

Ratified Agreements with Indian Tribes

Number and Date	Tribes	Commissioners	Citations
1. Sept. 26, 1872; ratified Dec. 15, 1874	Eastern Shoshone	Felix R. Brunot	Kappler, 1:153–55; 18 Stat. pt. 3: 191–92
2. May 2 and 19, 1873; ratified June 22, 1874	Sioux: Sisseton, Wahpeton	Moses N. Adams; William H. Forbes; James Smith, Jr.	Kappler, 2:1059–63 (replaced agreement of Sept. 20, 1872, Kappler, 2:1057–59); 18 Stat. pt. 3: 167 (Indian Appropriation Act for 1875)
3. Sept. 13, 1873; ratified Apr. 29, 1874	Ute	Felix R. Brunot	Kappler, 1:151–52; 18 Stat. pt. 3: 36–41
4. June 23, 1874; ratified May 3, 1875	Eastern Shawnee	H. W. Jones	Kappler, 1:158n; 18 Stat. pt. 3: 447 (Indian Appropriation Act for 1876)
5. Sept. 23–Oct. 27, 1876; ratified Feb. 28, 1877	Sioux; Northern Cheyenne; Northern Arapaho	Manypenny Commission	Kappler, 1:168–78; 19 Stat. 254–64
6. Nov. 21, 1876; ratified Feb. 20, 1893	Puyallup and Northern Pacific Railroad Company	R. H. Milroy; J. W. Sprague (for railroad)	Kappler, 1:465–67n; 27 Stat. 468
7. Mar. 6, 1880; ratified June 15, 1880	Confederated Ute		Kappler, 1:180–86; 21 Stat. 199–205
8. May 14, 1880; ratified Feb. 23, 1889	Northern Shoshone; Bannock; Sheepeater		Kappler, 1:314–16; 25 Stat. 687–89

No.	Date	Tribes	Commissioners	Citation
9.	June 12, 1880; ratified Apr. 11, 1882	Crow		Kappler, 1:195–97; 22 Stat. 42–43
10.	July 18, 1881; ratified July 3, 1882	Northern Shoshone; Bannock	Joseph K. McCammon	Kappler, 1:199–201; 22 Stat. 148–50
11.	Aug. 22, 1881; ratified July 10, 1882	Crow	Llewellyn A. Luce; William H. Walker; Charles A. Maxwell	Kappler, 1:201–4; 22 Stat. 157–60
12.	Sept. 2, 1882; ratified July 4, 1884	Flathead; Kutenai; Lower Pend d'Oreille	Joseph K. McCammon	23 Stat. 89–90 (Indian Appropriation Act for 1885)
13.	July 7, 1883; ratified July 4, 1884	Indians of Columbia and Colville Reservations	Henry M. Teller	Kappler, 2:1073–74; 23 Stat. 79–80 (Indian Appropriation Act for 1885)
14.	Jan. 13, 1885; ratified Mar. 3, 1893	Yakima	Robert S. Gardner	Kappler, 1:486–89n; 27 Stat. 631–32 (Indian Appropriation Act for 1894)
15.	Dec. 14, 1886; ratified Mar. 3, 1891	Arikara; Gros Ventre; Mandan	John V. Wright; Jared W. Daniels; Charles F. Larrabee	Kappler, 1:425–28; 26 Stat. 1032–35 (Indian Appropriation Act for 1892)
16.	Dec. 28, 1886– Feb. 11, 1887; ratified May 1, 1888	Gros Ventre; Piegan; Blood; Blackfeet; River Crow	John V. Wright; Jared W. Daniels; Charles F. Larrabee	Kappler, 1:261–66; 25 Stat. 113–33

Ratified Agreements with Indian Tribes

Number and Date	Tribes	Commissioners	Citations
17. Mar. 18, 1887; ratified July 13, 1892	Spokane	John V. Wright; Jared W. Daniels; Henry W. Andrews	Kappler, 1:453–54n; 27 Stat. 139 (Indian Appropriation Act for 1893)
18. Mar. 26, 1887; ratified Mar. 3, 1891	Coeur d'Alene	John V. Wright; Jared W. Daniels; Henry W. Andrews	Kappler, 1:419–22; 26 Stat. 1026–29 (Indian Appropriation Act for 1892)
19. May 27, 1887; ratified Sept. 1, 1888	Northern Shoshone; Bannock	Robert S. Gardner; Peter Gallagher	Kappler, 1:292–97; 25 Stat. 452
20. Jan. 19, 1889; ratified Mar. 1, 1889	Creek	William Vilas	Kappler, 1:321–24; 25 Stat. 757–59
21. July 8 – Nov. 21, 1889	Chippewa of Minnesota	Henry M. Rice; Martin Marty; Joseph B. Whiting	approved by president, Mar. 4, 1890, according to stipulations in 25 Stat. 642–46; *House Ex. Doc.* no. 247, 51-1, serial 2747, pp. 27–66
22. Sept. 9, 1889; ratified Mar. 3, 1891	Coeur d'Alene	Benjamin Simpson; John H. Shupe; Napoleon B. Humphrey	Kappler, 1:422–24; 26 Stat. 1029–32 (Indian Appropriation Act for 1892)
23. Dec. 12, 1889; ratified Mar. 3, 1891	Sioux: Sisseton, Wahpeton	Eliphalet Whittlesey; D. W. Diggs; Charles A. Maxwell	Kappler, 1:428–32; 26 Stat. 1035–39 (Indian Appropriation Act for 1892)
24. May 20, 1890; ratified Feb. 13, 1891	Iowa	Jerome Commission	Kappler, 1:393–98; 26 Stat. 753–59
25. June 12, 1890; ratified Feb. 13, 1891	Sac and Fox	Jerome Commission	Kappler, 1:389–93; 26 Stat. 749–53

Date	Tribe	Commission	Citation
26. June 25, 1890; ratified Mar. 3, 1891	Citizen Band of Potawatomi	Jerome Commission	Kappler, 1:409–11; 26 Stat. 1016–18 (Indian Appropriation Act for 1892)
27. June 26, 1890; ratified Mar. 3, 1891	Absentee Shawnee	Jerome Commission	Kappler, 1:411–14; 26 Stat. 1018–21 (Indian Appropriation Act for 1892)
28. Oct. 13 – Nov. 13, 1890; ratified Mar. 3, 1891	Cheyenne; Arapaho	Jerome Commission	Kappler, 1:415–18; 26 Stat. 1022–26 (Indian Appropriation Act for 1892)
29. Dec. 8, 1890; ratified Mar. 3, 1891	Crow	J. Clifford Richardson; Charles M. Dole; Rockwell J. Flint	Kappler, 1:432–36; 26 Stat. 1039–43 (Indian Appropriation Act for 1892)
30. May 9, 1891; putatively ratified, June 21, 1906	Indians of Colville Reservation	Mark A. Fullerton; W. H. H. Dufur; James F. Payne	27 Stat. 62–64; confirmed, 420 U.S. 194–222 (1975); printed in *Senate Ex. Doc.* no. 15, 52-1, serial 2892, Pp. 13–20
31. June 4, 1891; ratified Mar. 2, 1895	Wichita and affiliated bands	Jerome Commission	Kappler, 1:560–65; 28 Stat. 894–99 (Indian Appropriation Act for 1896)
32. June 21 – Sept. 9, 1891; ratified Mar. 3, 1893	Kickapoo	Jerome Commission	Kappler, 1:480–84; 27 Stat. 557–63
33. Oct. 21, 1891; ratified Mar. 3, 1893	Tonkawa	Jerome Commission	Kappler, 1:495–96n; 27 Stat. 643–44 (Indian Appropriation Act for 1894)

Ratified Agreements with Indian Tribes

Number and Date	Tribes	Commissioners	Citations
34. Dec. 19, 1891; ratified Mar. 3, 1893	Cherokee	Jerome Commission	Kappler, 1:490–92n; 27 Stat. 640–43 (Indian Appropriation Act for 1894)
35. Aug. 27, 1892; authorized July 13, 1892	Crow	Elbert D. Weed; Fellows D. Pease; Fred. H. Foster	Kappler, 1:450–53n; 27 Stat. 137 (Indian Appropriation Act for 1893)
36. Oct. 21, 1892; ratified June 6, 1900	Comanche; Kiowa; Apache	Jerome Commission	Kappler, 1:708–13; 31 Stat. 676–81
37. Oct. 22, 1892[2]; amended version ratified Apr. 21, 1904	Turtle Mountain Chippewa	Peter J. McCumber; John W. Wilson; W. Woodville Flemming	Kappler, 3:39–41; 33 Stat. 194–96
38. Oct. 31, 1892; ratified Aug. 15, 1894	Alsea and others, Siletz Reservation	Reuben P. Boise; William H. Odell; H. H. Harding	Kappler, 1:533–35; 28 Stat. 323–26 (Indian Appropriation Act for 1895)
39. Nov. 23, 1892; ratified Mar. 3, 1893	Pawnee	Jerome Commission	Kappler, 1:496–98n; 27 Stat. 644 (Indian Appropriation Act for 1894)
40. Dec. 31, 1892; ratified Aug. 15, 1894	Yankton Sioux	J. C. Adams; John J. Cole	Kappler, 1:523–29; 28 Stat. 314–19 (Indian Appropriation Act for 1895)
41. Jan. 3, 1893; ratified Feb. 20, 1893	Seneca and William B. Barker		Kappler, 1:468; 27 Stat. 470

Date	Tribe/Reservation	Commissioners	Citation
42. May 1, 1893; ratified Aug. 15, 1894	Nez Perce	Robert Schleicher; James F. Allen; Cyrus Beede	Kappler, 1:536–41; 28 Stat. 326–32 (Indian Appropriation Act for 1895)
43. Dec. 4, 1893; ratified Aug. 15, 1894	Yuma	Washington J. Houston; John A. Gorman; Peter R. Brady	Kappler, 1:542–45; 28 Stat. 332–36 (Indian Appropriation Act for 1895)
44. Jan. 8, 1894; ratified Aug. 15, 1894	Yakima	John Lane; Lewis T. Erwin	Kappler, 1:529–31; 28 Stat. 320–21 (Indian Appropriation Act for 1895)
45. Feb. 7, 1894; ratified Aug. 15, 1894	Coeur d'Alene	John Lane	Kappler, 1:531–32; 28 Stat. 322–23 (Indian Appropriation Act for 1895)
46. Sept. 26, 1895; ratified June 10, 1896	Indians of Blackfeet Reservation	William C. Pollock; George Bird Grinnell; Walter M. Clements	Kappler, 1:604–9; 29 Stat. 353–58 (Indian Appropriation Act for 1897)
47. Oct. 9, 1895; ratified June 10, 1896	Indians of Ft. Belknap Reservation	William C. Pollock; George Bird Grinnell; Walter M. Clements	Kappler, 1:601–4; 29 Stat. 350–53 (Indian Appropriation Act for 1897)
48. Feb. 25, 1896; ratified June 10, 1896	Indians of San Carlos Reservation	Province McCormick	Kappler, 1:609–11; 29 Stat. 358–60 (Indian Appropriation Act for 1897)
49. Apr. 21, 1896; ratified June 7, 1897	Eastern Shoshone; Arapaho	James McLaughlin	Kappler, 1:624–27; 30 Stat. 93–96 (Indian Appropriation Act for 1898)

Ratified Agreements with Indian Tribes

Number and Date	Tribes	Commissioners	Citations
50. Dec. 3, 1896; ratified June 7, 1897	Seneca and William B. Barker		Kappler, 1:622–23; 30 Stat. 89–90 (Indian Appropriation Act for 1898)
51. Apr. 23, 1897; ratified June 28, 1898	Choctaw; Chickasaw	Dawes Commission	Kappler, 1:646–56; 30 Stat. 505–13
52. Sept. 27, 1897; ratified June 28, 1898	Creek	Dawes Commission	Kappler, 1:656–62; 30 Stat. 514–19
53. Dec. 16, 1897; ratified July 1, 1898	Seminole	Dawes Commission	Kappler, 1:662–65; 30 Stat. 567–69
54. Feb. 5, 1898; ratified June 6, 1900	Northern Shoshone; Bannock	Benjamin F. Barge; James H. McNeely; Charles G. Hoyt	Kappler, 1:704–8; 31 Stat. 672–76
55. Mar. 1, 1898; ratified Mar. 3, 1899	Lower Brulé Sioux	James McLaughlin	Kappler, 1:688–90; 30 Stat. 1362–64
56. Mar. 10, 1898; ratified Mar. 3, 1899	Sioux, Rosebud Reservation	James McLaughlin	Kappler, 1:690–92; 30 Stat. 1364–66
57. Aug. 14, 1899; ratified Apr. 27, 1904	Crow	Benjamin F. Barge; James H. McNeely; Charles G. Hoyt	Kappler, 3:87–97; 33 Stat. 352–62
58. Oct. 7, 1899; ratified June 2, 1900	Seminole	Dawes Commission	Kappler, 1:702–3; 31 Stat. 250–51
59. Mar. 8, 1900; ratified Mar. 1, 1901	Creek	Dawes Commission	Kappler, 1:729–39; 31 Stat. 861–73
60. Apr. 9, 1900; ratified Mar. 1, 1901	Cherokee	Dawes Commission	Kappler, 1:715–29; 31 Stat. 848–61

Date	Tribe / Reservation	Negotiator	Citation
61. June 17, 1901; ratified June 21, 1906	Klamath; Modoc; Northern Paiute or Snake (Yahuskin Band)	James McLaughlin	Kappler, 3:234–36; 34 Stat. 367–68 (Indian Appropriation Act for 1907)
62. June 27, 1901; ratified Apr. 28, 1904	Indians on Grand Ronde Reservation	James McLaughlin	Kappler, 3:105–7; 33 Stat. 567–70
63. Sept. 14, 1901; ratified Apr. 23, 1904	Sioux, Rosebud Reservation	James McLaughlin	Kappler, 3:71–75; 33 Stat. 254–58
64. Nov. 2, 1901; ratified Apr. 27, 1904	Sioux: Sisseton, Wahpeton, Cuthead, Devils Lake Reservation	James McLaughlin	Kappler, 3:83–87; 33 Stat. 319–24
65. Feb. 8, 1902; ratified July 1, 1902	Kansa		Kappler, 1:766–70; 32 Stat. 636–41
66. Mar. 10, 1902; ratified Feb. 20, 1904	Red Lake and Pembina Chippewa	James McLaughlin	Kappler, 3:28–33; 33 Stat. 46–50
67. Mar. 21, 1902; ratified July 1, 1902	Choctaw; Chickasaw	Dawes Commission	Kappler, 1:771–87; 32 Stat. 641–57
68. June 30, 1902; ratified June 30, 1902	Creek	Dawes Commission	Kappler, 1:761–66; 32 Stat. 500–505
69. Apr. 21, 1904; ratified Mar. 3, 1905	Eastern Shoshone; Arapaho	James McLaughlin	Kappler, 3:117–23; 33 Stat. 1016–22
70. May 28, 1904; ratified Mar. 3, 1905	Indians of Port Madison Reservation	James McLaughlin	Kappler, 3:155–56; 33 Stat. 1078–79 (Indian Appropriation Act for 1907)

Ratified Agreements with Indian Tribes

Number and Date	Tribes	Commissioners	Citations
71. Feb. 27, 1909; ratified Apr. 4, 1910	Sac and Fox of the Mississippi (Oklahoma and Iowa)	F. C. Campbell	36 Stat. 289; *Senate Doc.* no. 358, 61-2, serial 5657, pp. 4–7
72. Mar. 16, 1909; ratified Apr. 4, 1910	Potawatomi of Kansas and Wisconsin	F. C. Campbell	36 Stat. 289; *Senate Doc.* no. 358, 61-2, serial 5657, pp. 7–9
73. May 10, 1911; ratified June 30, 1913	Southern Ute (Wiminuche Band)	F. H. Abbott; James McLaughlin	Kappler, 3:566–68; 38 Stat. 82–84 (Indian Appropriation Act for 1914)

Unratified Treaties

This volume deals primarily with Indian treaties that were approved by the Senate and ratified by the president of the United States, thus becoming effective as the "supreme law of the land." Although some cases of rejection by the Senate or of failure of the president to ratify and proclaim the treaty have been noted, no attention has been paid to the large bulk of documents that might be classified as unratified treaties.

Ratified treaties are reasonably easy to define, despite a few problem cases, for the process usually included congressional authorization, formally appointed and instructed commissioners, submission to the Senate by the president for its constitutional action (often with attached recommendations from the commissioner of Indian affairs, the secretary of war or interior, and the president), Senate resolutions of approval (sometimes with amendments), assent of the tribes to any amendments, and proclamation by the president attested by the secretary of state. For many treaties, journals of proceedings exist. If the Senate voted to reject the treaty, the document is easy to identify as an unratified treaty. But the ratification process could be interrupted also at other stages; the president could refuse or neglect to submit it to the Senate or fail, in the last instance, to ratify and proclaim the document even though it had been approved by the Senate.

The great majority of the treaties included an article that clearly stated when the treaty would be binding, in some such words as these: "This treaty shall take effect and be obligatory on the contracting parties, as soon as it is ratified by the President of the United States, by and with the advice and consent of the Senate of the same." In a few instances special conditions were set; for example, that the treaty would take effect only when approved by the tribe in full council, that rejection of specified articles by the president or the Senate would not invalidate the rest of the treaty, or that changes could be made in the treaty by the government (a blanket authority not dependent upon Indian assent).[1]

In addition, there are numerous cases in which agreements were made with the Indians by Indian agents, military personnel, or others, which may never have entered, and certainly did not get through, the formal ratification process. There are no set criteria for determining just what makes an "unratified treaty," and lists that have been compiled vary greatly in number of items. Robert M. Kvasnicka, long-time curator of Indian records in the National Archives, produced a list in the 1970s that had 150 entries, but Kvasnicka admitted that the list was not definitive. "Unratified treaties," he said, "are scattered throughout the BIA and military records, since unauthorized persons frequently made agreements with Indian groups and tried to pass them off as treaties. I tried to capture as many of these as I could, but I couldn't begin to cover all the pertinent military records."[2]

Vine Deloria, Jr., in drawing up a list of Indian treaties and agreements in 1973, faced the same problem and found no easy solution. "The Apaches, for example," he noted, "were continually making agreements with officers of the Army in the field during the period in which they fought against the United States for the possession of the American Southwest. Are these field agreements considered treaties, which they certainly were in a political and military sense, or are they simply agreements of the period since they were rarely ratified by Congress according to its Constitutional powers?" Deloria argues for the inclusion of some documents as "treaties" even though they were not ratified. "Because they were signed by the tribes concerned *in good faith*," he writes, "we consider them as valid treaties which must be included in any book on Indian treaties and agreements. That the United States did not uphold their validity in the final analysis does not mean either that the tribes did not consider them seriously or that the United States did not gain a great benefit from them."[3]

1. Kappler, 2:32, 134, 627, 884.
2. Letter of Kvasnicka to author, November 18, 1983, with "List of Unratified Indian Treaties (Revised)" attached.
3. *A Chronological List of Treaties and Agreements Made by Indian Tribes with the United*

The compilation of documents by the National Archives from Record Group 75 entitled Documents Relating to the Negotiation of Ratified and Unratified Treaties with Various Indian Tribes, 1801–1869 (T494) devotes eight of its ten rolls of microfilm to unratified treaties, 1821–1869. In many cases this file contains the original treaty with signatures. There is, unfortunately, no list of the treaties included, but Kvasnicka's list shows eighty-seven treaties from these rolls of microfilm.

The index for the State Department Ratified Indian Treaties file includes thirty-two cards for treaties listed as unratified, but the treaties themselves are not present except for seven included in the file under no. 274a.[4]

Charles J. Kappler, in volumes 2–5 of *Indian Affairs: Laws and Treaties*, prints forty-seven unratified treaties. His prefaces to the various volumes refer to these treaties as "several old Indian treaties which it was not possible to procure when the volume containing the treaties was prepared" or "a number of unratified treaties with Indians in whose behalf legislation has been enacted or is pending in Congress and which treaties have a bearing on such acts of Congress or pending legislation."[5]

The treaty substitutes known as agreements that were used after the end of treaty making in 1871 also faced the problem of nonapproval by Congress after they had been formally negotiated with Indian tribes. In one notable case concerning the Colville Reservation, it was not clear whether Congress had ratified an agreement of 1891 or not, until the Supreme Court in 1975 decided that it had.[6]

There is no doubt that failure to ratify treaties or agreements caused considerable confusion and hardship. In some cases, however, the government fulfilled the stipulations despite the lack of ratification and proclamation.

States (Washington: Institute for the Development of Indian Law, 1973), 1–2. It is clear that I have not followed his list in this work.

4. Ratified Treaties (M668, roll 1; roll 10, frames 447ff.).
5. Kappler, 3:iii; 4:v. A similar statement is in 5:v.
6. See discussion of the case, pp. 323–24 above.

Sources for the Study of
American Indian Treaties

Collections of Indian Treaties

Ratified Indian Treaties File (National Archives).

The official copies of ratified Indian treaties were originally kept in a Ratified Indian Treaties file in the Department of State. This file is now in the National Archives, General Records of the United States Government, Record Group 11. In nearly all cases these are the original manuscript treaties signed by the United States commissioners and the Indian chiefs and warriors. The file has been microfilmed as microcopy M668, sixteen rolls, of which the first is a sixteen-millimeter roll that reproduces card file indexes to the treaty series.

The treaties are arranged chronologically by date of signing, and each bears a serial number. The first seven numbered treaties are copies and predate the formation of the United States government. The United States treaties begin with no. 8 (the treaty of September 17, 1778, with the Delaware Indians) and end with no. 374 (the treaty of August 13, 1868, with the Nez Perce Indians). For most treaties, the file contains accompanying papers, such as the Senate's resolution of ratification (with amendments, if any), documents recording Indian assent to amendments, the proclamation of the treaty by the president (to which the treaty is often fastened to indicate that it is incorporated in the proclamation), and printed copies of the treaties, including proclamation formulas. In addition, one occasionally finds copies of correspondence, instructions to the treaty commissioners, a journal of the treaty negotiations, and the like. In the latter part of the file there are typewritten copies of correspondence (usually from the Department of the Interior and the Department of State) relative to the treaties. In a few cases the original treaty is missing.

Indian Treaties, and Laws and Regulations Relating to Indian Affairs: To Which
   is Added an Appendix, Containing the Proceedings of the Old Congress, and
   Other Important State Papers, in Relation to Indian Affairs. Washington:
   Way and Gideon, 1826.

This volume, compiled by Chief Clerk Samuel S. Hamilton at the direction of
Secretary of War John C. Calhoun and Thomas L. McKenney, head of the
Indian Office in the War Department, prints the full text of treaties from the
Delaware treaty of September 17, 1778, to the Creek treaty of January 24,
1826. The treaties are arranged alphabetically by tribe, except that there is a
special section devoted to treaties to which several tribes are parties. Brief
summaries of the provisions are entered in the margins. The final fifth of the
volume contains laws and other documents relating to Indian affairs, and there
is a general index at the end. The volume was intended for use by Indian
department officials and field officers, and it is valuable for the numerous
explanatory notes entered in brackets or as footnotes throughout the volume.
A second printing, with the same title page, was issued in 1831, containing a
supplement of additional treaties, 1826–1831, and other documents, pp. 531–
661.

Treaties between the United States of America, and the Several Indian Tribes, from
   1778 to 1837: With a Copious Table of Contents. New Edition, Carefully
   Compared with the Originals in the Department of State. Compiled and
   Printed by the Direction, and under the Supervision, of the Commissioner
   of Indian Affairs. Washington: Langtree and O'Sullivan, 1837. Reprint,
   Millwood, N.Y.: Kraus Reprint Company, 1975.

This volume includes treaties, arranged chronologically, from the treaty with
the Delawares, September 17, 1778, to the treaty with the Choctaws and
Chickasaws, January 17, 1837. It includes some treaty documents not included
in the State Department's file and not printed in the *United States Statutes at
Large* or by Charles J. Kappler; for example, contracts and conventions made
by New York Indians in disposing of their lands to the state or to private
individuals. Some of the later treaties in the volume print the original treaty as
it was signed and then append to it the specific amendments made by the Senate,
rather than print simply the amended treaty.

   The volume has its own usages in punctuation, capitalization, and spelling
of proper names. Despite the title page's declaration that the treaties were
"carefully compared with the originals in the Department of State," that apparently was not the case, for the preface to the volume states that "after trial it
was found that the differences were altogether unimportant, and were occasioned, principally, by the punctuation, which was generally incorrect."

United States Statutes at Large.

Treaties with foreign nations and with the Indian tribes are "the supreme law
of the land" and are on a par with statute laws. They are, accordingly, published
in the official compilations of laws known as the *United States Statutes at Large.*

Before volume 18 (1873–75), the *Statutes* were published by private publishers under the authority of Congress, the most important of which was the series published by Little, Brown and Company (1845–73). Volume 7 of this series, published in 1846 and edited by Richard Peters, is devoted completely to Indian treaties, from 1778 to 1842. Thereafter, Indian treaties, intermingled with treaties with foreign nations, were printed at the end of appropriate volumes. Indian treaties thus appear in volumes 9–16 and 18. In general, the treaties are printed chronologically, by date of signing, but delay in ratification or clerical mistakes occasionally required printing at later times, out of the strict chronological sequence. A few treaties are printed twice. Beginning with volume 10, which includes treaties starting in 1851, the *Statutes* prints the full presidential proclamation form, with the introductory preamble, the full text of the original treaty, the Senate resolution of advice and consent (often with amendments), the assent of the Indians to amendments, and the final ratification formula. There are no special titles supplied by an editor, but there are marginal notations of date of signing, date of proclamation, and contents by paragraph.

A Compilation of All the Treaties between the United States and the Indian Tribes Now in Force as Laws. Washington: Government Printing Office, 1873.

This bulky volume was prepared in accordance with congressional legislation of March 3, 1873, entitled "An act to provide for the preparation and presentation to Congress of the revision of the laws of the United States, consolidating the laws relating to postroads, and a code relating to military offenses, and the revision of treaties with the Indian tribes now in force." It prints the treaties arranged alphabetically by tribe with little editorial explanation. The texts are taken from the *Statutes at Large*, but the volume includes some, like the contract between the Senecas and Robert Morris of 1797 and the Fort Laramie Treaty of 1851, which are not in the regular series in the *Statutes*. The date of proclamation is given but not the date of signing, except in cases where there was no proclamation. The printed lines throughout the volume, including titles and proclamation dates, are numbered serially in the left-hand margin—up to number 46,946. This publication is of little, if any, value for modern students of the treaties.

Kappler, Charles J., comp. *Indian Affairs: Laws and Treaties*, volume 2, *Treaties*. Washington: Government Printing Office, 1904. (*Senate Document* no. 319, 58th Congress, 2d session, serial 4624.)

This volume is the standard collection of Indian treaties and the easiest to use. It is a second edition of a compilation published in 1903. Signatures on the treaties, omitted in 1903 to save space, are now included, and some treaties unavailable earlier are inserted. It follows a chronological arrangement and relies for its texts on the *Statutes at Large* (although it prints the Fort Laramie Treaty of 1851, which the *Statutes* omits), and in most cases it prints the treaty *as amended* instead of the original treaty with amendments printed at the end, as the *Statutes* does. Kappler notes in his preface to the original edition: "At the suggestion of the Commissioner of Indian Affairs, the current modern spelling of Indian names, as decided by the Indian Office and the Bureau of Ethnology, has been introduced and adopted in the headlines to the treaties, but in the text it was found expedient to follow the orthography of the Statutes." The list of "revised spelling of names of Indian tribes and bands" is printed in appendix I in the second edition, p. 1021. Kappler follows the marginal editorial notes of the *Statutes*, adds useful footnotes from time to time, and indicates date of proclamation as well as date of signing. Kappler's *Treaties* is part of a larger work, *Indian Affairs: Laws and Treaties*, 5 volumes, 1904–1941, which includes some valuable material on treaties and which prints agreements and a number of unratified treaties.

There are two recent compilations of the texts of treaties. One, edited by George E. Fay, was published as Occasional Papers, Miscellaneous Series or Ethnology Series, of the Museum of Anthropology, University of Northern Colorado, Greeley. The other was published by the Institute for the Development of Indian Law, Washington, D.C. Both simply print the standard texts by tribes rather than chronologically.

Lists of Indian Treaties and Agreements

A number of lists have been compiled of treaties and agreements made with the Indian tribes. For the most part, these are based on the documents printed in the *Statutes at Large* or in Kappler's *Treaties*. Some are arranged chronologically, others alphabetically by tribe.

"List of all Indian treaties and agreements made with the several tribes of Indians in the United States which have been ratified (alphabetically arranged), with the date of each treaty and where the same appears in the Statutes at Large." *Laws of the United States Relating to Indian Affairs Compiled from the Revised Statutes of the United States*, pp. 341–50. Washington: Government Printing Office, 1884.

This is an adequate list of treaties, but the listing of agreements is incomplete.

"Treaties made with Indian tribes in the United States which have been ratified by the Senate" (arranged by dates).
"Agreements with Indians which have been ratified by Congress" (arranged by dates).
"Agreements with Indians which have been ratified by Congress" (arranged alphabetically by tribe).

These three lists are printed in Report of the Commissioner of Indian Affairs,

1903, in *House Document* no. 5, 58th Congress, 2d session, serial 4645, pp. 469–79. All three lists provide dates and citations to the *Statutes at Large*.

"List of Indian treaties and agreements made with the several tribes of Indians in the United States which have been ratified (alphabetically arranged), with the date of each treaty and where the same appears in the Statutes at Large." Cyrus Thomas, "Treaties," in Frederick Webb Hodge, ed., *Handbook of American Indians North of Mexico*, 2:805–13. 2 vols. Washington: Government Printing Office, 1907–1910.

Although Thomas cites the 1903 Indian Office list as his source, he actually follows that in the 1884 *Laws of the United States Relating to Indian Affairs*.

"A chronological list of the ratified treaties made with Indians, with dates of negotiation of treaties indicated." *House Report* no. 2503, 83d Congress, 2d session, serial 11582, pp. 1556–59. Washington: Government Printing Office, 1953.

This list cites as its source Kappler's *Treaties* as originally published in 1903. It provides citations to the *Statutes at Large*.

List of Indian Treaties. Committee on Interior and Insular Affairs, House of Representatives, 88th Congress, 2d session, Committee Print no. 33. Washington: Government Printing Office, 1964.

This brief publication was intended for ready reference to Indian treaties; it reprints three items:

1. "Treaties made with Indian tribes in the United States" (arranged chronologically), from the Report of the Commissioner of Indian Affairs, 1903.
2. "List of all Indian treaties and agreements made with the several tribes of Indians in the United States which have been ratified with the date of each treaty and where the same appears in the Statutes at Large," from Cyrus Thomas, "Treaties," in Hodge's *Handbook*, 805–13.
3. Index of Kappler's *Treaties*, 1903 edition.

In addition there is a brief list of "selected references" on Indian treaties.

A Chronological List of Treaties and Agreements Made by Indian Tribes with the United States. Washington: Institute for the Development of Indian Law, 1973.

This list, compiled by Vine Deloria, Jr., is divided into "Chronological List of Treaties" and "Agreements with Indian Tribes," arranged chronologically. Both include some unratified items.

Records of the National Archives

There are Indian-related materials scattered through a great many Record Groups of the National Archives. The following Record Groups are most useful. Microfilm numbers are indicated in parentheses.

Record Group 11, General Records of the United States Government.
    Ratified Indian Treaties, 1722–1869 (M668).

Manuscript original treaties signed with Indian tribes, arranged chronologically by serial number. See description above on p. 521.

Record Group 46, Records of the United States Senate.
    Records of Executive Proceedings, Presidents' Messages—Indian Relations.

Arranged by congress, these records pertain to the Senate's ratification of Indian treaties. They contain the presidents' messages transmitting the treaties to the Senate for its constitutional action, together with a good many related documents. Some files pertain to single treaties, others to groups of treaties submitted together by the president. A typical file number, e.g., Sen 25B-C3, indicates 25th Congress, Executive Proceedings (B), Indian Relations (C), and sequential number in that file (3).

Record Group 48, Records of the Department of the Interior.
    Records of the Indian Division, 1828–1907.
    General Records, 1838–1907.
        Letters Received, 1849–1880.
        Letters Sent, 1849–1903.
        Register of Treaties, 1859–1866.

I have not researched these records exhaustively but have depended on documents to and from the secretary of the interior found in other files.

Record Group 59, General Records of the Department of State.
    Domestic Letters, 1789–1906 (M40)
    Miscellaneous Letters, 1789–1906 (M179).

These files contain some correspondence relating to Indian treaties. I have used only the typed copies of letters from these collections that are filed with the pertinent treaties in Ratified Indian Treaties, Record Group 11 (M668).

Record Group 75, Records of the Bureau [Office] of Indian Affairs.
    Letters Sent by the Secretary of War Relating to Indian Affairs, 1800–1824
        (M15).

Letters Received by the Secretary of War Relating to Indian Affairs, 1800–
1823 (M271).
Letters Sent by the Bureau [Office] of Indian Affairs, 1824–1881 (M21).
Letters Received by the Bureau [Office] of Indian Affairs, 1824–1881
(M234).
Report Books, 1838–1885 (M348).
Documents Relating to the Negotiations of Ratified and Unratified Treaties
with Various Indian Tribes, 1801–1869 (T494).

The documents in the last item, a microfilmed compilation, come largely from
the incoming correspondence of the Office of Indian Affairs and of the War
Department relating to Indian affairs. Present are journals of treaty commissioners, proceedings of councils, copies of treaties, reports, and other records
relating to the negotiation of the treaties—both ratified and unratified. The
ratified treaties are arranged by the State Department Ratified Indian Treaties
file number; the unratified treaties are arranged simply chronologically. The
items in John H. Martin's *List of Documents Concerning the Negotiation of Ratified Indian Treaties* that are marked with an asterisk are generally to be found in
this microfilm collection.

Government Publications

The following publications are of special value for studying the treaties
or specific categories of treaties.

Journals of the Continental Congress. 34 vols. Washington: Government
Printing Office, 1904–37.

These volumes allow one to follow the government's actions on treaty matters
before the Constitution.

American State Papers: Indian Affairs. 2 vols. Washington: Gales and Seaton,
1832–34.

These volumes cover material from May 25, 1789, to March 1, 1827. Included
is a mass of documentation concerning treaties, with treaty texts and numerous
related documents, such as instructions to commissioners, reports of commissioners and other pertinent correspondence, and journals of proceedings. The
grouping of documents relating to a given treaty or series of treaties makes this
a tremendously valuable and convenient source for the early treaties.

Serial Set of Congressional Documents.

The series begins with the Fifteenth Congress (1817), and the volumes are
shelved by serial numbers, assigned consecutively to volumes of documents
produced by each session of Congress.

There is considerable Indian treaty material in the series, in particular in reports of the secretary of war, the secretary of the interior, and the commissioner of Indian affairs attached to the annual messages of the president and in various committee reports of the House and Senate. There are abundant materials on the agreements that replaced treaties after 1871. The chief index to the Serial Set is *CIS US Serial Set Index*, 36 vols. (Washington: Congressional Information Service, 1975–79); see also Steven L. Johnson, *Guide to American Indian Documents in the Congressional Serial Set: 1817–1899* (New York: Clearwater Publishing Company, 1977).

Senate Executive Documents and Reports.

When the Senate considered Indian treaties for ratification, the treaties, supporting documents submitted by the president, and committee reports dealing with the treaties were printed confidentially for use by the senators. Although many of these documents are available in other form (e.g., Ratified Indian Treaties file in National Archives Record Group 11, Records of Executive Proceedings of the Senate in National Archives Record Group 46, the Serial Set of Congressional Documents, and the *Journal of the Executive Proceedings of the Senate*), these printed documents and reports are a useful source. The extant ones are now listed conveniently in *CIS Index to US Senate Executive Documents and Reports, Covering Documents and Reports Not Printed in the US Serial Set, 1817–1969*, 2 vols. (Washington: Congressional Information Service, 1987). There is an accompanying collection of the full texts on microfiche. The index and the microfiche also cover treaties with foreign nations and Senate consideration of presidential nominations.

Journal of the Executive Proceedings of the Senate.

Because the executive proceedings of the Senate, in which treaty matters were considered, were secret, information on the action taken on treaties does not appear in the regular House and Senate journals or in published congressional debates. From time to time, however, the Senate has authorized the publication of these proceedings. Amendments and votes on treaties can be found here, but there is no transcription of debates. Senate action in confirming appointment of treaty commissioners is also in these proceedings.

Congressional Debates.

Debates in the House and Senate about Indian affairs often touched on treaty matters. These debates can be followed in the four series of published debates: *Annals of Congress* (1789–1824); *Register of Debates in Congress* (1825–37); *Congressional Globe* (1833–73); and *Congressional Record* (1873—).

United States Statutes at Large.

A continuing series from 1789 to the present, these volumes print laws of Congress in chronological order. Authorization of treaty negotiations, appropriations to implement treaties, and some other treaty-related actions are printed here, as are Indian agreements and their confirmation. Indian treaties also appear in the *Statutes*. See description of the publication of the treaties above, pp. 442–45.

Decisions of Federal Courts.

Many of the Indian cases decided by the United States Supreme Court and lower federal courts rest on treaty stipulations. The Supreme Court decisions are found in *United States Reports*, the first 90 volumes of which are generally cited by the names of the reporters: Dallas, Cranch, Wheaton, Peters, Howard, Black, and Wallace. Cases in lower federal courts can be found in *Federal Cases*, *Federal Reporter*, and *Federal Supplement*.

Executive Orders.

Executive orders relating to Indians are printed in Charles J. Kappler, comp., *Indian Affairs: Laws and Treaties*, 5 vols. (Washington: Government Printing Office, 1904–41). See also these compilations: *Executive Orders Relating to Indian Reservations from May 5, 1855, to July 1, 1912.* (Washington: Government Printing Office, 1912); *Executive Orders Relating to Indian Reservations from July 1, 1912, to July 1, 1922* (Washington: Government Printing Office, 1922); *Executive Orders Relating to Indian Reservations, 1855–1922* (Wilmington, Del.: Scholarly Resources, 1975)—this volume reprints the two previous items.

Special Publications

Carter, Clarence E., ed. *The Territorial Papers of the United States*. 26 vols. Washington: Government Printing Office, 1934–56; National Archives, 1958–62. Continued by John Porter Bloom, ed., vols. 27, 28. Washington: National Archives and Records Service, 1969–75.

These volumes cover the territories from the Northwest Territory through Wisconsin Territory. Even though Indian affairs are not a topic of special emphasis, these transcriptions of documents from the National Archives are rich in material relating to Indian treaties. The annotations of the editors are often of great value.

Cohen, Felix S. *Handbook of Federal Indian Law, with Reference Tables and Index*. Washington: Government Printing Office, 1942.

This volume has useful material on the history and scope of Indian treaties. Included (pp. 485–605) are "Annotated Tables of Statutes and Treaties," which contain a wealth of references to earlier and later statutes and treaties, federal cases, and other documents related to treaties.

An amended version of Cohen's *Handbook* was issued by the Office of the Solicitor, Department of the Interior, as *Federal Indian Law* (Washington: Government Printing Office, 1958). A modern revision that is truer to the spirit of the original work is *Felix S. Cohen's Handbook of Federal Indian Law*, 1982 ed. (Charlottesville, Va.: Michie Bobbs-Merrill, 1982).

Decisions of the Indian Claims Commission, microfiche ed. (New York: Clearwater Publishing Company, 1973–78).

Because so many Indian claims rested on treaty provisions, these documents give a valuable perspective on treaty making. An alphabetical list of cases and an index by docket number are given in *United States Indian Claims Commission, August 13, 1946—September 30, 1978: Final Report* (Washington: Government Printing Office, 1979).

Martin, John H. *List of Documents Concerning the Negotiation of Ratified Indian Treaties, 1801–1869*. Special List No. 6. Washington: National Archives, 1949.

This is a careful and extensive listing of documents pertaining to the negotiation of Indian treaties. It is arranged by the numbers assigned the treaties in the State Department Ratified Indian Treaties file, but it begins with no. 30. Most of the documents identified are available in the various microfilm publications of Indians materials issued by the National Archives.

A comparable compilation by Martin, "List of Documents Concerning the Negotiation of Ratified Indian Agreements," provides information on documents pertaining to sixty-seven ratified agreements. It has not been published but is available at the National Archives.

Royce, Charles C., comp. *Indian Land Cessions in the United States*. Eighteenth Annual Report of the Bureau of American Ethnology, 1896–1897, part 2. Washington: Government Printing Office, 1899.

This essential reference work provides an abstract of land cession provisions of treaties and agreements and maps showing the cessions by state.

Smith, E. B., comp. *Indian Tribal Claims Decided in the Court of Claims of the United States, Briefed and Compiled to June 30, 1947*. 2 vols. Washington: University Publications of America, 1976.

These volumes contain cases arranged alphabetically by tribe and provide information on jurisdictional acts, location and population of tribes, amounts claimed, nature of the claims, and court action. A brief statement of each case is given by Smith.

Smithsonian Institution. *Handbook of North American Indians*. General editor, William C. Sturtevant. 20 vols. projected. Washington: Smithsonian Institution, 1978—.

These volumes, arranged by culture areas and special topics, have detailed anthropological information about Indian tribes, but they also provide some historical information, including accounts of tribal treaties with the United States.

Vaughan, Alden T., ed. *Early American Indian Documents: Treaties and Laws, 1607–1789*. 20 vols. projected. Washington: University Publishers of America, 1979—.

Although these volumes pertain chiefly to the European colonial period, some of the documents are from the early national period of the United States.

Studies of Treaties and Treaty Making

This is a selected list of books and articles that deal with Indian treaties in general or with individual Indian councils and treaties. Preference has been given to more recent studies.

Almost every work on United States Indian policy, almost every history of an Indian tribe, and many biographies, of necessity, deal with aspects of Indian treaty making. In addition, law journals, especially in recent decades, are filled with articles that touch on treaty rights and related topics. See the citations in the footnotes for titles of many such works, particularly those that have been of use in the present study. Published bibliographies on American Indian affairs are also useful for directing readers to treaty materials.

Abele, Charles A. "The Grand Indian Council and Treaty of Prairie du Chien, 1825." Ph.D. dissertation, Loyola University of Chicago, 1969.

Anderson, George E., W. H. Ellison, and Robert F. Heizer. *Treaty Making and Treaty Rejection by the Federal Government in California, 1850–1852*. Socorro, N. Mex.: Ballena Press, 1978.

Anderson, George E., and Robert F. Heizer. "Treaty-making by the Federal Government in California 1851–1852." In *Treaty Making and Treaty Rejection by the Federal Government in California, 1850–1852*, pp. 1–36. Socorro, N. Mex.: Ballena Press, 1978.

Anderson, Harry. "The Controversial Sioux Amendment to the Fort Laramie Treaty of 1851." *Nebraska History* 37 (September 1956): 201–20.

Balman, Gail. "The Creek Treaty of 1866." *Chronicles of Oklahoma* 48 (Summer 1970): 184–96.

Barce, Elmore. "Governor Harrison and the Treaty of Fort Wayne, 1809." *Indiana Magazine of History* 11 (December 1915): 352–67.

Barnes, Lela. "Isaac McCoy and the Treaty of 1821." *Kansas Historical Quarterly* 5 (May 1936): 122–42.

Bischoff, William N., and Charles M. Gates, eds. "The Jesuits and the Coeur

D'Alene Treaty of 1858." *Pacific Northwest Quarterly* 34 (April 1943): 169–81.

Boyd, Mark F. "Horatio S. Dexter and Events Leading to the Treaty of Moultrie Creek with the Seminole Indians." *Florida Anthropologist* 11 (September 1958): 65–95.

Brugge, David M., and J. Lee Correll. *The Story of the Navajo Treaties.* Window Rock, Ariz.: Research Section, Navajo Parks and Recreation Department, Navajo Tribe, 1971.

Burns, Robert Ignatius, ed. "A Jesuit at the Hell Gate Treaty of 1855." *Mid-America* 34 (April 1952): 87–114. Report of Adrian Hoecken.

Bushnell, David I., Jr. "The Virginia Frontier in History—1778." Part 5, "The Treaty of Fort Pitt." *Virginia Magazine of History and Biography* 24 (April 1916): 168–79.

Campisi, Jack. "From Stanwix to Canandaigua: National Policy, States' Rights, and Indian Land." In *Iroquois Land Claims*, ed. Christopher Vecsey and William A. Starna, pp. 49–65. Syracuse: Syracuse University Press, 1988.

———. "The Oneida Treaty Period, 1783–1838." In *The Oneida Indian Experience: Two Perspectives*, ed. Jack Campisi and Laurence M. Hauptman, pp. 48–64. Syracuse: Syracuse University Press, 1988.

Clifton, James A. "Chicago, September 14, 1833: The Last Great Indian Treaty in the Old Northwest." *Chicago History* 9 (Summer 1980): 86–97.

Cohen, Fay G. *Treaties on Trial: The Continuing Controversy over Northwest Indian Fishing Rights.* Seattle: University of Washington Press, 1986.

Danziger, Edmund J., Jr. "They Would Not Be Moved: The Chippewa Treaty of 1854." *Minnesota History* 43 (Spring 1973): 174–85.

Decker, Craig A. "The Construction of Indian Treaties, Agreements, and Statutes." *American Indian Law Review* 5, no. 2 (1977): 299–311.

DeMallie, Raymond J. "American Indian Treaty Making: Motives and Meanings." *American Indian Journal* 3 (January 1977): 2–10.

———. "Touching the Pen: Plains Indian Treaty Councils in Ethnohistorical Perspective." In *Ethnicity on the Great Plains*, ed. Frederick C. Luebke, pp. 38–53. Lincoln: University of Nebraska Press, 1980.

Dustin, Fred. "The Treaty of Saginaw, 1819." *Michigan History Magazine* 4 (January 1920): 243–78.

Edmunds, R. David. "'Nothing Has Been Effected': The Vincennes Treaty of 1792." *Indiana Magazine of History* 74 (March 1978): 23–35.

Ellison, William H. "Rejection of California Indian Treaties: A Study in Local Influence on National Policy." In *Treaty Making and Treaty Rejection by the Federal Government in California, 1850-1852*, pp. 50–70. Socorro, N. Mex.: Ballena Press, 1978.

Ferguson, Clyde R. "Confrontation at Coleraine: Creeks, Georgians and Federalist Indian Policy." *South Atlantic Quarterly* 78 (Spring 1979): 224–43.

Ferguson, Robert B. "Treaties between the United States and the Choctaw Nation." In *The Choctaw before Removal*, ed. Carolyn Keller Reeves, pp. 214–30. Jackson: University Press of Mississippi, 1985.

Fielder, Betty. "The Black Hawk Treaty." *Annals of Iowa* 32 (January 1955): 535–40.

Fisher, Robert L. "The Treaties of Portage des Sioux." *Mississippi Valley Historical Review* 19 (March 1933): 495–508.

Fixico, Donald L. "As Long As the Grass Grows . . . The Cultural Conflicts and Political Strategies of United States–Indian Treaties." In *Ethnicity and War*, ed. Winston A. Van Horne, pp. 128–49. Milwaukee: University of Wisconsin System, American Ethnic Studies Committee/Urban Corridor Consortium, 1984.

Foreman, Carolyn Thomas. "The Lost Cherokee Treaty." *Chronicles of Oklahoma* 33 (Summer 1955): 238–45.

Foreman, Grant. "The Texas Comanche Treaty of 1846." *Southwestern Historical Quarterly* 51 (April 1948): 313–32.

———, ed. "The Journal of the Proceedings of Our First Treaty with the Wild Indians, 1835." *Chronicles of Oklahoma* 14 (December 1936): 394–418.

Franks, Kenny A. "An Analysis of the Confederate Treaties with the Five Civilized Tribes." *Chronicles of Oklahoma* 50 (Winter 1972–73): 458–73.

———. The Implementation of the Confederate Treaties with the Five Civilized Tribes." *Chronicles of Oklahoma* 51 (Spring 1973): 21–33.

Gates, Charles M., ed. "The Indian Treaty of Point No Point." *Pacific Northwest Quarterly* 46 (April 1955): 52–58.

Gerwing, Anselm J. "The Chicago Indian Treaty of 1833." *Journal of the Illinois State Historical Society* 57 (Summer 1964): 117–42.

Hagan, William T. "The Sauk and Fox Treaty of 1804." *Missouri Historical Review* 51 (October 1956): 1–7.

Haines, Francis. "The Nez Perce Tribe versus the United States." *Idaho Yesterdays* 8 (Spring 1964): 18–25.

Halbert, Henry S. "The Story of the Treaty of Dancing Rabbit." *Publications of the Mississippi Historical Society* 6 (1902): 373–402.

Harmon, George D. "The North Carolina Cherokees and the New Echota Treaty of 1835." *North Carolina Historical Review* 6 (July 1929): 237–53.

Hawkinson, Ella. "The Old Crossing Chippewa Treaty and Its Sequel." *Minnesota History* 15 (September 1934): 282–300.

Hayden, Ralston. *The Senate and Treaties, 1789–1817: The Development of the Treaty-Making Functions of the United States Senate during Their Formative Period*. New York: Macmillan Company, 1920.

Heilbron, Bertha L. "Frank B. Mayer and the Treaties of 1851." *Minnesota History* 22 (June 1941): 133–56.

Heizer, Robert F. "Treaties." In *Handbook of North American Indians*, vol. 8, *California*, ed. Robert F. Heizer, pp. 701–4. Washington: Smithsonian Institution, 1978.

Henderson, Archibald. "The Treaty of Long Island of Holston, July, 1777." *North Carolina Historical Review* 8 (January 1931): 55–116.

Henslick, Harry. "The Seminole Treaty of 1866." *Chronicles of Oklahoma* 48 (Autumn 1970): 280–94.

Hill, Burton S. "The Great Indian Treaty Council of 1851." *Nebraska History* 47 (March 1966): 85–110.

Hoover, Herbert T. "The Sioux Agreement of 1889 and Its Aftermath." *South Dakota History* 19 (Spring 1989): 56–94.

Horsman, Reginald. "The British Indian Department and the Abortive Treaty of Lower Sandusky, 1793." *Ohio Historical Quarterly* 70 (July 1961): 189–213.

Hough, Franklin B., ed. *Proceedings of the Commissioners of Indian Affairs, Appointed by Law for the Extinguishment of Indian Titles in the State of New York.* 2 vols. Albany: Joel Munsell, 1861.

Hryniewicki, Richard J. "The Creek Treaty of November 15, 1827." *Georgia Historical Quarterly* 52 (March 1968): 1–15.

———. "The Creek Treaty of Washington, 1826." *Georgia Historical Quarterly* 48 (December 1964): 425–41.

Humphreys, A. Glen. "The Crow Indian Treaties of 1868: An Example of Power Struggle and Confusion in United States Indian Policy." *Annals of Wyoming* 43 (Spring 1971): 73–90.

Ibbotson, Joseph D. "Samuel Kirkland, the Treaty of 1792, and the Indian Barrier State." *New York History* 19 (October 1938): 374–91.

Jennings, Francis, ed. *The History and Culture of Iroquois Diplomacy: An Interdisciplinary Guide to the Treaties of the Six Nations and Their League.* Syracuse: Syracuse University Press, 1985. Accompanies an extensive microfilm edition of Iroquois treaty documents.

Jones, Dorothy V. *License for Empire: Colonialism by Treaty in Early America.* Chicago: University of Chicago Press, 1982.

Jones, Douglas C. "Medicine Lodge Revisited." *Kansas Historical Quarterly* 35 (Summer 1969): 130–42.

———. *The Treaty of Medicine Lodge: The Story of the Great Treaty Council As Told by Eyewitnesses.* Norman: University of Oklahoma Press, 1966.

Josephy, Alvin M., Jr. "A Most Satisfactory Council." *American Heritage* 16 (October 1965): 26–31, 70–76. A treaty with Pacific Northwest tribes in 1855.

Kane, Lucile M. "The Sioux Treaties and the Traders." *Minnesota History* 32 (June 1951): 65–80.

Keller, Robert H. "America's Native Sweet: Chippewa Treaties and the Right to Harvest Maple Sugar." *American Indian Quarterly* 13 (Spring 1989): 117–35.

———. "An Economic History of Indian Treaties in the Great Lakes Region." *American Indian Journal* 4 (February 1978): 2–20.

———. "On Teaching Indian History: Legal Jurisdiction in Chippewa Treaties." *Ethnohistory* 19 (Summer 1972): 209–18.

Kellogg, Louise Phelps. "The Menominee Treaty at the Cedars, 1836." *Transactions of the Wisconsin Academy of Sciences, Arts and Letters* 26 (1931): 127–35.

Kelsey, Harry. "The California Indian Treaty Myth." *Southern California Quarterly* 55 (Fall 1973): 225–38.

Kessell, John L. "General Sherman and the Navajo Treaty of 1868: A Basic and Expedient Misunderstanding." *Western Historical Quarterly* 12 (July 1981): 251–72.

Kickingbird, Kirke, and others. *Indian Treaties*. Washington: Institute for the Development of Indian Law, 1980.

Kickingbird, Lynn, and Curtis Berkey. "American Indian Treaties—Their Importance Today." *American Indian Journal* 1 (October 1975): 3–7.

Kinnaird, Lucia Burk. "The Rock Landing Conference of 1789." *North Carolina Historical Review* 9 (October 1932): 349–65.

Kvasnicka, Robert M. "United States Indian Treaties and Agreements." In *Handbook of North American Indians*, vol. 4, *History of Indian-White Relations*, ed. Wilcomb E. Washburn, pp. 195–201. Washington: Smithsonian Institution, 1988.

Lambert, Paul F. "The Cherokee Reconstruction Treaty of 1866." *Journal of the West* 12 (July 1973): 471–89.

Lane, Barbara. "Background of Treaty Making in Western Washington." *American Indian Journal* 3 (April 1977): 2–11.

Lanehart, David. "Regaining Dinetah: The Navajo and the Indian Peace Commission at Fort Sumner." In *Working the Range: Essays on the History of Western Land Management and the Environment*, ed. John R. Wunder, pp. 25–38. Westport, Conn.: Greenwood Press, 1985.

Larson, Gustive O. "Uintah Dream: The Ute Treaty—Spanish Fork, 1865." *Brigham Young University Studies* 14 (Spring 1974): 361–81.

Lehman, J. David. "The End of the Iroquois Mystique: The Oneida Land Cession Treaties of the 1790s." *William and Mary Quarterly*, 3d ser., 47 (October 1990): 523–47.

Leonard, Stephen J. "John Nicolay in Colorado: A Summer Sojourn and the 1863 Ute Treaty." *Essays and Monographs in Colorado History*, no. 11 (1990), 25–54.

Lindquist, G. E. E. "Indian Treaty Making." *Chronicles of Oklahoma* 26 (Winter 1948–49): 416–48.

Litton, Gaston L., ed. "The Negotiations Leading to the Chickasaw-Choctaw Agreement, January 17, 1837." *Chronicles of Oklahoma* 17 (December 1939): 417–27.

McCullar, Marion Ray. "The Choctaw-Chickasaw Reconstruction Treaty of 1866." *Journal of the West* 12 (July 1973): 462–70.

McKenney, Thomas L. *Sketches of a Tour to the Lakes, of the Character and Customs of the Chippeway Indians, and of Incidents Connected with the Treaty of Fond du Lac*. Baltimore: Fielding Lucas, Jr., 1827.

McNeil, Kinneth. "Confederate Treaties with the Tribes of Indian Territory." *Chronicles of Oklahoma* 42 (Winter 1964–65): 408–20.

Mahan, Bruce E. "The Great Council of 1825." *Palimpsest* 6 (September 1925): 305–18.

———. "Making the Treaty of 1842." *Palimpsest* 10 (May 1929): 174–80.

Mahon, John K. "The Treaty of Moultrie Creek, 1823." *Florida Historical Quarterly* 40 (April 1962): 350–72.

———. "Two Seminole Treaties: Payne's Landing, 1832, and Ft. Gibson, 1833." *Florida Historical Quarterly* 41 (July 1962): 1–21.

Manley, Henry S. "Buying Buffalo from the Indians." *New York History* 28 (July 1947): 313–29. Buffalo Creek Treaty, 1838.

―――. *The Treaty of Fort Stanwix, 1784*. Rome, N.Y.: Rome Sentinel Company, 1932.

Parker, Arthur C. "The Pickering Treaty." *Rochester Historical Society Publication Fund Series* 3 (1924): 79–91.

Partoll, Albert J., ed. "The Blackfoot Indian Peace Council." *Frontier and Midland: A Magazine of the West* 17 (Spring 1937): 199–207.

―――. "The Flathead Indian Treaty Council of 1855." *Pacific Northwest Quarterly* 29 (July 1938): 283–314.

Phillips, Edward Hake. "Timothy Pickering at His Best: Indian Commissioner, 1790–1794." *Essex Institute Historical Collections* 102 (July 1966): 185–92.

Quaife, Milo M., ed. "The Chicago Treaty of 1833." *Wisconsin Magazine of History* 1 (March 1918): 287–303.

Rakove, Jack N. "Solving a Constitutional Puzzle: The Treatymaking Clause As a Case Study." *Perspectives in American History*, n.s., 1 (1984): 233–81.

Roberts, Gary L. "The Chief of State and the Chief." *American Heritage* 26 (October 1975): 28–33, 86–89. Creek Treaty of New York, 1790.

Rutland, Robert A. "Political Background of the Cherokee Treaty of New Echota." *Chronicles of Oklahoma* 27 (Winter 1949–50): 389–406.

Satz, Ronald N. *Chippewa Treaty Rights: The Reserved Rights of Wisconsin's Chippewa Indians in Historical Perspective*. Transactions of the Wisconsin Academy of Sciences, Arts and Letters, vol. 79, no. 1. Madison: Wisconsin Academy of Sciences, Arts and Letters, 1991.

Schwartzman, Grace M., and Susan K. Barnard. "A Trail of Broken Promises: Georgians and the Muscogee/Creek Treaties, 1796–1826." *Georgia Historical Quarterly* 75 (Winter 1991): 697–718.

Silliman, Sue I. "The Chicago Indian Treaty of 1821." *Michigan History Magazine* 6, no. 1 (1922): 194–97.

Smith, Dwight L. "The Land Cession Treaty: A Valid Instrument of Transfer of Indian Title." In *This Land Is Ours: The Acquisition of the Public Domain*, pp. 87–102. Indianapolis: Indiana Historical Society, 1978.

―――. "Wayne and the Treaty of Greene Ville." *Ohio State Archaeological and Historical Quarterly* 63 (January 1954): 1–7.

Smith, Ralph A. "The Fantasy of a Treaty to End Treaties." *Great Plains Journal* 12 (Fall 1972): 26–51. Treaties with the Southern Plains Indians.

Stanley, Henry M. "A British Journalist Reports the Medicine Lodge Peace Council of 1867." *Kansas Historical Quarterly* 33 (Autumn 1967): 249–320.

Stern, Theodore. "The Klamath Indians and the Treaty of 1864." *Oregon Historical Quarterly* 57 (September 1956): 229–73.

Taylor, Alfred A. "Medicine Lodge Peace Council." *Chronicles of Oklahoma* 2 (June 1924): 98–117.

Trafzer, Clifford E., ed. *Indians, Superintendents, and Councils: Northwestern Indian Policy, 1850–1855*. Lanham, Md.: University Press of America, 1986.

Vipperman, Carl J. "The Bungled Treaty of New Echota: The Failure of Cherokee Removal, 1836–38." *Georgia Historical Quarterly* 73 (Fall 1989): 540–58.

Watts, Charles W. "Colbert's Reserve and the Chickasaw Treaty of 1818." *Alabama Review* 12 (October 1959): 272–80.

Wells, Samuel J. "International Causes of the Treaty of Mount Dexter, 1805." *Journal of Mississippi History* 48 (August 1986): 177–85.

——— "Rum, Skins, and Powder: A Choctaw Interpreter and the Treaty of Mount Dexter." *Chronicles of Oklahoma* 61 (Winter 1983–84): 422–28.

Wilkinson, Charles F., and John M. Volkman. "Judicial Review of Indian Treaty Abrogation: 'As Long As Water Flows, or Grass Grows upon the Earth'—How Long a Time Is That?" *California Law Review* 63 (May 1975): 601–61.

Wright, J. Leitch, Jr. "Creek-American Treaty of 1790: Alexander McGillivray and the Diplomacy of the Old Southwest." *Georgia Historical Quarterly* 51 (December 1967): 379–400.

Wrone, David R. "Indian Treaties and the Democratic Idea." *Wisconsin Magazine of History* 70 (Winter 1986–87): 83–106.

Wunder, John R. "No More Treaties: The Resolution of 1871 and the Alteration of Indian Rights to Their Homelands." In *Working the Range: Essays on the History of Western Land Management and the Environment*, ed. John R Wunder, pp. 39–56. Westport, Conn.: Greenwood Press, 1985.

Index

Abbott, Lyman, 346–47
aboriginal title, 232. *See also* title to land
abrogation of treaties, 18, 269, 324, 349, 352, 356, 386, 407–8. *See also* broken treaties
Absentee Shawnee Indians, 318
acculturation, 87. *See also* civilization, promotion of
ACE. *See* All Citizens Equal
activism for treaty rights, 409–28
Adair, William P., 268
Adams, John, 76, 88–89
Adams, John Quincy, 145, 149–50, 157
Adams, Margaret, 216
advice and consent of Senate, 73, 169–70. *See also* ratification of treaties
Advisory Council on Indian Affairs, 374
agency interpreters, 213
agents. *See* Indian agents; special agents
agreement of amity, 266–67
agreements with Indian tribes, 313–26, 350–52; table of, appendix C; unratified, 519
agriculture, promotion of, 9–12, 139–40, 237, 239, 257, 258–59, 270, 277, 278
AIM. *See* American Indian Movement
AIPRC. *See* American Indian Policy Review Commission
Alabama-Creek conflict, 172–74
Albany, N.Y., 27

Albany Plan of Union, 37
Alcatraz Island, 411
All Citizens Equal, 425
Allegany Reservation, 202
alliance, treaty of, 32–33
Allison, William B., 317
allotment of land in severalty: before the Dawes Act, 11, 173, 197, 233, 242, 275, 277, 278; provisions for, in Dawes Act, 319, 328–29, 348
amendments to treaties, 278, 434, 435–42
American Bar Association, 350
American Board of Commissioners for Foreign Missions, 158
American Indian Chicago Conference, 410
American Indian Defense Association, 373, 379
American Indian Magazine, 368
American Indian Movement, 412, 424
American Indian Policy Review Commission, 416–17
American law, 349–50
Anadarko Indians, 256
annuities, 86, 88, 96, 111, 122, 230, 242; commutation of, 322; dependence of Indians on, 119, 199, 239–40; perpetual, 93, 124, 139, 322; policy concerning, 138–39. *See also specific treaties*

Picture Credits

1. Treaty no. 17, Ratified Indian Treaty File, Record Group 11, National Archives. 2. Drawing by John Trumbull, Charles Allen Munn Collection, Fordham University Library, Bronx, New York; photograph from Frick Art Reference Library (FARL negative 21170). 3. Negative no. 111-SC 94145, Still Pictures Branch, National Archives. 4. Treaty no. 23, Ratified Indian Treaty File, Record Group 11, National Archives. 5. Engraved by Joseph Richardson, Jr.; photograph from R. Henry Norweb. 6. Portrait by Charles Willson Peale, courtesy, Independence National Historical Park. 7–9. Negative nos. 111-SC 94159, 94155, 94193, Still Pictures Branch, National Archives. 10. Treaty no. 96, Ratified Indian Treaty File, Record Group 11, National Archives. 11–12. Lithographs from Lewis, *Aboriginal Port Folio* (1835—); negative nos. USZ62-32586 and USZ62-32588, Prints and Photographs Division, Library of Congress. 13. Lithograph from McKenney and Hall, *History of the Indian Tribes of North America* (1836–1844); negative no. 998-a-1, National Anthropological Archives, Smithsonian Institution. 14. Frontispiece from McKenney, *Memoirs, Official and Personal* (1846); photograph by Photographic Services, Marquette University. 15. Treaty no. 152, Ratified Indian Treaty File, Record Group 11, National Archives. 16. Pen and pencil sketch by George Winter, Tippecanoe County Historical Association, gift of Mrs. Cable G. Ball. 17. Treaty no. 214, Ratified Indian Treaty File, Record Group 11, National Archives. 18. Painting by Frank Blackwell Mayer, Minnesota Historical Society, St. Paul. 19. Montana Historical Society, Helena. 20–22. Drawings by Gustav Sohon, Washington State Historical Society, Tacoma. 23. Frontispiece of Stevens, *The Life of Isaac Ingalls Stevens*; photograph by Photographic Services, Marquette University. 24–25. Drawings by Gustav Sohon, Washington State Historical Society, Tacoma. 26. Treaty no. 291A, Ratified Indian Treaty File, Record Group 11, National Archives. 27. Negative no. 690-B, National Anthropological Archives, Smithsonian Institution. 28. Negative no. 111-SC 87714, Still Pictures Branch,

National Archives. 29. From sketch by J. Howland, *Harper's Weekly*, November 16, 1867; negative no. USZ62-92503, Prints and Photographs Division, Library of Congress. 30–31. Photographs by William S. Soulé; negative nos. 1375 and 1380-a, National Anthropological Archives, Smithsonian Institution. 32. Watercolor by Hermann Stieffel, National Museum of American Art, Smithsonian Institution, gift of Mrs. T. T. Brown. 33–34. Photographs by Alexander Gardner, negative nos. 3686 and 3235, National Anthropological Archives, Smithsonian Institution. 35. Negative no. 55766, National Anthropological Archives, Smithsonian Institution. 36. Photograph by W. H. Jackson, negative no. 1663-a, National Anthropological Archives, Smithsonian Institution. 37. Photograph by C. M. Bell, negative no. 1704-b, National Anthropological Archives, Smithsonian Institution. 38. Negative no. LC-BH 82601-29312, Prints and Photographs Division, Library of Congress. 39. Assumption Abbey Archives, Richardton, North Dakota. 40. Larry Dion/*Seattle Times*. 41. Richard S. Heyza/*Seattle Times*. 42. Mike Gryniewicz, Photographic Services, Marquette University. 43. Courtesy of Great Lakes Indian Fish and Wildlife Commission.